IFIP Advances in Information and Communication Technology 314

IFIP – The International Federation for Information Processing

IFIP was founded in 1960 under the auspices of UNESCO, following the First World Computer Congress held in Paris the previous year. An umbrella organization for societies working in information processing, IFIP's aim is two-fold: to support information processing within its member countries and to encourage technology transfer to developing nations. As its mission statement clearly states,

> *IFIP's mission is to be the leading, truly international, apolitical organization which encourages and assists in the development, exploitation and application of information technology for the benefit of all people.*

IFIP is a non-profitmaking organization, run almost solely by 2500 volunteers. It operates through a number of technical committees, which organize events and publications. IFIP's events range from an international congress to local seminars, but the most important are:

- The IFIP World Computer Congress, held every second year;
- Open conferences;
- Working conferences.

The flagship event is the IFIP World Computer Congress, at which both invited and contributed papers are presented. Contributed papers are rigorously refereed and the rejection rate is high.

As with the Congress, participation in the open conferences is open to all and papers may be invited or submitted. Again, submitted papers are stringently refereed.

The working conferences are structured differently. They are usually run by a working group and attendance is small and by invitation only. Their purpose is to create an atmosphere conducive to innovation and development. Refereeing is less rigorous and papers are subjected to extensive group discussion.

Publications arising from IFIP events vary. The papers presented at the IFIP World Computer Congress and at open conferences are published as conference proceedings, while the results of the working conferences are often published as collections of selected and edited papers.

Any national society whose primary activity is in information may apply to become a full member of IFIP, although full membership is restricted to one society per country. Full members are entitled to vote at the annual General Assembly, National societies preferring a less committed involvement may apply for associate or corresponding membership. Associate members enjoy the same benefits as full members, but without voting rights. Corresponding members are not represented in IFIP bodies. Affiliated membership is open to non-national societies, and individual and honorary membership schemes are also offered.

Luis M. Camarinha-Matos   Pedro Pereira
Luis Ribeiro (Eds.)

Emerging Trends in Technological Innovation

First IFIP WG 5.5/SOCOLNET Doctoral Conference on
Computing, Electrical and Industrial Systems, DoCEIS 2010
Costa de Caparica, Portugal, February 22-24, 2010
Proceedings

 Springer

Volume Editors

Luis M. Camarinha-Matos
Pedro Pereira
Luis Ribeiro
New University of Lisbon
Faculty of Sciences and Technology
Campus de Caparica, 2829-516 Monte Caparica, Portugal
E-mail: {cam, ldr}@uninova.pt, pmrp@fct.unl.pt

CR Subject Classification (1998): C.2, H.1, C.4, I.2.9, C.3, J.2

ISSN   1868-4238

ISBN-13   978-3-642-26242-5 Springer Berlin Heidelberg New York

springer.com

© IFIP International Federation for Information Processing 2010
Softcover reprint of the hardcover 1st edition 2010

Typesetting: Camera-ready by author, data conversion by Scientific Publishing Services, Chennai, India
Printed on acid-free paper   SPIN: 12844760   06/3180   5 4 3 2 1 0

Preface

Identifying Emerging Trends in Technological Innovation

Doctoral programs in science and engineering are important sources of innovative ideas and techniques that might lead to new products and technological innovation. Certainly most PhD students are not experienced researchers and are in the process of learning how to do research. Nevertheless, a number of empiric studies also show that a high number of technological innovation ideas are produced in the early careers of researchers. The combination of the eagerness to try new approaches and directions of young doctoral students with the experience and broad knowledge of their supervisors is likely to result in an important pool of innovation potential.

The DoCEIS doctoral conference on Computing, Electrical and Industrial Engineering aims at creating a space for sharing and discussing ideas and results from doctoral research in these inter-related areas of engineering. Innovative ideas and hypotheses can be better enhanced when presented and discussed in an encouraging and open environment. DoCEIS aims to provide such an environment, releasing PhD students from the pressure of presenting their propositions in more formal contexts.

The first edition of DoCEIS, which was sponsored by SOCOLNET, IFIP and IEEE Industrial Electronics Society, attracted a considerable number of paper submissions from a large number of PhD students (and their supervisors) from 15 countries. This book comprises the works selected by the International Program Committee for inclusion in the main program and covers a wide spectrum of topics, ranging from collaborative enterprise networks to microelectronics. Thus, novel results and ongoing research in the following areas were presented, illustrated, and discussed:

- Value systems alignment in enterprise networks
- Collaborative networks governance and support
- Information modelling and management
- Risk assessment and decision support based on imprecise information
- Evolvable manufacturing systems and cooperative robotics
- Systems modelling and control
- Advances in telecommunications and electronics
- Sensorial perception and signal processing
- Energy systems and novel electrical machinery

As a gluing element, all authors were asked to explicitly indicate the (potential) contribution of their work to technological innovation.

We expect that this book will provide readers with an inspiring set of promising ideas, presented in a multi-disciplinary context, and that by their diversity these results can trigger and motivate new research and development directions.

We would like to thank all the authors for their contributions. We also appreciate the dedication of the DoCEIS Program Committee members who both helped with the selection of articles and contributed with valuable comments to improve their quality.

February 2009   Luís M. Camarinha-Matos
                                                                              Pedro Pereira
                                                                              Luis Ribeiro

First IFIP / SOCOLNET Doctoral Conference on COMPUTING, ELECTRICAL AND INDUSTRIAL ENGINEERING
Costa de Caparica, Portugal, 22–24 February 2010

Program Committee Chair

Luis M. Camarinha-Matos (Portugal)

Program Committee

Marian Adamski (Poland)
Hamideh Afsarmanesh (The Netherlands)
Juan Jose Rodriguez Andina (Spain)
Helder Araujo (Portugal)
Amir Assadi (USA)
José Barata (Portugal)
Arnaldo Batista (Portugal)
Luis Bernardo (Portugal)
Xavier Boucher (France)
António Cardoso (Portugal)
Wojciech Cellary (Poland)
David Chen (France)
Fernando J. Coito (Portugal)
Luis M. Correia (Portugal)
José Craveirinha (Portugal)
Rui Dinis (Portugal)
Mischa Dohler (Spain)
Pedro Faia (Portugal)
Ip-Shing Fan (UK)
Maria Helena Fino (Portugal)
José M. Fonseca (Portugal)
Leopoldo Garcia Franquelo (Spain)
Alfredo Álvarez García (Spain)
Rafael Martínez Gasca (Spain)
Paulo Gil (Portugal)
João Goes (Portugal)
Henrique Leonel Gomes (Portugal)
Luis Gomes (Portugal)
Antoni Grau (Spain)
Paul Grefen (The Netherlands)
Tarek Hassan (UK)
Tomasz Janowski (Macau)
Ricardo Jardim-Gonçalves (Portugal)

Bojan Jerbic (Croatia)
Pontus Johnson (Sweden)
Stephan Kassel (Germany)
Bernhard Katzy (Germany)
Xu Li (Canada)
João Martins (Portugal)
Maria do Carmo Medeiros (Portugal)
Paulo Miyagi (Brazil)
Eduardo Mosca (Italy)
Jörg Müller (Germany)
Horacio Neto (Portugal)
Mário Ventim Neves (Portugal)
Rui Neves-Silva (Portugal)
Mauro Onori (Sweden)
Manuel D. Ortigueira (Portugal)
Angel Ortiz (Spain)
Luis Palma (Portugal)
Kulwant Pawar (UK)
Willy Picard (Poland)
Hervé Pingaud (France)
Paulo Pinto (Portugal)
Ricardo Rabelo (Brazil)
Hubert Razik (France)
Sven-Volker Rehm (Germany)
Yacine Rezgui (UK)
Rita Ribeiro (Portugal)
Luis Sá (Portugal)
Ricardo Sanz (Spain)
Gheorghe Scutaru (Romania)
Adolfo Steiger-Garção (Portugal)
Klaus-Dieter Thoben (Germany)
Manuela Vieira (Portugal)
Antonio Volpentesta (Italy)

Organizing Committee Co-chairs

Luis Gomes (Portugal), Ricardo J. Gonçalves (Portugal)

Organizing Committee (PhD Students)

Carla Viveiros
Carlos Matos
Carlos Agostinho
David Inácio
Ezequiel Carvalho
Filipe Barata
Graça Almeida
João Sarraipa
João Mendes

José Carlos Ribeiro
José Inácio Rocha
Luis Ribeiro
Luis Moita Flores
Pedro Pereira
Ruben Costa
Rui Lino
Tiago Ferreira
Vitor Holtreman

Technical Sponsors

 Society of Collaborative Networks

IFIP WG 5.5 COVE
Co-Operation infrastructure for Virtual
Enterprises and electronic business

 IEEE–Industrial Electronics Society

Organizational Sponsors

Organized by:

PhD Program on Electrical and Computer Engineering FCT-UNL.
In collaboration with PhD Programs in: Electrical and Computer Engineering -
FCT-U Coimbra and Electronics and Telecommunications - U Algarve.

Table of Contents

Part 4: Assessment and Decision Support

Part 5: Evolvable Factory Automation

Part 6: Cooperative Robotics

Part 7: Robots and Manipulation

Part 8: Petri Nets Based Modeling

Part 9: Advances in Telecommunications

Part 10: Sensorial Perception – I

Part 11: Sensorial Perception – II

Part 12: Signal Processing – I

Part 13: Signal Processing – II

Part 14: Advances in Energy Systems

Part 15: Dedicated Energy Systems

Part 16: Advances in Electrical Machinery

Part 17: Electronic Circuits Layout and Optimization

Part 18: Microelectronic Circuits Design

Part 1

Enterprise Networks and Strategic Alignment

Applying Causal Reasoning
to Analyze Value Systems

Patrícia Macedo[1,2] and Luis M. Camarinha-Matos[1]

[1] Faculty of Sciences and Technology, Universidade Nova de Lisboa, Portugal
pmacedo@est.ips.pt
[2] Polytechnic Institute of Setubal, Portugal
cam@uninova.pt

Abstract. Collaborative networked organizations are composed of heterogeneous and autonomous entities. Thus it is natural that each member has its own set of values and preferences, as a result, conflicts among partners might emerge due to some values misalignment. Therefore, tools to support the analysis of Value Systems in a collaborative context are relevant to improve the network management. Since a Value System reflects the set of values and preferences of an actor, which are cognitive issues, a cognitive approach based on qualitative causal maps is suggested. Qualitative inference methods are presented in order to assess the potential for conflicts among network members and the positive impact between members' Value Systems. The software tool developed, in order to support the proposed framework and the qualitative inference methods, is briefly presented.

Keywords: Collaborative networks, value systems, causal reasoning.

1 Introduction

Collaborative networked organizations (CNO) are formed by heterogeneous and autonomous entities. Thus, it is natural that each member has its own set of values and preferences; as a result, they will have different perceptions of outcomes, which might lead to non-collaborative behaviour. In recent years some studies have explored the importance of Value Systems in the context of networked organizations [1-4]. Furthermore, some efforts have been done to develop methods to analyze Value Systems in collaborative environments [5, 6]. These preliminary efforts have revealed that a cognitive approach based on causal maps was a promising way; however, a consistent qualitative approach has not yet been explored. Behavioural researchers [7, 8] have concluded that a qualitative approach has the advantage of being close to natural language; thus, decisions makers and experts can understand the model easily, which will increase the confidence on the outputs. Departing from the work developed on cognitive maps by Eden [9], and the work done on qualitative operators for reasoning maps by Montibeller and Belton [10], a qualitative inference approach has been developed in order to assess the potential for conflicts among network members and the positive impact between members' Value Systems.

L.M. Camarinha-Matos, P. Pereira, and L. Ribeiro (Eds.): DoCEIS 2010, IFIP AICT 314, pp. 3–13, 2010.

2 Contribution to Technological Innovation

Collaborative networks constitute an important organizational structure to promote innovation, namely in the context of small and medium size enterprises. This research aims to contribute to technological innovation in the way that it will provide new methods and tools to support CNO management in the scope of Value Systems management and analysis. The presented qualitative approach is a step forward in the area of the analysis of Value Systems alignment, since it proposes applying qualitative causal reasoning to infer qualitative indicators about Value Systems alignment in a collaborative context. Another contribution to technological innovation is the development of a prototype that implements the analysis framework and the qualitative reasoning methods in an integrated and distributive mode, which may boost the development of new consulting services in the management of collaborative networks.

3 Related Work on Values Alignment

Values alignment in an organizational context is a topic that has been studied essentially by social sciences researchers. Brian Hall [11] and Richard Barrett [12] developed models of values in organizations and analyzed the importance of values management for the success of organizations. Richard Barrett also studied the alignment between employees' core-values and enterprise's core-values. On the other hand, Eden [9] used causal maps to represent the cognitive structure of core-values, also establishing the relationships between organizational goals and core-values. Another cognitive approach was proposed by Rekom and his colleagues [13] as a method to identify the core-values held by organizations based on their employees daily actions.

4 Core Value System Analysis Extended-Framework

The base concepts on Value Systems and Core Value System analysis are briefly described, in order to facilitate the understanding of the proposed approach.

Core Value System: base concepts. The adopted Core Value System (CVS) conceptual model assumes that core–values are the core characteristics of the organization (or network of organizations) to be evaluated. The Value System is decomposed in two subsystems. The first subsystem - core value objects subsystem (COS) - is represented by the organization (or networked organization) itself. The second one - core evaluation subsystem (CES) - represents the mechanisms of evaluation, such as the functions to evaluate the organization's core-values, the core-evaluation perspective and the core-values themselves.

The set of core-values and respective preferences of an actor are represented according to this conceptual model by the core-evaluation perspective. The core-evaluation perspective will be the main structural element in the proposed approach. A detailed and formal description of these concepts can be found in [6, 14].

Core Value System analysis extended-framework. In order to analyze core-values in a collaborative network, a model that supports the analysis of the relationships among: core-values, organizations, and collaborative networks, is required. This kind of relationships can be modelled using graphs. The idea is to represent a network in symbolic terms, abstracting reality as a set of linked nodes. In this case, each node represents an element (a network, an organization, or a core-value) and the directed arcs specify the relationships. The causal modelling method is used to model the causal relationships among core-values in order to analyze the influence among them. Considering the nature of this analysis, a combination of these two modelling techniques was suggested in the framework proposed by Camarinha-Matos et al. [5]. However, the mentioned framework does not support the actor's preferences. As preferences are one of the main elements of a Core Value System it is fundamental to consider them in the Core Value System analysis process. Although the preferences were first modelled in a crisp mode (see [14]), in this approach it is proposed to represent them in a qualitative way.

Although, the previous framework considered that all influences among core-values had a similar strength, it may be also important to be able to model different intensities of influence. Thus, it is proposed to extend the CVS analysis framework in order to add the following properties to the maps (see Fig. 1): (i) in core-values influence map the width of the direct-edge represents the strength of the influence; (ii) in organisations' core-values map and CNO's core-values maps the edges of the graphs have different widths according to the degree of importance of the core-value.

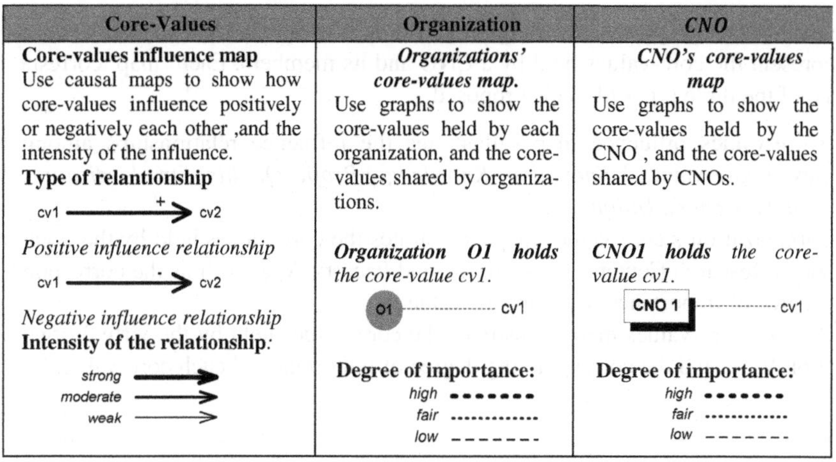

Core-Values	Organization	CNO
Core-values influence map Use causal maps to show how core-values influence positively or negatively each other ,and the intensity of the influence. **Type of relantionship** cv1 ——+——> cv2 *Positive influence relationship* cv1 ——·——> cv2 *Negative influence relationship* **Intensity of the relationship:** strong ⟹ moderate → weak →	*Organizations' core-values map.* Use graphs to show the core-values held by each organization, and the core-values shared by organizations. ***Organization O1 holds the core-value cv1.*** O1 ·············· cv1 **Degree of importance:** high ▪▪▪▪▪▪ fair ············ low – – – – – –	*CNO's core-values map* Use graphs to show the core-values held by the CNO , and the core-values shared by CNOs. **CNO1 holds the core-value cv1.** CNO 1 ·············· cv1 **Degree of importance:** high ▪▪▪▪▪▪ fair ············ low – – – – – –

Fig. 1. Core Value System analysis extended-framework

Formally, the three types of maps proposed in the extended-framework are formally specified as direct graphs.

Definition 1 (Organization's core-value map) – The organization's core-value map is defined as an ordered pair , $OCVM = (V, OW)$

- $V = CV \cup O$, CV is the set of core values, O is the set of organizations
- OW is a set of relations (edges).
  $OW = \{ow_{ij} = (o_i, cv_j, p): o_i \in O \wedge cv_j \in CV \wedge p \in DI = \{low, fair, high\}\}$. The preference operator is defined as: $preference: OW \rightarrow DI, preference(o, cv, p) = p$.

Definition 2 (CNO's core-value map) – The CNO's core-value map is defined as an ordered pair, $CCVM = (V, CW)$.

- $V = CV \cup CNO$, CV is the set of core values, CNO is the set of networked organizations.
- CW is a set of relations (edges).
  $CW = \{cw_{ij} = (cno_i, cv_j, p): cno_i \in CNO \wedge cv_j \in CV \wedge p \in DI = \{low, fair, high\}\}$. The preference operator is defined:
  $preference: CW \rightarrow DI, \ preference(cno, cv, p) = p$.

Definition 3 (Core-values influence map) – A core-values influence map is defined by an ordered pair : $CVIM = (CV, E)$ where,

- CV is the set of core values.
- E is the set of influences (edges)
  $$E = \{e_{ij} = (cv_i, cv_j, p, s): cv_i \in CV \wedge cv_j \in CV \wedge p \in P$$
  $$= \{weak, moderate, strong\} \wedge s \in S = \{+1, 0, -1\}\}.$$
- The following operators are defined:
  $influenceValue: E \rightarrow P \times S, \ influenceValue(cv_i, cv_j, p, s) = (p, s), signal: E \rightarrow S,$
  $signal(cv_i, cv_j, p, s) = s, intensity: E \rightarrow P, intensity(cv_i, cv_j, p, s) = p$.

The example maps presented in Fig. 2 illustrate how to use the extended framework to represent the core-values held by a CNO and its members. Each map corresponds to one of the three types of maps proposed:

1. Core-values influence map –illustrates the influence relationships among the seven core-values {*Innovation, Knowledge, Profit, Quality, Standardization, Social Awareness, Uniqueness*}.
2. Organization's core-values map - illustrates the core-values held by the organizations Research Center, University A, and Factory A, as well as the corresponding degree of importance of each core-value.
3. CNO's core-values map - illustrates the core-values held by the virtual organization VO1, and the corresponding degree of importance of each core-value.

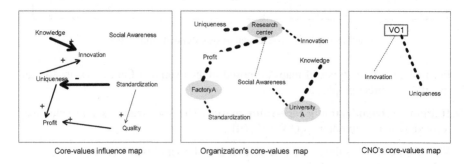

Fig. 2. Extended-framework maps- example

5   Core Value System Analysis Methods

Observing the example represented in the causal map of Fig. 2, we can notice that *Standardization* influences *Quality* positively in a direct way. Nevertheless, as on one hand *Standardization* influences *Quality*, and *Quality* influences *Profit*, and on the other hand *Standardization* influences *Uniqueness*, and *Uniqueness* influences *Profit*, we can also deduce that *Standardization* influences *Profit* in an indirect way.

Thus, we can define two kinds of influence relationships: the direct influence and the indirect influence.

Definition 4 (Direct influence) – A core-value cv_i is said to have a direct influence on a core-value cv_j if there is a direct link from the node cv_i to the node cv_j.

Definition 5 (Indirect influence) – A core value cv_i is said to influence indirectly cv_j, if there is a node cv_k, such that cv_i has a direct influence in cv_k and cv_k has an influence (direct or indirect) on cv_j.

In order to infer the composite influence relationship between two core-values, the following operations have to be performed (see Fig. 3):

1. Determine all **indirect influences**.
2. Determine the result from **joining all indirect influences**, calculated in (1).
3. Determine the result of the **composition** of the direct influences with the joint influences, calculated in (2).

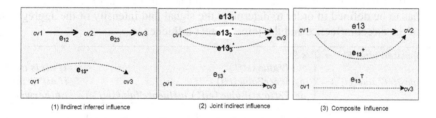

Fig. 3. Inference Operations

In order to characterize each inferred influence relationship, it is necessary to specify how its intensity and signal can be determined. In order to determine the resulted intensity of the indirect influence a recursive approach is used and it is assumed that there is a decision table *decT1* (see Table 1 as an example) with the following specification, $decT1: P^2 \rightarrow P$ (for P specification see Definition 3).

Table 1. Decision Table (decT1) example

decT1(p1,p2)	weak	moderate	strong
weak	weak	weak	weak
moderate	weak	moderate	moderate
strong	weak	moderate	strong

Thus, the indirect influence value is recursively defined as:

$$
\begin{aligned}
&indirectIValue\colon E^* \to P \times S \\
&indirectIValue(eij_n{}^*) \\
&= \begin{cases} influenceValue(eij) & \textbf{if } cv_i \textbf{ has a direct influence in } cv_j \\ (decT1(intensity(eik), intensity(ekj_n{}^*)), signal(eik) \times signal\,(ekj_n{}^*)) & \textbf{otherwise} \end{cases}
\end{aligned}
$$

Definition 6 (Joint indirect influence) – Joint indirect influence of cv_i on cv_j is the result of the "junction" of one or more indirect influences of cv_i on cv_j. The intensity and signal of the joint influences can be inferred as suggested below.

Let us assume that: $eij_n{}^+ <=> $ *Joint indirect influence($\{eij_1{}^*, eij_2{}^*, \ldots eij_n{}^*\}$)* and a decision table $decT2\colon (P \times S)^2 \to P \times S$ (of the kind of decT1 defined above) was defined in order to determine the signal and intensity of the aggregation of two indirect influences.

So, the intensity and signal of the joint indirect influence is defined recursively.

$$
\begin{aligned}
&jointIValue\colon E^C \to P \times S \\
&jointIValue(eij_n{}^+) = \begin{cases} indirectIValue(eij_n{}^*) & \textbf{if } n = 1 \\ decT2((indirectIValue(eij_n{}^*), jointIValue(eij_{n-1}{}^+)) & \textbf{otherwise} \end{cases}
\end{aligned}
$$

Definition 7 (Composite influence) – The composite influence is determined by the aggregation of two components: the direct influence and the joint indirect influence. The intensity and signal of the composite influence can be inferred as it is suggested below:

- $eij^C =$ Composite influence(eij, eij^+).
- A decision table (of the kind of decT1 defined above) $decT3\colon (P \times S)^2 \to P \times S$ has to be defined in order to determine the signal and intensity of the aggregation of the direct influence and the joint indirect influence.

$$
\begin{aligned}
&compositeIValue\colon E^C \to (P \times S) \\
&compositeIValue(eij^C) = \begin{cases} jointIValue\,(eij^+) & \textbf{if } eij \textbf{ is null} \\ influenceValue(eij) & \textbf{if } eij^+ \textbf{is null} \\ decT3(jointIValue\,(eij^+), influenceValue(eij)) & \textbf{otherwise} \end{cases}
\end{aligned}
$$

After the composite influence between two core-values has been calculated, it is possible to determine the two alignment metrics introduced in[5]: (i) the number of positive impacts between two Core Value Systems; (ii) the number of potential conflicts between two Core Value Systems.

Definition 8 (Positive impact) – There is a positive impact between two Core Value Systems, CVS_x and CVS_y, if there is a core-value cv_i that belongs to CVS_x and a core-value cv_j that belongs to CVS_y, such that cv_i influences positively cv_j.

Let us consider PI_{xy} as the set of positive impacts of CVS_x in CVS_y:

$$
PI_{xy} = \{eij^C : signal(eij^C) = 1 \ \wedge cv_i \in CVS_x \wedge cv_j \in CVS_y\}
$$

The impact intensity depends on two factors: (i) the intensity of the influence relationship; (ii) the degree of importance of the value (in the example of Fig. 2, *Knowledge* has a positive impact on *Innovation*, but as *Innovation* has a low degree of importance to VO1, the University's CVS has not a high positive impact on VO1's CVS).

The combination of these two factors is defined through a decision table (see Table 2), $decT4: P \times DI \rightarrow DI$. (for PI specification see definition 3 and for DI specification see definition 2). Thus, the impact intensity is defined as:

$$impactIntensity: E^C \rightarrow DI = \{low, fair, high\}.$$
$$impactIntensity(eij^C) = decT4(intensity(eij^C), preference(ow_{yj})).$$

Table 2. Decision Table (decT4) example

decT4 (x,y)	low	fair	high
weak	low	low	fair
moderate	low	fair	high
strong	low	fair	high

Definition 9 (Potential for conflict) – It is considered that a conflict between CVS_x and CVS_y exists if there is a core-value cv_i that belongs to CVS_x and a core-value cv_j that belongs to a CVS_y, such that cv_i influences negatively cv_j, or cv_j influences negatively cv_i.

Let's define CI_{xy} as the set of conflicts between CVS_x and CVS_y:

$$CI_{xy} = \{eij^C : signal(eij^C) = -1 \wedge (cv_i \in CVS_x \wedge cv_j \in CVS_y)\}$$
$$\cup \{eji^C: signal(eji^T) = -1 \wedge (cv_i \in CVS_x \wedge cv_j \in CVS_y)\}$$

Like the positive impact intensity, the intensity of the conflict also depends on the intensity of the influence and the degree of importance of the core value. Thus, a similar inference process is suggested to determine the conflict intensity.

Application example: The mentioned inference methods were implemented in SWI-Prolog. Fig. 4 shows the main rules to implement the positive impacts assessment and the potential for conflicts assessment.

```
p_impact(E1, E2, CV1,CV2,I) :-        p_conflict(E1, E2, CV1,CV2,I):-
   value(E1, CV1, _),                    value(E1, CV1, _),
   value(E2, CV2, DI),                   value(E2, CV2, DI),
   CV2\==CV1,                            (jointComposite(CV1,CV2,neg,In);
   jointComposite(CV1,CV2,pos,I1),      jointComposite(CV2,CV1,neg,In)),
        decT4(I1,DI,I).                       decT4(In,DI,I).

positiveImpacts(E1,E2,LC) :-          potencialConflicts(E1,E2,LC) :-
   findall([CV1,CV2,I],                  findall([V1,V2,I],
   p_impact(E1,E2,CV1,CV2,I), LC).       p_conflict(E1,E2,V1,V2,I), LC).
```

Fig. 4. Prolog implementation

Let us take Fig. 2 to exemplify the use of the inference methods explained above. The positive impact of each member's CVS in the VO1's CVS is computed and from the results obtained (see Table 3), we can observe that University A's CVS and Research Center's CVS have a positive impact on VO1's CVS.

Table 3. Positive Impact results

	N° positive impacts	Positive impacts
Factory A	0	
University A	1	The *knowledge* value has a **high** positive impact on *innovation* value.
Research Center	1	The *uniqueness* value has a **fair** positive impact on *innovation* value.

The analysis of the potential for conflicts among CNO members (see Table 4) shows that there is a potential for conflict between Factory A and the Research Center due to the fact that Factory A considers *Standardization* has an important core-value, which has a negative influence in *Innovation* and *Uniqueness*, both core-values of the Research Center.

Table 4. Potential for conflict results

Pair of Members		# Potential Conflicts	Core-Values Conflicts	
Factory A	University A	0		
Factory A	Research Center	2	*standardization* and *uniqueness*	high
			standardization and *innovation*	low
Research Center	University A	0		

6   Core Value System Management Tool

In the previous section, the process of core-value definition and analysis was briefly described. In order to be able to implement this in a real world context, a tool to support the CVS management and to assist the analysis process was developed. The purpose of the tool is not to fully automate the process of Core Value System analysis, but rather to assist the analysis process during the VO and VBE management.

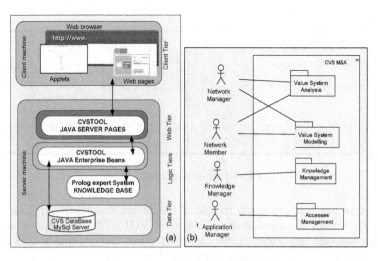

Fig. 5. (a) CVS Tool Technological Architecture (b) – CV Use Case Diagram

Essentially, the Core Value System analysis can be performed among CNO members' Core Value Systems, or between the CNO's Core Value System and the Core Value System of a partner or a potential partner. In order to be able to support these main features, four components are implemented (see Fig 5b):

- **Core-values knowledge management** – To be used by the knowledge experts, in order to specify core-values and their characteristics.
- **Core Value System management** – To be used by brokers, network managers and network member in order to define their Core Value Systems.
- **Core Value System Analysis** – To be used by brokers, network managers and network members in order to analyze their Core Value Systems.
- **Access management tool** – Provides features that allow the application manager to configure accesses to the application according to the user profiles.

As this application was developed to be used in a network context, where users are disperse, a web access to the application is a requirement. For its implementation a client server multitier architecture was adopted, as it is illustrated in Fig. 5a. The application was developed using the J2EE platform. The database was implemented in MySql. In order to implement the graphical features to support the causal maps and the graphs, the JUNG API is used. The implementation of a reference knowledge base is done using SWI-Prolog, and all the reasoning methods are implemented in Prolog and accessed via Java Enterprise Beans.

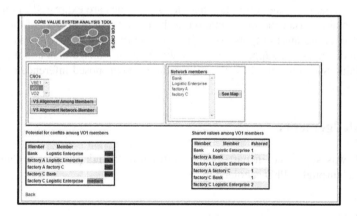

Fig. 6. CVS Analysis tool for CNO's – CVS analysis

Two screen-shots of the application are presented, in order to give a brief view of its features. The results of the qualitative inference for the Core Value System alignment among CNO members are shown in Fig. 6. The map that represents the core-values held by the network members is shown in Fig. 7.

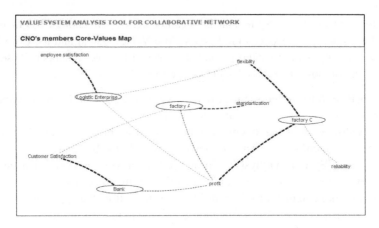

Fig. 7. CVS Analysis tool for CNO's – Analysis Maps

7 Conclusion

A qualitative reasoning approach to analyze Core Value Systems in collaborative environments has been proposed. The reasoning methods presented were supported in an analysis framework based on qualitative causal maps and graphs. This approach has the following main advantages: (i) facilitates the representation of knowledge about core-values; (ii) increases the "transparency" and the understandability of the reasoning mechanisms due to the fact that decision tables are expressed in qualitative terms; (iii) makes easier the interpretation of the outputs for all agents of the decision making process, because outputs are expressed totally in qualitative terms. The web application developed to support the core-Value System management and the analysis of Core Value Systems will allow the validation of the proposed inference methods in real world scenarios.

Acknowledgements

This work was supported in part by the Portuguese "Fundação para a Ciência e a Tecnologia" through a PhD scholarship.

References

1. Zineldin, M.A.: Towards an ecological collaborative relationship management A "co-opetive" perspective. European Journal of Marketing 32, 1138–1164 (1998)
2. Macedo, P., Sapateiro, C., Filipe, J.: Distinct Approaches to Value Systems in Collaborative Networks Environments. In: Network-Centric Collaboration and Supporting Frameworks, vol. 224, pp. 111–120. Springer, Boston (2006)
3. Abreu, A., Camarinha Matos, L.M.: On the role of value systems to promote the sustainability of collaborative environments. International Journal of Production Research 46, 1207–1229 (2008)

4. Afsarmanesh, H., Camarinha-Matos, L.M., Ermilova, E.: Vbe Reference Framework Methods and Tools for Collaborative Networked Organizations, pp. 35–68. Springer, Heidelberg (2008)
5. Camarinha-Matos, L., Macedo, P., Abreu, A.: Analysis of Core-values Alignment in Collaborative Networks. In: Camarinha-Matos, L.M., Picard, W. (eds.) Pervasive Collaborative Networks, pp. 52–64. Springer, Poznan (2008)
6. Abreu, A., Macedo, P., Camarinha-Matos, L.M.: Elements of a methodology to assess the alignment of core-values in collaborative networks. International Journal of Production Research 47, 4907–4934 (2009)
7. Budescu, D.V., Wallsten, T.S.: Consistency in interpretation of probabilistic phrases. Organizational Behavior and Human Decision Processes 36, 391–405 (1985)
8. Olson, D., Moshkovich, H., Schellenberger, R.: Consistency and Accuracy in Decision Aids: Experiments with Four Multiattribute Systems. Decision Sciences 26, 723–747 (1995)
9. Eden, C.: The Analysis of Cause Maps. Journal of Managemnet Studies 29 (1992)
10. Montibeller, G., Belton, V.: Qualitative operators for reasoning maps: Evaluating multicriteria options with networks of reasons. European Journal of Operational Research 195, 829–840 (2009)
11. Hall, B.: Values Shift: A Guide to Personal and Organizational Transformation. Twin Lights Publishers, Rockport (1995)
12. Barrett, R.: Building a Vison-Guided, Values-Driven organization. Butterworth-Heinemann (2006)
13. Rekom, J.V., Riel, C.B.M.V., Wierenga, B.: A Methodology for Assessing Organizational Core Values. Journal of Management Studies 43, 175–201 (2006)
14. Camarinha-Matos, L., Macedo, P.: A conceptual model of value systems in collaborative networks. Journal of Intelligent Manufacturing (2008)

Assessment of the Willingness to Collaborate in Enterprise Networks

João Rosas and Luis M. Camarinha-Matos

Universidade Nova de Lisboa, Faculty of Sciences and Technology,
2829-516 Monte Caparica, Portugal
{jrosas,cam}@uninova.pt

Abstract. The success of a partnership depends fundamentally on the partners' active and vigorous participation in the achievement of the common goals. The commitment to these goals is associated to each partner's attitudes and intentions. These intentions, in turn, are linked to the partner's beliefs concerning the expected outcomes of a collaboration opportunity. This work proposes an approach to assess organizations' willingness to collaborate. This approach follows a behavioral perspective, which is based on the Theory of the Planned Behavior. A tool named Intentions Query Mechanism selects a number of appropriate questions from a knowledge-base, from which the answers allow to estimate the level of an organization's willingness to collaborate.

Keywords: Organization's behavior, willingness to collaboration, collaborative networks, Theory of the Planned Behavior.

1 Introduction

Willingness to collaborate in a networked organization is related to the partner's attitudes and intentions towards concrete collaboration situations. It is dependent on a variety of aspects, which are basically related to the expected outcomes of a collaboration opportunity, such as increased profits, achieving new markets, or obtaining some competitive advantages. When a partner perceives a collaboration opportunity as beneficial, its intention or willingness to collaborate increases, otherwise it decreases. Other aspects which account for willingness to collaborate are the perceived risks, external incentives, or the presence of a fierce competition.

This work proposes an approach to assess organizations' willingness to collaborate. It follows a behavioral perspective, based on the Theory of the Planned Behavior [1]. The approach involves the assessment of an organization's attitudes towards collaborating, the external influences, or social incentive/pressure to collaborate, and the perceived control over factors that might facilitate/impede the partner's ability to collaborate. Assessing the willingness to collaborate helps to foresee how well an organization is likely to perform in a partnership.

2 Contribution to Technological Innovation

In spite of its value, this subject has not been well explored yet. An innovative aspect of this work is that it bases the notion of collaboration willingness on the idea of

L.M. Camarinha-Matos, P. Pereira, and L. Ribeiro (Eds.): DoCEIS 2010, IFIP AICT 314, pp. 14–23, 2010.

behavioral beliefs, attitudes and intentions concerning collaboration opportunities. Additionally, a systematic approach for collaboration willingness assessment, with automatic inquiring selection, is also proposed. This concept of collaboration willingness is part of a larger collaboration readiness model [2], as illustrated in Fig. 1.

Fig. 1. The collaboration readiness concept

Each component of the readiness model is characterized as follows:

- **Preparedness** – is based on the concept of organization's character. It aims at assessing whether an organization is likely to display reliable behavior inside partnerships [3]. The greater this likelihood, the greater the preparedness level.
- **Competences fitness** – This concept is seen as a soft versus hard competencies dichotomy. Hard competencies are associated to the achievement of concrete or "physical" outcomes, while soft competencies are more associated to more abstract or intangible ones. Competencies fitness aims at assessing how well an organization uses its hard competencies in a partnership. Their effective use might also require the exercise of certain soft competencies, such as the ability to share knowledge [4].
- **Willingness** – It corresponds to the topic of this paper, and aims at assessing partners' attitudes and intentions to participate in a collaboration opportunity.

Similarly to willingness, an innovative aspect of this collaboration readiness model is that it assumes a behavioral perspective aiming at assess partners readiness to collaborate, helping to increase the likelihood of partnerships success. The establishment of this conceptual basis is fundamental for the development of a new generation of tools to support partner's selection for collaborative networks.

3   Related Research

At first sight, willingness to collaborate should have taken much attention by collaborative networks researchers, given its potential importance for partnerships success. As a matter of fact, a more generic problem, which can be referred as willingness to perform a particular behavior is already a common subject in human behavior studies [5]. However, such is not the case for the area of collaborative networks, as research works addressing organizations' willingness to collaborate are scarce. An example of such a research is [6] where willingness to collaborate is defined as a new communication trait. As such, willingness to collaborate is positively related to a number of traits, such as willingness to communicate, argumentativeness, verbal aggressiveness, interpersonal communication competency, and a relaxed, friendly and attentive communicator style. In [7] it is analyzed the influence of organization's corporate culture, and perceived culture of a particular partner, in order to undertake a shift from a transactional buyer-seller relationship to an intensified collaboration. If there is fitness between own and peer's culture, then willingness to cooperate increases.

Other works could be mentioned here, but are not related to collaboration. The research from [8] is concerned with a firm's willingness to engage in innovation. The research in [9], addresses a firms' willingness to adopt cleaner technologies.

The topic of willingness to collaborate seems to be an unexplored subject in the field of collaborative networks.

4   Modeling Willingness to Collaborate

As mentioned before, willingness to collaborate is concerned with assessing a partner's attitudes and intentions towards concrete collaboration situations. A theory that seems to be useful here is the Theory of the Planned Behavior (TPB) proposed by Ajzen [1]. Therefore, before introducing the proposed approach, a brief introduction to *TPB* is made.

The Theory of the Planned Behavior. Many works from social sciences aiming at predicting people's behavior are based on the Theory of Planned Behavior. This theory aims at predicting the people's willingness to engage in a particular behavior. According to this theory, human action is guided by three kinds of considerations:

- Behavioral beliefs, which correspond to beliefs about the likely outcomes from performing such behavior, and the evaluation of these outcomes.
- Normative beliefs, which correspond to beliefs about the normative expectations of the surrounding environment (other people, the group, or society) and the motivation to comply with these expectations.
- Control beliefs, which correspond to beliefs about the presence of factors that may facilitate or impede the performance of the behavior, and the perceived power of these factors.

In their respective aggregates, the behavioral beliefs produce a favorable or unfavorable attitude towards the behavior in question; normative beliefs result in perceived social pressure or subjective norm towards performing the behavior; and control beliefs give rise to perceived behavioral control. In combination, these factors lead to the formation of a behavioral intention. According to TPB, this intention is assumed to be the immediate antecedent or predictor of the behavior [1].

The adopted assumption is that *TPB* can also be considered suitable for predicting the organizations' behaviors. This suitability lies in the assumption that organizations behave like rational agents, making systematic use of the available information, in order to decide which goals to pursuit. These goals are achieved through corresponding business processes, usually established at a strategic level. Assuming that organization's strategic planning is based on goals to be achieved suggests that these goals can be seen as organizations' intentions to perform the corresponding behaviors. In other words, they correspond to the organizations' planned behavior [8]. As a result, if an organization's intentions are based on goals to be achieved, and if organization's behaviors are in turn a consequence of these intentions, then the TPB can be applied to organizations in order to predict their behavior. Consequently, TPB can be used to assess organizations' willingness to collaborate.

The collaboration willingness model. The assessment of the willingness to collaborate depends on the perception of an organization's intentions concerning a particular collaboration opportunity *(CO)* and other factors, named as background factors, which are illustrated in Fig. 2. These intentions in turn depend on the organization's attitudes, social influence or incentives, and the perceived control over the collaboration opportunity and these factors. The proposed model for willingness to collaborate follows a structure that is compliant with TPB.

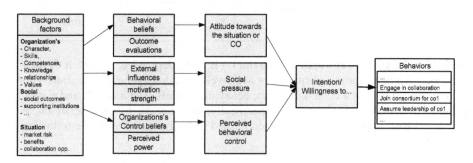

Fig. 2. Willingness to collaborate model

In order to keep the presented model as generic as the *TPB* in the definitions below, we consider not only the "willingness to collaborate" behavior, but also other behaviors related to collaboration, as illustrated on the right side of Fig. 2. Additionally, in order to illustrate the definitions below, some examples of queries are presented near each definition. These examples aim at assessing an organization's willingness to "engage in a partnership".

Definition 1 (Background factors) – Are the aspects relevant to the perception of an organization's intentions to collaborate in a specific collaboration opportunity.

Definition 2 (Organization's Behavioral beliefs) – Correspond to beliefs that a behavior (e.g. engaging in a partnership) will provide a number of expected outcomes (e.g. higher profit or the access to an extended market). Each behavioral belief is specified by a subjective probability that the corresponding outcome will be achieved. It can be specified as a set of tuples $\{(bb_i, v_i) \mid bb_i \in BB, v_i \in [0,1]\}$, in which:

- bb_i - identifies a belief about an outcome from the behavior in question.
- v_i – corresponds to a belief strength, or subjective probability, of the corresponding outcome being achieved.
- $BB=\{bb_1, bb_2, ...\}$ – represents the set of identified behavioral beliefs concerning collaboration behaviors.

The organization believes that engaging in the partnership will allow growing abroad.							
Extremely unlikely					X			Extremely likely
	1	2	3	4	5	6	7

Definition 3 (Outcome appraisal) – It represents how an organization values the outcome associated to each behavioral belief in *Definition 2*. It can be specified as a set $\{(oa_i, v_i) \mid oa_i \in OA, v_i \in [0,1]\}$, in which for each tuple:

- oa_i, - specifies the outcome associated to the behavioral belief bb_i in *Definition 2*.
- v_i - represents a subjective appraisal of the expected outcome.
- $OA=\{oa_1, oa_2, \ldots\}$ – represents the set of outcomes, each related one-by-one to a behavioral belief specified in *Definition 2*.

The organization thinks growing abroad is							
Not important					X			Very important
	1	2	3	4	5	6	7

Definition 4 (Attitude towards a behavior) – It is the degree 'A_b' to which the performance of a behavior b is positively or negatively valuated by the organization. This value is determined as a composite of the behavioral beliefs (*Definition 2*) and corresponding evaluations (*Definition 3*). Specifically, the strength of each belief bb_i is weighted by the appraisal oa_i of the outcome, and then aggregated using the following equation:

$$A_b = \frac{1}{n \times (\#scale)^2} \times \sum_{i=1}^{n} \pi_2[(bb_i, v_i)] \times \pi_2[(oa_i, v_i)] \tag{1}$$

The first part of the above equation, and for the next ones, transforms the result into a percentage format. The symbol (#scale) stands for the size of the used scale. For instance, if the scale is defined as scale=$\{1, 2, 3, 4, 5, 6, 7\}$, then (#scale)=7. Additionally, π_2 stands for the algebraic projection, which retrieves the second element of the corresponding tuple given as argument.

Definition 5 (External stimulus or influences) – Are used to represent external influences, which favor or disfavor the performance of the behavior in question, such as engaging in a partnership. It can be specified as a set $\{(es_i, v_i) \mid es_i \in ES, v_i \in [0,1]\}$, in which for each tuple:

- es_i – identifies an external stimulus for the behavior in question
- v_i – specifies the degree of belief in that stimulus.
- $ES=\{es_1, es_2, \ldots\}$ – represents the external stimulus or influences, which potentially influence the organization in the performance of the considered behavior.

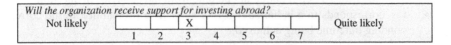

Will the organization receive support for investing abroad?							
Not likely			X					Quite likely
	1	2	3	4	5	6	7

Definition 6 (Motivation to comply) – Establishes the degree or strength of motivation to which an organization complies with the external influences (*Definition 5*) over the performance of the behavior. It can be specified as a set $\{(mc_i, v_i) \mid mc_i \in MC, v_i \in [0,1]\}$, in which for each tuple:

- mc_i – identifies a motivation to comply with the external stimulus es_i specified in *Definition 5*.
- v_i – Its corresponding motivation strength.
- $MC=\{mc_1,mc_2, ...\}$ – The motivators associated to the performance of a behavior.

How important is receiving support to invest aboard for this organization?							
Not important						X		Very important
	1	2	3	4	5	6	7

Definition 7 (Social influence) – It corresponds to the composite aggregation of each external stimulus with the corresponding motivations to comply. Specifically, the strength of each external stimulus es_i is weighted by motivation to comply mc_i, using the following equation:

$$SI_b = \frac{1}{n \times (\#scale)^2} \sum_{i=1}^{n} \pi_2[(es_i, v_i)] \times \pi_2[(mc_i, v_i)] \qquad (2)$$

Definition 8 (Organization's control beliefs) – It is concerned with the beliefs an organization has got on the factors that may facilitate or impede the performance of the behavior. It can be specified as a set $\{(cb_i, v_i) \mid cb_i \in CB, v_i \in [0,1]\}$, in which for each tuple:

- cb_i – identifies a control factor that may facilitate, or impede, the performance of the behavior.
- v_i – the subjective probability that the corresponding factor is present.
- $CB=\{cb_1, cb_2, ...\}$ – The identified control beliefs set associated to the performance of the behavior.

Is the organization prepared to operate abroad?							
Not likely				X				Quite likely
	1	2	3	4	5	6	7

Definition 9 (Perceived power) – Corresponds to the perceived value of each control factor, as specified in *Definition 8*. It can be specified as a set $\{(pp_i, v_i) \mid pp_i \in PP, v_i \in [0,1]\}$, in which for each tuple:

- pp_i – identifies the perceived power for the control factor in the corresponding control belief cb_i specified in *Definition 8*.
- v_i – the value for the corresponding pp_i.
- $PP=\{pp_1,pp_2, ...\}$ – The identified perceived power set associated to the performance of the behavior.

Is preparedness to operate abroad a main concern?								
much						X		Not much[1]
	1	2	3	4	5	6	7	

Definition 10 (Perceived behavioral control) – It refers to the organization's perceptions on its capability to perform the behavior. This element is determined by the
aggregation of the control beliefs with the perceived power of each one. Specifically,
the strength of each control belief cb_i is weighted by the perceived power pp_i, and the
products are aggregated using the following equation:

$$PBC_b = \frac{1}{n \times (\#scale)^2} \sum_{i=1}^{n} \pi_2[(cb_i, v_i)] \times \pi_2[(pp_i, v_i)] \tag{3}$$

Definition 11 (Organization's willingness to collaborate) – According to TPB,
intention to collaborate can be taken as a direct measure of the willingness to collaborate. Intention is based on the attitude toward the behavior (*Definition 4*), the social
influences (*Definition 7*), and perceived behavioral control (*Definition 10*). Each of
these factors is weighted or adjusted taking into consideration the behavior or situations. Its value can be computed by a function

$$I = F(ATB, SI, PBC) = w_1*ATB + w_2*SI + w_3*PBC. \tag{4}$$

$$W \sim I$$

The weights w_1, w_2 and w_3 represent correlation coefficients. They indicate to which
extent the values of *ATB*, *SI* and *PBC* influence the willingness to collaborate level.
Their determination requires a separated pilot study, in which a questionnaire sent to
organizations, which participated in previous partnerships, would allow determine the
correlation between these values and the the willingness to collaborate level. This
determination is typically made using correlation or regression analysis.

The values of attitude A_b, social influence SB_b and perceived behavioral control PCB_b
for the provided examples can be obtained, using the above definitions, as following:

$$\begin{cases} A_{\text{engage in the partnership}} = \dfrac{1}{1 \times 49} \times 4 \times 5 = 0.41 \\[2mm] SI_{\text{engage in the partnership}} = \dfrac{1}{1 \times 49} \times 3 \times 6 = 0.37 \\[2mm] PCB_{\text{engage in the partnership}} = \dfrac{1}{1 \times 49} \times 4 \times 6 = 0.49 \end{cases} \tag{5}$$

Assuming the weight values as $w_1=0.33$, $w_2=0.33$ and $w_3=0.33$, the level of the willingness to collaborate is

$$W \sim I_{\text{engage in the partnership}} = 0.33*(0.41 + 0.37 + 0.49) = 42\% \tag{6}$$

The Intentions Query Mechanism. In order to provide a systematic way of assessing
the willingness to collaborate, a tool named Intentions Query Mechanism (*IQM*) was

---

[1] The scale used in this example is inverted to ensure that the right side always reflects a positive attitude.

developed. From the description of a collaboration opportunity, this tool selects the a set of possible questions to be asked, in order to assess willingness to collaborate. The approach used to develop the *IQM* is based on a Prolog knowledge-base, which manages an experts' repository of questions. These questions are used to enquire partners' attitudes towards collaboration-related behaviors and expected outcomes. From the text description of a given collaboration opportunity, the tool detects the semantic relationships between the terms used in the CO description and the questions stored in the repository. Each time the tool finds a match, the corresponding term is highlighted, as illustrated in Fig. 3. The discovery of the semantic relationships is performed with using WordNet, a large network of semantic relations between English words [10]. An example of a semantic relationship is between the words "listen" and "perceive", for which WordNet stores the fact that "to perceive" is a *hypernym* of "to listen".

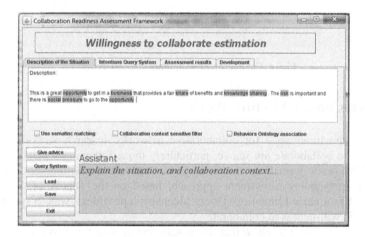

Fig. 3. Describing the collaboration opportunity

The highlighted terms are subsequently used to select the specific questions from the knowledge-base, which is presented to a concerned user for the necessary answers, as illustrated in

Fig. 4. These questions are specified according to the definitions presented in previous section. As they aim at evaluating subjective behavioral beliefs, the corresponding answers do not require strict crisp values.

Finally, these values are provided as input to the TPB part and the result is a number, which represents the organization's willingness level to collaborate, as specified in *Definition 11*. Using this definition, the willingness to collaborate level for the organization in the example is 50.96%, as shown in Fig. 5. An interpretation of this result for a concrete organization could be that this organization's willingness to engage in a given collaboration opportunity is not appreciably high.

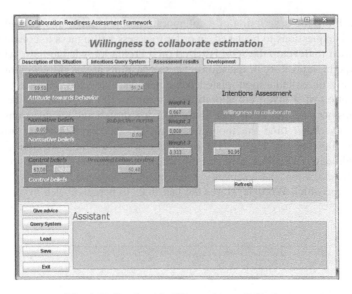

Fig. 4. Estimation of willingness to collaborate

5   Conclusions and Future Work

In spite of the importance for collaborative networks, research works concerning willingness to collaborate are scarce, particularly those following a behavioral perspective. This work formalized this concept of collaboration willingness, and introduced a corresponding assessment approach, based on the Theory of the Planned Behavior. A tool named Intentions Query Mechanism provides a way to systematically assess this willingness to collaborate.

The preliminary results show that this assessment approach is feasible and promising. Nevertheless, further research is needed to improve it into a more complete assessment model.

Acknowledgments. This work was supported in part by the Portuguese "Fundação para a Ciência e a Tecnologia" through PhD scholarship.

References

1. Ajzen, I.: The theory of planned behavior. Organizational behavior and human decision processes 50, 179–211 (1991)
2. Rosas, J., Camarinha-Matos, L.M.: An approach to assess collaboration readiness. International Journal of Production Research 47, 4711–4735 (2009)
3. Rosas, J., Camarinha-Matos, L.M.: Modeling collaboration preparedness assessment. In: Collaborative Networks: Reference Modeling. Springer, US (2008)
4. Rosas, J., Macedo, M., Camarinha-Matos, L.M.: An Organization's extended (Soft) Competencies Model. In: Camarinha-Matos, L.M., Paraskakis, I., Afsarmanesh, H. (eds.) PRO-VE 2009. IFIP AICT, vol. 307. Springer, Heidelberg (2009)

5. Ajzen, I.: From intentions to actions: A theory of planned behavior. In: Kuhl, J., Beckmann, J. (eds.) Action control: From cognition to behavior, pp. 11–39. Springer, New York (1985)
6. Anderson, C.M., Martin, M.M., Infante, D.A.: Decision-making collaboration scale: Tests of validity. Communication Research Reports 15, 245–255 (1998)
7. Claudia, K., Michael, L.: Philipps: Corporate culture and its impact on the willingness to cooperate in the distribution channel: conceptualization and empirical finding in the German hospital industry. University of Marburg
8. Corral, C.M.: Explaining and predicting the innovative behaviour of the firm: a behavioural approach
9. Montalvo Corral, C.: Sustainable production and consumption systems—cooperation for change: assessing and simulating the willingness of the firm to adopt/develop cleaner technologies. The case of the In-Bond industry in northern Mexico. Journal of cleaner production 11, 411–426 (2003)
10. George, A.M.: WordNet: a lexical database for English. Commun. ACM 38, 39–41 (1995)

Business and IS/IT Strategic Alignment Framework

Llanos Cuenca, Angel Ortiz, and Andres Boza

Research Centre on Production Management and Engineering, Universidad Politécnica de
Valencia, Camino de Vera, s/n 46022 Valencia, Spain
{llcuenca,aortiz,aboza}@cigip.upv.es

Abstract. Incorporating information systems and information technology
(IS/IT) in the organizations have considerable risks, and these risks are increased when a strategic plan for its incorporation is not done. The objective of
this research is to contribute in the alignment between business and IS/IT
strategies using concepts and techniques from engineering and enterprise architecture. To achieve this objective, this research proposes to define a modeling
framework for business and IS/IT strategic alignment. The implementation of
this proposal in a ceramic tile company has helped to validate its usefulness.

Keywords: Strategic alignment, framework, business, IS/IT, enterprise
engineering.

1 Introduction

The current economic conditions and the high level of market uncertainty, forces the
companies to be in a continuous adaptation to respond constant changes. Information
systems and information technology (IS/IT) are crucial, bringing added value to business or even changing the way we carry them out. Enterprise architecture, considered
as the foundation of enterprise systems engineering, has emerged as a 'tool' to help
stakeholders to manage system engineering and changes. It is not only an IT issue, but
first of all a strategic and organizational challenge [1]. Aligning IS/IT and business
strategy is a key in maintaining business value [2], [3], [4], [5]. This alignment is not
easy, neither in its conceptualization [6], [7], [8], nor in its accomplishment [7]. In
fact, the lack of this alignment has been the reason for not achieve the improvement
expected through their investments in IS/IT [9], [2], [10], [11].

The main purpose of this research is to improve the alignment between business
and IS/IT strategies, making use of enterprise engineering. Modeling IS/IT by building blocks allows facilitating alignment with the business since the early phases of life
cycle and incorporating the building blocks in enterprise architectures.

2 Contribution to Technological Innovation

Technological innovation can improve competitiveness of a company. This competitiveness improves when add value is included in all business process. IS/IT allows

L.M. Camarinha-Matos, P. Pereira, and L. Ribeiro (Eds.): DoCEIS 2010, IFIP AICT 314, pp. 24–31, 2010.
© IFIP International Federation for Information Processing 2010

making better this value chain improving the enterprise processes or defining new processes changing the way companies do business. In this sense, it is important to define and to align business and IS/IT strategy. In this paper two disciplines are combined, IS/IT strategic planning and enterprise architecture.

3 Related Work

Enterprise Engineering (EE) allows understanding, defining, specifying, designing, analyzing, and implementing business processes for the entire life cycle, so that the enterprise can achieve its objectives [12], [13]. Enterprise Architecture (EA) is the discipline of designing enterprises guided with principles, frameworks, methodologies, requirements, tools, reference models and standards. EA is a set of descriptive representations that are relevant for describing an enterprise such that it can be produced to management's requirements and maintained over its period of useful life [14], [15]. The alignment is the degree of fit and integration among business strategy, IT strategy, business infrastructure, and IT infrastructure [2]. The works analyzed in this research include enterprise architecture (Zachman [14], TOGAF [16], EAP [17], DoD AF [18], CIMOSA [19], GERAM [20] e IE-GIP [21]), strategic alignment models (Henderson y Venkatraman [2], Luftman [22], Maes [23], Santana [24]) and works on both subjects [25], [26], [27], [28], [29], [30], [31], [32].

3.1 Critical Analysis

Enterprise architecture frameworks organize, manage and interrelates a wide variety of models used to structure and operate an enterprise by taking into account all possible views. A modeling view is a representation of a whole system from the perspective of a related set of concerns [33], [20]. All the analyzed Enterprise Architectures contain views in their frameworks, however, life cycle, building blocks, and how the building blocks fit together, is not defined by all of them. Life cycle is related to the life cycle of the entity being modeled. The life cycle of an enterprise model is the result of the model development process by which models are created, made operational and finally discarded [34]. A building block is a primitive component (with syntax and semantics) of a modeling language [12].

This analysis has allowed defining different views: Business, Resource, Organization, Information, Data, Application and Technological Views. The proposal maintains, in most cases, a definition according to the architectures analyzed. In case of differences between similar views of different architectures its redefinition has been necessary. Business View contains business process and business entity in a company; Resource View contains capabilities and resources; Organization View includes organization levels, authority and responsibility; Information View contains input and output process; Data View defines types and data sources needed to support the information view; Application View identifies the application needs and data presentation; Technological View determines the technology to use and defines how this technology should be used. The starting point for the analysis of the life cycle phases was CIMOSA, IE-GIP, EAP and TOGAF, because they are the most complete. CIMOSA and IE-GIP do not provide concepts related to information systems and technologies in earlier phases. Neither do they include aspects related to the conceptualization of IS/IT. Moreover, the business model of EAP does not include TO-BE process definition and does not establish an action plan. In this sense, IE-GIP is more complete. This action plan is partially covered in TOGAF but is mainly directed by business strategy.

Formal definition is less common in strategic alignment models, in this sense; they do not include building blocks nor life cycle phases. Hence, it is not possible its definition under the enterprise engineering approach, which is solved in this proposal.

4   Business and IS/IT Strategic Alignment Framework

The proposed business and IS/IT strategic alignment framework has been included in the CIMOSA [19] and IE-GIP [21] modeling framework, new life cycle phases and building blocks. Three new phases have been defined: Business and IS/IT conceptualization, Business Process and IS/IT definition and Business and IS/IT master plan. New building blocks are defined for these phases and integrated with the other building blocks [36] (Fig.1).

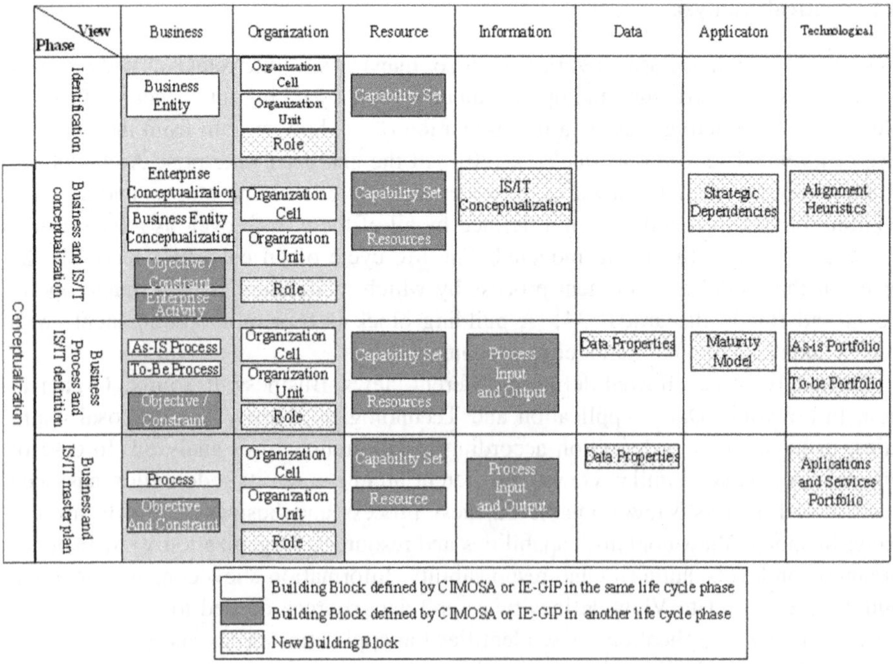

Fig. 1. Business and IS/IT strategic alignment framework

The definition of the building blocks of CIMOSA and IE-GIP is detailed in [19] and [21]. The new building blocks are:

- Role: Represents the profile required to undertake a task. It can be assigned to an organizational unit, a business process or an enterprise activity building block. The roles will be used in the modeling phases where these building blocks will be used. The roles are assigned to the organization view.
- IS/IT Conceptualization: Indicates whether the IS/IT strategy and its alignment with the business has been completed. The constructor is used in the conceptualization phase and it is associated with the information view.
- Alignment heuristics: The purpose is to detect possible failures in the alignment. The constructor is used in the conceptualization phase and it is associated with the technological view.
- Strategic dependencies: It is based in I * framework [37]. The purpose is to detect dependencies between actors, roles, organization unit, organization cell or set of roles that depends on another role. The constructor is used in the conceptualization phase and it is associated with the application view.
- As-IS portfolio: The purpose of the as-is portfolio is to support the information associated with each application and its relationship with as-is business objectives. It is used in the business process and IS/IT definition phase. It is associated with the technological view.
- To-Be portfolio: The purpose of the to-be portfolio is to support the information associated with each application and its relationship with to-be business objectives. There must be at least a relationship with a business objective. It is used in the business process and IS/IT definition phase. It is associated with the technological view.
- Maturity Model: It is based on the maturity models of Luftman [22] and Santana [24] and allows you to define the maturity level of strategic alignment. It is used in the business process and IS/IT definition phase. It is associated with the application view. The alignment will be assessed using a rating scheme of five levels. Level 1: No Alignment, Level 2: Beginning Process, Level 3: Establishing Process, Level 4: Improved Process, Level 5: Complete Alignment.
- Data properties: It defines the properties for the inputs and outputs of process, identifying the type and source of data and storage, retrieval and data availability. It is used in the business process and IS/IT definition phase. It is associated with the data view.
- Application and services portfolio: The applications and services portfolio include those that have been identified in the to-be portfolio and those who remain in the as-is portfolio. It is used in the master plan phase and is associated with the application view.

4.1 Building Block Templates and Relations

Each building block is represented with a template [34], [35]. Figure 2 shows the maturity model building block.

Type:
Name:
Identification: MM-
Design Responsible: U- responsible for designing and maintaining this building block

Stakeholder: U- o C- stakeholder of the business entity on which the maturity analysis takes place
Business Entity: Name or ID
Criterion: Criteria selected
Attribute: Attributes of criteria analyzed
Level: [1..5] Level assigned
Responsible: U- o C- responsible for assigning the attribute level
Review Date: The date that is discussed or reviewed and the corresponding attribute is assigned a
    level of maturity.
Final assigned level: Nil or level.
Average level of criteria for stakeholder: value
Average level of criteria for the business entity: value

Fig. 2. Maturity model template

In addition, to ensure the modeling framework integrity, the building blocks are related to each other. The following figure shows the relationship in the business and IS/IT conceptualization phase and the contents of some building blocks.

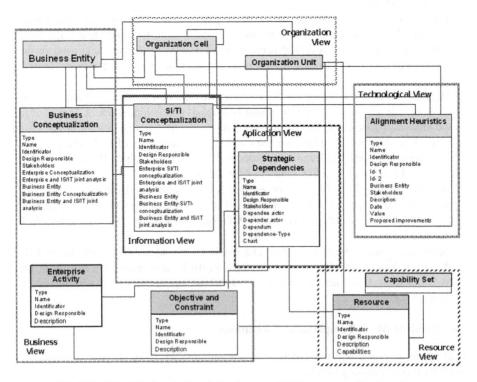

Fig. 3. Building blocks relations in business and IS/IT conceptualization phase

5 Case Study

The proposed modeling framework has been applied in a ceramic tile company. It was necessary several interviews with the managers appointed by the company, and the outcome of these interviews was concretized in the templates associated with each building block. The business entity selected was the collaborative order management because is a critical process for the company. Information systems and information technology are essential to support this process.

The business and IS/IT conceptualization was carried out after identifying business entity. With the definition of the alignment heuristic at this stage was possible to identify aspects that had not been well resolved in the conceptualization. The strategic dependencies model has helped to identify the dependencies between macro-level actors, which have allowed detecting bottlenecks and vulnerabilities. The business processes and IS / IT definition phase started when the conceptualization phase was concluded. Among other benefits, the application and services portfolio has enabled linking the enterprise business processes to applications and services at the macro level through goals. Also, this has allowed a prioritization of the applications. The maturity model has allowed a detailed analysis of the alignment between business and IS / IT, with an allocation of values from one to five, where one represents the lowest value. For the company, the result was less than two, which represents an emerging alignment. This encouraged the company to improve some aspects. An example of a template (the Portfolio application template) is shown below (Fig 4).

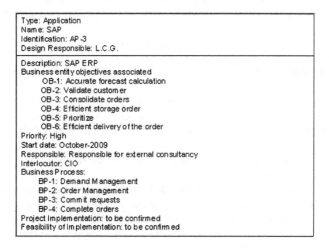

Fig. 4. Portfolio application template

6 Conclusions and Future Lines

This paper puts forward the needs for a consistent and integrated modeling framework to incorporate the information, resources, data, and technological views in the early life cycle phase to facilitate strategic alignment. The analysis of strategic alignment models has allowed to identify the elements needed for strategic planning of IS/IT and its alignment with the business strategy. These elements have been defined by building blocks and incorporated into CIMOSA and IE-GIP modeling frameworks.

This research presents a significant contribution to enterprise architecture field. The application to a ceramic tile company has helped to validate the usefulness of the proposed modeling framework. This research is part of ongoing research in enterprise engineering field. Future lines of work are raised by the definition of ontology for the proposed modeling framework. A second line of work is proposed to integrate this proposal with the performance measurement architecture and its associated information system, ensuring alignment with business strategy. Finally life cycle phases can be extended to those aspects based on a cyclical methodology for business reengineering.

References

1. Chen, D., Doumeningts, G., Vernadat, F.: Architectures for enterprise integration and interoperability: past, present and future. Computers in industry 59, 647–659 (2008)
2. Henderson, J.C., Venkatraman, N.: Strategic alignment: Leveraging information technology for transforming organizations. IBM systems journal 32(1), 472–484 (1993)
3. Hirschheim, R., Sabherwal, R.: Detours in the Path toward Strategic Information Systems Alignment. California Management Review, Fall 44(1), 87–108 (2001)
4. Sabherwal, R., Chan, Y.: Alignment between Business and IS Strategies. Information Systems Research 12(1), 11–33 (2001)
5. Peppard, J., Breu, K.: Beyond Alignment: A coevolutionary view of the information systems strategy process. In: Twenty-fourth International Conference on Information Systems (2003)
6. Ciborra, C.U.: De profundis? Deconstructing the concept of strategic alignment. Scandinavian journal of Information Systems 9(1), 67–82 (1997)
7. Scott, G.M.: Still not solved: the persistent problem of IT strategic planning. Communications of the Association for Information Systems 16, 904–936 (2005)
8. Silvius, G.A.J.: Business and IT alignment in theory and practice. In: Proceedings of the 40th Hawaii International Conference on Systems Sciences, Hawaii (2007)
9. King, W.R.: Strategic Planning for Management Information Systems. MIS quarterly 2(1), 27 (1978)
10. Papp, R.: Business-IT alignment:productivity paradox payoff? Industrial Management & Data Systems 99(8), 367–373 (1999)
11. Bleistein, S.J., Cox, K., Verner, J., Phalp, K.T.: B-SCP: A requirements analysis framework for validating strategic alignment of organizational IT based on strategy, context, and process. Information and Software Technology 48, 846–868 (2006)
12. Vernadat, F.: Enterprise Modeling and Integration. In: Principles and applications. Chapman & Hall, Boca Raton (1996)
13. Berio, G., Vernadat, F.: Enterprise modelling with CIMOSA: Functional and organizational aspects. Production Planning Control 12(2), 128 (2001)
14. Zachman, J.A.: Concepts of the framework for enterprise architecture. Zachman International Inc.,
    http://members.ozemail.com.au/~visible/papers/zachman3.htm
15. Zachman, J.A.: Enterprise architecture — a framework, http://www.zifa.com
16. TOGAF The Open Group Architecture Framework,
    http://www.opengroup.org/togaf/

17. Spewak, S.: Enterprise Architecture Planning: Developing a Blueprint for Data, Applications, and Technology. Wiley, Chichester (1993)
18. DoD Architecture Framework. Version 1.5. Volume I: Definitions and Guidelines,. DoD Architecture framework Version 1.5.,
    http://www.defenselink.mil/cio-nii/docs
19. CIMOSA: Open System Architecture for CIM. 2nd extended revised version. Springer, Berlin (1993)
20. IFIP-IFAC Task Force, GERAM: Generalized Enterprise Reference Architecture and Methodology, Version 1.6.2, Annex to ISO WD15704, IFIP-IFAC Task Force (1999)
21. Ortiz, A., Lario, F., Ros, L.: IE-GIP. A proposal for a Methodology to Develop Enterprise Integration Program. Computers in Industry 40, 155–171 (1999)
22. Luftman, J.: Assessing business-it alignment maturity. Communications of the association for information systems 4(14) (2000)
23. Maes, R.: A Generic Framework for Information Management. Prime Vera Working Paper, Universiteit Van Amsterdam (1999)
24. Santana, R.G., Daneva, M., van Eck, P.A.T., Wieringa, R.J.: Towards a business-IT alignment maturity model for collaborative networked organizations. In: Proceedings of the International Workshop on Enterprise Interoperability Munich, Germany, pp. 70–81 (2008)
25. Wilton, D.: The Relationship Between IS Strategic Planning and Enterprise Architectural Practice, pp. 100–107 (2004)
26. Wegmann, A., Balabko, P., Le, L., Reveg, G., Rychkova, I.: A Method and Tool for Business-IT Alignment. In: Enterprise Architecture Proceedings of the caise, Porto Univ., Porto, Portugal (2005)
27. Pereira, C., Sousa, P.: Enterprise Architecture: Business and IT Alignment. In: ACM Symposium on Applied Computing (2005)
28. Lindström, A.: An Approach for Developing Enterprise-Specific ICT Management Methods – from Architectural Principles to Measures (2006)
29. Versteeg, G., Bouwman, H.: Business architecture: A new paradigm to relate business strategy to ICT. Inf. Syst. Front 8, 91–102 (2006)
30. Plazaola, L., Flores, J., Silva, E., Vargas, N., Ekstedt, M.: An Approach to Associate Strategic Business-IT Alignment Assessment to Enterprise Architecture. In: Conference on Systems Engineering Research, Stevens Institute of Technology Campus, USA (2007)
31. Gammelgård, M., Simonsson, M., Lindström, A.: An IT management assessment framework: evaluating enterprise architecture scenarios. Inf. Syst. E-Business Management 5(4), 415–435 (2007)
32. Wang, X., Zhou, X., Jiang, L.: A method of business and IT alignment based on enterprise architecture (2008)
33. Martin, R., Robertson, E.: Frameworks: comparison and correspondence for three archetypes (2002)
34. EN/ISO 19439 Enterprise integration — Framework for enterprise modeling (2006)
35. EN/ISO 19440 Enterprise integration — Constructor for enterprise modeling (2007)
36. Cuenca Ll., Ortiz A., Boza, A.: Marco arquitectónico para la propuesta IE-GIP. Extensión de la Arquitectura CIMOSA. Aplicación a una empresa del sector cerámico. Universidad Politécnica de Valencia. PhD thesis (2009)
37. Yu, E.: Modeling Strategic Relationships for Process Reengineering. PhD thesis (1995)

Part 2

Issues in Information Systems

Introduction of Empirical Topology in Construction of Relationship Networks of Informative Objects

Hesam T. Dashti[1], Mary E. Kloc[2], Tiago Simas[3], Rita A. Ribeiro[3]
and Amir H. Assadi[1,*]

[1] Department of Mathematics, University of Wisconsin, USA
dashti@wisc.edu, ahassadi@wisc.edu
[2] Department of Applied Mathematics and Computer Science,
Weizmann Institute of Science, Israel
mary-elizabeth.kloc@weizmann.ac.il
[3] CA3, Uninova, Campus New University of Lisbon/FC, Portugal
tms@uninova.pt, rar@uninova.pt

Abstract. Understanding the structure of relationships between objects in a given database is one of the most important problems in the field of data mining. The structure can be defined for a set of single objects (clustering) or a set of groups of objects (network mapping). We propose a method for discovering relationships between individuals (single or groups) that is based on what we call the *empirical topology*, a system-theoretic measure of functional proximity. To illustrate the suitability and efficiency of the method, we apply it to an astronomical data base.

Keywords: Euler method for differential equation, clustering, network mapping, genetic algorithm, computational astronomy.

1 Introduction

Determining the interrelationships of objects belonging to either a given data set (clustering) or networks (network mapping) is a central problem in many fields, including data mining (web mining, unsupervised classification) [1][2], computational biology (quantitative trait loci, analysis of gene expression profiles [3] and protein-protein interaction networks [7]), and computational astronomy (clustering profiles of variable stars, determining types of planets by luminosity clustering [4][5][6]). This motivates research groups in diverse areas to develop new practical methodologies.

The process of clustering or network mapping requires a similarity measure for grouping individuals; this measurement should be defined on the space of attributes of the individuals. The manner in which databases are constructed and individuals are grouped is strongly dependent on the aim of the researchers; for example, for finding similar types of stars in computational astronomy [8] [9], the individuals could be the

---

* The author gratefully acknowledges partial financial support through NSF Grants DMS-0923296 and DBI-0621702.

L.M. Camarinha-Matos, P. Pereira, and L. Ribeiro (Eds.): DoCEIS 2010, IFIP AICT 314, pp. 35–43, 2010.
© IFIP International Federation for Information Processing 2010

observed objects in the sky and the attributes could be the parameters that describe the individuals. Alternatively, for determining the most significant parameters (a feature reduction problem, in general), the individuals could be the parameters and the attributes could be the different types of stars. Hence, the similarity measure is strongly dependent on the types and roles of individuals and attributes in the given problem.

When analyzing data sets pertaining to individuals and attributes, two main issues must be considered: the level of noise in the data, and the size of the data sets. In general, noise reduction methods are database-dependent; there is no practical noise reduction algorithm for all types of databases and all types of noise. Some algorithms [10][11] focus on specific kinds of databases (and associated noisy data), while others incorporate some flexibility in order to deal with different kinds of noisy data. Also, there are now many improved clustering algorithms that are suitable for use on very large data sets, as designing algorithms with lower time complexity has been a central focus in computer science from the beginning [12].

In this paper, we propose a new method for Discovering Relationship Networks based on Empirical Topology (*ET-DRN*). The ET-DRN method is a procedure for grouping individuals (in both clustering and network-mapping problems) that can deal with many types of noisy data. It is a hierarchical clustering procedure that composed of three different algorithms: 1) the Euler algorithm is used to assign the individuals to groups, 2) a Genetic algorithm is used to increase density (as measured using the Shannon entropy) of individuals inside group and, 3) the dissimilarity of the groups is determined using the Kullback-Leibler (KL) divergence. One can easily generalize and adapt this procedure by replacing KL-divergence by a different information-theoretic variant. The ET-DRN algorithm clusters a given data set by dividing it into groups of objects where elements of each group have minimum possible entropy and the groups have maximum distance between them.

We use an astronomy database to evaluate the suitability of the ET-DRN; in this case, the aim is to discover relationships between stars observed by the OGLE project [13]. The objects (individuals) are observed in a special period of time and positions of the objects rather than the earth construct a time series in its dynamic space. Based on the time series and the color of the objects in the sky, 13 attributes are determined for each object, as shown in Table 1. A comprehensive description of the attributes can be found in [14]. As described in Table 1, the attributes are basically calculations of different layers (e.g. first frequency of first harmonic, first frequency second harmonic), so normalization of the data is necessary to obtain a single feature space. The ET-DRN algorithm uses heuristic algorithms that treat the individuals as a discrete collection of measurements and optimize various statistical criteria. It takes advantage of a system-theoretic measure of functional proximity (called *empirical topology*) and applies it to the computational astronomy case study by comparing the different observed objects with space-like snapshots (intervals) of the complex dynamical system. Each snapshot is determined by using the Euler method on one attribute a_i. The Shannon entropy is computed for attributes a_{i+1} through a_{13}. Then ET-DRN rearranges the objects of each snapshot to reduce the snapshot's system entropy. Finally, hierarchical clustering is performed on attribute a_{i+1}.

The empirical topology imposes an organization of the astronomical observations that is analogous to the subdivision of a topological space into its connected components. This allows the data to be organized into a network with far fewer nodes (snapshots), where each node encodes the measurements of a particular class of stars. Considering individuals in a high dimensional space and analyzing them as objects of a digital geometry allows us to construct a sensible mathematical structure (to which all of the approaches of computational geometry can be applied) where noisy data and outliers are clearly detectable. In a more general setting, digital geometries can be regarded as finer mathematical structures that are imposed on sets of points arising from discrete samples. *Neighborhood relationships* of collections of observations could be regarded as sets of points in a digital space.

The ET-DRN algorithm handles all objects in the database according to their positions in the space of features. As mentioned, ET-DRN is a hierarchical clustering algorithm that, in each step, reduces the entropy of the system to just one dimension of the feature space and finds intervals of similar objects in the corresponding feature space. Unlike other iterative hierarchical clustering algorithms, the ET-DRN algorithm iterates with attention to the distribution of objects in other dimensions, so in each step it is working on only a small part of the database, focusing on one of the features while paying attention to this feature's relationship with all other features. During the process of reducing the system entropy, the ET-DRN algorithm increases the distance of classes using the Kullback-Leibler divergence which incorporates the probability of connectivity of the objects to determine the more significant classes.

As mentioned before, we applied the ET-DRN algorithm to an astronomical data set, where Simas et. al. [9] had already performed comprehensive study on appropriateness and accuracy of several clustering algorithms to the same set. In their study, they examined the performance of the algorithms at hand based on testing six desirable features; but *none of the outcomes of six algorithms could produce satisfactory results on tests of all six features.* Here we show that beside precision of the ET-DRN algorithm, it satisfies all of the desired features, thus demonstrating a different level of performance that was not hitherto achievable. Therefore, the failure of previous algorithms on the proposed features in [9], is sufficient grounds that we need not compare our algorithm with the other ones, and just demonstrate the ET-DRN properties for satisfying those features.

The Methodology section describes the empirical topology and outlines each step of the algorithm in detail. Section 3 presents results using experimental data that demonstrate the suitability of the ET-DRN for this problem.

2 Contribution to Technological Innovation

Non-supervised clustering algorithms have proved to be of great value in the increasingly data-dependent technological advances. An illustration of this statement is in applications to new and improved medical instrumentation, especially in brain surgery as applied to devastating diseases such as Parkinson's Disease. One of the senior co-authors have two one US patent and another international patent for application of the unsupervised clustering of data formed from brain signals, such as spiking of neurons collected by multi-electrodes [18][19][20]. The specific applications to Deep Brain Stimulation (DBS) are particularly noteworthy, and the results to relieve severe symptoms in Parkinson's patients are truly remarkable and highly praised in literature. Unfortunately, as in all other complex diseases of the nervous system, the applicability of the DBS for Parkinsonian patients through DBS is limited to individual circumstances of the patient and types of the insult to the brain. Nonetheless, such algorithms provide much more precise tools for the neurologists and neurosurgeons to utilize advanced medical instrumentation to advantage.

The unsupervised algorithms in the ET-DRN class presented in this article also fall in that category, as shown in the previously referenced algorithms [18]. The advantages of the ET-DRN approach to design of biomedical data clustering algorithms are in versatility and applicability to massive data sets, thus opening the potential for on-line and real-time analysis of massive data sets that must use many more (neuronal signal) recording channels for improved biomedical applications.

3 Methodology

The ET-DRN algorithm considers objects as points in a digital geometry of the high-dimensional space of their attributes. The process of the hierarchical clustering to reduce the dimension of the space is done by determining snapshots (intervals) of similar objects on each dimension. In other words, on each level of attributes, ET-DRN determines the groups of objects and then finds subgroups on higher levels of attributes. The snapshots are determined by using the Euler method. The Euler method of interpolating a function is applied to a given set of sample points (e.g. two dimensional) of a function and uses no apriori knowledge of the function. It starts from first sample node (start-point) and defines a straight line from the start-point to another point (end-point) where the line connecting these two points satisfies the constraint on slope change. Iteratively, the end-point then becomes the start-point for the next step, and the method is repeated until the last sample point. The groups of points between the start-points and end-points show snapshots (intervals) of the points. These groups, upon definition of the employed constraints, can represent clusters of objects in a given data base, where each sample point is associated with two attributes of an object. The following pseudocode describes the implementation of the Euler method and the employed constraints on it.

```
program EulerConstrain (slope)
    {Assume 'fabs(X)' function returns absolute value of
X. input: FirstIndex, FirstValue, SecondIndex,
SecondValue };
    const  NeperNumber = 2.71;
    var    Power;
begin
    Power = fabs(FirstValue - SecondValue)
*fabs³(FirstIndex - SecondIndex);
    slope = (0.5)*(NeperNumber^Power-1);
end.

program EulerMethod (NumberClasses)
    {Assuming NumberClasses shows number of classes;
ObjectIndex traces on all objects in the given data
```

```
set; this program renews ClassID of all objects. Input:
DataSet};
  const  MaxYears = 10;
  var    ClassNum: Integer;
  begin
    For all ObjectIndex on DataSet
        begin
         if EulerConstrain(ObjectIndex.Index,
            ObjectIndex.Value, ObjectIndex->Next.Index,
            ObjectIndex->Next.Value) > Threshold
            begin
             NumberClasses = NumberClasses + 1;
            end.
          ObjectIndex->Next.ClassID
        end.
  end.
```

As mentioned, the ET-DRN algorithm gradually reduces the dimension of the space of objects using the Euler method. The ET-DRN considers the influence of all attributes on the arrangement of objects (sample points in the Euler method). In each step of the hierarchical clustering, the ET-DRN rearranges the objects of the intervals calculated in the previous step. In each interval, the optimal arrangement is that closest objects settle beside each other, where the measure of closeness of two objects is the L_2 norm of their unreduced attributes. In order to find the best arrangement, ET-DRN assumes that the objects in their digital geometry are cities of the Traveling Salesman Problem (TSP) in high-dimensional space [15]. In fact, the ET-DRN reduces the problem to the TSP and tackles the TSP using the Genetic Algorithm (GA). GA is notable heuristic approach; its convergence was proven by [16]. The topology of the employed GA is described in the comments of the following GA pseudocode:

```
program GA (NewArrangment)
  {Input: Dataset};
  const  MaxYears = 10;
  var    Population: two dimensional array of integer;
  begin
              Population[PopNum];//Population[i]represents
                                 //an arrangement for
                                 //elements of the Dataset

  for i:1..PopNum
    begin
              Fill(Population[i]);//the "Fill" function,
                                 //fills Population[i]
                                 //with a random arrangement
                                 //in normal distribution.

    end.
  While (satisfaction)//will stop when min entropy of
                      //the system reaches to a
```

```
                    //predetermined value or iterates
                    //for a predetermined times.
      begin
            Entropy(Population);//for each arrangement
                                //of the Population
                                //calculates L2 distance
                                //of objects, where
                                //objects are distributed
                                //in the space of
                                //attributes.
            Evolution(Population, EPopulation);
            Entropy(EPopulation);
            RolledWheel(Population, EPopulation);//Based
                            //on rolled wheel method
                            //replace the Population
                            //with a combination of
                            //previous Population and
                            //EPopulation.
  end.
```

The clustering process of ET-DRN is completely flexible and based on a selected threshold in the constraint of Euler method; this allows the clustering approach to find a wide range of numbers of clusters. Typically, this ability is mentioned as a benefit of clustering algorithms, where the algorithm does not need any apriori information about the number of clusters. However, finding an automated approach for monitoring the number of clusters is very important to avoid obtaining insignificant clusters. Cluster monitoring and the ability to merge insignificant classes in order to get a smaller number of meaningful clusters are considered in the ET-DRN algorithm by calculating the Amount of Weights of Relation (AWR) of the clusters.

The AWR of the clusters is the same as distance of clusters from each other and could also be employed for network mapping problems, since this value is a measure of the connectivity of the clusters. In the case of clustering problems, this value is employed to find close clusters and merge them in order to discover significant groups of objects. The ET-DRN calculates the AWR by applying an alternative to the standard Kullback-Leibler divergence formula that we call "Entropic Kullback-Leibler" [Formula.1] to avoid confusion with the established terminology. The Entropic Kullback-Leibler uses entropy values where the traditional Kullback-Leibler formula utilizes probability values. The entropy value for each class comes from result of the GA procedure from previous step.

$$\text{Divergence}(i, j) = \text{Entropy\_i} * \log(\text{Entropy\_i}/\text{Entropy\_j}) \qquad (1)$$

The Kullback-Leibler formula is not symmetric, so the matrix of the AWR values is an asymmetric matrix. One can look at this asymmetric matrix as a weighted directed graph, and any kind of clustering algorithm can be employed for the network mapping problem.

In clustering algorithms, one problem that appears during the process of merging classes is deciding, when two classes are close together, which class should be merged to another one. In the ET-DRN algorithm, this problem is solved by using the attitude of the AWR matrix, where attractions of two classes differ from one class to another: the class more attractions will be absorbed by another class. The following pseudocode shows the method for constructing the AWR matrix:

```
program AWR_Matrix (Matrix: in dimension of
NumberClasses by NumberClasses)

{for a given array "Entropy" that includes entropy
values of all classes}
    var   i: 1..NumberClasses; j:1..NumberClasses

begin
    Matrix[i][j] = Divergence(i, j);
end.
```

4   Experimental Results

To evaluate the ET-DRN algorithm, we started by applying it to a labeled astronomical database [13]. The precision of the algorithm was computed based on the previous labels. In both databases, objects are represented by 13 attributes (Table 1), a discussion of which can be found in [14]. The labeled database includes approximately 10,000 objects, categorized into 9 classes.

Table 1. Name and description of the employed attributes

Name	Description
Log-f1	log of the first frequency
Log-f2	log of the second frequency
Log-af1h1-t	log amplitude first harmonic first frequency
Log-af1h2-t	log amplitude second harmonic first frequency
Log-af1h3-t	log amplitude third harmonic first frequency
Log-af1h4-t	log amplitude fourth harmonic first frequency
Log-af2h1-t	log amplitude first harmonic second frequency
Log-af2h2-t	log amplitude second harmonic second frequency
Log-crf10	amplitude ratio between harmonics of the first frequency
Pdf12	phase difference between harmonics of the first frequency
Varrat	variance ratio before and after first frequency subtraction
B-V	color index
V-I	color index

The precision values were calculated using the well-known True Positive formula (Formula 2). In this formula, "True Positive" is the number of correctly clustered objects and "False Positive" is the number of objects that were clustered incorrectly. This value is computed for each class separately, as listed in Table 2.

$$Precision = True\ Positive/(True\ Positive + False\ Positive) \tag{2}$$

Table 2. Precision values for each class

Class ID	Precision
Class 1	0.987053
Class 2	0.993354
Class 3	0.956856
Class 4	0.690141
Class 5	0.861775
Class 6	0.7625
Class 7	0.520392
Class 8	0.641975
Class 10	0.8610

5   Conclusion

In this paper, we introduced a novel algorithm for constructing relationship networks of data sets of individuals based on a system-theoretic measurement of *functional proximity* (called *empirical topology*).

The method, called ET-DRN, uses heuristic algorithms and performs a hierarchical clustering process on the representative attributes of the individuals. The ET-DRN algorithm was applied to an astronomical database, and its calculated precision was very promising for the de novo clustering problem. In addition, this algorithm was able to discover new relationships within ambiguous and incomplete databases such as the astronomical database using its hierarchical clustering procedure.

The ET-DRN algorithm also allows for the merging of classes based on the value of the Kullback-Leibler divergence, thus increasing its usability and making it independent of any apriori information about the data base. We believe this method can be applied to any kind of database. Since it would be easy to transform into a parallel processing platform, the ET-DRN algorithm can be applied to very large databases, such as biological databases and future astronomical databases from European Space Agency (10^8) [17].

Acknowledgments. We gratefully acknowledge Luis Maro Sarro for discussions that led to an improved understanding of the problem characteristics, and for providing the database and permitting the comparison of our results with his excellent work. Amir Assadi gratefully acknowledges partial financial support through NSF Grants DMS-0923296 and DBI-0621702.

References

1. Han, J., Kamber, M.: Data Mining: Concepts and Techniques. Morgan Kaufmann, San Francisco (2000)
2. Srivastava, J., Cooley, R., Deshpande, M., Tan, P.-N.: Web usage mining: discovery and applications of usage patterns from Web data. ACM SIGKDD Explorations Newsletter 1, 12–23 (2000)

3. Dashti, H.T., Kloc, M., Lee, T., Michelotti, G., Zhang, T., Assadi, A.: InfoMax gene networks constructed from intervention in the animal models of Parkinson's disease. BMC Neuroscience 8, 134 (2007)

4. Zheng-zhong, H., Yu-hua, T.: The fuzzy classification and activity prediction of solar active regions. Chinese Astronomy and Astrophysics 27, 89–93 (2003)

5. Thomas, J., Schulz, H.: Classification of multifluid CP world models. A&A 366, 395–406 (2001)

6. Christlieb, N., Wisotzki, L., Grabhoff, G.: Statistical methods of automatic spectral classification and their application to the Hamburg/ESO Survey. A&A 391, 397–406 (2002)

7. Stelzl, U., Worm, U., Lalowski, M., Haenig, C., Brembeck, F., Goehler, H., Stroedicke, M., Zenkner, M., Schoenherr, A., Koeppen, S., Timm, J., Mintzlaff, S., Abraham, C., Bock, N., Kietzmann, S., Goedde, A., Toksöz, E., Droege, A., Krobitsch, S., Korn, B., Birchmeier, W., Lehrach, H., Wanker, E.E.: A human protein-protein interaction network: a resource for annotating the proteome. Cell 122, 957–968 (2005)

8. Sarro, L.M., Debosscher, J., Aerts, C., López, M.: Comparative clustering analysis of variable stars in the Hipparcos, OGLE Large Magellanic Cloud and CoRoT exoplanet databases. Accepted for publication is Astronomy and Astrophysics (2009)

9. Simas, T., Silva, G., Miranda, B., Moitinho, A., Ribeiro, R.: Knowledge Discovery in Large Data Sets. In: Proceedings of the International Conference: Classification and Discovery in Large Astronomical Surveys, vol. 1082, pp. 196–200 (2008)

10. Peters, R.A.: A new algorithm for image noise reduction using mathematical morphology. IEEE Transactions on Image Processing, vol 4, 554–568 (2002)

11. Brailean, J.C., Kleihorst, R.P., Efstratiadis, S., Katsaggelos, A.K., Lagendijk, R.L.: Noise reduction filters for dynamic image sequences: a review. Proceedings of the IEEE 83, 1272–1292 (2002)

12. Cormen, T.H., Leiserson, C.E., Rivest, R.L., Stein, C.: Introduction to Algorithms, 3rd edn. MIT Press, Cambridge

13. The OGLE official web site, http://ogle.astrouw.edu.pl/

14. Soszynski, I., Udalski, A., Szymanski, M., Kubiak, M., Pietrzynski, G., Wozniak, P., Zebrun, K., Szewczyk, O., Wyrzykowski, L.: The Optical Gravitational Lensing Experiment. Catalog of RR Lyr Stars in the Large Magellanic Cloud. Acta Astronomica 53 (2003)

15. Applegate, D.L., Bixby, R.E., Chvátal, V., Cook, W.J.: The Traveling Salesman Problem: A Computational Study. Princeton University Press, Princeton (2006)

16. Goldberg, D.E.: Genetic Algorithms in Search, Optimization, and Machine Learning. Addison-Wesley Professional, Reading (1989)

17. European Space Agency-GAIA,
http://sci.esa.int/science-e/www/area/index.cfm?fareaid=26

18. Montgomery, E., Huang, H., Assadi, A.: Unsupervised Clustering Algorithm for N-dimensional Data. Journal of Neuroscience Methods 144, 19–24 (2005a)

19. Montgomery, E., Huang, H., Assadi, A.: US Patent No: P04257US. New method that allows unsupervised cluster analysis in n-dimensional space (2005b)

20. Montgomery, E., Huang, H., Assadi, A.: US Patent No: P04257WO. Methods and devices for analysis of clustered data, in particular action potentials (i.e. neuron firing signals in the brain) (2005c)

The TSTS Method in Cultural Heritage Search

Mirosław Stawniak and Wojciech Cellary

Department of Information Technology, Poznań University of Economics
{stawniak,cellary}@kti.ue.poznan.pl

Abstract. In cultural heritage content management systems in which cultural objects are described with the use of their semantic, temporal and spatial properties, the search capabilities taking all those properties into consideration are very limited. The difficulty comes from the fact that concepts evolve over time and depend on location. In this paper the TSTS search method is presented based on the TST similarity measure that allows assessing the similarity factor between different resources in a knowledgebase. A ranked search result is generated basing on the semantic distance between the fuzzy set created for the user query and fuzzy sets describing potential results in the time-space continuum.

Keywords: Semantic web, semantic search, cultural objects, cultural heritage.

1 Introduction

In recent years increasing interest in creating virtual museums is observed. Virtual museum objects are stored in heritage content management systems. Detailed descriptions of the objects include e.g. the dates and places of their creation, storage and renovation. In many content management systems objects are also mutually linked according to their semantic conceptual relationships. Current heritage content management systems usually allow users to search for cultural objects, however, the search capabilities provided are quite limited. The problem is that concepts related to cultural objects are dependent on time and geographical location, can evolve over time, and may have different meaning in different locations. As a result, search methods developed so far, both keyword-based and semantically oriented, fail because of the imprecision of data - on the one hand contained in museum knowledgebases, and on the other hand used in the queries by users.

In this paper a TSTS (Theme-Space-Time Search) method of semantic search is proposed that takes into account three factors to answer a user query: relations between concepts in context of their temporal and spatial properties. Contribution of the TSTS method to technological innovation in the domain of semantic search in the cultural heritage field is presented in Section 2. In Section 3, current solutions for cultural objects search engines are discussed. In Section 4, the TSTS method is presented, including the TST concept similarity measure and its application in search. The characteristics of the TSTS method are discussed in Section 5. Finally, Section 6 concludes the paper.

L.M. Camarinha-Matos, P. Pereira, and L. Ribeiro (Eds.): DoCEIS 2010, IFIP AICT 314, pp. 44–51, 2010.

2 Contribution of the TSTS Search Method to Technological Innovation

To present contribution of the TSTS search method to technological innovation consider the following example of a fragment of a cultural heritage domain presented in Figure 1. This domain deals with cultural objects, geographical places, and historical periods. Rectangles represent concept instances, while ovals – their properties. For the sake of clarity, only properties describing time spans (denoted by t) and geographical coordinates (denoted by g) in literal values are presented. In this example some of the concept instances are directly described by the time and space information (e.g. Vase 1 was created in time t_1 and place g_1), while for others time/space information is expressed by references to other concept instances (e.g. Vase 2 was created in time t_2 in Greece). Moreover, some concept instances can be linked with more than one pair (time, place) since they evolved over time or appeared in different places at different times. Greece is an example of an evolving concept instance, because the borders of Greece have changed many times. As a result, location and area of 'Greece' depend on the date considered. As a consequence, when the term 'Greece' is used in a query, time has to be specified to obtain a precise response. Similarly, term 'Archaic Period' is not bound to only one period in time, but depending on place may refer to different time spans. For example the archaic period occurred in Egypt between 3100-2600 BC, but in Greece between 750-480 BC.

A typical query issued by an archaeologist is: *find all the vases originating from Greece created in the archaic period.*

There are two types of search methods that could be used to answer such a query: keyword search and semantic search. Keyword search is the simplest and the most common search method. In the cultural heritage context, where terms are ambiguous, results obtained using this method are usually inaccurate. This method is able to return only those objects for which a given keyword occurs inside their textual description.

Semantic search methods are usually more accurate than keyword based methods, because they are able to analyze relations between concepts and their instances. However, if a purely semantic search method was used in the example above, it

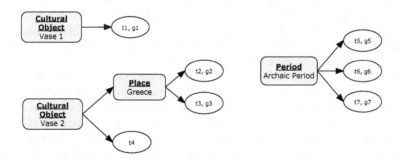

Fig. 1. A fragment of a simplified semantic model instance for a cultural heritage domain

would also return inaccurate results, because some concepts are not explicitly connected to each other, but they relate only through their temporal and geographical coincidence (e.g. 'Archaic period' and 'Vase 1' are related because they both occurred in the same place at the same time).

The TSTS method of semantic search presented in this paper takes into account three factors to answer a user query: relations between concepts together with their temporal and spatial properties. As the majority of users are accustomed to expressing their information needs in terms of keywords, the TSTS method allows users to ask questions using a traditional 'Google like' interface. However, the TSTS uses semantic information concerning the application domain to obtain results that are not possible to be found when traditional search methods are applied.

The TSTS method is based on the TST similarity measure that allows assessing the distance between different concepts in a semantic, spatiotemporal database. During the evaluation of this measure, for each concept a fuzzy set of points in the time-space continuum is constructed. In such a fuzzy set, the more closely a point is related to the analyzed node, the higher degree of membership it receives. In the next step fuzzy set operations such as intersection and union are applied to the fuzzy sets that correspond to the concepts from the user query. As a result, another fuzzy set is obtained that represents the region in space and time that the user is interested in.

In the example above, in a user query three concepts 'Vase', 'Greece' and 'Archaic Period' are mentioned. The concept 'Vase' yields the set containing points in the time-space continuum that correspond to all acts of the creation of a vase. For the concept 'Greece', a set is generated including all the points in space in which Greece has ever existed. Finally, the concept 'Archaic Period' yields the set of points in which that period occurred. Intersection of these three fuzzy sets is a region in time and space matching the user's query. Finally, cultural objects that are 'closest' to that region are found and presented as the query result.

3   Searching Cultural Objects

A number of different approaches to cultural object searching have been developed and presented in the literature.

Fitzwilliam Museum [1] website makes its collection accessible through the standard OPAC (Online Public Access Catalog) search interface. The search is based on keywords. Although, it is possible to issue a query limiting search results to a certain place and time period, search is performed on textual basis. Mainly due to data inconsistency, search results are prone to be inaccurate, which is a common disadvantage of search methods based on keywords.

Heritage 4 [2] is a system for storing and presenting cultural objects used to build the virtual Museum of Copenhagen [3]. In this system users can conduct searches choosing textual, geographical and/or, temporal criteria or through relations between objects. Although in the Heritage 4 system search is made via an appealing interface, it does not support complex queries such as the one presented in Section 1. The spatiotemporal search can only operate on objects that are directly described by space and time properties and those properties cannot be inferred through relations with other objects. Therefore, this system does not indirectly support the evolving concepts.

Semantic search is a process used to improve searching capabilities by using semantic networks to disambiguate queries in order to generate more relevant results. The semantic search methods are divided into two categories: exact methods and approximate methods.

The SPARQL language is devoted to the exact semantic search methods. SPARQL is a language for querying the RDF semantic networks developed by RDF Data Access Working Group (DAWG) [4]. SPARQL is designed for finding patterns in semantic graphs. Although the SPARQL language is very powerful, initially it was not designed to answer the queries that deal with time and space . Some extensions to SPARQL exist [5] that allow querying for time and space, but they make the use of this language even more sophisticated.

Another interesting approach to the exact semantic search is proposed in [6], in which spatial and temporal query operators have been formalized and evaluated. Although the proposed framework was designed to deal with queries containing references to time and space, there is no direct support for the changing or evolving entities.

In general, the exact search methods have two disadvantages. First disadvantage concerns the relationship with a knowledgebase. The exact search methods either require a user to know the structure of a knowledgebase and then the search system may cooperate with different knowledgebases, or the search system is strictly bound to knowledgebases of a single structure fixed a priori. The second disadvantage of the exact search methods is their inability to return the results that do not meet a given search criterion, but which are close to meet it. Although this property is not considered to be a disadvantage in certain applications, in the cultural heritage domain it is a disadvantage. In the cultural heritage domain spatiotemporal data in the knowledgebase and in the user query can be imprecise, so the possibility to find objects that are close to meeting a given criterion and ranking the results is very important.

Approximate semantic search methods are based on similarity measures. These methods usually do not require a user to know the structure of the semantic network and they permit to rank the results. Although there has been a number of such measures proposed [7-8], none of them takes both time and space information into consideration.

The TSTS method presented in this paper can be categorised as an approximate semantic search method, because it is based on a similarity measure, namely the TST (Theme-Space-Time). The main feature of the TSTS method, as opposed to the existing methods, is its ability to seamlessly deal with the concepts evolving or changing in time and space. Also, the TSTS method does not require a user to know the structure of the searched knowledgebase. Finally, the TSTS method is able to operate on imprecise data and rank the search results.

4   The TSTS Method

In this section, the word *node* is used to denote a concept or a concept instance in a semantic network; the word *edge* – to denote a relation instance, and the word *graph* – to denote the semantic network.

4.1 Concept Similarity Measure

The TST (Theme-Space-Time) measure presented in this paper indicates similarity between two concept instances in a semantic network. The computation of this measure in done in three steps: weight mapping, fuzzy set creation, and distance measuring.

4.1.1 Weight Mapping

In a classical semantic network each edge has only a label associated to it. Therefore, it is only possible to indicate the presence or absence of a relation between two concept instances. The computation of the TST measure requires additional numerical value associated with the relation instances expressing their strength. Different ideas can be found in literature for devising a calculation that can generate a formula for the strength of each existing relation instance in the knowledgebase. However, despite the research, a formula that outperforms all the others in a large set of experiments, or proves to be the best for all application domains has not been found. In this paper the technique of calculating a numerical weight value based on analysis of link structure, called *weight mapping,* presented in [8] has been applied. The following specificity measure was used:

$$W_{ij} = \frac{1}{\sqrt{n_j}} . \tag{1}$$

The value n_j is equal to the number of instances of a given relation type that have concept C_j as its destination node. Therefore, the weight of the relation is inversely proportional to the number of relations with the concept C_j. The more concepts with the same type as C_i and related to C there are$_j$, the higher W_{ij} is.

4.1.2 Fuzzy Set Creation

In the fuzzy sets theory each element is given a degree of membership. Mathematically it is described with the aid of a membership function valued in the real unit interval [0,1]. Operations on fuzzy sets are generalizations of crisp set operations such as union or intersection. There is more than one possible generalization. Fuzzy intersection and fuzzy union are the functions that map the degree of membership from given sets into a new degree of membership.

The TSTS method requires that for each concept being measured the fuzzy set of points representing the concept in space-time continuum is created. The main idea is that if a given concept is related to other concepts that are positioned somewhere in time and space, there is a great possibility that the concept itself is also related to the same point.

For concept C_i the membership function expressing the fuzzy set is expressed by the following recursive formula:

$$\mu_i(x) = \bigcup_j (1-k)\alpha_i(x) \oplus_{W_{ij}} \mu_j(x) . \tag{2}$$

Function μ_i denotes the fuzzy set for the concept C_i. Function α_i represents the region in the space-time continuum defined by the properties immediately defined for node C_i. Function μ_j denotes the fuzzy set for the concept C_j being the neighbouring node of the node C_i.

Operator $\oplus_{Wij}$ is able to interpolate between the fuzzy union and fuzzy intersection depending on the weight W_{ij} of the relation between nodes C_i and C_j. This operator is defined by the following function:

$$\mu_{i\oplus j}(x) = W_{ij}s_{i\cup j}(x) + (1 - W_{ij})t_{i\cap j}(x)$$

(3)

$$s_{i\cup j}(x) = \mu_i(x) + \mu_j(x) - \mu_i(x)\mu_j(x), \quad t_{i\cap j}(x) = \mu_i(x)\mu_j(x)$$

The s and t are the functions that were chosen for computing fuzzy union and fuzzy intersection, respectively.

During the process of computing the fuzzy set, for each propagation through an edge the degree of membership is reduced. The process repeats until newly visited nodes do not add any significant information or there are no further nodes to be processed. The k value corresponds to the percentage of the degree of the membership value that the membership function is decreased by every time an edge is processed, effectively functioning as an attenuation factor.

4.1.3 Measuring Distance

The TST measure is the distance between two nodes and it is the compound of the semantic distance in the semantic network, and the distance in time and space. It is defined by the following formula:

$$TST(C_i, C_j) = \lambda_s d_s(C_i, C_j) * \lambda_g d_g(\mu_i, \mu_j) * \lambda_t d_t(\mu_i, \mu_j).$$

(4)

Function $d_s(C_i, C_j)$ is the semantic similarity between concepts C_i and C_j. Computing the semantic similarity is widely discussed in the literature, where many different formulas were proposed. For the TSTS method, a function that simply counts the intermediate nodes on the shortest path between C_i and C_j was chosen.

The functions $d_g(\mu_i, \mu_j)$ and $d_t(\mu_i, \mu_j)$ are the distances between points in the fuzzy sets computed for concepts C_i and C_j in the geographic coordinates and time dimension respectively, expressed by the formulas:

$$d_g(\mu_i, \mu_j) = \int_0^1 \min_{(t_i, g_i) \in \mu_i^{>\alpha}, (t_j, g_j) \in \mu_j^{>\alpha}} \left(\left|g_i - g_j\right|\right) d\alpha$$

(4)

$$d_t(\mu_i, \mu_j) = \int_0^1 \min_{(t_i, g_i) \in \mu_i^{>\alpha}, (t_j, g_j) \in \mu_j^{>\alpha}} \left(\left|t_i - t_j\right|\right) d\alpha,$$

(5)

where $\mu_i^{>\alpha}$ is a set of points from the fuzzy set described by function μ_i for which the degree of membership is greater then α. Value g_i is the geographical part of an element in the fuzzy set. Value t_i denotes the time part of an element in the fuzzy set. Parameters λ_s, λ_g, λ_t are the scaling factors that allow the end user to weight which part of the measure is the most important.

4.2 Answering User Queries

Searching for cultural objects that satisfy a query specified by a user is performed in three phases: the resolving phase, the fuzzy set building phase, and the measuring phase. In the resolving phase each keyword or a phrase from the user query is mapped to an existing node in the underlying semantic network. In many cases a keyword alone cannot be used to unambiguously identify the node. In such case the user is presented with a list of matching nodes and is asked to indicate the concept or its instance of his/her interest.

In the next phase, a fuzzy set of points in the time-space continuum is created from the nodes contained in the user query. The nodes from the user query are joined through the three most common relations: *and, or* and *not*. The resulting fuzzy set is constructed using appropriate fuzzy set operations on the fuzzy sets corresponding to the nodes in the query – fuzzy intersection for *and*, fuzzy union for *or*, and fuzzy complement for *not*.

Finally, for each cultural object in the underlying knowledgebase the TST distance between the node representing the cultural object and the user query is computed. If the user query contains only one node, the TST distance has the form described in Section 4.1.3. If the user query consists of more than one concept, the semantic distance d_s in the presented formula needs to be computed differently. The value d_s is obtained by combining semantic distances between nodes referenced in user query and the currently analysed cultural object node using the same functions that were used to join the fuzzy sets. On the base of the TST measure the results are ranked. Those cultural objects for which the TST distance is the lowest are the best match.

In the presented TSTS method, the results can be shown as a flat list, because the TST measure is a numerical value. However, the final value of TST measure is compounded of three distances – in semantic, temporal and geographical dimension. All those distances can be separately visualized for each object found, giving a user a better understanding of why a particular cultural object was considered. Moreover, the fuzzy set constructed from the user query can also be visualized, indicating the actual area in time and space that was covered by the user query.

5 Discussion

The TSTS method responses to the problem of searching objects in the cultural heritage domain, where concepts are dependent on time and geographical location. As a result, those concepts are imprecise both in the knowledgebases describing cultural heritage subdomains and in the query expression. Imprecision concerns rivers, seashores, islands, countries, periods, as well as artistic, literary and intellectual movements, etc. The use of fuzzy sets to represent concepts in the time-space continuum permits to deal with this imprecision. The TSTS method is independent of the knowledgebase schema. The search results may be ranked, as they have numerical values of the TST similarity measure attached.

6 Conclusions

The TSTS search method is particularly important in case of multinational and multicultural audience visiting a virtual museum. In such case, queries are imprecise more than ever, as searchers do not have background knowledge of the heritage domain. The TSTS method provides information that contributes to acquiring that knowledge, because it locates the concepts searched in time and space. Thanks to that location, the objects found may be presented in a clear and attractive way on maps and time scales.

Future research on the TSTS search method will be focused on the comparison of different measures. Generalization and specialization of concepts has to be taken into account to improve accuracy of the TSTS method, when applied in closed cultural heritage subdomains.

References

1. Fitzwilliam Museum, http://www.fitzmuseum.cam.ac.uk/
2. Snizek, B., König, T.: Heritage 4 – A 4D Cultural Heritage Management System. In: 15th Int. Conf. on Virtual Systems and Multimedia VSMM 2009, Vienna, Austria (2009)
3. Museum of Copenhagen, http://absalon.nu/
4. SPARQL Query Language for RDF (2008),
   http://www.w3.org/TR/rdf-sparql-query/
5. Dodds, L.: SPARQL Geo Extensions (2006),
   http://xmlarmyknife.com/blog/archives/000281.html
6. Perry, M., Hakimpour, F., Sheth, A.: Analyzing theme, space, and time: an ontology-based approach. In: Proc. 14th Annual ACM Int. Symp. on Advances in Geographic Information Systems. GIS 2006, Arlington, Virginia, USA, November 10-11, pp. 147–154. ACM, New York (2006)
7. Rocha, C., Schwabe, D., Aragao, M.P.: A hybrid approach for searching in the semantic web. In: Proceedings of the 13th international Conf. on World Wide Web. WWW 2004, May 17 - 20, pp. 374–383. ACM, New York (2004)
8. Ziegler, C., Simon, K., Lausen, G.: Automatic computation of semantic proximity using taxonomic knowledge. In: Proc. 15th ACM Int. Conf. on Information and Knowledge Management. CIKM 2006, pp. 465–474. ACM, New York (2006)

Representing User Privileges
in Object-Oriented Virtual Reality Systems

Adam Wójtowicz and Wojciech Cellary

Department of Information Technology, Poznań University of Economics
{awojtow,cellary}@kti.ue.poznan.pl

Abstract. In virtual reality systems which are collaborative and dynamic, i.e. where at run-time mutually interactive objects can be added or removed in different contexts and where their behavior can be modified, the problem of data security and privacy protection is renewed. In such virtual worlds operations on objects should or should not be allowed to users playing particular roles with respect to inter-object interactions. In this paper a method called VR-PR is presented, where privileges are represented by pairs: object – semantic operations induced from object interactions. Semantic operations are generated using automatic analysis of the object method call graphs. Then they are used in the privilege creation and modification process. Privileges based on semantic operations are expressive, flexible and consistent with permanently evolving set of objects composing the virtual world, interactions between the objects, and a set of users.

Keywords: User privileges, virtual reality, data security, data privacy, semantic operations.

1 Introduction

Today virtual worlds are dynamic environments where multiple objects interact with each other by calling methods in reaction to internal and external events. Virtual worlds are also creative environments, where at run-time users create new objects, modify them, assemble them into more complex objects, extend their functionality etc. In such dynamic and creative environments the problem of data privacy protection is renewed. From the business perspective, intellectual property rights of creators and publishers of objects in virtual worlds must be protected, as they are source of revenues. Thus, flexible access control using privileges based on interactions existing in a persistently running virtual world should be installed. Privileges granted to a user for a given object should be represented in a way that is compatible with the representation and semantics of intellectual property rights issued for this object. Also, the semantics of interactions between objects owned by different users should be taken into account by the privilege system. Moreover, the privilege system should automatically encompass newly created objects. In virtual worlds objects may be created from scratch by a user who becomes their sole owner, but also as compositions of preexisting objects coming from different sources. The privilege system should be expressive

L.M. Camarinha-Matos, P. Pereira, and L. Ribeiro (Eds.): DoCEIS 2010, IFIP AICT 314, pp. 52–61, 2010.

enough to handle such dependencies. Methods of privilege modeling developed so far, which are presented in Section 3, are either geometry-centric with no advanced interaction support or coarse-grained with no privilege semantics modeling capabilities. Those methods however are not sufficient for highly dynamic creative virtual worlds.

In this paper, a method called VR-PR is proposed of flexible user privilege representation for virtual world objects, maintaining compatibility with access control standards and the data model. The concept of this method is presented in Section 2. In Section 3 the state of the art in the field of access control models which can be applied to multi-user virtual worlds is presented, followed by critical remarks. In Section 4 VR-PR approach is presented to privilege representation and generation of semantic operations used to express privileges. In Section 5 the main issues concerned in this paper are discussed. Section 6 concludes the paper.

2   Contribution of the VR-PR Method to Technological Innovation

The VR-PR method concerns flexible user privilege representation for virtual world objects. The VR-PR method consists of automatic analyses of relationships and interactions between objects of a dynamic virtual world constructed according to the object-oriented data model, such as the one presented in [7]. To this end, a semantic layer is inserted between the access control mechanism and the object-oriented data model. The semantic layer reflects real interactions between objects, represented by a set of abstract semantic operations. The set of semantic operations may slowly evolve over time. Its evolution is, however, much more stable than transformations of the virtual world objects, interactions and structure. In the VR-PR method two phases are alternately performed during virtual world run-time: the phase of automatic generation of semantic operations and the phase of privilege creation and modification. To guarantee consistency of semantic operations used during the second phase in the first phase semantic operations are created basing on automatic analysis of object method call graphs.

The following is an innovative contribution of this paper to the area of virtual world security. First, an access control model is proposed appropriate to a virtual world containing very large number of VR classes, objects and methods that is understandable and manageable for non-IT professional users who may express their will in terms of intuitively understandable semantic operations instead of object methods.

Second, a privilege system is proposed that strictly controls the allowed range of virtual world penetration by behavioral method calls. Third, an algorithm for automatic regeneration of semantic operations used in privileges is proposed, which assures privileges consistency with the data model and its integrity. It increases the security level of the security policies defined using privileges containing semantic operations.

Fourth, a two-phase induce-and-use approach is proposed, which makes the process of privilege management stable: operation set is updated on-demand, but the updates do not change as fast as the data model evolves. Semantic operations can be regenerated without modifying the existing privileges, as well as without role-privilege and user-role assignment modifications.

3 State of the Art

When designing virtual worlds, to control access to objects Role-Based Access Control (RBAC) model [16], Attribute-Based Access Control (ABAC) [17], extensions of these models or their combinations may be applied. Although they are useful in the virtual worlds domain as far as roles, users and their credentials are concerned, they do not solve the problem of privilege granting in highly dynamic virtual worlds.

Research on data privacy protection in virtual environments is derived from the output of either CAD or VR communities. The majority of research effort on advanced privileges modeling in virtual environments is based on the CAD achievements as there is a need in the industry for CAD systems providing data privacy protection while enabling safe collaboration. In [1] a role-depended access model to 3D environments is proposed. In this approach each design feature of an object is assigned to one of predefined access levels representing modes of detail reduction. The role is defined by selecting access level for each object. It protects object geometry only – protection does not concern interactions and behaviors. Users update objects independently, then objects are synchronized by the central system. Such asynchronous approach is justified in some CAD collaborative applications, but it does not meet virtual worlds practice. In [2] an access control model for distributed 3D collaborative engineering systems is proposed. In this model RBAC extension is used which consists of a partial data sharing mechanism and fine grained access control. Access granularity is supported on different levels: assembly, component, feature and surface, which form a hierarchy. Dynamic geometric and non-geometric constraints can be modeled, but inter-object interactions and their different semantics are not supported as an element of the privilege system. Only basic operations such as read, write and modify are used to form privileges. In [3] FACADE system is proposed, which is synchronous collaborative 3D virtual environment enabling selective sharing of 3D objects. FACADE authors classify their work as both data- and interaction-centric, however, interaction is regarded here only as inter-user design-time interaction and not inter-object dynamic behavior. There are cross-hierarchy relations between objects called "need-to-know requirements" but their nature is static and they are explicitly defined by designers. This concept provides role-based views on modeled data with read/write privileges granularity. Read privilege is extended to a continuous scale of mesh resolutions, but since only geometry is considered, there is no support for a whole spectrum of semantic operations that could form privileges.

From among non-CAD-based approaches, the most distinguished are rule-based access control models developed for the multimedia domain as a whole. Such models have even been a subject of standardization as a part of MPEG-21 – Right Expression Language (REL) [18]. Unfortunately, Digital Item (DI) representation which lies under it is not expressive enough to support complex behavior-rich 3D objects. Other access control standards, such as Extensible Access Control Modeling Language (XACML) [19], are even more general in the multimedia context.

An interesting rule-based access control model has been developed for and implemented in the DEVA system [5]. In the DEVA approach, execution of a given operation is controlled by access rules expressed by a source code defined in so-called *keys*. However, both operations and keys have to be explicitly defined by users. There is no automatic induction of operation dependencies, so users are responsible for maintaining access rules consistency. In [5] there is no explanation of how the DEVA approach is integrated with standard access control or how privileges are represented.

A number of papers are devoted to methods of modeling virtual worlds not only as a set of geometrical objects, but also semantically [8,9,10,11]. Such approaches enable application of algorithms automatically exploring the content of the virtual world, reusing objects in different contexts and taking advantage of domain knowledge stored in external ontologies. However, there has been no effort to integrate semantic virtual world models with user privileges control to protect data privacy. The next research field related with this paper is structured design of virtual worlds [7]. It focuses on methods of building VR applications in which content is dynamically configured from high-level elements, thus it can be relatively easily created and modified by domain experts and common users. Nevertheless, those reusable elements lack integrated user privilege support as well.

4   VR-PR Approach

4.1   Concept of the VR-PR Approach

Interactive virtual worlds admit content dynamically generated by users. In such virtual worlds the structure of the data model evolves which entails specific requirements for the access control model. In standard access control models such as RBAC and its extensions, *privileges* are formed as a pair *operation – resource*. However, in dynamic virtual worlds based on object oriented paradigm a question arises: how to build an access control model appropriate to a very large number of dynamic classes, objects and methods that is understandable and manageable for users? In such virtual worlds resources have to be objects, however, operations may be defined differently. If an operation is an object method, privileges are too dependent on the data model. When a method changes, or a new class is added, the operation set used to define privileges has to be changed accordingly. If an operation represents all the object's methods, i.e. privileges are defined with the object granularity, another problem arises: different methods of an object usually have diametrically different semantics and they call different methods (i.e. have different call graphs), so their range of penetration of the virtual world is different, which is not reflected by such privilege system. Moreover, it is also very dependent on data model changes. If an operation is a primitive, such as "read" or "write", privilege system is independent of data model changes, but it does not follow the evolution of the virtual world, so it is useless in case of dynamic virtual worlds that constantly evolve. If the set of operations is not fixed but is updated by human operators according to data model changes, the risk of inconsistencies grows drastically.

In the VR-PR approach, *semantic operations* are used. A semantic operation is a conceptual extension of the operation from the standard access control models. Similarly to a regular operation, it is used to define privileges in conjunction with objects. But the main innovation is its semantics that is automatically induced from the object-oriented data model, instead of being defined arbitrarily. In other words a semantic operation is a set of bindings to semantically similar object methods induced from method call graphs. Each semantic operation is assigned to a given type and it has its place in the semantic operations hierarchy. Semantic operations reflect all the method calls, i.e. all in-world interactions of the objects, which may be complex, diverse, and dynamic. A semantic operation set is generated in a way assuring that each method call is bound to at least one induced semantic operation. Semantic operations are intuitively understandable by virtual content authors, publishers, administrators or other users authorized to create new privileges or modify existing ones.

In the VR-PR approach the privileges are processed in two phases. The *Semantic Operations Generation Phase* (SOGP) follows the virtual world data model evolution by regenerating a semantic operation set on each change. It is performed by the induction process basing on the analysis of the similarity of virtual object's method call graphs, as well as on the analysis of relationships between elements of the data model (cf. Subsection 4.2). A set of available semantic operations is generated from potential method calls known at design-time (inter-object relationship: uses-a), and from the static class hierarchy and object set structure (relationships: is-a, instance-of, part-of). During the SOGP phase semantic operation type categorization and generalization hierarchies are built.

Semantic operations are induced by *semantic unification* of different methods. This means that methods with similar call graphs are logically bound to a common semantic operation in the privilege system, whereas in the virtual world they are still recognized as separate ones.

From the data security and privacy point of view, measuring the level of similarity of the methods by measuring the level of similarity of their call graphs is justified. A semantic operation which groups methods with similar call graphs describes well the range of the penetration of the virtual world by a set of calls. In the VR-PR approach, the allowed range of virtual world penetration by method calls is controlled by the privilege system. As a result, the privilege function of protecting objects is satisfactory fulfilled – the system is protected against non-authorized deep method calls in a dense net of variable behavioral dependencies.

The second phase of the approach is the *Privilege Creation and Modification Phase* (PCMP), which is described in Subsection 4.3. Semantic operations induced during the first phase are used to form privileges by assigning them to objects. This process is controlled by an access control mechanism which makes the process consistent with the data model.

4.2 The SOGP Phase

In the VR-PR approach semantic operation induction is based on static *call graph* – a graph whose nodes are methods and edges are all possible calls of other methods. A node represents a method in the context of a given object, which means that if a given class has many instances, then for each method of this class there are as many nodes as instances. The call graph is created from the source code of virtual world objects. Global and local call graphs are distinguished. The *global call graph* contains all the methods and all the potential calls of other methods included in the source code of all the objects composing a virtual world at a given moment. It is updated incrementally when the data model changes. A *local call graph* is developed for each method. It is a subgraph of the global call graph built with a given method as the starting point and containing all the methods that are called by these methods, and all their callees.

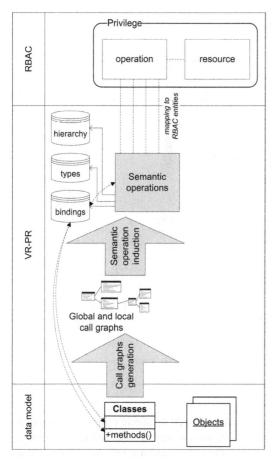

Fig. 1. SOGP: semantic operations generation

Semantic operations have types assigned. The types reflect the way semantic operations have been induced. When a given semantic operation is based on the methods with identical local call graphs, its type is called *fully-matching*. When call graphs of two unified methods cover methods belonging to the same classes (but they are based on different objects sets), the semantic operation is called *class-matching*.

The first phase of the VR-PR approach is composed of the following five steps (Fig. 1):

1. Construct the global call graph. This graph is a basic data structure for the process of automatic generation of semantic operations.
2. Induce semantic operations. The induction of each semantic operation is preceded by local call graph pre-selection. Each semantic operation is generated by semantic unification of different methods, basing on the analysis the similarity of local call graphs of methods and on the analysis of the static class hierarchy and object set structure. Metadata descriptions of the software modules, classes, objects and methods are taken into account during semantic unification if they are available.
3. Assign types to semantic operations.
4. Store bindings between each semantic operation and a set of methods which have been the base of its induction for further use during the PCMP phase.
5. Build semantic operations hierarchy according to composability criterion. It is orthogonal both to the role hierarchy and to the class inheritance hierarchy.

Potentially, semantic unification can be performed on two methods which are: different methods of different classes (but having similar calls); the same method, but in different object context (parameterized or using non-static field values); different methods of the same class. The aforementioned cases are distinguished during the selection of methods to be unified, as well as during call similarity analysis. Metadata descriptions of the software modules, classes, objects and methods taken into account during semantic unifications are useful in excluding semantically incoherent unifications, as well as in providing semantic labeling for the semantic operations.

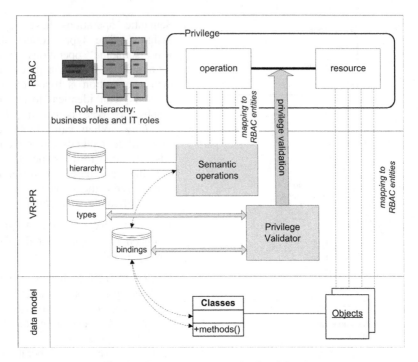

Fig. 2. PCMP: privilege creation/modification

4.3   The PCMP Phase

In the PCMP phase of the VR-PR approach the induced semantic operations are used
to create privileges by assigning semantic operations to objects and binding so created
privileges to roles (Fig. 2). Whether a given semantic operation may be assigned to a
given object or not, depends on the *privilege validation* mechanism. Privilege validation can work in two modes: *strict privileges* and *potential privileges*. In the strict
privileges mode a privilege may be created only if a given semantic operation has
been induced from the requested object. In the potential privileges mode a given
semantic operation can be assigned to an object even if the operation has not been
induced from any of the object's methods. Such privileges are used when it can be
anticipated that taking into account data model dynamism some objects will gain new
competences. However, at the moment of the creation of such privileges they do not
make any new method calls allowed, because those methods are as yet inexistent.

Since all the calls which are triggered by a given operation, including all the call
dependencies (represented by a call graph), are known before each iteration of the
privilege creation phase, during privilege assignment this knowledge can influence
final decision whether a given privilege can be assigned or not. Thus, after privilege
assignment, during run-time it is guaranteed that no access error will arise related to
the lack of privileges to any of dependent methods called. This follows from the fact
that each semantic operation stores all the bindings to the methods which were the
base of its induction.

5   Discussion

The SOGP and PCMP phases described in Section 4 are following each other at run-time. Creating privileges is not a static task performed only during the virtual world creation, but a dynamic process following virtual world evolution. Users, roles and virtual world data model naturally evolve, while access control model core structures as semantic operations hierarchy remains persistent. In earlier approaches the operation set was static, though operations allowed on resources were defined with different semantics and complexity, i.e. read/ write, or execute/ modify/ insert/ append, or activate/ play/ reorganize. In some cases the operation set could evolve via non-automated changes following data model modifications, which does not assure privileges consistency. In the VR-PR approach, dynamism of the virtual world is inherently taken into account. Defining privileges using automatically regenerated semantic-based operations makes the process of role creation and management consistent, because of semantic operation set internal consistency and consistency with currently used data model. In the VR-PR approach semantic operations layer introduces stability into the process of privilege management. It is updated on-change (i.e. when new objects or new interactions appear), but updates do not change the semantic operations set significantly – especially when semantic operations are induced hierarchically and form a tree structure. Thus, access to semantic operations provides a safe tool to a role manager or any user who is not a 3D modeling expert nor a programmer but who is eligible to create or modify a privilege.

The VR-PR approach makes it possible to avoid unwanted frequent redefining and proliferation of roles. It may happen when privilege changes are not driven by business processes (e.g. a virtual world user gains new duties), but are forced by low level data model activity modification (e.g. when competences of the object to which privileges have been already granted are changed). The advantage of the VR-PR approach is that in this approach semantic operations can be regenerated without modifying the privileges assigned, as well as without role-privilege and user-role assignment modifications.

As an additional benefit, descriptive possibilities of semantic operations can be used in the role-mining process which is performed for security auditing purposes. In the VR-PR approach each semantic operation forming privilege assigned to a role expresses meaningful information about privilege semantics with an explicit representation. Semantic operations used in privileges can be treated as metadata unambiguously describing the role to which those privileges have been assigned. Having such metadata, role-mining process is much more straightforward.

Generally, in object-oriented virtual worlds applications during their lifetime there is a drift towards decreasing the size of the methods and increasing the number of calls. Along with increasing the number of calls, inter-object dependencies become more complex. Thus, a need for automatic analysis for security purposes becomes critical. This is yet another motivation for applying the VR-PR approach to the object-oriented virtual worlds.

6 Conclusions

In the VR-PR approach presented in this paper to provide data security and privacy a security mechanism is proposed based on the concept of semantic operations. They are derived at run-time from the virtual world's current data model and are applicable to access a control model as a part of a privilege. Semantic consistency of the security policies composed of privileges using semantic operations is forced by the two-phase regeneration and validation mechanism. On the other hand, this challenging functionality does not preclude expressing user rights in a precise, accurate, and flexible way.

The VR-PR approach bridges the semantic gap between abstract roles, both business roles and IT roles of virtual world users, and low-level operations executed on virtual world objects. Development of an abstract layer of semantic operations reduces the risk of inconsistent privilege modifications. It does not violate the RBAC access control model nor the object-oriented data model – it constitutes a middle layer placed between these two models developed for different purposes and it is designed with respect to 3D virtual worlds specificity.

References

1. Qiu, Z.M., Kok, K.F., Wong, Y.S., Fuh, J.Y.: Role-based 3D visualisation for asynchronous PLM collaboration. Comput. Ind. 58(8-9), 747–755 (2007)
2. Wang, Y., Ajoku, P., Brustoloni, J., Nnaji, B.J.: Intellectual Property Protection in Collaborative Design through Lean Information Modeling and Sharing. Comput. Inf. Sci. Eng. 6, 149 (2006)
3. Cera, D.D., Kim, T., Han, J., Regli, W.C.: Role-based viewing envelopes for information protection in collaborative modeling. Computer-Aided Design 36(1), 873–886 (2004)
4. Fang, C., Peng, W., Ye, X., Zhang, S.: Multi-level access control for collaborative CAD. In: Proceedings of the Ninth International Conference on Computer Supported Cooperative Work in Design, vol. 1, pp. 643–648 (2005)
5. Pettifer, S., Marsh, J.: A Collaborative Access Model for Shared Virtual Environments. In: Proceedings of the 10th IEEE international Workshops on Enabling Technologies: infrastructure For Collaborative Enterprises. WETICE, pp. 257–262. IEEE Computer Society, Washington (2001)
6. Bullock, A., Benford, S.: An access control framework for multi-user collaborative environments. In: Proceedings of the international ACM SIGGROUP Conference on Supporting Group Work, pp. 140–149. ACM, NY (1999)
7. Walczak, K.: Structured Design of Interactive VR Applications. In: The 13th International Symposium on 3D Web Technology Web3D, Los Angeles, California, USA, pp. 105–113. ACM Press, NY (2008)
8. Latoschik, M.E., Biermann, P., Wachsmuth, I.: Knowledge in the Loop: Semantics Representation for Multimodal Simulative Environments. In: Butz, A., Fisher, B., Krüger, A., Olivier, P. (eds.) SG 2005. LNCS, vol. 3638, pp. 25–39. Springer, Heidelberg (2005)
9. Lugrin, J., Cavazza, M.: Making sense of virtual environments: action representation, grounding and common sense. In: Proceedings of the 12th international Conference on intelligent User interfaces, IUI 2007, pp. 225–234. ACM, NY (2007)
10. Pittarello, F., De Faveri, A.: Semantic description of 3D environments: a proposal based on web standards. In: Proceedings of the Eleventh international Conference on 3D Web Technology. Web3D 2006, pp. 85–95. ACM, NY (2006)

11. Gutierrez, M., Vexo, F., Thalmann, D.: Semantics-based representation of virtual environments. IJCAT 23, 229–238 (2005)
12. Sallés, E.J., Michael, J.B., Capps, M., McGregor, D., Kapolka, A.: Security of runtime extensible virtual environments. In: Proceedings of the 4th International Conference on Collaborative Virtual Environments, CVE 2002, pp. 97–104. ACM, NY (2002)
13. Tolone, W., Ahn, G., Pai, T., Hong, S.: Access control in collaborative systems. ACM Comput. Surv. 37(1), 29–41 (2005)
14. Izaki, K., Tanaka, K., Takizawa, M.: Authorization model based on object-oriented concept. In: Proceedings of the the 15th international Conference on information Networking. ICOIN, pp. 72–77. IEEE Computer Society, Washington (2001)
15. Wong, R.K.: RBAC support in object-oriented role databases. In: Proceedings of the Second ACM Workshop on Role-Based Access Control, Fairfax, Virginia, United States, RBAC 1997, pp. 109–120. ACM, New York (1997)
16. Sandhu, R., Ferraiolo, D., Kuhn, R.: The NIST model for role-based access control: towards a unified standard. In: Proceedings of the Fifth ACM Workshop on Role-Based Access Control, RBAC 2000, pp. 47–63. ACM, NY (2000)
17. Priebe, T., Dobmeier, W., Schläger, C., Kamprath, N.: Supporting Attribute-based Access Control in Authentication and Authorization Infrastructures with Ontologies. Journal of software: JSW 2(1), 27–38 (2007)
18. Wang, X., Demartini, T., Wragg, B., Paramasivam, M., Barlas, C.: The mpeg-21 rights expression language and rights data dictionary. IEEE Transactions on Multimedia 7(3), 408–417 (2005)
19. Moses, T. (ed.): eXtensible Access Control Markup Language (XACML) Version 2.0., http://docs.oasis-open.org/xacml/2.0/ access_control-xacml-2.0-core-spec-os.pdf

Survey of Media Forms and Information Flow Models in Microsystems Companies

Christopher Durugbo, Ashutosh Tiwari, and Jeffery R. Alcock

School of Applied Science, Cranfield University, Cranfield, United Kingdom
{c.durugbo,a.tiwari,j.r.alcock}@cranfield.ac.uk

Abstract. The paper presents the findings of a survey of 40 microsystems companies that was carried out to determine the use and the purpose of use of media forms and information flow models within these companies. These companies as 'product-service systems' delivered integrated products and services to realise customer solutions. Data collection was carried out by means of an online survey over 3 months. The survey revealed that 42.5% of respondents made use of data flow diagrams and 10% made use of design structure matrices. The survey also suggests that a majority of companies (75%) made use of textual and diagrammatic media forms for communication, analysis, documentation and representation during design and development processes. The paper also discusses the implications of the survey findings to product-service systems.

Keywords: Information flow, Modelling, Services, Product-service systems, Microsystems.

1 Introduction

This study focuses on a sample of microsystems companies to consider accessibility issues for product-service systems (PSS) but in particular information flow by means of media forms and models. Determining the use and purpose of use of media forms and information flow models could be useful in improving the delivery of products and services realised from microsystems production. This is because a PSS applies 'social constructs' that require information flow to manage the delivery of value propositions based on closely linking and offering products and services [1]. Further-more, information flow knowledge is key to the implementation of standards for quality, efficiency, and financial performance in the delivery of customer solutions as defined by ISO 9000 and ISO 14000 [2].

The main aim of this paper is to capture industry practice in the use of media forms and information flow models for the delivery of product-service systems.

The remainder of this paper has been structured as follows. Section 2 describes the novelty of the research while Section 3 identifies common information flow models in literature. Section 4 outlines the methodology for the research. Section 5 presents the findings of the study while Section 6 discusses the implication of the study for PSS.

L.M. Camarinha-Matos, P. Pereira, and L. Ribeiro (Eds.): DoCEIS 2010, IFIP AICT 314, pp. 62–69, 2010.

2 Contribution to Technological Innovation

As microsystems production moves from a 'surprise to enterprise' [3] phase, it is important to examine current applied tools. This paper investigates information flow modelling in microsystem companies that apply PSS and seeks to contribute to technological innovation by:

1) establishing if there are correlations in the information flow models for PSS proposed in literature and those actually employed in industry
2) comparing and contrasting the various media forms employed for information flow during microsystem production

To the best of our knowledge, no previous study of this kind has been undertaken for the microsystems domain.

3 Information Flows for Product-Service Systems

A Product-Service System (PSS) has been defined as 'an integrated product and service offering that delivers value in use' [4]. Value in use for a PSS is realised in a function-oriented business model highlighting the importance of *information flow* for the delivery of products and services by a manufacturer to a costumer [5].

Information flow is based on information gathering [1] by means of textual, audio, video and graphical media forms [6]. These media forms are used for communication within an organisation [7], for description of processes [8], for analysis of systems [9] and for the documentation of ideas, activities and processes [10].

A useful way of representing information flow in a system or an organisation is by means of information flow models that depict system functions and architectures [5]. Diagrammatic tools in particular have been suggested for information flow modelling because these tools require less storage and are processed more efficiently in humans [11]. Function-oriented diagrammatical information flow models such as data flow diagrams (DFD), Integrated DEFinition (IDEFØ), Graphes à Résultats et Activités Interreliés (GRAI) grids, Petri nets, Input-Process-Output (IPO) charts and Design Structure Matrices (DSM), provide useful means for representing information flow in a PSS [5]. DFD can be used in organisations to propose information flow paths (logical view) and to represent actual flows (physical view). DFD depict processes, external entities, data stores and flows in sequential representations. Information flows in manufacturing can be highlighted by the IDEFØ approach by means of boxes that depict processes, and arrows that indicate inputs, controls, outputs, and mechanisms associated with a function. GRAI grids provide information flow descriptions to support decision making processes in an organisation or a system. Petri-Nets deliver representations of information flow in the development and simulation of event-driven and automated manufacturing systems. IPO charts offer information flow descriptions in programs but can also be extended to describe systems with varying complexity. DSM offer compact, visual, matrix representations for systems analysis to offer a roadmap of system level knowledge.

4 Research Methodology

This study was undertaken in four stages: literature review, state-of-the-art in industry, online questionnaire and data representation.

The research began with a literature review of function-oriented diagrammatic models for product service systems [5]. The second stage considered the state-of-the-art in industry for product-service systems within the microsystems industry based on a sample of 100 microsystems companies [12]. The sample was made up of a random selection of members of organisations (MEMS Industry Group, IVAM and SEMI) for companies aiming to carry out business transactions within the microsystems industry. These companies are headquartered at locations in Europe (56%), North America (38%) and Asia (6%). For the third stage, a questionnaire was developed and distributed with pre-defined responses (and the option of a user-defined response) from participants over a period of 3 months. The questionnaire inquired about the use and the purpose of use of media forms and information flow models in microsystems production through questions such as 'What are the major considerations in the choice of media forms?' and 'What modelling techniques have you used as part of your duties?' Responses to the questionnaires were solicited in three ways: firstly, via electronic mail containing the questionnaire, secondly, by means of an online survey site for which participants were allocated a unique ID to maintain traceability and confidentiality, and thirdly, by means of follow up telephone calls. *40 companies completed the questionnaire.* A breakdown of the types of companies that completed the questionnaire is presented in Table 1.

Table 1. Breakdown of survey respondents

Type of Company	Number of Survey Respondents
Microsystems foundry	8
Microsystems manufacturer	22
Computer-Aided Design (CAD) developer	3
Intellectual Property (IP) company	2
Consulting firm	2
Microsystems distributor	3

For the fourth stage, data representation was undertaken by means of column charts that show the results of the study. Responses to each question in the survey were aggregated and presented in a column chart that compared the aggregated responses.

5 Research Findings

In terms of media forms, the survey revealed that 40 of the respondents made use text formats (electronic mail, facsimile and text files) while 34 of the respondents applied graphical representations (diagrams and charts) for the flow of information. Audio and video formats, on the other hand, were used by 16 and 21 of the respondents respectively as shown in Fig. 1.

What media forms are used in the flow of information?

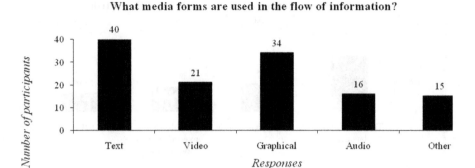

Fig. 1. Media forms for microsystems production

15% of the respondents noted the use of software based simulation and 3D simulation /animation by means of Computer-aided design (CAD) tools as key to information flow during design and development. 12.5% of the respondents noted that popular information technology formats especially slide presentations, video conferencing and internet/intranet websites were crucial to the flow of information for the design and development of microsystems. 1 of the respondents noted the use of physical prototypes as a means of information flow. 10% of the respondents also noted that information flow by face-to-face and word of mouth was applied to complement their companies' media forms because they were small and new companies to the microsystems industry.

When are these media forms used?

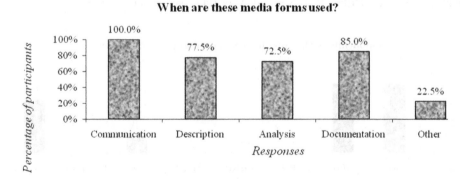

Fig. 2. Purpose of use for media forms during microsystems production

In terms of the purpose for using media forms (the question posed was 'When are these media forms used?'), 100% of the respondents chose various media forms based on use for communication, 77.5% for description of functions and processes, 72.5% for analysis of systems and 85.0% for documentation (as shown in Fig. 2). Other uses of media forms captured by 22.5% of the survey respondents included: for presenting results and for conversations to clarify concepts or rectify issue.

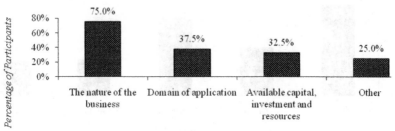

Fig. 3. Major considerations for selecting media forms during microsystems production

In relation to major considerations for selecting media forms, the study revealed that 75.0% of the respondents chose various media forms because of the nature of their business, 37.5% because of the domain of application, and 32.5% because of available capital. Other considerations for the choice of media forms include: standard industry practice, ease of communication, effort required to generate the material vs. the communication value, ease of use and convenience. These other considerations were noted by 25.0% of the survey respondents as shown in Fig. 3.

For information flow models, the survey showed that 17 of the respondents applied DFD as part of their duties, 4 respondents made use of DSM while 17 of the respondents did not make use of any of the information flow models identified in Section 2. All respondents that made use of DSM also made use of DFD. None of the respondents made use of IDEFØ, Petri Nets, GRAI or IPO charts as shown in Fig. 4.

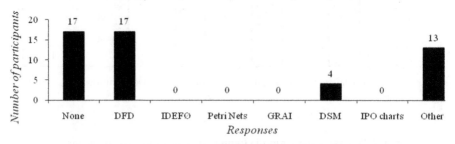

Fig. 4. Diagrammatic models for microsystems production

32.5% (13 from 40) of the respondents noted the use of other forms of diagrammatic tools such as engineering block diagrams, Gantt charts, timing diagrams, software development tools, enterprise resource planning (ERP) tools and project management tools based on methodologies such as PRINCE2 (**PR**ojects **IN**

Controlled Environments). 5% of the respondents also noted the use of intuitive and individual approaches for generating diagrams to carry out tasks.

The study revealed that when asked what diagrammatic tools were used to model, 50% (20 from 40) of the respondents answered for products while 17.5% (7 from 40) answered for services. 12.5% (5 from 40) of the respondents made use of diagrammatic tools to model both products and service.

In relation to the purpose of using modelling tools, the study showed that 50% of respondents applied modelling tools for the design and development of products as shown in Fig. 5. 15% of respondents made use of modelling tools to design services while 17.5% of respondents made use of modelling tools to develop services. Other purposes of use identified by 12.5% of respondents include: for customer support, for quality planning, for managing the life of software development, to explain products and services to customers, for research and quality control, and for the delivery of services and products.

When are these modelling tools used?

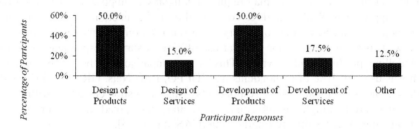

Fig. 5. Purpose of use for diagrammatic models during microsystems production

6 Implications for Product-Service Systems

The implications of this study are threefold: emphasis on business-driven information flows, simplicity of information flows and trade-offs between creativity/conformity in approaches to managing information flow.

With regards to *business-driven information flows,* the study suggests that most companies (75.0% of survey respondents) considered the nature of their business the major consideration for choice of media forms. The microsystem businesses studied included foundries, manufacturers, CAD developers, IP companies, consulting firms and distributors. Consequently, the decision by a microsystem company to make use of media forms is dependent on the type of products and services offered. For instance, a CAD developer could prefer information flow by means of software based simulation whereas microsystems distributors could lay greater emphasis on information flow by means of internet websites. Furthermore, the use of modelling tools as highlighted in the study, supports product/service design, product/service development and in one case product/service delivery.

In terms of *simplicity of information flow,* the study highlights two key themes: ease of use and informal information flows. As suggested by this study, text and graphical forms (the simpler media forms) scored higher among respondents. Furthermore, in Perry *et al.* [6] the use of face-to-face or word of mouth, though not media forms, are identified as common and informal forms of communications. Consequently, although this was not asked as part of the questionnaire, it is assumed that this is the case for all participating companies for two main reasons. Firstly, information flow by face-to-face contact and word of mouth are natural forms of information exchange and secondly, these forms of communication offer useful avenues for informal flow of information.

The study also highlights the importance of considering *trade-offs between creativity and conformity* in approaches to managing information flow. This is because the study identified cases (5% of the survey respondents) in which information flow was individual-focused i.e. companies allowed designers and engineers to make use of intuitive and individual approaches for modelling information flow. This attitude for analysing and managing information flow on one hand could foster timely delivery of a PSS. This is because approaches based on individual initiatives may allow individuals to apply approaches best suited to their mode of operation thereby fostering timeliness in the individual's results or output. On the hand, issues of compatibility and continuity in functions of a PSS may require a company to impose standard information flow approaches. With regards to compatibility in the functions of a PSS, the use of common tools such as DFD could serve as a starting point for modelling information flow. This study suggests the popular use (42.5% of survey respondents) of DFD for modelling products and services. This is in comparison to the DSM approach which was used by 10% of respondents and IDEFØ, Petri Nets, GRAI or IPO charts which were not used by any of the respondents. This suggestion correlates with assertions in literature that highlight the common use and wide spread support for DFD by most Computer-Aided Software Engineering (CASE) tools [5].

7 Conclusions

The paper presents the findings of a survey to capture information flow for product-service systems (PSS) based on a sample of 100 microsystems companies. In literature, textual, audio, video and graphical media forms of nature have been identified for maintaining information flow and for exchanging ideas among system developers and implementers. Furthermore, the use of modelling tools has been promoted in research for defining and representing information flow in organisations and systems.

As indicated by the results of 40 respondents to the survey, information flow in terms of communication, analysis, description and documentation of microsystem functions, is largely motivated by the nature of businesses. In addition, the survey showed that 17 of the respondents have used Data Flow Diagrams and 4 respondents have used Design Structure Matrices. None of the respondents made use of Integrated DEFinition (IDEFØ), Graphes à Résultats et Activités Interreliés (GRAI) grids, Petri nets or Input-Process-Output (IPO) charts. The study also highlights the importance of emphasis on business-driven information flows, simplicity of information flows and trade-offs between creativity/conformity in managing information flow.

Future work will focus on the implications of this study to propose techniques for simplifying and emphasising business-driven information flow for microsystem companies within the context of PSS. This study presents an initial attempt to investigate information flow modelling in microsystem companies. Further studies are therefore recommended to evaluate how the findings of the survey compare with other domains and the wider implications of modelling information flow for PSS in terms of promoting creativity and conformity in companies.

Acknowledgements. The authors would like to extend their sincere thanks to the Engineering and Physical Sciences Research Council (EPSRC), for its support via the Cranfield Innovative Manufacturing Research Centre (IMRC), towards the work carried out in the preparation of this paper. Also the authors would like to thank all the participants that took part in the survey.

References

1. Morelli, N.: Developing new product service systems (PSS): methodologies and operational tools. J. Clean Prod. 14, 1495–1501 (2006)
2. Fujita, H.: Two decades of MEMS – from surprise to enterprise. In: IEEE MEMS Conf., pp. 1–6 (2007)
3. Durugbo, C., Tiwari, A., Alcock, J.R.: An Infodynamic Engine Approach to Improving the Efficiency of Information Flow in a Product-Service System. In: Proceedings of the 1st CIRP IPS2 Conference, pp. 107–112 (2009)
4. Baines, T.S., Lightfoot, H.W., Evans, S., Neely, A., Greenough, R., Peppard, J., Roy, R., Shehab, E., Braganza, A., Tiwari, A., Alcock, J.R., Angus, J.P., Basti, M., Cousens, A., Irving, P., Johnson, M., Kingston, J., Lockett, H., Martinez, V., Michele, P., Tranfield, D., Walton, I.M., Wilson, H.: State-of-the-art in product-service systems. P I Mech. Eng. B-J. Eng. 221, 1543–1552 (2007)
5. Durugbo, C., Tiwari, A., Alcock, J.R.: A Review of Information Flow Diagrammatic Models for Product-Service Systems. Submitted to Int. J. Adv. Manuf. Tech. (2009)
6. Perry, M.J., Fruchter, R., Spinelli, G.: Spaces, traces and networked design. In: P Ann HICSS, pp. 112–121 (2001)
7. Doumeingts, G.: GRAI Approach to Designing and Controlling Advanced Manufacturing Systems in CIM Environment. In: Nof, S.Y., Moodie, C.L. (eds.) Advanced Information Technologies for Industrial Material Flow Systems. NATO ASI Series, pp. 461–529. Springer, Berlin (1989)
8. Martin, J., McClure, C.: Diagramming Techniques for Analysts and Programmers. Prentice Hall, Englewood Cliffs (1985)
9. DeMarco, T.: Structured Analysis and System Specification. Yourdon Press, New Jersey (1979)
10. Katzan, H.: Systems Design and Documentation: An Introduction to the HIPO Method. Van Nostrand Reinhold, New York (1976)
11. Hungerford, B.C., Hevner, A.R., Collins, R.W.: Reviewing software diagrams: a cognitive study. IEEE T Software Eng. 30, 82–96 (2004)
12. Durugbo, C., Tiwari, A., Alcock, J.R.: State-of-the-art in Product-Service Systems based Microsystems Production. Submitted to Int. J. Adv. Manuf. Tech. (2009)

Part 3

Collaborative Networks Support

The Virtual Enterprise from a Governance Perspective

David Romero[1], Ana Inês Oliveira[2],
Luis M. Camarinha-Matos[2,3], and Arturo Molina[1]

[1] Tecnológico de Monterrey, Campus Monterrey & Ciudad de México, México
david.romero.diaz@gmail.com, armolina@itesm.mx
[2] UNINOVA, Portugal
[3] Universidade Nova de Lisboa, Portugal
aio@uninova.pt, cam@uninova.pt

Abstract. Virtual Enterprises (VEs) are temporary alliances of enterprises that share a common goal towards responding to a competitive collaboration or business opportunity. VEs need suitable governance principles that can only be achieved if during the VE creation they have been properly defined through a negotiation process. This paper presents the VE from a governance perspective and how fundamental the negotiation process in the VE creation phase can be.

Keywords: Virtual Enterprise, Governance, Negotiation, Agreements, Contract.

1 Introduction

Virtual Enterprise (VE) governance principles can be understood as a set of guidelines to adapt, coordinate and safeguard autonomous actions, performed by different VE actors, collectively working in a joint plan determined by a collaboration or business opportunity, where risks, resources, responsibilities and rewards are shared to achieve a common goal during the VE lifecycle. In this sense, VE governance is defined as the ground rules and principles by which a Virtual Enterprise will be governed and managed during its lifecycle, i.e. creation, operation/evolution and dissolution. Furthermore, it is important to mention that the VE governance approach and rules for each Virtual Enterprise will be negotiated and agreed between the VE partners during its creation process. Considering the VE creation process within the context of a VE Breeding Environment (VBE) [1], most of the VE governance principles will be instantiated from the common principles adopted in the VBE and some will be defined by the VE partners (if need) taking into account the collaboration or business opportunity requirements and the VE model characteristics. As a result of this "inheritance" from the VBE, the VE set-up time will be reduced noticeably by decreasing the number of governance issues to be negotiated and agreed regarding the VE governance structure, including the supervision, control and coordination mechanisms related to the VE management. Therefore, authors propose to use the VBE governance model defined by Romero et al [2] as a starting base to instantiate a VE governance model that will inherited the most important principles, bylaws and rules to define a governance framework for the VE management, which will provide to the VE planner/coordinator a set of guidelines to make decisions, negotiate and assign/allocate tasks and resources among VE partners aiming to optimize the VE performance (Fig. 1).

L.M. Camarinha-Matos, P. Pereira, and L. Ribeiro (Eds.): DoCEIS 2010, IFIP AICT 314, pp. 73–82, 2010.
© IFIP International Federation for Information Processing 2010

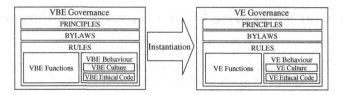

Fig. 1. From a VBE Governance Model to a VE Governance Model [2]

The following sections will introduce a set of guiding principles to support the design and management of an effective VE governance model founded on the results of an empirical research study based on 10 collaborative networks (CNs): IECOS (MX), ISOIN (ES), ORONA (ES), Virtuelle Fabrik (DE/CH), CeBeNetwork (FR/DE/UK), Virfebras (BR) Swiss Microtech (CH/CN), Torino Wireless (IT), Virtual Enterprise Network (UK), and Supply Network Shannon (IE).

The methodology followed for this research study included an extensive literature review on available knowledge on governance in the CNs domain[1] and a set of interviews/study cases to the CNs listed.

2 Contribution to Technological Innovation

For the accurate operation of a Virtual Enterprise, its creation represents a crucial phase, because it is at this stage that most of the VE details are defined. The fact that the VE creation is supposed to happen in the context of a VBE also gives a good indication of the level of the desired agility of the collaboration system, as it provides the suitable environment for such collaborations, such as collaboration history, trust and similarity of ICT infrastructure. Moreover, in order to have an effective operation of a Virtual Enterprise, proper governance principles and models have to be settled during the VE creation negotiation. Hence, this paper intends to contribute in this direction. Simultaneously, some examples of technological tools that may help the process are also suggested.

3 Virtual Enterprise Governance

Virtual Enterprise Principles. *VE principles* are defined as the values that should govern the VE partners' behaviour during their involvement in collaboration or business opportunities. Table 1 introduces some of the values understood as social attitudes which will impact the VE partners' collaborative performance.

Virtual Enterprise Bylaws. *VE bylaws* underline the VE actors' roles, rights, responsibilities and procedures for participating in collaboration or business opportunities (VE creation), and the manner for conducting proper VE management as a set of supervision, control and monitoring activities to guarantee reaching the

---

[1] The present ideas are based on a number of papers that cannot be referred due to the restricted space.

goals settled for a collaboration opportunity. In addition, VE bylaws may include some other governance mechanisms aimed at rewarding good performance, sanction opportunistic behaviours, providing guidelines for conflict resolutions, and managing intellectual property rights in collaborative endeavours.

VE Actors' Roles, Rights and Responsibilities. In a Virtual Enterprise several *roles* can be played by a number of actors. A VE actor can be represented either by an enterprise or by an individual representing an enterprise. Some of these *roles* can be assumed simultaneously by the same enterprise or individual. Each actor's participation in a VE is related to a specific *role,* including a set of *rights* and *responsibilities* associated to that *role.* Each of these *roles* requires assigning different *rights* and *responsibilities.* Table 2 describes the main roles, rights and responsibilities for each VE actor in order to define certain levels of responsibility and information access associated to each role.

Table 1. VE Principles (VE Partners' Expected Behaviours)

Principle	Description
Honesty	• When providing profiling and competency information. • When providing trust criteria information for trustworthiness evaluation.
Trust / Integrity	• When acting loyalty with good faith for all VE stakeholders. • When playing different VE roles always avoiding opportunistic behaviours.
Openness	• When sharing risks, resources, responsibilities and rewards. • When negotiating different VE related issues.
Performance Orientation	• When performing the tasks assigned by the VE coordinator, always meeting or even exceeding the cost, time and quality frames expected. • When collaborating, always trying to enhance collaborative performance by improving reliability, flexibility, responsiveness and communication.
Responsibility	• When attempting to keep promises such as delivery times and quality levels.
Mutual Respect	• When diverse opinions may arise during negotiation processes.
Commitment	• When complying with agreements reached. • When meeting the VE contracts terms.

VE Membership Policies. Once a collaboration or business opportunity has been identified, a set of enterprises will be selected from a VBE to form a VE according to the collaboration opportunity requirements [1]. The *VE membership policies* refer then to the governance of all activities related to the VE partners search and selection process, following certain regulations to guarantee the VE partners fair selection under equal opportunity bases and based-on transparent criteria. In this direction, a 'template' for providing detailed/updated information about the potential VE partners' competences should be provided, so the candidates can provide on equal bases their related information about processes capabilities, free resources capacities, production costs and conspicuous proof of the validity of the provided information [4]. Thus, the VE planner may have the proper information to select the best-fit VE partners for a new VE according to the collaboration opportunity (CO) requirements. Moreover, the VE broker should make public the collaboration opportunity requirements under a definition of the necessary competences to perform certain activities/tasks concerning the VE work breakdown structure. In this way, the potential VE partners may compare their available competences against specific activities/tasks that need certain

Table 2. VE Actors' Roles, Rights and Responsibilities

Broker	• **Role.** Performs as identifier and/or designer of new collaboration or business opportunities. • **Rights.** Access to information about new collaboration or business opportunities; Access to VE partners profiling & competency information. • **Responsibilities.** Identify, acquire and design collaboration opportunities; Market the VE competences; Negotiate with VBE customers; Discover competency gaps as weak points and missing competences when evaluating collaboration or business opportunities or when VE creation failed due to lack of competences.
Planner	• **Role.** Performs as designer of the VE rough plan and as the integrator of potential VE partners to fulfil a collaboration or business opportunity, being responsible for setting-up the consortium. • **Rights.** Access to information about new collaboration opportunities; Access to VE partners profiling & competency information; Access to VE partners past performance record. • **Responsibilities.** Search for the most suitable VE partners according to the collaboration or business opportunity requirements; Create, configure and negotiate the VE rough plan structure by scheduling activities and assigning tasks to VE partners to achieve the required time, cost and quality frames requested by the VE customer.
Coordinator	• **Role.** Performs as coordinator/manager of a VE during its operation and dissolution phases. • **Rights.** Access to VE partners profiling & competency information; Access to VE partners past performance record; Access to VE inheritance information; Access to the VE related information. • **Responsibilities.** Define the VE profiling and competency information; Coordinate the VE partners in order to fulfil the goals settled in the creation phase; Monitor the VE activities status according to the VE plan; Supervise the VE performance; Intervene on VE corrective actions.
Partner	• **Role.** Performs the tasks assigned by the VE coordinator according to VE contract and/or agreement(s). • **Rights.** Access to VE related information. • **Responsibilities.** Keep updated own VE partner profiling and competency information; Negotiate contracts and/or collaboration agreements; Report on tasks progress.
Customer	• **Role.** May perform as the trigger of a new VE by originating a business opportunity. • **Rights.** Depending on the VE business, the customer may access to VE activities status to track progress. • **Responsibilities.** Describe the product (good and/or service) to be delivered according to preferences and constrains (e.g. time, cost and quality).

processes capabilities and resources capacities to be carried out and apply to perform them during the VE operation [4]. Depending on the CO constrains, the VE planner may also use other assessment/selection approaches as performance indicators, and/or trust level, to filter and select the potential VE partners [3].

VE Management Recommendations. VE management can be defined as a set of activities, measures and operations needed to guide the VE partners and to control the VE operational processes and their interdependencies in order to achieve the VE objectives without breaking any legal, contractual and governance agreement [5]. In a VE context, both the governance and management activities are devoted to support the VE coordinator in its responsibility of ensuring that all VE partners will contribute and perform according to plan during the VE lifecycle. Nevertheless, the VE management activities cannot be to fully regulated. Therefore, the VE governance principles can provide, in this sense, some common basis to guide the VE partners' behaviours in any situation that could not be regulated in the consortium agreement. Consequently, the VE governance principles as the VE partners' expected behaviours (Table 1) will motivate a proactive conduct towards the VE objectives achievement and good relationships among the VE partners.

VE Incentives & Sanctions. Incentives & sanctions can influence the motivation and performance of VE partners. For example, if a VE partner is always performing within a certain collaborative performance level, this should be recognized and rewarded, perhaps during the VE partners search and selection process. On the other hand, if a VE partner is not performing at the expect level, having long delivery times and bad quality during the VE operation, it should be positioned in a passive role (e.g. poor VE involvement) for a certain period of time, till the enterprise demonstrates an improvement in its readiness for collaboration [3].

VE Security Issues (Confidentiality of Information). A Virtual Enterprise can be simply based-on trust relationships, informal knowledge and intellectual property sharing. Nevertheless, it is recommended to establish interchange agreements and confidentiality agreements to safeguard the confidential information and intellectual property at the necessity of their disclosure and sharing. During the VE creation process, potential VE partners may be required to provide some confidential information regarding their competences to the VE planner and even to other potential VE partners in order to promote themselves towards VE involvement and also to facilitate the VE configuration. Therefore, a preliminary 'confidential agreement' should be put in place in order to protect any information that may be disclosed during the VE creation process in order to maintain the necessary level of secrecy regarding all information that will reach all parties involved, both during the course of negotiations and afterwards for an unlimited time period. When a VE is created in the context of a VBE it is likely that such principles have been part of the VBE bylaws. Furthermore, during the VE operation, VE partners should establish an 'interchange agreement' to delimitate the use of intellectual property shared by any VE partner for the purpose specified and the time period defined in the agreement. Also, a confidentiality agreement should establish bilateral non-disclosure agreements that will facilitate the communication between VE partners and the information provision to the VE coordinator for decision making. Finally, as part of the VE dissolution, VE partners should establish an agreement for the right use of the know-how gained during the VE lifecycle, under the condition that they should maintain secrecy regarding those outside of the former VE partners. General templates for all these agreements can be established at the VBE level and thus avoiding lengthy negotiations at the VE creation phase.

VE Lifecycle Support Tools – Use Guidelines. This *bylaw* is related to the use of technology as a supporting mean to provide access to the information and interactions required by each VE actor to perform its duties. As mentioned before, VE partners have different rights and responsibilities, according to their roles, that demand the use of different *software tools* and access to different *information repositories* for supporting their activities in which they enrol during VE lifecycle. Table 3 introduces some of the examples of software tools developed in ECOLEAD [1] [6] aimed at supporting the VE lifecycle and the actors that directly interact with them.

VE Conflict Resolution Policies. Possible *conflicts* and *disputes* that may arise among VE partners will be worked out by a steering committee headed by the VE coordinator, and if necessary by an advisor according to the conflict domain. In case of not solving the problem according to internal VE bylaws, VE partners may proceed to take case into legal statements.

VE Financial Policies. Being a VE shareholder (a VE partner) means to provide resources: financial, physical, technological and/or knowledge in order to support the VE existence and benefit from dividends as a result of getting involved and respond to collaboration or business opportunity identified in the market. In the VE context, payments and the accounting structure must be defined during VE creation in order to guarantee a fair distribution of the revenues according to the roles played, contributions made and tasks performed by each VE partner during the VE operation. Additionally, the *VE financial policies* should include other financial obligations like tax payments and insurance coverage for the VE customer after the VE dissolution.

Table 3. Examples of VE Lifecycle Tools

Creation	• **Broker** - The *Collaboration Opportunity Identification (CO-Finder)* is a supporting tool for the identification of new COs available as call for tenders in e-marketplaces [1]. • **Planner** - The *Collaboration Opportunity Characterization* and *VE rough planning (COC-Plan)* is a supporting tool for identifying the required competences to respond to an identified CO, as well as for defining a rough structure of the potential VE [1]. • **Planner** - The *VE Partners Search and Selection (PSS)* is a supporting tool devoted to the identification of potential VE partners, their assessment and selection by matching their competences with the required competences to respond to an identified CO [1]. • **Planner/Coordinator & VBE members** - The *Agreement/Contract Negotiation Wizard (WizAN)* is a supporting tool aimed at assisting the VE planner and the potential VE partners during the negotiation processes towards the VE constitution. It includes features for the formulation and modelling of internal consortium contracts and agreements [1] [6].
Operation/Evolution	• **Coordinator** - The *VO Modelling Environment (VO-MOD)* is a supporting tool for modelling the VE structure and its related information such as: VE topology, VE work breakdown structure, budget elements, key performance indicators, etc. [7]. • **Coordinator** - The *Supporting Indicator Definition (SID)* is a supporting tool for configuring a set of key performance indicators for case-specific applications [7]. • **Coordinator** - The *Distributed Indicator Information Integrator (DI3)* is a supporting tool for information retrieval from different repositories namely belonging to different partners [7]. • **Coordinator** - The *Monitor and Finance Functionalities (MAF)* is a supporting tool for monitoring the VE performance during its lifecycle [7]. • **Coordinator** - The *Decision Support System (DSS)* is a supporting tool for re-scheduling and reconfiguration of the VE rough plan structure [7].
Dissolution	• **Coordinator** - The *Virtual Enterprise Information Management System (VIMS)* is a supporting tool for managing all VE related information as well as the VE inheritance information [5].

VE Financial Policies. Being a VE shareholder (a VE partner) means to provide resources: financial, physical, technological and/or knowledge in order to support the VE existence and benefit from dividends as a result of getting involved and respond to collaboration or business opportunity identified in the market. In the VE context, payments and the accounting structure must be defined during VE creation in order to guarantee a fair distribution of the revenues according to the roles played, contributions made and tasks performed by each VE partner during the VE operation. Additionally, the *VE financial policies* should include other financial obligations like tax payments and insurance coverage for the VE customer after the VE dissolution.

VE IPR Policies. The *VE IPR policies* deal with the intellectual rights shared during the VE lifecycle, but in special with the intellectual property (IP) created during the VE operation (e.g. a patent). Proper IP agreements should depict that the involved VE partners will share reasonable legal fees, costs and expenses related to the filing, prosecuting and maintaining a patent protection. Also, the respective share to obtain revenues from the invention licensing or commercialization should be considered.

VE Amendments to Bylaws. Bylaws are subject to *amendment* at any regular meeting of the Virtual Enterprise. Consensus and approval by the majority of the VE partners must occur so an amendment can be modified.

Following paragraphs will introduce some key **VE rules** identified in this work:

VE Behavioural Rules. VE behavioural rules refer to those guidelines for VE partners to properly act and conduct during the VE lifecycle, including the VE ethical code and culture. The *VE ethical code* intends to define the core-values, ethical principles and ethical standards to guide the VE partners' decision making and conduct during the VE lifecycle, so VE partners have common bases for acting in all situations. Furthermore, the *VE culture* aims to create a collaborative culture where a shared belief between potential VE partners is promoted under the premise that by working together the VE partners can best accomplish a common goal that would not be possible, or would have higher cost, if attempted individually.

VE Functional Rules. VE functional rules are aimed at supporting both *operational* and *administrative processes* along the VE lifecycle. Most important functional rules for VE management may include: guidelines for configuration and launching; VE operation guidelines for collaborative business processes management, including collaborative performance measurement; VE evolution guidelines for activities re-scheduling and resources reallocation; and VE dissolution guidelines for inheritance information management.

4   Supporting VE Creation Process: Negotiation and Contracting

To guarantee that during the VE lifecycle phases everything is performed in a proper and legal manner, the VE creation phase is of extreme importance, since during this phase it is essential to carry out a *negotiation process* with all the VE partners until final agreements related to the VE consortium formation, VE rough plan structure and VE governance model (Section 2) are achieved. The establishment of collaboration commitments, represented by *contracts* and/or *agreements,* corresponds then to the most crucial step in a VE creation process [1] [6]. During the VE creation phase, negotiation is an iterative process to reach agreements and it can be seen as complementary to the VE rough planning and VE partners' selection processes, and might in fact require going back to previous steps if a solution cannot be found with the current the VE partners' configuration.

The VE creation process is not as simply as selecting the right VE partners and matching their competences to the CO requirements; there are many other factors which can also affect the VE creation process. The contract/agreement(s) negotiation shall then proceed in parallel with the other VE creation phases. In each step, specific elements for the contract/agreement(s) should be collected as a result of a focused negotiation process. Table 4a describes the VE creation process when a contract for a new collaboration or business opportunity is already guaranteed, while in contrast, Table 4b describes a scenario where the collaboration or business opportunity is not yet acquired. In each case different negotiation agreements should be reached.

Table 4. VE Creation Phases according to Its Trigger

(a) VE Creation Phases for acquired Collaboration or Business Opportunity
Preparatory Planning: (1) CO/BO Identification and Characterization - Identification and characterization of a new collaboration or business opportunity (CO/BO) that can be detected by a broker or promoted as part of the VBE business strategy. **(2) VE Rough planning** - Identification of the required VE partners competences, as well as the VE possible configurations as work breakdown structure structures to execute the VE tasks. At this stage it is crucial to define the VE partnership form and its cooperation agreements.
Consortium Formation: (3) Partners Search & Selection - Identification of potential VE partners and their assessment and selection. **(4) VE Composition** - Iterative process to reach agreements and align needs with offers.   It can be seen as complementary to the other steps in the VE creation process.
VE Launching: (5) Detailed VE plan - Once the VE partners have been selected and agreements are reached, it is necessary to refine the VE rough plan and its governance principles. **(6) Contracting & Set-up** - Formulation of contract and agreement models and set-up the necessary infrastructures to start the VE operation.
(b) VE Creation Phases for Quotation/Bidding
Quotation/Bidding Phase: (1) CO identification, (2) VE rough plan, (3) VE partners selection, (4) Prepare bid - When an opportunity is identified it is necessary to prepare a bid/quotation in order to try to get a contract with the customer. For the preparation of this bid, it is necessary to make a rough plan of the foreseen VE and also to select the core VE partners. The bid is often prepared by the initial VE consortium.
Contract Attainment (5a) - In case the bid is "unsuccessful", the core VE consortium dissolves; otherwise the VE creation continues.
Final VE Creation: (5b) Revise VE rough plan, (6) Select additional VE partners, (7) VE details & contracting, (8) VE set-up - In case the bid is "successful", the VE rough plan needs to be revised based-on the specific contract conditions with the customer; new additional VE partners might be necessary, and the VE will be detailed and launched.

Contracts/Agreements: Classes, Topologies and Lifecycle. In a VBE context, which offers a common ground for the establishment of cooperation agreements, common operation principles and mutual trust, the VBE members (potential VE partners) can take advantage of the breeding environment to prepare themselves to collaborate in potential VEs that will be established when a collaboration or business opportunity arises. Nevertheless, being VEs temporary alliances triggered by specific opportunities, their structure and governance may differ from one to another, therefore several and/or different *classes of contracts* and/or *agreements* may be required to support its creation. Most VE related agreements rely on the number of parties involved and on the implied promises. Regarding the first case, the number of parties involved may imply 'bi-lateral' or 'multi-lateral' contracts, while in the second case, contracts can be classified according to their promises as (a) 'adhesion contracts' - recognized as standardized contracts that in general are offered without affording a realistic opportunity to bargain/negotiate and under such conditions the only way to obtain the desired result is by accepting all the contract terms; (b) 'internal contracts' - understood as contracts that do not include any supply to third parties (although the partners' goal might include it); and (c) 'external contracts' - understood as contracts that represent a joint activity with third parties [1] [6].

The most suitable application for these types of contracts in relation to a VE creation process within a VBE would be: (a) the VBE members adhesion contract to join the breeding environment and inherit/accept the VBE governance principles; (b) the internal contract as the agreements that will regulate the VE consortium behaviour, in which the VE governance principles and rules will be explicitated; and (c) the external contract where the VE commitment to the customer will be detailed.

Table 5 describes different types of VE governance according to the *VE topology*. In addition to the traditional supply-chain topology, the most typical solution for the consortium internal contract/agreement are the cases of (1) explicit consortium - the collaboration is regulated by a contract between the VE customer and the VE consortium that clearly describes the VE consortium composition; the VE consortium by itself is regulated by an internal agreement, and (2) internal consortium - there is a contract between the VE customer and one VE partner, which does not necessarily explicit the VE consortium composition; in this case there is only one VE partner that is committed to the VE customer, being the other VE partners committed to the one that signs the contract.

Table 5. VE Governance Topologies

Supply-Chain: Process Oriented	• **Topology:** In a supply-chain topology, partners' interaction pattern follows a value chain. • **Governance Characteristics:** Long-term partnerships; Inexistence of a leader; Linear relations (one-to-one); Independent decision-making; Limited organisational flexibility depending on the value chain. • **Governance Implication:** Limited communication; Limited information exchange; Alignment of activities so that more efficient results can be achieved; Partners' relations limited to their pairs (neighbour partners); Organisational integration limited to pairs; Bilateral agreements.
Hub & Spoke: Main Contractor	• **Topology:** In a star topology, partners interact through a central hub or strategic operation centre, allowing a more rapid configuration of the partners' network. • **Governance Characteristics:** Medium-term partnerships; one leader; centralized relations (all-to-one); centralized decision-making; limited organisational flexibility determined by a leader. • **Governance Implication:** Limited communication and information exchange restricted by the power centralization; division of labour among partners coordinated by the strategic operation centre; the central hub (contractor) assumes the responsibility for the group; some tools available to share information; possibility to limit the potential participation of partners; association agreements.
Peer-to-Peer: Project Oriented	• **Topology:** In a peer-to-peer topology, partners' interaction pattern relies on personal networks and social relationships. • **Governance Characteristics:** Short-term partnerships; Multiple relations (all-to-all); Democratic decision-making; High organisational flexibility determined by the possible network configurations. • **Governance Implication:** Partners share: risks, resources, responsibilities, benefits, etc; Partners' preparation to play/assume multiple roles; Clear definition of the roles, rights and responsibilities; Extensive use of tools to share information; Multiple kinds of agreements.

Similar to VEs, contracts also have a lifecycle that includes several phases, starting with the intention of establishing a contract and ending with its actual enactment. This last phase, the contract enactment, is the fulfilment of the promised obligations of the parties involved (the VE partners) and the corresponding benefits. Nevertheless, the relevance of this work is put into the contract establishment phase that is when the process of finding suitable contracting parties and negotiating contract/agreement(s) with them happen. With the purpose of illustrating a tool that intends to support the negotiation process during the VE creation phase, below, it is briefly described the WizAN tool that was developed within the ECOLEAD project.

Agreement Negotiation (WizAN) Tool. The WizAN [1] [6] is an example of a tool to support the negotiation process during the VE creation process and its operation/ evolution phase in case a VE partner might be replaced. The WizAN aim is not to fully automate the negotiation process, but rather to assist the human actors in the process itself. WizAN tool inputs are collected along the steps of the VE creation phase (e.g. rough plan, scheduling, budgets, needed competences, suitable partners, shared assets, liability allocation, etc.). The full negotiation process involves a number of elementary negotiations in order to reach the necessary agreements to accomplishing a VE internal agreement. The VE internal consortium contract is then the synthesis of all agreements established among the VE partners that will regulate and govern their collaboration.

Table 6. WizAN's Main Functionalities

Functionality	Description	Outputs	Actors
Contract Editor	• Uses the contract editor repository and agreed negotiation items/clauses to add sections to contracts.	Contracts/ agreements	VE Planner
Virtual Negotiation Room	• Virtual place where negotiation participants can access the various items/clauses being negotiated and can "discuss" them in order to reach agreements	Agreed Negotiation items / clauses	VE Planner & VE partners
Support for Agreement Establishment	• Facilities for contract signing, notification of events or new agreement documents relevant to parties, and repository/ archive for its storage (e.g. eNotary).	Signed Contracts Repository	VE Planner & VE partners
Contract System	• Collection of contract and negotiation clauses templates to support the contracts creation.	Contracts Skeletons	VE Planner

5   Conclusions

The need of a VE governance model arises from the necessity of having common operating principles and rules to allow an effective communication and coordination between VE partners during the VE lifecycle. This paper provides a set of guidelines to define a VE governance model by presenting its main elements (principles, bylaws and rules), and introduces a supporting tool (WizAN) for the negotiation of those contracts and/or agreements needed to formalize a VE collaboration.

Acknowledgments. The joint research presented in this document is a contribution the "Collaborative Networks and Distributed Industrial Systems" Research Group, from UNINOVA and the "Technological Innovation" Research Chair of TESM.

References

1. Camarinha-Matos, L.M., Oliveira, A.I., Sesana, M., Galeano, N., Demsar, D., Baldo, F., Jarimo, T.: A Framework for Computer-assisted Creation of Dynamic Virtual Organisations. International Journal of Production Research 47(17), 4661–4690 (2009)
2. Romero, D., Giraldo, J., Galeano, N., Molina, A.: Towards Governance Rules and Bylaws for Virtual Breeding Environments. In: Camarinha-Matos, L.M., Afsarmanesh, H., Novais, P., Analide, C. (eds.) Establishing the Foundation of Collaborative Networks, vol. 243, pp. 93–102. Springer, Heidelberg (2007)
3. Romero, D., Galeano, N., Molina, A.: Mechanisms for Assessing and Enhancing Organisations' Readiness Collaboration in Collaborative Networks. Journal of Production Research Production Research 47(17) (2008)
4. Ermilova, E., Afsarmanesh, H.: Competency Modelling Targeted on Promotion of Organizations towards VO Involvement. In: Camarinha-Matos, L.M., Picard, W. (eds.) Pervasive Collaborative Networks, vol. 283, pp. 3–14. Springer, Heidelberg (2008)
5. Jasson, K., Karvonen, I., Ollus, M., Negretto, U.: Governance and Management of Virtual Organizations. In: Camarinha-Matos, L.M., Afsarmanesh, H., Ollus, M. (eds.) Methods and Tools for Collaborative Networked Organizations, pp. 221–238. Springer, Heidelberg (2008)
6. Oliveira, A.I., Camarinha-Matos, L.M.: Agreement Negotiation Wizard. In: Camarinha-Matos, L.M., Afsarmanesh, H., Ollus, M. (eds.) Methods and Tools for Collaborative Networked Organizations, pp. 191–218. Springer, Heidelberg (2008)
7. Negretto, U., Hodík, J., Král, L., Mulder, W., Ollus, M., Pondrelli, L., Westphal, I.: VO Management Solutions. In: Camarinha-Matos, L.M., Afsarmanesh, H., Ollus, M. (eds.) Methods and Tools for Collaborative Networked Organizations, pp. 257–274. Springer, Heidelberg (2008)

Negotiation and Contracting in Collaborative Networks

Ana Inês Oliveira[1] and Luis M. Camarinha-Matos[1,2]

[1] UNINOVA, Instituto de Desenvolvimento de Novas Tecnologias, Campus da Caparica,
Quinta da Torre, 2829-516 Monte Caparica, Portugal
[2] Faculty of Sciences and Technology, New University of Lisbon, Campus da Caparica, Quinta
da Torre, 2829-516 Monte Caparica, Portugal
{aio,cam}@uninova.pt

Abstract. Due to the increasing market turbulence, companies, organizations
and individuals need to tune their actuation forms so that they can prevail. It is
particularly essential to create alliances and partnerships for collaborative
problem solving when responding to new businesses or collaborative
opportunities. In all types of alliances it is necessary to establish agreements
that represent the rights and duties of all involved parts in a given collaboration
opportunity. Therefore, it is important to deeply understand the structures and
requirements of these alliances, i.e. what kind of members does the alliance
have, what kind of protocols may be implied, how conflicts may possibly be
resolved, etc. Moreover to these requirements, also the required support tools
and mechanisms have to be identified. For that, this paper presents a research
work that is being carried in the negotiation and contracting field, in order to
promote agility in collaborative networks.

Keywords: Collaborative networks, negotiation, agreement, virtual organization
creation, virtual organization breeding environment, agility, reliability.

1 Introduction

Due to the persistent market instability it is increasingly mandatory that companies
and organizations increase their agility and promptly react and respond to business or
collaboration opportunities that occur. Occasionally, they might not be able to react
and respond by themselves, and consequently, have to collaborate with their peers.
For that, the topic of collaborative networks (CNs) appears significantly promising. If
the enterprises or the organizations share a common interoperable infrastructure,
common operating principles, common cooperation agreements, and a base of trust
among them, then their ability to rapidly form a virtual organization (VO) is increased
[9]. Nevertheless, to form a VO, besides the important mission of selecting the
adequate partners with the most suitable competencies to respond to the collaboration
opportunity (CO) characteristics, it is also of extreme importance to have a robust and
reliable negotiation mechanism that enables the possible VO partners to negotiate in
order to achieve a consensus VO agreement during the VO creation process. This VO
agreement will then be the basis for the governing principles of the VO during its
operation phase.

L.M. Camarinha-Matos, P. Pereira, and L. Ribeiro (Eds.): DoCEIS 2010, IFIP AICT 314, pp. 83–92, 2010.

Furthermore, depending on the different domains or on the different objectives, CNs, and specifically, VOs may appear in a variety of forms with a variety of behavioral patterns [8]. Thus, it is also important to have into account that each environment must be treated accordingly to its context and to its fundamental characteristics. This also applies to the negotiation process that will also have to be *adaptable* to each specific case. Therefore, although significant work has already been carried out in the area of *CNs* and in the area of *electronic contracting*, one gap still exists that leaves space for additional research work, that is:

How can different collaborative environments be characterized in terms of their negotiation space, and how can the electronic negotiation process for consortia creation be handled to increase agility and reliability?

2   Contribution to Technological Innovation

Whenever a business or collaboration opportunity appears, if the interested entities are clustered into VO Breeding Environments (VBEs), the chance of acquiring the business opportunity is higher. Nevertheless, although the mechanisms and models provided by the VBE to its members already facilitate the VO formation, one important stage that is specific for each case is the negotiation between possible VO partners due to the numerous differences that those partners might have, for example, cultural differences. Thus, having into account this background, the motivation of this work is on the negotiation process that happens during the VO creation phase, which certainly has a relevant impact on the agility and reliability of the process, and can ensure the proper functioning of the VO during its operation phase. From this negotiation process the main outcome will be the VO consortium agreement that will represent the governing rules and principles of the consortium during its operation phase and it can include negotiation of rights and duties of all partners involved, but also can include for example, some sections on intellectual property rights, partners' benefits and shared risks.

For this significant topic on collaborative networks, proper technological support must be provided. For that, this work contributes with an identification and preliminary characterization of technological tools that can be related to the topic and for the consolidation of important characteristics of the negotiation process in the formation of collaborative consortia.

3   Related Work

As mentioned in the previous sections, the most important fields of this work are: the collaborative networks, in particular virtual organization creation and its related environment; and the negotiation and contracting. Therefore, in the next two subsections a brief outline and discussion on these areas is described.

Virtual Organization Creation and its Related Environment. The Virtual Organization (VO) paradigm constitutes one of the first manifestations of the collaborative networks. Being the concept developed and applied in several domains and areas, many contributions for the characterization and modeling of the paradigm can be found in the literature, as exemplified by [7] and [9]. The main idea behind this concept is basically of a temporary consortium of enterprises and/or organizations, geographically dispersed, that strategically join their competencies to rapidly respond to a business or collaboration opportunity. Typically VOs are supported by computer networks [4] [5]. Nevertheless, to enable the rapidness in the VO creation process, it is necessary that enough information is available about potential partners and that they are ready and prepared to participate in such collaboration. This readiness includes the existence of common models and infrastructures that can be achieved if the VO creation happens in the context of a VO Breeding Environment (VBE). Contrary to the VO that is a temporary collaboration, the VBE is a long-term alliance of the member organizations that provides the necessary means for the VO creation [3] [9]. Therefore, the VO creation process, that is triggered by a CO during the operation phase of a VBE, is well identified and characterized, including its structure, requirements, working flow, actors involved, and technological tools that can be used for each phase [10].

For most of the phases of the VO creation, a negotiation process might be required, for example to settle on agreements among possible VO partners. In this context, negotiation and agreement establishment appears as a major issue for VO, namely during its creation phase, but also potentially in its evolution phase, for example if during the VO operation phase a VO partner might need to be added or replaced [6] or to resolve some conflicts among network participants, that are inevitable [14].

Negotiation and Contracting. Negotiation is an interactive communication and decision-making process between two or more parties who seek a consensus decision and cannot apply unilateral actions to achieve their objectives [19].

As negotiation processes involve a transversal, multi- and inter-disciplinary approach, it is necessary to have a holistic view of the problem, making use of multiple methodologies and paying attention to the practical details [12]. So, a negotiation process can rely on several mechanisms such as: auctions, game theory, intelligent agent mechanisms, etc. [17]. Nevertheless, such process if often conducted by human actors that in the last instance are the ones responsible for decision-making. Although some works try to insert some automation into the negotiation process [13], this continues to be a rather difficult issue. The main obstacle is to produce a context-independent solution [2], and thus only partial and very specific solutions and prototypes with practical relevance are available, as is for example the case of the eLegal project [20] where the main goal was to develop solutions to legal issues related to VOs in the area of the civil construction. Nevertheless this framework would be prepared specifically for each project. Furthermore, the legal and contractual issues associated to each contract/agreement concentrated on the ICT perspective can be found in [21].

Focusing on the contract or agreement being established among the partners that will form a VO, that is, the internal consortium agreement, its relevance is to establish the necessary clauses to regulate the consortium behaviour during the VO operation phase. In this way, special attention should be put into e-contracting forms as they can capture and describe the rights and duties of all VO partners [18], as well as specification of penalties to apply to those that do not satisfy the agreement.

Computer assisted negotiation and e-contracting is expected to provide a faster and cheaper solution than traditional contracting for geographically distributed consortia formation. Several significant characteristics of the e-contracting process can be found in [1]. Moreover, an electronic contract can have both a machine readable and human readable representation, that is usually required when the contract creation and management involves the participation of human beings.

Moreover, the advances in the negotiation domain stem from the use of information systems and communication media to support negotiation processes and decisions. Negotiation Support Systems (NSS) are interactive, computer-based tools intended to support negotiating parties in reaching agreements. These systems provide varying levels of structured communications and decision support; and offer both dispute resolution mechanisms (i.e. dealing with infringements of existing contracts) as well as contract formation services (i.e., creating new agreements) [19].

Progress in this area during the last years has highlighted a number of important topics that need to be considered when developing processes and methodologies for negotiation and e-contracting, including *Contract Models*, *Ontology*, *Contract Framework*, *Electronic Institutions*, and *Digital Signature*.

Procedures for e-contracting and negotiation are also important in relation to the ISO 9000 certification as they can ensure clearly defined and repeatable procedures within the CN as a whole and not only within the companies that are members of a collaborative network [16].

However, further research in this area is mandatory due to the evolution on technology and new requirements that are constantly challenging the current processes. Some of these challenges are related to communication channels, use of artificial intelligence methods, intellectual property rights, electronic institutions, etc.

4   Research Contribution and Innovation

The rapid formation of VOs to respond to a business opportunity is crucial in order to enable organizations and companies to survive in turbulent market conditions. Nevertheless various empirical studies still show a very high percentage of failures in collaborative consortia. If they succeed it is then an indicator of *agility* and *reliability* that are two factors that are increasingly more important. It is thus in the VO creation process that additional effort has to be done if organizations / companies want to be successful. For that, among other factors the consortium negotiation process among partners is essential since it is where partners reach agreements and commitments to regulate the future collaboration.

When a VO is created in the context of a VO Breeding Environment (VBE), most of these aspects are agreed at the VBE level prior to any consortia formation. On the VOs perspective, negotiation mechanisms might be applied in different stages, namely: (i) during VO creation either for negotiating with the potential customer, or to negotiate an internal VO agreement; or (ii) for VO agreement amendment, meaning that it can be used for partners' inclusion or replacement, and changes of roles. The establishment of internal agreements is one of the foremost negotiation needs as they will determine the behavior of the networks, and thus represents an issue of special relevance during the VO creation process [11]. Table 1 summarizes the main phases of VO creation, highlighting the ones that require some negotiation level when a CO is already guaranteed. The case when there has to be a quotation process can be found in [11].

Table 1. VO creation phases

VO creation phase		Main focuses
Preparatory planning	CO identification and characterization	Who? Where and how? Which patterns of collaboration? How to structure the VO? Any initial template model?
	Rough VO planning	
Consortia formation	Partners search and suggestion	Who? Where? Which criteria? Which base information? Profiles? Decision support?
VO launching	Detailed VO planning	Who? Negotiation process? Contracts, rules templates? Agreements? Common infrastructure? Governing principles? Detailed plans?
	Contracting	
	VO setting up	

Due to the geographical distribution of potential participants in a VO, various attempts have been made to use some form of electronic support to the negotiation processes. Nevertheless past experiences demonstrate that the willingness of some parties to participate in online negotiations is difficult to achieve [19]. As a first step, it is important to ensure to all involved negotiating parties that by the introduction of electronic negotiation mechanisms no full automation is aimed but rather some computerized assistance. Furthermore, when the electronic negotiation fails, meeting face-to-face will still have to be considered as an option. So, in an electronic negotiation context, performance improvement includes enhancement of efficiency and effectiveness of both the process and the outcome, together with the flexibility of human intervention in decisions. Moreover, with the rapid growth of web-based services and global trade, there is also some commercial potential for web-based Negotiation Support Services (WNSS), as already supported by [19].

Negotiation Services. Becoming clear that the negotiation plays an important role in the process of the formation of collaborative consortia, it is important to create an environment that is the more explicit and traceable as possible.

To build a system capable of performing such negotiation during VO creation, the current work proposes some areas that need to be considered, namely the interaction with other systems and the negotiation support modules. In terms of interaction with other systems, a robust negotiation process will have to directly interact with the VBE information system to have access mainly to the VBE members profile and competencies as well as collaboration history. Regarding negotiation support modules, the ones identified (so far, more will appear during the accomplishment of this research work) are the following:

- Agreement editor that will enable: agreement templates generation; agreements templates instantiation; agreement configuration to current situation/context;
- Virtual negotiation room (VNR) that is a virtual space (online) where each participant will be able to negotiate and/or discuss certain issues/clauses of the agreement; and
- Support for notary services to guarantee on one hand the authenticity and validity of the agreements, and on the other hand to provide a safe deposit for documentation. The functionality to support auditing and supervision is also foreseen.

Fig. 1 illustrates the negotiation modules represented by the described application services together with a characterization of a CO and a partner's search engine. Also data bases services have to be considered in the process. Moreover, Fig1. also represents the main interactions with the VBE information system and with the relevant actors involved (the VBE members that will be the potential VO partners and the VO planner). All of the users can have access to negotiation services with correct authentication means through their web browsers.

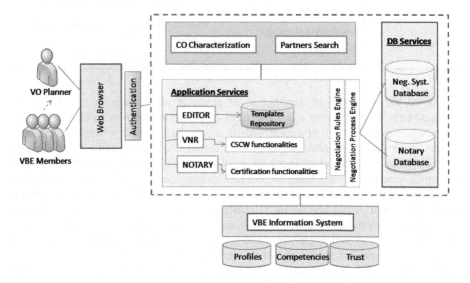

Fig. 1. Negotiation modules and interactions

Negotiation Model. With regards to the identified modules and interactions, it is necessary to reflect on new models of negotiation agreements since many different environments and participants might be considered. For that it is important to characterize those differences and model them. By doing this, it will be possible to instantiate the proper mechanisms for negotiation depending on different contexts. Thus, fundamental topics emerge, such as:

- Identifying network members whose agreement is necessary;
- Identifying the scope and (legal) jurisdiction of the network;
- Addressing issues of the network's legitimacy;
- Negotiating the ground rules;
- Discussing administration and allocation of responsibilities;
- Negotiating the decision rules for closure of an issue;
- Identifying a system for resolving impasses; and
- Identifying a decision process for ending the network.

In Fig. 2 it is then illustrated a negotiation process in VO creation that takes into account the previous topics.

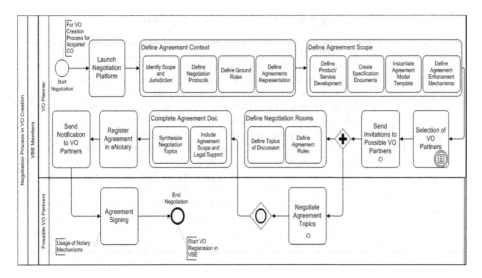

Fig. 2. Negotiation process in VO creation

Experiment Case: WizAN. To support some of the previous concepts, an Agreement Negotiation Wizard (WizAN) was developed [15]. The assumption is to use the tool for the VO creation process to assist in the agreement establishment in the VBE context. Also, the tool is aimed at assisting the human users in their decision making; therefore, it was designed with computer-assisted functionalities and not as a fully automated system. The main outcome of WizAN is then the internal consortium agreement summarizing the results of the negotiations / discussions that are performed during the VO creation process.

The full negotiation process is guided by an agreement template composed of a number of sections where each one refers to a specific topic to be negotiated. When a negotiation topic is created a virtual negotiation room (VNR) is "opened" in the system, and it is associated to a specific section of the agreement where a link to the topic is kept. Several VNRs might be created to negotiate all the topics that require discussion. Once all topics are agreed by the participants, the composite agreement can be assembled into a document that represents a compilation or integration of the agreements reached on all VNRs.

The actors involved in the process are therefore: VO planner who is responsible for the configuration and creation of the VO; and the VBE members that will act at this stage as potential VO partners. To assist the human actors in these processes, WizAN includes four main modules, namely: Contract Editor (CE), Virtual Negotiation Room (VNR), Support for Agreement Establishment (eNotary), and Assisted Contract Elaboration System (ACE). Table 2 illustrates the main functionalities of each of these modules.

Discussion of Results. Although this research is still in its initial stage, the preliminary study that led to the tool described in the illustrative case was developed in the scope of an European project, ECOLEAD, and positively evaluated in a real

Table 2. WizAN's main functionalities [15]

Functionality	Description
Contract Editor (CE)	Users can find the base information regarding the agreements being established among the VO partners. Through CE the VO planner is able to initiate, conduct, and monitor the VO creation; as it deals with the general part of the agreement that is being established.
Virtual Negotiation Room (VNR)	Is a virtual 'place' where the negotiation takes place. Through the VNRs each participant can access the various negotiation topics and discuss with the other involved participants in order to reach agreements. For each negotiation topic one VNR is created.
Support for Agreement Establishment	Is a module that allows clients to exchange information with a warranty of authenticity and validity as well as providing them a safe repository to save and request documentation. Furthermore it provides the functionality for partners to (digitally) sign agreements.
Assisted Contract Elaboration System	Collection of contract and negotiation object templates to support the contracts creation.

scenario with a Swiss and a Chinese VBE supporting negotiations between partners from the two geographical areas [16]. As a result, it is possible to draw some positive conclusions, namely in terms of the *focused negotiation process* due to the usage of the VNRs and the possibility to use attached documents that also prevent misunderstandings, making the process more *reliable*. Moreover, a degree of *authenticity* is also guaranteed due to the existence of an *eNotary* service. Also, the system ensures the privacy of the information exchanged in the VNRs, guaranteeing that partners have access only to authorized information. Finally, by using such system, it is possible to reduce the negotiation time of the VO creation process, which increases the *agility* indicator.

Although the preliminary work has already developed some facilitates for the negotiation process in the VO creation, the process can still become more effective, but always depending on the availability of adequate information about the potential partners and their level of interestingness in the VO involvement. For instance, considering indicators of readiness of each partner to collaborate or their trustworthiness level can lead to a higher level of assistance during the negotiation process. Moreover, considering the three situations, already identified, in which negotiation can take place (during VO creation to negotiate with the potential customer, or to negotiate the internal VO agreement; and to do VO agreement amendments); it is necessary to investigate if it is possible to use the same negotiation methodology in all of them and how to evaluate the VO partners readiness and preparedness in each case. Depending on the results, a negotiation taxonomy can also be adjusted. Another research line of extreme importance is the eNotary service which is one of the key factors in this work mainly due to its safety and authenticity properties, and aim to extend its functionalities with support for auditing and supervision.

Another direction is to increase the level of intelligence of the negotiation wizard by analyzing some behavioral and emotional patterns (an aspect of affective computing) and reacting accordingly. On one hand, the patterns that may be analyzed are for example: delays in communication, language usage, etc., and on the other hand, the reactions that the system can have depending on the required automation level, could vary from alerts for human users of the system to automatic responses. In the last case (the more autonomous one), the multi-agent paradigm is one of the appropriated implementation directions.

5   Conclusions and Further Work

In collaborative environments, the process of consortium/team creation can become more agile and reliable if there is a framework that can rapidly create the appropriate conditions to electronically achieve a consortium agreement. This framework should consider the concepts already established in collaborative networks and create an environment that is customizable according to the different collaboration levels. The framework should also be able to let the involved participants clearly assume their duties, responsibilities and rights according to their defined roles.

Nevertheless, there are some areas where some research challenges remain. As an interesting topic for research is how to improve and better adapt the negotiation wizard to multidisciplinary and multicultural environments that are used by people and organizations with different business practices, languages, objectives and terminologies. Another promising direction is the application of machine learning and affective computing to take into account patterns of behavior and emotions of the involved parties. Thus, although several works already mention the negotiation phases and taxonomy, a research challenge is the definition and formalization of more specific negotiation protocols for collaborative networks. Negotiation with customer during the acquisition for a collaboration opportunity might also be considered in future. Nevertheless, through all of these conclusions, it is possible to assume that if the characteristics of a specific VBE are well defined, as well as its governance principles, the negotiation process can then be tuned accordingly and thus the agility in the VO creation process can increase.

Acknowledgments. This work has been supported by the *Collaborative Networks and Distributed Industrial Systems* Research Group of Uninova.

References

1. Angelov, S.: Foundations of B2B Electronic Contracting. PhD, Technische Universiteit Eindhoven, Eindhoven (2006) ISBN 90-386-0615-X
2. Angelov, S., Grefen, P.: An Approach to the Construction of Flexible B2B E-Contracting Processes. Technical Report TR-CTIT-02-40, Centre for Telematics and Information Technology, University of Twente, Enschede (2002) ISSN 1381-3625
3. Afsarmanesh, H., Camarinha-Matos, L.M.: A Framework for Management of Virtual Organization Breeding Environments. In: Camarinha-Matos, L.M., Afsarmanesh, H., Ortiz, A. (eds.) Collaborative Networks and their Breeding Environments, pp. 35–48. Springer, Heidelberg (2005)
4. Camarinha-Matos, L.M., Afsarmanesh, H.: Elements of a base VE infrastructure. J. Computers in Industry 5(2), 139–163 (2003)
5. Camarinha-Matos, L.M., Silveri, I., Afsarmanesh, H., Oliveira, A.I.: Towards a Framework for Creation of Dynamic Virtual Organizations. In: Camarinha-Matos, L.M. (ed.) Collaborative Networks and their Breeding Environments, pp. 69–80. Springer, Heidelberg (2005)

6. Camarinha-Matos, L.M., Oliveira, A.I.: Contract Negotiation Wizard for VO Creation. In: Cunha, P.F., Maropoulos, P.G. (eds.) Digital Enterprise Technology, pp. 333–342. Springer, Heidelberg (2007)
7. Camarinha-Matos, L.M., Afsarmanesh, H.: Related work on reference modeling for collaborative networks. In: Camarinha-Matos, L.M., Afsarmanesh, H. (eds.) Collaborative Networks: Reference Modeling, pp. 15–28. Springer, Heidelberg (2008)
8. Camarinha-Matos, L.M., Afsarmanesh, H.: Collaboration Forms. In: Camarinha-Matos, L.M., Afsarmanesh, H. (eds.) Collaborative Networks: Reference Modeling, pp. 51–66. Springer, Heidelberg (2008)
9. Camarinha-Matos, L.M., Afsarmanesh, H., Ollus, M.: ECOLEAD and CNO Base Concepts. In: Camarinha-Matos, L.M., Afsarmanesh, H., Ollus, M. (eds.) Methods and Tools for Collaborative Networked Organizations, pp. 3–32. Springer, Heidelberg (2008)
10. Camarinha-Matos, L.M., Oliveira, A.I., Demsar, D., Sesana, M., Molina, A., Baldo, F., Jarimo, T.: VO Creation Assistance Services. In: Camarinha-Matos, L.M., Afsarmanesh, H., Ollus, M. (eds.) Methods and Tools for Collaborative Networked Organizations, pp. 155–190. Springer, Heidelberg (2008)
11. Camarinha-Matos, L.M., Oliveira, A.I., Sesana, M., Galeano, N., Demsar, D., Baldo, F., Jarimo, T.: A framework for computer-assisted creation of dynamic virtual organisations. International Journal of Production Research 47(17), 4661–4690 (2009)
12. Gimpel, H., Jennings, N.R., Kersten, G.E., Ockenfels, A., Weinhardt, C.: Negotiation, Auctions, and Market Engineering. In: International Seminar (Revised Selected Papers), Dagstuhl Castle, Germany, November 12-17. Springer, Heidelberg (2008)
13. Jennings, N.R., Norman, T.J., Faratin, P., O'Brien, P., Odgers, B.: Autonomous Agents for Business Process Management. Journal of Applied Artificial Intelligence 14, 145–189 (2000)
14. O'Leary, R., Bingham, L.B.: A Manager's Guide to Resolving Conflicts in Collaborative Networks, IBM Center for the Business of Government, Washington D.C (2007)
15. Oliveira, A.I., Camarinha-Matos, L.M.: Agreement Negotiation Wizard. In: Camarinha-Matos, L.M., Afsarmanesh, H. (eds.) Methods and Tools for Collaborative Networked Organizations, pp. 191–218. Springer, Heidelberg (2008)
16. Oliveira, A.I., Camarinha-Matos, L.M., Pouly, M.: Agreement Negotiation Support in VO Creation. In: Camarinha-Matos, L.M., Picard, W. (eds.), pp. 107–118. Springer, Heidelberg (2008)
17. Rocha, A.P., Oliveira, E.: An Electronic Market Architecture for the Formation of Virtual Enterprises. In: Proceedings of the IFIP TC5 WG5.3 / PRODNET Working Conference on Infrastructures for Virtual Enterprises: Networking Industrial Enterprises, October 27-28, pp. 421–432 (1999)
18. Rocha, A.P., Cardoso, H., Oliveira, E.: Contributions to an electronic institution supporting virtual enterprises' life cycle. In: Putnik, G.D., Cunha, M.M. (eds.) Virtual Enterprise Integration: Technological and Organizational Perspectives, pp. 229–246. Idea Group Publishing, London (2005)
19. Turel, O., Yuan, Y.: User Acceptance of Web-Based Negotiation Support Systems: The Role of Perceived Intention of the Negotiating Partner to Negotiate Online. Group Decision and Negotiation 16(5), 451–468 (2007)
20. Carter, C., Hassan, T., Mertz, M., White, E.: The eLegal project: specifying legal terms of contract in ICT environment. International Journal of Information Technology in Construction 6, 163–174 (2001)
21. Shelbourn, M., Hassan, T., Carter, C.: Legal and Contractual Framework for the VO. In: Camarinha-Matos, L.M., Afsarmanesh, H., Ollus, M. (eds.) Virtual Organization Systems and Practices, pp. 167–176. Springer, Heidelberg (2005)

Pro-Active Asset Entities in Collaborative Networks

Tiago Cardoso and Luis M. Camarinha-Matos

Faculty of Science and Technology, Universidade Nova de Lisboa,
Quinta da Torre, Caparica, Portugal
{tomfc,cam}@uninova.pt

Abstract. In a Collaborative Network (CN) scenario it would be desirable that CN members could be able to start collaboration within their Virtual Organization Breeding Environments or Professional Virtual Communities in a short time-frame, whenever a new Business Opportunity appears.

As a contribution towards such dynamic scenario, this paper proposes the concepts of Assets Entity, Pro-Active Assets Entity and Integrated Market of Pro-Active Assets Entities. The first concept can be used to model attributes and all functional and intelligent content elements a CN member can provide (its Assets). The second is responsible for the representation and promotion of an Assets Entity. The later offers an adaptation of the market place concept where each Pro-Active Assets Entity registers itself, brokers post their needs and try to find the best providers, through a bidding and negotiation process.

Keywords: Collaborative Networks, Assets, Virtual Organization Breeding Environment, Professional Virtual Community, Interoperability.

1 Introduction

The area of Collaborative Networks (CNs) has consolidated its conceptual baseline, namely in terms of Reference Modeling, as well as Methods and Tools, identifying distinct perspectives of this scientific discipline, as presented in [1, 2]. Nevertheless, important critical issues remain regarding the fast creation of such organizations.

Whenever a new Business Opportunity (BO) appears, the CN members, either companies, other organizations and / or professionals; should be able to start collaboration, within their Virtual Organization Breeding Environment (VBE) or Professional Virtual Community (PVC), in a short time-frame. In the typical, case one of the CN members – the initiator, or a broker, identifies the needed competencies and takes care of selecting all the needed CN members in order to create a Virtual Organization (VO) that will satisfy the requirements of the BO.

From the CN members' perspective, when they join this organizational structure, they are already willing to collaborate, adding their value to Virtual Organizations. Two main forms can be identified for this value: 1 - through the provision of services; 2 - through the provision of Intelligent Content. Depending on the economic area of the CN, different examples can be found for these two kinds of **Assets**: an example of Service Asset can be an assembling process or a consultancy service; an example of

L.M. Camarinha-Matos, P. Pereira, and L. Ribeiro (Eds.): DoCEIS 2010, IFIP AICT 314, pp. 93–102, 2010.

Intelligent Content Asset can be a business Process Model, a CAD document or even a Multimedia cultural documentary on a given city, for the case of a tourism CN.

Nevertheless, as the CN evolves, the number of members gets bigger and the chances of an Asset from a specific CN member to be chosen are reduced. Moreover, current approaches, lack mainly in two perspectives:

1. Passive Entities - Web Services, or content available through WebPages, are passive entities in the sense they stay still waiting for a client initiative instead of behaving in an auto-initiative manner in order to look up for new Business Opportunities and pursue negotiations in order to achieve commitments.
2. No Aggregation - The Assets a CN member can provide are treated in an independent form - no aggregation is made. If, for example, a Business Opportunity BO1 can be satisfied by 5 distinct assets (A1 ...A5), taking into account that there may be CN members able to provide more than one of the needed assets, the selection of CN members to form a VO that will satisfy BO1 can range from 1 up to 5 distinct CN members. The reduction of the number of CN members would reduce the needed agreements and potentially improve the work flow but, with current approaches, this reduction remains a coincidence.

Given this context, the following question arises: "Is it possible to create a new conceptual framework able to model the value of CN members within the organization, composed of new constructs that behave in a social and auto-initiative manner, representing and promoting all the elements that CN member can provide, in order to improve the tackled Business Opportunities, as well as the business success chances?"

This paper introduces four concepts aligned with this research question:

1. Assets - This concept is the abstraction of distinct kinds of elements a CN member can provide. With this "uniformization", as a base modeling mechanism, the two kinds of assets identified can be treated in the same way whenever a model is created for the formation of a Virtual Organization. For example, the assembling service and some needed CAD document are two assets that can be treated as building blocks in the corresponding VO model - one is a Service and the other is an Intelligent Content.
2. Asset Entities (AE) - The aggregation of all the Assets a CN member provides, improving the possibilities to reduce the number of CN members needed for the formation of a VO, as well as the corresponding negotiation effort.
3. Pro-Active Asset Entities (PAE) - Here, auto-initiative is added to the AE concept through the introduction of behavior elements. This concept is inspired in the Multi-Agent Systems (MAS) applied to the AE concept within a CN context. The main objective is to represent an AE and lookup for Business Opportunities where one or more of the represented Assets can be included.
4. Integrated Market (IM) - Finally, in the context of a CN, the concept of an Integrated Market where all the PAEs register themselves and where brokers model and post client's needs – the Business Opportunities (BO). This structure will be the place where PAEs look up for BOs where they can match the Assets they represent. Whenever a match happens, the PAE is responsible for pursuing the needed activities to achieve an agreement, in a bidding-like negotiation process. The scope of an IM can be the one of a VBE (or PVC).

2 Contribution to Technological Innovation

Information and Communication Technology evolution is moving towards autonomy of existing systems and devices, giving them the capacity to observe the surrounding environment, cooperate with neighbors and behave independent of human interaction.

Intelligent Manufacturing, where machines provide their functionality and behave in an auto-initiative basis towards collaborative work, is an example of this reality.

The Internet of Things, where sensorial ability, along with processing and storage, in an auto-initiative social behavior of The Things, is another example.

The contribution of this paper to technological innovation is made through the introduction of four concepts aligned with these trends. These concepts support a development framework aiming the creation of collaborative platforms through an active representation and promotion of CN member's Assets. This representation provides built-in functionality to carry out tasks like business opportunity search, bidding and negotiation, all in an auto-initiative semi-automated basis.

3 Related Work

The proposal of Pro-Active Assets Entity to model Enterprises and Free-lancers assets within Collaborative Networks is mainly inspired in Service Oriented Computing (SOC) and Multi-agent Systems (MAS).

Baseline Concepts and Definitions - Web Services in particular and Service Oriented Computing in general introduced a new abstraction paradigm in software development facilitating inter-enterprises' collaboration. This approach evolved through three main phases that can be identified by their main keywords: Publish – when enterprises became able to "wrap" some functionality and wait for worldwide potential clients to call them; Register / Find – when UDDI registries appeared and web-services became "findable" and finally Compose – when the creation of "Value Added Services" became possible, as a result of the integration of simpler services through mechanisms like workflow or technologies like BPEL4WS. This paradigm presented "a design principle intended for the construction of reliable distributed systems that deliver functionality as a service, with an additional emphasis on loose coupling between interacting services" [4].

Other initiatives, like OSGi, coming from software components research area, provide standard interoperability functionality to compose and change composition of services dynamically. The framework proposed by OSGi Alliance, has already other proposals built on top of it, like Apache FELIX, providing the interoperability means to integrate distinct applications / bundles.

Nevertheless, the Web-Service approach is limited in the sense that services are entities that stay still waiting for a clients' call. Nothing is done by the Web Services themselves to "attract" clients or make "promotions", for example. Furthermore, some authors defend that Web-Services will evolve to big groups, or "Service Parks", "owned" by big players who define the groups' rules [5]. It is not clear yet if this will become the reality, but if it does Small and Medium Enterprises may see their possibility of adoption of this paradigm restricted / subjugated to major players' rules – a potential near-future limitation of this paradigm. However, the organization of SMEs as a long term cooperation alliance (such as a VBE or PVC) opens the possibility of creating "service parks" or "service markets" within the alliance.

Recently, in [6, 7] the concept of Service Entities (SE) is proposed "as constructs that may help structural and functional CNO modeling". Here, a group of Web-Services can belong to one SE and be enriched with attributes towards better interoperability.

On the other hand, the usage of Multi-agent Systems, as a second inspiration area, represents "a promising approach to both model and implement the complex supporting infrastructures required for virtual enterprises and related emerging organizations" [8]. This work points out the main limitation of this approach as the lack on robustness of current solutions in Wide Area Networks, like the Internet.

Nevertheless, the agents approach presents promising characteristics for this domain. In [9], Wooldridge defines the top 4 Software Agents' properties that constitute important inspiration points for the PAE architecture: autonomy (agents operate without the direct intervention of human or others and have control over their actions and internal state), social ability (agents are able to cooperate with humans or other agents in order to achieve their tasks), reactivity (agents perceive their environment and respond in a timely fashion to changes that occur in it) and pro-activeness (agents do not simply act in response to their environment, they are able to exhibit goal-directed behavior by taking the initiative).

In the case some PAE interaction is needed, typically the case when a single Asset cannot apply to a business opportunity by itself, the production of Value-Added-Assets (VAA) can take place, following workflow interaction patterns between distinct PAEs. Here, inspiration ideas have been retrieved from Multi-agent Systems (MAS), through the existing interaction between distinct Software Agents. [10].

This proposal also extends ideas from the evolution of the Semantic Web, namely the Intelligent Content (I-Content) concept, defined as "information content with explicit semantic description through which machines and people can share meaning and value" [11]. Although the I-Content concept adds semantic to content, it still remains static content. Pro-Active Assets Entity extends the I-Content concept adding pro-activeness and auto-initiative behaviors.

Concerning the little interaction between MAS and SOC research communities; although this is a reality, some initiatives start to connect them. One example is a new trend on the Semantic Web with the introduction of Pro-Activity information in the description of Web Services. Nevertheless, the few initiatives addressing this approach mainly exist in the MAS research area.

In the case of the "Proactivity Layer of the Smart Resource Platform" proposed in [12] or the "Proactive Self-Maintained Resources", described in [13], Semantic Web Languages are used, illustrating this benefit applied to MAS. In both cases, the "agentification" of resources, or smart-devices, is made through this approach. In the first case, the objective was their integration. In the second case, the aim was the definition of an ontology-driven rules' approach for modeling context-sensitive agent behavior.

Web Services and Agent Technologies on Collaborative Networks - In [5], an early proposal was made, defending that "as Web Services become more sophisticated, they effectively will become software agents themselves". The authors defend that WSDL and UDDI are insufficient to support service discovery and composition, mainly because of the lack on semantics. The authors argue that importing ideas from

Multi-Agent Systems would provide the means to create such sophisticated "Service Agents", needed in the formation of dynamic Virtual Enterprises. This work also points out research directions, like the combination of DAML-S and UDDI approaches.

Another example of work integrating the two paradigms is presented in [14]. There, the authors propose an "embedded Web service architecture (EWSA), inspired in the Software Components' research area, which allows agent-based applications to be integrated into enterprise application environments using Web Services". The main objective of this solution is the reduction of time-to-market of the agent-based applications. Nevertheless, EWSA together with the proposal made in [6] mainly target the formation and evolution life cycle phases of an organization like a CN. Furthermore, these two proposals focus on functional perspectives of enterprises and lack on other kinds of Assets. For example, an enterprise that sells a business process model or an individual that provides touristic multimedia content on European cities, are not covered by any of these approaches.

4 Research Contribution and Innovation

Given the assumption of Asset as: anything an enterprise, organization or a free-lancer member of a CN can provide and that can be represented / triggered by a software component; and the assumption of Value Added Asset as: an asset that results from the composition of simpler Assets, or other VAA; the concept of Service Entity, presented in [7], can be extended as Assets Entity – a concept that includes the Assets an entity can provide, as well as a set of Attributes from that entity (an enterprise, another organization or a free-lancer member of a CN).

Definition 1 (Assets Entity (AE)) –is a tuple AE=(AT, AS), where:

- $AT = \{attr_i \mid i \in N\}$ – the set of Attributes of the corresponding entity.
- $AS = \{a_i \mid i \in N\}$ – the set of Assets the corresponding entity can provide.

Within a context of an increasing number of AEs, new mechanisms to "promote" each AE become useful and needed. The concept of Pro-Active Assets Entity is introduced as a software component responsible for the representation and promotion of an AE, looking for Business Opportunities and behaving in a social manner for the provision of all the Assets of the corresponding Entity. The PAE is defined as follows:

Definition 2 (Pro-Active Assets Entity (PAE)) – is a tuple PAE=(AE, PS, BF), where:

- AE – The Assets Entity represented and promoted by PAE;
- $PS = \{ p_1, p_2, p_3 \}$, a set of 3 Properties defined as follows:
  - ○ p_1 (**Pro-activity**) – enabling the PAE to look for Business Opportunities (BOs);
  - ○ p_2 (**Negotiation-ability**) – enabling the PAE to make bids for discovered BOs in a semi-automated manner, as well as carry out negotiation processes in order to improve previously made bids;

o p_3 (**Social-ability**) - enabling an interaction with other PAEs to support the creation of VOs through IMPs, whenever Asset composition means are needed to
apply to a given BO.

- BF={$f_{g,i}$ | g ∈ {1 - General, 2 - I-Content, 3 - Service}, i ∈ N} – The Built-In
Functionality from the PAE, divided into three groups whether the functionality is
specific to one of the two kinds of assets (I-Content or Service) or it is common to
any kind of asset, as exemplified in Table 1.

Table 1. Example of Pro-Active Assets Entity built-in functionality

$f_{1,1}$ – Find Correlated PAEs
$f_{1,2}$ – Look up in IMPs for BOs
$f_{1,3}$ – BID on BOs
$f_{1,4}$ – Promote Asset
$f_{1,5}$ – Negotiate Asset for BO
$f_{2,1}$ – Open / Show I-Content
$f_{2,2}$ – Extract Info / Knowledge from I-Content
$f_{3,1}$ – Call / Execute / Call-Back the service Asset
$f_{3,2}$ – Create / Edit VAA.

From a provider's perspective, a PAE will work like a promotion helper for its assets, finding Business Opportunities, performing negotiation, and eventually promotions, towards the inclusion of the represented asset in VOs.

Finally, the concept of Integrated Market of PAEs is the place where PAEs register
themselves, typically one IMP *per* VBE / PVC. As an IMP might have a large number
of PAEs registered, finding potential compatible Assets within that space is an easier
process and improves all the pre-collaboration negotiation effort, as well as guarantees ICT compatibility. These factors improve the possibility of a collaboration to
start in a short time-frame window. Furthermore, the IMP performs monitoring and
certification functionality on the registered PAEs in order to provide accurate information to support brokers' choices.

Definition 3 (Integrated Market of Pro-Active Assets Entities (IMP)) – is a tuple
IMP = (PE, BO, PM, CR, BF), where:

PE={pae_i | i ∈ N} – the set of registered Pro-Active Assets Entities,

BO={bo_i | i ∈ N} – the set of announced business opportunities,

PM={$pm_{i,j}$ | (∀ $pm_{i,j}$ ∃ pae_i ∈ PE □ ∃ bo_j ∈ BO)} – a set with Performance Measure-
ment (PM) information,

CR={cae_i | (∀ cae_i ∃ pae_i ∈ PE)} – a set with Certification information on Assets
Entities and,

BF={ f_1, f_2, f_3 ,f_4} – 4 Built-In Functionality, where:

f_1 (**PAE Registration**) – enabling distinct PAEs to register themselves, as well as the
set of assets from the entity they represent;

f_2 (**BO Posting**) – enabling brokers to post their needs / BOs;

f_3 (**Performance Measurement**) – providing automated PAE performance measuring mechanisms, as well as enabling brokers to grade their performance, in order to increase the information on every registered PAE. As a result, more accurate data becomes available for future CN members selection processes.

f_4 (**Certification**) – based on PM info, an IMP can certify some PAE's quality (introducing the notion of conspicuity associated to a Pro-Active Assets Entity).

From the broker's perspective an IMP is a "place" where he can specify some need and wait for distinct bids or proposals. There, instead of asking for the catalogue of some service or content providers, the broker only has to post the need, or Business Opportunity. Furthermore, the IMP concept extends the base ideas from UDDI registry systems, as well as blackboard architectures. The former provides the means needed to give registration functionality for PAEs and the later provides the means needed for Brokers to post their needs – the Business Opportunities.

Process / Motivating Scenario – One of the main contributions of the usage of the proposed concepts come from the changes in the interaction between CN members and brokers that only start the process specifying a need – the Business Opportunity. After that, the initiative goes to the other side for a specified amount of time where distinct PAEs submit their BIDs. Figure 1 shows a simplified BPMN diagram representing the interaction process between a broker and PAEs through the IMP.

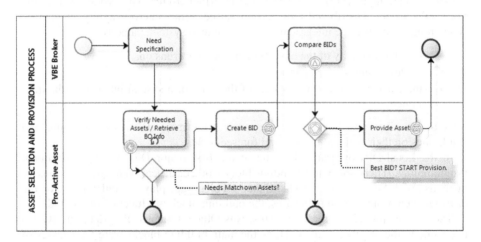

Fig. 1. Broker / PAE Interaction Bidding Process trough IMP

This simplified version of this process is divided into the 5 Tasks T_1 through T_5.

T_1 (**Broker Need Specification**) – The VBE / PVC broker divides the BO in simple Asset needs posting them in the IMP. For example "Enterprise A needs a watch production service" or "Person X wants to go on a tour in the country Y and is looking for multimedia cultural content concerning city K, as well as accommodation and travelling services". In both cases a composed asset can be considered and the broker that gathers this BO forms the VO that will provide a "Value Added Asset".

T_2 (**BO Analysis**) - PAEs gathers BO info, analyze it and decide whether or not to bid. For the first example, PAEs from enterprises with a watch assembling service, for example, analyze the posts while in the second example, PAEs of tourism agents or free-lancers with touristic I-Content from the desired city, perform the same actions.

T_3 (**Bidding**) – Each Pro-Active Assets Entity that finds the posting suitable make a bid and sends it to the broker.

T_4 (**Best Bid Choice / START**) –The broker compares the received bids and chooses the best one. After the choice is made, the selected PAE is notified and the task execution or I-Content transfer can start.

- This choice can go through longer negotiation process between brokers and PAEs, like logistic details definition, for the first example.

T_5 (**Asset Provision End**) – Finally, the process is concluded with the service end or the content provision finishing.

5   Discussion of Results and Critical View

Software development history can be divided into two major groups of distinct Development Paradigms (DP): Local-DPs and Distributed-DPs. The evolution from the Local-DPs to the Distributed-DPs' group raised some interoperability challenges concerning the parts to be integrated in the distributed system, namelly:

- the heterogeneity of the environment each part runs on,
- the autonomy of each part and
- the existence of distinct owners of the parts of a system intended to be integrated.

Nevertheless, it is possible to compare some of the major DPs of each group, find similarities on their main constructs and foresee trends.

In the Local-DPs programming, one of the first major DPs was the Functional Programming. There the main building blocks or constructs were the functions or methods. Web-Services, in the Distributed-DPs' group, play a similar role, for the distributed environment. In both cases, the building block is a function or method.

The next major DP, in the Local-DPs, was Object Oriented Programming (OOP) that came in the 60s with Simula. Here, the main building blocks were the Classes of Objects with many methods within a single construct, together with Attributes to store information concerning the modeling elements – the objects. Simula also added some useful features like the Encapsulation, Inheritance and the Polymorphism. Again, a parallel can be established with the Distributed-DPs' group. In 2008 the Service Entities (SE), proposed in [6, 7], play a similar role, putting together many web-services with attributes within a single construct – the Service Entities. This time, the keywords in the software development were Functions / Methods and Attributes.

More or less at the same time as the OOP, the Multi-Threaded Programming (MTP) appeared with the corresponding mechanisms for communication and synchronization among distinct processes, needed for parallel execution. These two DPs (OOP and MTP) opened the way for the Multi-Agent Systems (MAS). Here, the main building blocks were Software Agents and the new construct was their behavior, other than their autonomy, social ability, reactivity and pro-activeness, as referred in section 3.1. In the Distributed-DPs' group, little before the SEs, technologies like OWL-S (former DAML-S) introduced the semantic constructs needed to "facilitate the automation of Web service tasks including automated Web service discovery, execution, interoperation, composition and execution monitoring".[15]

Establishing a relation between the Local-DPs evolution and the actual reality in the Distributed-DPs, the SE and OWL-S open now a new way for the proposal of solutions that add auto-initiative and behavior constructs to the Functions / Methods and Data Fields / Attributes ones.

Figure 2 synthesizes this comparison exercise on the evolution of Local and Distributed Development Paradigms. The concepts presented in this paper provide a proposal aligned with these trends. The Pro-Active Assets Entity concept represents all the Assets form an enterprise or professional behaving in an auto-initiative manner, looking for business opportunities in Integrated Markets.

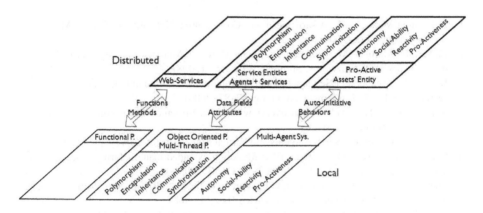

Fig. 2. From Functional Programming to Pro-Active Assets

6   Conclusions and Future Work

In this paper a new approach for modeling CN member's Assets was presented – Assets Entities, Pro-Active Assets Entities and Integrated Markets of Pro-Active Assets Entities. The proposal is based on the concept of Asset as something an enterprise, another organization or an individual can provide. This concept extends the functional abilities covered by current approaches, like web-services, to any other kind of Intelligent Content, like a Process Model, for example. On top of this Asset concept, the concept of Assets Entity provides a single construct able to put together all the Attributes and Assets of an Entity (member of a CN). The concept of Pro-Active Assets Entity acts like an envelope that carries the Assets Entity, providing the means to represent it, finding suitable Business Opportunities for it.

This is done through the introduction of the Integrated Markets. There, the PAEs register themselves and brokers become able to post some needs – the Business Opportunities. The Pro-Active Assets Entities, always looking for suitable Business Opportunities, check for a matching and if the result is positive start a Bidding Process. Finally, the client chooses the BID that best fits the needs.

In section 5, a simple analysis of the evolution of the trends on Development Paradigms shows that this proposal is aligned with the identified directions. In fact, Auto-Initiative and Autonomy are two important keywords for systems development.

The ongoing work aimed at the development of a prototype with the base pro-activeness and auto-initiative mechanisms. The next phase of the work will target the evaluation of this proposal framework in Collaborative Networks and extend the mode to cover those cases in which no PAE submits a bid to a given Business Opportunity. In this last case, the broker needs to take some other initiatives, namely to convince some PAEs to change their current priorities or alternatively changing BO requirements.

References

1. Camarinha-Matos, L.M., Afsarmanesh, H.: Collaborative Networks: Reference Modeling. Springer, New York (2008)
2. Camarinha-Matos, L.M., Hamideh, A., Ollus, M. (eds.): Methods and Tools for Collaborative Networked Organizations. Springer, New York (2008)
3. Brazier, F.: Agents and Service-Oriented Computing for Autonomic Computing - A Research Agenda. IEEE Internet Computing, 82–87 (2009)
4. Srinivasan, L., Traedwell, J.: An overview of service-oriented architecture, web services and grid computing (2005)
5. Petrie, C., Bussler, C.: Service Agents and Virtual Enterprises: A Survey, pp. 68–78 (2003)
6. Franco, R.D., Bas, Á.O., Esteban, F.L.: Modeling extended manufacturing processes with service oriented entities. Service Business 3, 31–50 (2008)
7. Franco, R.D., Bas, Á.O., Burguera, G.P., Varela, R.N.: MANBREE: Supporting Structural and Functional CNO Modeling With Service-Based Entities
8. Camarinha-Matos, L.M.: Multi-Agent Systems in Virtual Enterprises. In: International Conference on AI, Simulation and Planning in High Autonomy Systems (AIS 2002), pp. 27–36. SCS (2002)
9. Wooldridge, M.: Agent-based computing. Interoperable Communication Networks (1998)
10. Rabelo, R.: Advanced Collaborative Business ICT Infrastructures. In: Methods and Tools for Collaborative Networked Organizations, pp. 337–370. Springer, Heidelberg (2008)
11. Intelligent Content (2008)
12. Khriyenko, O.: Proactivity Layer of the Smart Resource in Semantic Web. In: ESWD (2006)
13. Terziyan, V.: SmartResource - Proactive Self-Maintained Resources in Semantic Web: Lessons Learned. IJSH (2007)
14. Ramirez, E.H., Brena, R.F.: Multi-Agent Systems Integration in Enterprise Environments Using Web Services. In: Protogeros, N. (ed.) Agent and Web Service Techn ologies in Virtual Enterprises, pp. 174–189 (2008)
15. DAML Services (2009)

Part 4
Assessment and Decision Support

Qualitative Model for Risk Assessment in Construction Industry: A Fuzzy Logic Approach

Abel Pinto[1], Isabel L. Nunes[1], and Rita A. Ribeiro[2]

[1] Universidade Nova Lisboa / FCT, Caparica, 2829-516 Portugal
abel.fnpinto@gmail.com, imn@fct.unl.pt
[2] Uninova, Campus UNL/FCT, Caparica, 2829-516 Portugal
rar@uninova.pt

Abstract. Risk Assessment for Health and Safety (RAH&S) of workers is a complex task that entails the consideration of many parameters which are, more often than not, difficult to quantify. RAH&S in the construction industry is rampant with inadequate data and/or imprecise and incomplete information, particularly in the design stage, for which traditional quantitative approaches do not give adequate answers. In this work we outline the basic aspects for a Qualitative Risk Assessment Model (QRAM) based on elicited data and using a fuzzy logic approach.

Keywords: Risk assessment, safety, fuzzy sets, construction industry.

1 Introduction

Safety is a prominent feature to be taken into account in the construction industry, and Risk Assessment for Health and Safety (RAH&S) is a key step to achieve it, particularly to support decision-making in safety programs (Ringdahl, 2001).

In general, risk assessment is a complex process that entails the consideration of many qualitative parameters which are difficult to quantify. Risk assessment in the construction industry, due the specific nature of the sector (Dedobbeleer e Beland, 1991; Ringen et al., 1995; Gillen et al, 1997; Laitinen, 1999; Loosemore, 2001; Tam et al., 2004), must deal with ill-defined and imprecise data and information. So far traditional approaches do not seem to provide adequate answers (Ringen et al., 1995) to deal with this issue. Moreover, using probability (classical or Bayesian) or statistics theories may mask other aspects of incomplete and imprecise knowledge and can lead to a false sense of accuracy and precision, thus leading to inadequate and/or inefficient decisions.

To overcome some of the mentioned problems in assessing safety risks, we propose a qualitative model for risk assessment, hereinafter denoted QRAM (Qualitative Risk Assessment Model), which based on elicited data and using a fuzzy logic approach. The goal is to contribute to work safety by improving risk assessment in construction sites.

L.M. Camarinha-Matos, P. Pereira, and L. Ribeiro (Eds.): DoCEIS 2010, IFIP AICT 314, pp. 105–111, 2010.

2   Contribution to Technological Innovation

The majority of quantitative traditional methods use probabilistic techniques and / or statistics to deal deal with the intrinsic uncertainty and imprecision in data and information. This implies some limitations, such as requiring analysts to estimate parameters, to ensure a sufficiently representative domain or make comparisons with other sites (which departs from the real system under study).

Recently, there are also qualitative approaches using fuzzy logic, proposed in the literature (see for example: Azadeh et al., 2008, Gurcanli, Mungen, 2009), but they lack having a systematic survey of all parameters that should be taken into consideration, together with a general formulation to obtain a complete risk assessment measure.

Hence, the main contributions of the proposed QRAM are: to provide a framework for factors that need to be evaluated in construction sites; to propose a formula expressing the relationships between the parameters (risk factors), thus obtaining an overall risk measure; to provide a simple semantic scale to facilitate the elicitation of information about the parameters. The final aim of QRAM is to obtain an overall measure of risk for the construction site as well as to obtain partial risk calssifications for important parameters included in the overall measure.

QRAM will focus on elicited data, thus avoiding estimates to allow assessment of actual risks of the site. The data and information will be obtained by direct observation, interviews with workers and foremen and also from consultation and review of documentation of the site (health and safety plan, reporting accidents and incidents, records of meetings, work procedures...), among others. After we transform the collected data, using fuzzy logic techniques, and then aggregate it to obtain the risks level classification for the site.

3   Background on Risk Assessment for Health and Safety (RAH&S)

Traditional RAH&S methods are typically based on information, which is subject to uncertainty (usually handled by probability and/or statistics theories) or is just ill-defined. Due to its intrinsic uncertainty and incompleteness traditional RAH&S methods present some limitations, as pointed by some authors [Karwowski & Mital, (1986); Cornell (1996); Wang et Ruxton. (1997); Pender (2001); Sii et al. (2001); Tixier (2002); Faber (2003); Nilsen (2003); Kentel et Aral. (2004)], such as:

o   Inherent imprecision in human-centered systems;
o   Difficult to generate a mathematical model due to intrinsic uncertainty in this type of problems. For instance, it is difficult to represent and describe the safety behavior, which causes work accidents involving operational procedures, human error and decisions taken by designer and management;
o   Difficult to quantify the effects and consequences of hazards because they involve many factors with a high level of uncertainty, even when the physical processes are clearly understood;

o   Large number of assumptions, judgments and opinions are involved in a risk quantification process, hence, it requires considerable skills from a safety analyst to interpret results;
o   Construction projects are unique by definition. This reduces the relevance and reliability of statistical aggregates derived from probability-based analysis;
o   Humans are limited in their ability to encompass and process the full range of information required for holistic decisions;
o   Uncertainty and ignorance may be found in temporal aspects of the flow of knowledge, which are important in project planning;
o   Project parameters and outcomes must be communicated to others and the imprecision of our language is not good to express these.

Considering all above statements, it is apparent that RAH&S in the construction industry is rampant with inadequate data and/or imprecise, ill-defined, and incomplete information, particularly in the design stage, for which traditional approaches do not give adequate answers. Fuzzy logic (Zadeh, 1965, Zimmerman, 1991) provides a natural way of modelling the intrinsic vagueness and imprecision of subjective assessments, while also allows the inclusion of human creativity and intuition, which is an essential ingredient for successful risk analysis (Ru, 1996). However, most qualitative approaches neither consider a systematic framework for all parameters that can influence the risk nor formalize the relationships between parameters (Liu et al., 2001, Tixier et al., 2002, Mure et al., 2006).

4   Proposed Qualitative Model: QRAM

In this section we outline the basic aspects that a model for RAH&S in the construction industry should account for. The knowledge acquisition (i.e. data elicitation) should be obtained by observation of reality, interviews with workers, foreman and engineers, responsible and consultation of site documents (working procedures, reports of work accident investigation ....). The collected data shall be transformed using fuzzy sets (Azadeh et al., 2008) and will be aggregated with specialized fuzzy operators, to obtain a ranking of risks in the construction site.

The starting point is the following formulation for risk assessment in construction sites, RAC, as shown in eq. 1. The risk is directly proportional to organizational inadequacies (O_I), which are not related with a specific hazard, and other direct factors (F_D), and additional factors (F_A). The direct and additional factors are inversely proportional to safety barriers factors (S_B), which are also dependent on some hazard.

$$RAC = O_I \otimes \frac{F_D \oplus F_A}{S_B} \qquad (1)$$

F_D are the main direct factors related with the hazard under analysis (for example, in falls from height, the factor is the height of the fall).

F_A are additional factors; they also depend on hazards under analysis and include a variable number of parameters. Examples of aditional factors (for the same hazard) are: tidiness of workplace, inclination of work floor, friction level between shoe´s soles and soil.

Both direct factors and additional factors include a variable number of parameters, which will depend on the site being evaluated. The risk specialist will choose which factors will be evaluated for the specific site. In general the formulation will be:

$$F_{(D \cup A)} = \oplus(f_1, f_2, ..., f_n) / N \tag{2}$$

Where N is the number of parameters that will be considered for any of the two factors.

O_I express organizational inadequacies and are a function of the lack (or poor): safety culture (S_c), safety organisation (S_o), work organisation (W_o), supervision (S), leadership (L), personal factors and communications (C). Formally,

$$O_I = \oplus(S_c, S_o, W_o, S, L, P, C) / N \tag{3}$$

with N being the number of parameters.

S_B represent the Safety Barriers implemented in the site for controling the risk. Their effectiveness should be measured by:

$$S_B = \oplus(M, A, S, I) / N \tag{4}$$

where (Hollnagel 1999):

o M -Material barriers physically prevent an action from being carried out or the consequences from spreading;
o A -Functional (active or dynamic) barriers work by impeding the action to be carried out, for instance by establishing a logical or temporal interlock.
o S -Symbolic barriers require an act of interpretation in order to achieve their purpose, hence an "intelligent" agent that can react or respond to the barrier.
o I -Immaterial barriers are not physically present or represented in the situation, but depend on the knowledge of the user to achieve their purpose.

The proposed process to obtain the final RAH&S measure, *RAC* (eq 1), will use concepts and techniques from fuzzy set theory (Zadeh, 1965, 1975, 1983).

In this first work we use a single discrete fuzzy set for classifying the factors and their respective parameters. The proposed fuzzy classification can be used to elicit classifications from different sources (e.g. workers, engineers, safety experts), for all parameters in a user-friendly semantic form. Formally, the general fuzzy parameter classification membership function, to be used in this preliminary model is:

$$ParameterClassification = \begin{Bmatrix} Excelent / 1, VeryGood / 0.8, Good / 0.6, \\ Satisfactory / 0.4, Mediocre / 0.2, Bad / 0.001 \end{Bmatrix} \tag{5}$$

At this stage, the terms and respective values considered are just indicative and in future work they will be validated and tuned. All parameters in eq. 2, eq. 3 and eq. 4

(e.g. material barriers M) will be classified using the above discrete fuzzy set. To obtain the values for the respective factors (e.g. S_B) we plan to use an aggregation operator, $\oplus$, such as arithmetic sum, average or any other compensatory operator (Zimmerman, 1991). Finally to obtain the overall risk measure for the construction site, we plan to use conventional arithmetic operators.

At this stage of the research work we are not yet sure about which operators are more suitable for obtaining the risk assessment in the construction industry, but a study about them is foreseen in the near future. Here, as mentioned, we just focused on the conceptual model for determining the risk assessment.

5 Illustrative Example

In order to illustrate the applicability of the method, we will use a simple illustrative case for the risk that causes more deaths in Portugal, in the sector: falls from height.

In this example we only describe the calculations for additional factors, F_A, because the process is similar for the other factors in eq. 1.

Consider a construction work on a scaffold with three meters high, thus the single direct factor, is $F_D = 0.001$, because we assumed the intervals: [0 to 0,5m] $F_D = 1$;]0,5 to 1m] $F_D = 0.8$;]1 to 1,4m], $F_D = 0.6$;]1,4 and 1,6 m] $F_D = 0.4$;]1,6 to 1, 8m] $F_D = 0.3$;]1,8 to 2m] $F_D = 0.2$, and > 2m $F_D = 0.001$.

The additional factors considered and the respective semantic classification, using the fuzzy membership semantic variables (eq. 5) are: (a little clean and tidy) = *mediocre*; (horizontal surface) = *good*; (foot boards, wood, presented in good repair) = *satisfactory*; (when dry, the material floor provides good traction on the sole of the shoe) = *satisfactory*; (lighting level well suited to work) = *good*, (irons waiting on the surface of the collision) = *bad*; (dry weather and no wind) = *good* (scaffolding meet all legal and regulatory requirements, was well fitted and properly anchored) = *good*.

Now, aggregating the classifications for the additional factors (eq. 2), using the membership values of eq. 5, we have:

$$F_A = (0.2 + 0.6 + 0.4 + 0.4 + 0.6 + 0.001 + 0.6 + 0.6)/8 = 0.4375$$

Notice that in this example we used arithmetic operators to aggregate the values, but in the future other operators will be tested to improve the method.

Although the six factors are appropriate, in various degrees: *good* (4) and *satisfactory* (2), there are two factors with inappropriate levels, one mediocre and another bad. Hence, the combination is only satisfactory (closest semantic level in the classification fuzzy set for the result 0.4375). This result means the site safety has to be improved, particularly to protect the irons on hold (*bad*) and clean and organize the workplace (*mediocre*).

Regarding the safety barriers S_B, the scaffold has railings around the outside perimeter of the platforms, properly fitted, good and robust (*very good*), the inner side is 20 cm from the construction (*very good*), the access to work platforms is appropriate and also well protected (*very good*). The company implemented a procedure for working at heights which includes work on scaffolding, the procedure is well prepared and written in language appropriate to their users (*very good*). The company provides training to all workers on scaffolding, however, the training records do not show the knowledge acquired by trainees is properly understood, hence the company did not prove the effectiveness of training (*mediocre*). Following the above calculation for additional factors and using eq. 4,

$$S_B = (0.8 + 0.8 + 0.8 + 0.8 + 0.2)/5 = 0.68$$

This result shows that the efficiency in the safety barriers is *good* (closest semantic value for the result 0.68) .

Regarding the organizational factors O_I (eq. 2) and for simplicity we consider an overall classification of *excelent* (membership value = 1).

Finally we can determine the level of risk assessment for the example, following eq. 1,

$$RAC = 1 \times \frac{0.1 + 0.4375}{0.68} = 0.79$$

Notice we used again arithmetic operators to improve clarity of method´ explanation. The final risk level in the construction site for the falling height, yields a value of *very good* (corresponding to the closest semantic variable).

Although the criteria for acceptability of risk is appropriate and very good there is room for improvements, namely implement new safety barriers and also improve some additional factors (e.g. improve some aspects related to training).

6   Conclusion and Further Work

Fuzzy approaches for human-centred problems seem to be quite flexible, hence in this work we introduce a preliminary version of a qualitative method for RAH&S, in the construction industry, using fuzzy logic concepts and techniques. From all pointed limitations and inadequacies of traditional RAH&S methods it seems that using this type of fuzzy approach, to evaluate work safety factors, yields a more realistic representation and solution for evaluation of risks in the construction industry.

The outlined qualitative model (QRAM) is still under development. It needs to be further improved and refined, such as identifying other types of hazards and further characterize all risks involved, as well as to set criteria for the tolerability of risk analysis in construction sites. After these improvements it needs to be tested and validated with real case studies to assess its suitability and generality for the construction sector.

References

1. Azadeh, A., Fam, I.M., Khoshnoud, M., Khoshnoud, M.: Design and implementation of a fuzzy expert system for performance assessment of an integrated health, safety, environment (HSE) and ergonomics system: The case of a gas refinery. Information Sciences 178, 4280–4300 (2008)

2. Cornell, M.E.P.: Uncertainties in risk analysis: Six levels of treatment. Reliability Engineering and System Safety 54, 95–111 (1996)
3. Dedobbeleer, N., e Beland, F.: A Safety Climate Measure for Construction Sites. Journal of Safety Research 22, 97–103 (1991)
4. Faber, M.H., Stewart, M.G.: Risk assessment for civil engineering facilities: critical overview and discussion. Reliability Engineering and System Safety 80, 173–184 (2003)
5. Gurcanli, G.E., Mungen, U.: An occupational safety risk analysis method at construction sites using fuzzy sets. International Journal of Industrial Ergonomics 39, 371–387 (2009)
6. Hollnagel, E.: Accidents and barriers. In: Proceedings of the European Conference on Cognitive Science Approaches to Process Control, CSAPC (1999)
7. Karwowski, W., Mital, A.: Potential Applications of Fuzzy Sets in Industrial Safety Engineering. Fuzzy Sets and Systems 19, 105–120 (1986)
8. Kentel, E., Aral, M.M.: Probabilistic-fuzzy health risk modeling. Stoch Envir. Res. and Risk Ass. 18, 324–338 (2004)
9. Laitinen, H., Marjamaki, M., e Paivarinta, K.: The validity of the TR safety observation method on building construction. Accident Analysis and Prevention 31, 463–472 (1999)
10. Liu, J., et al.: Fuzzy Rule-Based Evidential Reasoning Approach for Safety Analysis. International Journal of General Systems 33(2-3), 183–204 (2004)
11. Loosemore, M., e Lee, P.: Communication problems with ethnic minorities in construction industry. International Journal of Project Management 20, 517–524 (2001)
12. Mure, S., Demichela, M., Piccinini, N.: Assessment of the risk of occupational accidents using a fuzzy approach. Cogn. Tech. Work 8, 103–112 (2006)
13. Nilsen, T., Aven, T.: Models and model uncertainty in the context of risk analysis. Reliability Engineering and System Safety 79, 309–317 (2003)
14. Pender, S.: Managing incomplete knowledge: Why risk management is not sufficient. International Journal of Project Management 19, 79–87 (2001)
15. Ringdahl, L.H.: Safety Analysis principles and pratice in occupational safety, 2nd edn. Taylor & Francis, London (2001)
16. Ringen, K., Englund, A., Welch, L., Weeks, J.L., Seegal, J.L.: Why construction is different. Occupational Medicine 10, 255–259 (1995)
17. Ru, W.G., Eloff, J.H.P.: Risk analysis modelling with the use of fuzzy logic. Computers & Security 15(3), 239–248 (1996)
18. Sii, H.S., Wang, J., Ruxton, T.: Novel risk assessment techniques for maritime safety management system. International Journal of Quality & Reliability Management 18(8/9), 982–999 (2001)
19. Tam, C.M., Zeng, S.X.E., Deng, Z.M.: Identifying elements of poor construction safety management in China. Safety Science 42, 569–586 (2004)
20. Tixier, J., et al.: Review of 62 risk analysis methodologies of industrial plants. Journal of Loss Prevention in the Process Industries 15, 291–303 (2002)
21. Wang, J., Ruxton, T.: A review of safety analysis methods applied to the design process of large engineering products. J. Eng. Design 8(2), 131–152 (1997)
22. Zadeh, L.A.: Linguistic variables, approximate reasoning and dispositions. Med. Inform. 8(3), 173–186 (1983)
23. Zadeh, L.A.: The concept of a linguistic variable and its application to approximate reasoning-part I. Information Sciences 8, 199–249 (1975)
24. Zadeh, L.A.: Fuzzy sets. Information and Control 8, 338–353 (1965)
25. Zimmerman, H.J.: Fuzzy Set Theory and its Applications, 2nd edn., pp. 36–43. Kluwer Academic Publishers, London (1991)

Decision Support for Life-Cycle Optimization Using Risk Assessment

Maria Marques[1] and Rui Neves-Silva[2]

[1] UNINOVA – Instituto de Desenvolvimento de Novas Tecnologias,
FCT Campus, 2829-516 Caparica, Portugal
Tel.: +351 212 947 832
mcm@uninova.pt
[2] FCT/UNL – Universidade Nova de Lisboa, FCT Campus, 2829-516
Caparica, Portugal
rns@fct.unl.pt

Abstract. The key idea of this work, is to use risk assessment to support the user in deciding which service should be used, from a set of services developed to support life-cycle optimization, in a specific situation. The risk of a specific situation affecting an industrial plant, characterized by the symptoms, is estimated from the information stored on the system concerning the probability of occurrence of the consequence and its impact. It is expected that this knowledge grows along the life-cycle of a industrial plant. Then, depending of the knowledge available and on the risk of the situation, the adequate service is suggested for promptly reaction in eliminating the problem or avoiding critical situations.[1]

Keywords: Risk Assessment, Decision Support, Life-cycle optimization.

1 Introduction

Life Cycle Management (LCM) has been developed as a business approach for managing the total life cycle of products and services. By learning how to more effectively manage this cycle, a company or organisation can uncover a wealth of business, environmental and social value - and make the choice to engage in more sustainable activities and production patterns.

Life Cycle Management is all about making more informed business decisions - and chances are that life cycle considerations are already influencing the decisions currently made. Life Cycle Management is simply about helping making these decisions in a more deliberate and systematic way - so a more sustainable production and consumption is possible, and clearly define and measure the business value gained by doing so [1]. Life-cycle management of industrial plants is about taking decisions on a daily basis. What configuration is best, what production pattern, when to replace a part, who should be involved in a maintenance process, etc. On the other side, an

---

[1] This work was partially supported by Commission of European Union within the project InLife (Integrated Ambient Intelligence and Knowledge-Based Services for Optimal Life-Cycle Impact of Complex Manufacturing and Assembly Lines), under the Sixth Research Framework Program of the European Union, with the contract NMP2-CT-2005-517018.

L.M. Camarinha-Matos, P. Pereira, and L. Ribeiro (Eds.): DoCEIS 2010, IFIP AICT 314, pp. 112–121, 2010.

industrial plant can produce, through the available instrumentation, a huge amount of information from where decisions can be supported if well interpreted.

Thus the central problem is on how to combine the existing information so that we can foresee what impact a specific decision will have. Most of the times the information is not structured and it is scattered along the plant making extremely difficult to correlate it and reach a consistent conclusion, i.e. a decision.

In terms of decision theory reaching a conclusion is choosing among a set of alternatives. The parameters involved in this process are treated as subjective judgments, expressing the decision-maker's knowledge, experience, and intuition [2]. Nevertheless, some research using naturalistic methods shows, that in situations with higher time pressure, higher stakes, or increased ambiguities, experts give a more important role to intuitive decision making rather than structured approaches, following recognition primed decision approach to fit a set of indicators into the expert's experience and immediately arrive at a satisfactory course of action without weighing alternatives [3]. Due to the large number of considerations involved in many decisions, computer-based decision support systems have been developed to assist decision makers in considering the implications of various courses of thinking. These systems can help reduce the risk of human errors due to cognitive and temporal limitations [4]. All these aspects become clear when the decision must be made in a noisy environment or in a distressing situation, which are very common conditions in industrial plants.

The work here presented was developed under the scope of the InLife project. One of the objectives of InLife was to develop a system that uses the data coming from different sources along the industrial plant to support decisions for lifecycle management [5]. From the analysis of the received data, and in case there are changes that may cause an increase of the risk level, the system is able to fire adequate services that suggest actions helping the user deal with the situation. Additionally the incoming data is used to compute life-cycle parameters, defined by the user. If any of the defined parameters exceed a predefined threshold, than the same strategy is applied, which will provide support to the life-cycle management.

2   Contribution to Technological Innovation

Approach for system development. The system comprises a service platform, which constitutes the user interface. Thus, the existing services will interact with the user presenting the information available in a structured and suitable way. The system supports the user by providing suggestions in terms of the most suitable service to be used in a specific situation, as well as in making a decision considering the relevant information for each case. Accordingly, the system is responsible for analysing the data received, process it and transform it into knowledge that is used to deliver services to the user. The generation/collection of knowledge is based on the use of Ambient Intelligence technology (AmI) [9],[10], Knowledge Management (KM) techniques [11] and the developed service platform [8].

Among the set of services offered three are in the core of the decision support approach: *Condition-based Maintenance, Online Remote Maintenance and Diagnostics,* and *Prevention of Hazardous Situations.* They were selected since they are seen as services to be used on a daily basis operation, especially the first two. Thus the level of decision involved and the impact those decisions will have is more interesting in terms of life-cycle management then the services used occasionally.

The services main function is to provide support for actions to achieve a specific service goal through recommendations to the human user of the system. These recommendations result from the understanding of the plant operation by the system which is the result of modelling cause effect relations (cause events/actions to consequence effects) achieved by an effective life-cycle parameter monitoring.

These relations are used for the establishment of cases that describe the effects of a certain cause. The collection of these cases is then used to select the best option, from the set of already available, for a specific situation. This is the strategy used to implement the decision support approach based on the utilization of the three above mentioned services.

System Entities. In order to have the system installed and running in several industrial plants there is the need for developing a model, general enough that comprises all the relevant information on plant operation. Nevertheless, and despite the generic character of the model it is also required that it includes several aspects of the operation. Thus the result requires a good balance between simplification of some aspects and the complexity that still is associated to the production process. Since the developed model to support the entire system includes some aspects that are not relevant for the work here described, we will focus on the entities that are vital for the application of the proposed approach.

Fig. 1 shows part of the developed model simply showing the entities that are directly involved on the risk assessment and in support to decision process.

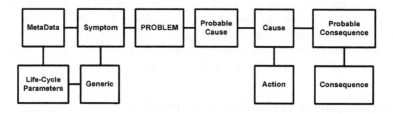

Fig. 1. Simplified developed model for saving data from plant

The entity **Problem** is the central part of the entire system, since any deviation on the defined normal behaviour of the plant will be stored has an instance of this entity. This entity is connected to **Symptom**, representing the firing event for the risk assessment process, and to **Probable Cause**, which is a set of possible causes for the occurred situation (among a list of predefined causes). The **Symptom** entity makes the connection between the lower level part of the model and the upper one. In the lower level we can find entities to represent the operating parts of the plant like **Generic** (representing machines involved in production, production processes or product parts) and **Life-Cycle Parameters** (representing the defined parameters that are seen as relevant for the plant). Additionally, **MetaData** is used to represent the *a priori* knowledge related with the plant (e.g. in terms of which **Generics** are related to which **Life-Cycle Parameters** so that an abnormal value of these latest generate a **Symptom**). In the upper part of the model the aim is to store the information associated to causes and actions that are related to the problems. Additionally the information on which are the probable causes for a specific problem and the probable consequences for each cause are also stored.

All these entities have several fields that are used to store the associated information, once again, and for the sake of simplicity, here we will only refer the ones that are used in the context of this work. Thus, and in what refers to **Problem,** the field *frequency* is used to represent the certainty of knowledge about a problem. The problems with frequency higher than 1 did not occurred, but they were artificially introduced at setup stage and are reference expected problems for each symptom.. Thus, when a similar problem occur the probability of the cause to be the same defined for the problem with higher *frequency* is higher than for other different problems that only occurred once.

In what concerns **Probable Cause** the fields *probability* and *risk* are used. The first one will store the probability of that cause to be the correct one, whereas the second will store the value of the calculated risk during risk assessment. Note that a **Probable Cause** is unique but two probable causes can be associated to the same cause. The **Probable Consequence** has a field to store the *probability* of a specific cause to induce a specific consequence. Finally, **Consequence** has a field to store the *impact* that that consequence will have (if occurs). On the other part of the model we find that **Symptom** has a field to identify the **Generic** where the abnormal life-cycle parameter value occurred (given by the connection between **Generic**, **Life-Cycle Parameter** and **MetaData**).

In terms of innovation three aspects are considered as major contributions: (i) the use of AmI and KM to collect and manage the information generated by the plant and its users; (ii) the developed model; and (iii) the use of the information to develop the risk assessment and provide support to decision to the user based on the results.

3   Risk Assessment

Risk is a concept that denotes a potential negative impact to an asset or some characteristic of value that may arise from some present process or future event. In everyday usage, "risk" is often used synonymously with "probability" of a loss or threat. Nevertheless, risk should combine the probability of an event occurring with the impact that the event would have and with its different circumstances [12],[13].

Risk assessment is considered as the initial and periodical step in a risk management process. Risk assessment is the determination of quantitative or qualitative value of risk related to a concrete situation and a recognised threat [14]. Thus, risk R is defined as the result of the product between the probability of occurrence of a specific incident E and the impact I of that incident (in money or injuries), i.e.

$$R = P_o(E) \times I(E)$$

If any of the relevant parameters defined for the plant crosses its threshold, the information provided by the system allows the probability of an incident to be estimated. Also, the estimated consequences of the incident allow the estimation of the level of risk that we are dealing with. The functions that describe both incident probability and losses are supposed to be known (even if with some level of uncertainty). This information is collected during set-up phase and during operation using operator knowledge in order to compute the risk.

Assessment Method. In what concerns InLife the calculated risk is presented in cost units. The values of threshold between risk levels are to be defined by the industrial users since they may not be adequate for all cases [6].

The use of Event Tree Analysis, using Bayesian networks [15], for assessing the probability of occurrence is seen as the most suitable method to achieve the final consequences. An Event Tree starts from an undesired initiator (loss of critical supply, component failure etc) and follows possible further system events through to a series of final consequences. As each new event is considered, a new node on the tree is added with a split of probabilities of taking either branch. The probabilities of a range of 'top events' arising from the initial event can then be seen [16]. The method described corresponds to the so called "Probabilistic Risk Assessment" and as an analytical tool includes the consideration of the following:

❑   Identification of the combinations of events that, if occur, could lead an undesired event;
❑   Estimation of the chance of occurrence for each combination; and
❑   Estimation of the consequences associated with each combination.

For instance, consider that an alarm is fired indicating that there is a deviation on the expected value of "mean-time-between-failure", expressing that this value exceeded some threshold that is considered normal. Assuming that the occurrence of this type of situation is known as generating a specific loss, that must be quantified, and that the probability of incident associated to the fired alarm is also known, than it is possible to calculate the risk associated to this situation.

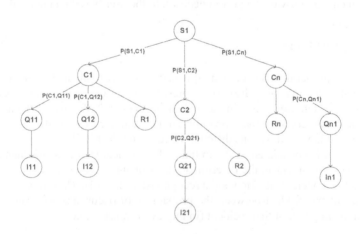

Fig. 2. Risk assessment based on probabilities

Fig. 2 shows the process of calculating the probabilities of consequences associated to the detection of a specific symptom (S). The symptom is the entity that enables the detection of some abnormal situation. Note that it is not the cause of the situation nor the situation it self. Thus the symptom may be caused by one or more possible causes (C). Each cause has one or more consequences (Q). For the sake of simplicity we establish that the measurement of impact I is associated with the consequences Q. The identification of the situation with the higher level of risk is done by navigation on the tree following the higher probabilities. The calculation of risk is done by using the formula:

$$R_i = P(S_i, C_i) \times P(C_i, Q_{ij}) * I_{ij}$$

For each combination the method computes a value of risk. The combination with the higher risk value is the one that must be considered, i.e. treated, in first place. Thus if we only considerer the higher risk value than:

$$R = \max\{R_i\}$$

Depending on the options made at the set-up phase there is also the possibility of presenting the several values of risks computed for the other consequences in order to guide the user on solving each of the associated causes [7]. This is an option for each company to decide since it is highly dependent on company policies.

Example. Let us consider two problems P_1, P_2 that are stored in the system, and classified as solved problems (i.e. the cause for each of them is already found and the problem was efficiently eliminated). For each one we also have information on "frequency" (f) and "Probable Cause" (PC_i). Now, Let us consider a new third problem P_3 which has just occurred and about which we only know that has the same symptoms of P_1, P_2. Assuming that: $f_1 > f_2$.

P_1		P_2		P_3	
f	f_1	f	f_2	f	1
PC_i	PC_1	PC_i	PC_3		
PC_i	PC_2	PC_i	PC_4		

Lets say that for problem P_1 we are pretty sure about its cause but in what concerns P_2 the possible causes are equally probable. Thus when defining the probabilities we must reflect these considerations, admitting that $p_1 > p_2$ and $p_1 + p_2 = 1$ and $p_3 = 0.5$.

P_1		P_2	
$p(PC_1)$	p_1	$p(PC_3)$	p_3
$p(PC_2)$	p_2	$p(PC_4)$	p_3

Note that $p(PC_i) = P(S_i, C_i)$.

Lets now associate the "Cause" (C_i) to each **Probable Cause**, assuming that two probable causes are associated to the same cause. This must be considered when computing the probable causes for the new problem.

PC_i	C_i
PC_1	C_1
PC_2	C_2
PC_3	C_3
PC_4	C_4

Finally we have to define the probability of "Cause" to degenerate in a specific "Consequence" (Q_{ij}) with an associated impact (I_{ij}). Assuming that: $p_4 + p_5 + p_6 = 1$, $p_7 + p_8 = 1$, $p_9 + p_{10} = 1$, and: $p_4 > p_5 > p_6 > p_7 > p_8$ and $p_{10} > p_9$.

C_1		C_2		C_3	
$p(Q_{11})$	p_4	$p(Q_{21})$	p_7	$p(Q_{31})$	p_9
$p(Q_{12})$	p_5	$p(Q_{22})$	p_8	$p(Q_{32})$	p_{10}
$p(Q_{13})$	p_6				

Note that $p(Q_{ij})=P(C_i,Q_i)$.

We are now able of computing the risk associated to this case. Let's start by building the table of the probability of the probable causes that depends o the values established for the frequency:

P_3	
$p(PC_1)$	$f_1p_1=p_{11}$
$p(PC_2)$	$f_1p_2=p_{12}$
$p(PC_3)$	$f_2p_3=p_{13}$
$p(PC_4)$	$f_2p_3=p_{13}$

The calculated values must be normalised so that the resulting sum is 1. Note that $p_{11}>p_{12}$. Remember that PC_4 is related with C_1, what results in having three different causes, thus we can sum the values p_{11} and p_{13} associated to $p(PC_4)$ and create a new value p_{14}.

Let us now build the table of the probability of specific consequence associated to a cause.

	$p(Q_{11})$	$p_{14}p_4=p_{15}$
C_1	$p(Q_{12})$	$p_{14}p_5=p_{16}$
	$p(Q_{13})$	$p_{14}p_6=p_{17}$
C_2	$p(Q_{21})$	$p_{12}p_7=p_{18}$
	$p(Q_{22})$	$p_{12}p_8=p_{19}$
C_3	$p(Q_{31})$	$p_{13}p_9=p_{10}$
	$p(Q_{32})$	$p_{13}p_{10}=p_{21}$

Considering the assumptions that we made previously, we have: $p_{15}>p_{16}>p_{17}>p_{21}>p_{18}>p_{20}>p_{19}$.

At this point we just have to multiply the defined impacts for each consequence, and we will have the different risk values. Note that each consequence Q_{ij} has an associated impact I_{ij}. Assuming that: $I_{11}>I_{12}>I_{13}>I_{21}>I_{22}>I_{31}>I_{32}$ we have:

R1	$p_{15}I_{11}$	R5	$p_{19}I_{22}$
R2	$p_{16}I_{12}$	R6	$p_{20}I_{31}$
R3	$p_{17}I_{13}$	R7	$p_{21}I_{32}$
R4	$p_{18}I_{21}$		

The selected risk value, following the defined methodology is R_1 since, considering the conditions imposed, it presents the higher risk value.

Reaching this point we can present the result to the user in terms of what is the most risky situation and which procedure should be applied to avoid it. Remember that we kept tracking of the cause associated to R_1, thus it is possible to suggest actions that will correct the situation.

In terms of system we need to keep track of what were the causes involved in the problem evaluation, since even if they were not elected, it is useful to have this information. But, how should this information be stored? Remember that P_1 and P_2 have four probable causes but two of them are associated to the same cause, C_1. Thus to set the probable causes of P_3 we have to consider that the probability associated to C_1 is higher that the other two. If we consider the four different probable causes the probability for each of them would be 0.25. Then, we will have 0.25 for the associated to C_2 and C_3 and 0.5 to the associated to C_1.

4 Support to Decision

Through the services developed the users have access to specific functionalities of the system prepared to provide a prompt acquisition and provision of knowledge using an adequate presentation for each type of user. Thus, let us consider again the case shown on Fig. 2 where it would be possible to compute the risk associated to a specific situation. Nevertheless we are able to improve this knowledge with the one that has already been gathered along the life-cycle of the plant. In fact, if we have specific knowledge of the plant it is possible to develop a more accurate and more useful support to decision. For instances if the system stores not only the data that constitutes the case but also the action that was performed to solve it, then it is possible to provide the user with this information which will help him to make a decision on what should be done. In this point of view the support to decision system correlates the past cases that match the current one, and assess the involved risk accordingly. On the top of this strategy each user has to establish what is considered as critical in the considered plant. This information is crucial since it is used to assess the risk for hazardous situations.

Fig. 3 shows the flowchart that describes how the risk is assessed and how this information combined with the information available is used to select the appropriate service. The situation begins while plant is operating normally and a symptom is detected by monitoring systems. After providing the system with a description of the detected symptom, the system will start searching for stored situations that involve symptoms with the same description provided. The stored situations have associated to them one or more symptoms. Each symptom has one or more probable causes (probability) associated and each cause one or more probable consequences (probability). This cascade of information relating the existing knowledge on the situation will be used to compute risk by means of Probabilistic Risk Assessment. Furthermore the existence of knowledge on how to solve the situation, i.e. actions, is also important for the launching of services since they are launched based on this knowledge.

Finally the system will support the user in solving the situation by providing information on which is the adequate service to be used. If the situation is well known, and was not assessed as critical, the system will select "Condition-based maintenance" service. Further the system will suggest the appropriate maintenance action that must be developed based on the information that was already available to cope with that situation. The service of *Condition-based maintenance* will also support the user to decide when the suggested action should be performed. This scheduling module will also use information of production in order to suggest non producing slots for scheduling the necessary action.

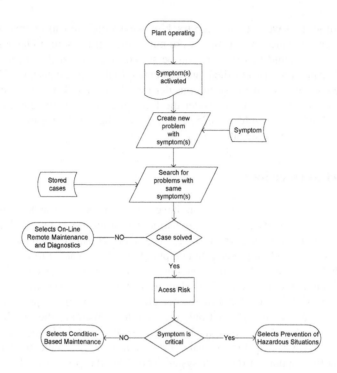

Fig. 3. Decision support using risk assessment

If the situation involves any of the parameters that were previously established as being critical for the plant and their operators, the system will select *Prevention of hazardous situations* service. Note that the main idea is to prevent the accidents from occurring thus, the actions should be preventive (e.g. operators training). If the situation does not fit in any of the previous categories the system will select *Online remote maintenance and diagnostics* service. This service aims not only at developing maintenance but also to provide diagnostics to the user. Thus the service uses InLife problem solving module to collect and correlate all the information available that may be related with the situation described. This information is presented to the user in a structured way in order to support him on finding an appropriate solution. If the user was able of finding a solution for the situation, which includes an action to be developed, than the system stores this information and use it if another symptom with the same description is detected or introduced by the user. The calculation of probabilities is highly dependent on this information update since the objective is to use the knowledge acquired during system operation to optimize system performance.

5   Conclusions and Future Work

This paper proposes a approach on how to collect information that is scattered along the manufacturing system. This information is then processed and the knowledge derived from it can be used to improve life-cycle management of the industrial plant. With the knowledge acquired it is possible to improve the decision making process by developing a set of services specifically focused on its support. The work here presented shows that by assessing the risk associated to the current status of the plant, it is possible to identify the cause for a certain problem and, based on that, propose, actions that support the user on the decision process. The impact of this kind of system is not assessable on a short term basis. Being a life cycle management system, the results need to be measured along time, on a long term approach. Nevertheless the level of structured information that is being gathered and stored and the support to decision offered is seen as very promising for a enhanced life cycle management of the industrial plant.

Future work, will include refinement of the risk assessment algorithm especially in what concerns the interrelation of symptoms and the inclusion of the time effect. Additionally, authors are also interested in exploring the relation of the method with the adaptive systems theory.

References

1. UNEP/SETAC. Draft Final Report of the LCM Definition Study Version 3.6. Life Cycle Initiative (2003)
2. Raiffa, H.: Decision Analysis: Introductory Lectures on Choices under Uncertainty. Addison-Wesley, Reading (1968)
3. Baker, D., Bridges, D., Hunter, R., Johnson, G., Krupa, J., Murphy, J., Sorenson, K.: Guidebook to Decision-Making Methods. In: WSRC-IM-2002-00002, Department of Energy, USA (2002)
4. Holsapple, C.W.: Decision Support Systems. DSIS Area, School of Management, UK (1999)
5. Marques, M., Neves-Silva, R., Stokic, D., Reimer, P., Agirre, J.: Life-Cycle Management of Complex Manufacturing and Assembly Lines. In: Proceedings of the 14th International Conference on Concurrent Enterprising, Lisbon (2008)
6. Marques, M., Neves-Silva, R.: Risk Assessment to Support Decision on Complex Manufacturing and Assembly Lines. In: Proceeding of the 5th International Conference on Industrial Informatics, Vienna (2007)
7. Marques, M., Neves-Silva, R.: Decision support system using risk assessment for life-cycle management of industrial plants. In: Proceeding of the 13th IFAC Symposium on Information Control Problems in Manufacturing, Moscow (2009)
8. InLife Consortium. InLife Public Concept- Report. InLife Project: Integrated Ambient Intelligence and Knowledge- Based Services for Optimal Life-Cycle Impact of Complex Manufacturing and Assembly Lines, the contract NMP2-CT-2005-517018U (2006)
9. IST Advisory Group. Scenarios for Ambient Intelligence in 2010, IPTS Seville (2001)
10. IST Advisory Group. Ambient Intelligence: from Vision to reality, IST (2003)
11. Bray, D.: Literature Review - Knowledge Management Research at the Organizational Level, Social Science Research Network (2007)
12. Holton, G.A.: Defining Risk. Financial Analysts Journal 60(6), 19–25 (2004)
13. Stamatelatos, M.: Probabilistic Risk Assessment: What Is It And Why Is It Worth Performing It? In: NASA Office of Safety and Mission Assurance (2000)
14. Anderson, K.: Intelligence-Based Threat Assessments for Information Networks and Infrastructures: A White Paper (2005)
15. Ben-Gal, I.: Bayesian Networks. In: Ruggeri, F., Kenett, R., Faltin, F. (eds.) Encyclopedia of Statistics in Quality and Reliability. John Wiley & Sons, Chichester (2007)
16. Russel, S., Norvig, P.: Artificial Intelligence – A modern Approach. Prentice Hall, Englewood Cliffs (2003)

A Clinical Decision Support System
for Breast Cancer Patients

Ana S. Fernandes[1], Pedro Alves[1], Ian H. Jarman[2], Terence A. Etchells[2],
José M. Fonseca[1], and Paulo J.G. Lisboa[2]

[1] Faculdade de Ciências e Tecnologia, Universidade Nova de Lisboa
{asff,jmf}@uninova.pt
[2] School of Computing and Mathematical Sciences, Liverpool John Moores University,
Byrom Street, Liverpool L3 3AF, UK
{T.A.Etchells,I.H.Jarman,P.J.Lisboa}@ljmu.ac.uk

Abstract. This paper proposes a Web clinical decision support system for clinical oncologists and for breast cancer patients making prognostic assessments, using the particular characteristics of the individual patient. This system comprises three different prognostic modelling methodologies: the clinically widely used Nottingham prognostic index (NPI); the Cox regression modelling and a partial logistic artificial neural network with automatic relevance determination (PLANN-ARD). All three models yield a different prognostic index that can be analysed together in order to obtain a more accurate prognostic assessment of the patient. Missing data is incorporated in the mentioned models, a common issue in medical data that was overcome using multiple imputation techniques. Risk group assignments are also provided through a methodology based on regression trees, where Boolean rules can be obtained expressed with patient characteristics.

Keywords: Breast cancer, survival analysis, decision support systems.

1 Introduction

Prognostic assessments as well as clinical indicators are the key issues to guide clinical oncologists to better define the treatments and to better assess the impact of prognostic factors on survival of operable breast cancer patients.

This paper presents a web decision support system for clinical oncologists, where three different survival models are considered: the commonly used NPI (Nottingham Prognostic Index), Proportional Hazards Modelling and PLANN-ARD (Partial Logistic Artificial Neural Network with Automatic relevance determination), such that each model provides an independent prognostic index. The prognostic indices (PI) for each of the models are derived from prognostic factors and allow stratification of patients by survival outcome. A patient stratification methodology is also introduced to separate the population into significantly different survival risk groups In addition, these risk groups can be characterized using explanatory rules obtained from the prognostic factors used in the analysis. Both, the patient's risk group and the explanatory rules can be incorporated in the Web decision support system. It is important to mention that the aim of the proposed decision support system is to enhance the oncologists'

L.M. Camarinha-Matos, P. Pereira, and L. Ribeiro (Eds.): DoCEIS 2010, IFIP AICT 314, pp. 122–129, 2010.
© IFIP International Federation for Information Processing 2010

current practices, rather than to replace them. Therefore, all the previous models are incorporated in the web interface.

Section 2 explains the current study's contribution to technical innovation, section 3 gives a description of the data set used to train the model and defines the predictive variables chosen for the analysis. Section 4 presents the prognostic models and the methodologies used for patient stratification into different survival groups and Section 5 presents the Web decision support system followed by the conclusions.

2 Contribution to Technical Innovation

The present work makes an important contribution to both technical innovation and clinical application as several important novelties were added or changed to current practice. Jarman et al (2008) have already presented a web decision support system as a relevant innovation [1]; this study improves upon this system by resolving and improving, some particular issues. Currently there are several survival models which are in use, such as NPI and other Cox proportional hazards models. It is intended to augment NPI by adding more variables considered to be important in the prognostic model, which selection is explained in section 4. Moreover, it was intended to define a prognostic model to become predictive rather than explanatory as well as modelling non-linear dependences, with PLANN-ARD. Previous research [2] on the dataset used for this study and mentioned on section 3, showed missing data to be missing at random (MAR): hence, it can be successfully imputed. Therefore this work also takes account of missing data and censorship within principled frameworks [2], applying multiple imputation in combination with neural network models for time-to-event modelling, where a new PI was also considered. It is important to note that survival models must take account of censorship, which occurs when a patient drops out of the study before the event of interest is observed or if the event of interest does not take place until the end of the study. Moreover a new stratification methodology was developed, based on decision trees, which adds a more robust path to identify the patient's risk group and the explanatory rules that characterize risk group membership, based on patient's characteristics. Finally, a new web decision support system contributes to technical innovation as it implements both the previously mentioned models, where all can be compared.

3 Data Description

The data set comprise 931 consecutive series of female patients recruited by Christie Hospital in Wilmslow, Manchester, UK, during 1990-94. The current study is specific to early operable breast cancer patients filtered using the standard TNM (Tumour, Nodes, Metastasis) staging system as tumour size less than 5 cm, node stage less than 2 and without clinical symptoms of metastatic spread. The event of interest is death to any cause, being a single risk model, where the study period for analysis is 5 years and the time-to-event was measured in months from surgery. All patients in this study were censored after 5 years of follow-up. 16 explanatory variables in addition to outcome variables were acquired for all patient records.

This study will only focus on Histological type lobular and ductal, therefore some records were withdrawn. Also, two of the 931 records in the training data were identified as outliers and removed. Finally, at the end of the analysis the data set ended up with 743 subjects. Missing data is a common problem in prediction research. After analysing the data set, information has been considered to be Missing at Random (MAR) where a new attribute may be created to denote missing information or the missing values can be imputed. The latter has been shown to be effective [3]. Therefore, the missing covariates were imputed following the method indicated in [3] and repeated 10 times. The choice of this number is a conservative one, as several studies have shown that the required number of repeated imputations can be as low as three for data with up to 20% missing information.

4   Breast Cancer Prognostic Models and Stratification Methods

This section explains both, the different prognostic models and the stratification methodology which were included in the web decision system. The following detailed methods bridge the gap between individual predictions for single patients and allocations of patients into risk groups.

4.1   Breast Cancer Prognostic Models

It is important to mention that historically, the purpose of prognostic models was to stratify patients into cohorts with distinct survival. The most widely used index is TNM, which is purely clinical, as it depends only on clinical investigations and palpation and takes account of metastatic spread of the disease but is not sufficiently detailed for early breast cancer. The Nottingham prognostic index (NPI) [4], a clinical prognostic index for breast cancer patients has been widely applied to inform the choice of adjuvant therapy. It is an indicator of breast cancer outcome and its score is calculated using the following formula:

$$NPI=0.2 \times pathological\ size + histological\ grade + nodes\ involved . \qquad (1)$$

Subsequently, from their NPI patients are allocated into prognostic groups from excellent prognostic group to poor prognostic group based on the cutpoints: <2.41; <3.41; <5.41 and ≥5.41. Predictive prognostic inference for individual patients was also introduced by the web-based interface for clinical oncologists which has expanded the covariate basis for prognostic inference. www.Adjuvantonline.com [5] is an interface format that appears to be readily accepted by practicing clinicians. This model has the advantage to infer the potential effect of different treatment choices and since its publication on the web, there is greater interest in making individualised predictions of survival. However, its predictions do not include confidence intervals, yet are likely to be subject to substantial uncertainties for particular groups of patients. Advances in therapy, detection technologies and health policy have skewed the patient population and additional prognostic indicators can be added to increase the predictive power of NPI. Consequently, the other two prognostic models are included and compared in this study.

In the survival analysis field, the proportional hazard model, also known as Cox regression is widely used. Cox regression factorises dependence on time and the co-variates, where the hazard rate is modelled for each patient with covariates x_p at time t_k, as follows:

$$\frac{h(x_p,t_k)}{1-h(x_p,t_k)} = \frac{h_0(t_k)}{1-h_0(t_k)} \cdot \exp(\sum_{i=1}^{N_i} bx_i). \qquad (2)$$

where h_0 is the baseline hazard function and x_i are the patient variables. Here the prognostic score is defined by the traditional linear index βx. However, for this study 10 imputed data sets were used, which means that the final prognostic score for each patient was determined as the mean of the 10 prognostic indices identified,

Model selection was carried out through Cox regression (proportional hazards) [2], where six predictive variables were identified: *age at diagnosis, node stage, histological type, ratio of axillary nodes affected to axilar nodes removed, pathological size* (i.e. tumour size in cm) and *oestrogen receptor count*. All variables are binary coded as 1-from-N.

The Partial Logistic Artificial Neural Network is a predictive model, rather than an explanatory model, such as the proportional hazards regression and also has the capability of capturing interactions between covariates as well as fitting the time dependence of the hazard function. It has a strong regularisation framework which has been added to avoid overfitting, using the method of Automatic Relevance Determination, hence the acronym PLANN-ARD [6]. For a single risk, such as overall mortality, this model has the structure of a multi-layer perceptron with a single hidden layer and sigmoidal activations in the hidden and output layer nodes. The number of hidden nodes was determined using cross-validation that is several networks were trained, each one with different hidden nodes and validated with cross-validation. It was concluded that 8 hidden nodes were sufficient to train the network and not lead to over-fitting.

Covariates and discrete time (monthly time increments) are introduced in the network as inputs, where the output is the hazard for each patient and for each time. Estimating the weights requires a likelihood term for the status of one patient at time t_k, by using an indicator when the patient status is observed alive at time t_k (labeled as 0) or have died (label as 1). The papers cited in [6] make a strict theoretical correspondence between this neural network model and classical statistical time-to-event models for censored data. To obtain patient information, that is appropriate to their prognostic risk group, it is important to define first this risk group as well as the relevant prognostic score, appropriated for non-linear models, as with the previous mentioned prognostic models. Therefore, the following expression is proposed:

$$PI(x_p) = (-\ln(1-CCI(t))) = \ln(-\ln(S(t))). \qquad (3)$$

where the CCI is the crude cumulative incidence, identified as the probability of the occurrence of a specific event of interest and *S(t)* is the estimated survival at the end of follow up. As a consequence of imputation, PLANN-ARD was computed 10 independent times, one to each imputed data set, which resulted in 10 different trained networks. The mentioned time independent PI was also computed for the 10 networks and averaged for each patient, producing a final PI.

4.2 Group Risk Stratification

In a clinical environment stratification of patients, in different risk groups, based on survival models is frequently used in the evaluation of treatments or to assess the impact of prognostic factors on survival. Therefore, a stratification methodology needs to be defined in order to separate the different patients in statistically significant risk groups by overall mortality. Previous studies [7] presented a comparison between different stratification methodologies, such as the bootstrap log-rank aggregation based on the log-rank test and a regression tree, based on CART algorithm [8], where the PI is now the target for regression using a rule-tree. The bootstrap log-rank aggregation was considered in order to diminish the log-rank cut-points overestimation [9]. All stratification methodologies were applied to both survival models: PLANN-ARD, a neural network for time-to-event data and Cox proportional hazards.

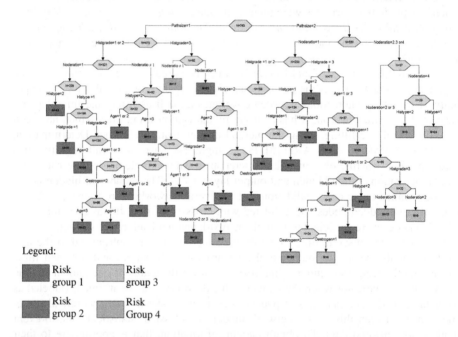

Fig. 1. Final regression tree, indicating the risk groups belonging for all the patients with different predictive variables, using the proportional hazards model as a prognostic model

However, a concern of many clinicians is the 'black box' nature of artificial neural networks (ANN) [10] which raises the important issue of explaining individual inferences by the network. This is a key stage in evaluating the clinical plausibility of inferences made by analytical models to enable clinicians to apply these inferences with confidence. Consequently, the regression tree can be a very well accepted stratification method in a clinical environment, as it gives simple explanatory rules, based on the predictive variables for all the risk groups considering all the existent possibilities, as it can be observed in figure 1. This figure represents the final regression tree, where, thanks to the pruning method, the final leafs define different risk groups. Each risk group is characterized by different rules based on the patient's characteristics which are defined by each branch of the regression tree.

5 Framework for Integrated Decision Support System

All the prognostic models, combined with the stratification methods described above can be integrated with decision supports for clinicians and patients, being used for personalized patient information systems. Figure 2 represents the framework web home page, where the three prognostic models can be computed and the output compared for a single patient. The framework's main goal is to assist the clinicians and patients in defining the appropriate information to their prognostic risk group, by way of a cross-matching matrix for all the different methodologies. The interface combines a group score (the NPI index) with two statistical models (one linear and one non-linear) to estimate breast cancer specific mortality. This provides a 'second opinion' for current users of Adjuvant! but using a single data-based model and hence with the potential to provide not just point estimates of survival but also theoretically derived confidence intervals for those estimates. The Kaplan Meier survival curves can also be available for each cell of the matrix in order to discover heterogeneity within a prognostic risk group. It is important to mention that the basis of this framework is to detail the prognosis risk group using different methodologies, rather then replacing one for another. The same idea of cross-tabulation can be extended to a scatter plot of the PI. It can also inform if some patients are outliers of the model or in the borderline between groups.

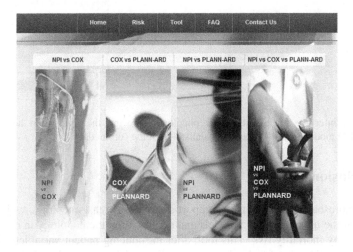

Fig. 2. Home page of a patient information system for breast cancer patients with the possibility to choose a 2D or 3D cross-matching visualisation for different risk group allocation

Patient's characteristics are submitted and the risk scores as well as risk groups are calculated. These are displayed in the web page, figure 3. The cross-matching can be visualized in two dimensional and three dimensional plots. As an example, figure 3 represents in the ordinate the currently used clinical risk score, namely the Nottingham Prognostic Index (NPI), while the abscissa is the PI derived from the PLANN-ARD. The result is that patients in NPI group 3 are shown in the plot to be stratified into different risk groups. Finally, this Web clinical decision support system also allows clinical oncologists to collect and save their patients prognosis as well as their clinical data. Therefore, supported by patient history, clinical oncologists have the possibility to compare prognosis and treatments and improve their medical decisions.

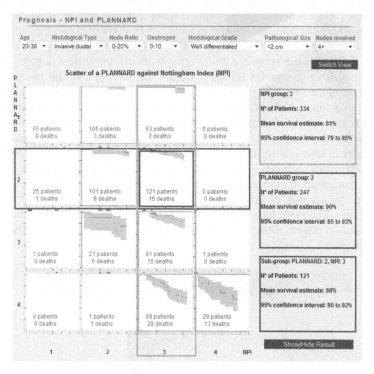

Fig. 3. User interface for breast cancer oncology, showing the risk group belonging for PLANN-ARD model and NPI PI and a visualisation of the patient data

6 Conclusions

This paper presents a web decision support system for breast oncology, which shows the value of the new prognostic models and stratification methodology in discriminating patients by mortality risk. This tool, after introducing patient variables, identifies the risk group allocation for the three prognostic models presented in this paper (NPI, Cox proportional hazards, PLANN-ARD) and consequently the rules that explain each risk group. A cross-matching matrix of grouped survival and the position a patient resides within the matrix it is also presented, leading to better insights if the risk group allocation for a specific prognostic model is more accurate. Moreover, as Adujantonline is gaining clinical support, a link to this web tool has been placed in the presented web decision support system. Future work on the prognostic model will include a detailed validation of the prognostic predictions by application to out-of-sample data collected by the British Columbia Cancer Agency. This is the same data set that was used to evaluate the Adjuvantonline system, thus enabling benchmarking. In order to improve the presented tool, for future work the different treatment choices for the data base used for training the prognostic model.

Acknowledgments. The authors gratefully acknowledge Mr. R. Swindell from Christie Hospital for making the anonymised modelling data set available for this study and members of the BC Cancer Agency's Breast Cancer Outcomes Unit for assembling the British Columbia data. This study was partially funded by the European Network of Excellence Biopattern (FP6/2002/IST/1-508803) and by Fundação para a Ciência e Tecnologia, through the POS_C(SFRH/BD/30260/2006).

References

1. Jarman, I.H., Etchells, T.A., Martín-Guerrero, J.D., Lisboa, P.J.G.: An integrated framework for risk profiling of breast cancer patients following surgery. Artificial Intelligence in Medicine 42, 165–188 (2008)
2. Fernandes, A.S., Jarman, I.H., Etchells, T.A., Fonseca, J.M., Biganzoli, E., Bajdik, C., Lisboa, P.J.G.: Missing data imputation in longitudinal cohort studies – application of PLANN-ARD in breast cancer survival. In: 2008 Seventh International Conference on Machine Learning and Applications, 2008, ICMLA 2008, pp. 644–649 (2008)
3. Clark, T.G., Altman, D.G.: Developing a prognostic model in the presence of missing data an ovarian cancer case study. Journal of clinical epidemiology 56, 28–37 (2003)
4. Haybittle, J.L., Blamey, R.W., Elston, C.W., Johnson, J., Doyle, P.J., Campbell, F.C., Nicholson, R.I., Griffiths, K.: A prognostic index in primary breast cancer. Brit J. Cancer 45, 3621 (1982)
5. Ravdin, P.M., Siminoff, L.A., Davis, G.J., Mercer, B.M., Hewlett, J., Gerson, N., Parker, H.L.: Computer Program to Assist in Making Decisions about Adjuvant Therapy for Women with Early Breast Cancer. J. Clin. Oncol. 74(4), 980–991 (2001)
6. Lisboa, P.J.G., Wong, H., Harris, P., Swindell, R.: A Bayesian neural network approach for modelling censored data with an application to prognosis after surgery for breast cancer. Artificial Intelligence in Medicine 28(1), 1–25 (2003)
7. Fernandes, A.S., Etchells, T.A., Jarman, I.H., Fonseca, J.M.: Stratification methodologies for neural networks models of survival. In: Cabestany, J., et al. (eds.) IWANN 2009. LNCS, vol. 5517, pp. 989–996. Springer, Heidelberg (2009)
8. Breiman, L., Friedman, J.H., Olsen, A.R., Stone, C.J.: Classification and Regression Trees. The Wadsworth & Brooks (1984)
9. Etchells, T.A., Fernandes, A.S., Jarman, I.H., Fonseca, J.M., Lisboa, P.J.G.: Stratification of severity of illness indices: a case study for breast cancer prognosis. In: Lovrek, I., Howlett, R.J., Jain, L.C. (eds.) KES 2008, Part II. LNCS (LNAI), vol. 5178, pp. 214–221. Springer, Heidelberg (2008)
10. Lisboa, P.J.G.: A review of evidence of health benefit from artificial neural networks in medical intervention. Neural Networks 15(1), 9–37 (2002)

Part 5

Evolvable Factory Automation

Evolvable Production Systems: Mechatronic Production Equipment with Evolutionary Control

Antonio Maffei[1], Mauro Onori[1], Pedro Neves[2], and José Barata[2]

[1] Royal Institute of Technology, Dept. Of Production Engineering,
Stockholm, Sweden
Tel.: 46-8-7906637
onori@iip.kth.se
[2] Universidade Nova de Lisboa /UNINOVA, Quinta da Torre,
Monte da Caparica, Caparica, Portugal
jab@uninova.pt

Abstract. Current major roadmapping efforts have all clearly underlined that true industrial sustainability will require far higher levels of systems' autonomy and adaptability. In accordance with these recommendations, the Evolvable Production Systems (EPS) has aimed at developing such technological solutions and support mechanisms. Since its inception in 2002 as a next generation of production systems, the concept is being further developed and tested to emerge as a production system paradigm. Characteristically, Evolvable systems have distributed control, and are composed of intelligent modules with embedded control. A concerted effort is being exerted through European research projects in collaboration with manufacturers, technology/equipment suppliers, and universities. After introducing EPS, this paper presents current developments and applications.

Keywords: Evolvable Production Systems, Modularity, Distributed Control.

1 Introduction

The major problems of manufacturing companies are all relate to uncertainty. First of all, it is very difficult for companies to predict the type and range of products that will have to be developed. The second uncertainty regards the production volumes and lifespan reached by these future products.

Evolvable systems, as a next generation of production systems, was first introduced in 2002 and has, since then, been developed and tested to emerge as a production system paradigm (see EUPASS, A3 projects). The essence of evolvability resides not only in the ability of system components to adapt to the changing conditions of operation, but also to assist in the evolution of these components in time such that processes may become self-X, x representing a property of the system such as reconfigurable, etc.

According to the results attained by many roadmaps, such as ManuFuture [1], ManVis [2], FutMan [3] and EUPASS [4], one of the most important objectives to be met by European industry is sustainability, which is multi-faceted: including

L.M. Camarinha-Matos, P. Pereira, and L. Ribeiro (Eds.): DoCEIS 2010, IFIP AICT 314, pp. 133–142, 2010.

economical, social and ecological aspects. The conclusion to this holistic problem is that future manufacturing solutions will have to deal with very complex scenarios.

This article gives a brief overview of the achievements attained by Evolvable Assembly Systems, EAS [5]. EAS represents one of the paradigms proposed as an opportunity to solve such threats. NOTE: the relation to Holonic Manufacturing Systems ([6], [7]) and Reconfigurable Manufacturing Systems will be described later.

Evolvable systems clearly approach the idea that system components may evolve to meet upcoming demands and needs. This inevitable bridges the fields of production engineering and computer science, but it also introduces aspects of computational evolution. Hence the link to a partial study of genetics and evolutionary principles (discussed later). Evolvable systems have characteristically distributed control, are composed of intelligent modules and are open in architecture: they go beyond the concept of embedded control and begin to suggest embedded intelligence. The technical and architectural aspects of the evolvable system development are supported by a comprehensive methodological framework. Evolvability being a system concept, it is envisaged to address every aspect of an assembly system throughout its life cycle, i.e., design and development, operation and evolution. The work has been and being implemented through large European research projects. Furthermore, integration of legacy subsystems and modules have been addressed in the methodology. It has, to date, resulted in several demonstrators and offered methodologies and architectures in support. This paper presents current developments and applications.

2 Contribution to Technological Innovation

As defined in [8] RMS incorporates principles of modularity, integrability, flexibility, scalability, convertibility, and diagnosability. These principles impose strong requirements to the control solution. In particular, centralized approaches become completely unsuited due to their intrinsic rigidity. Decentralised solutions must be considered that take into account the fundamental requirements of plugability of components, which includes the aspects related to dynamic addition /removal of components, as well as adaptation in the sense that the system does not need to be reprogrammed whenever a new module is added/ removed. This is a fundamental aspect behind any control solution approach to solve the defined requirements. Moreover, diagnosability also demands a decentralized approach, in particular if the manufacturing system is considered as a set of manufacturing components, each with diagnosis capability. The overall diagnosis of the system is obtained considering all the diagnosis information obtained from the individual modules. Due to these requirements, a particular and relevant aspect in the system being considered is the "intelligent" nature of its components, i.e., each component is considered as having computational power that will support individual diagnosability, dynamic plugability, adaptation, etc.

Therefore, the major challenge in the control solution is how to guarantee proper coordination and execution in a system in which both its components and working conditions can be dynamically changed. This is a challenge that needs a completely new approach and this is why in the context of EPS a solution based on concepts inspired from the Complexity Theory and Artificial Life is being developed. The next section covers what concepts from non traditional manufacturing research domains are being used to create truly dynamic control solutions.

Nevertheless, in the context of this paper it is important to clarify what are the big differences between the approach being proposed here and Holonic Manufacturing. The genesis of holonic manufacturing was very much a biological inspired approach and it was very close to the concepts of bionic and fractal. However, succeeding implementations along the years have drifted more and more from the original inspiration, and, in many aspects, the systems became more hierarchical.

Hence, the control approach to be developed in the context of EPS wants to go back to the basics, that is to say relying stringy on the original idea of considering each component as a distributed intelligent unit that may aggregate in order to create a complex system. In this context, concepts such as emergence and self-organisation become more and more important to be applied to new generation control solutions. Interestingly enough other researchers are proposing a self-organisation view in manufacturing enterprises [9]. However, true implementations of these new concepts within shop floor are still very few.

Considering what was stated above, one may view Evolvable Production Systems (EPS) as a development of the Holonic Manufacturing Systems (HMS) approach; however, a closer looks reveals that, although there are similarities in the exploitation and implementation phases, the paradigms differ quite substantially in their perspective (or trigger issue), and that only EPS achieves fine granularity. By granularity it is considered the level of complexity of the component that compose a manufacturing system. For instance, when a line is composed of several cells and these cells are modules that can be plugged in and out, this is thick granularity. If, on the other hand, the components that can be plugged in or out are grippers, sensors, or pneumatic cylinders, this is fine granularity. This issue is in fact a very important one in terms of distinguishing the paradigms.

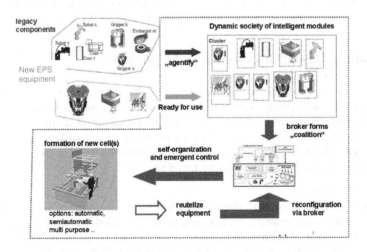

Fig. 1. Basic Overview of EPS Approach

The main difference in the EPS paradigm is that it was created from a more dynamic, industrially-relevant perspective (trigger issue): EPS is mainly concerned with what occurs in a production system when a production change-over is called for; that is, whenever the current production system needs to undergo some change in its physical, control, or productivity layout [10]. Such changes occur at ramp-up, product change-over, or demand surges. This is where the biological inspiration to EPS first makes itself apparent: it is change that drives the adaptability/evolution of the EPS systems, not the current or known scenarios. Furthermore, as will be detailed later, the adaptability is dictated by real evolvability principles such as "survival-of-the-fittest" at algorithm level. This biological approach becomes even more evident when one studies the way modularity is achieved within EPS. In most approaches, modularity is set by either known mechanical subdivisions, or by taking the classical subdivisions that exist within manufacturing; for example, in reconfigurable assembly, the modules are most often set by the transport/handling/joining/placing/packaging processes. There is no biological link and the RMS and HMS paradigms tend to try to achieve a general, top-level solution.

EPS is radically different in this respect as it will focus on the predicted and unpredictable changes that may occur within a very limited product range (genus). The first solution will be limited and specific, and may, if successful, gradually be applied to the associated product family (species). Hence EPS is not a generic solution but a specific approach that may be adopted by other "species" if its evolutionary capabilities denote a high rate of success.

Furthermore, EPS takes a hybrid and not top-down approach to the definition of its modules. The EPS modules are defined by precise sub-processes that have been identified for a given product range: the taxonomy of the sub-processes is very detailed and therefore results in fine granularity. This is a low-level approach, and gives modules with very optimised performance characteristics: process-oriented modules [11]. Note that since it is specific, and focuses on the given evolutionary demands of a product range and its sub-processes, it may also be closely linked to product design issues. This is unique among current paradigms, which clearly underlines the contribution.

3   Enabling Research Domains and Concepts

The main issue to be addressed in this section is describing the areas in which EPS control systems are getting inspiration to solve the requirements for adaptability at fine granularity. Numerous scientific domains investigating phenomena which EPS also exhibit have emerged in the last few years, which can provide helpful tools and valuable theoretical background to cope with the complexity of manufacturing systems. A more detailed definition may be found in [12].

Complexity Theory
Complexity Theory looks for simple causes leading to complex behaviours [13]. Complex systems are spatially and/or temporally extended non-linear systems with many strongly-coupled degrees of freedom. They are composed of numerous in themselves often simple elements and are characterized by collective properties. EPS consist of numerous equipment modules which are connected to each other and have multi-lateral interactions. Each of them has some degrees of freedom, which are

constraint by other system parts. Together, the modules form a system with the desired global behaviour.

Artificial Life

Taking natural life and its characteristics as an example, scientists attempt to create life-like behaviors with the capability of evolution on computers and other "artificial" media. EPS are very similar to artificial living systems, with a modifiable structure, will exhibit some kind of self-organization, can adapt to their environment, and react to stimuli. They are capable of evolving according to the circumstances, namely in terms of equipment states, and can incorporate newly available technology.

Autonomic Computing

Although at another level than the other areas described above, Autonomic Computing is a fundamental concept for EPS. The vision of Autonomic Computing [14] refers to the tendency of computers to become ubiquitous. Forming large networks and having complex and multiple interactions, they become increasingly difficult to manage. As a consequence, software will be designed to take care of itself. User interaction will be minimized and reprogramming avoided. Note that the more modules of fine granularity include computational power, the more is necessary to find new ways of coordination and automatic plugability, which is exactly what EPS want to address.

Agents

Depending on the context, an agent can be a human person, an association, an animal, or a piece of software, eventually connected to some hardware. The fundamental characteristics are identity, intelligence and the ability to act and react in order to persecute goals. Agents have at least a certain degree of autonomy and can compete or collaborate with others.

There are numerous successful experiences with agent-based systems in industry [15]. Rockwell Automation even develops agent-based systems where the agents run inside the PLC itself [16] instead of on separate computers.

Self-Organization

Reasons for implementing self-organization in EPS are to minimize and facilitate user interaction, i.e. to hide complexity and increase system autonomy. Building and configuring a system composed of numerous entities with multi-lateral interactions is a highly complex task; the more autonomy the system has, the easier it gets for the user. Agents need the capacity of organizing their collaboration themselves, in according to the needs, without passing through a central coordination point.

Emergence

Complex systems most often consist of at least two different levels: the macro-level, considering the system as a whole, and the micro-level, considering the system from the point of view of the local components. Local components behave according to local rules and based on preferably local knowledge; a representation of the entire system or knowledge about the global system functionality is neither provided by a central authority nor reachable for the components themselves. They communicate, interact with each other and exchange information. From the interaction in this local world emerge global phenomena, which are more than a straight-forward composition of the local components' behaviors and capabilities. Typically, there is not only a global behavior dependent on the local parts, but their behavior is also influenced by the system as a whole. Emergent phenomena are scalable, robust, and fault-tolerant, i.e. insensitive to small perturbations and local errors as well as component failure, thanks to redundancy. They exhibit graceful degradation, meaning that there is no total break-down because of minor local errors.

Evolution

EPS implies, at least partially, evolutionary behavior according to Darwinian theory. It intends to do so by applying complex adaptation behaviour at control level, and by subdiving the system equipment into specific modules. According to scientific results in the fields of Computational Ecology and Genetics ([17], [18]), the idea to adopt a modular approach is very similar to natural selection. Hence the analogy of applying modularity at system level, based on process constraints, to that of a genotype-modularity used in nature to limit the combinatorial explosion. The challenge in EPS, as with computational adaptation, is to "code" the events correctly and create the correct representations. Hence the need to study emergence and complexity theory.

4   Architectural Aspects behind Methodology

The EPS Methodology [19] provides the references architecture, enablers, and modeling formalisms. In the following section brief description of the methodology is given. Note that a full description of the Methodology and associated Reference Architecture is available through the EUPASS project framework (http://www.eas-env.org). The EPS formalised concepts (ontology) and definitions are represented using a set of descriptive tools such as:

- Definitions of the most important concepts: module, process, product, EPS module, skills, EPS system (which is a composition of modules), etc.
- Diagrams (UML, etc) where the interactions between the concepts defined are shown. This enables to show how the EPS architecture generates assembly systems. The interaction may show the global system behaviour

The domain ontology indeed captures the concepts in the system with their specifications (consensual semantic) i.e., what the concepts are and how they are related to each other in the domain. However, it does not capture the logic behind the relationships and the how's in the synthesis and functionality of the system.

A full description of the EAS ontology, and its associated Knowledge Model, is given in [20].

4.1   Reference Architecture, RA

The EPS Reference Architecture (EPS_RA) describes the essential features of an Evolvable System which means the reference architecture specifies the necessary features that a system should have to be an evolvable system. The reference architecture is composed of three main elements: Principles, Technical Positions and Templates. *Principles:* EPS has two fundamental principles which lay the foundation and guide the development process of an evolvable system. These principles can be considered as a description of the core ideas of the evolvable system paradigm.

Principle 1: *the most innovative product design can only be achieved if no assembly process constraints are posed. The ensuing, fully independent, process selection procedure may then result in an optimal assembly system methodology.*

Principle 2: *Systems under dynamic conditions need to be evolvable, i.e., they need to have an inherent capability of evolution to address the new/changing requirements.*

The enabling models include the development process model, the business model and the knowledge model. These models are constructed using the formalisms described above and most notably the EPS ontology. The figure below depicts the first proposed EPS_RA using IDEF0. The is a simplified high level activity model showing the main activities in the development process and their input, output, control and mechanisms needed to generate or modify instances of the architecture.

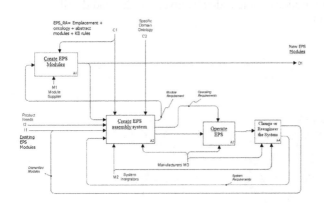

Fig. 2. The simplified EPS_RA

The traditional top-down system design is feasible only in cases where the emergent behaviour is fully describable; [21]. If emergent behaviour has to be investigated even at design and development stages, then a heterarchical or a network approach are the options.

Concepts that are formalised in the EPS Ontology are used to capture the stakeholders understanding of their own domain. The EPS knowledge model is thus a structured and formalised collection of such knowledge capturing representations of the domains. The main objective of the EPS knowledge model is to provide an environment that supports the development and operation of evolvable systems.

The domain knowledge captured using the EPS ontology and the EPS knowledge templates are the two entities used to develop the knowledge model. The knowledge models are used among other things how each module in a system should address for a new set of conditions.

The elements in the EPS knowledge model consists of the knowledge domains:

1. The enterprise knowledge domain - globalizes knowledge of the system and represents the business, organizational and global knowledge models. Enterprise knowledge enables environment recognition and maintenance of associations.
2. The product knowledge domain – captures the knowledge related to product specification and design to assembly tasks.
3. The execution knowledge domain: capturing knowledge elements related to communications, planning and scheduling
4. The learning knowledge domain: containing knowledge elements that are used to incorporate case based reasoning.

The EPS RA is ultimately be viewed from different perspectives addressing the different concerns of the stakeholders. The stakeholders include:

- those who build the system (structure and communication views),
- those who use it (functional view),
- those who are concerned with control (control view).

5 Practical Developments

Initial evaluations were carried out in the test cell shown below (fig.3.0a). More industrially viable evaluations are currently being deployed within a new system being developed at KTH (fig.3.0b). For obvious reasons, reconfigurability may be illustrated by videos and is more arduous via text-details given in [22] and detailed (videos, etc.) on www.Eas-Env.Org.

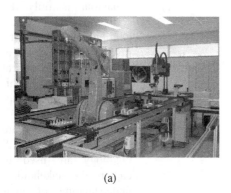 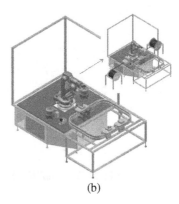

(a)   (b)

Fig. 3. (a) The Evaluation Test Case. (b) Industrial Test Case.

At present the EPS paradigm is only just starting to take a practical form, and the control solution, ontologies, and methodologies only partially describe the most recent developments. These ideas are now being put into real industrial scenarios within the EUPASS project [19], and through the participation of Electrolux Home Products Italy SpA and UNINOVA. The layout given in figure 3.0b is being setup for two industrial products (self-configuring & reconfiguring).

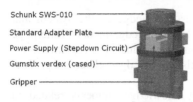

Schunk SWS-010
Standard Adapter Plate
Power Supply (Stepdown Circuit)
Gumstix verdex (cased)
Gripper

Fig. 4. The Intermodular Receptacle

The project has now demonstrated that legacy equipment may be modified to Evolvable Production System [22]. An intelligent interface was developed out of an old Schunck gripper, as shown below, and the EUPASS project has now developed a full Evolvable Production System in Windisch, Switzerland.

5 Conclusions

EPS, as with other similar approaches, offers great opportunities for attaining true agility and cost-effective, stepwise automation. The technologies for achieving this are available and there are several partners willing to partake in this endeavour (for detailed list see website cited below: FESTO, BOSCH, ELECTROLUX, TQC, KIT, etc.); however, it is vital to point out that EPS does imply that the manner in which we develop and create projects for the development of assembly systems are radically changed, assuming a more synthesis-based approach.

In order to stimulate the further development and update of the paradigm and its applications, a collaborative web space has been developed, in which the architecture, standards, equipment modules and other details are detailed and made accessible: www.Eas-Env.Org. This EAS Environment web space is currently being expanded to include work from related projects.

References

1. Strategic Research Agenda-assuring the future of manufacturing in Europe; Manufuture Platform-Executive Summary, December 2005, EC (2005)
2. MANVIS, Manufacturing Visions-Integrating Diverse Perspectives into Pan-European Foresight; FP6 Support Action, NMP2-CT-2003-507139 (2006)
3. The Future of Manufacturing in Europe 2015-2020-The Challenge for Sustainability; Fut-Man, Institute for Prospective Technological Studies, European Commission Joint Research Centre, EUR 20705 EN (2007)
4. EUPASS Adaptive Assembly Roadmap 2015-deliverable 1.5f; Del. 1.5f, EUPASS-Evolvable Ultra Precision Assembly, NMP-2-CT-2004-507978 (2008)
5. Barata, J., Onori, M., Frei, R.: ISIE 2006 -IEEE International Symposium on Industrial Electronics. IEEE, Montreal (2006)
6. Van Brussel, H., Wyns, J., Valckenaers, P., Bongaerts, L., Peeters, P.: Reference Architecture for Holonic Manufacturing Systems: PROSA. Computers in Industry 37, 255–274 (1998)
7. Bussmann, S., Mcfarlane, D.C.: Rationales for Holonic Manufacturing. In: Second Int. Workshop on Intelligent Manufacturing Systems, Leuven, Belgium (1999)
8. Elmaraghy, H.A.: Flexible and Reconfigurable Manufacturing Systems Paradigms. Int. Journal of Flexible Manufacturing Systems 17, 261–276 (2006)
9. Tharumarajah, A.: A Self-organising View of Manufacturing Enterprises. Computers in Industry 51, 185–196 (2003)
10. Maffei, A., Dencker, K.: From Flexibility to Evolvability: ways to achieve self-reconfigurability and full-autonomy. In: Proceedings of the IFAC/SYROCO 2009 Conference, Gifu, Japan (2009)
11. Maraldo, T., Onori, M., Barata, J., Semere, D.: Evolvable Assembly Systems: Clarifications and Developments to Date. In: CIRP/IWES 6th International Workshop on Emergent Synthesis, Kashiwa, Japan (2006)
12. Barata, J., Onori, M., Frei, R., Leitão, P.: Evolvable Production Systems – Enabling Research Domains. In: Proceedings of the 2nd Int. Conf. on Changeable, Agile, Reconfigurable and Virtual, Proc. CARV 2007, Toronto, Canada (2007)

13. Delic, K.A., Dum, R.: On the Emerging Future of Complexity Sciences. ACM Ubiquity 7 (2006)
14. Kephart, J.O., Chess, D.M.: The Vision of Autonomic Computing. IEEE Computer 0018-9162/03, 41–50 (2003)
15. Monostori, L., Váncza, J., Kumara, S.R.T.: Agent-Based Systems for Manufacturing. CIRP Annals 55 (2006)
16. Mařík, V., Vrba, P., Hall, K.H., Maturana, F.P.: Rockwell automation agents for manufacturing. In: AAMAS, Utrecht, NL. ACM Press, NY (2005)
17. Wagner, P.G., Altenberg, L.: Complex Adaptations and the Evolution of Evolvability. Evolution 50, 967–976
18. Bowers, C.P.: Simulating Evolution with a Computational Model of Embryogeny, PhD Thesis, The University of Birmingham (2006)
19. Lohse, N., Ferreira, P., Ratchev, S.: Multi-Agent Architecture for Self-Configuring Modular Assembly Systems. In: Proceedings of the IFAC/SYROCO 2009 Conference, Gifu, Japan (2009)
20. Ueda, K.: Journal of Artificial Intelligence in Engineering 15, 319–320 (2001)
21. Hofmann, A., Siltala, N.: Emplacement and Blue Print - An Approach to Handle and Describe Modules for Evolvable Assembly Systems. In: Proceedings of the IFAC/SYROCO 2009 Conference, Gifu, Japan (2009)
22. Adamietz, R.: Development of an Intermodular Receptacle- A First Step in Creating EAS Modules, MSC Thesis, KTH, Stockholm, Sweden (2007)

The Meaningfulness of Consensus
and Context in Diagnosing
Evolvable Production Systems

Luis Ribeiro, José Barata, and João Ferreira

Universidade Nova de Lisboa, Faculdade de Ciências e Tecnologia, Campus da FCT-UNL,
Monte de Caparica 2829 – 516, Caparica, Portugal
{ldr,jab}@uninova.pt, jpf19013@fct.unl.pt

Abstract. An Evolvable Production System (EPS) is a complex and lively entity composed of intelligent modules that interact, through bio-inspired mechanisms, to ensure high system availability and seamless reconfiguration. The diagnosis of such dynamic systems, characterized by constant change, presents new diagnostic challenges and opportunities that can hardly be tackled by traditional approaches. On the one hand, given the decoupled nature of the system, fault interaction and propagation are harder to detect and contain, as is the development of a global diagnostic model, on the other hand local intelligence and careful characterization of the interactions, between the modules, can be explored to emerge the diagnostic functionalities. The impact of simple consensus mechanisms (majority voting) and fault context analysis (module and its current interactions states) is assessed in a multiagent-oriented application in the assembly domain to understand the validity and contribution of this approach in emerging useful self-diagnostic properties in EPS.

Keywords: Diagnosis, Evolvable Production Systems, Multi-agent Systems, Interaction Diagnosis, Hidden Markov Models.

1 Introduction

Mass Customization has been perceived as the excellence paradigm in industry and services however, as pointed out by [1], "we are now entering the era of network competition". This has led enterprises to seek innovative organizational paradigms [1, 2]: Supply chains, Extended Enterprises, Virtual Enterprises, Collaborative Networks, etc. In this context, industrial installations require improved agility to face the socio-economic challenges ahead and effectively contribute to network competitiveness. Researchers in production paradigms, acknowledging this dynamic business environment, increasingly suggest and envision lively shop floors which are aggregations of intelligent and distributed interacting entities. Evolvable Production Systems (EPS) [3, 4] relying is such intelligent environments will allow quicker ramp-up times once both product design and shop-floor reconfiguration adjust to meet a balanced compromise These systems, however, are inherently complex and present significant diagnostic challenges and opportunities. Fault interaction and propagation are harder

L.M. Camarinha-Matos, P. Pereira, and L. Ribeiro (Eds.): DoCEIS 2010, IFIP AICT 314, pp. 143–150, 2010.

to detect and contain as it becomes more difficult to devise the diagnostic model of a system that, in the limit, can be in constant change and is highly heterogeneous. Nonetheless, local intelligence can be explored to circumvent these problems and enhance the diagnosis capabilities of the system by indirectly inferring the local state from the behaviour fault behaviour of other devices.

Being agile is also a matter of preventing breakdowns, incidents and developing sustainably. Intelligent automation such as required for future production systems must involve diagnostic capabilities that match the performance of the control solution.

Traditional diagnostic approaches often require a full model of the system and are not directly applicable to modern production paradigms like EPS. In fact, to avoid corrupt the control functionalities, the diagnostic system should be embedded in the paradigm and designed accordingly.

This has not been the case. Most diagnostic methods have been developed targeting a specific shop-floor component or a subsystem (manipulators, electrical motors, rotary equipment), or even the entire plant, rather than an evolving entity. The approach proposed in this paper is being developed under the framework of EPS whose control and design principles been investigated in the EUPASS[1] project. Intelligent interaction is explored as a fundamental diagnostic feature in EPS. The main concept is the design of local (module level) diagnosers that evaluate their internal status is respect to a given interaction type taking into consideration their operational context and their sensorial perceptions. The objective is to, through this local interaction, emerge polarized consensus regarding disturbances in the shop floor. The presented experiments report some preliminary results of the ongoing research.

2   Contribution to Technological Innovation

Networked information systems are the cornerstone of today's society [5, 6]. The pervasive nature of such system ensures seamless, and often unnoticed, everyday-life interaction. The natural evolution of these human-machine networks is towards complexity. This is manifested in the size of the network and in the interconnectivity degree. Industrial networks are not immune to this effect as the complexity of the installation grows more and more devices require communications and more processes need to be synchronized. There is a considerable set of industrial network standards that ease the integration of traditional logic based control devices. However, in the era of network competition, the flux of information between shop floor components and higher level management tools is increasingly important [7]. To meet these requirements there is an ongoing generalized research effort to change the nature and interfacing of the industrial devices in order to make them more pluggable and seamlessly available to other systems.

Research in this area will enable industry to effectively instantiate powerful production paradigms such as EPS at the cost of increased interaction complexity between the architectural building blocks (automation modules). As earlier detailed conventional shop floor diagnostic methods, alone, will not encompass this dramatic shift. This is the context addressed by the present work.

---

[1] EUPASS project http://www.eupass.org/

The main contributions of the ongoing research can be summarized as follows: propose a diagnostic architecture that is suitable for intelligent automation system instantiating the EPS concept and in that context ensure the co-evolution of the diagnostic system while improving the overall sustainability of the installation; Capture the dynamics of fault propagation and interaction in distributed industrial systems composed of a high number of interaction modules and Enhance the traditional device-customized diagnostic approaches by introducing the network dimension and incorporating it in the local diagnosis.

3 Related Literature

A complete review on diagnostic methods derived from the automatic control community can be found in [8] where the application of: parameter estimation, evaluation of parity relations, state estimation and principal component analysis methodologies is properly covered.

A review of quantitative and qualitative history based methods where diagnosis is performed based on the previous system's faulty behaviour can be found in [9] where the application of artificial neural networks, probabilistic inference methods and expert system is discussed. Qualitative logic based diagnostic methods are covered in [10].

The research being reported in this paper, however, has a close connection with the authors' previous work developed under the Inlife Project[2] where web services were applied to a pilot assembly cell and functionalities including self-monitoring/ diagnosis/reporting were implemented at device and process levels [11, 12]. A preliminary version of ACORDA [13], a prospective logic engine, that enables the revision of results, trough the encoding of preference rules was used. Although the engine provided an efficient platform to formalize the diagnostic models, the used version did not support modeling uncertainty. Probabilistic methods applied in the diagnosing industrial systems are reported in [14], [15] and in [16]. The first work proposes the application of Hidden Markov Models and principal component analysis to diagnose chemical processes. The second work uses Bayesian Networks to diagnose and study processes in a caravan manufacturing line. The third solution relies on a structured representation of the domain to tackle fault scenarios with multiple causes and fault propagation. The present work rather than considering the entire shop floor or subsystems focuses on the intelligent modules and their interactions with purpose of emerging at network level consistent fault propagation patterns.

4 A Diagnostic Method Proposal

The main goal of the proposed method is to, through stigmergy, emerge a coherent diagnostic perspective at network level. For that purpose each agent will evaluate its own internal state based on a sequence of observations that it performs as the fault event develops in the system. Each individual agent should be only able to observe its direct neighbours and its sensorial equipment. This constraint is to ensure that the

---

[2] InLife project http://www.uninova.pt/inlife/

diagnostic system scales in highly dynamic environments with a considerable number of nodes.

A common interaction semantic is required to enable consistent diagnosis. In this context, the interactions between the agents have to be characterized. For the problem considered a suitable representation is the following $I = (D, N)$ where I denotes an interaction, D an interaction's direction and N its nature. The system can therefore be envisioned as a directed graph where each agent is a node and each link is a specified interaction. While the nature of the interaction can be any symbol with an associated semantic, the direction is either: inbound, outbound or both ($d \in \{I_b, O_b, B\}$). Distinct networks are considered for each interaction nature (n).

Internally each agent can be in one of the following states: OK – the module abstracted by the agent is working normally; NOK – the module has a fault, PFO – the module is propagating a fault, that he has generated, through its outbound connections; PFOther – the module is affected by a propagating fault on its inbound connections and PFOPFOther – the module is being affected by a fault that is propagating through its inbound connections and that it is propagating over it is outbound connections. The last state may raise some confusion of whether the propagated fault is from an inbound neighbour and is transmitting to outbound neighbours or is the summed effect of this interaction with a self-generated fault however, the relevant aspect to consider is the propagation itself. Once the origin of the fault is eliminated the agent will exhibit a state that is either OK or PFO accordingly to the fault's context and disambiguate the previous occurrence as depicted in Fig 1.

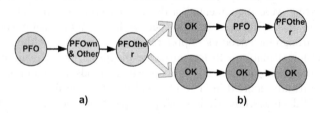

a)   b)

Fig. 1. The agents' states during a fault (a) and after that fault has been resumed in its origin (b) where the system can emerge two distinct configurations according the presence of fault summing effects

Fig. 1 also details a fundamental aspect which is the polarization of the agents' state. The agent's observations enable the emergence of a polarized consensus on the network's state. A note on how the agents perform their observations is worth at this point. Rather than polling information from its direct neighbours they push it asynchronously when their internal state changes.

The quality and type of the observations play a major role on the convergence of the system to a useful diagnosis (the network emerging a consensus for any given fault context). In the next section the present diagnostic method will be formalized using Hidden Markov Models (HMM) and the impact of the observations in ensuring the converge of the network will be assessed in two scenario where the influence of other agents state weighted differently.

5 Preliminary Experiments and Results

The diagnostic model proposed can be formalized as HMM [17] which is the following tuple $\lambda = (A, B, \pi)$. Where A is a $N \times N$ matrix (N is the number of states in the model) denoting the state transition probabilities $P(q_{t+1} = S_j \mid q_t = S_i) = a_{ij}$, B is a $N \times M$ matrix (M is the number of observation symbols) that encloses the observation probabilities $P(O_t = k \mid q_t = S_i) = b_i(k)$ (i.e. the probability that the observation k happens given the state S_i), π represents the starting state probabilities (in the model considered in this paper the initial state of the model is always OK P=1). In the present case $N=5$ where each state has the semantic described in the previous section. Concerning M, two scenarios are considered $M=8$ (Table 1) and $M=18$ (Table 2). For brevity not all the observation symbols are represented in the second case.

Table 1. Observation alphabet for M = 8

Symbol	Agent Internal State	Inbound Interactions	Outbound Interactions
OOO	0	0	0
OOF	0	0	1
OFO	0	1	0
OFF	0	1	1
FOO	1	0	0
FOF	1	0	1
FFO	1	1	0
FFF	1	1	1

To clarify the reading of the tables in Table 1 the symbol OOF implies that the agent observes that its sensor readings are normal as well as its neighbours with inbound connections. On the contrary, the neighbours with outbound connections are affected with faults. Both models share the A matrix. For brevity both A, B_1 and B_2 matrices have been omitted. Table 2 considers more observation symbols that enrich

Table 2. Observation alphabet for M = 18 note that some of the symbols have been omitted and some combinations denoting simultaneously inbound minority and majority are impossible

Symbol	Own Fault	Inbound Minority	Inbound Majority	Outbound Minority	Outbound Majority
Ok	0	0	0	0	0
IMaj	0	0	1	0	0
IMin	0	1	0	0	0
OF	1	0	0	0	0
OF_OMin	1	0	0	1	0
OF_IMaj	1	0	1	0	0
OF_ IMaj_OMin	1	0	1	1	0
OF_IMin	1	1	0	0	0
OF_IMin_OMaj	1	1	0	0	1
OF_IMin_OMin	1	1	0	1	0

the model and allow agents a finer granularity control over the inbound and outbound observations. Further they allow the proper balance of B matrices supporting changes in opinions as larger number of neighbours are affected by a fault.

To test both models a simple experiment comprising four agents was set up. Two pneumatic valves (V_1 and V_2) controlling the compressed air flow from a robotic manipulator (R_1) which provides air to a gripper (G_2). One of the valves allows air in the gripper and the other expels the air when it is not used as shown in Fig.2. Tables 3 and 4 summarize the sequence of observations each agent performs for the cases where $M=8$ and $M=18$ respectively

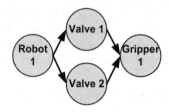

Fig. 2. Network of agents under study

The robot detects a fault using its sensor information. That information is passed on to its direct neighbours V_1 and V_2. Soon V_1 and V_2 will also fail causing a change in the agents' observations. In this example the differences in the observations are felt by G_1 which in the first model is limited basic inbound fault detection. As shall be seen in Table 5 ignoring minorities and majorities, ultimately the fault context, impacts the final consensus on the network.

Table 3. Sequences of observations per agent with M = 8 for eight consecutive instants

Agent	t_0	t_1	t_2	t_3	t_4	t_5	t_6	t_7	t_8
R_1	OOO	FOO	FOO	FOO	FOF	FOF	FOF	FOF	FOF
V_1	OOO	OOO	OFO	FFO	FFO	FFO	FFO	FFO	FFO
V_2	OOO	OOO	OFO	OFO	FFO	FFO	FFO	FFO	FFO
G_1	OOO	OOO	OOO	OFO	OFO	OFO	OFO	OFO	OFO

Table 4. Sequences of observations per agent with M = 18 for eight consecutive instants

Agent	t_0	t_1	t_2	t_3	t_4	t_5	t_6	$\cdot\cdot$	t_8
R_1	Ok	OF	OF	OF	OF OMin	OF OMaj	OF OMaj	$\cdot\cdot$	OF OMaj
V_1	Ok	Ok	IMin	OF_IMin	OF IMin	OF IMin	OF IMin OMin	$\cdot\cdot$	OF IMin OMin
V_2	Ok	Ok	IMin	IMin	OF IMin	OF IMin	OF IMin OMin	$\cdot\cdot$	OF IMin OMin
G_1	Ok	Ok	Ok	Ok	IMin	IMaj	IMaj	$\cdot\cdot$	IMaj

Table 5 clearly illustrates that the M = 18 model better captures the fault propagation dynamic in the network. The final result is always biased by the B matrix set up. When learning the model parameters from sample data the second diagnostic model has also the advantage of being able to capture system's details such as the relation

Table 5. Evolution of agents' internal as new observations are processed

Observations	t_0	t_1	t_2	t_3	t_4	t_5	t_6	⋯	t_8
M = 8									
R_1	Ok	NOk	NOk	NOk	PFO	PFO	PFO	⋯	PFO
V_1	Ok	Ok	Ok	PFOther	PFOther	PFOther	PFOther	⋯	PFOther
V_2	Ok	Ok	Ok	Ok	PFOther	PFOther	PFOther	⋯	PFOther
G_1	Ok	Ok	Ok	Ok	Ok	Ok	Ok	⋯	Ok
M = 18									
R_1	Ok	NOk	NOk	NOk	PFO	PFO	PFO	⋯	PFO
V_1	Ok	Ok	Ok	PFOther	PFOther	PFOther	PFOPFOther	⋯	PFOPFOther
V_2	Ok	Ok	Ok	Ok	PFOther	PFOther	PFOPFOther	⋯	PFOPFOther
G_1	Ok	Ok	Ok	Ok	Ok	PFOther	PFOther	⋯	PFOther

between the reliability of the agent's sensor and indirect fault inference (inferring the agent's own fault behaviour considering its neighbours response to faults.). In the present test the first model failed in diagnosing G_1 as it is highly unlikely that if both valves fail the gripper will remain operational (state OK) whether in the second model G_1 detected that it was under the effect of fault propagation. If G_1 had been connected to another device the error would propagate and affect the emerged network consensus.

6 Conclusions and Future Work

The presented preliminary experiments testing the proposed diagnostic method suggest that there significant differences in the emergence of coherent diagnostic consensus at network level when ignoring the fault context. Further testing is required to study the behaviour of the proposed method in networks with a high number of interacting agents and distinct levels of connectivity. Also, the fault update dynamics of the agents (propagation of error messages) needs to be addressed to understand of synchronous versus asynchronous update can influence the overall outcome. Although is still early to conclude the results obtained are encouraging and suggest that the proposed method may be suitable to support diagnosis under the framework of the EPS paradigm.

References

1. Christopher, M.: The Agile Supply Chain: Competing in Volatile Markets. Industrial Marketing Management 29, 37–44 (2000)
2. Camarinha-Matos, L.M., Afsarmanesh, H., Novais, P., Analide, C. (eds.): Establishing the Foundation of Collaborative Networks, vol. 243. Springer, New York (2007)
3. Alsterman, H., Barata, J., Onori, M.: Evolvable Assembly Systems Platforms: Opportunities and Requirements. In: Molfino, R. (ed.) Intelligent Manipulation and Grasping, IMG 2004, Genova, vol. 1, pp. 18–23 (2004)
4. Barata, J., Onori, M., Frei, R., Leitão, P.: Evolvable Production Systems: Enabling Research Domains. In: CARV 2007 - 2nd International Conference on Changeable, Agile, Reconfigurable, and Virtual Production, Toronto - Canada (2007)

5. Amaral, L.A.N., Ottino, J.M.: Complex networks: Augmenting the framework for the study of complex systems. The European Physical Journal B 38, 147–162 (2004)
6. Newman, M.E.J.: The structure and function of complex networks. SIAM Review 45, 167–256 (2003)
7. Colombo, A.W.: Industrial Agents: Towards Collaborative Production Automation, Management and Organization. IEEE Industrial Electronics Society Newsletter 52, 17–18 (2005)
8. Isermann, R.: Fault Diagnosis Systems: An Introduction from Fault Detection to Fault Tolerance. Springer, Berlin (2006)
9. Venkatasubramanian, V., Rengaswamy, R., Kavuri, S.N.: A review of process fault detection and diagnosis Part III: Process history based methods. Computers and Chemical Engineering 27, 327–346 (2003)
10. Venkatasubramanian, V., Rengaswamy, R., Kavuri, S.N.: A review of process fault detection and diagnosis Part II: Qualitative models and search strategies. Computers and Chemical Engineering 27, 313–326 (2003)
11. Barata, J., Ribeiro, L., Colombo, A.W.: Diagnosis using Service Oriented Architectures (SOA). In: International Conference on Industrial Informatics. IEEE, Vienna (2007)
12. Ribeiro, L.: A Diagnostic Infrastructure for Manufacturing Systems. Electrical and Computer Science Engineering, vol. MSC. New University of Lisbon, Lisbon, 121 (2007)
13. Lopes, G., Pereira, L.M.: Prospective Programming with ACORDA. Empirically Successful Computerized Reasoning, Seattle, USA (2006)
14. Zhou, S., Zhang, J., Wang, S.: Fault diagnosis in industrial processes using principal component analysis and hidden markov models. In: American Control Conference, Boston, USA (2004)
15. Rodrigues, M.A., Liu, Y., Bottaci, L., Rigas, D.I.: Learning and diagnosis in manufacturing processes through an executable Bayesian network. In: 13th international conference on Industrial and engineering applications of artificial intelligence and expert systems: Intelligent problem solving: methodologies and approaches, New Orleans, Louisiana, United States, pp. 390–395 (2000)
16. Son, J.P., Park, J.H., Cho, Y.Z.: An integrated knowledge representation scheme and query processing mechanism for fault diagnosis in heterogeneous manufacturing environments. Robotics and Computer Integrated Manufacturing 16, 133–141 (2000)
17. Lawrence, R.R.: A tutorial on hidden Markov models and selected applications in speech recognition. Readings in speech recognition, pp. 267–296. Morgan Kaufmann Publishers Inc., San Francisco (1990)

Applications of Dynamic Deployment of Services in Industrial Automation

Gonçalo Candido[1], José Barata[1], François Jammes[2], and Armando W. Colombo[3]

[1] UNINOVA – Universidade Nova de Lisboa, Portugal
{gmc,jab}@uninova.pt
[2] Schneider Electric – Corporate R&D, 38TEC – Grenoble, France
francois2.jammes@schneider-electric.com
[3] Schneider Electric Automation GmbH, BU Automation, SysCo, Germany
armando.Colombo@schneider-electric.com

Abstract. Service-oriented Architecture (SOA) is becoming a de facto paradigm for business and enterprise integration. SOA is expanding into several domains of application envisioning a unified solution suitable across all different layers of an enterprise infrastructure. The application of SOA based on open web standards can significantly enhance the interoperability and openness of those devices. By embedding a dynamical deployment service even into small field de- vices, it would be either possible to allow machine builders to place built- in services and still allow the integrator to deploy on-the-run the services that best fit his current application. This approach allows the developer to keep his own preferred development language, but still deliver a SOA- compliant application. A dynamic deployment service is envisaged as a fundamental framework to support more complex applications, reducing deployment delays, while increasing overall system agility. As use-case scenario, a dynamic deployment service was implemented over DPWS and WS-Management specifications allowing designing and programming an automation application using IEC61131 languages, and deploying these components as web services into devices.

Keywords: Service-oriented Architecture, Device Model, Services Dynamic Deployment, DPWS, WS-Management.

1 Introduction

Service-oriented Architecture (SOA) is a major focus of interest from device level to high level IT [1] [2] [3] [4]. SOA promises to lead to near-perfect applications in which every function is implemented and exposed as a service possible to be discovered and used by other network element. SOA establishes an architectural model that aims to enhance the efficiency, agility, and productivity of an enterprise by positioning services as the primary means through which solution logic is represented in support of the realization of strategic goals associated with service-oriented computing. The continuous convergence between computing and networking areas, enabled by the advances in semiconductor and transmission technology, allows new approaches to communication between systems and devices, in particular, embedded devices. The expansion of SOA

L.M. Camarinha-Matos, P. Pereira, and L. Ribeiro (Eds.): DoCEIS 2010, IFIP AICT 314, pp. 151–158, 2010.

approaches into different domains of application promises to deliver a complete cross-level and cross-domain connectivity over the same technology paradigm.

At crescent rhythm, Internet technology is emerging as the basic carrier for inter-connecting electronic devices in widely diverse domains of application [5] [6] [7]. One of the most promising approaches concerns the application at device level where the usage of high level service-based communications infrastructure allows completely innovative advances. Some research opportunities were already mapped in [8].

The goal of this document is to summarize a SOA-based solution for the industrial automation domain evidencing the role of the services dynamic deployment feature as a fundamental tool to enhance systems agility at device level. The concept of agility in this context implies being more than flexible or lean. Flexibility refers to a company that can easily adapt itself to produce a mostly predetermined range of products, while lean essentially means producing without waste. On the other hand, agility corresponds to operating efficiently in a competitive environment dominated by change and uncertainty [9]. Agility is a fundamental requirement for modern production companies in order to face challenges provoked by the globalization, environmental and working conditions regulations, improved standards for quality and fast technological mutation [10]. However, global company agility is always limited by its least agile building block – all levels of the CIM pyramid, from ERP to field device level, need to be agile and interact in a seamless and synchronized manner.

At organization level, managers already noticed that they need to cooperate with other organizations in order to remain competitive [11]. Although several work has been done on the topics of virtual organizations agility of production and/or collaboration to deal with unexpected demands and volatile markets at level [12] [13], this agility can only be achieved if all organization levels are also equally agile. The automation devices level plays a fundamental role, since a device is the last frontier where high level process workflows are transformed into a structured collection of physical actions to be performed in a particular sequence – device control and management aspects are here crucial to support above levels agility.

The next section clarifies the importance of this work as an innovative contribution to future exploitations in the domain SOA-ready devices in industrial automation; section 3 exposes a device model comprising the dynamic deployment feature; section 4 pictures the overall architecture comprising the previous device model features; section 5 summarizes a dynamic deployment prototype implementation for the industrial automation domain; and, at last, the final conclusions and future perspectives are presented.

2 Contribution to Technological Innovation

The approach exposed in this document represents a new trend input concerning SOA-ready devices. Specifically, in the industrial automation domain it is fundamental to understand the concrete requirements and progress expectations – how can SOA paradigm provide its own contribute here?

In the industrial automation domain, and more concretely in manufacturing systems, the major goal is to produce fast, cheap, and quality products in line with current and expected client demands while remaining agile enough to handle constant output fluctuations, in terms of form and quantity. The interoperability and easy access to a device plays a major role when trying to accomplish previous goal.

Since the majority of high level business IT is already based over SOA technologies, it is important to research the field device domain and make it effortlessly compliant with the above infrastructure, while providing the expected functionality and performance to domain experts. Although the device model present in this document is most focused over the industrial domain, it remains abstract enough to fit other domains of application, as well as the envisaged applications of this device model in an involving infrastructure. By deploying an SOA-based middleware that already provides, besides others, discovery, identification, services invocation and eventing functionalities over an open standard, any developments over it will only need to focus on application behaviour since compliance and openness are already implicitly embedded. So, by allowing to manage and to deploy services into a device in a generic way, the system agility is increased while remaining compliant with open standards which also increase device interoperability across different vendors.

In summary, this work is expected to increase overall system agility by providing a new device model enriched with a dynamic deployment of services feature laying over open web standards possible to be extended and mapped to new domains of application.

3 Device Model

3.1 Overview

In this context, a device is to be seen as the main logical entity that abstracts an application element, while its services represent the functionalities that a particular element allows others to exploit to accomplish its own goals. A service will encapsulate a function or behavior that can be discovered and employed by any other network element in order to execute a particular task. However, it's possible to define a logical device that can be defined whenever there is a need to abstract a particular system component not explicitly associated to a physical entity. The definition remains abstract enough to be mapped to a wider range of application domains. Also, the application can be composed of several devices that interact between them through the services hosted on those with no imposed control architecture envisaged a priori.

3.2 Built-in vs. Deployed Services

The device model in Fig. 1 represents the device itself as a real-world physical entity. This physical device will already embed some built-in services that allow deploying applications but also other added-value services that allow the integrator to setup, monitor, and diagnose that particular device. These services are deployed by the device builder, being immediately available when taking a new device out from the box. They cannot be removed or modified by the end-user – if the end-user wants to add its own services, he can do it through dynamic deployment. This collection of services is considered generic to every particular range of devices. The dynamic deployment service is itself a built-in service, which allows the systems integrator to deploy its own resources i.e. logical devices and its services.

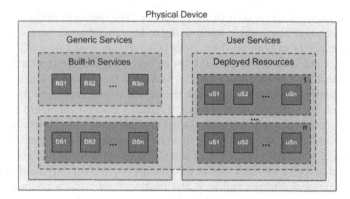

Fig. 1. Device Model

The user application will be dynamically deployed in a form of logical devices. These logical devices will represent the logical entities that can be observed from the current application, exposing their hosted services as their capabilities that others can make use of. An application can even compose several of these logical devices into several layers of increasing abstraction, in an orchestration or choreography manner – application construction based on existing building blocks. Still, it would be possible to deploy services that will enhance the functionality already provided by the current built-in services – these services are also considered generic to that particular range of devices, although they are not considered mandatory to the majority of applications. This approach allows a higher level of device customization. Also, some application functionalities can be considered generic enough and be reused across several applications, being deployed whenever they are required. For example, it would be possible to deploy into a PLC device some services that can control some common system components. This approach will avoid the need to recode those components every time they are needed and still remain consistent with previous implementations or development guideline.

4   Infrastructure

The device model presented in previous section will then fit in a bigger infrastructure that will make use of its embedded capabilities. These features at device level will subsequently enhance overall system ability in terms of interoperability and agility by laying over open web standards and allowing a fast deployment of services whenever system requirements changes oblige to. Since implementation details are encapsulated by the service itself under its interface, it will be possible to retrieve and connect to a device without knowing its current IP address, but simply searching for the required functionality - transparent interoperability. The integrator has also the ability to manage the complete lifecycle of these resources, as described in [14].

Deployed services can either be developed by the integrator or retrieved under an online repository of services - offered by device manufacturer or any other partner (see Fig. 2). When built-in services are not enough to current system requirements, there is a need to deploy extra services that might allow a more complex control over the device, or implement a common function to a particular domain of application. This infrastructure opens the door to new business models, where a disparate range of developers sell their own services to fill common needs. Although users can develop and deploy their own devices and services resources, it would be also possible to build an application only by combining resources developed by partners and/or reused from previous projects. Besides, the clear separation between hardware and software layers will allow the same service to be deployed across dissimilar physical devices. Even if implementation changes due to variations on device firmware capabilities, the service interface remains the same for the same concrete function – a service can be substituted by an equivalent one without changing anything only by keeping the service interface.

Whenever there is a need to connect to a particular device for configuration, maintenance, monitoring or diagnosis purposes, it can be used a device with any web standards-compliant tools, such as a PDA or a tablet PC with wireless access. This allows the user motion along the platform to better check equipment status and behavior.

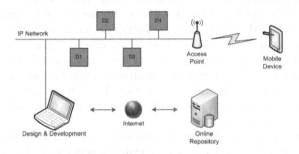

Fig. 2. Network topology example

The device generic built-in services will provide basic discovery, management and connection operations even on a new device. In the same way, the actual application will be easily discoverable and directly interoperable in the network since it is deployed in the form of several logical devices deployed across different physical devices. From the end-user point of view, the application is totally independent from the actual hardware platform – logical view of the system.

5   Industrial Automation Scenario

In the industrial automation domain, systems integrators are used to their own processes and programming languages. IEC61131 programming languages are the most used within this domain, due to its simplicity and run-time performance. The challenge is then how to turn this reality compatible with a complete SOA environment, while increasing system capacity in terms of agility, interoperability and robustness.

Devices Profile for Web Services (DPWS) is a common web services middleware and profile for devices [15], being currently ongoing a standardization process by OASIS. WS-Management [16] specification describes a general WS* based protocol for managing systems such as PCs, servers, devices, Web Services, applications, and other manageable entities. The implementation summarized in this chapter, firstly shown in SODA project industrial demonstrator [17], will be further exploited in SOCRADES project industrial pilot application. It joints DPWS and WS-Management specifications in a single application that supports the dynamic deployment of services, besides other features already described in [14].

The automation control application is developed by abstracting different system components and coding its behavior using IEC61131 programming languages. The original component IEC61131 code is translated to PLCOpen format, being embedded in a service template that will then be deployed into the device (see Fig. 3). It should be noted that this template is independent from particular implementation details, which will be comprised in a parameter value that can be run or interpreted by device firmware. Once the component is made available and active, it will be possible to retrieve it and its services invoked or events subscribed in the network as any other DPWS device – using DPWS, the discovery and identification features are already supported in a distributed manner.

As example, operating systems "Windows Vista" and "Windows 7" are already DPWS-compliant by default, being possible to use the available device explorer to discover and interact effortlessly with any DPWS device available in the network. It is then possible to retrieve its individual metadata values, comprising not only some catalog parameters but also available services contract and a link to the device web server where the user is able to define a collection of setup, monitoring and diagnostic parameters through any traditional web browser. This simple feature already represents a major input to enhance out-of-the-box device connectivity and setup – one of the biggest customer demands.

Even though this implementation focused over industrial automation domain, it remains abstract enough to adapt to other domains of application since the implementation details are isolated from the process to deploy new services into devices.

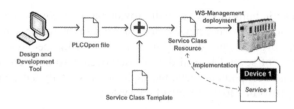

Fig. 3. Dynamic deployment process

6 Conclusions

SOA paradigm is envisaged to expand and become an essential aspect at device level, including in industrial automation domain. It is then important to create models and methodologies to extract the major inputs from this paradigm to face domain requirements.

The existence of a dynamic deployment service embedded on a device can al- low more complex applications plus the creation of new business opportunities. It increases device interoperability and overall system agility whenever there is a need to update, manage or connect to it due to behavior adjustments or occasional downtime. Implementation intricacies are hidden under services interfaces that remain compliant with the overall SOA infrastructure, allowing an end-to-end interoperability across the different levels of the global application. These devices and services can be retrieved and used in a distributed manner across a common IP network in a transparent way.

Still, there is an important need to create new tools and methodologies to provide an easier development under this new paradigm compliant with the major open web standards. Also, training and clarification activities are also of major importance when pushing a new paradigm into a domain known to be particularly restrict as the industrial automation domain. Security and semantic aspects, as possible adaptation to other domains of application can be envisaged as future research topics over this same subject.

Acknowledgments. The work present here was developed within the scope of the European IST FP6 project "Service-Oriented Cross-layer infRAstructure for Distributed smart Embedded deviceS" (see http://www.socrades.eu).

References

1. Bloomberg, J., Schmelzer, R.: Service orient or be doomed. Wiley, Chichester (2006)
2. Erl, T.: Service-oriented architecture: concepts, technology, and design. Prentice Hall PTR, Upper Saddle River (2005)
3. Rosen, M., Lublinsky, B., Smith, K., Balcer, M.: Applied SOA: Service-Oriented Architecture and Design Strategies. Wiley India Pvt. Ltd., Chichester (2008)
4. Bell, M.: Service-oriented modeling: service analysis, design, and architecture. Wiley, Chichester (2008)
5. Jammes, F., Smit, H.: Service-oriented paradigms in industrial automation. IEEE Transactions on Industrial Informatics 1(1), 62–70 (2005)
6. Karnouskos, S., Baecker, O., De Souza, L., Spiess, P.: Integration of SOA-ready networked embedded devices in enterprise systems via a cross-layered web service infrastructure. In: 12th IEEE Conference on Emerging Technologies and Factory Automation, pp. 293–300 (2007)
7. Barata, J., Ribeiro, L., Colombo, A.: Diagnosis using Service Oriented Architectures (SOA). In: 2007 5th IEEE International Conference on Industrial Informatics, vol. 2 (2007)
8. Candido, G., Barata, J., Colombo, A., Jammes, F.: SOA in reconfigurable supply chains: A research roadmap. Engineering Applications of Artificial Intelligence (2009)
9. Goldman, S., Nagel, R., Preiss, K.: Agile competitors and virtual organizations: strategies for enriching the customer. Van Nostrand Reinhold Company (1995)
10. Lin, C., Chiu, H., Chu, P.: Agility index in the supply chain. International Journal of Production Economics 100(2), 285–299 (2006)
11. Vernadat, F.: Interoperable enterprise systems: principles, concepts, and methods. Annual Reviews in Control 31(1), 137–145 (2007)

12. Camarinha-Matos, L., Afsarmanesh, H.: A modeling framework for collaborative networked organizations. In: Network-centric collaboration and supporting frame- works. IFIP working conference on virtual enterprises, pp. 3–14. Springer, Heidelberg (2006)
13. Camarinha-Matos, L.: ECOLEAD-Achievements in Collaborative Networked Organizations. In: IFIP Working Conference on Virtual Enterprises, Guimarães, Portugal (2007)
14. Cândido, G., Jammes, F., Barata, J., Colombo, A.: Generic Management Services for DPWS-enabled devices. In: Proceedings of IECON 2009 Annual Conference of the IEEE Industrial Electronics Society (2009)
15. OASIS: Devices profile for web services version 1.1 specification (2009),
    http://www.oasis-open.org/committees/ws-dd
16. DMTF: Web services for management (ws-management) specification (2008),
    http://www.dmtf.org/standards/wsman/
17. SODA: Soda project industrial demonstrator (2008),
    http://www.soda-itea.org/Demonstrators/Industrial/
    default.html

Improving Energy Efficiency in the Production Floor Using SoA-Based Monitoring Techniques

Daniel Cachapa[1,2], Robert Harrison[1], and Armando Colombo[2]

[1] Wolfson School of Mechanical and Manufacturing Engineering, Loughborough University, Loughborough, LE11 3TU, United Kingdom
{D.Cachapa-Vieira,R.Harrison}@lboro.ac.uk
[2] Schneider Electric Automation GmbH, Industry Business Unit, Steinheimer Str. 117, 63500 Seligenstadt, Germany
{Daniel.Cachapa,Armando.Colombo}@de.schneider-electric.com

Abstract. Modern manufacturing systems are struggling to remain competitive under the pressures of and increasingly demanding society. The advent of SoA-based production systems is presented as the solution to facing those difficulties. In order to support this new production paradigm, new tools have to be developed for the benefit of the production engineers of who will be implementing and deploying the SoA-based factory floor. This entails the development of Smart Devices, which while being autonomous are able to communicate and cooperate in an open and standardized way with other participants in the production system. These capabilities can be exploited in order to implement a next-generation production monitoring system that is not only able to monitor production status, but also energy usage, eventually leading to much greener and more efficient factories.

Keywords: SoA, Web Services, Production Monitoring, Simulation.

1 Introduction

Modern industrial manufacturing is facing pressure from all directions: governments want greener and safer products, while costumers demand quality, customization and lower prices. In order to face these challenges in an age of technological boom, companies are turning more and more to machines to accomplish the tasks previously made by human.

The field of factory automation has been a pioneer in this area and has evolved much in the past few years as machines get ever more sophisticated and efficient. Nevertheless, these changes have also raised the complexities involved in maintaining and controlling them. Implementing a modern factory floor is an incredibly expensive and time-consuming labour as production specifications must be transformed into the machine code connecting all of the devices together. Likewise, a monitoring framework must also be implemented so that production engineers can have a real-time view of the machine's status, production flow, energy usage, stock management, as well as other essential production indexes.

L.M. Camarinha-Matos, P. Pereira, and L. Ribeiro (Eds.): DoCEIS 2010, IFIP AICT 314, pp. 159–166, 2010.

It is expected that the event-based, high-level and decoupled nature of SoA-enabled production devices will allow for easier integration, configuration and maintenance of factory monitoring systems, while at the same time improving the performance and capabilities over traditional systems. The study of monitoring and energy efficiency issues in SoA-based factory automation relies not only on following current state-of-the-art in the relevant areas, but also on the building of prototype engineering solutions that demonstrate the proposed methodologies. Those solutions should be engineered based on existing use-cases that represent current industrial needs.

2   Contribution to Technological Innovation

The flexible production line requires the development of modular devices which can be plugged into the production line and participate in a cooperative network configured to accomplish a given task. The devices themselves should be autonomous in the sense that they don't depend directly on any of the other participants in the network to achieve their full functionality, which means that the devices are individually programmed and tested before reaching the production line.

This entails:

- Developing building blocks - Intelligent functions embedded into devices (profiles, HMI, tools, web, agents).
- Making the blocks work together - Design of networked autonomous and fault adaptive systems (protocols, robust, security).
- Assuring a common objective - Concepts, methods and tools for building robust, reconfigurable intelligent systems and guarantee expected overall system behaviour.

Also important is that the devices are able to communicate in a standards-based manner with the other participants in the network. Standardization guarantees better flexibility for the system builder in mixing and matching parts from different suppliers, creating a fairer market for device builders and thereby reducing costs through the power of healthy competition in the marketplace.

The requirements described above are embodied in the tenants of SoA as it describes a standards-based network of autonomous participants which work together in order to reach a common goal. Specifically, the use of SoA and Web Service technology from the enterprise level all the way down to the device level yields the following benefits:

- Easy adoption: it is possible to deploy the technology incrementally either by gradually replacing components, or using middleware solutions in older equipment (Priyantha, Kansal, Goraczko, & Zhao, 2008).
- Easy integration: made possible by the standards-based nature of SoA and WS technology.
- Easy to develop new applications: SoA and Web Services are at the heart of new programming paradigms heavily endorsed by influential software companies such as Microsoft® and Sun®.
- Reduced time for setup: made possible by the high-level nature of Web Services, and facilities such as discovery and eventing.

Bringing SoA into the production line requires a careful design in order to keep a clean architecture with clear hierarchical separation between different levels and usage patterns. The implementation must account for the requirements of the current production runs, as well as being ready to quickly incorporate changes in the production process, while at the same time supporting use cases that can range from production control to production monitoring, to business process management (Karnouskos, Baecker, de Sousa, & Spieß, 2007).

With energy prices are on the rise, and environmental concerns coming from both consumers and governmental agencies, the industry is concerning itself greatly with energy savings on the shop floor, which not only have the potential of yielding savings directly on the energy bills and environmental taxes, but also having an impact on sales as the marketing department is allowed to stick a "green" label on the end-user packaging.

The research presented here aims to develop a SoA-based framework for decoupled factory devices, and use it to perform monitoring of production data, with a particular emphasis on energy usage, in order to research viable energy management strategies for the factories of the future.

3 State-of-the-Art / Related Literature

Many SoA-based frameworks have been proposed, such as in (Colombo, 2008), where the author separates the production system into three hierarchies: the embedded components (TEC), composed into embedded machines (TEM), which themselves are arranged into embedded production systems (TES). In (Lastra, 2004), the author presents a similar approach dubbed Actor-based Assembly Systems in which simple SoA-based devices with limited functionality are composed together to build complex production systems. In {Document Not In Library} the authors present a similar framework of SoA-based devices using the OPC Unified Architecture. These frameworks have many things in common, which represent the central tenets of the SoA-based production system: a society of autonomous devices which cooperate in order to achieve the functionality required for the production objectives.

The research presented here builds upon the same basic procedures and techniques in order to build a fully functional production system. Much of the work follows the groundwork laid down in the SIRENA (Jammes & Smit, 2005) and in the SOCRADES (de Souza et al., 2008) projects, as well as the RI-MACS project {Document Not In Library}. It is also closely related to the objectives put forward by the CONET {Document Not In Library} research project.

The developments and tools developed in support of the research are mainly supported upon the Devices Profile for Web Services (DPWS) communication stack (Jammes, Mensch, & Smit, 2005) under the development umbrella of the SoA4D group {Document Not In Library}, and the Delmia Automation CAD suite {Document Not In Library} as a simulation/visualization tool. The results of the early experiments with these sets of tools are described in (Cachapa, Colombo, Feike, & Bepperling, 2007) and (Leitão et al., 2009).

4 Research Contribution and Innovation

The research plan for the work presented here is separated in two stages: the development of a SoA-based framework for factory devices, and the leveraging of that framework in order to perform event-based monitoring of production and energy data.

The first and most essential step in the creation of a test production line based on the SoA paradigm is the availability of "smart devices". The concept of a Smart Device is used to describe a device that is designed from the ground up to be autonomous and cooperative. Smart devices integrate the kinematics; the behaviour, which is exposed to the outside as services; and, in the case of a virtual device, the geometry, or physical dimensions of the device it represents. Smart Devices can thus be brought into the production line, connected to the network, and have their full functionality immediately available for the controller to exploit with minimal configuration. The procedure of developing a virtual smart device in the Delmia Automation environment with a DPWS-based service interface which is identical to the one available from the corresponding real device is described in (Cachapa, Colombo, Feike, & Bepperling, 2007).

The Smart Devices feature fixed input and output ports at its physical boundaries, so that different devices can be connected at their ports in order to build a continuous sequence of machines that can transport work pieces inside the production cell. The ports themselves are intimately connected to the device's internal functionality and exposed as individual services, meaning that the physical composition of devices is also reflected in the functional composition of the respective services associated to those ports. Two or more devices can be composed in this manner in order to form composed devices, which abstract the interactions between the individual devices and whose resulting characteristics may be different from the simple sum of the capabilities and limitations of each component. The composed devices can be themselves composed into new composed devices of an even higher hierarchy.

By linking and composing smart devices together, a full, SoA-based production system can be assembled. This technique was demonstrated in (Leitão et al., 2009) where a virtual SoA-based production cell, shown in Fig. 1a) was built according to an existing physical cell, shown in Fig.1b), and used to aid the development of the production controller.

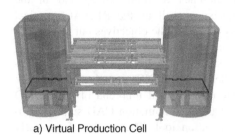

a) Virtual Production Cell   b) Real Production Cell

Fig. 1. Virtual and real representations of a SoA-based production cell

Since all participants in the production line share the same network and high-level functionality, and the components in both the virtual and the real environments appear in the network as autonomous devices, there is no difference in functionality between them from the controller's point of view, which allows replacing some of the virtual components for real ones for testing purposes. The outcome is an open architecture where all the participants can communicate freely according to their function, as seen in Fig. 2.

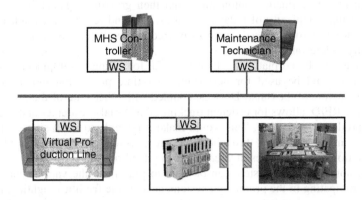

Fig. 2. Virtual SoA-based production system with hardware in the middle

Thanks to the high-level nature of the services provided by the smart devices, the device operations have a one-to-one mapping between both the real and virtual worlds, meaning that as long as all the devices are accessible in the network, the same controller is able to perform the same set of operations in the virtual and real worlds without the need for any specific platform dependencies. Fig. 3 shows an example of this mapping during a transfer operation from one smart device to another.

Fig. 3. Mapping operations in the real world to the virtual world using SoA-based real and virtual smart devices

This technique allows the production engineer to validate the production cell's layout and process control on the virtual production floor, and later replace the virtual devices for real ones as necessary for testing until the control software is running the full, physical, production cell. Similarly, the installation of a new device can be tested offline by first connecting it to the virtual model, and replacing it with the real device only after the new configuration has been validated.

4.1   Event-Based Monitoring of Production and Energy Data

The initial steps towards a SoA-based production monitoring system for factory automation begin with a study of existing systems and a gathering of the requirements for such a system, as well as a wish list for improvements. The results of this study were as expected: monitoring systems are proprietary, in-house solutions, and are based on a patchwork of barely compatible and sometimes outdated technologies.

This is the outcome of the systems having been built many years ago to face the growing pains of production automation, and then growing organically to face the ever increasing complexity of today's factories. The end result is a complex system layout featuring multiple closed networks interconnected by data exchangers, bridges and various middleware solutions.

The same SoA-based platform which is useful for aiding development of production systems could be used for performing real-time production monitoring. The event-based nature of the Smart Devices, coupled with other state-of-the-art technologies, such as RFID, allows for efficient tracking of materials, resources and operations over the production lifecycle. This would make it possible to use a single, open and standards compliant network throughout the entire factory floor, which would facilitate integration of new devices in already existing facilities.

Furthermore, the same system can be used to plug in to the various energy consumers participating in the production system, such as the facilities, lighting, heating, and others. Having detailed real-time and historical energy data will go a long way towards finding energy inefficiencies in the production process and researching ways of optimizing or eliminating them.

5   Discussion of Results and Critical View

The results achieved so far demonstrate that a SoA-based engineering tool can support the production engineer by greatly simplifying the process of production line layout and configuration. The simulation capabilities offered by the tool are indispensible for quick prototyping and testing of the capabilities, performance and throughput of the production process.

Furthermore, both the high-level nature the Web Service-based components and the generic support of the virtual 3D platform enable the quick development of new components and their adaptation into an existing production environment, where they can be thoroughly tested before deployment.

After deployment, the same technologies can serve as the base to a next-generation production monitoring system, replacing the current proprietary ones which face enormous limitations due to their complexity and forced support for legacy technologies.

The open and standard nature of the technologies and protocols used in the communication between the different devices enable a future where factories don't have to rely on a limited set of vendors for all of their production or control devices, but instead, benefit from an ecosystem where competing companies which all develop their products targeting the same standards, giving rise to a modular factory floor where the different machines are mixed-and-matched according to their quality, capabilities and price.

That's not to say that a new system would solve all the problems overnight. Initially, the SoA-based production monitoring system would either function parallel to the existing systems, or legacy technology would have to be adapted through the use of middleware software.

6 Conclusions and Further Work

It is unquestionable that the current tools for production engineering aren't capable of supporting the advent of SoA in the factory floor. For this reason, new tools and techniques will have to be developed.

The research presented here lays the groundwork for developing SoA-based virtual production lines based on proven industrial standards. These tools are an essential platform for conducting further research in the fields of production control and monitoring.

The first glimpses on the current state of production monitoring in use today show that there is much that can be improved. The event-based and open nature of the SoA-based production system makes it ideal for tackling the problem of monitoring the factory floor. It is hoped that the research into these issues culminates in a standard, extensible set of guidelines for production monitoring systems which follow closely current industrial requirements.

Acknowledgments. The authors would like to thank the European Commission and the partners of the EU IST FP6 project "Service-Oriented Cross-layer infrastructure for Distributed smart Embedded devices" (SOCRADES) and the EC ICT FP7 NoE project "Cooperating Objects" (CONET) for their support. Further recognition is due to the brilliant engineers at the Ford Motor Company in Dunton UK.

References

1. Priyantha, N., Kansal, A., Goraczko, M., Zhao, F.: Tiny Web Services: Design and Implementation of Interoperable and Evolvable Sensor Networks. In: Proceedings of the 6th ACM Conference on Embedded Network Sensor Systems, pp. 253–266. ACM, New York (2008)
2. Karnouskos, S., Baecker, O., de Sousa, L., Spieß, P.: Integration of SOA-ready Networked Embedded Devices in Enterprise Systems via a Cross-Layered Web Service Infrastructure. In: Proceedings of the 12th IEEE Conference on Emerging Technologies and Factory Automation, pp. 293–300. IEEE Computer Society, Los Alamitos (2007)
3. Colombo, A.: Integration of Web-Services and Agent Technology: A Service-Oriented Architecture-based Automation Framework. In: Workshop Agenten in der Automatisierungstechnik (2008)
4. Lastra, J.: Reference Mechatronic Architecture for Actor-Based Assembly Systems. Doctoral thesis, Tampere University of Technology (2004)
5. Jammes, F., Smit, H.: Service-oriented Architectures for Devices - the SIRENA view. In: 3rd IEEE International Conference on Industrial Informatics, pp. 140–147. IEEE Computer Society, Los Alamitos (2005)

6. de Souza, L., Spiess, P., Guinard, D., Kohler, M., Karnouskos, S., Savio, D.: SOCRADES: A Web Service Based Shop Floor Integration Infrastructure. In: Floerkemeier, C., Langheinrich, M., Fleisch, E., Mattern, F., Sarma, S.E. (eds.) IOT 2008. LNCS, vol. 4952, pp. 50–67. Springer, Heidelberg (2008)
7. Jammes, F., Mensch, A., Smit, H.: Service-oriented Device Communications Using the Devices Profile for Web Services. In: Proceedings of the 3rd International Workshop on Middleware for Pervasive and Ad-hoc Computing, pp. 1–8. ACM, New York (2005)
8. Cachapa, D., Colombo, A., Feike, M., Bepperling, A.: An Approach for Integrating Real and Virtual Production Automation Devices Applying the Service-oriented Architecture Paradigm. In: IEEE Conference on Emerging Technologies and Factory Automation, pp. 309–314. IEEE Computer Society, Los Alamitos (2007)
9. Leitão, P., Mendes, J., Bepperling, A., Cachapa, D., Colombo, A., Restivo, F.: Engineering Tools for the Integration of Service-oriented Production Systems. In: 13th IFAC Symposium on Information Control Problems in Manufacturing (2009)

Part 6

Cooperative Robotics

Dual-Arm Robot Motion Planning Based on Cooperative Coevolution

Petar Ćurković and Bojan Jerbić

Faculty of Mechanical Engineering and Naval Architecture, Department of Robotics
and Manufacturing Systems Automation, University of Zagreb, Ivana Lučića 5,
10000 Zagreb, Croatia
{petar.curkovic,bojan.jerbic}@fsb.hr

Abstract. This paper presents a cooperative coevolutionary approach to path planning for two robotic arms sharing common workspace. Each arm is considered an agent, required to find transition strategy from given initial to final configuration in the work space. Since the robots share workspace, they present dynamic obstacle to each other. To solve the problem of path planning in optimized fashion, we formulated it to multi-objective optimization domain and implemented co-evolutionary algorithm to simultaneously optimize four conflicting objectives. End-effector trajectory length, end-effector velocity distribution, total rotate angle and number of collisions are the objectives to be optimized. Simulation results for two 2-R type robots are presented.

Keywords: Co-evolution, path planning, multi-objective optimization.

1 Introduction

Over the last two decades, evolutionary algorithms have been applied in a variety of fields, namely: robotics, scheduling, construction engineering, speech recognition, space engineering, image processing etc. An augmentation of evolutionary computation, coevolutionary computation, drives the inspiration from natural processes of coevolution between different (animal) species. The main difference between coevolutionary and standard evolutionary algorithms is in the nature of individuals' fitness evaluation. While the former uses a static fitness function for evaluation of individuals from a single population, the latter employs non-stationary fitness function for evaluating individuals from multiple populations, based on their interactions with individuals from other populations [1].

Coordinated path planning for multiple robots is difficult because the problem is NP-complete, whose complexity grows exponentially as the number of DOF increases [2] [3]. Required is to plan not only for the paths of individual robots, but also for the order of their consecutive movements, in order to prevent the robots from colliding with one another. The path planning problem for multiple manipulators sharing common work space have been studied for some time now [4].

L.M. Camarinha-Matos, P. Pereira, and L. Ribeiro (Eds.): DoCEIS 2010, IFIP AICT 314, pp. 169–178, 2010.

2   Contribution to Technological Innovation

Current industrial control approaches are on the edge of becoming obsolete. While the processes inducted by the globalization have opened the door for a worldwide market, at the same time, competition is additionally boosted. In this context, traditional, deterministic automation approaches are cost ineffective, inflexible and unreliable in the conditions of short-termed business opportunities.

In this line of thought, employing dual-arm robots in decentralized control fashion, for solving complex assembly tasks receives recent attention in the first line in research community. Such robots should be able to decompose complex assembly tasks to several simpler ones, simultaneously change end effectors, reduce facilities costing, total assembly time and spare area.

However, theory about motion planning of this type of robots is not perfect. The problem is twofold; from the one hand, feasible collision free paths between two intermediate points should be calculated prior the movement of each robot begins. From the other hand, it is difficult to achieve synchronization of the two hands in context of industrial communication protocols, i.e. fast Ethernet, due to its stochastic nature and time delays.

This work was motivated bearing in mind that the two hands of the robots could be to some extent autonomous, being controlled by two controllers in decentralized fashion. Each controller should be governed by one evolutionary algorithm, and the communication between the two controllers should take place at the time controllers are checking for collisions, for the case when the objective is to find collision free paths.

Some of the technological benefits of the proposed approach: assembly speedup and efficiency increase due to asynchronous and parallel computation. Scalability – it should be possible to add additional agents and represent them in form of new co-evolving population. Modularity and cost reduction, it is easier and most cost effective to rearrange system that is based on decentralized control principles.

Problem of synchronization of the two hands at the level of execution of complex tightly coupled assembly tasks is beyond the scope of this paper and considered for future work.

3   Related Literature

Many important contributions to the problem of path planning in recent years have been made, each one possessing its own merits and disadvantages. Comprehensive survey can be found in [5]. Practical multi-robot motion planning problems are often decoupled in the sense that the robots trajectories are planned for only one robot at a time in priority order. Then in the second phase, velocities are modulated so that collisions between the robots are avoided. If a problem of path planning is represented as an optimization problem, robust optimization techniques, such as evolutionary algorithms have proven suitable for finding solution for such formulated problems.

Rana and Zalzala [6] [7] propose an evolutionary planner to evolve near time-optimal collision-free trajectories for multi-arm robot manipulators. In this study, planning is carried out in joint space of the manipulator, and the path is represented as a string of via points connected by cubic polynomial splines. Davidor [8] also applies evolutionary algorithms to the trajectory generation by searching the inverse kinematics solutions to pre-defined end effector robot paths. Pires, Machado and Oliveira [9] employ multi objective genetic algorithm to evolve joint-space strings of manipulator configurations. Five indices, namely manipulator joints travelling distance, joint velocity, cartesian distance, cartesian velocity and energy are used to qualify the evolving trajectories. Toyoda and Yano [10] used multi-purpose genetic algorithm to optimize movement of multi-joint robotic arms in presence of stationary obstacles. Optimum solutions with smooth trajectories and minimal joint rotation were obtained. Venegas and Marcial-Romero [11] present preliminary results of Constructive Solid Geometry based approach to path planning of multiple robot arms. They used two phase genetic algorithm to obtain a plan for the robotic arms by using a strategy that combines the exploration of the free collision space while looking for the target position from each previously explored area.

Majority of papers dealing with evolutionary – based path planning consider either single agent operating in an environment without presence of obstacles, or in an environment containing static, point obstacles. The problem then boils down to finding suitable set of interior points, to be interpolated to formulate the polynomial of given order representing the trajectory.

The method presented in this paper considers concurrent development of robot trajectories for two 2R type robots sharing common work space. Each robot is considered an agent that is to find appropriate strategy for moving from given initial to final configuration. Since one agent presents dynamical obstacle to the other, and vice versa, often it is necessary for the agents to detour away from optimal, shortest paths, to find feasible strategies. It is also necessary to check for collisions between the links of the two robots in each consecutive time step.

Cooperative coevolutionary algorithms (CEAs) offer great potential for concurrent multiagent domains. Two populations, each representing set of configurations of one robot in joint space, co-evolve to minimize number of collisions between interacting individuals, at the same time minimizing distance traveled, total joint rotation angle, and equalizing end-effector velocity profile. Best collaborators are sought and preserved to achieve memory effect in subsequent populations, and to bias coevolutionary search for optimal strategies.. The paper is organized as follows: In section 2, impact on technological innovation is discussed. Section 3 presents related literature and recent work, with focus on implementation of evolutionary algorithms to path planning. Problem and proposed algorithm are discussed in the section 4. Section 5 presents simulation and result for one given scenario. In section 5 some coevolutionary modifications are described. Finally, we discuss results and give insights for future work in sections 6 and 7.

4   Problem and Algorithm Formulation

In this paper, two 2-R type robots with two links and two joints are considered. The end-effector is considered to move in the horizontal plane. The configuration spaces of the two robots are: $C_1 = q_{11} \times q_{21} \in R^2$ for the first robot and $C_2 = q_{12} \times q_{22} \in R^2$ for the second. The two manipulators are to move from given initial to a given final configuration. The lengths of all links are set to 1 m, with distance between the robots of 2.1 m. The links are free to rotate in the range $[0, \pi]$ rad .

4.1   Individual Representation

An individual in a population is encoded as real-valued vector in the joint space:

$$\left[\left\{ q_{11}^{(\Delta t,G)}, ..., q_{ij}^{(\Delta t,G)} \right\}, \left\{ q_{11}^{(2\Delta t,G)}, ..., q_{ij}^{(2\Delta t,G)} \right\}, ..., \left\{ q_{11}^{((n-2)\Delta t,G)}, ..., q_{ij}^{((n-2)\Delta t,G)} \right\} \right] \tag{1}$$

Where i denotes the robot $i=1,2$, j is the number of *DOF*, Δt is sampling time between two consecutive configurations, q is angle between the link and positive x axis, G is current generation. At the beginning of the evolutionary process, joint values are randomly initialized, whereby the initial and final configurations are not encoded into the string because they remain constant throughout the search process. Without the lost of generality, adopted is normalized sampling time with $\Delta t = 0.1$ s.

4.2   Operators of the Coevolutionary Algorithm

The algorithm starts with random initialization of two populations, each representing set of configurations for one robot. The performance of each robot's configuration depends on the current state of the robots from other population, since the two must coordinate the motion, to achieve continuous collision free movement. In the canonical CCEA, each individual from the first population should be evaluated by all individuals from other population, what is extremely time-consuming. To speed-up the evolution process, modified co-evolution is considered. In the modified version, each individual is evaluated by a finite set of the top collaborators from the other population, based on scores from previous generation. In this study, we evaluated the top 10 % of the populations, which is a modification of the approach proposed by the Sims [12], where "...the most "interesting" results occurred when the all vs. best competition pattern was used". The sizes of both populations were same and set to 60 individuals. In what concerns the selection operator, the successive generations are reproduced on the basis of roulette wheel selection. Standard single point crossover operator is used. The mutation operator replaces one allele with a given probability using the equation, where rand gives random number from the given interval:

$$q_{ij}^{(\Delta t,G+1)} = q_{ij}^{(\Delta t,G)} + rand \in (0, \pi / 5] \Big| q_{ij}^{(\Delta t,G+1)} < \pi \tag{2}$$

4.3 Fitness Criteria

Fitness criteria should take into account number of collisions between the two robotic arms, trajectory length, velocity profile, and total rotate angle. The most important criterion is the collision number, since collisions should be avoided at all costs. To check for collisions, in each time step Δt, linear system is solved that describes current positions of all links of the two robots.

4.4 Collision Penalty

Collision penalty depending on collision between Robot 1 and Robot 2 in corresponding configurations is given by:

$$C_1 = \sum_{k=1}^{k=n-2} C_k, C_1 \to \min \tag{3}$$

where:

$$C_k = \begin{cases} 1 \text{ if R1 and R2 collide in } i^{th} \text{ generation} \\ 0 \text{ otherwise.} \end{cases} \tag{4}$$

It is important to note that the evaluation of the eq. 3 needs representatives from other co-evolving population and here is where cooperative coevolution makes contribution.

4.5 Total Distance of the End-Effector Movement

$$C_2 = \sum_{k=1}^{k=n} dist\left(p_j, p_{j-1}\right), C_2 \to \min \tag{5}$$

where p_j is the robot's intermediate end-effector position. In the case where no obstacles are present in the environment, optimal value of the function is length of the straight line connecting initial and final end-effector position. For all other cases, $C_2 > C_{2optimal}$.

4.6 Total Rotation Angle

Since the robots are redundant systems even in this simple form of 2 *DOF*, resulting in possibilities of reaching the same point in the space in elbow-up and elbow-down configurations, criterion of minimizing the total distance is not enough. Additionally, it is necessary to minimize the total rotation angle, to ensure no oscillations between the elbow-up and elbow-down configurations occur. Following expression defines total angle for one joint of one robot. Each robots' total angle should be minimized:

$$C_3 = \sum_{i=1}^{n} |\alpha_i - \alpha_{i-1}| \rightarrow \min \qquad (6)$$

where α_i is the angle between the limb of the robot and positive horizontal axis.

4.7 End-Effector Velocity Distribution

To ensure even distribution of passing points along the robots' trajectory, the distance between two adjoining points in unit time should be equal:

$$C_4 = \left\{ dist\left(p_j, p_{j-1}\right)_{\max} - dist\left(p_j, p_{j-1}\right)_{\min} \right\} \rightarrow \min \qquad (7)$$

Optimal value for C_4 is equal to 0, what means that all passing points are equally distant from each other.

4.8 Objective Function Calculation

Objective (fitness) function for each candidate is calculated as weighted linear combination of above equations.

$$F = f\left(w_1 \cdot C_1 + w_2 \cdot C_2 + w_3 \cdot C_3 + w_4 \cdot C_4\right) \rightarrow \min \qquad (8)$$

Where values of weight factors w_i are constants. Values of weight constants have significant impact on the overall behavior of the algorithm. Namely, since objective criteria are in conflict, i.e. shortest distance criterion conflicts collision penalty criterion, proper tuning of these parameters is very tedious and time demanding. We are considering implementing non-linear functional relationships in weight parameters in the future. To address this problem in this paper, we implement dynamic weight factors and show the effectives of proposed approach.

5   Simulation Results

Several experiments were conducted to test the performance of the proposed algorithm. It was observed that, beside the parameters of the fitness function, the success ratio of the algorithm depends on the initial and final configurations of the robots. The easiest scenario is when configurations of the robots result with no collisions. Most difficult scenarios occurred for configurations when significant detouring from shortest paths was necessary, (to ensure collision free motion).

Fig. 1 shows evolved motions for two robots sharing work space. In the above case, all lengths of robot links are 1 m, and the distance between bases of the robots is set to 1.5 m. The algorithm successfully evolved trajectories for given start and end

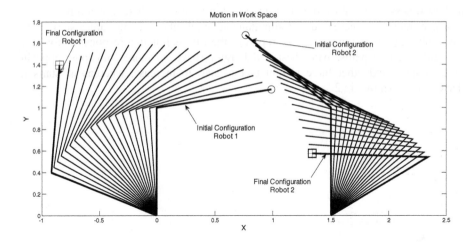

Fig. 1. Trajectories evolved for two robots simultaneously. Trajectories are optimized in terms of length, end-effector velocity distribution, total rotation angle, and number of collisions.

configurations of the robots. Trajectory of the left robot could be further optimized in terms of length, since it is obvious that end-effector performs arc motion, while linear motion would result in reduced trajectory length.

Operation of the coevolutionary algorithms is very complex and theoretical background is still developing in the research community [13] [14]. For example, it is not possible to employ simple elitist function to the coevolutionary algorithm, as it is in the case of standard algorithm. The reason is that each individual from one population is, in canonical case, evaluated by each individual from coevolving population. The consequence is that performance of the individuals from first population depends on the structure of the other population(s). That means that individual, that had high fitness value and was good in one generation, may suddenly become not so good in the next generation. The fitness vs. time function is not monotonously growing in that case.

6 Modified Coevolution

Standard evaluation each individual by each individual from other populations is time consuming. To speed up the evolutionary process, we save top 10% individuals from both populations and evaluate them by each individual from other population. By doing so, we hope to only increase the speed of the convergence, without hindering the ability of the algorithm for finding solutions near Pareto front. Other issue is biasing coevolutionary search towards optimal solutions. Taking in consideration the nature of the problem, we introduce dynamic fitness function. Since it is very difficult to find proper combination of weight factors, we employ following procedure:

The search starts with weight parameters having initial values chosen either by random or by some previous experience. Afterwards, number of collisions is monitored for the pair of individuals we call *best collaborators* – the pair receiving the highest fitness value. Since the most important criterion is to find collision free trajectories, weight w_l is increased and simultaneously all other weight values start to decay. This way, importance is given to part of the fitness function responsible for finding collision free paths. After best collaborators have no more collisions, opposite process starts and other three weight factors start to increase, whereas w_l starts to decay, as shown by Fig 2.

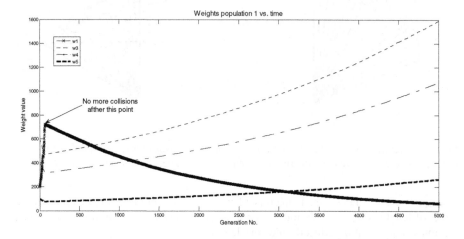

Fig. 2. Non-stationary weight factors over generations

If, in any moment, best collaborators start to collide, the first process begins, increasing the importance of avoiding collisions.

Such way, after individuals are evolved, which generally do not collide with each other, they are fine-tuned afterwards. If stationary fitness function is used, it is very difficult to evolve satisfactory strategies for the robots. There are numerous possibilities to improve this process of tuning fitness function. For example, we monitor only best collaborators i.e. one individual from the first and one individual from the second population to determine when to change fitness function. At the other hand, gradients of the growth of weight factors are chosen after several experiments were conducted. It is very important parameter, whose behavior should be determined with more care.

7   Discussion

As it is already mentioned, there are many possibilities to improve presented approach. There are two critical factors: speed of the convergence and completeness of the solution i.e. number of satisfying configurations developed by the algorithm before stopping criterion is matched. In what concerns speed of the convergence, it is proposed to evaluate a finite representative set from each population. This way, number of evaluations of the algorithm is decreased, but some, possibly good combinations of individuals might get lost. In what concerns completeness of solution, we propose dynamic weight factors for the fitness function. In such way, we are able to adapt the evolutionary process according to current state in the population. It is rather rough idea, how the process should look like, since only two individuals are monitored, and based on their interaction it is decided on the values of the weight factors. Simple method for changing fitness factors is adopted, namely, they are increased or decayed by adding or subtracting some fixed increment. The values of the increments remain fixed over the evolutionary process, but are different for each weight factor.

8 Conclusion and Future Work

Our long-term goal is to develop a framework based on described principles and implement it to a pair of real robots, probably of SCARA configuration. To do so, many important questions should be answered. First of all, algorithm should be further optimized in terms of speed of execution, although off-line planning with combination of machine learning is possible. No real physical properties of the robot are taken into consideration in this work, i.e. maximal acceleration etc. what is another important issue. At the level of execution of the algorithm, problem of synchronization of two hands based on Ethernet protocols is issue for itself and beyond the scope of this paper, but certainly an issue to be cleared before implementation to real robots would be possible.

Acknowledgments. The author kindly acknowledge Croatian Ministry of Science, Education and Sports for the Grant No. 120-1201948-1941, *Autonomous Multiagent Assembly.*

References

1. Paredis, J.: Coevolutionary Computation. Artificial Life Journal 2(4) (1996)
2. LaValle, S.M.: Planning Algorithms. Cambridge University Press, Cambridge (2006)
3. Canny, J.: The Complexity of Robot Motion Planning. MIT Press, Boston (2006)
4. Erderman, M., Lozano-Perez, T.: On multiple moving objects. In: Proceedings of the IEEE Conference on Robotics and Automation, San Francisco, California, USA, pp. 1419–1424 (1986)
5. Latombe, J.C.: Robot Motion Planning. Kluwer Academic Publishers, Boston (1991)
6. Rana, A.S., Zalzala, M.S.: An Evolutionary Algorithm for Collision Free Motion Planning of Multi-arm Robots. In: IEEE Genetic Algorithms in Engineering Systems: Innovations and Applications (1995)
7. Rana, A.S., Zalzala, M.S.: An Evolutionary Planner for Near Time-Optimal Collision-Free Motion of Multi-Arm Robotic Manipulators. In: UKACC International Conference on Control (1996)
8. Davidor, Y.: Genetic Algorithm and Robotics; A Heuristic Strategy for Optimization. World Scientific, Singapore (1991)
9. Solteiro Pires, E.J., Tenreiro Machado, J.A., Moura Oliveira, P.B.: Robot Trajectory Planning Using Multi-objective Genetic Algorithm Optimization. In: Deb, K., et al. (eds.) GECCO 2004. LNCS, vol. 3102, pp. 615–626. Springer, Heidelberg (2004)

10. Toyoda, Y., Yano, F.: Optimizing Movement of A Multi-Joint Robot Arm with Existence of Obstacles Using Multi-Purpose Genetic Algorithm. Ind. Eng. Man. Sys. 3, 78–84 (2004)
11. Venegas Montes, H.A., Raymundo Marcial-Romero, J.: An Evolutionary Path Planner for Multiple Robot Arms. In: Evo Workshops. LNCS. Springer, Heidelberg (2009)
12. Sims, K.: Evolving 3D Morphology and Behavior by Competition. In: Artificial Life IV Proceedings. MIT Press, Cambridge (1994)
13. Bucci, A.: Emergent Geometric Organization and Informative Dimensions in Coevolutionary Algorithms. PhD thesis, Brandeis University (2007)
14. Panait, L., Luke, S., Harrison, J.F.: Archive-based Cooperative Coevolutionary Algorithms. In: Proceedings of the GECCO (2006)

Comparative Study of Self-organizing Robotic Systems Regarding Basic Architecture

Irina-Gabriela Lolu and Aurelian Mihai Stanescu

Faculty of Automatic Control and Computers,
University POLITEHNICA of Bucharest, Romania
lolu_irina@yahoo.com, ams@cpru.pub.ro

Abstract. Self-organization has become an intensely researched area, being considered the new control system science. Different self-organizing algorithms (bio and non-bio inspired) have been developed by scientist worldwide with general applicability in autonomous systems, multi-robot systems, autonomic networking, sensor and actor networks and mobile ad hoc networks. This paper presents a comparative analysis of basic architectures for multi-robot systems from the point of view of self-organization capabilities. We identify requirements for implementing efficiently self-organization mechanisms with high applicability in multi-robot systems.

Keywords: Self-organization, robotic systems, architecture.

1 Introduction

Nature has always inspired scientists to develop techniques, algorithms and mechanisms and to apply them in artificial systems. This is also the case of self-organization; inspired from biology, physics and chemistry and used in computer science and robotics. This paper presents a critical analysis of basic architectures for robotic systems from the point of view of self-organization capabilities. We also propose a simple architecture that enables efficient implementation of self-organizing mechanisms.

Since it was introduced in 1947 by W. Ross Ashby[1], self-organization has caught the interest of the research community in various fields (ex. autonomous systems, autonomic networking, sensor and actor networks, mobile ad hoc networks), including robotics. The generally accepted definition for self-organization is: the mechanism enabling a system to change its internal organization according to environmental changes without explicit external command.

There are two approaches in self-organization: stigmergy and social. The concept of stigmergy was introduced by Grassé [2] to explain the social behavior of termites. It was demonstrated that coordination in ants and termites colonies is achieved through indirect communication by the means of a chemical substance, pheromone, deposited in the environment. The important characteristics of pheromones that have to be kept in mind when implementing stigmergy are: they evaporate in time (evaporation), the concentration increases when new pheromones are released at a marked

L.M. Camarinha-Matos, P. Pereira, and L. Ribeiro (Eds.): DoCEIS 2010, IFIP AICT 314, pp. 179–186, 2010.

location (aggregation) and they propagate through environment (propagation). The bio-inspired stigmergy mechanisms aim to achieve self-organization trough simple rules and interactions between robots/agents, using indirect communication by the means of artificial "pheromones". Stigmergy has been used in applications for hierarchical task networks[3], manufacturing control [4], coordination of unmanned vehicles[5] a.s.o.

In contrast with stigmergy, the social approach uses direct communication,. These techniques are inspired from natural social behaviors encountered in human societies, business organizations and even economic systems. The most popular social self-organization mechanisms are market-based (in which entities act to increase their profit)[8] and delegation based mechanisms (in which delegation is based on trust or reputation level, authority and voting)[9].

2   Contributions to Technological Innovation

The adaptive and robust self-organizing systems are an increasing trend nowadays, especially in software application, although the developers have to face great challenges: non-linearity, unpredictability, instability and sensitivity. When designing a self-organizing robotic system the challenges are even more difficult due to hardware limitations and time restrictions. Our work is a contribution to the design of such systems and concerns with one of the first steps of developing a robotic system: choosing the basic architecture. We are contributing with an analysis of existing architectures and we also propose a new architecture that ensures the implementation of different types of self-organizing mechanisms. We hope this paper will encourage further research in self-organizing robotic systems, enabling the development of the future robot societies.

3   Comparative Analysis of Basic Architectures

In this chapter we will discuss several robot architectures from the point of view of self-organization capabilities. Even though there are essential differences between stigmergy and the social approach, both have the same following proprieties:

- Absence of external control
- Decentralization
- Emergence
- Self-maintenance
- Self-building
- Adaptive
- Sensitivity
- Low predictability
- Robustness.

There are two different types of implementation for stigmergy: software and hardware. The software implementation has no special requirements (small processing power, shared memory for environment simulation), but the hardware implementation is restricted by the physical proprieties of pheromones. Still some solutions have been proposed by Johansson and Saffiotti [6], [7].

The social techniques are agent-oriented, thus the basic requirement is an agent-oriented architecture. Therefore we will concentrate on studying architectures based on multi-agent systems (MAS). For efficient implementation we also consider the following requirements: fast, long distance communication capabilities and considerably more processing power and memory than necessary for implementing stigmergy.

While the social approach is mostly used in more complex heterogeneous systems that require hierarchy, social learning, and knowledge propagation through gossiping [10], the stigmergy approach has some important advantages:

- Simplicity (robots/agents don't need a complex deliberative mechanism to implement the simple rules of stigmergy)
- Asynchrony (robots/agents act asynchronous according to the information found in the environment)
- Anonymity(robots/agents are not aware of each other)
- Public knowledge (all knowledge is public and can be found in the environment)
- Low –cost

We are considering the following criteria for analyzing existing MAS architectures for robotic systems: coordination – centralized/decentralized, resource requirements and communication capabilities.

There have been designed architectures for self-organizing multi-robot systems, but they implement a simple, specific self-organization mechanism using none or very little direct communication. From this category we mention ALLIANCE [11], Cebot[12], SWARM-bots[13] and ABBA[14]. These architectures cannot be used for developing more complex applications that require a social self-organization mechanism demanding high-level, message-oriented communication.

The first category of architectures that we present is the layered architectures category, depicted in Figure 1.These architectures have two [15], three [16] or even eight layers [17], that can communicate only with the neighboring layers using an inter-layer communication protocol (ex. TCP/IP). The drawback of this architecture is that the superior layers have to use the intermediate layers to communicate with the inferior layers, causing latencies which could be significant in real-time applications.

The top layer is usually called the Cognitive Layer and is represented by one or more deliberative agents that could enable self-organization, if chosen properly. These architectures were designed for cooperative robots, but were not meant especially for self-organization mechanisms, thus even if they have a multi-agent system these agents were not chosen in a way that enables emergent behavior.

Most of the architectures have a single agent that coordinates and controls the other agents ("Global Manager" or "Coordinator" [15],[18]), which means centralizing the decision, contrary to the distributed coordination essential for self-organization. Table 1 summarizes the studied architectures.

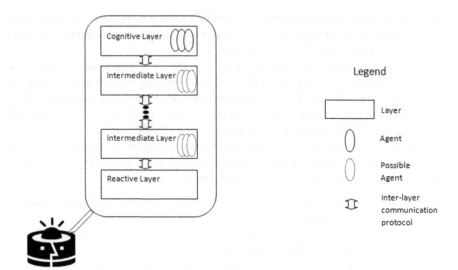

Fig. 1. Generic layered architecture

Table 1. Layered architectures examples

Name	No. of layers	Description	Disadvantages
Physical Robot Agent [15]	2	• Action Layer: Executor, Repository of Tasks and State Monitor • Cognitive Layer: Decision Maker, Coordinator and Negotiator	• Centralized control
Acromovi [19]	4	• Applications and Middleware Layer - multi-agent systems implemented in Java • ARIA and Saphira Layers – implemented in C++	• Inter-layer communication – Java JNI and Java RMI • High resource requirements
ARA [16]	3	• Reflexive Layer – on the robot • Reactive and Cognitive Layers - on another machine • High-level behaviors composed of elementary behaviors	• Separation on two machines
Busquets [18]	2	• Executive and Deliberative systems • Coordination through bidding executed by a Coordinator	• Centralized control

Another category of architectures are the architectures with one layer composed of different types of agents: Body Agents, Deliberative Agents, Service Agents, Behavioral Agents a.s.o.(Figure 2) We mention here the ARMADiCO[20] architecture which has distributed coordination among agents (based on a utility function) that could enable emergent behavior.

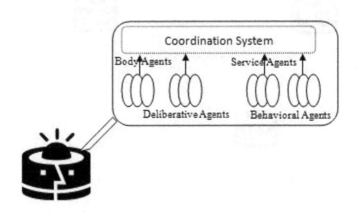

Fig. 2. One layer architecture based on multi-agent system

4   An Architecture for Self-organizing Robotic Systems

The disadvantages we identified in our analysis of the above architectures motivated us to design a simple, flexible architecture, with low resource requirements and decentralized control. Therefore we propose the two layered architecture with simple inter-layer communication (plain function call) depicted in Figure 3. Removing the intermediate layers we eliminate message passing, we reduce inter-layer communication (by embedding the intermediate layers in the superior or inferior layers), although at the cost of increasing intra-layer communication.

The Action Layer is a simple implementation of tasks (reactive) and its design does not influence the self-organization capabilities, but it has an impact over the performance of the system. The top layer (Cognitive Layer) is a multi-agent system with three or more agents, depending on the self-organization mechanism we want to implement. This ensures the flexibility of the architecture.

The DF and AMS agents implement the analogue components defined in the FIPA standard [21], and they are necessary to ensure self-organization in a multi-robot system. The DF agent is responsible for maintaining a list of all agents and their services in the system and offers the following services: updating and search. The AMS agent is responsible for registering and unregistering agents.

Choosing the other agents depends directly on the application and on the robots capabilities. In our opinion there is no need for "body" agents corresponding to sensors, but agents that control actuators could be useful for resolving resource

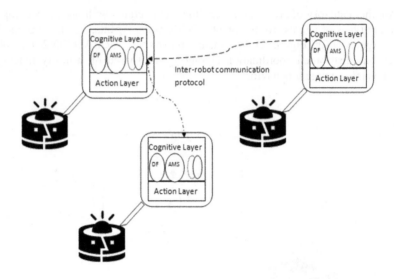

Fig. 3. A two layered architecture for self-organizing multi-robot systems

concurrency. An example for emergent behavior that could be implemented using this architecture is navigation with obstacle avoidance. In this case we must define the following agents: motor control agent – controls the motors and decides which agent has priority, move forward agent – moves forward the robot, avoid obstacle agent – when sensing an obstacle stops the robot and changes the direction of the robot.

Our current implementation of this architecture is on a Lego NXT robot (we wanted to underline the advantages of this architecture by implementing it on a machine with low computational power), using leJOS NXJ (a Java programming environment). We implemented a simple agent platform that uses shared memory for local communication and Bluetooth communication for inter-robot communication (a Bluetooth Agent). In our system every robot has an agent platform and the agents have the possibility of registering on multiple platforms (when agents communicate they use the local platform's communication service). At the moment we are developing a practical application that gives the possibility to test different self-organization algorithms in different scenarios in order to have consistent results.

5   Conclusions

In this paper we presented our analysis of the studied architectures for self-organizing robotic systems with respect to the identified requirements for the implementation of self-organizing mechanisms. The problems we encountered are: centralized coordination, high resource requirements and inter-layer slow communication protocols. Therefore we proposed an architecture that haves none of these disadvantages. We intend to further develop this architecture and test it with different self-organization mechanisms in our further work.

References

1. Ashby, W.R.: Principles of the Self-Organizing Dynamic System. Journal of General Psychology 1947 37, 125–128 (1947)
2. Grassé, P.P.: La reconstruction du nid et les coordinations interindividuelles chez Bellicositermes natalensis et Cubitermes sp. La théorie de la stigmergie: essais d'interprétation du comportement des termites constructeurs. Insectes Sociaux 6, 41–84 (1959)
3. Parunak, H.V., Belding, T., Bisson, R., Brueckner, S., Downs, E., Hilscher, R.: Stigmergic Reasoning over Hierarchical Task Networks. In: Decker, Sichman, Sierra, Castelfranchi (eds.) Proc. of 8th Int. Conf. on Autonomous Agents and Multiagent Systems (AAMAS 2009), pp. 1195–1196 (2009)
4. Karuna, H., Valckenaers, P., Saint-Germain, B., Verstraete, P., Zamfirescu, C.B., Van Brussels, H.: Emergent Forecasting Using a Stigmergy Approach in Manufacturing Coordination and Control. In: Brueckner, S.A., Di Marzo Serugendo, G., Karageorgos, A., Nagpal, R. (eds.) ESOA 2005. LNCS (LNAI), vol. 3464, pp. 210–226. Springer, Heidelberg (2005)
5. Parunak, H.V., Brueckner, S., Sauter, J.A.: Digital pheromone mechanisms for coordination of unmanned vehicles. In: International Conference on Autonomous Agents and Multi-Agent Systems (AAMAS 2002), pp. 449–450. ACM Press, New York (2002)
6. Johansson, R., Saffiotti., A.: Navigating by Stigmergy: A Realization on an RFID Floor for Minimalistic Robots. In: Proc of the IEEE Int. Conf. on Robotics and Automation (ICRA), Koba, Japan (2009)
7. Edelen, M.R.: Swarm intelligence and stigmergy: Robotic implementation of foraging behavior. Master of Science thesis, University of Maryland, College Park, Maryland, USA (2003)
8. Hassas, S., Castelfranchi, C., Marzo, D., Karageorgos, A.: Self-organizing Mechanisms from Social and Business/Economics Approaches. Informatica 30(1) (2006)
9. Schillo, M., Fley, B., Florian, M., Hillebrandt, F., Hinck, D.: Self-organization in multi-agent systems: from agent interaction to agent organization. In: Proceedings of the 3rd International Workshop on Modeling Artificial Societies and Hybrid Organizations (MASHO 2002), Workshop at KI 2002, the 25th German Conference on Artificial Intelligence Aachen, pp. 47–56 (2002)
10. Jelasity, M.: Engineering emergence through gossip. In: Edmonds, B., Gilbert, N., Gustafson, S., Hales, D., Krasnogor, N. (eds.) Proceedings of the Joint Symposium on Socially-Inspired Computing, pp. 123–126. Hatfield (2005)
11. Parker, L.E.: ALLIANCE: An Architecture for Fault Tolerant Multi-Robot Cooperation. IEEE Transactions on Robotics and Automation 14(2) (1998)
12. Fukuda, T., Kawauchi, G.: Cellular robotic system (CEBOT) as one of the realization of self-organizing intelligent universal manipulator. In: Proceedings of the 1990 IEEE Conference on Robotics and Automation, pp. 662–667 (1990)
13. Dorigo, M., Trianni, V., Şahin, E., Groß, R., Labella, T.H., Baldassarre, G., Nolfi, S., Deneubourg, J.-L., Mondada, F., Floreano, D., Gambardella, L.M.: Evolving self-organizing behaviors for a swarm-bot. Autonomous Robots 17(2-3), 223–245 (2004)
14. Jung, D., Zelinsky, A.: An architecture for Distributed Cooperative Planning in a Behavior-Based Multi-Robot System. Journal of Robots and Autonomous Systems 26(2-3), 149–174 (1999)
15. Eze, J., Ghenniwa, H., Shen, W.: Distributed Control Architecture for Collaborative Physical Robot Agents. In: IEEE International Conference on Systems, Man & Cybernetics, Washington, DC, pp. 2977–2982 (2003)

16. Neves, M.C., Oliveira, E.: A multi-agent approach for a mobile robot control system. In: Proceedings of Workshop on Multi-Agent Systems: Theory and Applications, pp. 1–14 (1997)
17. Shaw, M., Garlan, D.: Software Architecture: Perspectives on an Emerging Discipline. Prentice-Hall, Englewood Cliffs (1996)
18. Busquets, D., Sierra, C., López de Mántaras, R.: A multiagent approach to qualitative landmark-based navigation. Autonomous Robots 15, 129–154 (2003)
19. Nebot, P., Cervera, E.: Agent-based Application Framework for Multiple Mobile Robots Cooperation. In: Proceedings of the 2005 IEEE International Conference on Robotics and Automation, Barcelona, pp. 1521–1526 (2005)
20. Innocenti, B., Lopez, B., Salvi, J.: Resource coordination deployment for physical agents. In: 6th Int. Workshop of AAMAS: From Agent Theory to Agent Implementation, pp. 101–108 (2008)
21. The Foundation of Intelligent Physical Agents, http://www.fipa.org

Laban Movement Analysis towards Behavior Patterns

Luís Santos and Jorge Dias

Instituto de Sistemas e Robótica,
Departamento de Engenharia Electrotécnica e de Computadores
Faculdade de Ciência e Tecnologia da Universidade de Coimbra
Pólo II, Pinhal de Marrocos, Coimbra, Portugal
{luis,jorge}@isr.uc.pt

Abstract. This work presents a study about the use of Laban Movement Analysis (LMA) as a robust tool to describe human basic behavior patterns, to be applied in human-machine interaction. LMA is a language used to describe and annotate dancing movements and is divided in components [1]: Body, Space, Shape and Effort. Despite its general framework is widely used in physical and mental therapy [2], it has found little application in the engineering domain. Rett J. [3] proposed to implement LMA using Bayesian Networks. However LMA component models have not yet been fully implemented. A study on how to approach behavior using LMA is presented. Behavior is a complex feature and movement chain, but we believe that most basic behavior primitives can be discretized in simple features. Correctly identifying Laban parameters and the movements the authors feel that good patterns can be found within a specific set of basic behavior semantics.

Keywords: Laban Movement Analysis, Behavior Patterns, Bayesian Networks, Movement Characterization.

1 Introduction

Social interaction is a key issue in human life and also a relevant area in psychology and cognitive science. Social psychologists have been researching social interaction for a long time and conclude that social signals strongly determine human behavior. The majority of these signals are consciously produced, in the form of spoken language. However human interaction also involves non-verbal elements which are extensively and mainly unconsciously performed during human interaction. The non-verbal communication occurs concurrently to spoken words, through aural cues (voice quality, tone and fluency of speech) and visual cues (gestures, body language or posture, facial expression and gaze). These non-verbal signals are intuitively used by humans to understand and predict each other's behavior, mood, personality, and social relations, in a very wide range of situations. This work will focus on body's own language and movements.

By keeping track of relevant body parts (hands and head) a computational system can determine relevant features, thus providing ground for the estimation of parameters that will allow a robust analysis of performed actions and its characteristics [3].

L.M. Camarinha-Matos, P. Pereira, and L. Ribeiro (Eds.): DoCEIS 2010, IFIP AICT 314, pp. 187–194, 2010.
© IFIP International Federation for Information Processing 2010

The acquisition method is accomplished using video sensing devices. Image processing uses mainly two algorithms: CAMshift and Haar-like features to keep track of body parts. Once Cartesian data of body part position is available, basic Low Level Features (LLF) that constitute the basis of the Bayesian Network are computed. Detailed description of this acquisition and tracking methods is out of the scope of this work, and detailed information can be found in [3, 4, 5].

To interpret and contextualize the resulting LLF, Laban Movement Analysis (LMA) [1], a method for observing, describing, notating, and interpreting human movement, is used. Based on [3] we will debate how Computational Laban Movement Analysis (C-LMA) implemented over Bayesian Networks provides a good movement classifier. Bayesian Network properties allow the independent implementation of models, one for each of the Laban Components. By merging each of the models into one global model, it is believable that it will maximize result expectation for movement identification.

It has been shown that, in many social situations, humans can correctly interpret non-verbal signals and can estimate the behavior with high accuracy. Some approaches to characterize behavior decompose it in small basic actions performed in time. These actions exhibit certain characteristics, with some of them being personal i.e. specific for each individual. However it is felt necessary to create a system with an enough abstraction degree to characterize behavior in general. This work presents LMA as a potential tool to establish the relationship of mathematical properties of acquired visual cues to higher level semantic behavior description. This work aims to provide in the future a system that will automatically analyze behavior in different situations using the developed models based on Laban Movement analysis.

2   Contribution to Technological Innovation

Laban Movement Analysis is a tool widely used in studies of dance and in physical and mental therapy. However its computational implementation had yet been superficial. This work presents a computational approach to LMA implementation based on Bayesian Networks. The nature of this probabilistic method provides the necessary flexibility to model each of LMA components individually. Other interesting properties relates to the ability of Bayesian Framework to deal with incomplete information, uncertainty, make predictions on future events and, most important, provides an embedded scheme for learning. This work aims to take Rett's [3] work on movement classification using partial LMA implementation and extend the global model to a higher level: Behavior. LMA provides a set of descriptors carrying a semantic that can intuitively be seen as basic behavior characteristics. By developing LMA remaining components, hence completing the LMA global model, this work expects it will provide a good set of behavior descriptors based on LMA semantics. Behavior approaches so far, rely on pure geometric approaches, i.e. they do not carry inherent semantics which can immediately be related to behavioral aspects of human actions. Literature states that LMA provides good descriptors for the emotional content of expressive movements, thus, this work aims to take advantage of those characteristics and the flexibility given by the Bayesian approach to develop models to robustly characterize behavior.

3 State of the Art

Laban Movement Analysis is a descriptive language to study dancing movements. The general framework is widely applied in physical and mental therapy [2] as well as studies on dance. However, it is finding little application in the engineering domain. Recently, researchers from neuroscience [6] started to investigate LMA as a tool to describe certain effects on the movements on animals and humans. [3] In his PhD Thesis within the Bayesian Approach to Cognitive Systems (BACS) project developed a social robot that could identify a set of movements within human-machine interaction. His robot interface interpreted movement using Bayesian models divided in abstraction levels based on Laban Movement Analysis.

Within behavior analysis are several studies based on probabilistic approaches. Despite the flexibility of the probabilistic approach, the majority of presented methods so far, lack the psychological aspects of behavior, focusing on purely geometrical approaches. Léon and Sucar [11] developed a Bayesian model to recognize different activities, with different speed of execution for different persons. They present a very small number of movements, characterized by the global trajectory of the movement between successive images. A few years later Hongeng et al. [8] presented a new method to recognize human activities. An activity is defined as being composed by events (simple or complex) executed by an individual, or through several events that model the interaction between individuals (multiple events). The event modeling, based on the body shape and trajectory of the subject is done through the hierarchical representation of activities Medioni [9], where events are organized in level of abstraction, allowing flexibility and modularity in activity modeling. Arsic [10] proposed a system to automatically detect abnormal behavior from passengers in public transport vehicles monitored by a fixed video camera. Environment constrains lead the authors to observe the passengers actions performed by the upper body. Arsic and their collaborators modeled behavior using Bayesian Networks, postulating that behaviors like nervous, aggressive and others could be described through the combination of a set of simple activities, performed by different body parts, which they called low level actions. Hence small actions like face expressions and global body movement (sitting, rising, etc.) constituted basic actions used by the system to identify high level behavior.

4 Laban Movement Analysis

Laban Movement Analysis (LMA) is a method to observe, describe, notate and interpret human movement, developed by Rudolf Laban (1879 to 1958). Foround et al. [6] states that LMA places emphasis on the underlying motor patterns by notating how the body segments are moving, how they are supported or affected by other body parts, as well as whole body movement. A recent study by Rett J. [3], explored how LMA can be used to classify human expressive movements within human-machine interaction. Rett's work also emphasizes that LMA, based in its inherent semantics, has the potential to analyze emotional content of human actions.

Laban theory consists of several major components, though the available literature does not set a standard regarding their total numbers. The work of Norman Badler's group [1, 7] mentions five major components: Body, Space, Effort, Shape and

Relationship, though the latter is more abstract and deals/emerges from the other four, leading some studies to consider only the first four.

4.1 Body

The *Body* component deals with relative motion of body parts and the body center as well as which are moving at all. This component also deals with issues like locomotion and kinematics. More specifically, the kinematic chains try to relate the spatial *Shaping* and the inherent *Effort* qualities. Laban chose the navel as the body center. The lower part of the body is used to study the global locomotion and the upper body deals with exploring, manipulation and gesturing.

4.2 Space

The Space component presents concepts to describe the trajectory executed by the observed actor's body parts while performing a movement. These concepts are measured relative to a frame of reference determined by the body of the actor. Whilst concepts may differ in complexity of expressiveness and dimensionality, they are all reproducible in the 3-D Cartesian system and discretized in form of direction symbols [4]. Using observed trajectories, discretized in frames I along time, Rett proposed the following Bayesian model [3, 4] to estimate the movement M knowing 8 possible directions symbols A in a 2-D plane.

$$P(M \mid A\ I) \tag{1}$$

This approach, whilst not presenting outstanding results (presented in section 5), was a good indicator regarding future developments. Hence *Effort* component was implemented.

4.3 Effort

What makes the framework of LMA so special is its ability to describe an additional 'expression' that accompanies the spatial trajectory (*Space* component). It relates low-level features like velocity, acceleration and curvature to *Effort* qualities like *Time* (*E.Ti*), *Space* (*E.Sp*), *Weight* (*E.We*) and *Flow* (*E.Fl*). By retrieving some evidences about the emotional state or the intention of the performer, the *Effort* component can be seen as the key descriptor to solve the task of analyzing 'expressive movements'. Table 1 shows the *Effort* qualities, the underlying cognitive process, the subject and the two extremes that characterize each quality has [2].

Table 1. *Effort* qualities and their subjects

Effort	Cognitive Process	Subject	Extremes
Space	Attention	The Spatial Orientation	Direct / Indirect
Weight	Intention	The impact	Strong / Light
Time	Decision	The urgency	Sudden / Sustained
Flow	Progression	How to keep going	Free or Careful

Movements are described and distinguished by those qualities close to an extreme, e.g. a *Punch* movement has *Strong Weight, Sudden Time* and *Direct Space*. When a person acts sudden and vigorous/strongly, socially humans interpret these signs as someone who might be angry or violent, thus estimating themselves each other's behavior. It is reasonable to state that *Effort* descriptors approach the semantic humans use to characterize each other's movements in terms of "'expressiveness'". Following Rett's work, [12] extends and implements the *Effort* model (equation 2).

$$P(M \mid E.sp \; E.ti \; E.fl) \tag{2}$$

Knowing the *Effort* qualities *Time E.ti, Space E.sp* and *Flow E.fl* the movement M can be estimated. Despite only *Effort* and *Space* have yet been implemented, one other component is now being studied that has special interest to the behavior concept is the Shape component. At this level of the Bayesian Network, movements are hand labeled with determined *Effort* characteristics, however in the lowest level, to decide which mathematical features are dominant in each of the *Effort* qualities, a probabilistic evaluation is made [3].

4.4 Shape

Bartenieff and Lewis [2] do not define Shape a component of its own but rather a set of qualities emerging from the Body and Space components. Two Shape qualities were mentioned particularly: Shape Flow describes movements that are focused on the body itself, going towards or away from the body center and using descriptors like shrinking and growing, bulging and hollowing (also including breathing). The term Spatial Shaping is used for movements that are going towards a goal in space (e.g. reaching). It is usually described in a Euclidean frame of reference that is aligned with an initial position of the egocentric frame of reference. Due to this, movements can be described by using the vertical, horizontal and sagittal axes and relating them to bipolar descriptors like sinking and rising, enclosing and spreading, and retreating and advancing. Fig 1. shows the descriptors (left) and some exemplary movements (right).

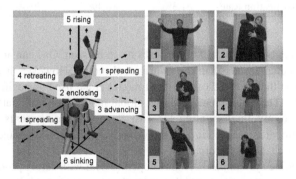

Fig. 1. The Shape component with its spatial qualities and some exemplary movements: 1. embracing, 2. hugging, 3. shake, 4. retreating 5.reaching and 6.ducking.

5 Practical Implementation

In the referred studies [4], to test the implemented *Space* model, the actor performed the movements facing one vision acquisition system. The available database encompassed eight previously learned movements, yielding this model to present 32 misclassification trials out of 95, yielding a positive classification rate of 66,31%.

To study *Effort* model [12] a database of 5 movements was designed. These movements were spatially similar, however characterized for having different combinations of *Effort* qualities. Table 2 summarizes the obtained results.

Table 2. Results for E*ffort* qualities

	Physical qualities					
	Space		Flow		Time	
	Ind	Dir	Free	Bound	Sud	Sus
Positive Results	79.3%	90.2%	61.2%	58.7%	84.8%	97.1%

In light of the presented results, LMA starts to present its true potential. It was demonstrated that spatial similar movements can be discretized using Effort parameters. The potential becomes clearer when the two already implemented models are fused in one global model (equation 3). Results are presented in Table 3.

$$P(M \mid A \mid E.sp \ E.ti \ E.fl) \tag{3}$$

Table 3. Results for *Effort* and *Space* combined

	Laban Components		
	Space	*Effort*	*Space + Effort*
Classification Rate	61.3%	86,4%	79.4%

An improvement of the overall classification can be seen. One can argue that Effort alone provides better results than the joint global model. However, it must be taken into consideration that the studies on Effort model alone used a specific database for proof of concept. The experiments with the global model took both databases used in Effort and Space. By implementing the two remaining components we expect to strengthen the global model, leading to a good movement/body language characterization in terms of Laban descriptors.

A robust tracking system has been developed to deal with actors pose changes. It is based on stereo camera system which allows the system to track body parts in 3-D space. The methodology is out of the scope of this work. Details can be found in [5].

6 Behavior Modeling

The previous section provided and debated LMA modeling results based on Bayesian network, demonstrating that the used probabilistic approach could potentiate a computational implementation of a this valuable tool for human movement characterization. Behavior has been studied [8, 10, 11] and the common fact these approaches have, is that behavior can be composed of small actions/events. With this concept in mind, this work proposed an approach based on Laban Movement Analysis, where behavior is divided in small movements and Laban parameters. Actions performed by human beings carry themselves emotion that can be expressed in form of visual cues: movements and body language. Rett [3] demonstrated that LMA could be used to identify movements. Literature [1, 2] states, that Laban semantics present a natural language to express body motion. Descriptors like sudden, strong, sinking or stretching can very well be applied when humans are trying to understand each other's behavior. Hence by knowing each of these characteristics, one can infer basic behavior actions. Using a Bayesian language, knowing movement M and Laban components *Comp* the behavior B can be estimated.

$$P(B \mid M\ Comp) \tag{4}$$

Equation (5) presents the possible space for the variable B

$$B \in \{Violent,\ Relaxed,\ Quiet,\ (...)\} \tag{5}$$

Equation (4) is the first approach to a behavior Bayesian model, and evolution of the presented work makes it a believable and innovative solution for an expected robust behavior probabilistic characterization.

6 Conclusions

The implemented LMA components presented positive results. As results demonstrated, the merging of two components improved classification, which leads to the expectation of further classification improvement with the implementation of the other Laban components in future work. Also Laban parameters are found to be good behavior descriptors with an enough abstraction degree to give models the necessary flexibility. Behavior can be divided in small events, and described through Laban parameters. Future work will lead to the final LMA global implementation and behavior parameterization with the aim to provide a robust behavior characterizer to be applied in areas like rehabilitation or surveillance.

References

1. Zhao, L.: Synthesis and Acquisition of Laban Movement Analysis Qualitative Parameters for Communicative Gestures. PhD Thesis, University of Pennsylvania (2002)
2. Bartenieff, I., Lewis, D.: Body Movement: Coping with the Environment. Gordon and Breach Science, New York (1980)

3. Rett, J.: Robot Human Interface Using Laban Movement Analysis Inside a Bayesian Framework. PhD Thesis, University of Coimbra (2009)
4. Rett, J., Santos, L., Dias, J.: Laban Movement Analysis using Multi-Ocular System. In: International Conference on Intelligent Robots and Systems, IROS (2008)
5. Prado, J., Santos, L., Dias, J.: Horopter based Dynamic Background Segmentation applied to an Interactive Mobile Robot. In: 14th International Conference on Advanced Robotics, ICAR (2009)
6. Foroud, A., Whishaw, I.Q.: Changes in the kinematic structure and non-kinematic features of movements during skilled reaching after stroke: A Laban movement analysis in two case studies. Journal of Neuroscience Methods 158, 137–149 (2006)
7. Chi, D., Costa, M., Zhao, L., Badler, N.: The emote model for effort and shape. In: SIGGRAPH 2000, Computer Graphics Proceedings. Annual Conference Series, ACM SIGGRAPH, pp. 173–182. ACM Press, New York (2000)
8. Hongeng, S., Nevatia, R., Bremond, F.: Video-based event recognition: activity representation and probabilistic recognition methods. Computer Vision and Image Understanding 96, 129–162 (2004)
9. Medioni, G., Cohen, I., Bremond, F., Hongeng, S., Nevatia, R.: Event detection and analysis from video streams. IEEE Transactions on Pattern Analysis and Machine Intelligence 23, 873–889 (2001)
10. Arsic, D., Wallhoff, F., Schuller, B., Rigoll, G.: Video based online behavior detection using probabilistic multi-stream fusion. In: Proceedings of the IEEE International Conference on Image Processing, vol. 2, pp. 606–609 (2005)
11. León, R.D., Sucar, L.E.: Continuous activity recognition with missing data. In: Proceedings of the 16th International Conference on Pattern Recognition, vol. 1, pp. 439–442 (2002)
12. Santos, L., Prado, J., Dias, J.: Human Robot Interaction Studies on Laban Human Movement Analysis and Dynamic Background Segmentation. In: 2009 IEEE/RSJ International Conference on Intelligent Robots and Systems, IROS (2009)

Self-adaptive Vision System

Tomislav Stipancic and Bojan Jerbic

University of Zagreb, Faculty of Mechanical Engineering and Naval Architecture,
Ivana Lucica 5, 10000 Zagreb, Croatia
{Tomislav.Stipancic,Bojan.Jerbic}@fsb.hr

Abstract. Light conditions represent an important part of every vision application. This paper describes one active behavioral scheme of one particular active vision system. This behavioral scheme enables an active system to adapt to current environmental conditions by constantly validating the amount of the reflected light using luminance meter and dynamically changed significant vision parameters. The purpose of the experiment was to determine the connections between light conditions and inner vision parameters. As a part of the experiment, Response Surface Methodology (RSM) was used to predict values of vision parameters with respect to luminance input values. RSM was used to approximate an unknown function for which only few values were computed. The main output validation system parameter is called Match Score. Match Score indicates how well the found object matches the learned model. All obtained data are stored in the local database. By timely applying new parameters predicted by the RSM, the vision application works in a stabile and robust manner.

Keywords: Active vision system, self adaptation, active behavioral scheme, experiment planning, response surface methodology.

1 Introduction

The development of robotics is dictated by increasing demands of humanity. Today's robots are involved in almost all areas of human activity, namely: medicine, technology, research and accessibility of hazardous or unclean areas, etc. Service Robotic is a term that appears to indicate just one step in robot evolution. This evolution moves from the simplest industrial robots and goes to the highly sophisticated personal robots, which aim to be universal. Such robots would be able to exist alone in the surroundings just like human beings, regardless of their original purposes. The prerequisite for intelligent behavior of any artificial system is thus the ability to perceive its environment [1]. To do that, it is necessary to establish some kind of active sensing structure which is able to deliver timely fresh information to the system. Such a structure has to have the capability to determine what to do with the acquired information and to make proper decisions with respect to timely appropriate actions. Information detection and determining what to do with the collected information in a controlled manner is an approach in robotics called Active Sensing [2]. Such systems can often contain different subsystems responsible for different behavioral schemes. There are trends in today's robotics which are suggesting that robotic systems have to include

L.M. Camarinha-Matos, P. Pereira, and L. Ribeiro (Eds.): DoCEIS 2010, IFIP AICT 314, pp. 195–202, 2010.
© IFIP International Federation for Information Processing 2010

the active sensing unit with one or more active behavioral schemes. Active Sensing Unit has to decide what behavioral scheme to choose according to an actual environmental savior or actual system needs and to seek optimal solutions to make desired actions. For example, Active Placement Scheme can be related to the vision sensor positioning, Active Vision Parameter Scheme can be related to the proper vision parameter determination, Active Calibration Scheme can be related to the timely calibration of vision sensors, Active Model Construction Scheme can be related to the 3D object interpretation, Active Illumination Scheme can be used for choosing proper light sources at the right moment, etc. [2]. In the proposed approach it is very easy to find similarities with human beings because they cannot imagine their life without the system of active perception. Humans collect new information with their vision sensors – eyes. The brain is constantly analyzing and triangulating its 3D environment combining collected information with previously collected experience and knowledge, defining distances and relationships between objects in the observed scene. Active eyes usage goes to such lengths that people sometimes automatically change the viewing angle and object distances in order to complement missing information.

This article describes one behavioral scheme as a part of the research related to the Active Sensing. The main task of this particular behavioral scheme is to take care of the active vision parameter adaptation and it will be the part of the robotic system which conducts two more schemes: Active Calibration Scheme and Active Positioning Scheme. Active Vision Parameter Adaptation Scheme provides the needed vision acquisition accuracy and decreases the level of noise which can occur in constantly changing environmental conditions. High accuracy and low level of noise are very important for robotic vision, especially in assembly or disassembly operations where robots have to precisely manipulate with small parts, often in poor light conditions. The proposed scheme decreases the need for special light sources and techniques which are the most common vision application ingredients. The main accent was set on an experiment planning by using Response Surface Methodology (RSM) to develop Active Vision Parameter Adaptation Scheme. RSM [3] was used to determine the connection between input and output parameters at the beginning. Luminance in the room was used as an input parameter value. Intrinsic vision sensor parameters, such as Brightness and Gain, were used as an output value. Great potential lies in experiment planning [4]. In order to have optimal application output results it is very important to see a picture large enough at the beginning. Such an approach enables us to have better understanding of parameters dependences and gives the opportunity to guide the experiment to produce better results at the end. The presented scheme can be also used as a framework for other applications, because almost all vision sensors have similar or the same input vision sensor parameters. Along with such a conclusion, the analyzed idea was presented like a framework in order to facilitate easier future reproduction of the concept for everyone.

2   Contribution to Technological Innovation

Traditional methods for machine vision to better interpret scenes are usually focused on post- image processing. Usually, these approaches deal with current states to extract more information about the object surfaces AFTER vision sensor taking the pictures. Approach proposed in this paper is focused on adaptation of the vision system to the current light conditions BEFORE vision sensor taking the pictures. Such an approach facilitates further vision analysis and saves time-consuming enhancement processing, which is very important in a machine vision system, especially for real-time applications [2].

3 Equipment and Software

A Basler scA1400-17fc camera was used to acquire images from the object in the scene. The main characteristics of this camera are relatively high resolution (1392 × 1040 px) and color image representation. It is rather small and suitable for mounting directly to the robot hand. In this application, the camera was connected with the NI Compact Vision System (NI CVS - 1456) which was used for image acquisition and later image processing. The CVS is an all-in-one vision system which comes from National Instruments Company and contains a processor, a memory, an operating system and an I/O interface. The vision application set-up was carried out by means of the NI Vision Builder for Automated Inspection (VBAI) software, based on NI LabView and containing a number of tools for image acquisition, image preprocessing and processing, system communication with other external devices, etc. This software has to be installed on a PC. After the application configuration, the next step was to upload all data from the PC into the CVS, responsible for all later actions regarding the vision application. Fig. 1 shows the equipment and the hardware system configuration used in the experiment.

Fig. 1. Equipment and hardware system configuration

The device for measuring the luminance is called a luminance meter. In this application the XYL-III All Digital Luminance-meter was used. To provide measurements and later data analysis this device can be connected to a PC via RS-232 interface. Luminance describes the amount of light leaving a surface in a particular direction and can be thought of as the measured brightness of the surface as seen by the eye or a vision sensor and it is very important for this particular application [5]. It is expressed in Candelas per square foot, or more commonly, Candelas per square meter (Cd/m^2).

4 Experiment Description

Reliability of scene inspection by a vision system is strongly connected to the set of parameters chosen for a specific vision application [1]. If environmental conditions change over time, these parameters should either be optimized at the beginning of the process or changed on-line constantly. By changing vision parameters on-line constantly, vision system attains fresh information during the time which results with relatively high robustness and precision. The first step of the Active Vision Parameter Adaptation Scheme development was to make an experiment which was crucial for dependence determination of inner parameters. Beside that, the experiment brings hidden information on the system response regarding different input values. Such information can help in determining weak points of the experiment enabling better process understanding and optimization. The relationship between input and output factors was provided by means of Response Surface Methodology (RSM). The RSM [6] can be found as a part of the Design Expert software [7] which was used in this particular case and it represents a collection of mathematical and statistical techniques used for process optimization and analysis. It consists of a group of techniques that can be used in the empirical study of relationships between one or more measured responses with an arbitrary number of input factors. It comprises: designing a set of experiments, determining a mathematical model and the optimal value of the response, thus providing a better understanding of the overall system behavior. The empirical relationship is frequently obtained by fitting polynomial models. The main purpose of the first and the second order experiment designs was data collection for fitting such models. The first order polynomial model can be expressed by the general Equation 1,

$$y = \beta_0 + \sum_{j=1}^{k} \beta_j x_j + \varepsilon \tag{1}$$

where y is response, β_0, β_1,... β_k are the unknown regression parameters, x_1, x_2,... x_k are the input factors, k is the number of input factors and ε is random error. The CCD (Central Composite Design) was used to describe responses and to estimate parameters in the model. This design consists of a factorial portion, an axial portion and a centre point. It's well suited for fitting a quadratic surface, which usually works well for the process optimization. If the distance from the center of the design space to a factorial point is ±1 unit for each factor (Table 1.), the distance from the center of the design space to a star point is ±α with |α| > 1. The precise value of α depends on certain properties chosen for the design and on the number of factors involved. Applied load and sliding distance were considered as model variables. So, with respect to the system input parameters (Luminance and Match Score), the system will use output factors (Gain and Brightness) previously predicted by means of the RSM.

Table 1. Factors for response surface study

Factor	Unit	Low Level (-1)	High Level (+1)
Luminance	Cd / m^2	0	300
Match Score	-	800	1000

A particular vision tool called Match Color Pattern Vision Tool (Fig. 2.) was used to detect an object in the field of view. This tool can be found as a part of the vision software (VBAI). In the beginning of the configuration, the tool has to learn a template which contains an object(s) or a feature(s) of interest in the first line. Later, with respect to the learned template, the vision tool searches for similarities in the field of view. The match score is a value that indicates how similar a potential match is to the template image and it ranges from 0 to 1000. A score of 1000 indicates the perfect match. It was determined that a value lower then 800 of the match score results with positioning error which was too large for the developed vision application. Such values were not taken into consideration. The presented method can be used in combination with different vision tools for different purposes.

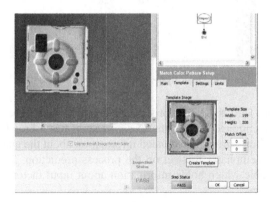

Fig. 2. Match Pattern Color Vision Tool setup

During the experiment, a luminance value ranged between 0 and 300 cd/m^2. The experiment was made far from windows. This resulted with relatively stabile light conditions without high values of sunlight illumination. To provide even more stabile conditions, windows were covered with curtains. It was very important to repeat the experiment in different light conditions to analyze as many possibilities as possible which resulted in a more robust application. A luminance measurement was taken with and without curtains on windows and neon lights switched on and off. A gain value represents the number of times a vision device amplifies a light input. It can be very useful in poor light conditions where it is necessary to make a more visible scene. Gain values ranged between 192 and 1023. An image brightness definition was connected with a pixel definition and it ranged between 0 and 255.

The Design-Expert software was used for the experiment design and analysis. The Design-Expert contains a set of statistical and numerical tools that can be used for processes optimizations, predictions, etc. The first step of the experiment design was to enter information about the Central Composite Design - CCD (Alpha Level, Center Points, etc.) and information about the analyzed vision application (Table 1). The software led us to define a missing portion of the CCD. By entering the data, the Design-Expert calculates the coded distance "alpha" for placement on the star points. The next step was to make a real experiment by combining data provided by the Design-Expert and to acquire responses. For the purposes of this experiment, 13 input factor variations (Figure 4) were collected and analyzed.

Std	Run	Block	Factor 1 A:Luminance cd/m2	Factor 2 B:Match Score -	Response 1 Gain -	Response 2 Brightness -
1	5	Block 1	0.00	800.00	856	223
2	11	Block 1	300.00	800.00	203	14
3	6	Block 1	0.00	1000.00	1004	232
4	1	Block 1	300.00	1000.00	260	83
5	13	Block 1	0.00	900.00	897	211
6	4	Block 1	362.13	900.00	241	11
7	9	Block 1	150.00	758.58	440	147
8	2	Block 1	150.00	1000.00	501	161
9	3	Block 1	150.00	900.00	444	152
10	12	Block 1	150.00	900.00	444	152
11	7	Block 1	150.00	900.00	444	152
12	10	Block 1	150.00	900.00	444	152
13	8	Block 1	150.00	900.00	444	152

Fig. 3. Design – Expert Layout Table

By filling values into the table, process of designing the experiment was completed. As it was mentioned before, the Design-Expert has a broad set of numerical and statistical tools for extracting extended information about the analyzed process. In this paper the main emphasis was set on the process prediction. Figure 5 shows the Point Prediction Table which holds information about input factor combinations and their related responses.

Factor	Name	Level	Low Level	High Level	Std. Dev.	Coding		
A	Luminance	158.11	0.000	300.00	0.000	Actual		
B	Match Score	862.16	800.00	1000.00	0.000	Actual		
Response	Prediction	SE Mean	95% CI low	95% CI high	SE Pred	95% PI low	95% PI high	
Gain	411.431	7.52	393.64	429.22	18.75	367.09	455.77	
Brightness	140.54	3.85	131.43	149.65	9.61	117.82	163.26	

Factors Tool
Gauges Sheet
Default
A Luminance +
B:Match Score +
158.108

Fig. 4. Design – Expert Layout Table along with Factors Tool Window

Input factor values can be changed by means of the Factor Tool Window. It is sufficient to move the slider placed at the Factors Tool Window to see new responses with respect to the input values. The Design – Expert Layout Table provides information used for future point prediction optimizations of this application. The next configuration step was related to the data storage into the database.

5 Vision Application Description

The Active Vision Parameter Adaptation Scheme described in this article contains: a vision application (NI Compact Vision System – software and hardware), a PC, a luminance meter and a database. The PC was used as a host of the Active Behavioral Unit and the vision software (VBAI). The main task of the Active Behavioral Unit was to provide communication and data management between all system components. It is a fact that the vision sensor takes pictures of the object from different angles and positions in the space. That results in timely different light conditions between picture shots. To ensure relatively similar conditions for taking pictures from different positions, the vision system gets new vision parameters from the database before taking new pictures. Information acquired from the luminance meter was the main criteria for determining which parameters to pick from the database. Figure 6 shows the active sensing flowchart which describes one common "pick-and-place" robot application.

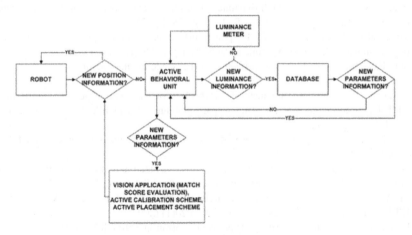

Fig. 5. Active Sensing flowchart

6 Conclusion

This paper provides a description of a particular Active Behavioral Scheme which is included in one bigger robotic system that relies on the Active Sensing paradigm. Described scheme enables the system to become much more robust and to become relatively resistant to timely new light conditions in the observed scene. The vision parameters determination is provided by means of Response Surface Methodology which can also be used for an experiment weak point determination. Instead of using the RSM, future work will be related to usage of neural networks in connections between input and output parameters determination. It would be interesting to analyze influence of other factors to vision application too (such as measuring of the room ambient light). The research described in this article will be a part of a PhD Thesis where the main emphasis will be set on Active Placement Scheme which is taking care of spatial positioning of the Vision Sensor [8].

References

1. Stipancic, T., Curkovic, P., Jerbic, B.: Robust autonomous assembly in environment with relatively high level of uncertainty. In: 10th International Conference on the Modern Information Technology in the Innovation Processes of the Industrial Enterprises, Prague, pp. 193–198 (2008)
2. Chen, S., Li, Y., Zhang, J., Wang, W.: Active Sensor Planning for Multiview Vision Tasks. Springer, Berlin (2008)
3. Box, G.E.P., Wilson, K.B.: The exploration and exploitation of response surfaces: some general considerations and examples. Biometrics 10, 16–60 (1954)
4. Stipancic, T., Curkovic, P., Jerbic, B.: Substantial vision application settings analysis. In: CIM 2009 - Computer integrated manufacturing and high speed machining, Biograd, pp. 217–220 (2009)
5. Inanici, M.: Evaluation of high dynamic range photography as a luminance data acquisition system. Lighting Research and Technology 38(2), 123–134 (2006)
6. Myers, R.H., Montgomery, D.C.: Response surface methodology: process and product optimization using designed experiments. John Wiley and Sons, New York (1995)
7. Stat–Ease, Inc., Users Guide: Multifactor RSM & General One-Factor, http://www.statease.com
8. Curkovic, P., Jerbic, B., Stipancic, T.: Hybridization of adaptive genetic algorithm and ART 1 neural architecture for efficient path planning of a mobile robot. Transaction of FAMENA, Zagreb (2008)
9. Khuri, A.I., Cornell, J.A.: Response surfaces: design and analyses. Marcel and Decker, New York (1997)
10. Gupta, S., Manohar, C.S.: An improved response surface method for the determination of failure probability and importance measures. Structural Safety 26, 123–139 (2004)
11. Li, Y.F.: Uncalibrated Euclidean 3-D Reconstruction Using an Active Vision System. IEEE Transaction on Robotics and Automation 20(1) (2004)
12. Raissi, S., Farsani, R.E.: Statistical Process Optimization Through Multi-Response Surface Methodology. In: Proceedings of World Academy of Science, Engineering and Technology, Hong Kong, vol. 51 (2009)
13. Denzler, J., Brown, C.: Information theoretic sensor data selection for active object recognition and state estimation. IEEE Transactions on Pattern Analysis and Machine Intelligence 24, 145–157 (2002)
14. Curkovic, P., Jerbic, B., Stipancic, T.: Cooperative Coevolutionary approach to dual arm robots' operation. In: Annals of DAAAM for 2008 & PROCEEDINGS of 19th International DAAAM Symposium, Vienna, pp. 341–342 (2008)
15. Curkovic, P., Jerbic, B., Stipancic, T.: Swarm-based Approach to Path Planning Using Honey-bees Mating Algorithm and ART Neural Network. Solid State Phenomena, 147–149 (2009)

Part 7

Robots and Manipulation

Right-Arm Robotic-Aided-Therapy with the Light-Exoskeleton: A General Overview

Luis I. Lugo-Villeda, Antonio Frisoli, Edoardo Sotgiu,
Giovanni Greco, and Massimo Bergamasco

Perceptual Robotics, Scuola Superiore Sant'Anna, via Rinaldo Piaggio, 34,
56025 - Pontedera (Pisa), Italy
{l.lugovilleda,a.frisoli,massimo.bergamasco}@sssup.it

Abstract. Rehabilitation robotics applications and their developments have been spreading out as consequences of the actual needs in the human activities of daily living (ADL). Exoskeletons for rehabilitation are one of them, whose intrinsic characteristics are quite useful for applications where repetitive, robustness and accurate performance are a must. As a part of robotic-mediated-rehabilitation programme into the worldwide, the exoskeletons are trying to improve the ADL of disable people through the fusion of several disciplines that lets to expand the capabilities of wearing a powered robotic exoskeletal device for rehabilitation tasks. This fact deserves to present this contribution from a general scope point of view, i.e., the technologies integration and its associated knowledge. So far, the Light-Exoskeleton which is intended for human arm rehabilitation in post-stroke patients is introduced. Preliminary experimental results as well as the involved stages about the system show the capabilities of using a robotic-constrained-rehabilitation for human arm.

Keywords: Exoskeletons, Robotic-Aided-Rehabilitation, Emerging Technologies Integration, Robotic Constrained Therapy.

1 Introduction

Robotic-Aided-Rehabilitation is one of the most multidisciplinary emerging fields that has been studied for several decades; it is due to the synergetic ability to use the interaction of robots into the disable humans-workspace as part of the rehabilitation robotics realm [4]. Actually, rehabilitation robotics belongs to the so-called program *Health Workforce* of the WHO (World Health Organization) wherein this technology is one of the forces driving such a program [12]. According to U.S. Centers for Disease Control and Prevention and the American Heart Association [2], 80,000,000 American adults (one in three) have one or more types of cardiovascular disease (CVD), of whom 38,100,000 are estimated to be age 60 or older, this represents as total direct and indirect amount of CVD for 2008 of $475.3 billion. Similar conditions are prevailing in Italy and EU countries; therefore, boosting the application of rehabilitation robotics for assisting people to recover their normal daily-living skills is quite essential. But what does rehabilitation robotics involve? The meaningful answer in our context leads to define it as follows:

L.M. Camarinha-Matos, P. Pereira, and L. Ribeiro (Eds.): DoCEIS 2010, IFIP AICT 314, pp. 205–214, 2010.
© IFIP International Federation for Information Processing 2010

Rehabilitation Robotics *is the multi-disciplinary field which concerns with restoring a disable person to an acceptable level of whether physical, mental or even social interaction with him/her environment by means of applied robotics, emerging technologies and health care areas.*

This definition helps to assess the robotic-mediated-therapy as an area of rehabilitation robotics, offering the capabilities to improve the gradual outcome of post-stroke patients engaged on rehabilitation of neuromotor control in comparison with conventional therapy [14]. Also the idea of robotic-mediated-therapy is an opportunity to innovate and improve trough new emerging fields the rehabilitation endeavour field. Here, we present some advantages by using our upper limb rehabilitation demonstrator in comparison with other approaches.

2 Contribution to Technological Innovation

Despite of these impressive achievements regarding exoskeletons, it has been said, they are in the early stage due to the involved fields that need being enhanced [15]. Nevertheless, as long as we unify important concepts with their associated technology, new trends along the technological innovation stream are arising for exploiting at maximum the application of such devices into rehabilitation fields.

Particularly, two of the foremost goals are presented as innovative:

1. The Robotic-Constrained-Therapy (RCT) which has been conceptualised as the application of constrained kinematics and constrained dynamics into a framework for treating the problem of upper limbs plasticity at the level of arm's joints.
2. The inclusion of nonlinear controllers that our best knowledge, they are practically unknown, but those present important characteristics managing the total energy of the closed-loop to be passive in every time and controlling the parametric and non parametric uncertainties induced by the patient's tremor.

2.1 Contribution to Technological Innovation Trough Emerging Fields

The contribution of this article is three-fold:

1. A robotic-aided-rehabilitation platform is generally presented under the rehabilitation robotics philosophy.
2. A general landscape of the novelty robotic constrained therapy is introduced.
3. Preliminary results are promising, such that the proposed platform is ready to undergo to real disable patients at the Cisanello hospital, Pisa, Italy, as the immediate future work.

2.2 Organization

The outline of this contribution is organized as follows. Section 3 shows the actual work into this field. The proposed system under the robotics rehabilitation trends is given into Section 4. Besides this a set of experimental results on healthy people is shown into Section 5. Section 6 presents, a set of discussions about the obtained results. Finally the conclusions and future work are given in Section 7.

3   Related Work

We describe the actual work driven by two major key approaches [11]:

3.1   Fixed-Frame Exoskeletons

In the first classification, we have the Armin II, an *exoskeleton* for human-arm rehabilitation whose 6 DoF have been used in conjunction with virtual environments,
suitable for helping post-stroke patients. The exoskeleton uses a simple *PD plus gravity compensation* controller to obtain apparently interactive forces, which are computed on the basis of the virtual environment interaction by an impedance controller
[5]. A 7-DoF upper-limb exoskeleton which can be used for therapeutic diagnostics
and for physiotherapy or as a haptic device in virtual reality simulation is presented in
[6], however it does not introduces neither the techniques for doing rehabilitation nor
the control scheme for assuring stability[1].

3.2   End-Effector Devices

In the second category, we have more devices to analyse, but all of them are very
competitive. Mostly of *end-effector devices* have been gone under the commercial
track, that is the case of the MIT Manus[7], A pantograph-based manipulator which
works into 2-D, it is constituted by a Stanford manipulator which trains patients who
have suffered an stroke and have lost arm motor skills. The main purpose of MIT-
Manus is guiding the human-arm and works in conjunction with a virtual environment for displaying the desired and real reaching exercise carried out by the patient.
Another example is the Mirror Image Movement Enabler system, [8], a PUMA 560-
based robot, which can impose bilateral 3-D force-position motions. Likewise, the
Bi-manu-track robot for upper-limbs rehabilitation uses active practise of forearm
movements, such as pronation/supination, and wrist flexion/extension into mirror
like fashion [9]. EU Gentle/s Project presents a 3 degree-of-freedom (DoF) haptic
device for right-handed subjects, which uses virtual environments for reaching exercises to tackle the arm tracking problem by using a path planning based on smooth
polynomials [10]. Finally, ARM-guide [11] drives the forearm along a linear position profile into 2-D space having guided force training in joint space. It is clear that
in robotic-mediated-rehabilitation devices either exoskeletons or end-effector devices, the virtual reality technology enhances the performance of upper-limb post-
stroke rehabilitation [3].

4   The Rehabilitation Robotics Platform

This section is devoted to present our proposed platform for carrying out the arm
therapy by using a right-arm exoskeleton.

---

[1] Notice that both exoskeletons belong to fixed-inertial frame exoskeletons.

4.1 The Light-Exoskeleton Architecture

The general scheme is presented in the Fig. 1.b). The system is clearly composed by the Light-Exoskeleton and its hardware/software integration; the therapist that handles the therapy session uses a workstation which contains the set of projected scenarios into the screen, following the clinical protocol and giving instructions to the patient during the rehabilitation sessions. The Light-Exoskeleton[2] is a right-arm assistant device, it is composed of five degree-of-freedom (DoF), it is capable of feeding the patient-arm with bio-mechanical force-feedback through the four-active DoF (using four-PWM controlled motors), and the last DoF is used for computing the exerted force direction in the operational space.

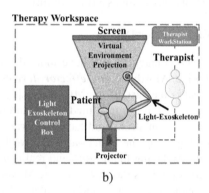

a)   b)

Fig. 1. The right–arm robotics rehabilitation platform. a) Light-exoskeleton architecture. b) Upper-part rehabilitation workspace.

The corresponding generalized coordinates are measured by digital encoders such that the vector $\mathbf{q} = \{q_1, q_2, q_3, q_4, q_5 \in \mathbb{R}\}$ corresponds with the human arm motions, i.e., adduction/abduction, flexion/extension, internal/external rotation, forearm flexion/extension and finally pronation/supination. In addition, one important variable is defined in order to analyse the arm's behaviour, the triplet $\mathbf{X}_h \in \mathbb{R}^3$ which stands as the temporal space variable of hand-palm; that vector is mapped onto the virtual scenario workspace for the interaction with video-game-like exercises. The exerted force by the patient's hand-palm is measured by means of a three-axial 100N force sensor, $\boldsymbol{\lambda} = \{\lambda_x, \lambda_y, \lambda_z \in \mathbb{R}\}$, see Fig. 1.a). One of the foremost goals of this platform is helping post—stroke (acute mild to moderate) patients handling their arm-stiffness and recovering the neurocontrol of their arm using the constrained kinematics and dynamics; also the brain plasticity through several kinesthetic coordination exercises is treated.

---

[2] Hereafter Light-Exoskeleton could be called for short L-Exos.

4.2   Involved Technologies, Knowledge and Their Trends to the Innovation

The performance of the rehabilitation platform depends on the application of several important areas such that innovative concepts and paradigms arise depending on the defined outcomes into arm rehabilitation as well as the patient's conditions. The set of relevant areas are described as follows.

- *Applied Robotics.* This field is quite important because trough the constrained kinematics and constrained dynamics we can handle the patient's limbs to move either a maximum or minimum angular displacement depending on the clinical protocol; for instance, the weighted-iterative inverse kinematics lets to get working more the internal/external rotation than arm adduction/abduction, but maintaining the angular position set $q \in \mathbb{R}^5$ in the Jacobian-null-space, whereas the dynamics of the system is modeled as a Differential-Algebraic-Equation (DAE index-2) yielded by the Lagrange formalism [13], representing the motion equations of the exoskeleton in non-free motion, i.e., including the contact of L-Exos with the patient. Likewise, these approaches are attempting in the best case to emulate the occupational therapist in contact with the patient arm; regulating force and position simultaneously or separately depending on the clinical procedure.

- *Applied Nonlinear Control.* This field is required and innovative into this platform; because of the applications of several nonlinear controllers have demonstrated better performance than linear ones as used on the related work [15]. The whole energy of the system should remain passive (controlled) all time, and these nonlinear controllers gather that condition. Also, the free-model nonlinear controllers are desirable and largely unknown at our best knowledge; it is due to many exoskeletons for rehabilitation have been designed for neuroscience or biomechanical groups, and with only a *proportional plus derivative with gravity compensation* controllers are used but neglecting all parametric non-modeled patient-induced uncertainties. Therefore, the next set of operation modes have it bases on the nonlinear controllers design:

  1. *Position Mode.* This mode lets the robot to take the control of the upper limbs transferring their position and perhaps their orientation; the patient—limbs are passive.
  2. *Triggered-Gains Position Mode.* In this mode, the patient starts applying a force for triggering the motion; the exerted force by the patient modules the percentage of the robot's help, adjusting the gains of the position controller which tracks the imposed trajectory in the task.
  3. *Composed Force/position Control Mode.* The patient is constrained by a defined task in terms of kinesthetic forces and positions onto his/her workspace; it induces active resistance to patient improving in this manner the patient coordination effort.
  4. *Direct Force Mode.* The patients can freely move their arm into a defined space wherein just the exerted force is controlled.
  5. *Open Loop Mode.* This option lets to patient interacting with the virtual environment trough several video-game-like applications; the patients use their actual skills for playing games but exerting forces and positions of their limbs according the game responses.

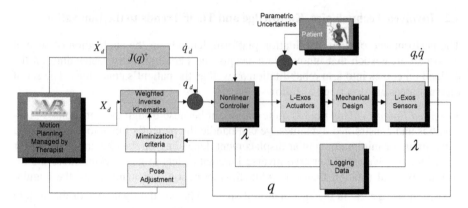

Fig. 2. The general closed-loop scheme, the path planning is generated according the virtual reality application into XVR software; afterwards the kinematics and dynamics establish the rehabilitation operation modes trough nonlinear controller described above.

- *Virtual Environments.* The virtual scenarios render more interactively the rehabilitation, attracting the full concentration of the patient, at the degree that they feel very comfortable in front of video-game-like applications for carrying out the session. Those scenarios include shapes to be tracked into spatial coordinates within the video-game-like virtual reality application, wherein the therapist can vary parameters like, the target distance, the number of trials, the timing, the maximum force, the depth, see Figure 3.
- *Bio-Signals*: The analysis of other signals coming from the muscles(EMG) different from the system's states are a good option for measuring the effectiveness and progress of the therapy[16]; even we could know whether the exoskeleton is not well-aligned with the patient-arm rotation axes.

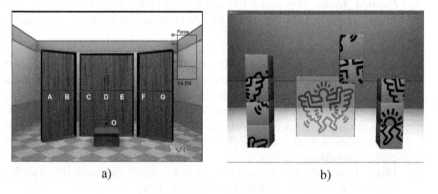

a)   b)

Fig. 3. Virtual reality applications with force sensing. a) The reaching video-game-like application, it will be used for our trials. b) Cubes application, it consists into a 3-dimensional puzzle to be organised by the patients.

- *Medical Assessment*: It includes several scales for assessing a rehabilitation session: a) The Fugl-Meyer scale, b) Modified Ashworth scale, (c) Range of Motion, etc.
- *Robotic Constrained Therapy (RCT)*: The main idea of this statement is to constrain from the kinematical and dynamical point of view the right-arm joints, such as the real therapist does; The magnitude of range motion depends on the clinical protocol and it is directly programmed and adjusted into the GUI (graphical user interface) of the therapist's workstation as long as the patient is able to perform an exercise.

5 Preliminary Experimental Results

Some preliminary experiments were carried out by a healthy people; nevertheless, similar results are expected on real disable people. We have chosen the presented task of the Fig.3.a) which is one of the most used tasks into rehabilitation, *the reaching task*. It consists into tracking from initial point to the final point and vice versa a spatial target in a determined lapse; in this experiment we used the first kind of operation mode[3] a virtual scenario and the minimum-jerk-criterion for the path planning. Firstly, notice that in Fig.4 the *constrained kinematics* is working with the same desired target but with different weights of shoulder joints; the main outcome relies on getting adduction/abduction arm motion to be minimum when varying its weight, $w_1 = 1, w_1 = 50, w_1 = 100;$ but the arm requires more effort for reaching the target on the external/internal rotation; thus constraining the first joint motion. Secondly, Fig. 5 shows the reaching task into spatial coordinates in terms of the hand-palm position $\mathbf{X}_h \in \mathbb{R}^3$ for one target, the constraining planes work like big potential fields that return the hand-palm of the patient when it tries to go away from the

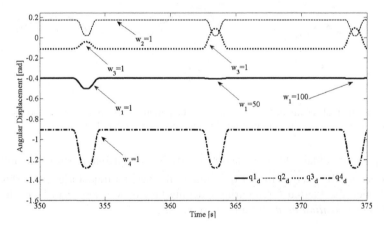

Fig. 4. The constrained kinematics using the weighted iterative inverse kinematics. Notice that the adduction/abduction is working less as long as its weight is bigger.

---

[3] The remaining operation modes are working with healthy people but not presented here.

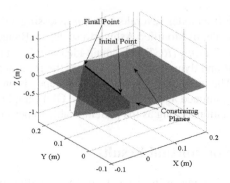

Fig. 5. The constrained dynamics is used into the nonlinear controller; we have constrained the hand-palm to move only onto the desired trajectory by introducing two constraining planes

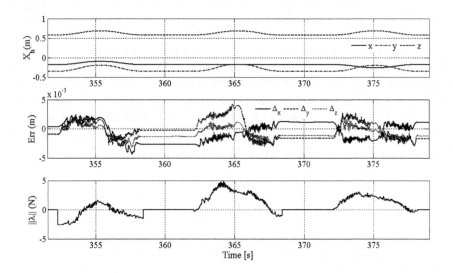

Fig. 6. Experimental results of the hand-palm of the patient, the Cartesian error and the exerted force along the trajectory during three-reaching targets in arm rehabilitation

desired position. Finally for three targets the desired and actual position, the low spatial errors, and the exerted force $\lambda \in \mathbb{R}^3$ along the desired trajectories have shown in Fig.6. Notice the exerted force during reaching task is not more than 5 Newton; we used the same *position mode* for all experiments.

6   Discussions

Until now, this contribution remains on the edge of performing the proposed approach on healthy patients and the other control modes deserve more attention; nowadays clinical pilot trials are actively working. The importance of presenting the required tools is a must. It is clear that many drawbacks are still being a challenge, because of the complexity of the L-Exos and the different behaviour of the patient to patient. The performance of getting a successful rehabilitation platform obeys to the correct use of the involved technologies and its associated knowledge; to our best knowledge, the constrained robotics presents the advantages so clear with respect to other works.

7 Conclusions and Future Work

We are presenting the involved disciplines for having stable right-arm rehabilitation. We introduce the Light-Exoskeleton which is intended for human arm rehabilitation suitable for post-stroke patients who present problems with normal arm skill motions. Several kinds of operation modes in non free motion make the system robust, accessible and feasible to be used in disable people. The constrained kinematics and dynamics foster the arm therapy to the robotic constrained therapy as innovative concept; thereby the robot represents the physician as long as we draw advantages from the emerging fields. Preliminary experimental results are shown as well as the involved stages about the system. The neuroplasticity can be managed via kinesthetic channel and coordinated motions imposed by the L-Exos, but always under the supervision of the physician or therapist. As near future work, the application on real patients is actually working as an eight-month clinical programme for assisting arm impaired people at Cisanello Hospital, Pisa, Italy. Also different scenarios are being programmed according to patients needs.

References

1. Hillman, M.: Rehabilitation robotics from past to present a historical perspective. In: Bien, Z.Z., Stefanov, D. (eds.) Advances in Rehabilitation Robotics. LNCIS, vol. 306, pp. 25–44. Springer, Heidelberg (2004)
2. Organization, W.H.: The world health report 2006: working together for health, Technical report 92 4 156317 6, WHO (2006)
3. The American Heart Association: Heart disease & stroke statistics, our guide to current statistics and the supplement to our heart & stroke facts 2009 update. Technical Report 1, American Heart Association (2009)
4. Prange, G.B., Jannink, M.J., Groothuis-Oudshoorn, C.G., Hermens, H.J., Ijzerman, M.J.: Systematic review of the effect of robot-aided therapy on recovery of the hemiparetic arm after stroke. J. Rehabil. Res. Dev. 43(2), 171–184 (2006)
5. Nef, T., Mihelj, M., Kiefer, G., Perndl, C., Muller, R., Riener, R.: Armin – exoskeleton for arm therapy in stroke patients. In: IEEE 10th International Conference on Rehabilitation Robotics, ICORR 2007, pp. 68–74 (2007)
6. Perry, J., Rosen, J.: Design of a 7 degree-of-freedom upper-limb powered exoskeleton. In: The First IEEE/RAS EMBS International Conference on Biomedical Robotics and Biomechatronics, BioRob 2006, pp. 805–810 (2006)
7. Krebs, H.I., Hogan, N., Volpe, B.T., Aisen, M.L., Diels, C.: Overview of clinical trials with mit-manus: a robot-aided neuro-rehabilitation facility. Technol. Health Care 7(6), 419–423 (1999)

8. Lum, P., Burgar, C., Van der Loos, M., Shor, P., Majmundar, M., Yap, R.: The mime robotic system for upper-limb neuro-rehabilitation: results from a clinical trial in subacute stroke. In: 9th International Conference on Rehabilitation Robotics, ICORR 2005, June-1 July 2005, pp. 511–514 (2005)

9. Schmidt, H., Hesse, S., Werner, C., Bardeleben, A.: Upper and lower extremity robotic devices to promote motor recovery after stroke -recent developments. In: 26th Annual International Conference of the IEEE Engineering in Medicine and Biology Society, IEMBS 2004, vol. 2, pp. 4825–4828 (2004)

10. Amirabdollahian, F., Loureiro, R., Harwin, W.: A case study on the effects of a haptic interface on human arm movements with implications for rehabilitation robotics. In: Proceedings of 1st Cambridge Workshop on Universal Access and Assistive Technology (CWUAAT) incorporating 4th Cambridge Workshop on Rehabilitation Robotics), pp. 17–24 (2002)

11. Reinkensmeyer, D., Dewald, J., Rymer, W.: Guidance-based quantification of arm impairment following brain injury: a pilot study. IEEE Transactions on Rehabilitation Engineering 7(1), 1–11 (1999)

12. Burdea, G.: Keynote address: Virtual rehabilitation-benefits and challenges. In: 1st International Workshop on Virtual Reality Rehabilitation (Mental Health, Neurological, Physical, Vocational) VRMHR 2002 Lausanne, Switzerland, pp. 1–11 (2002)

13. Spong, M.W., Hutchinson, S., Vidyasagar, M.: Robot Modeling and Control, 1st edn. John Wiley and Sons, USA (2006)

14. Lugo-Villeda, L.I., Frisoli, A., Parra-Vega, V., Bergamasco, M.: Robust tracking of the light–exoskeleton for arm rehabilitation tasks. In: IEEE-IFAC 9th International Symposium of Robot Control 2009, pp. 823–828 (2009)

15. Lugo-Villeda, L.I., Frisoli, A., Parra-Vega, V., Bergamasco, M.: Regressor–free force/position control of fixed–base exoskeletons for rehabilitation tasks. In: Conference on Intelligent RObots and Systems. The 2009 IEEE/RSJ International (IROS 2009), pp. 1639–1645 (2009)

16. Lugo-Villeda, L.I., Frisoli, A.,, Sandoval-Gonzalez, B.M., et al.: Haptic Guidance of Light-Exoskeleton for Arm-Rehabilitation Tasks. In: Symposium on Human Interactive Communication (RO-MAN 2009). The 8th IEEE/RAS International, p. 189 (2009)

Grasp Exploration for 3D Object Shape Representation Using Probabilistic Map

Diego R. Faria, Ricardo Martins, and Jorge Dias

Institute of Systems and Robotics,
Department of Electrical Engineering and Computers, University of Coimbra – Polo II,
3030-290 Coimbra, Portugal
{diego,rmartins,jorge}@isr.uc.pt

Abstract. In this work it is shown the representation of 3D object shape acquired from grasp exploration. Electromagnetic motion tracking sensors are used on the fingers for object contour following to acquire the 3D points to represent its shape using a probabilistic volumetric map. It is used the object referential for its representation. For that, it is found the center of mass of the 3D object through the moments to define its referential. The occupancy of each individual voxel in the map is assumed to be independent from the other voxels occupancy. The posteriori achieved from Bayes' rule is the probability distribution on the occupations percentage for each voxel. The probabilistic map in a Cartesian system is converted to the spherical coordinate system for visualization with more details on its surface.

Keywords: Grasp exploration; Probabilistic map; Object shape representation.

1 Introduction

Applications of service robots will require advanced capabilities of grasping objects and skills that allow a robot to recognize the object also through the grasp exploration. Human uses the hand for recognizing some objects properties such as size, texture, etc. The skills of grasp exploration to acquire objects properties are important also in the robotic field to complement others sensors such as vision and laser to obtain more information of an object. The in-hand exploration strategies performed by humans motivated the development of analogous approaches to promote the exploration of surfaces of objects by robotic hands. These exploratory procedures are used to created internal representations of objects in order to proceed to its identification and integrating its 3D spatial and physical characteristics distribution to control the interaction with it.

In this work, it is generated the representation of the shape of a 3D object extracted from the data acquired during the human hand exploration of the object (by contour following). The representation of the object shape is built using a probabilistic volumetric map. The referential associated to the representation of the shape of the object is located in the estimated center of the mass of the object.

L.M. Camarinha-Matos, P. Pereira, and L. Ribeiro (Eds.): DoCEIS 2010, IFIP AICT 314, pp. 215–222, 2010.

2 Contribution to Technological Innovation

Nowadays, there is a tendency to move the development of robotic manipulators from simple grippers towards more natural human inspired articulated robotic hands, with integrated multimodal sensing technologies. This new generation of autonomous dexterous robotic hands is playing an important contribution to the evolution of the robotic research paradigms. The field of robotics is moving to the development of new systems adapted to be introduced in new environments far from the traditional robotic applications in the industrial production lines. There is an emerging trend in the development of methods and strategies to endow these robotic platforms with the ability to autonomously explore these environments, proceed to the characterization of objects, use them as tools or interact with them. This work intends to contribute to the development of autonomous dexterous robotic hands by developing methods to extract a representation of the manipulated object in order to estimate the object shape and size. These methods are developed using contact points acquired from demonstrations performed by humans during the in-hand exploration. The developed methodology will be then transferred to robotic dexterous hands in order to estimate the shape and size of a manipulated object, from contact points acquired by a robotic hand through contour following. Achieving the 3D object shape estimation, it is possible to determine, through its geometrical properties, the best region of the object to perform the grasp. Using this knowledge (object representation) it is possible to endow a robot to grasp different types of objects including unknown objects.

3 Related Work

Researches about human perception concerning haptic exploration disclose that contour following is an ordinary way of "exploratory procedures" that people use for determining the geometry of an object [1]. Many approaches have been proposed regarding robot haptic exploration for object recognition and object shape representation. In [2] the authors present haptic object recognition using a dexterous robot hand with a manipulator arm. Through the hand contact by enclosing the objects at predefined positions was possible evaluate joint angles and force readings. The object shape recovery was performed using sparse contact points from hand. The point clouds were fitted to superquadric models defined by a set of parameters describing shape and pose. In [3] the authors developed a framework for haptic exploration by contour following that can be used with robot or human hand. The object shape contour is acquired by a human hand using a data glove where the human operator visually guides the contact sensor along the contours of the object by the index fingertips. It is used an extended superquadric function for primitive modeling which can represent a variety of cubical and spherical geometries. They address modeling of basic superquadric shapes. The authors have used stereo vision for wrist tracking by particle filter. They have used a marker bracelet attached to the wrist of the subject with the data glove for its tracking. The proposed work in [4], the authors have used superquadric functions for shape recovery from haptic exploration with multi-fingered robot hands using fingertip tactile sensors. They have applied a hybrid minimization method utilizing a genetic algorithm by considering the contact normal information to recover superquadric primitives from synthetic exploration data. In a previous work [5] we developed a method to extract basic shapes (primitives) from data acquired from grasp exploration. Gaussian Mixture Models was used for points clustering and outlier removal. After a learning phase, the object shape was classified through Bayesian techniques. It was used least square minimization of a distance metric to find the shape orientation and scale for its representation.

4   Research Contribution and Innovation

In this section is described the methodology adopted for object representation using probabilistic map. Mapping techniques as occupancy grid [6], [7] has been used tin robotics field to describe an environment of a mobile robot. Two-Dimensional grid has been very used for static indoor mapping [8]. The idea is to verify the probability of each cell to be full or empty after the sensors observation. In [8] is described the standard grid mapping algorithm that is a version of Bayes filter. This filter is used to calculate the posterior over occupancy of each cell. Probabilistic volumetric maps are also useful as presented in [9] for data fusion (visual and auditory perception). The main idea of using the probabilistic map is due to: reach a simpler way of static object reconstruction and representation and the uncertainty of sensor noise due to real world (the sensor probability model depends on the characteristics of the sensor and the object being sensed). In the next subsections are presented the detailed content about the employed methodology for object representation through grasp exploration by contour following.

4.1.1   Probabilistic Volumetric Map for Object Representation

This work presents a model for grasp exploration, but it also can be used for data fusion. Our intention is to acquire the 3D shape of the object so that instead of work in an egocentric way, we will work with object-centric representation in a spherical coordinate system to reach more resolution on the object surface. The volumetric map is updated along the exploration in discrete intervals. The proposed methodology will be used for data fusion (multimodal perception) in a future work, e.g. using vision and touch. The occupancy of each individual voxel is assumed to be independent from the other voxels' occupancy and thus O_C is a set of independent random variables: $C \in M$ - index a cell on the Map; O_C - probability value describing the occupancy of the cell C; Z_{grasp} - grasp exploration measurement that influences the cell C. It represents 5 sensors which each one returns the 3D position of a movement; $P(O_C)$ - Probability distribution of preliminary knowledge of coverage value describing the occupancy of the cell C, initially is an uniform distribution; $P(Z_{grasp} \mid O_C)$ - probability distribution corresponding to the set of measurement Z_{grasp} that influences the cell C taken from the grasp exploration data. This distribution is taken from occupancy model. In case of data fusion from different sensors, it is necessary to declare the variables that represent the distribution of the measurement, e.g. working also with vision, then $P(Z_{vision} \mid O_C)$ represents the sensor model. In case of different sensors the joint distribution decomposition of the relevant variables shows the dependency assumptions according to Bayes' rule as follows:

$$P(Oc\, Z_{vision}\, Z_{grasp}) = P(Oc \mid C)P(Z_{vision} \mid Oc)P(Z_{grasp} \mid Oc) \tag{1}$$

The *posteriori* is the probability distribution on the occupation's percentage $P(O_C \mid Z_{vision}\, Z_{grasp})$ for each voxel:

$$P(Oc \mid Z_{vision}\, Z_{grasp}) = \alpha P(Oc \mid Z_{vision})P(Oc \mid Z_{grasp}) \tag{2}$$

Since this work is just for grasp sensor model, it is possible to simplify the estimation model of occupancy, so that the *posteriori* in this case is the probability distribution on the occupation's percentage $P(O_C \mid Z_{grasp})$ for each voxel. The occupation's probability is given by:

$$P(O_C \mid Z_{grasp}) = \frac{P(Z_{grasp} \mid O_C)P(O_C)}{P(Z_{grasp} \mid O_C)P(O_C) + (1 - P(Z_{grasp} \mid O_C))(1 - P(O_C))} \tag{3}$$

where $P(O_C \mid Z_{grasp})$ is the posteriori value; $P(Z_{grasp} \mid O_C)$ is acquired by the sensor measurement (likelihood); $P(O_C)$ is the *priori* information (at the beginning it is a uniform distribution representing the state full or empty) and subsequently the last *posteriori* becomes the *prior* for the next computation.

4.1.2   Grasp Exploration Occupancy Model

For the data acquisition (grasp exploration), we are using the Polhemus Liberty system [10]. It is used one magnetic sensor on the fingers (thumb, index and middle) to acquire the shape of an object by contour following. Each sensor return the 3D coordinates based on Polhemus Liberty referential. The frame rate of each sensor was configured to be up to 15Hz. During the data acquisition, it is defined a workspace $(35\times35\times35\text{cm}^3)$ in the experimental area to place the object for mapping. This space is subdivided in $0.5\times0.5\times0.5\text{cm}^3$ cells. During the displacement of each sensor in the workspace area, each one gives the information about its 3D position and it is possible to identify in which cell that the measurement is inserted. Due to the size of each cell relatively to the standard deviation of the magnetic tracking sensors measurements (until 0.2 cm for linear movements of 10cm), it is defined inside each cell a 3D isotropic Gaussian probability distribution, $P(Z_{grasp} \mid Oc)$, centred at the cell central point with standard deviation 0.2 and mean value equal to the cell central point coordinates of the cell. The probability of a measurement belongs to that cell is given by the equation (4). The values are normalized in order to consider that the probability value assigned to a point located at the centre of the cell is equal to 1.

$$P(Z_{grasp} \mid O_C) = \frac{1}{(2\Pi)^{3/2} \mid \Sigma \mid^{1/2}} \exp\left(-\frac{1}{2}(\mathbf{x} - \boldsymbol{\mu})^T \Sigma^{-1}(\mathbf{x} - \boldsymbol{\mu})\right) \tag{4}$$

In (4) $|\Sigma|$ represents the determinant of Σ (sensor noise variation). It can also represent a scalar value. Due to the normalization used, the equation (4) takes the form:

$$P(Z_{grasp} | O_C) = \exp\left(-\left(\frac{(x-u_x)^2 + (y-u_y)^2 + (z-u_z)^2}{2\sigma^2}\right)\right) \tag{5}$$

4.1.3 Object Referential and Representation in Spherical Coordinate System

To have a better representation of the object and to reach more details on its surface we are working with object-centric representation. To find the object referential and represent it centred in a sphere, it is computed the center of mass of the object. As long as the center of mass of the object is determined, it is possible to define the object referential. The center of mass of the points' distributions that represents the object is found along the grasp exploration in the workspace. While the data is acquired during the exploration, the center of mass the object is changing due to the amount of data and the object surface growing (Fig. 1(a)). The axes of the tracker device referential are kept, so that we just need to translate the points in the tracker referential to the object referential. Through the centroid, it is possible to define the radius of a sphere is the center of mass of the object, thus it is possible to center the object inside a sphere for its volumetric representation as shown in Fig.1 (b). To compute the center of mass of a 3D object shape we compute the discrete moments. The moments are a measure of the spatial distribution of the mass of a shape. The centroid is reached through some steps, computing the zero moment (summation of the voxels); first moments for x, y and z and then it is computed the centroid for each axis. The moments are computed in an iterative way, at some discrete intervals, after a new exploration the center of mass of the object is updated.

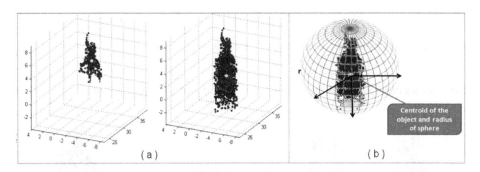

Fig. 1. (a) The center of mass of the object changes along the grasp exploration; (b) Illustration of the object representation in spherical coordinate system

4.1.4 Experimental Results

The magnetic sensors were attached to a glove to perform the object contour following to acquire the contact points. For this experiment, it was decided to use just the thumb, index and middle fingers to explore the object surface due to be enough to cover the object shape through the movements around it. The setup for the experiments is composed of a wooden table, without any metallic parts, since the electromagnetic tracker is sensitive to nearby ferromagnetic materials. The rigid 3D object is fixed on the tabletop in a defined workspace for all experiments having the object in the same area. The magnetic tracker emitter unit that determines the frame of reference for the motion tracking system is placed on the tabletop at ~30cm near to the object. A workspace of 35x35x35cm³ was defined on the table for the object mapping. The referential of the workspace was defined to be parallel to the sensor referential and then a simple translation is enough to convert the 3D points on the sensors referential to the workspace referential. Fig. 2 (a) shows the experimental setup area. Each voxel of the volumetric map was defined to represent an area 0.5x 0.5x0.5cm³ due to the good precision of the sensor position resolution at 30cm range (less then 1mm). The chosen exploratory procedure is performed during 90 seconds. The volumetric map is updated with the new sensors measurements every 15 seconds. The contour following movements have no pattern, that is, it is not necessary to follow some pre-defined rules such as making movement just in one direction. The subject is allowed to do movements in any direction, but for better representation it is suggested to perform horizontal and vertical movements around the object until to contour all surface. The chosen object for this experiment was a bottle of wine. Fig. 2 (b) and (c) shows the results achieved in the end of the exploration.

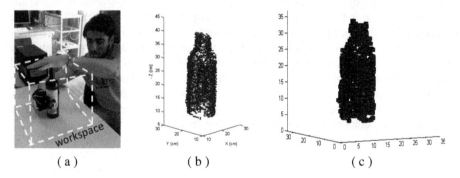

(a)   (b)   (c)

Fig. 2. (a) Experimental area for the in-hand exploration; (b) raw data; (c) representation of the object shape (just voxels with probability higher than 0.7)

Fig.3 shows other views of the object centered in the estimated center of mass.

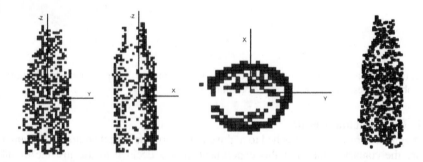

Fig. 3. Representation of the occupied cells with probability higher then 0.7 (object centered in the estimated center of mass)

5 Discussion of the Results

This approach for shape representation has a limitation: the rigid object need to be fixed in the specified workspace. If the object abruptly moves many times during the exploration, the reconstruction of the object can be less precise. The idea of this methodology is to do not represent the points with low probability so that the reach-to-grasp movement before the object contour following starts are not represented because the hand trajectory reaching the object have very few points and that points are not repeated (i.e. do not pass in the same cell twice) to increase the probability of the cells that the movement has occupied. The application ignores all points outside of the workspace where the object is placed. The adopted method uses a unique global map, where all the fingertips data are represented e.g. if one or more sensors passed through the same cell the probability increases. Other method could be applied; instead of building a unique map for all sensors, it could be built a local map and then fusing them into a global map through a Bayesian filter. The exploration was done with the sensors on right hand. During the trials, the subject that was performing the exploration usually hold with the left hand the top of the object to guarantee that it does not move, thus it is possible to reach better results, but at least a small variation of the object position can happen. After analyzing the exploration performance of some subjects, it was possible to see that the object shape influences the exploratory procedure, e.g. the bottle of wine was more explored in the middle due to the cylindrical shape. The top and bottom of the explored object is poorer in the representation due to the subject explore less those parts. The retrieved object attributes such as shape and size were satisfactory. The raw data, i.e., fingers movements inside the workspace were 6169 points. We have considered all cells with probability higher than 0.7 to represents the object shape. After computing the probabilistic volumetric map, the object shape has occupied 723 cells (probability $>= 0.7$). The use of tactile sensors for contact points could facilitate and improve the results, e.g. using tactile sensor would be possible to know when the fingers are in contact to the object to initialize the tracker device points acquisition, avoiding to start the application with the hand on the object or to fill some voxel on the workspace during the reach-to-grasp. In this work we have introduced the idea of work with multimodal perception. Our future directions is also to use the visual perception to acquire more information of the object and then through sensors fusion we can reach better results for the probabilistic representation of the object to be used for features extraction for its characterization.

6 Conclusion and Future Work

In this work is shown the probabilistic representation of a 3D object model achieved by grasp exploration through probabilistic volumetric map due to the simplicity to recover, by this method, a shape given the sensors measurements. The center of mass of the object is computed to define the object referential for its representation in the spherical coordinate system. As future work, it will be used the extended model for sensor fusion using stereo vision and grasp exploration for better representation of the object. For that, it is necessary sensors calibration, and it is necessary a joint distribution decomposition of the relevant variables to show the dependency assumptions according to Bayes' rule for the data fusion. The experiments will be performed with non-fixed object (in-hand exploration using two hands). For that, it is necessary to have an initial position of the object to be used as reference, and then it will be computed a transformation between the object referential when it is moving to the initial position referential. This will be done every time that the object moves to be possible to map all points in the origin to have the object model representation. After acquiring the representation of the object will be possible to recognize and characterize it.

Acknowledgments. This work is partially supported by the European project HANDLE (23-16-40). Diego Faria is supported by the Portuguese Foundation for Science and Technology (FCT).

References

1. Klatzky, R.L., Lederman, S.: Intelligent exploration by the human hand. In: Dextrous robot hands, ch. 4, pp. 66–81. Springer-Verlag New York, Inc., New York (1990)
2. Allen, P.K., Roberts, K.S.: Haptic object recognition using a multi-fingered dextrous hand. In: IEEE International Conference on Robotics and Automation, pp. 342–347 (1989)
3. Bierbaum, A., Welke, K., Burger, D., Asfour, T., Dillmann, R.: Haptic Exploration for 3D Shape Reconstruction using Five-Finger Hands. In: IEEE/RAS International Conference on Humanoid Robots (2007)
4. Bierbaum, A., Gubarev, I., Dillmann, R.: Robust shape recovery for sparse contact location and normal data from haptic exploration. In: IEEE/RSJ International Conference on Intelligent Robots and Systems, pp. 3200–3205 (2008)
5. Faria, D.R., Prado, J.A.S., Drews Junior, P., Dias, J.: Object shape retrieval through grasp exploration. In: ECMR-European Conference on Mobile Robots (2009)
6. Moravec, H.: Sensor fusion in certainty grids for mobile robots. AI Mag. 9, 61–74 (1988)
7. Elfes, A.: Using occupancy grids for mobile robot perception and navigation. Computer 22, 46–57 (1989)
8. Thrun, S.: Robotic mapping: a survey. In: Exploring artificial intelligence in the new millennium, pp. 1–35. Morgan Kaufmann Publishers Inc., San Francisco (2003)
9. Ferreira, J.F., Pinho, C., Dias, J.: Active exploration using bayesian models for multimodal perception. In: Campilho, A., Kamel, M.S. (eds.) ICIAR 2008. LNCS, vol. 5112, pp. 369–378. Springer, Heidelberg (2008)
10. Polhemus Liberty Electromagnetic Motion Tracking System,
    http://www.polhemus.com

Movement Speed Models of Natural Grasp and Release Used for an Industrial Robot Equipped with a Gripper

Mihai Stoica[1], Gabriela Andreea Calangiu[1], and Francisc Sisak[2]

[1] PhD Students of Transilvania University of Brasov, Electrical Engineering Departament
[2] Professor of Transilvania University of Brasov,
Electrical Engineering Departament, Romania
{mihai-V.stoica,gabriela.calangiu,sisak}@unitbv.ro

Abstract. In this paper, movement speed models of a robotic manipulator are presented according to the mode of operation of the human hand, when it wants to grasp and release an object. In order to develop the models, measurements on a human agent were required regarding the movement coordinates of his hand. The movement patterns have been approximated on the intervals, using first and second degree functions. The speeds were obtained by deriving these functions. The models obtained are generally presented; for their implementation in models applied for a certain robot, specific changes from case to case have to be made.

Keywords: Speed, Models, Robot, Grasp, Gripper.

1 Introduction

Robots became more powerful and more intelligent in the last decade and they are developing in the direction of services. Being used by people without technical knowledge, it's important for them to be easily operated using a flexible programming system. A great importance, concerning the robotics, is the way the robots catch and manipulate objects. The research is in the direction of the development of models for natural grasp of objects, like the human model.

In its functioning, the human hand has a completely natural movement with the sensorial ability for a subtle manipulation. Biological subtleties can be ignored since they contribute little to natural hand modeling [2, 9]. In [11] van Nierop et al. a model of the human hand is presented, which has natural movement and constraints due to the biomechanical joints of the skeleton and the skin of the hand. They present their research in modeling and provide a description of anatomic nomenclature. For the evaluation of the model, they realize the taxonomy of elementary tasks which describe the movements of the hands into a 2-dimensional parametric space.

Many papers have focused on the construction of a firm grasp [4]. In [1] R. Abu-Zitar and A.M. Al-Fahed Nuseirat present a heuristic technique used for solving the linear complementary problems (LCP). Their research consists in the determination of minimal force required for the grasp an object with a multi-finger gripper. The contact is assumed to be frictionless. A numerical algorithm, Lemke, can be used for solving the problem. Lemke is a direct method, deterministic, used for finding precise

L.M. Camarinha-Matos, P. Pereira, and L. Ribeiro (Eds.): DoCEIS 2010, IFIP AICT 314, pp. 223–230, 2010.

solutions using a few constraints. The authors propose the neural network technique for obtaining the largest number of precise solutions, in positions that can be solved and good solutions for position in which Lemke method fails. Using inequality theory, the problem is composed like a LCP. The research of the authors had to convert the problem into a heuristic search problem, using the architecture and learning capabilities of a single two layered neural network.

In their research, Alexandra Constantin et al. present a method for quality assessment in terms of arm movement imitation. They propose a segmentation and comparison algorithm based on the angle rotation of the joint [3]. Here, they describe an empirical study designed to validate the algorithm, comparing it with human assessment of imitation. The results show that automatic metric evaluation does not differ significantly from the human evaluation.

The work on automatic grasp synthesis and planning is a relevant idea [6, 7, 8]. In [10] is presented a method for automatic grasp based on shape primitives of an object, using a programming by demonstration platform. Initially, the system recognizes the grasp from a demonstrator and then generates the grasping strategies for the robot. The authors of this paper began by presenting how the grasp is modeled and learned and how it is mapped at the robot hand. They continued with the accomplishment of a dynamic simulation of the grasp execution, with focus on objects that must be grabbed whose position is not completely known.

Humanoid robotic requires new programming tools. The programming by demonstration method is good for simple movements, but until now the adaption for subtle moves is very difficult for it. The mathematical models have been realized only for simple hands or objects. In [5] Michele Folgheraiter et al. tried to use the information obtained directly by a human teacher. They have developed a glove which they used for collecting the information from the different experiments and generalized it into a neuronal network.

In this paper several elements derived from a research regarding natural grasp of an object by man, will be presented. In our research, we made some measurements on a human agent regarding the movement coordination of the hand and his finger when he wants to grasp and release an object. The basic idea was to translate these measurements into a model of movement speeds which can be used by an industrial robot equipped with a gripper.

2   Contribution to Technological Innovation

Humanoid and mobile robots development is heading in the direction of imitating the human behavior attempt. The objects grasp and manipulation is a significant domain even in the industrial robots field. In nowadays, industrial robots work with constant speeds when they have to grasp and release objects. This paper presents theoretical models of movement speed of an industrial robot manipulator simulating the human hand model. The usage of the proposed models for the movement speed of an industrial robot gripper improves the grasping quality, respectively the releasing quality of an object and minimizes the accomplishment time. Currently, the gripper of an industrial robot passes through three distinctive steps when a grasp or a release has to be done: the first step in which the gripper is positioned in the grasp point, respectively the release point; the second step in which the gripper closes, respectively it opens;

and the third step in which the robots continues his movement with or without object. The proposed models determine that the three steps above defined to intertwine: thus they improve the quality of grasping and releasing and the time in which these are accomplished is minimized. Both the gripper speed movement model and the closing/opening speed model have relatively large periods of time for opening and closing of the gripper. This shows that the models approach to human hand model and reduce the force shocks, caused by the inertial force, as it happens when the industrial robots currently used manipulate objects.

Therefore, in this paper speed models of an industrial robot gripper are proposed, in order to improve the object grasping and releasing, using human hand model simulation.

3   Measurement Procedures

The measurements have been made using the OptiTrack system, using the camera displacement like in Fig. 1 a). For improving the precision, the work volume was reduced to approximately 1 cubic meter.

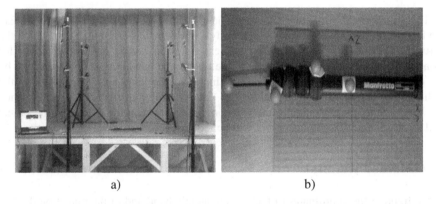

a)   b)

Fig. 1. a) The displacement of the camera; b) The object used to accomplish the measurements

The measurements were made on the object presented in Fig. 1 b). On this object there were attached four markers, which were selected for achieving a ``rigid body", named ``body" using the ARENA software.

The object is placed in the XOZ plane, like in Fig. 1 b). In this figure, the object is placed on worktable. If the object is lifted from the table, then OY coordinate of the four markers will increase; if it will be put down then it will decrease. In the measurement made the object is considered to be dot-like, being represented only by the coordinates of the rightmost marker.

The measurement operation consisted in capturing the human hand and the object coordinates when a human agent grasps an object from the workbench, lifts this object to a certain height, puts down the object on the workbench and releases it, lifts once again the hand without the object (open hand), than puts down the hand to grab again the object and starts again a new cycle.

For tracking the human hand those three markers disposed like in Fig. 2 were used. The markers are attached to a rigid support, as is it shown in the below picture.

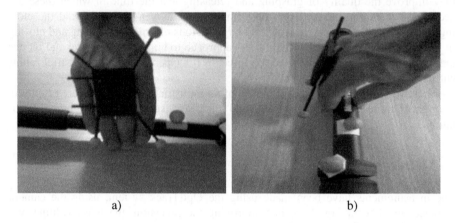

a)   b)

Fig. 2. Markers arrangement on the human agent

The arrangement of the markers on the hand surface has been tried. Due to the fact the four fingers do not constitute a rigid body a problem was encountered in which the software did not recognize the three markers as "rigid body", this is the reason for using the rigid support. As in the case of the object, the hand is considered dot-like by the coordinate's point of view. The coordinates of the hand are represented by the right-bottom marker coordinates in the Fig. 2.a. According to figures 1.b) and 2 when the hand opens, the distance on the OZ coordinate between the hand and the object will increase, and when it closes this will be reduced.

4   Obtained Results

In the figure 3 the coordinates of the human agent's hand and of the object on the OY direction, in a complete grab-release object cycle, are represented with green (A, B).

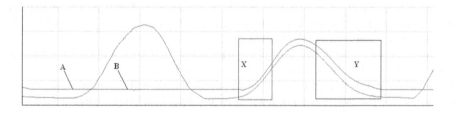

Fig. 3. The difference between the grip and the release of the object

The area where the object is lifted from the workbench is enclosed in a red rectangle (X), and the area where it is standing still on the workbench is enclosed in a blue rectangle (Y). It can be observed that the time which is needed in order to lift the object from workbench is smaller than the time which is needed for it to be still. The human agent, in the phase of placing the object back on the workbench, is more careful and the motion has a much higher precision.

The green lines (A, B) represent the coordinates at equal moments in time. The slope of the lines in every point is the speed in the corresponding point.

It can be observed that the speed of rise and descent isn't constant in either cases, not for the free hand and neither for the hand with an object. With other words the human agent's hand doesn't moves with a constant speed, which is usually the case in robotics, but according to a curve like the one presented in figure 3.

In figure 4 the blue lines (A, B) represent the OZ coordinates of the human hand, and also the object which has to be handled (coordinates through which the grabbing and releasing motions can be highlighted). The green ones (C) represent the OY coordinates of the hand and of the object.

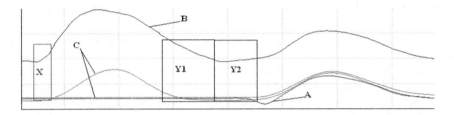

Fig. 4. The OZ and OY coordinates of the hand and object for an entire cycle

Just like it was the case with the horizontal movement, in the case of the closing and opening motion of the hand of the human agent, we have to deal with a motion which has a variable speed. The area inside the red rectangle (X) represents the release zone of the object. The area inside the black rectangles (Y1, Y2) represents the grabbing zone of the object. As it can be observed the time for grabbing the object is longer than time needed for releasing it.

Its grabbing starts in a moment before the moment in which the hand is at the level of the workbench. In the first black rectangle (Y1) the proper grasp of the object is presented. The second rectangle of the same color (Y2) follows an area of post-grabbing, an area where the human agents tests the grip. In this moment he checks whether the grip is stable and he ensures that it's the correct one. Only after realizing this, he begins to lift the object.

5   The Established Models

The results obtained in the previous chapter are used for constructing models of the movement speed on the vertical axis (in the direction of grabbing the object) and of the speed of closing-opening of the industrial robot's gripper. These models are obtained based on the actions of the human hand.

In the graphics from the previous figure the coordinates for vertical movement and for the closing-opening of the human hand are presented, at equal moments in time.

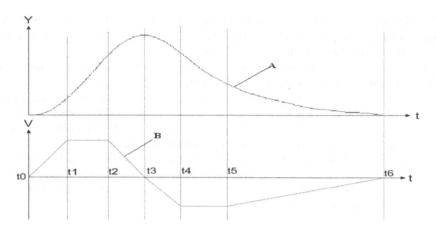

Fig. 5. Modeling of the vertical speed (in the direction of grabbing the object) of the gripper

By deriving these curves the movement speeds for the corresponding directions can be obtained.

In figure 5, on the upper graph, the vertical coordinate of the human agent's hand (A) is presented, when he lifts and lowers the object. In the interval t0 – t1 the curve can be approximated with a 2nd grade curve. By deriving the 2nd grade function a 1st grade function is obtained, thus the speed on this section can be approximated by a straight line segment. In the interval t1 – t2 the curve can be approximated with a straight line segment. For this reason the speed in this interval is constant. In the same way the other intervals are analyzed and in the end the speed's graph is obtained which is presented in the lower part of figure 5.

The graph at the lower part of figure 5 can represent an approximately model of the movement speed on the vertical (in the direction of the grabbing) of the gripper of an industrial robot. In this model the intervals t0-t1, t2-t3 and t3-t4 can be considered equal to T. In the t5-t6 interval (the interval for placing the object back to the work-bench) is big. It can be considered as being equal to 3T. The intervals t1-t2 and t4-t5 depend on the distance between the coordinates in which the robot has to act.

In conclusion the model presented above can be used on another scale, in a real system, considering the shape and some proportions of the speed-graph.

In figure 6, on the top graph the coordinates of the human hand and of the object are presented, when the object is released, the hand is raised without the object, the hand is lowered and the object is grabbed. The area in the yellow frame (X) is not used for establishing this model. When the object is released, the hand can have a relative motion on the OZ direction towards the object and because of this the coordinate difference on the OZ between hand and object is not the same as when the hand was opened. In the interval t4-t5 it is considered that the opening of the hand is constant. In the vicinity of the moment when the hand begins to rise and the moment in which it reaches the surface of the workbench, the difference on the direction OZ between the hand and the object, is approximately equal to the displacement of the thumb towards the other four fingers of the human hand (the opening of the hand).

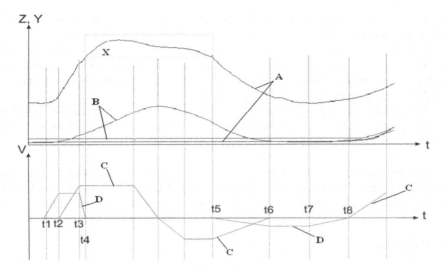

Fig. 6. Modeling the vertical speed of the robot's gripper and the closing-opening speed of the gripper

The vertical movement coordinates are presented in green (B), while the movement coordinates in the direction of the opening of the hand are blue (A). In the lower graph, the approximate model of the vertical movement speed of the robot's gripper is represented in red (C). The brown line (D) is the model which is used for closing and opening the gripper of the robot. These models were used in the same way as the one in figure 5. The interval t1-t4 is the interval in which the object is released. The robot's gripper opens with a growing speed until the moment t2. In this moment the robot begins to move the gripper on the vertical. For a brief period of time, t2-t3 the gripper opens with a constant speed, and in a very short time-period the gripper's speed reaches 0. In the periods of time: t1-t2 and t2-t3, in order to establish the model they can be considered to be T1. The deceleration period t3-t4 can be considered to be T1/3. The interval t5-t8 is the interval in which the object is grabbed. The gripper begins to close with an accelerating speed before it moves the proper grabbing position of the object. When it reaches the corresponding position, it closes with a constant velocity, and after a while the speed begins to drop until it reaches 0. This last phase is the period in which the robot tests whether the grip is stable.

An exact relationship between the intervals t5-t6, t6-t7 and t7-t8 can't be established, but they can be considered approximately equal to 2-3 times T1.

6 Conclusions

The obtained models are only approximations. They are not general, but they can be used for specific type of actions. In the shown models, the magnitude of acting speeds is intuitively chosen; it is important in which way this can be modeled. The speeds have been modeled with line segments: oblique and horizontal. Linear models have been used for simulating the human hand model in order to obtain simple and easy to use models. Others functions and techniques of measured data synthesis for the models improvement might be used, but those involve larger processing time.

In the models that have been presented only proportions between the time interval in which the speed is described by an oblique line segment, and in the time intervals with constant speed the time depends on distance between the point's coordinates in which the manipulator has to act are established.

These models have been realized for a two finger gripper, but they can be used also for manipulators with more than two fingers. In the future we want to implement and test these models on an industrial robot equipped with a three finger gripper.

Acknowledgements. This paper is supported by the Sectoral Operational Programme Human Resources Development (SOP HRD), financed from the European Social Fund and by the Romanian Government under the contract number POSDRU/6/1.5/S/6.

References

1. Abu-Zitar, R., Al-Fahed Nuseirat, A.M.: A Neural Network Approach to the Frictionless Grasping Problem. Journal of Intelligent and Robotic Systems 29, 27–45 (2000)
2. Bando, Y., Kuratate, T., Nishita, T.: A simple method for modeling wrinkles on human skin. In: Proceedings of the 10th Pacific Conference on Computer Graphics and Applications, pp. 166–175. IEEE Computer Society, Washington (2002)
3. Constantin, A., Hall, B.: Evaluating Arm Movement Imitatio. American Journal of Undergraduate Research 4(4) (2006)
4. Faverjon, B., Ponce, J.: On computing two-finger force-closure grasps of curved 2D objects. In: Proceedings of the IEEE International Conference on Robotics and Automation, Nice, France, pp. 2290–2295 (1991)
5. Folgheraiter, M., Baragiola, I., Gini, G.: Teaching Grasping to a Humanoid Hand as a Generalization of Human Grasping Data. In: López, J.A., Benfenati, E., Dubitzky, W. (eds.) KELSI 2004. LNCS (LNAI), vol. 3303, pp. 139–150. Springer, Heidelberg (2004)
6. Miller, A.T., Knoop, S., Allen, P.K., Christensen, H.I.: Automatic grasp planning using shape primitives. In: Proceedings of the IEEE International Conference on Robotics and Automation, pp. 1824–1829 (2003)
7. Morales, A., Chinellato, E., Fagg, A.H., del Pobil, A.: Using Experience for assessing grasp reliability. International Journal of Humanoid Robots 1(4), 671–691 (2004)
8. Platt, R., Fagg, A.H., Grupen, R.A.: Extending fingertip grasping to whole body grasping. In: Proceedings of The International Conference on Robotics and Automation (2003)
9. Rhee, T., Neumann, U., Lewis, J.P.: Human hand modeling from surface anatomy. In: Proceedings of the ACM SIGGRAPH Symposium on Interactive 3D Graphics and Games, pp. 27–34. ACM Press, New York (2006)
10. Tegin, J., Ekval, S., Kragic, D., Wikander, J., Iliev, B.: Demonstration-based learning and control for automatic grasping. Intel Serv. Robotics 2, 23–30 (2009)
11. Van Nierop, O.A., van der Helm, A., Overbeeke, K.J., Djajadiningrat, T.P.J.: A natural human hand model. The Visual Computer 24(1), 31–44 (2008)

Part 8

Petri Nets Based Modeling

Petri Net Based Engineering and Software Methodology for Service-Oriented Industrial Automation

J. Marco Mendes[1], Francisco Restivo[1], Paulo Leitão[2], and Armando W. Colombo[3]

[1] Faculty of Engineering of the University of Porto,
Rua Dr. Roberto Frias s/n, 4200-465 Porto, Portugal
{marco.mendes,fjr}@fe.up.pt
[2] Polytechnic Institute of Bragança, Quinta Sta Apolónia,
Apartado 134, 5301-857 Bragança, Portugal
pleitao@ipb.pt
[3] Schneider Electric Automation GmbH, Steinheimer Str. 117,
D-63500 Seligenstadt, Germany
armando.colombo@de.schneider-electric.com

Abstract. Collaborative industrial systems are becoming an emergent paradigm towards flexibility. One promising solution are service-oriented industrial automation systems, but integrated software methodologies and major frameworks for the engineering are still missing. This paper presents an overview of the current results on a unified and integrated methodology based on intrinsic and novel features of Petri nets. These nets are applied to the modeling, analysis, service management, embedded software controllers, decision support system and monitoring, to improve the fundamentals in the engineering of service-oriented automation systems. The solution may contribute to the reduction of the design, operational and reconfiguration phases in the life-cycle of novel automation environments. Results were obtained and discussed from simulations and real industrial demonstrators.

Keywords: Service-oriented Architecture, Service-oriented Computing, Industrial Automation, Software engineering, Petri Nets.

1 Introduction

In Service-oriented Architectures (SoA) for industrial automation [1] several research directions and solutions have been presented, but overwhelmingly directed to a specific part of the whole engineering problem that SoA reflects in industrial automation. Thus, an inroad is required for integrated solutions of engineering, respecting users, developers, available hardware and software. Petri nets (PN) were identified as being part of the solution by presenting a set of useful characteristics supporting the life-cycle of service-oriented systems. With the choice over Petri net based formalism, the research question and motivation of this work follows as: "How does Petri Nets based methodology's features contribute as a unified tool to the integration and collaboration of autonomous service-oriented automation control components and support their life-cycle management?".

L.M. Camarinha-Matos, P. Pereira, and L. Ribeiro (Eds.): DoCEIS 2010, IFIP AICT 314, pp. 233–240, 2010.

This work focuses on the actual results in terms of research, development and application of the integrated methodology for the engineering of service-oriented automation systems using Petri nets. This paper is organized in the following sections: Section 2 describes the contribution to technological innovation, section 3 presents an overview on related literature and state of the art, section 4 explains the overall engineering approach and software for service-oriented automation systems using as core methodology Petri nets, the application is resumed and discussed in section 5 and finally conclusions and future work are exposed in section 6.

2   Contribution to Technological Innovation

The present research work by using Petri nets for the engineering of service-oriented automation systems offer several novel aspects that already were reviewed by international committees (see e.g. the SOCRADES project at http://www.socrades.eu) and recent disseminations. Note that the aspects discussed here are part of the individual research work used in the context of the project. From the SoA side, it is well known that it represent a future trend in the automation and production world, but from the software engineering and also end-user perspective, integrated solutions are missing. As such, the research work focus on a Petri net based solution for those systems, for the design, analysis and also operation. Contributions are in a form of an open methodology for developing custom and feature-full Petri net applications and control solutions, an engineering process based on Petri nets and several runtime features such as distributed orchestration, composition and active conflict resolution.

3   Overview on Related Literature and State of the Art

In SoA, the main objective is the interoperability between different participants in the system by providing and using resources in form of services via an open protocol based communication platform (e.g. Web Services). In automation and manufacturing, service providers and requesters include also industrial devices, manufacturing equipment and products (besides the typical software agents that run on normal computers and servers). Several efforts are being done in integrating and managing these new systems. The first visible application resulted from the SIRENA project [1] with the objective to develop a service infrastructure for real-time embedded networked applications. Other projects in the same research area are currently in advance research and development state, such as the SOCRADES project.

Important subjects are still related to engineering solutions of service-oriented systems from the software/hardware and user point of view, and also to stimulate the industrial adoption. In service-oriented automation systems, a formal and unified method is required to provide design facilities, with the ability to validate models and to be also used as an integration middleware at runtime with enough flexibility and features. Previous works in the domain report some advances with engineering methodologies. Main research directions are related to SoA device integration and Device Profile for Web Services (DPWS) [1] [2] [3], orchestration and semantics of devices and systems [1] [4], the use of Business Process Execution Language (BPEL) and other formalisms [5] [6], process optimization [7], business integration (for example [8], integration of SoA and Multi-agent Systems (MAS) [9] and virtual SoA enabled production environments [10].

Petri net is a language for design, specification, simulation and verification of systems. Petri nets are a graphical and mathematical modeling tool applicable to any systems. They are a promising tool for describing and studying information processing systems that are characterized as being concurrent, asynchronous, distributed, parallel, nondeterministic, and/or stochastic [11]. Petri Nets can be applied to many areas, including the industrial automation and control. Since the formal Petri nets are very basic in the application point of view, numerous extensions nets have been introduced over the years, normally designated by high-level Petri net. Logic controllers of Petri nets have also been developed (see the sequence controllers developed in the early 80's by Hitachi Ltd. [12] and the application of fuzzy Petri net controllers [13]) or converted into other formalisms (such as the industrial standard languages of IEC 61131) that can be understood by the devices [14].

The traditional application of Petri nets in SoA environments seems to be orchestration and choreography, to define sequences, conditions, interactions and compositions of services. Petri nets and high-level Petri nets are used in orchestration and choreography for modeling processes/composition [15] [16], analysis purposes [17] [18] and negotiation [19]. However, the OASIS standard of Web Services Business Process Execution Language (WS-BPEL) is the most prominent standard for orchestration of services. The application of BPEL directly in automation environment can be discussed. From one side, it has already a well defined syntax in XML that can be used directly with Web services. From the other side, BPEL is a specification mainly targeting business requirements, it is unknown to automation system engineers, too complex and descriptive to be interpreted by resource constrained devices (typically used in automation), not suitable for internal service process description based on device/software capabilities, technology dependent on Web services and missing direct analysis and validation support. However, some efforts have been done in terms of the application of BPEL and orchestration in general for industrial automation with results (see for example [5]).

4   Research Contribution and Innovation

Especially for service-oriented industrial automation, the application of Petri nets must be open to several specifications, requirements and methodologies for engineering that will possibly come in future. Considering the several aspects, an approach was specified for a concrete Petri nets methodology that is feasible and customized for the studied needs. The resulting open methodology for the definition of Petri net based applications permits the construction of custom software using a ground basis made of several elementary packages. This includes the Petri net formalism (according to [11]), analysis routines and conflict management. Besides the required openness, another requirement is the introduction of the time factor when evolving the Petri net. Consequently, the basis of the Petri nets is guaranteed, except that the doors are open in terms of delays that can be used for customized operations. Over this, a modular property system was specified and a novel approach for the creation of token games (an "engine" that runs a Petri net) based on a customized template. Please consult the documentation of [20] for more information.

Having the basis for Petri nets applications and engineering, the next step would be identify what are the characteristics that can be extracted from them to be used in service-oriented automation systems. Most of these required or welcome features were already researched and documented. The remaining ones can be considered as future research work and possibly will also generate new characteristics. Table 1 lists the features and applications of Petri nets (and extensions) that are considered and also references to some publications with more detail over them.

Table 1. Features and applications of Petri nets and reference publications

Features and applications	Ref.	Features and applications	Ref.
Open methods for PN token games	[20]	Migration and virtual environments	[23]
Property system	[20]	Knowledge extraction from PN	-
Analysis and validation	[21]	PN interchange format (XML)	-
Petri net modularization/interfaces	[21]	Petri net-based engineering	[24]
Petri net service association	[20]	Application software tools for PC	[24]
Composition of Petri nets	[21]	Petri net controller for devices	[24]
Decision support system for PN	[22]		

The use of Petri nets can be presented in the life-cycle of processes as modeling, analysis (simulation) and execution (control). For the development of the required software applications, there are several needs since an integrated engineering approach and resulting software. Based on the requirements of physical hardware and users, it was decided that the basic building blocks that compose the distributed system should be configurable software components assuming different tasks. Therefore, the software components were designated as "*bots*" (that have the so called "orchestration engine" embedded inside) and are able (in a service-oriented fashion) coordinate their activity and proceed also to collaboration processes with other components in the system. The central part of Fig. 1 has represented the concept, where the domain of autonomy of the bot is, for example, a transfer unit (conveyor). Communication to other software components in the system (e.g. other bots) is done via the exposition of services as well as the requesting of necessary services from others. To design, configure and maintain bots, there is a need of specific tools, that are user-friendly and speed-up the development, using a high-level programming approach (visual languages, such as Petri nets).

Since SoA-based automation systems are lacking in dedicated software applications and methodologies, effort where done in the development of several software packages for the demonstrator. In any case, system engineering and associated tools are required to facilitate the developer's intervention. From the Petri nets side, the practical usage is limited by the lack of computer tools which would allow handling large and complex nets in a comfortable way. The project was baptized *Continuum Development Tools* (CDT), named after the continuum concept used in physics and philosophy. First developments were started by integrating already developed software components, in special the old editor called *PndK* (Petri nets development toolKit), under the same umbrella. Along with the integration, it was identified that several software packages are needed, namely: a framework for developing bots, engineering tools for the design and managing of bots and several utilities (mainly libraries) for supporting activities (e.g. such as communication and interface for devices). The main component is the Continuum Bot Framework (CBF) for the development of bots and their functional modules, inspired in the anatomy of living beings. Another component, the Continuum Development Studio (CDS) that is based on an extensible Document/View framework, provides an engineering tool for service-oriented bots, for example, supporting the visual description, analysis and simulation of their behavior (for now, in Petri nets formalism). The utilities package includes several reused software libraries and tools, some developed internally others adopted from the outside, such as the SOA4D DPWS library (available at https://forge.soa4d.org) providing facilities for the development of Web services and the Qt toolkit (see http://qt.nokia.com/products/), used mainly as a graphical toolkit for human interaction in the CDS.

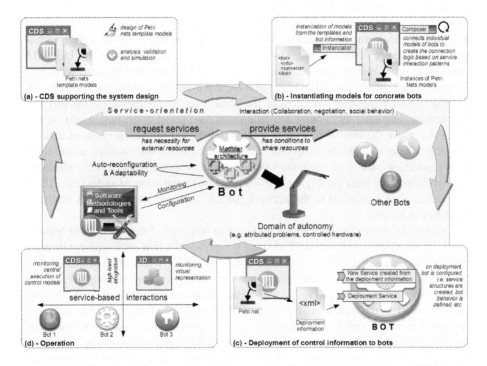

Fig. 1. Concept of the automation bot and engineering process (adapted from [24])

The engineering is overviewed in the external boxes of Fig. 1. The CDS is employed for designing and analyzing the Petri nets template models for describing the behavior of the bots (Fig. 1.a). When importing the device/connection information, several steps are done by the CDS: 1) instantiate Petri nets models for each bot based on the designed template models, 2) create the necessary properties of the Petri nets models so that several parameters of the given device/connection information and 3) based on the "enrichment" of the Petri nets models, composition of models can be done for creating connection logic and for the overall system analysis (Fig. 1.b). After the analysis and simulation (that can be done with the CDS), bots must now be configured. The process of deploying a service that encapsulates its logic as a Petri nets model to a bot that provides an embedded Petri Nets Kernel Module is depicted in Fig. 1.c. The deployment functionality is a standard feature of the DPWS and is exposed as a dynamic deployment service. The target and the deployment service can be discovered by stacks built-in discovery service. After deployment, a new service endpoint has been added and the execution of the services logic has been initiated. Deployment information includes the Petri nets behavior model, connection information of neighbors (required services), provided services by the bot and also extra configuration information for the other modules of the bot. The bot will configure itself (and its modules) and is then ready for operation (Fig. 1.d).

5   Application and Discussion

The implementation and evaluation of the current methodology is done using a virtual and real hardware demonstrator. The virtual one was modeled using the DELMIA solution to provide a simulation environment based on the real system. A service framework was added to DELMIA so that the environment can be controlled by the exposition and request of services, in the same way as pretended by the physical counterpart. The assembly equipment compromises a set of conveying modules, two lifters that make the interface between the two levels and two assembly workstations. The objective is to route the incoming pallets to the correct workstation, according to their production plan. The equipment is controlled by automation devices where the bots (including the Petri net engine, DPWS framework and other modules) run. These devices are then connected to the network, so that they can be configured, and their services can be used.

First results show the applicability and correct behavior of the system and reduced efforts in development. However and since it represents a first prototype application, there are some tasks of improvement on both methodology and application. One requirement is the previous knowledge about Petri nets, SoA and the engineering approach. This information has to be transmitted to the users and developers that are normally used to the traditional automation systems. The software part has to be improved in terms of stability, performance (e.g. improving response form embedded devices) and user-friendliness (mostly the engineering procedures using the CDS). Not less important is the automatic integration into higher level IT-systems, especially dealing with production orders and business needs.

This approach is used actively in the SOCRADES project for the specified demonstrator and has been evaluated by experts in the field. More information can be seen on the public available video at YouTube ("IP SOCRADES Demonstration of Service-Oriented Architecture integrating Real and Virtual Devices in the Electronic Assembly Scenario") that shows some of the application results of this approach.

6 Conclusions and Further Work

The current contributions of this work can be resumed by the specification of unified service-oriented engineering method that can be used in a collaborative automation environment and prove features of Petri net-based solution in service-oriented automation and production systems as a unified methodology and integration middleware. In the end, it should contribute to the reduction of the design, operational and reconfiguration phases in service-oriented automation systems. New features of this work can be addressed by the combination of the methodology itself, especially the token game template for customized implementations, conflict management, property system and also some aspects of engineering in service-oriented industrial automation. Worth of mention is that it concludes also in a new form of engineering that is different form the traditional used in automation systems.

Acknowledgements. The authors would like to thank the European Commission and the partners of the EU IST FP6 project "Service-Oriented Cross-layer infrastructure for Distributed smart Embedded devices" (SOCRADES), the EU FP6 "Network of Excellence for Innovative Production Machines and Systems" (I*PROMS), and the European ICT FP7 project "Cooperating Objects Network of Excellence" (CONET) for their support.

References

1. Jammes, F., Smit, H.: Service-oriented paradigms in industrial automation. IEEE Transactions on Industrial Informatics 1, 62–70 (2005)
2. Bobek, A., Zeeb, E., Bohn, H., Golatowski, F., Timmermann, D.: Device and service templates for the Devices Profile for Web Services. In: Proceedings of the 6th IEEE International Conference on Industrial Informatics, pp. 797–801 (2008)
3. Li, Q., Shu, Y., Tao, C., Peng, X., Shi, H.: Service-Oriented Embedded Device Model in Industrial Automation. In: Proceedings of the Workshop on Intelligent Information Technology Applications, pp. 525–529. IEEE Computer Society, Los Alamitos (2007)
4. Delamer, I.M., Lastra, J.L.M.: Self-orchestration and choreography: towards architecture-agnostic manufacturing systems. In: Proceedings of the 20th International Conference on Advanced Information Networking and Applications, vol. 2, p. 5 (2006)
5. Puttonen, J., Lobov, A., Lastra, J.L.M.: An application of BPEL for service orchestration in an industrial environment. In: Proceedings of the IEEE International Conference on Emerging Technologies and Factory Automation, pp. 530–537 (2008)
6. Lobov, A., Puttonen, J., Villasenor, V., Andiappan, R., Lastra, J.L.M.: Service oriented architecture in developing of loosely-coupled manufacturing systems. In: Proceedings of the 6th IEEE International Conference on Industrial Informatics, pp. 791–796 (2008)
7. Rahman, M., Ahmad, H.F., Suguri, H., Sadik, S., Longe, H.O.D., Ojo, A.K.: Supply chain optimization towards personalizing web services. In: 4th International IEEE Conference on Intelligent Systems, vol. 3, pp. 17–22 (2008)
8. Nguyen, D., Savio, D.: Exploiting SOA for adaptive and distributed manufacturing with cross enterprise shop floor commerce. In: Proceedings of the 10th International Conference on Information Integration and Web-based Applications & Services, pp. 318–323. ACM, New York (2008)

9. Ribeiro, L., Barata, J., Mendes, P.: MAS and SOA: Complementary Automation Paradigms. In: IFIP International Federation for Information Processing, Innovation in Manufacturing Networks, vol. 266, pp. 259–268. Springer, Boston (2008)
10. Cachapa, D., Colombo, A., Feike, M., Bepperling, A.: An approach for integrating real and virtual production automation devices applying the service-oriented architecture paradigm. In: Proceedings of the IEEE Conference on Emerging Technologies & Factory Automation, pp. 309–314 (2007)
11. Murata, T.: Petri nets: Properties, analysis and applications. Proceedings of the IEEE 77, 541–580 (1989)
12. Murata, T., Komoda, N., Matsumoto, K., Haruna, K.: A Petri Net-Based Controller for Flexible and Maintainable Sequence Control and its Applications in Factory Automation. IEEE Transactions on Industrial Electronics 33(1), 1–8 (1986)
13. Gomes, L., Steiger-Garção, A.: Petri net based Programmable Fuzzy Controller targeted for distributed control environments. In: Proceedings of the the International Joint Conference of the Fourth IEEE International Conference on Fuzzy Systems and the Second International Fuzzy Engineering Symposium, pp. 1427–1434 (1995)
14. Uzam, M., Jones, A.H., Ajlouni, N.: Conversion of Petri net controllers for manufacturing systems into ladder logic diagrams. In: Proceedings of the IEEE Conference on Emerging Technologies and Factory Automation, vol. 2, pp. 649–655 (1996)
15. Hamadi, R., Benatallah, B.: A Petri net-based model for web service composition. In: Proceedings of the 14th Australasian database conference, pp. 191–200. Australian Computer Society, Inc. (2003)
16. Bing, L., Huaping, C.: Web Service Composition and Analysis: A Petri-net Based Approach. In: Proceedings of the First International Conference on Semantics, Knowledge and Grid (2005)
17. Yang, Y., Tan, Q., Xiao, Y.: Verifying web services composition based on hierarchical colored petri nets. In: Proceedings of the first international workshop on Interoperability of heterogeneous information systems, pp. 47–54. ACM Press, New York (2005)
18. Martens, A., Moser, S., Gerhardt, A., Funk, K.: Analyzing Compatibility of BPEL Processes. In: Proceedings of the Advanced International Conference on Telecommunications and International Conference on Internet and Web Applications and Services, p. 147 (2006)
19. Jiang, H., Gu, J., Yu, Q.: Modeling of Web-based collaborative negotiation systems using colored Petri net. In: Proceedings of the 12th International Multi-Media Modelling Conference, 8 p. (2006)
20. Mendes, J.M., Restivo, F., Leitão, P., Colombo, A.W.: Customizable Service-oriented Petri Net Controllers. Accepted for the 35th Annual Conference of the IEEE Industrial Electronics Society (2009)
21. Mendes, J.M., Leitão, P., Colombo, A.W., Restivo, F.: High-Level Petri Nets Control Modules for Service-Oriented Devices: A Case Study. In: Proceedings of the 34th Annual Conference of the IEEE Industrial Electronics Society, pp. 1487–1492 (2008)
22. Leitão, P., Mendes, J.M., Colombo, A.W.: Decision Support System in a Service-oriented Control Architecture for Industrial Automation. In: Proceedings of the 13th IEEE International Conference on Emerging Technologies and Factory Automation, pp. 1228–1235 (2008)
23. Leitao, P., Mendes, J.M., Colombo, A.W.: Smooth Migration from the Virtual Design to the Real Manufacturing Control. In: Proceedings of the 7th IEEE International Conference on Industrial Informatics (2009)
24. Mendes, J.M., Bepperling, A., Pinto, J., Leitão, P., Restivo, F., Colombo, A.W.: Software Methodologies for the Engineering of Service-Oriented Industrial Automation: The Continuum Project. In: Proceedings of the 33rd Annual IEEE International Computer Software and Applications Conference (2009)

Properties Preservation in Distributed Execution of Petri Nets Models

Anikó Costa[1], Paulo Barbosa[2], Luís Gomes[1], Franklin Ramalho[2],
Jorge Figueiredo[2], and Antônio Junior[2]

[1] Universidade Nova de Lisboa, Portugal
{akc,lugo}@uninova.pt
[2] Universidade Federal de Campina Grande, Brasil
{paulo,franklin,abrantes,antonio}@dsc.ufcg.edu.br

Abstract. Model-based development for embedded system design has been used to support the increase of system's complexity. Several modeling formalisms are well matched for usage within this area. One of the goals of this work is to contribute to the usage of Petri nets as system specification language within model-based development of embedded systems having MDA proposals as a reference for the development flow. Distributed execution of the Petri net model is achieved through model partitioning into sub-modules. System decomposition is obtained through net splitting operation. Two types of implementation platforms were considered: compliant and non-compliant with zero time delay for communication between modules. Using model-checking techniques, properties associated with the execution of the distributed models in both types of platforms were compared with the execution of the initial (centralized) Petri net model.

Keywords: Petri net, model decomposition, distributed execution, model checking.

1   Introduction

The sustained growing of system's complexity has not been followed by the increase of the designer's productivity due to the lack of adequate methods and tools. The Model-based development approach can adequately support improvements in this area. In the past few years the research on embedded system design has been increasing. Most of the works use UML (Unified Modeling Language) as system design language. However, UML can be used for system specification, but not for analysis and syntheses. For that purposes is need to add specific profiles and included them into the tools which uses UML for system development. For example in [1] is proposed an UML profile for Modeling and Analysis of Real-Time and Embedded. Another work [2] is based on high-level UML design of system components and use SystemC for system behavior's validation.

Using Petri nets [3] [4] as system specification language for modeling the control part of the embedded system, the development process can be improved. Petri nets are

L.M. Camarinha-Matos, P. Pereira, and L. Ribeiro (Eds.): DoCEIS 2010, IFIP AICT 314, pp. 241–250, 2010.

an adequate formalism for modeling concurrency, parallelism and synchronization. These characteristics are commonly found when dealing with complex systems.

When one faces a complex system model, it is natural to want to decompose it into several sub-models due to the growing role that distributed systems are playing nowadays. The net splitting operation was introduced for this purpose [3], allowing to divide a Petri net model into several sub-nets. By using formal verification techniques we can obtain a reliable way to ensure that the execution of the original model and the parallel execution of the several sub-nets that were produced by the net splitting operation produce the same behavior, considering a selected set of properties (examples of selected properties include liveness, boundness, and relevant traces). In this way, we should get distributed models that can be implemented using different approaches:

- Implementing the global system model as a centralized controller;
- Using model decomposition to obtain several components, considered as independent controllers and implementing them in the same platform using synchronous communication channels for the communication between the components with zero time delay in the communication;
- Implementing the above referred components on different platforms where considering zero time delay for the communication becomes unfeasible (as they are in regions having different time domains, for instance).

This paper intends to prove that a specific set of properties associated with different distributed implementation models are preserved after the referred splitting transformations be implemented according to the Model Driven Architecture (MDA) approach [6] [7] [8]. The selected set of properties (liveness, boundness, and relevant traces) will be evaluated considering the execution behavior when different types of implementation platforms are considered.

The structure of the paper is the following. Section 2 discusses the main contributions on technological innovation issues. In the Section 3, the methodology overview of the MDA approach is presented. In Section 4, a running example is used to illustrate the usability of the proposed methodology. In Section 5, verification issues are addressed, concluding that all the proposed implementation models have the same behavior. Finally, in Section 6 conclusions are presented.

2 Contribution to Technological Innovation

The ultimate goal of the works where the presented one is included is to contribute to the usage of Petri nets as a system level specification language for embedded system design. In particular, the innovative contribution is to use the net splitting operation to formally support a technique to start from global system Petri net model and be able to obtain parallel components, which would be executed in heterogeneous platforms. As will be shown in the following sections, a set of properties of the global system model will be preserved after the described transformation, even when different types of platforms are considered for implementation.

The contribution of this paper is to introduce a MDA based methodology for embedded system design, when distributed execution of the model is a concern and where Petri nets are used as system specification language. The main focus is given to the properties verification of the transformed models.

3 Methodology Overview and Objectives

Our reference methodology for embedded system design using hardware-software co-design techniques starts with the description of the system's functionalities through UML (Unified Modeling Language) use cases. Afterwards, these use cases are manually translated into a set of operational formal models, where Petri nets are considered as the reference model formalism. These models are amenable to support property verification and to be automatically translated into code, after being partitioned into components and mapped into specific implementation platforms.

Our intention is to improve that methodology introducing the MDA philosophy of development. In this approach, the effort is focused on models, metamodels, and model transformations. In MDA, an application can be characterized by several models at different levels of abstraction. The relations between those models are defined as transformations between models.

The highest considered abstraction level is the Platform Independent Model (PIM). In such level, the models represent the system requirements and are independent of any specific implementation platform. The MDA approach emphasizes that a correct model at the PIM level should maintain its correctness independently of selecting different technology mappings afterwards.

The next level of abstraction is the Platform Specific Model (PSM). At this level, the models reflect the specific system characteristics. In this level, specific constructs of each platform are considered, although, as emphasized before, the behavior of the original PIM model must be preserved.

Finally, as the lowest level of abstraction, we are considering the implementation code, reflecting the concrete syntax of a specific implementation platform. This artifact does not insert any specific abstraction to the models, just being a straightforward representation of the PSM concepts.

In this work, the emphasis is on the PSM level. To illustrate these different abstraction levels and the model transformations between them, we use Petri nets (see Fig. 1), as we want to emphasize the usage of Petri nets as a system level specification formalism. However, from the point of view of the proposed methodology flow, Petri nets can be replaced by any other behavioral formalism with similar characteristics, without loss of generality of the proposed methodology flow.

Using Petri net as system level specification language, in the first level of abstraction we apply a transformation in order to decompose the model into several sub-nets using the net splitting operation [5]. These operations are introduced in our MDA approach by transformation rules that define how to transform a global Petri net model into partitioned Petri net sub-models (subnets). Afterwards, PSMs are generated from these subnets. In the case of a decomposed PIM model, we can consider two types of PSMs to be generated. One of them is where the communication between

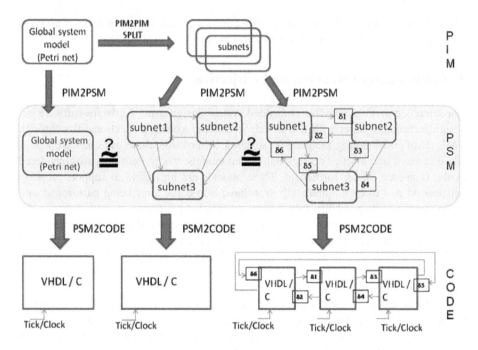

Fig. 1. From PIMs to code: an MDA-based approach

the models is made using synchronous communication channels [9] and the zero delay time paradigm can be applied. On the other hand, it is also possible to consider the case where the zero delay time paradigm does not hold and the communication between the models is made using a random time delay on the communication channels.

As the lowest level of abstraction those models are mapped into implementation code for a specific platform. Two types of implementation platforms for the distributed model are considered: those having a global clock/tick and where a synchronous communication between the components is possible according with the zero delay time paradigm, and those having different time regions (heterogeneous platforms) and where the synchrony paradigm does not apply and the communication is modeled using a delay between the components.

The objective of this paper is to present the way to demonstrate that the generated PSM models associated with different platforms have the same execution behavior.

The expected benefits of using an MDA approach for generating the models and respective code of the partitioned components are twofold: The first one is to lower the cost of deploying a given component and corresponding code on multiple platforms through reuse; The second one is to reach a higher level of automation in the code generation process, through the specification of transformations among those models.

In the next section we will present a running example to illustrate the application of the proposed methodology.

4 Running Example

We consider a simple example of application introduced by [10] with two cars going back and forth, as shown on the Fig. 2

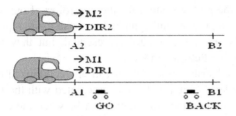

Fig. 2. Application example

Their movements are synchronized at the end points (in A[i] and B[i], respectively). The cars start moving when both are in the initial position (in A1 and A2) and the button GO is activated. They stop when reach the end point B1 and B2, respectively. To go back to the initial position both cars have to be in the respective positions B[i] and the button BACK has to be activated. A possible Petri net PIM model for this simple control problem is presented in Fig. 3 a). As PIM2PIM model transformation we can use the net splitting operation [5] to decompose the Petri net and obtain a set of distributed controllers (to be deployed one for each car). This can be done by choosing a set of nodes (transitions GO and BACK for the example) from

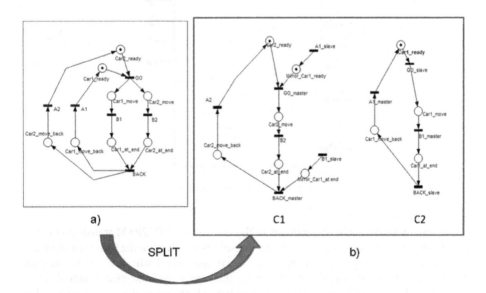

Fig. 3. Petri net models for two cars system: a) global controller; b) distributed controllers

where the net will be splitted. As the result of this operation we obtain four sub-nets, corresponding to the control of the movement in each direction of the cars. To obtain the model of the controller for each car we have to map two sub-nets to each controller (which are combined using the net addition operation [11]). The resulted models are shown in the Fig. 3 b).

As PSM model of the global system for the controller of our system is shown on Fig. 4 where the input and the output signals of the system are represented (dependencies on output signals are not explicitly represented, but they are associated with "Cari_move" places of the Petri net model).

When we consider a distributed model instead of a centralized model, as shown on Fig. 3 b) we can consider different behaviors associated with the PIM2PSM transformation. One of them is when the communication between the components is represented by synchronous communication channels. This means that pairs of transitions belonging to different sub-nets (one with attribute master and other one with attribute slave, as presented in Fig. 3b)) are synchronized through a synchronous communication channel and will fire at the same time, considering the same tick. The corresponding model is represented in Fig. 5. This model is composed of two sub-models. The sub-model where the transition with the attribute master is included generates an output event which is read by the other sub-model where a transition with the same name and attribute slave is included. Execution of both sub-models will satisfy the synchrony paradigm.

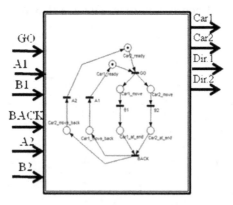

Fig. 4. Global system model

Another possible modeling attitude in the case of the PIM2PSM transformation is to consider firing in different instants for transitions involved in the same communication channel, resulting in a non-zero time delay associated with the communication between the two components. Considering that our communication channel, even when considering synchronous firing, is directed (which means that an output event is

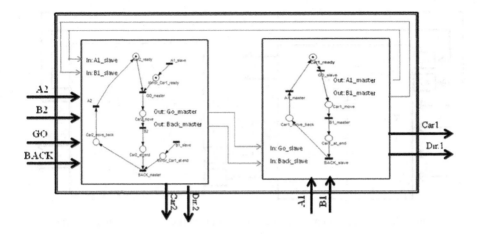

Fig. 5. Distributed system model implementation considering zero time delay

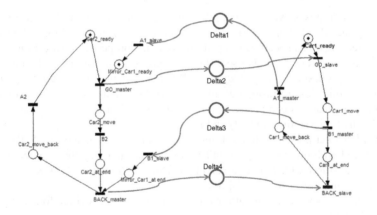

Fig. 6. Distributed system model including the communication between the components

generated by the master transition firing, which is read as an input event by the slave transition), it is possible to explicitly include this dependency as a delay δ into the model, and represent the delay as a place between the transition master and transition slave, as in the Petri net model of Fig. 6. It is easy to verify that, for this new model, those places are safe (limited to only one token).

The model of Fig. 6 corresponds to the system implementation where each sub-model is in execution in a different platform with different execution ticks (different time regions). In this way, we can not guarantee the synchronous firing of transitions belonging to different components. In this case the component with the master transition generates an output event which will be connected to the component to which the respective slave transition belongs as an input signal associated to that transition. This view of the model is represented in Fig. 7.

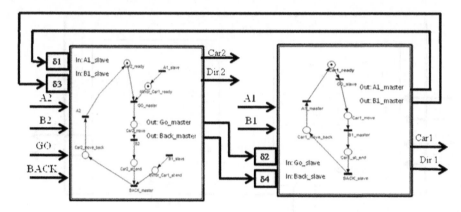

Fig. 7. Distributed system model implementation considering different platforms

5 Verification

For verification purposes, we are using rewriting logic and model checking techniques, supported by the Maude framework [12] [13] and Linear Temporal Logic (LTL) language [14], relying on its specification patterns to define properties verification.

Due to space restriction we choose to include here analysis on the verification only on the following question goals: *if an event P happens between two events Q and R*. The choice for this class of properties allows us to show that two models involved in proposed transformations can preserve, at least the partial order, the same behavior P bounded by the limits of the events Q and R.

For each Petri net presented in the figures Fig. 3 a), Fig. 3 b), and Fig. 5, the equations associated with the events Q, R and P are defined in a way that Q is equivalent to firing of transition GO, P is equivalent to firing of transition BACK , and P is equivalent to firing of transitions B[i] or A[i].

By applying the specification patterns in this scenario, we used the following temporal logic formula:

```
[](Q and !R -> (!R W (P and !R)))
```

In this sense, our objective is to demonstrate that a specific firing sequence associated with the initial model of the global system is verified for all cases of the different implementation models. One possible trace is the following:

$$Go \rightarrow (B1 \text{ and } B2) \rightarrow Back \rightarrow (A1 \text{ and } A2) \rightarrow Go$$

The semantics of this trace states that the order of firing of B1 and B2 is indifferent, the same way as the order of firing of A1 and A2. The important constraint to be checked is the firing of those transitions before firing transitions BACK and Go respectively.

By using the Maude 2.4 toolset, where we have defined the Petri nets presented in the figures Fig. 3 a) and b) and Fig. 5 and the equations needed for the verification purposes, the result in the above presented case is TRUE for all execution models as was defined in the previous section.

In this sense, preservation of this trace propriety is preserved along presented transformations.

On the other hand, in the case when the event P is defined as a non-observable sequence, the result of the verification is a counterexample. One of the non-observable sequences is Go $\rightarrow$ (B1) $\rightarrow$ Back, (considering no occurrence of B2). For this case we obtained for all our nets a result as a counterexample.

The associated codes and results are available in the institution's web site at http://www.uninova.pt/~mda-veritas.

6 Conclusions

The paper presents an MDA approach for verification of properties preservation of the transformed models. As reference modeling formalism was used Petri net and the net splitting operation for model decomposition. It was demonstrated using model checking techniques that all models associated with our running example keep the same behavior when mapped into implementations platforms with different constraints.

Complementary the different models were coded in VHDL and deployed into Spartan 3 FPGA platforms. It was validated that the different physical implementations keep the same behavior for relevant situations.

Acknowledgments. The work presented was partially supported by the collaborative project Verificação Semântica em Transformações MDA Envolvendo Modelos de Redes de Petri (MDA-VERITAS - Semantic Verification in MDA Transformation using Petri nets models), funded by FCT - Fundação para a Ciência e a Tecnologia (Portugal) and CAPES - Coordenação de Aperfeiçoamento de Pessoal de Nível Superior (Brazil) (http://www.uninova.pt/~mda-veritas).

References

1. Brisolara, L.C.B., Kreutz, M.E., Carro, L.: UML as Front-End Language for Embedded Systems Design. In: Gomes, L., Fernandes, J.M. (eds.) Behavioral Modeling for Embedded Systems and Technologies: Application for Design and Implementation, pp. 1–23. Information Science Reference, Hershey (2009)
2. Gargantini, A., Riccobene, E., Scandurra, P.: Model-Driven Design and ASM Validation of Embedded Systems. In: Gomes, L., Fernandes, J.M. (eds.) Behavioral Modeling for Embedded Systems and Technologies: Application for Design and Implementation, pp. 24–54. Information Science Reference, Hershey (2009)
3. Girault, C., Valk, R.: Petri nets for systems engineering: A Guide to Modeling. Verification and Applicatons. Springer, Heidelberg (2003)
4. Reisig, W.: Petri nets: An Introduction. Springer, New York (1985)
5. Costa, A., Gomes, L.: Petri net Partitioning Using net Splitting Operation. In: 7th IEEE International Conference on Industrial Informatics (2009)
6. OMG: Object Management Group (2009), http://www.omg.org
7. Miller, J., Mukerji, J.: Mda guide version 1.0.1. Object Management Group, OMG (2003)

8. Barbosa, P., Ramalho, F., Figueiredo, J., Junior, A., Costa, A., Gomes, L.: Checking Semantics Equivalence of MDA Transformations in Concurrent Systems. Journal of Universal Computer Science (JUCS) 15(11), 2196–2224 (2009),
    http://www.jucs.org/jucs_15_11/checking_semantics_equivalence_of
9. Christensen, S., Hansen, N.D.: Coloured Petri Nets Extended with Channels for Synchronous Communication. In: Valette, R. (ed.) ICATPN 1994. LNCS, vol. 815, pp. 159–178. Springer, Heidelberg (1994)
10. Silva, M.: Las Redes de Petri: En la Automática y la Informática. Editorial AC, Madrid (1985)
11. Barros, J.P., Gomes, L.: Net Model Composition and Modification by Net Operations: A Pragmatic Approach. In: 2nd IEEE International Conference on Industrial Informatics, Berlin, Germany, June 24-26 (2004)
12. Maude system and tools, http://maude.cs.uiuc.edu/maude1/tutorial/
13. Clavel, M., Durán, F., Eker, S., Lincoln, P.: Martí -Oliet, N., Meseguer, J., Quesada, J.F.: Maude: Specification and programming in rewriting logic. Theoretical Computer Science (2001)
14. Specification patterns for temporal logic model-checking. SAnTos Laboratories, http://patterns.projects.cis.ksu.edu/documentation/patterns/ltl.shtml

Semantic Equations for Formal Models in the Model-Driven Architecture

Paulo Barbosa[1], Franklin Ramalho[1], Jorge Figueiredo[1],
Anikó Costa[2], Luís Gomes[2], and Antônio Junior[1]

[1] Universidade Federal de Campina Grande, Brasil
{paulo,franklin,abrantes,antonio}@dsc.ufcg.edu.br
[2] Universidade Nova de Lisboa, Portugal
{akc,lugo}@uninova.pt

Abstract. Semantic equations are important pieces of the denotational semantics approach that enable the translation of syntactic constructs of models to semantic domains. In a previous work, we have extended the Model-Driven Architecture (MDA) four-layer proposal of architecture in order to incorporate formal semantics to its artifacts. Thus, semantic equations are key elements in this extended architecture. In this paper, we propose an approach to incorporate semantic equations described by model transformations in the MDA infrastructure. As a result, we automatically generate semantic models from the syntactic models involved in the MDA transformations. Therefore, the semantic equations play an important role in the MDA architecture since they allow the construction of tools for automated reasoning for several purposes, such as: (i) verification of semantics preservation in model transformations; (ii) choice of the best format to represent meaning and behavior of models and (iii) automatic generation and production of quality compilers. For instance, we claim that in the scenario of model transformations involving concurrent models described using Petri nets, semantic concepts can be more easily and appropriately handled in the MDA architecture. We have evaluated our approach by applying semantic equations to Petri nets models in a project for embedded systems codesign.

Keywords: Model-Driven Architecture, Petri nets, Denotational Semantics, Transformations, Semantic Equations.

1 Introduction

In the Model-Driven Architecture (MDA) [1] [2], a model is an abstract or concrete representation of a domain. They are described by metamodels that express the elements of the language. Model transformations process these elements through a set of definition rules that describe how to generate an output model from an input model. Although MDA promises to overcome important gaps in the software engineering, it has not specified ways to ensure that its artifacts are correctly represented. Particularly, the lack of a formal representation of the involved models in the four-layer MDA architecture leads to undesirable situations of ambiguity and low reliability.

L.M. Camarinha-Matos, P. Pereira, and L. Ribeiro (Eds.): DoCEIS 2010, IFIP AICT 314, pp. 251–260, 2010.
© IFIP International Federation for Information Processing 2010

In [3], we have proposed an extension of the four-layer MDA architecture in order to incorporate formal semantics in its infrastructure. We introduced semantic metamodels and models, and other artifacts to verify semantics equivalence between the input and output models involved in MDA transformations and to prove properties about them. This proposal was evaluated in the concurrent systems domains, through models represented using Petri nets [4] in a project of embedded systems co-design [5].

Assuming the importance of formal semantics in the modeling domain, to apply it to a model it is necessary the assignment of meanings to its sentences or components.

This needs to be treated in the proposal of the extension of the MDA architecture. This assignment should be given by a mathematical model that represents every possible computation in the language that describes the model. It is expected with the semantic description of a model the following benefits: (i) the development of partial evaluation techniques for interpreting and compiling models in the MDA architecture; (ii) the automatic generation of compiler semantics definitions; (iii) a foundation for understanding and evaluating the design issues; and (iv) a valuable reference for transformations that involve this model. In this sense, the formal definition is necessary to guarantee the preservation of properties in the output model after a transformation, which is the main goal of a PhD thesis that guides this work.

The denotational semantics [6] is one of the most employed approaches to provide formal semantics. It is specially addressed for the case in which the necessity of constructing mathematical objects to represent meaning of models emerges, as is in this work. In this approach, the meaning is given by functions that map syntactic elements to mathematically well-defined sets. This mapping is usually named as semantic equations.

Although semantic models are considered as important pieces for a formal architecture, in the extension of the MDA architecture they make sense only in the case of being automatically generated from the syntax. Most approaches based on semantic models depend on the expertise of a domain engineer, demanding costs, low reliability and very imprecise specifications as representations of what of most precise a model should have [7].

In this paper, we claim that the extraction of semantic models in MDA must be responsibility of the semantic equations, following declarative formal rules using automated tools according to the MDA standards. Semantic models can be described by a metamodel with the same expressive power as the metalanguage of denotational semantics. This fills the necessity of compiler generators guided by semantics as a unified framework. Denotational semantics specifications may have the format of a MDA transformation, providing this unification as mathematical objects and turning modeling languages closer to this metalanguage of formal semantics.

The structure of this paper is as follows. Section 2 discusses how this work can contribute to innovation in the specific MDA technology. Section 3 and 4 presents the main background issues necessary for understanding this work, namely our previous proposal of the extending the MDA architecture and the denotational semantics concepts involved. Section 5 gives details about our proposed approach to specify semantic equations illustrating and evaluating for specific models. Section 6 discusses related works. Finally, Section 7 discusses about the benefits and possible drawbacks of the presented work, and the final remarks.

2   Contribution to Technological Innovation

In this work, we propose and discuss an approach to introduce semantic equations as formal specifications in the MDA architecture. Considering MDA transformations as the pivotal element to specify semantic equations, some issues emerge to be answered, as pragmatic aspects of the transformation language and some theoretical aspects related to computability. These issues are addressed and discussed in this work.

We evaluate this proposal with a well-established and appropriate extraction from the syntactic constructs to semantic domains in the concurrent domain with Petri nets models. This allowed the verification of semantics preserving transformations as well as an on-the-fly occurrence graph generation system for it. Moreover, with the proposal of a representation to semantic equations, semantic properties of models can be checked for several purposes.

3   The Extended MDA Four-Layer Architecture

The current MDA architecture, shown in Figure 1, consists of four layers: (i) M0 involves executable representations of models as code; (ii) M1 describes the concrete syntax representation of a given model; (iii) M2 provides the metamodel which serves as a grammar to describe the model syntax developed at the layer M1; and (iii) M3 describes the layer M2 by using MOF, the Meta-Object Facility [2]. Since MOF describes itself, it is not required further metamodels. The model transformations are able to automatically generate output models from input models at the layer M1. They are defined in terms of metamodel descriptions and cope only with syntactic/structural aspects.

Our proposal of an extended MDA architecture for incorporating formal semantics is shown in Figure 2 as gray modules at the layers M1 and M2. Semantic equations, which are the focus of this paper is highlighted and will be discussed. Briefly, the other new inserted parts are:

- Semantic metamodel, which defines (i) the state configuration of a model or a program according to the semantic specifications; and (ii) the dynamic semantics capturing the state infrastructure of language constructs as well as how they use or change an existing state. It serves as a concretization for theories of formal semantics.
- Semantic model, which instantiates the state configuration metamodel. Since semantic metamodels represent theories of formal semantics, semantic models are representations according to these theories.
- Simplification rules, which are able to perform the inference and computation of state configurations. They instantiate the dynamic semantics. These rules are implemented according to the chosen computation mechanism.
- Formal checker, which is complementary to the simplification rules, also instantiates the dynamic semantics, and it is required to prove properties about the equivalence of the verified input and output models.

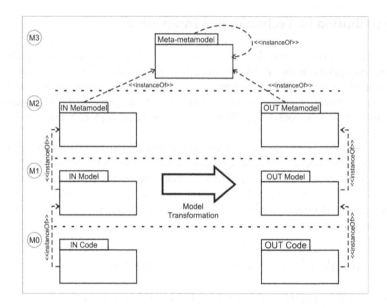

Fig. 1. The current MDA Architecture

The role of semantic equations in this architecture is to define mappings, from the language's abstract syntax structures to meanings drawn from semantic models. They are illustrated as the small arrows from the syntactic models to the semantic models in the layer M1.

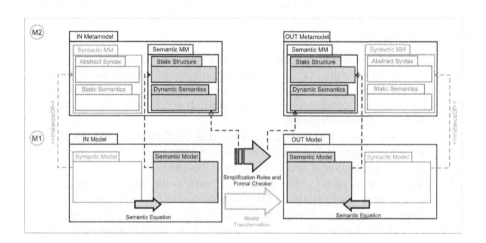

Fig. 2. The extended architecture to incorporate formal semantics

4 Denotational Semantics for Petri Nets

The main aim of denotational semantics is to provide a proper mathematical foundation for reasoning about programs and programming languages. It is based on a set of
denotations, i.e., a function with arguments that represent expressions before and after
executing. Denotations can inductively be defined by using any formal mapping to
specify how the denotations of components are combined.

To give the denotational semantics of a language, a suitable collection of meanings
is necessary. The most used theory is called Domain Theory, which employs structured sets, called domains, and their operations as data structures for semantics. These
domains plus their operations constitute a semantic algebra. According to [8], the
semantic algebra: (i) clearly states the structure of a domain and how its elements are
used by the functions; (ii) modularizes and provides reuse of semantic definitions; and
(iii) makes analysis easier.

We have chosen the Petri nets formalism as the description language of the involved models because this language is already well-accepted in the MDA community [9] and has a good support to formal semantics. It was designed as a graphical
and mathematical formalism for modeling concurrent systems. Moreover, this work is
inserted in the context of a project that proposes the use of Petri nets for the co-design
of embedded systems.

We take the nets analyzed in [10] which are shown in Figure 3 and refers to the
model of a parking lot controller when considering a centralized implementation or a
distributed implementation relying in two components (synchronized through transition firing) after applying the Splitting Operation.

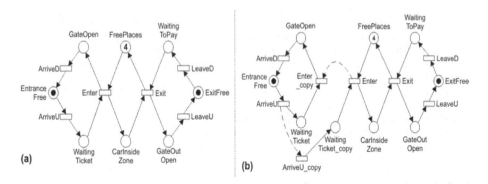

Fig. 3. Two nets that represent models before and after the Splitting Operation

In [11], Meséguer and Montanari use the category theory to claim that a Petri
net model is to be translated to an ordinary, directed graph equipped with two algebraic operations. These operations correspond to the sequential and parallel composition of transitions (representing behavior), with a distributive law between these
compositions.

The model has to provide the generators of the algebraic structure which the responsibility of the automatic mapping is given to the semantic equations.

The understanding of concurrency in terms of algebraic structures over graphs is very important for Petri nets modelers. It has the potential of unifying several views of semantics formalisms. Moreover, this structure can be manipulated by formal methods tools to be employed in several sorts of analysis and satisfying some requirements that are hard to solve by most editors and tools available for this domain. As an example, several formal tools could afford to the state space explosion problem, by providing an on-the-fly way of reasoning over occurrence graph structure of the Petri net model if it is seen as this algebraic structure.

By using more specific terms, this ordinary graph has a set of nodes as a commutative monoid $S^\oplus$ generated by the set S of places and the empty marking as identity. The sum + of transitions represents the parallel firing of transitions, and the sequential firing of transitions is denoted by the operation. By the guarantee of the closure property, we are representing computations through simple transitions.

For example, we have that the next code fragment is a representation of the semantic model for the Maude System [12] from the net before the Splitting Operation of Figure 3 as an illustration of the role that semantic models can play after extracted from the semantic equations. The Commutative operation + is present in line 7 with the specified properties. This semantic model may be used for several verification purposes, such as model-checking or theorem proving.

```
1: mod INPUT_NET is
2:   sorts Place Marking .
3:   subsort Place < Marking .
4:   ops GateOpen EntranceFree WaitingTicket CarInsideZone
5:    GateOutOpen ExitFree WaitingToPay FreePlaces : -> Place.
6:   op empty : -> Marking.
7:   op _+_:Marking Marking->Marking [assoc comm id:empty].
8:   rl [ArriveD]:GateOpen=>EntranceFree.
9:   rl [ArriveU]:EntranceFree=>WaitingTicket.
10: rl [Enter]:WaitngTicket + FreePlaces=>CarInsdeZone +
GateOpen.
11: rl [Exit]:CarInsdeZone + WaitingToPay=>GateOtOpen + Free-
Place.
12: rl [LeaveU]:GateOutOpen=>ExitFree.
13: rl [LeaveD]:ExitFree=>WaitingToPay.
14:endm
```

5   MDA Semantic Equations

In order to incorporate semantic equations into the extended MDA architecture, it is necessary to cope with pragmatic and formal issues. The former concerns requirements related to the language and tools that will represent semantic equations whereas the latter deals with theoretical aspects to ensure composition and recursion as is required by denotational semantics specifications.

Focusing on the pragmatic issues, there are three requirements that must be observed on the language used to represent semantic equations:

i.   It must be able to represent the functional characteristics of classical defini-
     tions for denotational semantics. Supporting the declarative paradigm allows
     pattern matching that is essential to describe functional operations. Moreover,
     this seems also necessary because the language that will describe the codo-
     main of semantic equations as in denotational semantics is completely based
     on functional constructs, such as functions definitions and applications.

ii. It must support the representation of actual features of most programming
     models, representing aspects of programming and modeling languages. Con-
     cepts such as sequentiality, concurrency, non-determinism and an infrastruc-
     ture to represent states are present whatever be the domain of the semantic
     equations application.

iii. It must manipulate and execute properly the semantic equations. This will en-
     able the integration with other formal methods tools. A powerful toolset of the
     language to support this seems to be essential to our solution.

On the other hand, there are two theoretical aspects of the language that must be
addressed:

iv. It must be fully (or partially) compositional. The understanding of composite
     expressions as transformations rules makes the proof of properties about se-
     mantics easier, allowing the translation of syntactic pieces to a semantic meta-
     language represented as a semantic algebra metamodel. This represents a
     challenge but also a useful improvement because there are usually proposi-
     tions, axioms and theorems that have been developed for this metalanguage.
     Finding such a compositional language allows us to reason using induction
     over the grammar of the modeling language, since this grammar can be de-
     scribed by metamodels.

v.   It must allow recursion over the grammatical structure (i.e. the metamodel) of
     the language it interprets. In other terms, it must enable to extract the current
     state of the model in terms of a meaningful representation (i.e. the semantic
     model). This is made by carrying a structure representing the environment of
     a program or of a model. When the input model (i.e. syntactic model) is given
     to the engine, the transformation explores it at the top-level term, creating any
     necessary context into an environmental structure, passes this structure into a
     recursive call for each of the subterms, and provides the terms able to be ana-
     lyzed based on what it gets back from the mapping that represents the seman-
     tic equations.

This work characterizes semantic equations as, essentially, MDA transformations. In
order to prove this, we choose a transformation language and MDA standards to accomplish the presented pragmatic and formal issues. This was evaluated through a
case study that we conducted for the mapping from syntactic structures to semantic
domains. For this, we have chosen the ATL language [13], because this language is
able to satisfy the mentioned requirements. Moreover we discuss this justification by
using Petri nets models.

Concerning the previously pragmatic addressed issues, we have a discussion about
each topic. About (i), classical definitions of denotational semantics are present requiring a declarative approach for the definition of functional algebraic concepts. In

(ii), we have that imperative fragments are necessary in when defining semantic equation, dealing with common concepts such as variables and sequencing. Finishing the first part of issues, we have that in (iii), ATL allows the manipulation of formal semantics concepts using an editor and an engine tool able to execute these specifications according to [13]. Concerning the theoretical issues, we see that in (iv), the compositionality of ATL enables the definition of the mapping into simpler parts, treating each algebraic structure as mathematics does and combining these rules for the whole. Finally the issue (v) is answered because ATL searches recursively in the language metamodel, dealing with the compositionality of the subterms, converting abstract syntax structures into the predefined algebraic structures responsible for the representation of meaning as semantic models.

6 Related Works

Regarding to related works we concentrate on the expected benefits of having semantic models using MDA standards through semantic equations. [14] proposes the use of Petri nets to simulate the behavior of models in MDA. The models are described in UML state chart Diagrams and then converted to a Colored Petri nets representation. In this case, Petri nets models act as semantic models. The work presented in [15] proposes the MOF formalization reusing the category theory modularization concepts from algebraic specification languages. This provides a graph-transformation-based formalization of MOF, upgrading MOF with new interfaces and a composition operator based on graph morphisms. It is the same idea reused here, however is a proposal for the meta-metalanguage of the MDA framework, and not for a specific domain as we made for Petri nets. In [16] the authors propose a novel approach for the definition of a formal semantics to languages based on the Alloy language. It intends to turn semantics definitions easier, encouraging the adoption of formal techniques. This work advocates that its approach provides two main advantages: uniform notation and a mechanism for analysis. Finally, [17] concentrates in some specific problems commonly found when using MDA such as refactorings and extraction of meanings of UML models. This work makes use of mathematical techniques, specially the lattices theory, to discover abstractions from a set of formal objects. This seems very useful for providing sound refactorings. The similarity with our work is that semantic equations can also be viewed as ATL transformations, when mapping a UML diagram to a formal context (the semantic model).

7 Final Remarks and Future Works

It is already known that MDA's artifacts and processes lack a semantic model, and that there is no way to ensure that its transformations preserve the semantics. The use of an underlying semantic model for verification purposes is a fundamental step in the MDA transformations, in order to have a formal definition of the involved artifacts in the transformation and be able to check its correctness by comparing whether the input and output models are consistent according to the semantic model definition.

Semantic models are also suitable for a compiler generation system for MDA. Currently, the models and metamodels built in this infrastructure can deal only with abstract and concrete syntax terms. Semantic equations are able to map to the denotational definition from a programming or modeling language. Concepts like semantic domains and semantic equations are specifications and the concrete implementation of a MDA compiler is encouraged. It enables dealing with semantic concepts such as scope, declarations, functions, type inference and type checking, control flow, exceptions and much more. Thus, the suitability of a semantic model is a promising step towards the automatic generation and production of quality compilers and processors.

We intend to analyze our approach in other scenarios than Petri nets modeling. Although each scenario have particular properties to be considered when providing semantic models by means of semantic equations, we advocate that our approach deserves special attention in all cases since: (i) the provided semantic metamodel may be reused; (ii) semantic models are required in any scenarios (iii) the pragmatic and theoretical issues raised in this work must be addressed.

Acknowledgments. This work was partially supported by the collaborative project Verificação Semântica em Transformações MDA Envolvendo Modelos de Redes de Petri (MDA-VERITAS - Semantic Verification in MDA Transformation using Petri nets models), funded by FCT - Fundação para a Ciência e a Tecnologia (Portugal) and CAPES - Coordenação de Aperfeiçoamento de Pessoal de Nível Superior (Brazil) (http://www.uninova.pt/~mda-veritas).

References

1. Miller, J., Mukerji, J.: MDA Guide Version 1.0.1. Object Management Group, OMG (2003)
2. OMG: Object Management Group (2008), http://www.omg.org
3. Barbosa, P., Ramalho, F., Figueiredo, J., Junior, A.: An Extended MDA Architecture for Ensuring Semantics-Preserving Transformations. In: Proceedings of 32nd Annual IEEE Software Engineering Workshop (2008)
4. Girault, C.V.R.: Petri Nets for Systems Engineering. In: XV, 607 p., Hardcover (2003)
5. Gomes, L., Barros, J.P., Costa, A., Pais, R., Moutinho, F.: Formal Methods for Embedded Systems Co-design: the FORDESIGN Project. In: ReCoSoC 2005- Reconfigurable Communication-centric Systems-on-Chip - Workshop Proceedings (2005)
6. Scott, D., Strachey, C.: Towards a Mathematical Semantics for Computer Languages. In: Proceedings of the Symposium on Computers and Automata. Microwave Research Institute Symposia Series, vol. 21 (1971)
7. Hausmann, J.: Dynamic Meta Modeling: A Semantics Description Technique for Visual Modeling Techniques. PhD thesis, University of Paderborn (2005)
8. Schmidt, D.A.: Denotational Semantics: a Methodology for Language Development. William C. Brown Publishers, Dubuque (1986)
9. Hillah, L., Kordon, F., Petrucci, L., Tréves, N.: Model Engineering on Petri nets for ISO/IEC 15909-2: API Framework for Petri Net types metamodels. Petri Net Newsletter, 22–40 (2005)

10. Barbosa, P., Costa, A., Ramalho, F., Figueiredo, J., Gomes, L., Junior, A.: Checking Semantics Equivalence of MDA Transformations in Concurrent Systems. Journal of Universal Computer Science, J.UCS (to appear, 2009), http://www.jucs.org/jucs

11. Meseguer, J., Montanari, U.: Petri nets are Monoids: a new Algebraic Foundation for Net Theory. In: Proceedings of the Third Annual IEEE Symposium on Logic in Computer Science (LICS 1988), pp. 155–164. IEEE Computer Society Press, Los Alamitos (1988)

12. Clavel, M., Durán, F., Eker, S., Lincoln, P., Martí-Oliet, N., Meseguer, J., Quesada, J.F.: Maude: Specification and programming in rewriting logic. Theoretical Computer Science (2001)

13. Bezivin, J., Breton, E., Valduriez, P., Dupr, G.: The ATL Transformation-Based Model Management Framework. Technical report, produced from IRIN (2003)

14. Hu, Z., Shatz, S.M.: Mapping UML Diagrams to a Petri Net Notation for System Simulation. In: SEKE, pp. 213–219 (2004)

15. Weisemöller, I., Schürr, A.: Formal Definition of MOF 2.0 Metamodel Components and Composition. In: Czarnecki, K., Ober, I., Bruel, J.-M., Uhl, A., Völter, M. (eds.) MODELS 2008. LNCS, vol. 5301, pp. 386–400. Springer, Heidelberg (2008)

16. Kelsen, P., Ma, Q.: A lightweight approach for defining the formal semantics of a modeling language. In: Czarnecki, K., Ober, I., Bruel, J.-M., Uhl, A., Völter, M. (eds.) MODELS 2008. LNCS, vol. 5301, pp. 690–704. Springer, Heidelberg (2008)

17. Arévalo, G., Falleri, J.R., Huchard, M., Nebut, C.: Building abstractions in class models: Formal concept analysis in a model-driven approach. In: Nierstrasz, O., Whittle, J., Harel, D., Reggio, G. (eds.) MoDELS 2006. LNCS, vol. 4199, pp. 513–527. Springer, Heidelberg (2006)

Part 9

Advances in Telecommunications

Delay Analysis for TDMA Schemes with Packet Recombining

Miguel Pereira[1,2,3], Luís Bernardo[1,3], Rui Dinis[1,2], Rodolfo Oliveira[1,3], Paulo Carvalho[1,3], and Paulo Pinto[1,3]

[1] FCT-UNL, Universidade Nova de Lisboa, Portugal
[2] IT, Instituto de Telecomunicações, Portugal
[3] UNINOVA, Monte da Caparica, Portugal
{miguelpereira,lflb,rdinis,rado}@fct.unl.pt,
pmc@uninova.pt, pfp@fct.unl.pt

Abstract. This paper considers the use of SC modulations (Single-Carrier) with FDE (Frequency-Domain Equalization) with low-complexity soft combining ARQ schemes (Automatic Repeat reQuest). With our technique, packets associated to different transmission attempts are combined in a soft way, allowing improved performances. Its low complexity makes it particularly interesting for the uplink of wireless systems. This paper proposes an accurate analytical model for a TDMA (Time Division Multiple Access) scheme where packet combining ARQ is applied. It evaluates the uplink non-saturated packet delay for a generic message arrival process. Our analytical results are validated using physical and MAC layer simulations.

Keywords: Delay analysis, ARQ schemes, Mac protocol and Markov Chains.

1 Introduction

Packet errors can be significant in wireless systems due to fading and shadowing effects, which may lead to significant decrease in the receiving power. The traditional approach to cope with an erroneous packet is to discard it, and ask for its retransmission, which corresponds to the conventional ARQ techniques (Automatic Repeat reQuest). The major problem with conventional ARQ techniques is that persistent unfavorable propagation conditions may originate a very high PER (Packet Error Rate). The individual packet error probability is not affected by the number of packet retransmissions because the information contained in signal of the discarded packets is not used. Hybrid ARQ/FEC (Forward Error Correction) strategies were proposed [1, 2] to cope with these scenarios. They retain the signal associated to an erroneous packet and they may ask for additional redundancy. The traditional H-ARQ (Hybrid ARQ/FEC) approach relies on a powerful error correcting code that is punctured, to increase the data rate. Successive retransmissions reduce the puncturing, and therefore increase the error correction capacities of the code. This limits the error correction capability to the base code capabilities. We proposed on [3] the use of soft packet combining techniques to implement H-ARQ on SC modulations (Single Carrier) with FDE (Frequency-Domain Equalization). It is based on repetition codes with soft decision, which is not bounded by the performance of the basic code. The use of H-ARQ

L.M. Camarinha-Matos, P. Pereira, and L. Ribeiro (Eds.): DoCEIS 2010, IFIP AICT 314, pp. 263–272, 2010.
© IFIP International Federation for Information Processing 2010

techniques improve the network throughput compared to conventional ARQ technique because the packet error probability after retransmission i (p_i) is usually lower than p_{i-1}. It also reduces the average packet delay.

In this paper we study the performance of H-ARQ techniques for SC-FDE schemes. SC-FDE schemes are generally accepted as one of the best candidates for the uplink of future broadband wireless systems [4]. We consider a TDMA (Time Division Multiple Access) scheme, where a station shares a multiple access communications channel by transmitting its messages during its dedicated time slots, and a generic packet arrival distribution function.

TDMA is used in several current wireless network systems (802.16 , 802.11s, etc.) when hard QoS (Quality of Service) guarantees are needed. TDMA was the focus of an extensive list of past works (e.g. [5, 6, 7]), which assumed a constant packet error probability for the different retransmissions. ARQ error control was analyzed in [5] for a Poisson distributed message arrival process. Rubin and Zhang [6] analyzed the message delay for TDMA using multiple contiguous-slot assignments, considering a generic message arrival process. Chen and Chang [7] proposed a delay analysis model for TDMA model where slot assignment is characterized by a random variable, for a Poisson distributed message arrival process.

2   Contribution to Technological Innovation

This paper is the first to propose an exact analytical model concerning the queue-size and the message delay analysis of the TDMA system with an H-ARQ technique, for a generic message arrival distribution. This model is validated for Poisson traffic using ns-2, showing a significant packet delay reduction compared to the conventional ARQ technique.

3   System Overview

In this paper we consider the uplink transmission in an SC-FDE system. The time-domain block associated to a given user (i.e., the corresponding packet) is $\{a_n; n = 0,1,...,N-1\}$, where a_n is selected from a given constellation and N is the DFT size (Discrete Fourier Transform). As with other block transmission techniques, a suitable cyclic prefix is added to each time-domain block.

If we detect errors in the packet we ask for its retransmission, but we store the signal associated to each transmission attempt. Although we could keep trying to transmit the packet until there were no errors, in practice there is a maximum number of transmission attempts N_R. If we fail after N_R attempts we need to change the transmission parameters (transmit power, carrier frequency, base station, etc.) since the channel is too bad.

The packet associated to r th attempt to transmit $\{a_n; n = 0,1,...,N-1\}$ is $\{a_n^{(r)}; n = 0,1,...,N-1\}$. Naturally, $a_n^{(1)} = a_n$; in the following it will be clear that we can use $a_n^{(r)} \neq a_n$ for $r > 1$ to improve the performance in the presence of strong in-band interference.

The received signal associated to the r th transmission attempt is sampled and the cyclic prefix is removed, leading to the time-domain block $\{y_n^{(r)}; n = 0,1,...,N-1\}$. If the cyclic prefix is longer than the overall channel impulse response then the corresponding frequency-domain block is $\{Y_k^{(r)}; k = 0,1,...,N-1\}$, where

$$Y_k^{(r)} = A_k^{(r)} H_k^{(r)} + N_k^{(r)} + I_k^{(r)}, \tag{1}$$

with $N_k^{(r)}$ denoting the channel noise and $I_k^{(r)}$ the corresponding interference. $\{A_k^{(r)}; k = 0,1,...,N-1\}$ is the DFT of $\{a_n^{(r)}; n = 0,1,...,N-1\}$ and $H_k^{(r)}$ is the overall channel frequency response for the r th transmission attempt.

Let us assume that we have R versions of the packet (i.e., there were R transmission attempts). Our receiver, which is based on the IB-DFE receivers proposed in [8, 9], is depicted in fig 1. We have an iterative frequency-domain receiver where, for a given iteration i, the frequency-domain samples at the output are given by

$$\tilde{A}_k^{(i)} = \sum_{r=1}^{R} F_k^{(r,i)} Y_k^{(r)} - B_k^{(i)} \overline{A}_k^{(i-1)} \tag{2}$$

where $\{F_k^{(r,i)}; k = 0,1,...,N-1\}$ $(r = 1,2,...,R)$ and $\{B_k^{(i)}; k = 0,1,...,N-1\}$ can be regarded as the feedforward and the feedback coefficients, respectively. $\{\overline{A}_k^{(i-1)}; k = 0,1,...,N-1\}$ denotes the DFT of the average data estimates $\{\overline{a}_n^{(i-1)}; n = 0,1,...,N-1\}$, where $\overline{a}_n$ denotes the average symbol values conditioned to the FDE output, which can be obtain as described in [10].

The optimum feedforward coefficients for a given iteration, can be written as (see [3]), $F_k^{(r,i)} = \breve{F}_k^{(r,i)} \Big/ \gamma^{(i)}$, with $\gamma^{(i)} = \dfrac{1}{N} \sum_{k=0}^{N-1} \sum_{r=1}^{R} \breve{F}_k^{(r,i)} H_k^{(r)}$ and

$$\breve{F}_k^{(r,i)} = \frac{H_k^{(r)*}}{\alpha + (1-(\rho^{(i-1)})^2) \sum_{r'=1}^{R} |H_k^{(r')}|^2}, \quad r = 1,2,...,R, \tag{3}$$

where $\alpha = \dfrac{E[|N_k^{(r)}|^2]}{E[|A_k|^2]}$ (i.e., α is the inverse of the SNR (Signal-to-Noise Ratio)) and the correlation coefficient $\rho^{(i)}$ is given by

$$\rho^{(i)} = \frac{1}{2N} \sum_{n=0}^{N-1} (|Re\{\overline{a}_n^{(i)}\}| + |Im\{\overline{a}_n^{(i)}\}|). \tag{4}$$

The optimum feedback coefficients (also to minimize the signal-to-noise plus interference ratio) are given by

$$B_k^{(i)} = \sum_{r'=1}^{R} F_k^{(r',i)} H_k^{(r')} - 1. \tag{5}$$

4 The System Model

In this section we present the exact message delay and queue-size analysis for the system.

4.1 System Characterization

We consider a communication channel on a TDMA basis. Time is divided into equal length slots, each of duration equal to 1 block data of 32 bytes. The start of a message transmission across the channel must coincide with the beginning of a slot. The success of an arriving message is given by q_l, $0 < q_l < 1$, with l, $1 \le l \le R$, representing the transmission number of each message and R the maximum number of retransmissions allowed for each message. Each packet contains 32 bytes, so that a packet transmission time is equal to 1 slot. N_n represents the number of messages arrivals at the station during the n th slot, according to a stochastic process. We assume that $\{N_n, n \ge 1\}$ is a sequence of i.i.d. random variables, and we set $a_m = P(N_n = m)$, $m \ge 0$, and $\alpha = E[N_n]$ where α is the mean number of messages arrivals per slot. The station is allocated a possible multiple contiguous slots per frame N, with $N \ge 1$. A frame contains $N + L$ slots, with $L \ge 1$, representing the group of slots allocated to other stations. Messages can only be transmitted in those N dedicated slots during a frame. This section proposes a complete solution for the delay with $N = 1$, and characterizes the system dynamics for a generic N value.

4.2 The Generating Function of the Queue Size

Let X_k represent the number of messages in the station's queue at the start of slot k (including message arrivals that will occur during slot $k - 1$), and let Z_k represent the number of transmissions of one message at the same slot. So, at the start of slot k we have X_k messages in queue, and we will transmit the corresponding message for the Z_k th time. The process $\{(X_k, Z_k)k \ge 1\}$ is not Markovian because it is time dependent. To make it Markovian we use one supplementary variable, Y_k, to represent the slot index in the frame, $1 \le Y_k \le N + L$. With this we define an embedded Markov Chain $\{(X_k, Y_k, Z_k), k \ge 1\}$.

It can be shown that the system is stable if the average number of messages arrivals per slot α is less than the average number of messages transmitted per slot. Under the stability condition, the conditional steady-state distribution $\{X_k\}$ given that $Y_k = j$ and $Z_k = l$ and the steady-state distribution of $\{X_k\}$ in the Cesaro sense exists. Denote

$$P_{j,i,l} = \lim_{k \to \infty} P(X_k = i \mid Y_k = j, Z_k = l) \tag{6}$$

$$\pi(i) = \lim_{J \to \infty} \frac{1}{J} \sum_{k=1}^{J} \sum_{j=1}^{N+L} \sum_{l=1}^{R} P(X_k = i \,|\, Y_k = j, Z_k = l) \tag{7}$$

Next, we define a set of z -transforms, $|z| \le 1$.

$$U_{j,l}(z) = \sum_{i=0}^{\infty} P_{j,i,l} z^i \qquad 1 \le j \le N+L, 1 \le l \le R \tag{8}$$

$$\Pi(z) = \sum_{i=0}^{\infty} \pi(i) z^i \tag{9}$$

$$A(z) = \sum_{i=0}^{\infty} a_i z^i \quad A'(1) = \alpha, \; A''(1) = \alpha_2 \tag{10}$$

The steady-state probabilities referred previously satisfy the following equilibrium equations. For $i \ge 0$

$$P_{1,i,l} = \sum_{m=0}^{i} a_m P_{N+L,i-m,l} \tag{11}$$

$$P_{j,i,l} = \sum_{m=0}^{i} a_m P_{j-1,i-m,l}, \qquad N+2 \le j \le N+L \tag{12}$$

$$P_{j,i,1} = a_i P_{j-1,0,1} + \sum_{l=1}^{R-1} q_l \sum_{m=0}^{i} a_m P_{j-1,i+1-m,l} + \sum_{m=0}^{i} a_m P_{j-1,i+1-m,R}, \qquad 2 \le j \le N+1 \tag{13}$$

$$P_{j,i,l} = (1-q_{l-1}) \sum_{m=0}^{i-1} a_m P_{j-1,i-m,l-1}, \qquad 2 \le l \le R, 2 \le j \le N+1 \tag{14}$$

Looking the fact that $P(Y_k = j) = (N+L)^{-1}$, for $1 \le j \le N+L$, we have

$$\pi(i) = \frac{1}{N+L} \sum_{j=1}^{N+L} \sum_{l=1}^{R} P_{j,i,l} \tag{15}$$

Considering (8) and (9) we then obtain

$$\Pi(z) = \frac{1}{N+L} \sum_{j=1}^{N+L} \sum_{l=1}^{R} U_{j,l} \tag{16}$$

The objective is to derive an expression for $\Pi(z)$. Multiplying the i th equation of (11) to (14) by z^i and summing over i, we obtain the following set of equations

$$U_{1,l}(z) = A(z) U_{N+L,l}(z) \tag{17}$$

$$U_{j,l}(z) = A(z) U_{j-1,l}(z), \qquad N+2 \le j \le N+L \tag{18}$$

$$U_{j,l}(z) = (1-q_{l-1}) A(z) \big(U_{j-1,l-1}(z) - P_{j-1,0,l-1} \big), \qquad 2 \le j \le N+1 \tag{19}$$

$$U_{j,1}(z) = A(z)P_{j-1,0,1} + \sum_{l=1}^{R-1} q_l A(z) z^{-1}(U_{j-1,l}(z) - P_{j-1,0,l}) + A(z) z^{-1} \times (U_{j-1,R}(z) - P_{j-1,0,R})$$

$$2 \leq j \leq N+1 \tag{20}$$

Henceforth this paper considers only the resolution of $\{X_k\}$'s steady-state distribution for $N = 1$. Using (17) to (20) iteratively, and due to the fact of $P_{1,0,l} = 0$ for $l \geq 2$ we obtain after some algebric manipulations

$$U_{2,1}(z) = \frac{f_0(z)}{g_0(z)} \tag{21}$$

where

$$f_0(z) = A(z)P_{1,0,1}\left[1 - z^{-1}\left(q_1 + Q_R A(z)^{(R-1)(L+1)} + \sum_{l=2}^{R-1} q_l Q_l A(z)^{(l-1)(L+1)}\right)\right] \tag{22}$$

$$g_0(z) = 1 - z^{-1}\left(q_1 A(z)^{L+1} + Q_R A(z)^{R(L+1)} + \sum_{l=2}^{R-1} q_l Q_l A(z)^{l(L+1)}\right) \tag{23}$$

and

$$Q_X = \prod_{m=1}^{X-1}(1 - q_m) \tag{24}$$

By the normalization condition, $\sum_{l=1}^{R} U_{2,l}(1) = 1$, we then obtain,

$$P_{1,0,1} = \left[\left(1 + \sum_{l=2}^{R} Q_l\right)\frac{D_z}{L_z} - \sum_{l=2}^{R} Q_l\right]^{-1} \tag{25}$$

where $U_{2,1}(1)$ is determined applying the L'Hôspital rule and is equal to

$$U_{2,1}(1) = \frac{f_1}{g_1} \tag{26}$$

and where

$$f_1 = P_{1,0,1} D_z \tag{27}$$

$$D_z = 1 + \alpha\left(1 - q_1 - Q_R[(R-1)(L+1)+1] - \sum_{l=2}^{R-1} q_l Q_l[(l-1)(L+1)+1]\right) \tag{28}$$

$$g_1 = 1 - (L+1)\alpha\left[q_1 + Q_R R + \sum_{l=2}^{R-1} q_l Q_l l\right] \tag{29}$$

From (16) we obtain the generating function

$$\Pi(z) = \frac{1}{L+1} \left(\sum_{j=0}^{L} A(z)^j \right) \left[U_{2,1}(z) + \sum_{l=2}^{R} P(z) \right]$$ (30)

where

$$P(z) = \left(Q_l A(z)^{(l-2)(L+1)+1} \right) \left(A(z)^L U_{2,1}(z) - P_{1,0,1} \right)$$ (31)

4.3 The Mean Queue Size

The mean the number of messages in the station's queue can be computed by taking the derivative of $\Pi(z)$ and letting z equal to 1. From (30) we obtain

$$\Pi'(1) = \frac{\sum_{j=0}^{L} j\alpha}{L+1} \left[U_{2,1}(1) + \sum_{l=2}^{R} Q_l \left(U_{2,1}(1) - P_{1,0,1} \right) \right] +$$

$$\left[U'_{2,1}(1) + \sum_{l=2}^{R} Q_l \left[(l-1)(L+1)\alpha U_{2,1}(1) + U'_{2,1}(1) - \left[(l-2)(L+1)+1 \right] \alpha P_{1,0,1} \right] \right]$$ (32)

To compute $U'_{2,1}(1)$ we apply twice the L'Hôpital's rule to obtain

$$U'_{2,1}(1) = \frac{f_2 g_1 - f_1 g_2}{2 g_1^2}$$ (33)

where

$$f_2 = P_{1,0,1} \left[2\alpha + \alpha_2 (1-q_1) - Q_R \left[(R-1) \times (L+1)+1 \right] \left[(R-1)(L+1)\alpha^2 + \alpha_2 \right] - \sum_{l=2}^{R-1} q_l Q_l \left[(l-1)(L+1)+1 \right] \left[(l-1)(L+1)\alpha^2 + \alpha_2 \right] \right]$$ (34)

$$g_2 = -q_1 (L+1) \left(L\alpha^2 + \alpha_2 \right) - Q_R R(L+1) \left(\left[R(L+1)-1 \right] \alpha^2 + \alpha_2 \right) - \sum_{l=2}^{R-1} q_l Q_l l(L+1) \left[(l(L+1)-1)\alpha^2 - \alpha_2 \right]$$ (35)

4.4 Delay Analysis

The message delay $E[D]$ is defined as the time interval elapsed between the message arrival and departure times. It can be calculated as the sum of the time elapsed between the message arrival and the beginning of the next slot (equal to one half-slot) plus the number of slots elapsed between the slot of its arrival and the instant it is fully transmitted from the system. For the general batch arrival case, this last component of the delay can be obtained using Little's formula assuming a first-come-first-served (FCFS) service discipline. That is,

$$E[D] = \frac{E[X]}{\alpha} + \frac{1}{2} \qquad (36)$$

where $E[X] = \Pi'(1)$ is given by (33). This equation can be used with any message arrival distribution, as long as the message arrival process, $A(Z)$, is defined.

The next section validates the proposed model, assuming arrivals to be governed by a Poisson process, so

$$A(z) = e^{-\lambda(1-z)}, A'(1) = \alpha = \lambda. \qquad (37)$$

5 Simulations

In this section, we present a set of performance results concerning the proposed packet combining ARQ scheme for a TDMA uplink channel. Each FFT (Fast Fourier Transform) block has N=256 data symbols and are selected from a QPSK constellation, with Gray mapping totalling 512 bits per data block. The data packets correspond to one FFT block, with 32 bytes. We consider an uncoded scenario where the channels for each packet retransmission remains fixed. To allow an efficient packet separation we consider the cyclic-shifted versions of the FFT-blocks for each retransmission attempt which formally is equivalent to have cyclic-shifted versions of the channel in each retransmission attempt [3].

We assumed perfect synchronization and channel estimation conditions. We consider, as referred earlier, one slot per station $(N = 1)$ and 8 stations $(L = 8)$ generating traffic following a Poisson process with λ packets/slot.

Fig. 1 shows the average PER of our interactive receiver when we have l transmission attempts (q_l). It shows a significant PER reduction with a l's increment, especially when the number of R is not too large (the E_b / N_0 gains for PER=0.5 are about 4dB when $l = 1$, 2dB when $l = 2$ and 1dB when $l = 3$). This is not surprising, since the total transmitted power grows with l and we take full advantage of all transmitted power.

We implemented the proposed packet combining approach in the ns-2 simulator [12]. We assumed that q_l for packets is a mean-ergodic process, and we modeled the PER variation with l using the average PER values measured in the first set of experiments, and represented in Fig. 1. The average q_l in function of E_b / N_0 is introduced as a matrix parameter for the simulations.

Fig. 2 depicts the simulation and the analytical model message delay in function of E_b / N_0 for different Poisson traffic load (when $1 / \lambda$ equal to 10, 20 and 30 packets), for $R = 4$ (it attempts up to 4 transmissions per packet). The analytical results were computed using 43 and 47. It shows that the measured delay follows the analytical model values, thus validating it. It also shows that message delay decreases as E_b / N_0 increases. Notice that packet combining allows a finite delay even for a initial very high PER ($q_1 \approx 0$ for 3dB), clearly showing its advantage compared to a classical TDMA scheme.

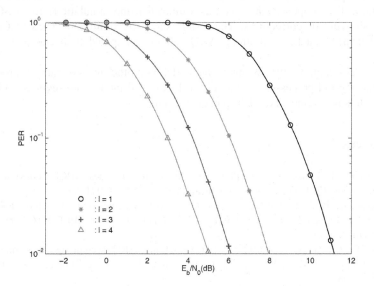

Fig. 1. PER performance for a single packet transmission

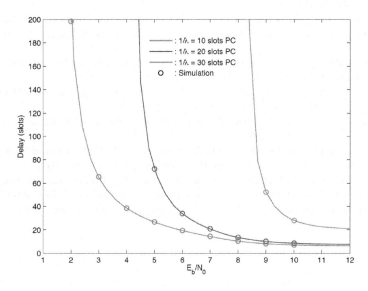

Fig. 2. Message delay with E_b / N_0 for Poisson traffic and $R = 4$

6 Conclusions

In this paper, we have carried out exact message delay and queue-size analysis for a single slot per frame packet-switched TDMA applying a packet combining ARQ scheme. We propose a generic analytical model that applies to any message arrival distribution. The proposed analysis was validated using simulations for a SC-FDE scheme, showing its correctness. The results show the significant gains that can be obtained using a packet combining ARQ scheme compared to a classical TDMA scheme.

Future work includes the testing of the model with other message arrival processes, including long-tail processes. At model level extended models are required to handle multiple slots per frame, and other queueing disciplines.

References

1. Hagenauer, J.: Rate-compatible Punctured Convolutional Codes (RPCP Codes) and Their Applications. IEEE Trans. on Communications 36(4), 389–400 (1988)
2. Gusmão, A., Dinis, R., Esteves, N.: Adaptive HARQ Schemes Using Punctured RR Codes for ATM-compatible Broadband Wireless Communications. In: IEEE VTC 2009 (Fall), Amsterdam (1999)
3. Dinis, R., Carvalho, P., Martins, J.: Soft Combining ARQ Techniques for Wireless Systems Employing SC-FDE Schemes. In: IEEE ICCCN 2008, St. Thomas U.S. Virgin Islands (2008)
4. Falconer, D., Ariyavisitakul, S., Benyamin-Seeyar, A., Eidson, B.: Frequency Domain Equalization for Single-Carrier Broadband Wireless Communications. IEEE Comm. Mag. 40(4), 58–66 (2002)
5. Saeki, B.H., Rubin, I.: An Analysis of a TDMA Channel Using Stop-and-Wait, Block, and Select-and Repeat ARQ Error Control. IEEE Trans. on Communications 30, 1162–1173 (1982)
6. Rubin, I., Zhang, Z.: Message Delay Analysis for TDMA Schemes Using Continous-Slot Assignments. IEEE Trans. on Communications 40(4), 730–737 (1992)
7. Chen, Y.J., Chang, J.F.: Per connection delay analysis of a frame-based TDMA/CDMA MAC protocol. Performance Evaluation 57, 19–55 (1992)
8. Benvenuto, N., Tomasin, S.: Block Iterative DFE for Single Carrier Modulation. IEE Elec. Let. 39(19), 1144–1145 (2002)
9. Dinis, R., Gusmão, A., Esteves, N.: On Broadband Block Transmission over Strongly Frequency-Selective Fading Channels. In: Proc. Wireless 2003, Calgary (2003)
10. Gusmão, A., Torres, P., Dinis, R., Esteves, N.: A Class of Iterative FDE Techniques for Reduced-CP SC-Based Block Transmission. In: Int. Symposium on Turbo Codes (2006)
11. The Network Simulator ns-2 (2.33), http://www.isi.edu/nsnam/ns/

Optoelectronic Oscillators for Communication Systems

Bruno Romeira and José Figueiredo

Centro de Electrónica, Optoelectrónica e Telecomunicações
Departamento de Física, Universidade do Algarve, 8005-139 Faro, Portugal
{bmromeira,jlongras}@ualg.pt

Abstract. We introduce and report recent developments on a novel five port optoelectronic voltage controlled oscillator consisting of a resonant tunneling diode (RTD) optical-waveguide integrated with a laser diode. The RTD-based optoelectronic oscillator (OEO) has both optical and electrical input and output ports, with the fifth port allowing voltage control. The RTD-OEO locks to reference radio-frequency (RF) sources by either optical or electrical injection locking techniques allowing remote synchronization, eliminating the need of impedance matching between traditional RF oscillators. RTD-OEO functions include generation, amplification and distribution of RF carriers, clock recovery, carrier recovery, modulation and demodulation and frequency synthesis. Self-injection locking operation modes, where small portions of the output electrical/optical signals are fed back into the electrical/optical input ports, are also proposed. The self-phase locked loop configuration can give rise to low-noise high-stable oscillations, not limited by the RF source performance and with no need of external optoelectronic conversion.

Keywords: Optoelectronic oscillators, resonant tunneling diodes, laser diodes, optical waveguides.

1 Introduction

Photonic radio-frequency (RF) systems use optical waves as carriers to transport RF signals through optical fibers to remote locations, taking the advantages of optical fibers low loss, light weight, high capacity, high security and immunity to electromagnetic interference [1]. This technology is beginning to be used in local access networks to provide private users ultra-wideband digital communications. Since optoelectronic oscillators (OEOs) can significantly simplify and augment the capacity of photonic RF systems they have attracted great attention in recent years. Their high-frequency and ultra-pure microwave signal generation capabilities allow the development of high-capacity photonic RF communication systems such as radio-over-fiber networks [2].

Here we introduce and discuss the operation modes of an innovative OEO circuit based on the integration of a resonant tunnelling diode (RTD) embedded within a semiconductor optical waveguide (RTD-OW), containing a photo-detecting region, with a laser diode (LD). The RTD-OEO is capable to produce both RF and optical

L.M. Camarinha-Matos, P. Pereira, and L. Ribeiro (Eds.): DoCEIS 2010, IFIP AICT 314, pp. 273–280, 2010.
© IFIP International Federation for Information Processing 2010

signals modulated at microwave frequencies, and opto-electronic/electro-optic conversion with potential applications on signal processing and communication systems such as radio-over-fiber networks [3]. The combination of a RTD-OW and a LD [4,5] gives rise to a new kind of five port OEO configuration that incorporates both electrical and optical input and output ports, and whose dynamics can be controlled by either electrical or optical injected signals.

This paper is organized as follows. Section 2 summarizes the contribution of this paper to the technology innovation by presenting the state of the art in optoelectronic oscillators for communication systems and introducing the RTD-OEO concept, by discussing its operation principle, configuration schemes and potential applications in photonic radio-frequency systems. Section 3 reports on recent progresses in the RTD-based transmitter and RTD-based receiver circuits. The conclusions and future work are presented in section 4.

2   Contribution to Technology Innovation

Generating pure high-frequency RF signals using simple, efficient, low-phase noise and low cost oscillators are being considered as the major requirements for next generation photonic RF communication systems. Since RF resonator-based oscillator technology can not match all advantages of photonic systems, there has been a great search of OEO configurations capable to generate ultra-pure RF carriers in both electrical and optical domains. Several OEO systems have been proposed over the last few years, including photonic oscillators based on InP monolithic oscillators [8], or using direct modulated semiconductor lasers and optical/optoelectronic injection schemes [9]. However, these configurations either are too complex or do not meet all the photonic RF systems OEO requirements.

An ideal OEO should involve the generation of ultra-pure RF signals in both electrical and optical domains with its operation being controlled by both electrical and optical injected signals. An OEO configuration that close match these requirements, capable to produce ultra-pure microwave signals, was proposed by Yao et al. [10]. However, such configuration is quite complex, containing an optical fiber delay line several kilometers long, a wide-band Mach-Zehnder (MZ) modulator to modulate non-linearly a semiconductor laser continuous-wave coherent light beam, a pre-amplified photodiode, a narrow microwave RF filter and a microwave amplifier.

The main contribution of this paper to the technology innovation is the proposal of a novel five ports OEO based on the integration of RTDs with optical waveguides and laser diodes. Since monolithic integration of an RTD with a laser diode was already demonstrated [4], we foresee the monolithic integration of the RTD-OW with a laser diode will lead to a major breakthrough, increasing the potential of the hybrid RTD-OEO as a reliable monolithic integrated optoelectronic oscillator. Our work points towards the demonstration of a full monolithic RTD-OEO by the end of the associated PhD program. Next, we present RTD-OEO concept, describing its operation principle and analyzing two self-phase locking configurations.

2.1 Novel Optoelectronic Oscillators for Photonic RF Systems

Resonant tunnelling diodes (RTDs) are nanoelectronic semiconductor structures with wide bandwidth negative differential conductance (NDC) region capable of producing electrical oscillations up to 831 GHz [6], which make them the fastest purely electronic devices operating at room temperature. When integrated within optoelectronic devices, such as optical waveguides and laser diodes, they can enhance the devices optoelectronic characteristics by reducing power consumption and offering significant improvements in the modulation/detection performance and functionality since they can operate as optical modulators and photo-detectors with built-in electrical amplifiers [4,5,7]. With especially interest are the recently demonstrated optoelectronic voltage controlled oscillators and optical controlled RF oscillators based on the hybrid integration of an RTD with a laser diode (RTD-LD) and an RTD with a semiconductor photo-conductive region, respectively [3].

The RTD-OEO proposed here combines the RTD-LD emission and RTD-OW photo-detection functionalities, see [3], in a single circuit leading to a five port circuit with both optical and electrical input and output ports, where the fifth port allows the voltage control of the electro-optical oscillations. Since the RTD-OEO emulates the RTD wideband NDC region, high frequency oscillations and generation of stable low-phase noise electrical and optical signals are expected, with both being controllable by electrical or optical injection signals. Figure 1 shows a typical RTD-OEO configuration.

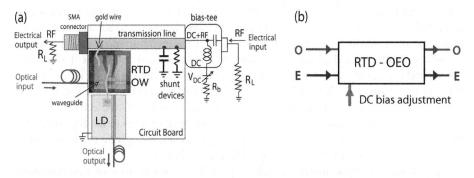

Fig. 1. RTD-OEO circuit schematics (not scaled). (a) RTD-OW connected in series with a laser diode with both electrical (E) and optical (O) output- and input-ports. (b) RTD-OEO diagram showing electrical and optical input and output ports plus the DC bias control port.

The schematic of Fig. 1(a) includes a shunt capacitor-resistor placed physically close and in parallel with RTD-OW and LD series connection to provide the appropriate resonant conditions for RTD operation as a microwave relaxation oscillator, with the relaxation frequency controlled by DC voltage. The RTD-OW photo-detection capability provides the circuit optical input port, allowing optical-to-electrical conversion. The laser diode acts as the circuit optical output port, which in combination with electrical input port allows electrical-to-optical conversion,

Fig. 1(a). The diagram of Fig. 1(b) summarizes the five port functions. The electrical and optical input ports act as injection ports to lock, optically or electrically, the OEO to reference sources. For detailed information on the RTD and LD, see [3] and [7].

This five port RTD based OEO circuit eliminates the need of discrete components such as RF amplifiers, RF couplers and filters, and corresponds to a significant simplification when compared to previously reported optoelectronic oscillators [8,9,12]. The RTD-OEO circuit proposed here aims to fulfill the needs of photonic RF systems and is much simpler and flexible due to RTD-OW optoelectronic nonlinearities and the RTD wide bandwidth negative differential conductance (NDC) characteristic. Since the wide-bandwidth NDC provides wide bandwidth electronic gain the RTD-OEO incorporates an intrinsically built-in RF amplification, which combined with the waveguide modulation/photo-detection and the laser diode emission capabilities, allows the implementation of low power consumption, high-frequency electrical and optical signal generators whose operation is controllable by both RF and optical injected signals. Moreover, its oscillation frequency can be tunable by a DC bias voltage.

2.2 RTD-OEO Self-phase Locking Operation

The RTD-OEO operates as follows. Without external perturbation, biasing the RTD-OEO in the RTD-OW negative differential conductance region generates current relaxation oscillations that drive the laser diode connected in series to the RTD-OW, which modulates the laser optical carrier. As mentioned, the oscillation frequency is controllable by the RTD-OW dc bias voltage, making the circuit to act as an optoelectronic voltage controlled oscillator (OVCO) [3,5]. This operation mode can be used to frequency synthesis and clock generation in both electrical and optical domains. When working in the OVCO mode, injecting a modulated optical signal in the photoconductive region of the RTD-OW the RTD-OEO current relaxation oscillations lock to the optical RF sub-carrier leading to simultaneously to optical-to-electrical conversion and to optical-to-optical modulation. In the presence of an external RF signal the relaxation oscillations can lock to the injected RF signal giving rise to electrical-to-optical conversion and to electrical-to-electrical modulation.

Optical and electrical injection locking provides a simple way of synchronizing and stabilizing optoelectronic oscillators but requires low-noise and high-stable RF sources. To overcome this limitation we propose an OEO self-phase locked loop configuration using the optical waveguide input port of the RTD-OEO, Fig. 2. The schemes include optical-to-electrical conversion, Fig. 2(a), and electrical-to-optical conversion, Fig. 2(b), based on a self-injection locking loop implemented with either an optical fiber or an optical waveguide loop. The optical self-injection forces the oscillator to be locked with its past, since a delayed replica of the RTD-OEO optical output is injected back to the oscillator reducing substantially fluctuations and eliminating the need of high-stable RF sources. The frequency stability is expected to be proportional to the length of the delay line. Also, a larger optical power injection will produce more phase noise reduction.

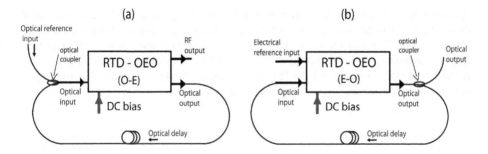

Fig. 2. Self-phase locking in (a) optical-to-electrical (O-E) and (b) electrical-to-optical (E-O) schemes. In both cases the optical delay also controls the RTD-OEO providing low-noise E/O conversions.

Because of configuration simplicity and flexibility the RTD-OEO is expected to find applications over a wide range of photonic and RF systems such as for time-frequency metrology, for the next generation of high-precision radar/sensors where extreme purity for reference microwave is crucial, to produce ultra-low jitter optical pulses at high bit rates (>10 GHz), to generate multi-wavelength and synchronized optical pulses, and to perform clock recovery, carrier recovery, signal modulation and demodulation, photonic signal up/down conversion, and distribute low-phase noise and high-stable RF carriers in communication links [13].

Next we present and discuss the recent results on the two main blocks of the RTD-OEO, specifically the electro-optical and the opto-electrical conversions.

3   RTD-OEO Modes of Operation Results and Discussion

In this section we describe the main results on RTD-OEO operation as optoelectronic voltage controlled oscillator, photo-detector, electrical/optical converter, and chaotic generator.

3.1   RTD-OEO Electro-Optical Conversion

When operated in the negative differential conductance region the RTD-OEO produces current relaxation oscillations that modulate the laser diode optical output, providing a simple way of producing optical sub-carriers with the relaxation oscillation frequency. Typical performance of implemented RTD-OEO biased in the RTD negative differential conductance region is shown in Fig. 3. Figure 3(a) shows RTD-OEO functioning as an optoelectronic voltage controlled oscillator (OVCO), with the oscillation frequency being tuned by the dc bias voltage. The photo-detected optical output power level remains practically unchanged over the entire tuning range. This mode of operation provides a simple way to tune optoelectronic oscillation frequency with high sensitivity when compared with other proposed voltage controlled oscillators [10].

The RTD-OEO can be locked by either optical or electrical signals. Injection locking due to an RF reference signal feed into the electrical port are presented in Fig. 3(b) [3,11]. In the presence of the RF injected carrier the RTD oscillator synchronizes either to the fundamental or harmonic frequencies modulating the laser diode. Figure 3(b) shows electrical-to-optical injection locking when the oscillator is locked to the 4th harmonic of RTD self-oscillations. The laser diode output is frequency modulated at ¼ of the injected signal (3 GHz frequency), corresponding to frequency division operation by 4 [5]. The frequency locking is controlled by tuning both the bias voltage and power of the injected signal.

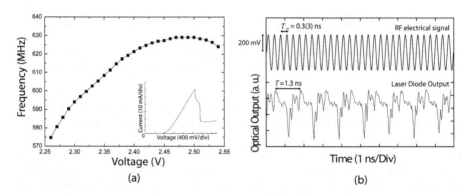

Fig. 3. (a) Optoelectronic voltage controlled oscillator. (b) Electro-optical conversion: injection locking at around 0.75 GHz measured in the laser output when a 3 GHz RF signal is injected in the RTD-OEO electrical input port

Under appropriate operating conditions, the strong nonlinearity of the RTD-OEO can produce aperiodic or chaotic signals as a result of frequency mixing between free-running relaxation oscillations and external RF signal [3,14]. In this regime the oscillator is not locked to the injected RF input (the injected frequency is outside the locking range). This behavior has interesting applications in optical chaos communications (see [14] and references therein).

3.2   RTD-OEO Opto-electrical Conversion

The RTD optical waveguide contains a photo-conductive region that is used to extract the RF-subcarrier from a modulated optical signal. When the RTD-OEO is DC biased in the NDC region, the presence of a modulated optical signal reduces the device's series resistance due to inter-band absorption and gives rise to current oscillations that emulates the RF signal that was used to modulate the incident optical beam. In this mode of operation we measured responsivity-gain up to 10 dB at 1550 nm [3,11].

Taking advantage of the photo-detection capabilities, the RTD-OEO can be remotely synchronized with an injected optical signal. Typical optical injection locking is presented in Fig. 4. Figure 4(a) shows the spectra corresponding to free running oscillation and optical injection locking. When the reference optical subcarrier signal is injected with a maximum single-side-band (SSB) noise of -120 dBc/Hz, the SSB measurements show a phase noise reduction of ~30 dB at 100 kHz carrier offset, Fig. 4(b). The phase noise reduction value approaches the phase noise of the reference source by increasing either the optical power or the modulation amplitude. The locking range as a function of injection power is shown in Fig. 4(c). The results shows that as the injection power decreases the locking range also decreases and the phase noise increases. Because the RF power of the free-running oscillator remains the same, this means the gain is effectively increased.

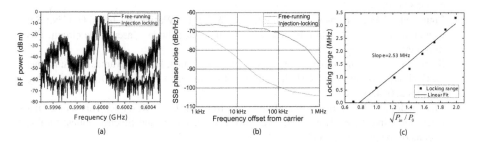

(a)   (b)   (c)

Fig. 4. (a) RTD-OEO free-running oscillation and locking to an 8 mW continuous wave optical signal modulated by an RF signal with 0.6 GHz and 500 mV amplitude. (b) Single Side Band phase noise measurements as function of the frequency offset. (c) Locking range as a function of the square root of the injection RF power P_{in}.

4   Conclusions and Future Work

In conclusion, we have proposed an innovative optoelectronic oscillator circuit based on the integration of a resonant tunnelling diode optical waveguide (RTD-OW) with a laser diode, the RTD-OEO. The RTD-OEO is a versatile and simple optoelectronic oscillator for microwave-photonic system applications because can be used for injection-locking, up-conversion, and down-conversion of both electrical and optical reference signals, and to produce RF and chaotic signals. Future work includes the monolithic integration of an RTD oscillator and a photo-conductive region with a laser diode, instead of using separated laser and RTD chips. This configuration could have applications in single chip OEO solutions for high-speed fiber-optic communication systems.

Acknowledgments. Bruno Romeira acknowledges the support of the Fundação para a Ciência e a Tecnologia, Portugal, through the grant SFRH/BD/43433/2008. This work is a result of a collaboration program with the group of Professor Charles N. Ironside of the Department of Electronics and Electrical Engineering of the University of Glasgow, United Kingdom.

References

1. Seeds, A.J.: Microwave Photonics. IEEE Trans. Microwave Theory Tech. 50, 877–887 (2002)
2. Sauer, M., Kobyakov, A.: Radio over fiber for picocellular network Architectures. J. Lightwave Techno. 25, 3301–3320 (2007)

3. Romeira, B., Figueiredo, J.M.L., Slight, T.J., Wang, L., Wasige, E., Ironside, C.N., Kelly, A.E., Green, R.: Nonlinear Dynamics of Resonant Tunneling Optoelectronic Circuits for Wireless/Optical Interfaces. IEEE J. Quant. Elec. 45, 1436–1445 (2009)
4. Slight, T.J., Ironside, C.N.: Investigation into the integration of a resonant tunnelling diode and an optical communications laser: model and experiment. IEEE J. Quant. Elec. 43, 580–587 (2007)
5. Figueiredo, J.M.L., Romeira, B., Slight, T.J., Wang, L., Wasige, E., Ironside, C.N.: Self-oscillation and period adding from a resonant tunnelling diode – laser diode circuit. Electron. Lett. 44, 876–877 (2008)
6. Suzuki, S., Teranishi, A., Hinata, K., Asada, M., Sugiyama, H., Yokoyama, H.: Fundamental Oscillation of up to 831 GHz in GaInAs/AlAs Resonant Tunneling Diode. Appl. Phys. Express 2, 054501 (2009)
7. Figueiredo, J.M.L., Romeira, B., Slight, T.J., Ironside, C.N.: Resonant Tunnelling Optoelectronic Circuits. In: Kordic, V. (ed.) Advances in Lasers and Electro Optics, In-Tech, Vienna (to be published, 2009)
8. Lee, K.H., Kim, J.Y., Choi, W.Y., Kamitsuna, H., Ida, M., Kurishima, K.: Low-Cost Optoelectronic Self-Injection-Locked Oscillators. IEEE Photon. Technol. Lett. 20, 1151–1153 (2008)
9. Sung, H.K., Zhao, X., Lau, E.K., Parekh, D., Hasnain, C.J.C., Wu, M.C.: Optoelectronic Oscillators Using Direct-Modulated Semiconductor Lasers Under Strong Optical Injection. J. Sel. Topics. Quantum Electron. 15, 572–576 (2009)
10. Yao, X.Y., Maleki, L.: Optoelectronic Oscillator for Photonic Systems. IEEE J. Quantum Electron 32, 1141–1149 (1996)
11. Romeira, B., Figueiredo, J.M.L., Slight, T.J., Wang, L., Wasige, E., Ironside, C.N.: Wireless/Photonics Interfaces Based on Resonant Tunneling Diode Optoelectronic Oscillators. In: Conference on Lasers and Electro-Optics (CLEO)/The International Quantum Electronics Conference (IQEC), OSA Technical Digest, paper CTuT4 (2009)
12. Chembo, Y.K., Larger, L., Colet, P.: Nonlinear Dynamics and Spectral Stability of Optoelectronic Microwave Oscillators. IEEE J. Quantum Electron 44, 858–866 (2008)
13. Lasri, J., Devgan, P., Tang, R., Kumar, P.: Ultralow timing jitter 40-Gb/s clock recovery using a self-starting optoelectronic oscillator. IEEE Photon. Technol. Lett. 6, 263–265 (2004)
14. Romeira, B., Figueiredo, J.M.L., Slight, T.J., Ironside, C.N.: Chaotic Dynamics in Resonant Tunneling Optoelectronic Voltage Controlled Oscillators. IEEE Photon. Technol. Lett. 21, 1819–1821 (2009)

Simulation Model for OBS Contention Avoidance Routing Strategies

Alvaro L. Barradas and Maria do Carmo R. Medeiros

Center of Electronics Optoelectronics and Telecommunications (CEOT),
Universidade do Algarve, Campus de Gambelas, 8005-139 Faro, Portugal
{abarra,cmedeiro}@ualg.pt

Abstract. Optical burst switching (OBS) provides a feasible paradigm for the next IP over optical network backbones. However, due to its bufferless nature, OBS efficiency can be reduced by resource contention leading to burst loss. Several methods have been proposed to address this problem, most of them relying on reactive mechanisms which increase the complexity of core nodes, hampering scalability. In this work we consider a preventive traffic engineering approach for contention resolution which provides source routing with the objective of minimizing contention at the transmission links considering only topological information. This paper presents a simulation model aimed at the evaluation of different offline routing strategies in terms of burst contention. The simulation model is used to compare the performance of different novel path selection strategies with the traditional shortest path routing approach. Results confirm that the proposed strategies are effective in reducing the overall blocking and the model is feasible for the proposed QoS evaluation.

Keywords: Optical networks, Network architecture and design, Optical burst switching, Contention avoidance, Routing strategies, Simulation.

1 Introduction

Optical burst switching (OBS) [1], [2] has emerged as an efficient switching paradigm for the core of IP over optical networks. OBS avoids the inefficient resource utilization of Optical Circuit Switching (OCS) and the requirements of buffers, optical logic processing and synchronization problems of Optical Packet Switching (OPS). In OBS the basic transport unit is the burst, an aggregate message that can be regarded as an optical ``super packet'' containing multiple IP packets going to the same egress node and (if used) grouped by some Quality of Service (QoS) criteria. Bursts are assembled at the ingress nodes and their transmission is preceded by dedicated setup messages, transmitted on a dedicated control channel with the purpose of reserving bandwidth along the path for the upcoming data bursts. Based on the information carried by the setup messages, the intermediate nodes reserve switching resources along a pre-configured path, providing an optical channel through which data bursts can be transmitted, after an adequate delay, from source to final destination without any optical-electrical-optical (OEO) conversion [2], [3]. OBS, like other switching paradigms, does not perform well in overloaded scenarios and can present low reliability

L.M. Camarinha-Matos, P. Pereira, and L. Ribeiro (Eds.): DoCEIS 2010, IFIP AICT 314, pp. 281–288, 2010.

since it generally uses one-way reservation protocols, where data bursts are transmitted without confirmation that resources along the path will be successfully reserved to establish the required end-to-end transparent connection. Consequently, whenever the number of simultaneous reservation attempts exceed the number of available resources some will fail and, owing to the lack of sophisticated optical buffers, will result in burst loss. Burst loss degrades the global OBS performance since dropping leads to rescheduling of lost data with significant impact on any end-to-end applications running in the network layers above, reducing its overall throughput. Therefore, minimizing burst loss is a key factor for the practical implementation of OBS networks.

Considerable effort has been devoted to the study of different methods to handle contention, including, burst scheduling, optical buffering, burst segmentation, wavelength conversion, and deflection routing [4], [5]. These are mainly reactive mechanisms driven by burst contention and requiring extra hardware and/or software components at each core node, significantly increasing their cost and complexity, leading to scalability impairments. A simple and cost efficient solution is to deploy contention mechanisms at the edge nodes. This approach has been followed by using burst assembly mechanisms [6], [7], by path selection and wavelength assignment [8], [9] or by balancing the traffic load between alternate paths [10], [11].

Path selection mechanisms at the ingress nodes can alleviate contention when compared with the shortest path (SP) routing. Although successfully used in both circuit switching and packet switching networks, SP routing does not take into consideration the traffic load offered to the network, and it often causes certain links to become congested while other links remain underutilized [10]. This is highly undesirable in bufferless OBS networks, since a few highly congested links can lead to unacceptably high burst loss values for the entire network, corroborating contention avoidance strategies as an important feature in the OBS field.

The paper is organized as follows. After an introductory section where some OBS intrinsic problems are considered together with a brief state of the art, Section 2 presents the objective of the paper and its main contribution to technological innovation. Section 3 presents the simulation model and describes the OBS network simulator. Section 4 evaluates the performance of a path selection strategy and Section 5 concludes the paper with final remarks and further work for the near future.

2   Contribution to Technological Innovation

The aim of this paper is to present a simulation model for the evaluation of preventive routing strategies intended to minimize the global network contention and the overall burst loss through the adoption of optimized path selection strategies. Our approach uses only topological information to be integrated in an integer linear programming (ILP) formulation from which optimized routes are obtained. These routes can be used alone, as single-path static routes to provide load-balancing without the need for additional control messages with regard to link status or, alternatively, combined with dynamic contention resolution schemes (deflection or segmentation) and used occasionally as a default routing scheme to assume whenever the network needs to recover from instability, favoring the network resilience.

This offline source routing approach presents the following a priori advantages: no extra hardware or software components are required on the core nodes and no network flooding with signaling messages resulting from (over)active link state update protocols. Moreover, with this approach there is also no place for out-of-order arrivals, a frequent disadvantage of multipath routing schemes typically requiring large memories at the edge nodes for re-ordering operations. These are distinguishing qualities to make the architecture of the OBS nodes less complex, contributing to reduce both their cost and scalability impairments.

3 Simulation Methodology

The simulation model described in this paper is deployed in two stages. The first stage, which comprises the determination of routing paths, is the optimization stage and was developed with the CPLEX optimizer. In this stage a routing problem is formulated using ILP, which is a widely used approach to address both high level and system level synthesis. Taking into account the computation times involved (which have been found in a range between tens of seconds and some minutes), the relatively infrequent update requests expected from changes in the OBS backbones whose topologies typically last for long time scales, and the quasi-stationary aggregate traffic demands at optical backbones, which are expected to change relatively slowly [12], this approach can be considered feasible for the real production of OBS networks by means of an operation process to be executed during its initial setup phase. The second stage, which comprises the application of the routing solution, is the simulation stage in *stricto sensu*, where the optimized paths produced on the first stage are incorporated into an OBS network simulation model.

3.1 First Stage - Routing Path Determination

Several optimization strategies for contention avoidance have been under evaluation for which different routing paths were calculated: minimizing the Max Congested Link (MCL), based on the idea that the more a certain link is included in the chosen paths for source-destination pairs, the highest the blocking probability can be [13]; minimizing the Maximum End-to-end Congested (MEC) path, based on the idea that blocking may occur at any link traversed by a burst along the path [13]; and two strategies considering the *streamline effect* [12], a reported phenomenon unique to OBS networks wherein bursts traveling in a common link are streamlined and do not contend with each other until they diverge. One of these strategies, entitled Streamline-Based Preplanned Routing with no Pre-determined Paths (SBPR-nPP) was recently published in [14] and, as an example, its ILP formalization will be succinctly presented next. The solution of this ILP problem will be used to drive source routing decisions on the second stage of this simulation methodology.

SBPR-nPP strategy. Let $G(N,L)$ be a network graph where N is the set of nodes and L is the set of links, and let us define a path over which a burst must travel, v, as a connected series of directed links, written as $v : s(v) \rightarrow d(v)$, from source node $s(v)$ to destination node $d(v)$. The set of paths that can be used by a burst from s to d is defined as $V_{s,d} = \{v : s(v) \rightarrow d(v) \mid s = s(v), d = d(v)\}$ and the set including all $V_{s,d}$ is defined as V. We also define $p_l^v = 1$ if link $l \in L$ is included in v, $p_l^v = 0$ otherwise. When taking a specific node as a reference point, a link coming out of that node can be denoted as l_{out} and a link coming into that node can be denoted as l_{in}. The total number of elements in N, L and V is denoted by N, L and V. In this strategy the algorithm must find a route for burst delivery between each $s \to d$ pair of nodes, which means that no pre-determined selection of routes exists. The main goal of the next objective function is to minimize ζ_{MAX}, a global bound that stores the highest number of routes competing for an output link. The second component of the objective function is a secondary goal to find routes having a small number of hops and also to avoid loops.

$$\text{Minimize} \, \zeta_{MAX} + \tfrac{1}{LN(N-1)} \sum_{s,d \in N} \sum_{l \in L} \theta_l^{s,d} \tag{1}$$

subject to

$$\sum_{l_{out} \in L:s(l_{out})=i} \theta_{l_{out}}^{s,d} - \sum_{l_{in} \in L:d(l_{in})=i} \theta_{l_{in}}^{s,d} = \begin{cases} 1 & \text{if } i = s \\ -1 & \text{if } i = d \\ 0 & \text{otherwise} \end{cases} , \tag{2}$$

$$\forall s,d \in N, \forall i \in N$$

$$\zeta_i \geq \sum_{s,d \in N} \theta_{l_{out}}^{s,d}, \forall i \in N, \forall l_{out} \in L : s(l_{out}) = i \tag{3}$$

$$\zeta_{MAX} \geq \zeta_i, \forall i \in N \tag{4}$$

$$\theta_l^{s,d} \in \{0,1\}; \text{non-negative integer}: \zeta_i, \zeta_{MAX} \tag{5}$$

where $\theta_l^{s,d}$ is a binary variable that indicates if the route for the s-d pair of nodes, used to carry bursts, uses link l. Constraint 2 guarantees flow conservation of every route. For a specific node i, constraint 3 stores in ζ_i the highest number of selected routes competing for an output link, and constraint 4 stores in ζ_{MAX} the maximum value of all ζ_i. The main goal of the objective function is to minimize ζ_{MAX}, the global bound.

3.2 Second Stage - Routing Path Application

The application of the routing paths calculated in the first stage is done by simulation using an OBS model developed within the OMNeT++ simulation environment [15] and some programming effort in C++.

The functional architecture of our OBS model has the same characteristics of the one presented in [3] assuming that each node can support both new input traffic generated by the client networks as well as *in transitu* traffic passing all-optically from source to final destination. This study uses the following three networks: ARPAnet, NSFnet, and COST239 whose topologies are presented in Fig. 1. The nodes are connected by optical fibers with 16 wavelengths per link and a transmission capacity of 10 Gbits per second (per wavelength). The adopted traffic assumes a Poisson pattern with a threshold-based assembly method, generating bursts with size 100 Kbytes. Bursts are forwarded through the core backbone reproducing the relevant actions of the Just-Enough-Time (JET) [2] scheduling scheme. The control information processing time is assumed to be 10 μs per core node, although other values from 12.5 μs to 1 μs could be adopted depending on the technology in place.

The model employs source routing, in which a complete routing decision is taken at the ingress edge node. The path over which the burst must travel is carried on the setup message that precedes the transmission of each data burst and will not be modified by downstream nodes. The adopted path is fetched from the edge node's routing tables previously populated by the results of the path selection strategy discussed in the Section 3.1. Core nodes do not employ any buffering in the data path and they do not use deflection, but full wavelength conversion is assumed. Thus, a burst is blocked only if there are no free wavelengths available to accomplish the 'next hop' on a predetermined path to a certain destination. If scheduling fails the burst is simply dropped and no further contention resolution method is adopted. Together with the network topology description, the simulation model is essentially composed of OBS capable nodes interconnected by optical fibers. The model is based on two main modules, Edge Node and Core Node, with snapshots depicted in Fig. 1. These modules will be presented next using their functional perspective.

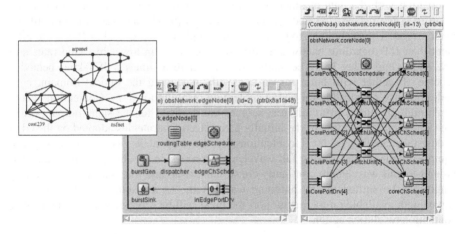

Fig. 1. Network topologies, and snapshots of edge node and core node (left to right)

Edge Nodes. Used to connect multiple subnetworks running on top of legacy link layer protocols to the OBS network. They can be considered either as ingress or egress nodes. When acting as ingress nodes, they are responsible for aggregating the incoming packets into bursts, for taking the initial (and here also permanent) routing decision, and for scheduling the bursts for transmission on outgoing channels. When acting as egress nodes, they perform the inverse operation, i.e., burst disassembly and packet forwarding to upper layers. In our model we assume the burst as the basic transport unit of interest. Hence, the issue of the packet aggregation policies is considered out of scope. Thus, whenever a Poisson process timer expires, a new burst is generated, a destination address is chosen at random between all other nodes in the network, a route to the destination node is taken from the source node's optimized routing table and an initial wavelength is randomly selected among the free ones. The burst is then retained on a system queue organized by destination address and the signaling process starts with the sending of a setup message on the appropriate dedicated channel. The setup message is always transmitted before the corresponding burst and apart from it by an adequate offset time. The model calculates this offset time in order to allow this message to be processed at each subsequent node before the burst arrival and in such a way that an optical path can be properly reserved for burst delivery.

Core Nodes. Responsible for processing setup messages, for switching the bursts from an input to an output port without OEO conversion and for handling contentions. Signaling in OBS is typically implemented using one out-of-band channel (λ_0 is used in this model). Several signaling schemes have been proposed for burst scheduling but Just-in-Time (JIT) and Just-Enough-Time (JET) are two of the most popular protocols in OBS networks. These are both one-way and source initiated signaling schemes, which means that bursts are sent to the core network without waiting for acknowledgments regarding the success or failure of the reservation attempts. Although closely related, they differ on the duration of the reservations. JIT uses immediate reservation with the data channel being reserved immediately since the moment the setup message reaches the node, while JET delays the channel reservation until the burst arrival. This technique, together with the implicit release, makes JET more efficient than JIT regarding bandwidth utilization, resulting in lower blocking rates and low end-to-end delay [5]. The study presented here assumes a JET-kind behavior scheme. Together with burst forwarding without leaving the optical domain, core nodes are also responsible for taking contention resolution actions. Contention occurs when multiple bursts from different sources are destined for the same output port at the same time [5]. Adding to the initially path selection strategies adopted on the edge nodes, the handling of burst contentions by the core nodes assume that they are equipped with devices having full wavelength conversion capability. This means that no end-to-end wavelength continuity constraint exists, and that any incoming wavelength can be shifted to any outgoing wavelength. As a result, only if there is no wavelength available on the output port the burst will be dropped without any further contention resolution action.

4   Performance Evaluation

For each network topology represented in Fig. 1 simulations were done using a specifically developed OBS simulator, assuming similar conditions with regard to the total amount of bursts generated per source node (10^6), arrival patterns and load variations. Results comparing the performance of the proposed path selection scheme with the SP routing are plotted in Fig. 2 with burst loss values normalized to the number of bursts that enter the network backbone against the average load. The plotted values of SBPR-nPP are always bellowing SP. This means that network performance can profit

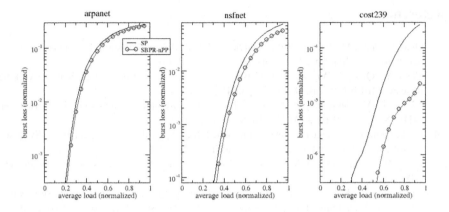

Fig. 2. Evaluation of SBPR-nPP vs. SP with normalized burst loss against average load

from balancing the potential path-load at the output links with these strategy. The graphics show also a progressively larger advantage for our algorithm following the increase of the physical connectivity parameter, with best results obtained for the COST239 European topology. This happens, because the higher connectivity of this network allows obtaining alternative paths to spread the potential traffic without extending them too much in terms of hop count. But even for the American ARPANET topology, which presents much lower connectivity values, a small benefit can be obtained with this approach.

5   Conclusion and Further Work

We consider the problem of routing path selection in OBS networks to minimize the overall burst loss due to resource contention of bursts aimed at the same output links. We take a preventive TE approach to provide source routing with minimized contention using only topological information and, in the case of the presented example, considering also the streamline effect. The proposed algorithm performs significantly better than the SP routing, with best performance obtained for networks characterized by having high physical connectivity.

Several research directions can be distinguished for future work. Among them, the adoption of combined routing strategies depending on traffic load variations can result in better performance. Another improvement can exploit the combined use of this static routing approach with the three basic deflection domains (time, space and wavelength) for contention resolution.

Acknowledgments. The work reported in this paper was supported in part by FCT within CEOT (unit 631) at the University of Algarve, Portugal, under the project PTDC/EEA-TEL/7168/2006.

References

1. Qiao, C., Yoo, M.: Optical Burst Switching (OBS): A New Paradigm for an Optical Internet. Journal of High Speed Networks 8(1), 69–84 (1999)
2. Chen, Y., Qiao, C., Yu, X.: Optical Burst Switching: A New Area in Optical Networking Research. IEEE Network 18, 16–23 (2004)
3. Xiong, Y., Vandenhoute, M., Cankaya, H.: Control Architecture in Optical Burst-Switched WDM Networks. IEEE JSAC 18, 1838–1851 (2000)
4. Li, J., Qiao, C.: Recent Progress in the Scheduling Algorithms in Optical-Burst-Switched Networks. OSA Journal of Optical Networking 3, 229–241 (2004)
5. Jue, J.P., Vokkarane, V.M.: Optical Burst Switched Networks. Springer, Heidelberg (2005)
6. Vokkarane, V.M., Jue, J.P.: Prioritized Burst Segmentation and Composite Burst-Assembly Techniques for QoS Support in Optical Burst-Switched Networks. IEEE JSAC 21, 1198–1209 (2003)
7. Jin, M., Yang, O.W.: Provision of Differentiated Performance in Optical Burst Switching Networks Based on Burst Assembly Processes. Computer Communications 30, 3449–3459 (2007)
8. Zhang, Q., Vokkarane, V.M., Jue, J.P., Chen, B.: Absolute QoS Differentiation in Optical Burst-Switched Networks. IEEE JSAC 22, 1781–1795 (2004)
9. Teng, J., Rouskas, G.N.: Wavelength Selection in OBS Networks Using Traffic Engineering and Priority-Based Concepts. IEEE JSAC 23, 1658–1669 (2005)
10. Teng, J., Rouskas, G.N.: Traffic Engineering Approach to Path Selection in Optical Burst Switching Networks. OSA Journal of Optical Networking 4, 759–777 (2005)
11. Li, J., Mohan, G., Chua, K.: Dynamic Load Balancing in IP-over-WDM Optical Burst Switching Networks. Computer Networks: The International Journal of Computer and Telecommunication Networking 47, 393–408 (2005)
12. Chen, Q., Mohan, G., Chua, K.: Route Optimization in Optical Burst Switched Networks Considering the Streamline Effect. Computer Networks (2008)
13. Barradas, A.L., Medeiros, M.C.R.: Edge-Node Deployed Routing Strategies for Load Balancing in Optical Burst Switched Networks. ETRI Journal 31(1), 31–41 (2009)
14. Barradas, A.L., Medeiros, M.C.R.: Pre-planned Optical Burst Switched Routing Strategies Considering the Streamline Effect. Photonic Network Communications (2009), doi:10.1007/s11107-009-021-y
15. Varga, A., Hornig, R.: An Overview of the OMNeT++ Simulation Environment. In: 1st Int. Conference on Simulation Tools and Techniques, SIMUTools 2008, Marseille (2008)

Transmission Performance of mm-Waves on Radio over Fiber Systems: Dispersion and Intermodulation Issues

Ricardo Avó, Paula Laurêncio, and Maria C.R. Madeiros

Center of Electronic, Optoelectronic and Telecommunications, Faculdade de Ciências e
Tecnologia, Universidade do Algarve, Campus de Gambelas,
8005-139 Faro, Portugal
{ricardoavo,plaurenc,cmedeiro}@ualg.pt

Abstract. Next generation wireless networks must provide high broadband
access, which can be achieved by combining the fiber optics and wireless
technologies. In this paper we analyze a mm-wave radio over fiber (RoF)
optical access network architecture, combining radio subcarrier multiplexing
techniques to improve system efficiency with fiber dispersion mitigation
provided by optical single sideband modulation techniques. Our results show
the system degradation introduced by the fiber link, namely fiber dispersion and
intermodulation effects.

Keywords: Radio over fiber, optical single sideband, subcarrier multiplexing,
intermodulation distortion.

1 Introduction

Consumer bandwidth requirements are increasing, driven by applications requiring
high speed data transmission such as regular file transfers which are becoming larger
and an increasing number of transparent applications, such as IP Television (IPTV)
and Voice over IP (VoIP). The consensus to overcome this bottleneck is to take
optical fiber closer to the consumer. Additionally, these needs are placing increasing
demands for more bandwidth allocation via wireless access networks. Nowadays, the
most used technologies for Wireless Local Area Networks (WLAN) are 802.11b/g/a
with throughputs up to ~27 Mbps, the 802.11n should ease the problem with ~100
Mbps throughput [1]. However, such speeds do not match the wireline home
networks provided by Fiber To The Home (FTTH) connections, such as 1 Gbit/s
Internet. Other problematic scenarios are in-home IPTV distribution, especially with
HDTV and future 3D HDTV, or even sharing content from a Personal Video
Recorder (PVR) with different TV sets. The scenario on the Wireless Wide Area
Networks (WWAN) connections is even worst, with theoretical maximum speeds of
14.4 Mbps with current High-Speed Packet Access (HSPA). The next generation
technologies provide 42Mbps in HSPA+ and 100Mbps with Long Term Evolution
(LTE).

L.M. Camarinha-Matos, P. Pereira, and L. Ribeiro (Eds.): DoCEIS 2010, IFIP AICT 314, pp. 289–296, 2010.

The increased bandwidth requirements cause spectral congestion at lower microwave frequencies, which are currently used in wireless access networks. In the millimeter-wave (mm-wave) region there is a large bandwidth available, with friendly regulation conditions, especially in the 60 GHz band, which has at least 5 GHz available bandwidth common thought out the main regions [2].

The reminder of this paper is organized as follows. In section 2 the contribution to the technological innovation is shown. In section 3, the network architecture is presented, emphasizing the effects of fiber dispersion and intermodulation introduced by the Optical Single Side Band (OSSB) modulator. Section 4 presents the simulation results for the downlink, and finally section 5 concludes the paper.

2   Contribution to Technological Innovation

Due to the small coverage area, 60 GHz networks require a large number of base stations (BSs) to cover a service area. This requirement has led to the development of system architectures where functions such as signal, routing, processing, handover and frequency allocation are performed at the central office (CO). The best solution for connecting the CO with BSs in such radio network is via an optical fiber network, now known as radio over fiber (RoF) [3]. RoF has proven to be a viable solution to transport analog signals, e.g. CATV on hybrid fiber-coax networks or on PON networks with the RF overlay. By exploiting high bandwidth wavelength-division multiplexing (WDM) networks, an integrated efficient fiber radio backbone network can be realized, where mm-wave carriers are modulated with data and placed on a particular wavelength channel and delivered to a specific BS.

In this paper we analyze the downlink operation of a RoF network that delivers directly the mm-wave signals from the CO to the BSs. The transmission of mm-wave signals over optical fiber is highly impaired by the fiber chromatic dispersion. To minimize this effect OSSB is used. To further improve the system efficiency Sub-Carrier Multiplexing (SCM) is employed, this allows for the use of multiple independent radio channels in each BS. We consider using four independent SCM channels feeding each BS.

3   System Description

The downlink basic configuration is shown in figure 1. At the central office, four base-band 1 Gbit/s data signals modulate four different microwave carriers (58.1 GHz, 60.3 GHz, 62.5 GHz and 64.7 GHz) by using Binary Phase Shift Keying (BPSK) modulation. The modulated subcarriers are combined and the composite signal is used to externally modulate a laser using OSSB modulation. The optical signal is then delivered to a specific BS through an optical fiber link. At the BS, a photodiode with a bandwidth greater than the subcarrier frequency is used to directly detect the composite signal. The electrical mm-wave signal is filtered, amplified and directly delivered to the BS antenna. This approach has the advantage of a simplified BS design but it is susceptible to fiber chromatic dispersion that severely limits the transmission distance [4]. For this reason the architecture considered here employs OSSB modulation.

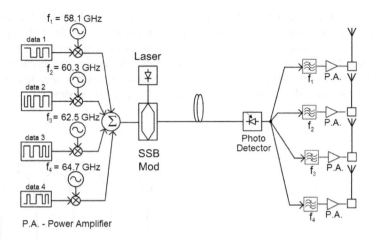

Fig. 1. Overall network architecture

The OSSB external modulator used in this work is the one proposed in [5]. The optical field at its output is given by:

$$E_{MZ\_SSB}(t) = E_{in}(t)\cos(x_c\pi m(t) - \pi/4)\exp\left(jx_c\pi\hat{m}(t)\right). \tag{1}$$

where $E_{in}(t) = \sqrt{2P_o}\,e^{j\omega_c t}$ is the optical field at the input of the MZ modulator, with optical angular frequency ω_c and average power P_o, x_c is the channel modulation parameter, $m(t)$ represents the applied SCM electrical signal composed by N channels using BPSK modulation and $\hat{m}(t)$ is its Hilbert transform. Assuming $m(t)$ to be a pure carrier at angular frequency ω_m, the optical field at the output of the OSSB modulator can be written as a series of Bessel functions [6]:

$$E_{MZ\_SSB}(t) = \sqrt{2P_0}\,e^{j\omega_c t} \sum_{n=-\infty}^{\infty} \cos\left[(n-1)\frac{\pi}{4}\right] J_n(m_I)e^{jn\left(\omega_m t - \frac{\pi}{2}\right)}. \tag{2}$$

where J_n is n order Bessel function, the modulation index $m_I = \sqrt{2}x\pi A_m$ and A_m is the $m(t)$ amplitude. For small values of m_I only the fundamental harmonic is significant, under this circumstances the modulator can be considered linear and intermodulation introduced by the modulator is not an issue. However, for high values of m_I other harmonics become relevant, as shown in figure 2a and may degrade the system performance, this is particularly important when combined with fiber dispersion.

3.1 The Effect of Fiber Dispersion

The ideal optical spectrum of a mm-wave over fiber is a signal which uses double sideband modulated (DSB), is composed by the optical carrier at optical frequency f_0 and by the mm-wave carrier f_i located at the optical frequency $\pm f_i + f_0$. When the mm-wave propagates through fiber modeled as a linear and dispersive link with a frequency response, $H_{LINK}(z,\omega) = exp(-j\beta_2\omega^2 z/2)$, ω is the angular modulation frequency, z is the longitudinal coordinate of the fiber, $\beta_2 = -\lambda^2 D/(2\pi c)$ denotes the group velocity dispersion, with D the dispersion parameter, c the light speed in vacuum and λ the carrier wavelength), the two optical field harmonics, $\pm f_i + f_0$, are affected by different phase changes due to the fiber dispersion. Furthermore, upon photodetection the two optical field harmonics interact in such a way leading to a detected photocurrent that change with distance and frequency, as shown in figure 2b.

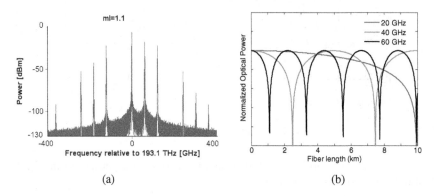

Fig. 2. a) Optical spectrum at the output of the OSSB modulator, for m_I=1.1. **b)** Normalized received optical power for an ideal optical system employing ODSB. Three RF carrier frequencies are considered, 20 GHz, 40 GHz and 60 GHz.

Theoretically, if optical single sideband modulation is employed, and the modulation index is small, dispersion does not affect the propagation of the mm-wave signal [6].

Note that, in practical systems the OSSB modulator, owing to its inherent nonlinearity, specially for higher values of m_I, generates other significant harmonic components as illustrated in figure 2a, and therefore the system behaviour approaches an Optical Double Side Band (ODSB).

3.2 The Effect of Intermodulation Distortion

For an OSSB/SCM system, intermodulation distortion mainly arises from the nonlinear characteristics of the optical modulator, the linear fiber dispersion and from the square law characteristics of the photodetection process. Here, we focus on the intermodulation distortion arising from the nonlinear characteristics of the optical modulator. Assuming $m(t)$ to represent the applied SCM electrical signal composed by N channels and $\hat{m}(t)$ is its Hilbert transform:

$$m(t) = A_m \sum_{i=1}^{N} u_i(t)\, sin(\omega_i t + \theta_i) \qquad \hat{m}(t) = A_m \sum_{i=1}^{N} -u_i(t)\, cos(\omega_i t + \theta_i) \qquad (3)$$

where ω_i represents the RF angular subcarrier of the i_{th} channel $u_i(t) = \pm 1$ for BPSK (+ for '1' and - for '0'), and θ_i is the subcarrier phase.

The optical field at the output of the OSSB modulator, $E_{MZ\_SSB}(t)$, can be expanded as a series of Bessel functions, for small channels modulation indexes (1) and can be rewritten as:

$$E_{MZ\_SSB}(t) = \sqrt{P_o/2}\exp[-j\pi/4]\left\{\prod_{i=1}^{N}\left\{1-j\frac{\sqrt{2}m_I}{2}[-s_i(t)-\hat{s}_i(t)]\right\}\right.$$
$$\left.+j\prod_{i=1}^{N}\left\{1-j\frac{\sqrt{2}m_I}{2}[s_i(t)-\hat{s}_i(t)]\right\}\right\}\exp(j\omega_c t) \tag{4}$$

with channel modulation index $m_I = \sqrt{2}x_c\pi A_m$.

The optical field at the output of a fiber link of length z is given by [7],

$$E_{out}(t) = \sqrt{P_o/2}\exp(-j\pi/4)\times\left\{\prod_{i=1}^{N}\left\{1-j\frac{\sqrt{2}m_I}{2}[-s_i(t)-\hat{s}_i(t)]\exp(-j\frac{\beta_2}{2}i^2\omega_i^2 z)\right\}\right.$$
$$\left.+j\prod_{i=1}^{N}\left\{1-j\frac{\sqrt{2}m_I}{2}[s_i(t)-\hat{s}_i(t)]\exp\left(-j\frac{\beta_2}{2}i^2\omega_i^2 z\right)\right\}\right\}\times\exp(j\omega_c t) \tag{5}$$

Furthermore, as the envelope of the optical field is detected by a photodetector with responsivity, R_λ, the detected photocurrent is proportional to the envelope of optical field at the fiber output. Considering the intermodulation products, the temporal expression of the detected current may be expressed as $i(t) \approx i_{DC} + i_{sig}(t) + i_{int}(t)$, where i_{DC} is the detected current DC term, $i_{sig}(t)$ is the SCM electrical signal, $i_{int}(t)$ accounts for the intermodulation products, which acts as noise.

In such systems it is important to consider the intermodulation effects between the sub-carriers as well as between sub-carrier and higher harmonics when high modulation indexes are considered.

For small modulation indexes intermodulation can be calculated using (5), however, for high values of m_I system simulation is necessary. When using system simulation the bandwidth of each channel and not just the carrier are taken into account.

4 Simulation Results

System simulations were performed using VPI TransmissionMaker™. The library blocks of the simulator were complemented when necessary with blocks implemented using MathWorks software tool MATLAB®. The light source considered in the simulation is an ideal laser, with 1 mW of emission power.

Figure 3 shows the simulation overview showing the signal at some system points. The 1 Gbit/s data which is filtered by a 100% roll over square root raised cosine filter. The filtered data modulates the mm-wave carrier using BPSK modulation. The 4 channels are mixed and used to modulate the optical carrier to OSSB with a m_I=0.2.

After transmission through standard singlemode fiber, operating at 1553 nm, 16 ps/(nm.km) dispersion coefficient, the signal is directly detected by a high speed PIN photodetector. The receiver considered introduces a noise current of $10e^{-12}$ $A/\sqrt{Hz}$. The photodetected channels are separated by mixing with the respective carrier and filtered by a 100% roll over square root raised cosine filter.

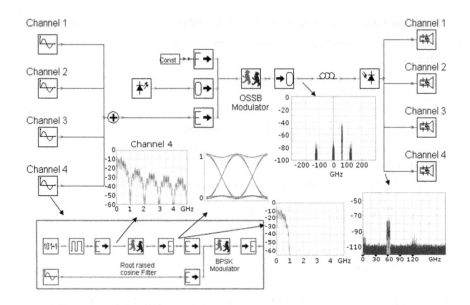

Fig. 3. Overall simulated system with illustrative signals

To measure the intermodulation distortion falling in a given channel, the channel under analysis is switched off, and the intermodulation power falling in the channel is measured. Figure 4a and 4b show the simulated received electrical spectrum when the 60 GHz channel is switched off, for two modulation indexes $m_I=0.44$ and $m_I=1.1$ respectively and a fiber length of 5 km. For $m_I=0.44$ the intermodulation power falling in the 60 GHz channel is not relevant whereas for $m_I=1.1$, the intermodulation power resulting from the sum of the different optical field harmonic beats is significant. Intermodulation power also depends on fiber length, since due to dispersion the different optical field harmonics suffer phase changes which depend on fiber length leading to total intermodulation power variations. In some situations, the intermodulation power falling in a given channel can even decrease with distance, as shown in figure 4c.

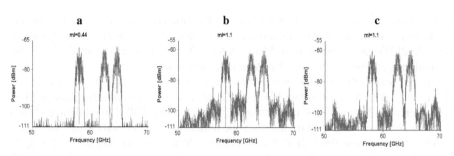

Fig. 4. Received electrical spectrum, showing intermodulation power falling on the 60 GHz channel. a) $m_I=0.44$ fiber length of 5 km. b) $m_I=1.1$ fiber length of 5 km. c) $m_I=1.1$ fiber length of 50 km.

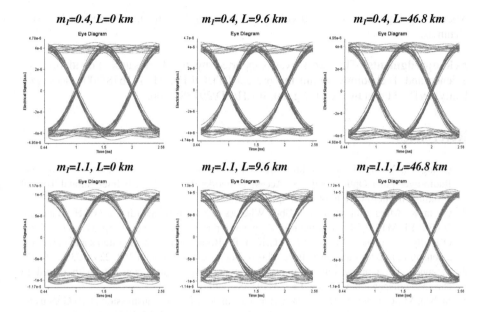

Fig. 5. Received eye diagrams for the 60 GHz channel considering different values of modulation index m_I and fiber lengths L

Figure 5 shows the eye diagrams of the received data of the 60 GHz channel corresponding to the two modulation indexes and different fiber lengths. For a fiber length of 0 km as expected for $m_I=1.1$, the received eye presents higher distortion when compared with $m_I=0.4$. For small values of m_I intermodulation is not relevant and the system performance is not significantly affected by dispersion, therefore the received eye diagrams are kept widely open when transmission distance increases. However, the most interesting results arise when the distortion introduced by the OSSB modulator is combined with fiber dispersion. For high modulation indexes $m_I=1.1$, the combined effect of dispersion and intermodulation give rise to oscillations on the system performance, for example for a fiber length of 46.8 km the eye is wider than for 9.6 km. Although not shown in this paper, we note that these results depend strongly on the mm-wave carrier frequency.

5   Conclusions

Although SSB improves the system reach, the intermodulation distortion and fiber dispersion are still the main issues, as shown by our numerical simulation. This implies a careful consideration when choosing the network architecture.

Other optical modulation techniques should be studied, such as optical carrier suppression or optical filtering, to compare the fiber chromatic dispersion effect with our OSSB system. The data transmission rate should be analyzed and its robustness should be compared to different modulation formats. Orthogonal Frequency Multiplexing (OFDM) could be a good candidate to improve the system performance when using high bit rates by dividing the transmission channel in several low rate channels.

Acknowledgments. This work was supported by the Portuguese Foundation for Science and Technology within the project PTDC/EEA-TEL/71678/2006, Research Unity, I&D 631 and by the PhD grant SFRH/BD/29138/2006.

References

1. Chang, G., Yu, J., Jia, Z.: Architectures and Enabling Technologies for Super-Broadband Radio-over-Fiber Optical-Wireless Access Networks. In: 2007 IEEE International Topical Meeting on Microwave Photonics, pp. 24–28 (2007)
2. Ohata, K., Maruhashi, et al.: 1.25Gbps Wireless Gigabit Ethernet Link at 60GHz-Band. In: 2003 IEEE MTT-S International Microwave Symposium Digest, vol. 1, pp. 373–376 (2003)
3. O'Reilly, J.J., Lane, P.M., Attard, J., Griffin, R.: Broadband wireless systems and networks: an enabling role for radio-over-fibre. Philos. Trans. R. Soc. London 358, 2297–2308 (2000)
4. Schmuck, H.: Comparison of optical millimeter-wave system concepts with regard to chromatic dispersion. Electron. Lett. 31, 1848–1849 (1995)
5. Sieben, M., Conradi, J., Dodds, D.E.: Optical single sideband transmission at 10 Gb/s using only electrical dispersion compensation. J. Lightwave Technol. 17, 1742–1749 (1999)
6. Laurêncio, P., Medeiros, M.C.R.: Dynamic range of optical links employing optical single side-band modulation. IEEE Photonics Technol. Lett. 15, 748–750 (2003)
7. Laurêncio, P., Simões, S., Medeiros, M.C.R.: Impact of the combined effect of RIN and intermodulation distortion on OSSB/SCM systems. J. Lightwave Technol. 24, 4250–4260 (2006)

Part 10

Sensorial Perception - I

Advances in Image Processing Techniques for Drusens Detection and Quantification in Fundus Images

André Mora[1,2], Pedro Vieira[3], and José Fonseca[1,2]

[1] Uninova, Campus da FCT-UNL, Monte da Caparica,
2829-516 Caparica, Portugal
[2] DEE-FCT-Universidade Nova de Lisboa, Campus da FCT-UNL, Monte da Caparica,
2829-516 Caparica, Portugal
`atm@uninova.pt, jmf@uninova.pt`
[3] DF-FCT-UNL, Campus da FCT-UNL, Monte da Caparica,
2829-516 Caparica, Portugal
`pmv@fct.unl.pt`

Abstract. Age-Related Macular Degeneration (ARMD) is considered the leading cause of irreversible blindness in developed countries. One of its risk factors is the presence of drusens, which are retina abnormalities appearing as yellowish spots in fundus images.

In this article a methodology using image processing techniques for the quantification of drusens is presented. The method uses splines combined with a contrast normalization to correct uneven illumination, followed by a drusen detection and modelling algorithm. The detection uses a gradient based segmentation algorithm that isolates drusens. They are then fitted by Gaussian functions, producing a model that is used to compute the area affected.

To validate the methodology, 22 images were marked by three ophthalmologists and compared to the automated method. The *sensitivity* and *specificity* for the automated process (*0.664* and *0.963*) were comparable to that obtained among the specialists (*0.656* and *0.971*). Also, the *Intraclass Correlation Coefficient* showed an agreement of *74.9%* between the processed images and the specialists' analysis.

Keywords: Image processing; retina imaging; automatic segmentation.

1 Introduction

Some ophthalmologic lesions have visible symptoms in the retina surface. Drusens, accumulations of extra-cellular materials beneath the retina surface, are one of those mentioned above. They are a risk factor for Age-Related Macular Degeneration, the leading cause of irreversible blindness in developed countries [1]. They appear in fundus images as speckles of higher intensity (see Fig. 1) and are qualitatively evaluated by the ophthalmologists by using fuzzy variables like: shape, size, location, etc. For this examination to be accurate, by quantifying the abnormalities, it requires a fastidious work from the expert that must be skilled for this task.

An accurate quantification of drusens in retina images using automatic procedures is one of the challenges for researchers who study medical imaging. This is a subjective

L.M. Camarinha-Matos, P. Pereira, and L. Ribeiro (Eds.): DoCEIS 2010, IFIP AICT 314, pp. 299–307, 2010.
© IFIP International Federation for Information Processing 2010

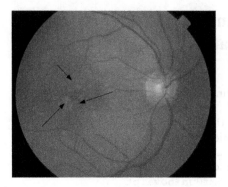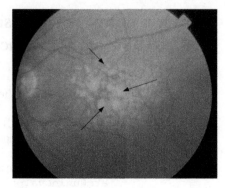

Fig. 1. Examples of retina images obtained by fundus photography

analysis and its criteria can differ among specialists and among analysis performed by one specialist at different moments. If we also consider that the design of an automatic diagnosis system is complex, then the development of such accurate procedure is a difficult task.

2   Contribution to Technological Innovation

Several studies have been published in the last twenty-years for drusens detection using image enhancement techniques. They included image pre-processing for illumination compensation and contrast improvement, and for the drusens segmentation have been proposed algorithms using adaptive local thresholds [2-7], global thresholds [8] or fuzzy logic thresholds [9]. Most of these techniques proved that good noise removal algorithm is required for getting reliable results. We have also contributed to this subject by introducing new image processing algorithms for illumination correction [10] and for drusens detection and modelling [11].

In this article it is proposed a methodology for automated drusens detection and quantification. The main goal is to create an algorithm which is as non-parametric as possible. Parameters should be calculated based on the image information, requiring less user intervention. The proposed methodology includes an image pre-processing step to compensate non-uniform illumination and contrast normalization; a detection algorithm that determines the number of drusens and an image modelling to quantify the area affected. The methodology was validated on a set of 22 images with the collaboration of three ophthalmologists.

3   Illumination Correction

In ophthalmologic imaging it is usually difficult to obtain good quality images. *Illumination* is not always uniform due to numerous factors: the retina surface is convex; the macula reflectance is lower than others parts of the retina; the patient eye is not stable, etc. The consequence is that the image has different contrast areas increasing

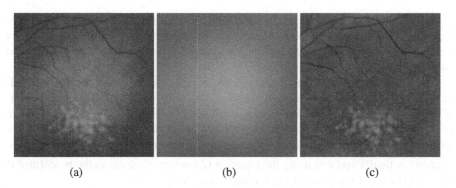

(a)   (b)   (c)

Fig. 2. *Illumination* correction: (a) Original image *f(x,y)*; (b) Estimated *illumination* model *i(x,y)*; (c) Corrected image

the complexity of the quantification methods. We propose to correct the non-uniformity of illumination and contrast before further processing.

The proposed technique is designed for gray scale images and since the retina images used are mostly in RGB format, a RGB to Gray conversion is applied to those. This conversion is obtained using the green channel information, which is a procedure widely used in other retina image works [4, 7, 12]. It is chosen by its better dynamic range, better contrast and less influence by the illumination differences, while it maintains all retina structures visible.

Using the gray scale image, and to correct the effects of non-uniform illumination, we then determine the image background intensity and correct the image accordingly. Several methods were tested (FFT, Gaussian fitting, Gaussian blurring, Splines) [10] and the smoothing spline fitting was the one to produce better contrasted images. This method fits the image background *f(x,y)* with a smoothing cubic spline (Fig. 2.b). This is a cubic spline *S(x,y)* that minimizes the function presented in equation (1), where *p* is a smoothing factor and $D^2S(x, y)$ is the second derivative of the cubic spline:

$$p \cdot \sum_{y=1}^{m} \sum_{x=1}^{n} |f(x, y) - S(x, y)|^2 + (1-p) \iint |D^2S(x, y)|^2 dxdy \qquad (1)$$

The smoothing factor *p*, defined in the interval [0..1], controls the relative weight between fitting all data points (*p*=1) and having a smooth spline (*p*=0). For *p=1* the spline is an interpolating spline that crosses every data point, while *p=0* it maximizes the smoothness generating a straight line. The reference value for *p* was determined empirically within our set of test images and obtained $p = 1e^{-6}$, for an image resolution of 12.5 *μm/pixel*.

The corrected image is obtained by dividing the original image by the illumination pattern, generating a unitary average intensity. To recreate a grey scale image with 256 levels a constant value, 85 (1/3 scale), is multiplied by the image. However, depending on the image contrast this value can generate out of scale values or low contrast images. To overcome this problem a contrast normalization procedure was introduced. It involves the determination of the standard deviation (σ) of the image intensity and its normalization to a predefined value.

The retinal vessels are one of the structures that are present in all images and provide good contrast with the background. We propose a method that evaluates locally the contrast between the vessels and the background and normalizes it to a predefined value.

Using a sliding window-based analysis the σ value and the mean intensity are calculated for each window. A window width of 1/8 of the optic disc diameter was considered to be adequate, as it can contain small vessel branches and background. Then from the 50 darker windows, that are typically windows containing vessels over a uniform background, is determined the median of the σ values (σ_{median}). The image intensity is finally updated using the equation (2), where $\sigma_{predefined}$ is the predefined σ value (0.15) and A the constant background value (85).

$$norm\_image(x, y) = A \cdot \left(\frac{\sigma_{predefined}}{\sigma_{median}} * (image(x, y) - 1) + 1 \right) \qquad (2)$$

4   Drusens Detection

Our Drusens detection and quantification algorithm is based on the modelling of Drusen spots to ensure a shape consistent image segmentation. For getting a better performance from the modelling algorithm it is recommended that an image preprocessing is applied to calculate the approximate number of Drusens, their location and optionally their size.

We propose a maximum detection algorithm based on labelling the maximum gradient path. In medium resolution images there are more then just one pixel pointing to each *intensity maximum*. Therefore, it is possible to follow one or more ascending paths that inevitably reach an *intensity maximum*.

The algorithm begins by determining the image gradient using a 3x3 Sobel operator which evaluates intensity changes in the horizontal and vertical axis. The pixel gradient is a vector which is oriented to the ascending pixel. The two-dimensional

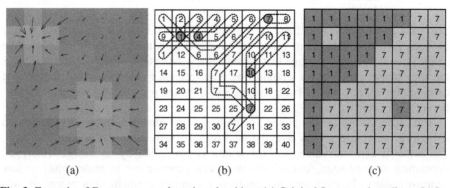

(a)   (b)   (c)

Fig. 3. Example of Drusens center detection algorithm. (*a*) Original Image and gradient; (b) Labelling 1st stage – *initial label propagation* – (with label propagation on the two upper rows); (*c*) Labelling 2nd stage – *apply compatibilities* - (two Drusens centered on the highlighted pixels).

gradient analyses the 3x3 neighbourhood of each pixel what eliminates several noise related artefacts. But when signal/noise ratio is low the algorithm can be significantly improved by changing every pixel gradient by the mean (vectors sum) of its neighbour's gradients. Fig. 3.a contains an example of an image after applying a 3x3 gradient mean. The original image represents two small Drusens.

In the first stage of the labelling procedure, *initial label propagation*, every pixel is examined in a top-left to bottom-right direction and is assigned a new label to all pixels that are not marked yet. Whenever a label is assigned to a pixel it is propagated to the neighbour pixel that is in the gradient azimuth direction. This labelling continues on the propagated pixels until the next pixel is already marked. Fig. 3.b presents the result of the labelling first stage. Every time the label propagation finishes on the same label that is being propagated, that pixel is marked as an *intensity maximum*. In the same situation when there is a different label the two labels are defined as being *compatibles*. This means that they belong to the same *intensity maximum*, i.e., the same Drusen spot.

The second stage of the labelling procedure is to apply the *label compatibilities* resulting on an image with as many labels as possible Drusens. The result is a segmented image where all pixels that contribute to a spot have the same label. It is important to notice that the algorithm is so far a non-parameterized algorithm.

But a problem arises when flat valleys or flat hills occur. In these cases not all gradient paths end on the same *intensity maximum* pixel since there might exist more then one pixel for that *intensity maximum*. Consequently, the algorithm will generate more *intensity maximums* then it really should. For solving this problem a merging strategy was followed. Using a connected components approach, the local *intensity maximums* are merged to other neighbour *intensity maximums* if they can be connected by a path that doesn't goes lower than a predefined amplitude.

At this stage drusens are detected and characterized by centre coordinates and size. This information will be used as the initial parameters for the modelling algorithm.

5 Drusens Modelling

The final phase is to analytically characterize the shape and intensity of the drusens, providing information to evaluate them quantitatively. The elevations shown on drusen areas on the tri-dimensional representation motivated us to create a model of the image intensity and from it extract the drusens dimensions. From the model it is computed the total affected area and drusens dimensions. This information can be valuable to an alongside comparison that evaluates sequence of images during a long term treatment.

In a three-dimensional view of the retina surface, as in Fig. 4.a, it can be seen a drusen that has a waveform similar to a Gaussian function superimposed to a flat background with low amplitude white noise. These observations and the possibility to describe the drusens by means of elementary functions motivated the use of Gaussian functions to model drusens. This approach allows the drusen modelling and its isolation from the background.

The modified Gaussian function used is given by:

$$G(x, y) = A * e^{-\left(\frac{X^2}{s_x} + \frac{Y^2}{s_y}\right)^{\frac{2}{d}}} + Z_0 \, .$$ (3)

where

$$X = (x - x_0) \cdot \cos(\theta) + (y - y_0) \cdot \sin(\theta)$$
$$Y = -(x - x_0) \cdot \sin(\theta) + (y - y_0) \cdot \cos(\theta)$$
$$s_y = s_F \cdot s_x$$ (4)

The Gaussian function used represented on equation (3) allows: translations in the xy plane (x_0, y_0) and in the background plane (Z_0), amplitude scaling (A), rotation (θ) and shape modifications (s_x, s_F, d). These latter defines the width in the x-plane (s_x), the shape factor (s_F) used to obtain the width in y-plane, allowing stretched shapes in the xy plane, and the shape factor (d) that controls the amplitude profile between square shape, round shape and thin shape.

For searching the function parameters that best fits the image we adopted the Levenberg-Marquardt non-linear least squares optimization algorithm with pre-defined parameters constraints ([13]). Because some Drusens are overlapped, a multiple function (one or more for each spot) simultaneous optimization must be used for studying the sum of all the Gaussian functions. In Fig. 4.b there is an example of superimposed Drusens *modeled* through multiple Gaussian functions.

Finally, for highlighting Drusen areas in the image it is shown the contour or the area of each detected spot at predefined percentage of its amplitude (without background).

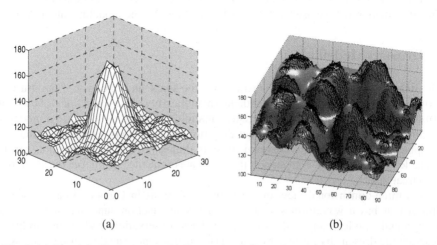

(a)   (b)

Fig. 4. (a) 3D original image view; (b) Drusens modeling using multiple Gaussian functions

6   Results

For evaluation of the drusen detection and quantification process a set of 22 images containing colour and greyscale fundus images was marked by three independent ophthalmologists. Our study was focused on the macula, as suggested by the Wisconsin Grading System [14] a circular *region of interest* centred in the macula with 3000µm diameter. The specialists marked this set of images using the computer assisted procedure with the software *MD3RI* [15] which were then used to compare the results produced by the proposed method (*AD3RI*) over the same images.

For the results analysis the percentage of drusen area, the *false positive* and *false negative* pixels, were computed. The results were then evaluated using the algorithm's *sensitivity* and *specificity* as well as using the *Intraclass Correlation Coefficient* (ICC) to evaluate the agreement between all the specialists and the *AD3RI* method and among each specialist.

The *sensitivity* and *specificity* indicators were obtained by comparing the processed image with each specialist marking. The average *sensitivity* and *specificity* were *0.664* and *0.963*, respectively. The same indicators were evaluated among the specialists as a comparative indicator and the average *sensitivity* and *specificity* were comparable to the previous ones, *0.656* and *0.971*, respectively.

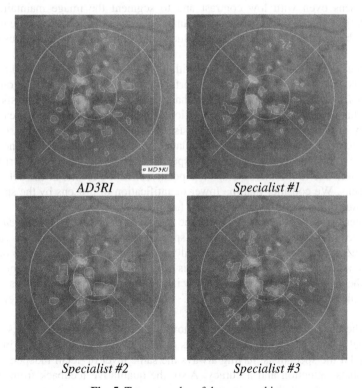

AD3RI   *Specialist #1*

Specialist #2   *Specialist #3*

Fig. 5. Two examples of drusens markings

As a comparative analysis method, the *ICC* with 95% confidence levels [16] evaluated the areas' values between specialists and the *AD3RI* (ICC_{AD3RI}) and among specialists (ICC_{Spec}). These indicators were all within the 95% confidence interval and obtained an average agreement of *74.9%* between the specialists and the *AD3RI* and an average agreement of *81.1%* among the specialists.

7 Discussion

The development of methods to quantitatively measure drusens in a reproducible and accurate procedure will improve the quality of the follow up of this disease and potentiate epidemiologic studies and clinical trials. In this article we presented a new method to quantitatively measure drusens and its' comparison with 22 images marked by three independent ophthalmologists. The algorithm is based on the detection and modelling of drusens to automatically calculate the affected areas including an image pre-processing for non-uniform illumination correction.

The presented non-uniform illumination correction algorithm was an important step to obtain a less parameterized methodology, since it is capable to deliver an image with normalized illumination and contrast to the following steps. The detection and modelling of drusens with Gaussian functions demonstrated to be capable to detect drusens even with low contrast and to segment the image maintaining the drusens typical shape. It also provides an analytical model which allows the determination of drusen indicators, such as confluence, average size, type of drusens and others.

From the statistical analysis of the algorithm with three specialists related to the 22 images was observed that the algorithm performs as do specialists. On the one hand, the *sensitivity* (*0.664*) was slightly higher than the one observed among the specialists (*0.656*). This is due to the algorithm detection of a higher overall area, increasing the probability of agreement with the specialists. On the other hand, the high *specificity* value (*0.963*) demonstrates that the automated process is very accurate and is also comparable to results obtained among the specialists (*0.971*). With the algorithm, the value is lower due to the increase of false positives, which results of the detection of more drusens. We consider that the lower quantification of drusens by the specialists is mainly due to the marking process being fastidious.

The other measure of agreement used, the *Intraclass Correlation Coefficient (ICC)*, demonstrated that the agreement among specialists on the overall areas values is approximately 81% and that the automatically processed images have *74.9%* of agreement when compared to specialists. This analysis showed a good concordance between the automated process and the specialists, verifying that the analysis is statistically significant, as all the obtained *ICC* values were within the 95% confidence levels.

From the above, the *AD3RI* method showed promising results to be tested by a wider panel of specialists and with new sets of images. It detected the most important drusen as did the specialists, having always the same level of detail independently of the specialists' attention and accuracy. Also, the qualitative feedback from the specialists confirmed that the results were accurate and that the software can play an important role in the follow-up of retina diseases.

Acknowledgments. This work was financed by the Fundação para a Ciência e Tecnologia, through the POCTI and POSI Research Programs (project n° POCI/SAU-ESP/57592/2004). The authors acknowledge the University of Aberdeen, Rudolfstiftung Hospital, Hospital Santa Maria and Faculdade de Ciências Médicas for supplying the retina images used in this work, for their valuable feedback on the software testing and for marking the sample images.

References

1. World Health Organization, International Agency for the Prevention of Blindness: State of World's Sight - Vision 2020: the right to sight (1999-2005) (2005)
2. Peli, E., Lahav, M.: Drusen Measurement from Fundus Photographs Using Computer Image Analysis. Ophtalmology 93, 1575–1580 (1986)
3. Kirkpatrick, J.N.P., Spencer, T., Manivannan, A., Sharp, P.F., Forrester, J.V.: Quantitative image analysis of macular drusen from fundus photographs and scanning laser ophthalmoscope images. Eye (Royal College of Ophthalmologists) 9, 48–55 (1995)
4. Rapantzikos, K., Zervakis, M., Balas, K.: Detection and segmentation of drusen deposits on human retina: potential in the diagnosis of age-related macular degeneration. Med. Image Anal. 7, 95–108 (2003)
5. Morgan, W.H., Cooper, R.L., Constable, I.J., Eikelboom, R.H.: Automated extraction and quantification of macular drusen from fundal photographs. Australian and New Zealand Journal of Ophthalmology 22, 7–12 (1994)
6. Phillips, R.P., Spencer, T., Ross, P.G., Sharp, P.F., Forrester, J.V.: Quantification of diabetic maculopathy by digital imaging of the fundus. Eye 5 (Pt 1), 130–137 (1991)
7. Shin, D., Javornik, N., Berger, J.: Computer-assisted, interactive fundus image processing for macular drusen quantitation. Ophthalmology 106, 1119–1125 (1999)
8. Smith, R.T., Nagasaki, T., Sparrow, J.R., Barbazetto, I., Klaver, C.C., Chan, J.K.: A method of drusen measurement based on the geometry of fundus reflectance. Biomed. Eng. Online 2, 10 (2003)
9. Thdibaoui, A., Rajn, A., Bunel, P.: A fuzzy logic approach to drusen detection in retinal angiographic images. In: 15th International Conference on Pattern Recognition, Barcelona, Spain, vol. 4, pp. 748–751 (2000)
10. Mora, A., Fonseca, J., Vieira, P.: Drusen Deposits Modelling with Illumination Correction. In: Biomed-2005, Innsbruck, Austria (2005)
11. Mora, A., Vieira, P., Fonseca, J.: Modeling of Drusen Deposits Based on Retina Image Tridimensional Information. In: Second International Conference on Computacional Intelligence in Medicine and Healthcare - CIMED 2005, Costa da Caparica, Portugal (2005)
12. Soliz, P., Wilson, M.P., Nemeth, S.C., Nguyen, P.: Computer-aided methods for quantitative assessment of longitudinal changes in retinal images presenting with maculopathy. In: Medical Imaging 2002: Visualization, Image-Guided Procedures, and Display, San Diego, CA, USA. SPIE, vol. 4681, pp. 159–170 (2002)
13. Marquardt, D.W.: An algorithm for least-squares estimation of non-linear parameters. Journal of the Society for Industrial and Applied Mathematics 11, 431–441 (1963)
14. Klein, R., Davis, M.D., Magli, Y.L., Segal, P., Klein, B.E., Hubbard, L.: The Wisconsin age-related maculopathy grading system. Ophthalmology 98, 1128–1134 (1991)
15. Mora, A., Vieira, P., Fonseca, J.: MD3RI a Tool for Computer-Aided Drusens Contour Drawing. In: Fourth IASTED International Conference on Biomedical Engineering - BIOMED 2006. ACTA Press, Innsbruck (2006)
16. McGraw, K.O., Wong, S.P.: Forming inferences about some intraclass correlation coefficients. Psychological Methods 1, 30–46 (1996)

A Novel Framework for Data Registration and Data Fusion in Presence of Multi-modal Sensors

Hadi Aliakbarpour[1,2], Joao Filipe Ferreira[1], Kamrad Khoshhal[1], and Jorge Dias[1]

[1] Institute of Systems and Robotics (ISR), University of Coimbra, Portugal
{hadi,jfilipe,kamrad,jorge}@isr.uc.pt
[2] IEEE student member

Abstract. This article presents a novel framework to register and fuse heterogeneous sensory data. Our approach is based on geometrically registration of sensory data onto a set of virtual parallel planes and then applying an occupancy grid for each layer. This framework is useful in surveillance applications in presence of multi-modal sensors and can be used specially in tracking and human behavior understanding areas. The multi-modal sensors set in this work comprises of some cameras, inertial measurement sensors (IMU), laser range finders (LRF) and a binaural sensing system. For registering data from each one of these sensors an individual approach is proposed. After registering multi-modal sensory data on various geometrically parallel planes, a two-dimensional occupancy grid (as a layer) is applied for each plane.

Keywords: Multi-modality, data registration, data fusion, Occupancy grid and Homography.

1 Introduction

Data registration and *data fusion* are two crucial issues in a multi sensory environment since heterogeneous sensors are substantially different. In this work we propose a novel framework for data registration and fusion in presence of various modalities such as image, range, sound and inertial data. This paper is structured as following. In Sec. 2 the main contribution is described. Sec. 3 is for related work. Sensors models are introduced in Sec.4. Sec. 5 is dedicated to registering data from different modalities and then applying a data fusion strategy. A preliminary result of an ongoing experiment is shown in Sec. 6. Then in Sec. 7 conclusion and future work are discussed.

2 Contribution to Technological Innovation

The use of surveillance systems is growing in different areas such as airports, banks and human behavior interpretation. Each particular sensor has its own drawbacks. Although to overcome that nowadays researchers are trying to use several sensors from different modalities instead of using just a single type, however data registration and data fusion are still two critical and determinant phases in surveillance systems. Our main contribution is to work on these subjects and make a framework based on geometric data registration and probabilistic data fusion.

L.M. Camarinha-Matos, P. Pereira, and L. Ribeiro (Eds.): DoCEIS 2010, IFIP AICT 314, pp. 308–315, 2010.

3   Related Works

Fusion of the sensors outputs is a crucial challenge related in such applications. A model namely JDL is proposed in [1] for data fusion. Armesto et al. in [2] presented an approach to model and fuse of non-linear data from multi-rate systems which have visual and inertial sensors. Bellotto and Hu also presented an approach in [3] to fuse the LRF data and vision data by PTZ camera. Chakravarty and Jarvis in [4] discussed a fusion method for LRF and panoramic vision data to track people from a stationary robot simultaneously. Khan et al. in [5] presented a new approach which fuse different views silhouette data form some.

4   Sensors Models

A pinhole camera model [6] is used in this work. The 3D LRF in this work is built by moving a 2D LRF along one of its axes. A detailed model of this configuration can be found in [7]. A detailed version of IMU model used in this paper can be seen in [12]. And eventually for the sound system, a Bayesian binaural system is considered for imitating human binaural system (see [8]). The Bayesian binaural system (described in [9]) composes three distinct and consecutive processors (Fig. 3-a): *the monaural cochlear unit*, which processes the pair of monaural signals $\{X_1, X_2\}$ coming from the binaural audio transducer system by simulating the human cochlea, so as to achieve a tonotopic representation (i.e. a frequency band decomposition) of the left and right audio streams; *the binaural unit*, which correlates these signals and consequently estimates the binaural cues and segments each sound-source; and, finally, *the Bayesian 3D sound-source localization unit*, which applies a Bayesian sensor model so as to perform localization of sound-sources in 3D space, using the egocentric frame of reference $\{\varepsilon\}$.

5   Multi-modal Data Registration and Data Fusion

In a multi-modal sensory environment, data registration and data fusion are two crucial issues. In this section we talk about these issues where there are four heterogeneous sensors. Prior to that, a coordinate reference $\{W\}$ and also a 3D plane π_{ref} inside this space will be introduced which are universal and common for all sensors inside the framework (see fig. 1-left). Let the origin of this coordinate frame be on our reference plane and also consider two coordinate vectors X and Y extending across (aligned) the plane (XY-plane of $\{W\}$ corresponds to π_{ref}). Moreover assume that the Z direction of this plane is parallel to the earth gravity vector but in an apposite direction. Having these definitions, π_{ref} becomes *a virtual horizontal plane* [10] which is considered a common geometrical plane for all sensors in this setup. The idea is to geometrically register data observed by sensors with different modalities (cameras, LRFs and microphones) onto this plane (in section 5.4 it is extended to some parallel planes). After having the registration structure, a BOF [14] will be applied to achieve the final framework.

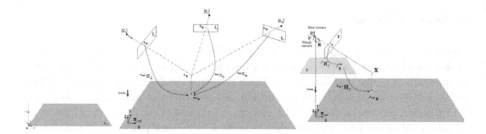

Fig. 1. *Left*: World coordinate system, W, and the reference plane, π_{ref}. *Middle*: Registering image points onto the reference plane π_{ref}. *Right*: Considering a virtual camera for each real camera. The principle axis of such a virtual camera is coincided to the gravity vector. The rotation matrix between real camera $\{C\}$ and virtual camera $_{\{C'\}}$ is given by the IMU [12].

5.1 Image Data Registration

The idea of this work is to have all data coming from different sensors registered on a common reference plane, namely π_{ref}. Fig. 1-*middle* shows a setup with n_c cameras, $C = \{C_i \mid i = 1..n_c\}$, and a reference plane π_{ref}. In this setup each camera is rigidly fixed with an IMU (Inertial Measurement Unit). The intention is to register a 3D point $^W X = (X,Y,Z)$ observed by camera C onto the reference plane π_{ref} as $^{\pi_{ref}} x$ using the IMU. The image plane of these cameras can be expressed as $I = \{I_i \mid i = 1..n_c\}$. A virtual image plane, $\{I'_i \mid i = 1..n_c\}$, is considered for each camera. Such a virtual plane is assumed to be a horizontal plane at a distance f below the camera sensor, f being the focal length [10]. In other words, it can be said that beside of each real camera C in the setup, a virtual camera C' is also considered whose center, $\{C'\}$, is coincided to the center of the real camera $\{C\}$. So that the transformation matrix between $\{C'\}$ and $\{C\}$ will just have a rotation part and the translation part is a zero vector. In order to have $^{\pi_{ref}} x$ from $^W x$ three consecutive steps are considered: Firstly, a 3D point $^W X$ is projected on the camera reference frame ($\{C\}$) using $^I x = P^W X$ (P is projection matrix). Secondly, $^I x$ (the imaged point on the camera's image plane) is projected to the corresponding virtual image plane as $^{I'} x$. This can be done by having the related homography transformation, namely $^{I'} H_I$. The corresponding equation is $^{I'} x = {}^{I'} H_I \, {}^I x$. Eventually, $^{I'} x$, the projected point on the virtual image plane, is reprojected to the main reference plane π_{ref} by having the related homography transformation matrix, called $^{\pi_{ref}} H_{I'}$. For the first step it is by the camera model described in the Sec. 4. The second and third steps are described in the following two sub-section. Assuming to already have $^{I'} H_I$ and $^{\pi_{ref}} H_{I'}$, the final equation for registering an image point $^I x$ onto the reference plane π_{ref} will be (see Fig. 1):

$$^{\pi_{ref}}x = {}^{\pi_{ref}}H_{I'}\,{}^{I'}H_I\,{}^Ix \tag{1}$$

Inertial Compensated Homography: Lets consider $^{I''}x$ as re-projection of a point ^Ix from image plane I of camera C onto the virtual image plane I' of camera C' (see figure 1-right). Then the following general equation can be used:

$$^{I'}x = {}^{I'}H_I\,{}^Ix \tag{2}$$

being $^{I'}H_I$ a 3×3 homography matrix between real image plane and its virtual plane. In this case H is called *infinite homography* since there is just a pure rotation between real camera and virtual camera centers [6]. In this case the equation for H will become as $^IH_I = K'RK^{-1}$ [9,13] being R as the rotation matrix between $\{C\}$ and $\{C'\}$ (real and virtual camera centers). Reminding that normal vector of the virtual camera's plane is coincided to the earth gravity vector, then the rotation matrix R can be achieved by using the *IMU* coupled to the camera. The *Camera Inertial Calibration Toolbox* is used in order to calibrate a rigid couple of a IMU and camera [12].

Homography Between Virtual Image Plane and π_{ref}: The homography matrix between the virtual image plane I' (the image of virtual camera) and π_{ref} needs to be computed. A homography matrix H can be represented by its axis and vertex and cross-ratio parameters:

$$H = I + (\mu - 1)\frac{va^T}{v^T a} \tag{3}$$

in which v is the vertex coordinates and a is the axis line [6,10,13]. For the case of a 3D plane being parallel to the image plane, like in our case, the Eq. 3 becomes a simple matrix by considering $a = (0,0,1)^T$ and $v = (v_x, v_y, 1)$. Then the result is [11]:

$$^{\pi_{ref}}H_{I'} = \begin{bmatrix} 1 & 0 & (\mu-1).v_x \\ 0 & 1 & (\mu-1).v_y \\ 0 & 0 & \mu \end{bmatrix} \tag{4}$$

which is the homography matrix between the reference plane π_{ref} and virtual image plane I'.

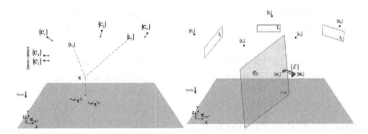

Fig. 2. *Left*: Range data registration. *Right*: Registration of azimuth plane of arrival of sound: The intersection of the arrival sound plane and π_{ref} will be registered as a line.

5.2 Range Data Registration

LRF is one of the interesting sensors in our multi-modal setup. The model of our LRF is described in [7]. Geometrical registration of range data is the goal of this section. The general intention is to be able geometrically registering data coming from LRF on the reference plane π_{ref} (see Fig. 2-left). More specifically, for a 3D point X in the scene which is observed in the LRF local reference frame as $^L x = (x, y, z, 1)$ (in its homogeneous form), its projection on π_{ref}, in homogeneous form $^{\pi_{\text{ref}}} x = (x, y, 1)$, can be expressed by

$$^{\pi_{\text{ref}}} x = \begin{bmatrix} 1 & 0 & 0 & 0 \\ 0 & 1 & 0 & 0 \\ 0 & 0 & 0 & 1 \end{bmatrix} {}^W T_L \, {}^L x \tag{5}$$

where $^W T_L$ is the transformation matrix between LRF's local reference and can be acomputed by the method described in [7].

5.3 Registration of Azimuth Plane of Arrival of Sound

In this work, we use a simplified version of the sensor model described in Sec. 4, taken the decomposition equation

$$P(\tau S_\theta \theta) = P(\theta)P(S_\theta \mid \theta)P(\tau \mid S_\theta \theta), \tag{6}$$

where τ is the interaural time-difference binaural cue [9], $\theta \in \{\theta_0, \cdots \theta_n\}$ denotes an azimuth angle taken from a discretised span of n angles, S_θ is a binary variable signaling the existence of a sound-source within the azimuthal plane at θ extending from the frame of reference $\{\xi\}$ (the so-called azimuth plane of arrival for the respective sound-waves), $P(\theta)$ is an uninformative uniform distribution, $P(S_\theta \mid \theta)$ is the prior on the existence of sound-sources for a given θ, also chosen to be a uniform distribution, and $P(\tau \mid S_\theta \theta)$ is the binaural sensor model, a set of normal distributions obtained through calibration (see [8]), which indicate the probability of the measurement of θ (i.e. the angle for the azimuth plane of arrival) knowing whether or not a sound-source is present in that plane. Using Bayes rule it is possible to invert the sensor model so as to obtain $P(S_\theta \mid \tau\theta)$; an auditory saliency map can then be constructed, and a MAP (maximum a posteriori) method can be used to extract the azimuth angle estimate for the most salient sound-source (see Fig. 3-b). Based on these definitions it is possible to also register sound information on the reference plane π_{ref} (see Fig 2). The idea for sound registering is to calculate the intersection between the π_{ref} and the plane of arriving sound. The result will be registered as a line on the π_{ref}.

5.4 Extension for Planes Parallel to π_{ref}

The idea for registering data coming from different sensors onto π_{ref} which was recently described can be extended to register them also on some other planes parallel

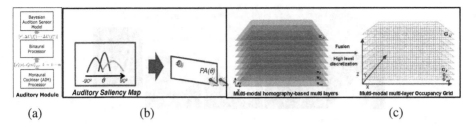

(a)	(b)	(c)

Fig. 3. (**a**): Bayesian binaural system. (**b**): Auditory saliency map and azimuth plane of arrival extracted for the most salient sound source. (**c**): Multi-modal multi-layer data registration and data fusion framework.

to π_{ref}. Fig. *3-c-left* represents a setup with *N-1* planes parallel to π_{ref}. Such an extension needs to be done for cameras, LRFs and microphones. For LRF it becomes simple since a general method to find the homogeneous transformation between LRF and {*W*} has been defined in Sec. 5.2. For arrival sound it is exactly the same method described in Sec. 5.3. Here we continue to describe this extension for images. The intention is to calculate homography for any of these layers having the homography of the reference layer $^{\pi_{ref}} H_I$. For doing so we use *Khan*'s approach described in [5].

5.5 Multi-layer Homography-Based Occupancy Grid

Fig. 3-c shows a schematic of the proposed multi-layer framework for data registration. The idea is to make an occupancy grid layer for each plane of the registration framework. In order to make the final data fusion a BOF grid [14] per each plane is proposed as an occupancy layer (see Fig. 3-(c)). It can be used as input of a classification algorithm in order to classify the objects inside the scene and then be used by a tracking algorithm. We use the concept and also the model described in [14] for using BOF in our case. Here the variables definition is the same as [14]. Using that the probability joint distribution for the model becomes also the same as what is defined in [14] (*l* being the layer index):

$$P(^lA_{c_l}^{t-1} \, ^lA_{c_l}^t \, O_{c_l}^t \, Z_1^t...Z_S^t) = P(^lA_{c_l}^{t-1})P(P(^lA_{c_l}^t \, |^l A_{c_l}^{t-1})P(O_{c_l}^t \, |^l A_{c_l}^{t-1})\prod_{i=1}^{S}P(Z_i^t \, |^l A_{c_l}^t O) \qquad (7)$$

6   Experiments

As a preliminary experiment result the image data registration part is performed for just one layer. We used the CVLab - EPFL dataset [15]. Fig. 4:(a)-(d) show four images from four views and their projection on the ground plane using homography concept. Then after background subtraction, they are combined and intersected in order to obtain the feet positions on the ground plane (Fig. 4-e).

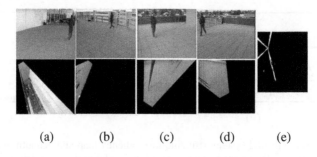

(a)   (b)   (c)   (d)   (e)

Fig. 4. (a) to (d): Images from different views and their projection on the ground plane using homography concept. e: combining four ground-projected images in order to have the feet intersection.

7 Conclusion and Future Work

Data registration and data fusion have been investigated in this paper where there are four heterogeneous sensors such as camera, microphone, laser range finder and inertial sensor. Then a multi-modal multi-layer framework is porposed. In such a framework firstly sensory data coming from different sensors are geometrically registered on different parallel planes, then an occupancy grid is applied for each layer. A prelimanry experiment result has been shown for image data registration in just one layer in Sec. 6. Data registration for other layers, range and sound data and also constructing an occupancy grid for each layer will be remained as our future work.

Acknowledgment. *Hadi Ali Akbarpour* and *Joao Filipe Ferreira* are supported by the **FCT** (Portuguese Fundation for Sceince and Technology). This work is partially supported by the European Union within the FP7 Project **PROMETHEUS**, www.prometheus-FP7.eu.

References

1. Smith, D., Singh, S.: Approaches to multisensor data fusion in target tracking: A survey. IEEE Transactions on Knowledge and Data Engineering 18, 1696–1710 (2006)
2. Armesto, L., Tornero, J.: On multi-rate fusion for non-linear sampled-data systems: Application to a 6d tracking system. Robotics and Autonomous Systems. Elsevier, Amsterdam (2007)
3. Bellotto, N., Hu, H.: Vision and laser data fusion for tracking people with a mobile robot. In: Proceedings of the 2006 IEEE International Conference on Robotics and Biomimetics, Kunming, China (2006)
4. Chakravarty, J.: Panoramic vision and laser range finder fusion for multiple person tracking. In: 2006 IEEE/RSJ International Conference on Intelligent Robots and Systems, IROS (2006)
5. Khan, S.M., Yan, P., Shah, M.: A homographic framework for the fusion of multi-view silhouettes. In: IEEE 11th International Conference on Computer Vision, ICCV 2007 (2007)

6. Hartley, R., Zisserman, A.: Multiple View Geometry in Computer Vision. Cambridge University Press, Cambridge (2003)
7. Aliakbarpour, H., Nunez, P., Prado, J., Khoshhal, K., Dias, J.: An efficient algorithm for extrinsic calibration between a 3d laser range finder and a stereo camera for surveillance. In: 14th International Conference on Advanced Robotics, ICAR 2009 (2009)
8. Ferreira, J.F., Pinho, C., Dias, J.: Implementation and calibration of a Bayesian binaural system for 3d localisation. In: IEEE International Conference on Robotics and Biomimetics (ROBIO 2008), Bangkok, Tailand, December 2008, pp. 14–17 (2008)
9. Pinho, C., Ferreira, J.F., BessiÃšre, P., Dias, J.: A Bayesian binaural system for 3d soundsource localisation. In: International Conference on Cognitive Systems (CogSys 2008), pp. 109–114 (2008)
10. Mirisola, L.G.B., Dias, J.: Tracking from a moving camera with attitude estimates. In: ICR 2008 (2008)
11. Mirisola, L.G.B.: Exploiting attitude sensing in vision-based navigation, mapping and tracking including results from an airship. PhD thesis (2009)
12. Lobo, J., Dias, J.: Relative pose calibration between visual and inertial sensors. International Journal of Robotics Research, Special Issue 2nd Workshop on Integration of Vision and Inertial Sensors 26, 561–575 (2007)
13. Criminisi, A.: Accurate visual metrology from single and multiple uncalibrated images. PhD thesis, Oxford (1999)
14. Mekhnacha, K., Mao, Y., Raulo, D., Laugier, C.: Bayesian occupancy filter based fast clustering-tracking algorithm. In: IROS 2008 (2008)
15. Fleuret, F., Jerome Berclaz, R.L., Fua, P.: Multi-camera people tracking with a probabilistic occupancy map. IEEE Transactions on Pattern Analysis and Machine Intelligence (2008)

Vector Sensor Arrays in Underwater Acoustic Applications

Paulo Santos, Paulo Felisberto, and Sérgio M. Jesus

Institute for Systems and Robotics, University of Algarve,
Campus de Gambelas, 8005-139 Faro, Portugal
{pjsantos,pfelis,sjesus}@ualg.pt

Abstract. Traditionally, ocean acoustic signals have been acquired using hydrophones, which measure the pressure field and are typically omnidirectional. A vector sensor measures both the acoustic pressure and the three components of particle velocity. Assembled into an array, a vector sensor array (VSA) improves spatial filtering capabilities when compared with arrays of same length and same number of hydrophones. The objective of this work is to show the advantage of the use of vector sensors in underwater acoustic applications such as direction of arrival (DOA) estimation and geoacoustic inversion. Beyond the improvements in DOA estimation, it will be shown the advantages of using the VSA in bottom parameters estimation. Additionally, is tested the possibility of using high frequency signals (say 8-14 kHz band), acquired during the MakaiEx 2005, to allow a small aperture array, reducing the cost of actual sub-bottom profilers and providing a compact and easy-to-deploy system.

Keywords: Vector sensor array, Direction of arrival estimation, Bottom properties estimation.

1 Introduction

Acoustic vector sensors measure both the acoustic pressure and the three components of particle velocity. Thus a single device has spatial filtering capabilities not available with pressure hydrophone. A Vector Sensor array (VSA) has the ability to provide information in both vertical and azimuthal directions allowing for a high directivity not possible with arrays of traditional hydrophone with same length and the same number of sensors. These characteristics have been explored during the last decade but most of the studies are related to direction of arrival (DOA) estimation. However, due to the VSA ability to provide directional information, this device can be used with advantage in other applications such as geoacoustic inversion. In this work it is shown that a reliable estimation of ocean bottom parameters can be obtained using a small aperture VSA and high-frequency signals.

This paper is organized as follows: in Section 2 is made a description of the contribution of this work to technological innovation. The state of the art and the related literature is presented in Section 3. Section 4 describes the vector sensor measurement

L.M. Camarinha-Matos, P. Pereira, and L. Ribeiro (Eds.): DoCEIS 2010, IFIP AICT 314, pp. 316–323, 2010.
© IFIP International Federation for Information Processing 2010

model and the theory related to the Bartlett estimator based on particle velocity for generic parameter estimation, enhancing the advantages of the VSA. In Section 5, the discussion of the results is made, showing that the VSA remarkably reduces the ambiguities presents in DOA estimation obtained with a hydrophone array and provide information both in vertical and azimuthal direction. Also, it is shown that VSA improves the resolution of bottom parameters estimation, such as sediment compressional speed, density and compressional attenuation based in matched-field inversion (MFI) techniques. The data herein considered was acquired by a four element vertical VSA in the 8-14 kHz band, during the Makai experiment 2005 sea trial, off Kauai I., Hawaii (USA) [1]. Finally Section 6 concludes this work.

2 Contribution to Technological Innovation

Vector sensors are long time used in underwater acoustic surveillance systems, mainly for DOA estimation. Only from the last decade the interest in VSA rose exponentially, influenced by electromagnetic vector sensor applications and developments in sensor technology that allowed building compact arrays for acoustic applications in the air. It is expected that in a near future will be also commercially available vector sensor devices well suited to develop compact underwater VSA at a reasonable costs. Beyond DOA estimation, it is likely that these new compact systems can be used with advantage over traditional hydrophone arrays in other underwater application fields, thanks to inherent spatial filtering capabilities of vector sensors. The advantage of use a VSA in DOA estimation is considered in this work to show the enhanced spatial filtering capabilities of a short aperture (4 elements) VSA. However, the main contribution is on using the short aperture VSA to improve inversion problems found in underwater acoustics, in particular geoacoustic inversion. The proposed geoacoustic inversion method based on MFI techniques shows the advantage of including particle velocity information that contributes to a better resolution of the estimated parameters, some of them with difficult estimation with traditional hydrophone arrays, even with larger aperture arrays. These methods were tested with field data acquired during Makai Ex 2005 [1], where probe signals in the 8-14 kHz band were used. The bottom estimates obtained are in line with the bottom characteristics known for the area. The band of the probe signal used is well above the band traditionally used in geoacoustic inversion (bellow 1 kHz), thus a systems based on a few elements VSA operating at such frequency band can be very compact, easy-to-deploy or to install in a light mobile platform like AUV, becoming a good alternative to actual profilers.

3 State of the Art

During the last decade, several authors have been conducting research on vector sensors processing, most of them theoretical works, suggesting that this type of device has advantage in DOA estimation and giving rise to an improved resolution. Nehorai and Paldi [2] developed an analytical model, initially for electromagnetic sources extending then to the acoustic case, to compare the DOA estimation performance of a

VSA to that of an array that measures only scalar acoustic pressure. At the beginning of 2000's, Cray and Nuttall [3], performed comparisons of directivity gains of VSA to conventional pressure arrays. Source bearing estimation was explored in [4], where the plane wave beamformer was applied to real data acquired by a four element VSA in the 8-14 kHz band, during Makai Experiment 2005, off Kauai I., Hawaii (USA). Increased spatial filtering capabilities gave rise to new applications where the VSA could be used with advantage over hydrophone arrays. Due to these characteristics the VSA is appearing in different fields like port and waterway security [5], underwater communications [6], underwater acoustic tomography and geoacoustic inversion [7,8]. The bottom parameter estimation results [9,10] using high-frequency signals acquired by the VSA during the Makai Ex 2005 are of considerable interest due to their uniqueness in this research area. Recently, some theoretical works [11,12] were published using quaternion based algorithms in order to more effectively process VSA data. These works are concerned to DOA estimation but in [10] it was suggested that quaternion based algorithms can be used with advantage also in geoacoustic inversions.

4   The Measurement Model

4.1   Particle Velocity Model Formulation

Solving inversion problems by MFI techniques, a propagation model to generate field replicas is required. Herein a ray tracing model – TRACE [13] – is considered to generate the particle velocity components, beyond the acoustic pressure.

Using the analytical approximation of the ray pressure [13], the particle velocity $\mathbf{v}(\Theta_0)$ for a generic set of environmental parameters (Θ_0) can be written as [14]:

$$\mathbf{v}(\Theta_0) = \mathbf{u}(\Theta_0)p , \qquad (1)$$

where the vector $\mathbf{u}$ is a unit vector related to the pressure gradient. The environmental parameter depends on the characteristics of the acoustic channel, including ocean bottom parameters.

4.2   Data Model

Assuming that the propagation channel is a linear time-invariant system, p is the pressure and v_x, v_y and v_z are the three particle velocity components, a narrowband signal at frequency ω (omitting the frequency dependency in the following formulas) due to a source signal s, for a particular set of channel parameters Θ_0, measured with an array of L vector sensors, can be written, for acoustic pressure as:

$$\mathbf{y}_p(\Theta_0) = [y_{p1}(\Theta_0),...,y_{pL}(\Theta_0)]^T , \qquad (2)$$

where $y_{pl}(\Theta_0)$ is the acoustic pressure at l^{th} vector sensor. The linear data model for the acoustic pressure is:

$$\mathbf{y}_p(\Theta_0) = \mathbf{h}_p(\Theta_0)s + \mathbf{n}_p,\tag{3}$$

where $\mathbf{h}_p(\Theta_0)$ is the channel frequency response measured on L pressure sensors and $\mathbf{n}_p$ is the additive noise. In the following formulation it is assumed that the additive noise is zero mean, white, both in time and space, with variance σ_n^2, uncorrelated between each sensor and uncorrelated with the signal s.

A similar definition has been adapted for the particle velocity:

$$\mathbf{y}_v(\Theta_0) = [y_{v_{x1}}(\Theta_0),...,y_{v_{xL}}(\Theta_0), y_{v_{y1}}(\Theta_0),...,y_{v_{yL}}(\Theta_0), y_{v_{z1}}(\Theta_0),...,y_{v_{zL}}(\Theta_0)]^T\tag{4}$$

becoming the data model for the particle velocity components, taking in account (1):

$$\mathbf{y}_v(\Theta_0) = \mathbf{u}(\Theta_0) \otimes \mathbf{h}_p(\Theta_0)s + \mathbf{n}_v,\tag{5}$$

where $\otimes$ is the Kronecker product and $\mathbf{n}_v$ is additive noise.

Taking into account (3) and (5), the VSA data model defined for a signal measured on L elements can be written as:

$$\mathbf{y}_{pv}(\Theta_0) = \begin{bmatrix} \mathbf{y}_p(\Theta_0) \\ \mathbf{y}_v(\Theta_0) \end{bmatrix} = \begin{bmatrix} 1 \\ \mathbf{u}(\Theta_0) \end{bmatrix} \otimes \mathbf{h}_p(\Theta_0)s + \begin{bmatrix} \mathbf{n}_p \\ \mathbf{n}_v \end{bmatrix}.\tag{6}$$

Data model (6) expands data model for the particle velocity components with acoustic pressure.

4.3 Bartlett Estimator

The classical Bartlett estimator is possibly the most widely used estimator in MFI parameter identification, maximizing the output power for a given input signal [15].

The Bartlett parameter estimate $\hat{\Theta}_0$ is given as the argument of the maximum of the functional:

$$P_B(\Theta) = E\left\{\hat{\mathbf{e}}^H(\Theta)\mathbf{y}(\Theta_0)\mathbf{y}^H(\Theta_0)\hat{\mathbf{e}}(\Theta)\right\} = \hat{\mathbf{e}}^H(\Theta)\mathbf{R}(\Theta_0)\hat{\mathbf{e}}(\Theta)\tag{7}$$

where the replica vector estimator $\hat{\mathbf{e}}(\Theta)$ is determined as the vector $\mathbf{e}(\Theta)$ that maximizes the mean quadratic power:

$$\hat{\mathbf{e}}(\Theta) = \arg\max_{\mathbf{e}}\{\mathbf{e}^H(\Theta)\mathbf{R}(\Theta_0)\mathbf{e}(\Theta)\},\tag{8}$$

where ^{H} represents the complex transposition conjugation operator, $E\{\}$ denotes statistical expectation and $E\left\{\mathbf{y}(\Theta_0)\mathbf{y}^H(\Theta_0)\right\}$ is the correlation matrix $\mathbf{R}(\Theta_0)$. The maximization problem is well described in [15], thus the Bartlett estimator when only pressure sensors are considered, can be written as:

$$P_{B,p}(\Theta) = \frac{\mathbf{h}_p^H(\Theta)\mathbf{R}_p(\Theta_0)\mathbf{h}_p(\Theta)}{\mathbf{h}_p^H(\Theta)\mathbf{h}_p(\Theta)}. \tag{9}$$

Appling the above formulation to the data model (5), it was shown in [14] that an estimator for particle velocity outputs is:

$$P_{B,v}(\Theta) = \frac{\left[\mathbf{u}^H(\Theta)\mathbf{u}(\Theta_0)\right]^2}{\mathbf{u}^H(\Theta)\mathbf{u}(\Theta)} P_{B,p}(\Theta) \propto \left[\cos(\Delta\theta)\right]^2 P_{B,p}(\Theta). \tag{10}$$

where $\Delta\theta$ is the angle between the vector $\mathbf{u}(\Theta)$ from the replica and the vector $\mathbf{u}(\Theta_0)$ from the data. Based on this equation, one can conclude that the particle velocity Bartlett estimator response is proportional to the pressure Bartlett estimator response by a directivity factor (gave by the inner product $\mathbf{u}^H(\Theta)\mathbf{u}(\Theta_0)$), which could provide an improved side lobe reduction or even suppression when compared with the pressure response.

For the data model (6), the VSA Bartlett estimator is given by [14]:

$$P_{B,v}(\Theta) \propto \left[1+\cos(\Delta\theta)\right]^2 P_{B,p}(\Theta) \propto \left(2\cos^2\frac{(\Delta\theta)}{2}\right)^2 P_{B,p}(\Theta). \tag{11}$$

One can conclude that when the acoustic pressure is included a wider main lobe is obtained (11), compared to the estimator with only particle velocity components (10). However, including the pressure on the estimator, can lead to reduce ambiguities when frequencies higher then the working frequency of the array are used.

5 Discussion of Results

5.1 DOA Estimation

One of the Bartlett estimator applications is the conventional beamformer for DOA estimation. The plane wave beamformer is applied to compare the performance of the VSA versus hydrophone arrays. In the case of plane wave DOA estimation, the search parameter Θ is the direction (θ_S, ϕ_S) and the replica vector is simple a combination of weights, which are direction cosines as weights for the particle velocity components and a unit weight for the pressure and is given by [4]:

$$\mathbf{e}(\theta_S, \phi_S) = \left[1, \cos\theta_S \sin\phi_S, \sin\theta_S \sin\phi_S, \cos\phi_S\right]^T \otimes \exp(i\vec{k}_S.\vec{r}), \tag{12}$$

where $\vec{r}$ is the position vector of the VSA elements (in this work the VSA used has four elements equally spaced with 10cm and located in the z-axis being the first one at the origin of the Cartesian coordinates system), $\vec{k}_S$ is the wavenumber vector corresponding to the chosen steered, or look direction (θ_S, ϕ_S) of the array, $\theta_S \in [-\pi, \pi]$ is the azimuth angle and $\phi_S \in \left[-\frac{\pi}{2}, \frac{\pi}{2}\right]$ is the elevation angle, Fig. 1.

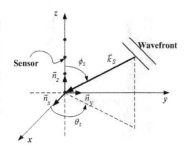

Fig. 1. The array coordinates and the geometry of acoustic plane wave propagation, with azimuth θ_S and elevation ϕ_S angles

Fig. 2 presents the simulation results obtained for the working frequency of the array, 7500Hz, and for a DOA of (45°, 30°). Fig. 2 (a) shows that when the acoustic pressure sensors are considered (9), only the elevation angle is obtained due to omnidirectionality of the sensors. On the other hand, Fig. 2 (b) shows that when the particle velocity components are introduced, the DOA is perfectly resolved due to the directivity factor obtained with the inner product in (10). Finally, when acoustic pressure is included, a wider main lobe is obtained, Fig. 2 (c), however the ambiguities are eliminated. This can be observed even when frequencies higher then the working frequency of the array are used. The main advantage of the VSA in the DOA estimation is that it resolves both vertical and azimuthal direction when compared with traditional hydrophones arrays. The results of the real data DOA estimation can be seen in [4].

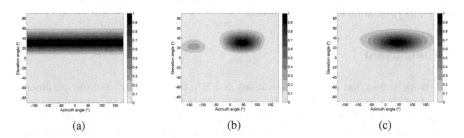

(a)   (b)   (c)

Fig. 2. DOA estimation simulation results at frequency 7500Hz with azimuth 45° and elevation 30° for Bartlett beamformer considering: only pressure sensors response (a), only particle velocity components response (b) and all elements of the VSA (p + v) (c)

5.2   Bottom Parameters Estimation

The ocean bottom parameters estimation is another subject where the VSA can be used with advantage. Fig. 3 shows the sediment compressional speed estimation obtained with pressure data only (a), particle velocity only (b) and both pressure and particle velocity (c). The estimation results for density and compressional attenuation can be found in [10].

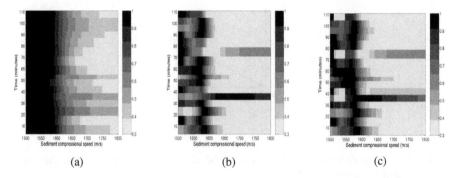

(a)   (b)   (c)

Fig. 3. Real data ambiguity surfaces for sediment compressional speed during the period of acquisition considering: pressure only (a), particle velocity only (b) and both pressure and particle velocity (c)

The ambiguity surfaces illustrated in Fig. 3 were obtained for the maximum values of estimator functions during almost 2 hours of data acquisition, showing the stability of the results. Fig. 3 (a) shows a wider main lobe obtained when only pressure data is considered (9), with poor resolution of the parameter estimation. Fig. 3 (b) and (c) were obtained considering the VSA Bartlett estimators (10) and (11), respectively without and with pressure. Comparing plots (b) and (c) clearly show that the estimate of sediment compressional speed is 1575 ± 5 m/s, but when the estimate function without pressure is considered, a narrower main lobe appears as well as some ambiguities, like in DOA estimation. The results obtained with the function that included all the vector sensor components are stable during the period of acquisition and show an increased resolution of the bottom parameters estimation, not possible with hydrophone arrays of same number of sensors.

6 Conclusion

This work shows the advantage of using a VSA for DOA and bottom parameters estimation. It was seen that the VSA reduces ambiguities in DOA estimation, when compared with hydrophone arrays, providing information in both vertical and azimuthal directions. Also, the VSA improves the resolution of the bottom parameters estimation allowing to access parameters, usually with difficult estimation using traditional hydrophone arrays.

One can remark that reliable estimates are obtained even with a small aperture array (4 elements only) and high frequency signals (say 8-14 kHz band). Thus the usage of VSA with high-frequencies can provide an alternative for a compact and easy-to-deploy system in various underwater acoustical applications.

Acknowledgments. The authors would like to thank Michael Porter, chief scientist for the Makai Experiment, Jerry Tarasek at Naval Surface Weapons Center for the use of the vector sensor array used in this work. The authors also thank Bruce Abraham at Applied Physical Sciences for providing assistance with the data acquisition and the team at HLS Research for their help with the data used in this analysis. This work was supported by project the FCT (ISR/IST plurianual funding U101/13) through the PIDDAC Program funds.

References

1. Porter, M., et al.: The Makai experiment: High-frequency acoustic. In: Jesus, S.M., Rodríguez, O.C. (eds.) 8th ECUA, Carvoeiro, Portugal, vol. 1, pp. 9–11 (2006)
2. Nehorai, A., Paldi, E.: Acoustic vector-sensor array processing. IEEE Trans. Signal Processing 42, 2481–2491 (1994)
3. Cray, B.A., Nuttall, A.H.: Directivity factors for linear arrays of velocity sensors. J. Acoust. Soc. Am. 110, 324–331 (2001)
4. Santos, P., Felisberto, P., Hursky, P.: Source localization with vector sensor array during Makai experiment. In: 2nd International Conference and Exhibition on Underwater Acoustic Measurements, Technologies and Results, Heraklion, Greece (2007)
5. Shipps, J.C., Abraham, B.M.: The use of vector sensors for underwater port and waterway security. In: Sensors for Industry Conference, New Orleans, Louisiana, USA (2004)
6. Abdi, A., Guo, H., Sutthiwan, P.: A new vector sensor receiver for underwater acoustic communication. In: Proceedings MTS/IEEE Oceans, Vancouver, BC, Canada (2007)
7. Peng, H., Li, F.: Geoacoustic inversion based on a vector hydrophone array. Chin. Phys. Lett. 24, 1997–1980 (2007)
8. Lindwall, D.: Marine seismic surveys with vector acoustic sensors. In: Proceedings of Soc. Exploration Geophysicists annual meeting, New Orleans, USA (2006)
9. Santos, P., Felisberto, P., Jesus, S.M.: Estimating bottom properties with a vector sensor array during MakaiEx 2005. In: 2nd International workshop on Marine Technology, MARTECH 2007, Vilanova I LA Geltrú, Barcelona, Spain (2007)
10. Santos, P., Rodríguez, O.C., Felisberto, P., Jesus, S.M.: Geoacoustic Matched-field inversion using a vertical vector sensor array. In: 3rd International Conference and Exhibition on Underwater Acoustic Measurements, Technologies and Results, Nafplion, Greece (2009)
11. Miron, S., Le Bihan, N., Mars, J.I.: Quaternion-MUSIC for vector sensor array processing. IEEE Transactions on Signal Processing 54(4), 1218–1229 (2006)
12. Wang, Y.H., Zhang, J.Q., Hu, B., He, J.: Hypercomplex model of acoustic vector sensor array with its application for the high resolution two dimensional direction of arrival estimation. In: I2MTC 2008 – IEEE International Instrumentation and Measurement Technology Conference, Victoria, Vancouver Island, Canada (2008)
13. Rodríguez, O.C.: The TRACE and TRACEO ray tracing programs. SiPLAB, FCT, University of Algarve (2008), http://www.siplab.fct.ualg.pt/models.shtml
14. Santos, P., Rodríguez, O.C., Felisberto, P., Jesus, S.M.: Geoacoustic Inversion with a vector sensor array. Submitted to J. Acoust. Soc. Am. (2009)
15. Krim, H., Viberg, M.: Two decades of array signal processing research. IEEE Signal Processing Magazine, 67–94 (1996)

An Approach to Modification of Water Flow Algorithm for Segmentation and Text Parameters Extraction

Darko Brodić[1] and Zoran Milivojević[2]

[1] University of Belgrade, Technical Faculty Bor, V.J. 12, 19210 Bor, Serbia
dbrodic@tf.bor.ac.rs
[2] Technical College Niš, Aleksandra Medvedeva 20, 18000 Niš, Serbia
zoran.milivojevic@vtsnis.edu.rs

Abstract. This paper proposes an approach to water flow method modification for text segmentation and reference text line detection of sample text at almost any skew angle. Original water flow algorithm assumes hypothetical water flows under only a few specified angles of the document image frame from left to right and vice versa. As a result of water flow algorithm, unwetted image frames are extracted. These areas are of major importance for text line parameters extraction as well as for text segmentation. Water flow method modification means extension values of water flow specified angle and unwetted image frames function enlargement. Modified method is examined and evaluated under different sample text skew angles. Results are encouraged especially due to improving text segmentation which is the most challenging process stage.

Keywords: Document image processing, Reference text line, Text line segmentation, Water flow algorithm.

1 Introduction

Previous work on text parameter detection can be categorized in few types:

- Histogram analysis,
- Docstrum (k-nearest neighbor clustering),
- Projection profile (Hough transform),
- Fourier transform,
- Cross-correlation,
- Other methods.

In [1] is mentioned previously proposed and accepted technique of reference line extraction based on identifying valleys of horizontal pixel density histogram. Method failed due to multi-skewed text lines.

The Docstrum method [2] is by product of a larger page layout analysis system, which assumed that only text is being processed. The connected components formed by the nearest neighbors clustering are essentially characters only. The method is suitable for finding skew angle. But, it is limited to Roman languages due to poor text line segmentation.

L.M. Camarinha-Matos, P. Pereira, and L. Ribeiro (Eds.): DoCEIS 2010, IFIP AICT 314, pp. 324–331, 2010.
© IFIP International Federation for Information Processing 2010

Another method proposed in [2, 3] deal with "simple" multi-skewed text. It uses as a basis simple type of Hough transform for straight lines. But, it's too specific.

The Fourier transform method is a representation in the Fourier domain of the projection profile method in the pixel domain. The results are mathematically identical, but Fourier transform is only different approach to the same text and document properties that projection profile is based upon [2].

The cross-correlation method calculates both horizontal and vertical projection profiles and then compares the shift inter-line cross-correlation to determine the skew rate. Although method can handle complex layout structure documents, applied range is limited to (-10°, 10°) [2].

Algorithm proposed by [4] model text line detection as an image segmentation problem by enhancing text line structure using a Gaussian window and adopting the level set method to evolve text line boundaries. Author specified method as robust, but rotating text by an angle of 10° has an impact on reference line hit rate.

Method of identifying words contour area as a start of detecting baseline point proposed in [5]. The assumptions made on the word elements definition are too specific.

Method [1] hypothetically assumed a flow of water in a particular direction across image frame in a way that it faces obstruction from the characters of the text lines. This method is adopted in [6, 7], but referent line hit rate is robust for rotating origin text from ±20° around x-axis In our paper, "water flow" method [1, 6, 7] is further adopted, implemented and examined on more complex text examples.

This paper is organized as follows: In section 2 contribution to technological innovation i.e. modification of water flow algorithm is presented. Section 3 includes definition of experiment under investigation. In section 4 experimental results are presented. Results are analyzed, examined, elaborated and discussed as well. In section 5 conclusions are made.

2   Contribution to Technological Innovation

Document text image identification procedure consists of three main stages. It is shown in Fig. 1.

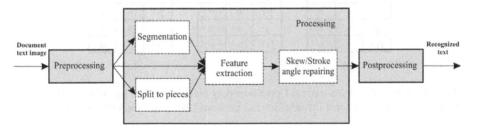

Fig. 1. Document text image identification procedure

In preprocessing stage, algorithm for document text image binarization and normalization is applied. Now, preprocessing text is prepared for segmentation, feature extraction and character recognition. During the processing stage, algorithms for text segmentation as well as for skew and reference text line identification are enforced. After that, reference text based on skew and stroke angle, is straightened and repaired. Finally, in postprocessing stage character recognition process is applied.

In this paper, some elements of preprocessing and processing stages are employed. A few assumptions should be made before defining algorithm. We suppose that there is an element of preprocessing. After preprocessing, document text image is prepared for segmentation and feature extraction. So, it represents distinct entity consists of group of words.

Document text image is an input of text grayscale image described by following intensity function:

$$I(l,k) \in [0,...,255] \quad , \tag{1}$$

where $l \in [0, N-1]$ and $k \in [0, M-1]$.

After applying intensity segmentation with binarization, intensity function is converted into binary intensity function given by:

$$I_{bin}(l,k) = \begin{cases} 1 & for \quad I(l,k) \geq I_{th} \\ 0 & for \quad I(l,k) < I_{th} \end{cases} \quad , \tag{2}$$

where I_{th} is given by Otsu algorithm [8].

Now, text lines are represented as digitized document image by matrix $\mathbf{X}$ with M x N dimension. Each word in document image consists of black points i.e. pixels. Every point is represented by number of coordinate pairs such as:

$$X(i,j) \in [0,1] \quad , \tag{3}$$

where $i = 1, ..., N$, $j = 1, ..., M$ of the matrix $\mathbf{X}$ [8, 9].

Original water flow algorithm assumes hypothetical water flows under only few specified angles of the document image frame from left to right and vice versa [1]. But, previously it needs to define pixel type from situation in Fig. 2.

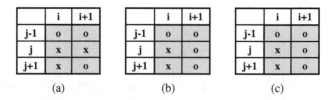

(a)   (b)   (c)

Fig. 2. Pixel type determination: (a) Upper boundary pixel, (b) Lower boundary pixel, and (c) Boundary pixel for additional investigation (x represents black and o represents white pixel)

Proposed algorithm verifies boundary pixel type in document image. After verification it makes unwetted areas around the words. Due to pixel type, i.e. upper or lower, slope is α or $-\alpha$. Additional investigation is made on pixel without complete location. It can be lower, upper or no boundary pixel. It depends on neighbor area of pixels. Apart from [8] and [9] enlarged window R x S pixels is defined as a basis. For analysis, it is proposed R = 5 and S = 7 [7]. Position of window is backwards from pixel candidate for additional investigation. After additional investigation pixel type is completely located [7]. Throughout previous decision making, unwetted areas algorithm simply draws area under specified angles. As a result words are bounded by unwetted dark stripes. These regions are mark out by lines defined as function:

$$y = k \cdot x , \tag{4}$$

where slope $k = tan(\alpha)$. Lines defined by slope make connection in specific pixel creating unwetted area defined as grey region in Fig. 3.

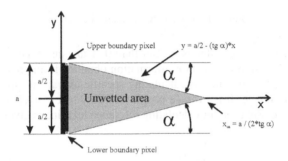

Fig. 3. Unwetted area definition

Basic water flow algorithm is proposed with water flow fixed angles of: 45°, 26.6°, 18.4° and 14° by masking out original document image [1]. First modification made on water flow algorithm is its extension in formulation of algorithm. Still, making straight lines from boundary pixel type and connecting each others in specified point makes unweted region as well. Hence, modified water flow algorithm is free to choose different α from 0° to 90°. Unfortunately, whole range of α isn't applicable due to impossibility of joining words to form text line regions.

Further improvement is made on defining water flow function from (4). From mathematical calculus it is known that (4) is special case of more universal function:

$$y = k \cdot x^n , \tag{5}$$

where (4) and (5) are equal for $n = 1$.

Using different n values from (5) rebuild different shape of unwetted areas around the words. The main achieving of unwetted area is to be exploited for text segmentation. The problem lies in broken words in text lines. Algorithm should join those words by unwetted areas. Unwetted areas can lengthen by using smaller angle α or different water flow function. Hence, another modification of algorithm function means more slow down of slope forming unwetted area. Expanded unwetted area is given in Fig. 4.

Water flow function is changed from (4) to (5) with power value $0 < n < 1$.

Basic and expanded water flow function zeroes are marked as x_{ua} and x_{eua}, respectively. Their difference $x_{diff} = x_{eua} - x_{ua}$ is given by:

$$x_{diff} = \frac{a}{(2 \cdot \tan \alpha)^{\frac{1}{n-1}}} . \tag{6}$$

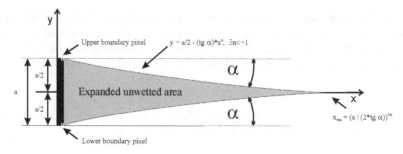

Fig. 4. Expanded unwetted area definition

For parameter $n < 1$, x_{diff} value is greater than 0. Thus, unwetted area is expanded. The skew angle detection is based on information obtained from presented algorithm. Defining reference text line means calculating specific average position of every column of document image. It is average position of only black pixels in every column of document image. Relation for calculating reference text line is given by [1]:

$$x_i = \frac{\sum_{j=1}^{L} y_j}{L} \quad i=1,...,K \quad , \tag{7}$$

where x_i is calculated point represent reference text line point, i is specified column, y_j is position of black pixel in column j and L is sum of black pixel in specified column j of the document image.

3 Experiment

For the experiment, sample text rotated from -45° to +45° by step of 5° around x-axis is used. Sample text is given in Fig. 5. Sample text reference line is represented by:

$$y = a \cdot x + b \quad . \tag{8}$$

After applying algorithm, calculated document image from (7), with only one black pixel per column, is obtained. That black pixel per column defines calculated reference text line and text line skewness. Calculated reference text line forms continuous or discontinuous line partly or completely representing reference text line.

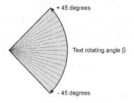

Fig. 5. Sample text rotating from –45° to +45° for the algorithm robustness investigation

To achieve continuous linear aspect of reference text line from point's collection, least square method is used. To find a first degree polynomial function approximation given by:

$$y = a' \cdot x + b' \quad, \tag{9}$$

number of data points is used as ndp and the slope a', and the y-intercept b' are calculated as [10]:

$$a' = \frac{\left(\sum y\right) \cdot \left(\sum x \cdot y\right) - ndp \cdot \left(\sum x \cdot y\right)}{\left(\sum x\right)^2 - ndp \cdot \left(\sum x^2\right)} \quad, \tag{10}$$

and

$$b' = \frac{\left(\sum x\right) \cdot \left(\sum x \cdot y\right) - \left(\sum y\right) \cdot \left(\sum x^2\right)}{\left(\sum x\right)^2 - ndp \cdot \left(\sum x^2\right)} \quad. \tag{11}$$

Further, referent line hit rate abbreviated by $RLHR$ is defined by:

$$RLHR = 1 - \frac{\beta_{ref} - \beta_{est}}{\beta_{ref}} \quad, \tag{12}$$

where β_{ref} is arctangent of a (origin) from (8) and β_{est} is arctangent of a' (calculated i.e. estimated) from (9). RMS values are calculated by [10]:

$$RMS = \sqrt{\frac{1}{R} \sum_{i=1}^{R} (x_{ref} - x_{est})^2} \quad, \tag{13}$$

where R is number of examined text rotating angles range from $\pm 60°$, x_{ref} is $RLHR$ for β_{est} equal to β_{ref} i.e. due to normalization equal to 1, and x_{est} is $RLHR$.

4   Results and Discussion

Benefit from extended algorithm is perceived in text segmentation process. Split up words in text line is presumably joined by unwetted areas from water flow function. Two word connections made by basic and extended algorithm are given in Fig. 6.

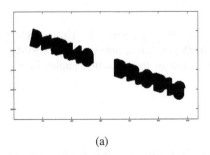
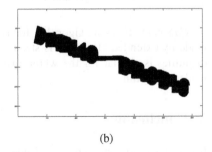

(a)   (b)

Fig. 6. Document text image with unwetted areas: (a) basic algorithm, and (b) extended algorithm (power $n = \frac{1}{2}$ from (5))

Sample text *RLHR* for basic and extended algorithm is given in Fig. 7.

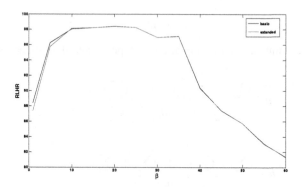

Fig. 7. Sample text *RHLR* (α from 10° to 30° by step 5°, β from 5° to 60° by step 5°): basic vs. extended algorithm ($n = \frac{1}{2}$)

RLHR for basic and extended algorithm are almost identical as can be seen from Fig. 7. For sample text rotating up to 40° *RLHR* is at least 90% or better. It proved robustness of both algorithms. *RLHR* isn't reduced due to better segmentation by extended algorithm. Sample text *RMS* for basic and extended algorithm is given in Fig. 8.

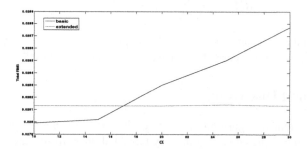

Fig. 8. Sample text *RMS* (α from 10° to 30° by step 5°, β from 5° to 60° by step 5°): basic algorithm vs. extended algorithm ($n = \frac{1}{2}$)

RMS made by basic algorithm for α from 10° to 30° is growing on. Unlike, *RMS* made by extended algorithm is steady. Due to *RMS* condition, magnitude of varying quantities is similar for the whole investigated region of the unwetted angles in extended algorithm.

5   Conclusion

In this paper an approach to modified water flow algorithm for text segmentation and reference text line extraction is presented. Water flow algorithm assumes hypothetical water flows under few specified angles of the image frame from left to right and vice versa. As a result of algorithm, unwetted image regions defined by function $y = kx$ are restored. Modified water flow algorithm made water to flow under whole range of different angles. Same way, it exchanges function defining unwetted image regions to $y = kx^n$. Those unwetted regions are corner stone needed for reference text line calculation. Using least square method on calculated reference text line, reference text line is defined and extracted. Modified water flow function proved better text segmentation preferences. Robustness of algorithm is examined and validated using sample text rotating in region of $\pm 60°$ around x-axis. Results confirmed good *RLHR* values for text rotating in region of $\pm 45°$. Further improvements of algorithm should be made on better *RLHR* in full region of $\pm 90°$. One way is algorithm throw out to strictly follow reference text line turn over.

References

1. Basu, S., Chaudhuri, C., Kundu, M., Nasipuri, M., Basu, D.K.: Text Line Extraction from Multi-Skewed Handwritten Documents. Pattern Recognition 40(6), 1825–1829 (2006)
2. Amin, A., Wu, S.: Robust Skew Detection in mixed Text/Graphics Documents. In: Proceedings of 8th International Conference on Document Analysis and Recognition (ICDAR 2005), Seoul, Korea, pp. 247–251 (2005)
3. Louloudis, G., Gatos, B., Pratikakis, I., Halatsis, C.: Text Line Detection in Handwritten Documents. Pattern Recognition 41(12), 3758–3772 (2008)
4. Li, Y., Zheng, Y., Doermann, D., Jaeger, S.: A New Algorithm for Detecting Text Line in Handwritten Documents. In: Proceedings of 18th International Conference on Pattern Recognition, Hong Kong, China, vol. 2, pp. 1030–1033 (2006)
5. Wang, J., Mazlor, K., Leung, H., Hui, S.C.: Cursive Word Reference Line Detection. Pattern Recognition 30(3), 503–511 (1997)
6. Brodić, D., Milivojević, Z.: Reference Text Line Identification Based on Water Flow Algorithm. In: Proceedings of ICEST 2009, SP-2 Sect, Veliko Tarnovo, Bulgaria (2009)
7. Brodić, D., Milivojević, Z.: Modified Water Flow Method for Reference Text Line Detection. In: Proceedings of ICCS 2009, Sofia, Bulgaria (2009)
8. Gonzalez, R.C., Woods, R.E.: Digital Image Procesing, 2nd edn., pp. 67–70. Prentice-Hall, New Jersey (2002)
9. Sonka, M., Hlavac, V., Boyle, R.: Image Processing, Analysis and Machine Vision, pp. 174–177. Thomson, Toronto (2008)
10. Bolstad, W.M.: Introduction to Bayesian Statistics, pp. 40–44, 235–240. John Wiley & Sons, New Jersey (2004)

Part 11

Sensorial Perception - II

A Face Attention Technique for a Robot Able to Interpret Facial Expressions

Carlos Simplício[1,2], José Prado[1], and Jorge Dias[1]

[1] Institute of Systems and Robotics, at Department of
Electrical Engineering and Computers of University of Coimbra, Coimbra, Portugal
{jaugusto,jorge}@isr.uc.pt
[2] School of Technology and Management of
Institute Polytechnic of Leiria, Leiria, Portugal
simplicio@estg.ipleiria.pt

Abstract. Automatic facial expressions recognition using vision is an important subject towards human-robot interaction. Here is proposed a human face focus of attention technique and a facial expressions classifier (a Dynamic Bayesian Network) to incorporate in an autonomous mobile agent whose hardware is composed by a robotic platform and a robotic head. The focus of attention technique is based on the symmetry presented by human faces. By using the output of this module the autonomous agent keeps always targeting the human face frontally. In order to accomplish this, the robot platform performs an arc centered at the human; thus the robotic head, when necessary, moves synchronized. In the proposed probabilistic classifier the information is propagated, from the previous instant, in a lower level of the network, to the current instant. Moreover, to recognize facial expressions are used not only positive evidences but also negative.

Keywords: Facial Symmetry, Focus of Attention, Dynamic Bayesian Network.

1 Introduction

Usually, human beings express their emotional states through paralinguistic cues, e.g., facial expressions, gaze, gestures, body positions or movements. Among all, our main work focuses specifically on human facial expressions.

Automatic facial expression recognition systems have many potential applications. They can be used in medicine / psychology, surveillance or in intelligent human-machine interaction. In this paper is proposed a human face focus of attention technique and a Dynamic Bayesian Network to classify human beings facial expressions. They will be incorporated in a companion robot, an autonomous mobile agent, whose hardware is composed by a robotic platform and a robotic head. The autonomous agent must observe and react according to the facial expressions of a person. This agent will be used in the context of assisted ambiance. The global project addresses the emergent tendencies of developing new devices to the elderly community.

L.M. Camarinha-Matos, P. Pereira, and L. Ribeiro (Eds.): DoCEIS 2010, IFIP AICT 314, pp. 335–342, 2010.
© IFIP International Federation for Information Processing 2010

2   Related Work and Contribution to Technological Innovation

A great part of the research done in facial expressions uses the tool FACS (Facial Action Coding System) proposed by Ekman [1]. FACS was developed to describe the visible "distortions" on the face produced by muscular activity.

Some studies about techniques to find automatically the vertical symmetry axis of human faces were published. Hiremath and Danti [2] proposed a bottom-up approach to model human faces. In this method a face is explained by various lines-of-separability, being one of them the axis of symmetry. Chen [3] proposed a method to automatically extract the face vertical middle line. In their method the histogram of gray level differences (between both sides of the face) is build. The symmetry axis corresponds to the line with maximal Y value (obtained as the relation between the number of events equals to the mean and the variance of the histogram). Nakao [4] applied the generalized Hough transform to find the vertical symmetry axis in frontal faces.

Various attempts have been done to develop a system classifying human facial expressions, but only a few through Bayesian networks. One of these classifiers was presented by Datcu and Rothkrantz [5]: it is a Bayesian belief network that handles behaviors along the time. A Bayesian network with a dynamic fusion strategy was developed by Zhang and Ji to classify six facial expressions [6].

Facial expressions recognition becomes easier if done in frontal face images. Normally, the image acquisition device is fixed and does not follow the head movements. To solve this problem, 3D models of the human face, projections of textures in the model and geometric transformations are used to obtain a image of a frontal face. In this paper a different method to get always a frontal face image is proposed: a robotic system is used to follow the human being movements. In the proposed technique of human face focus of attention, the robotic platform navigate, running an arc centered in the human, to keep always targeting the face frontally. If necessary, the robotic head rotates in synchronization with the platform. The approximated symmetry presented by human faces is the attribute to support the extraction of information to control the tasks of movement.

Facial expressions recognition is performed by a Dynamic Bayesian Network (DBN). With this classifier, one of six emotional states (anger, fear, happiness, sadness, neutral or other) will be assigned to the human being. The evidences provided to the DBN are derived from some Action Units as defined by Ekman [1]. However, unlike other authors, positive and negative evidences are used explicitly to obtain the probability associated with each facial expression (for the neutral facial expression are used just negative evidences, therefore it is an exceptional case). There is another difference from previous works: the information is propagated along time in a low level, near the nodes which collect the evidences from the sensors.

3   Autonomous Mobile Agent (AMA)

The Autonomous Mobile Agent (AMA) architecture is presented in Fig. 1. At hardware level, the AMA consists in a Robotic Head and a Robotic Platform. The commands (*head movement* and *platform movement*), to put the AMA frontally to the human being face, are sent to the hardware by the Robotic Systems Controller (RSC).

This module (it is briefly described in sub-section 3.1) receives an input, *face pose*, coming from the module Face Pose Identification System (FPIS). As is explained in sub-section 3.2, FPIS processes an image to provide the respective output, *face pose*. With the Robotic Head positioned "face-to-face" with the human being, the module Automatic Facial Expression Recognition System (AFERS) takes an image and provides the respective Emotional State in probabilistic terms. This output is associated with a discrete random variable with six events (*anger, fear, happy, sad, neutral* and *other*). Specifically, the system output is composed by six probabilities: *p(anger)*, *p(fear)*, *p(happy)*, *p(sad)*, *p(neutral)* and *p(other)*. In sub-section 3.3 is presented the Dynamic Bayesian Network which provides this module output.

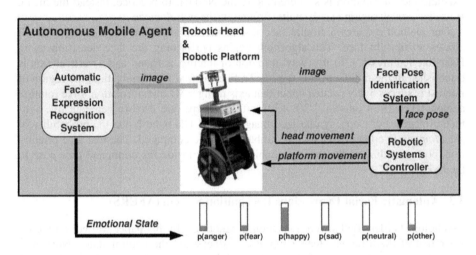

Fig. 1. Autonomous Mobile Agent (AMA) - principal modules

3.1 Robotic Systems Controller (RSC)

The Robotic Platform does three types of movements (longitudinal or transversal translations and rotations) following the commands provided by the RSC.

Longitudinal translations are performed to approach or move away the AMA from the human being. The objective is keeping the image of the human being face with the same number of pixels. Transversal translations are performed to keep always the face in the centre of the image.

Rotations correspond to an arc of circle centered in the human being. These movements are performed to follow the rotation movements done by the human being, getting always an image of a frontal face.

The Robotic Head can move in synchronization with the platform when it is necessary.

3.2 Face Pose Identification System (FPIS)

In a perfect bilateral symmetric image, the difference between a pixel value and the respective symmetric counterpart is zero. By nature, human faces do not present a perfect bilateral symmetry and it is reflected in the acquired images. Moreover, the "imperfections" in the images are worsened by the noise associated to the acquisition process or due to lights distribution. Despite this, gray-level differences can be used to detect the bilateral symmetry axis of a human face.

The theoretical method used to identify the axis of symmetry is based on rather simple principles but is very effective. A vertical axis is defined to divide the face image region in two parts with equal number of pixels and a Normalized Gray-level Difference Histogram (NGDH) is built. When the face is frontal, this vertical axis bisects it and the information collected in the NGDH is strongly concentrated near the mean. If the camera is fixed, when the face rotates the defined axis is not a symmetry axis and the information is scattered along the NGDH. In practice, instead the mean, is used a narrow region (+/- 10 units) around it: the *pseudomean*.

Our method requires a frontal face just in the initialization, but it assumes in all phases an upright face. The algorithm begins performing the face detection using Haar-like features [7]. In this way, a region of interest is found and a vertical axis is established in the middle of this region. To find the real face orientation, the region of interest is successively rotated about that axis using a 3D transformation. Five rotation angles, taken from interval [-30; +30] with 15° steps, are used to generate five synthetic images. For every synthesized image, the NGDH is built and the probability of *pseudomean* is computed. The five probabilities are compared. The real face orientation, corresponding to the great probability, is sent inside the command *face pose* to the module RSC.

3.3 Automatic Facial Expressions Recognition System (AFERS)

Psychologists identified seven transcultural emotions. In this paper we will only consider five of them (anger, fear, happiness, sadness and the neutral state). Normally, every emotional state has a characteristic facial expressions associated to it. In Fig. 2 are presented examples of facial expressions.

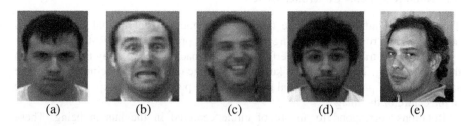

(a)   (b)   (c)   (d)   (e)

Fig. 2. Facial expressions associated to some transcultural emotional states: (a) anger, (b) fear, (c) happiness, (d) sadness and (e) neutral

The AFERS try to recognize local facial actions as defined in FACS [1]. FACS defines a total of 52 Action Units (Aus). Eight of them are related with the head pose. The remainder 44 concern to facial expressions. Each of these AUs is anatomically related to the activity of a specific set of muscles which produces changes in the facial appearance (in our work, only a sub-set of these AUs is used). A facial expression can be interpreted as a set of specific AUs, which cause "distortions" in facial features (i.e., mouth, eyes, eyebrows or noise). Identified these "distortions", facial expressions can be recognized.

Inside the AFERS, there is a specific module to classify the facial expressions: a Dynamic Bayesian Network (DBN). Fig. 3 presents part of the structure of this classifier of 6 levels.

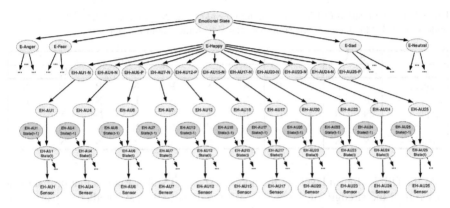

Fig. 3. Dynamic Bayesian Network (DBN) - partial structure. Light nodes are of the present time slice, while dark nodes belong to the previous one (*t-1*). The dashed arrows connect nodes of different time slices: from past to present and from here to future (these nodes are not represented).

At the DBN's first level there is only one node. The overall classification result is provided by the random variable associated with this node: *Emotional State* ∈ *{anger, fear, happy, sad, neutral, other}*. First five events correspond to emotional states that actually are intended to classify. The sixth (*other*) is used for completeness when the facial expression does not fit the five preceding categories.

In the second level there are five nodes, one for every facial expression associated to an emotional state to recognize. To each node is associated one of the following variables: *E-Anger* ∈ *{no, yes}*, *E-Fear* ∈ *{no, yes}*, *E-Happy* ∈ *{no, yes}*, *E-Sad* ∈ *{no, yes}* or *E-Neutral* ∈ *{no, yes}*; where two events are associated with each variable.

After the second level, the structure presented in Fig. 3 is not complete. The figure only shows, from top to bottom, all the nodes and arcs used to classify the facial expression corresponding to happiness (since a similar structure is used to the other emotional states, we avoid to overcharge the figure). In the following, description will only be made to the happiness emotional state.

To the happiness, in the third level of the DBN, there are eleven nodes which are associated with the following variables: *EH-AU1-N* ∈ *{no, yes}*, *EH-AU4-N* ∈ *{no, yes}*, *EH-AU6-P* ∈ *{no, yes}*, *EH-AU7-N* ∈ *{no, yes}*, *EH-AU12-P* ∈ *{no, yes}*, *EH-AU15-N* ∈ *{no, yes}*, *EH-AU17-N* ∈ *{no, yes}*, *EH-AU20-N* ∈ *{no, yes}*, *EH-AU23-N* ∈ *{no, yes}*, *EH-AU24-N* ∈ *{no, yes}* and *EH-AU25-P* ∈ *{no, yes}*. The events associated with these variables are related to the absence or presence of "distortions" (respectively on eyebrows, eyes and mouth) that are relevant to the facial expression.

The probabilities assigned to events of these third level variables depend on evidences (positives and negatives) strength.

In table 1 are discriminated, for every facial expression, the AUs that lead to positive or negative evidences. For example, to happiness, the AU6 is positive evidence, but AU7 is negative evidence. From this table it is possible to reconstitute completely the structure of the DBN.

Table 1. Discrimination of the AUs that are considered as Negative evidences (N) or Positive evidences (P) for the facial expressions associated to some emotional states

	Brows		Eyes		Mouth						
	AU1	AU4	AU6	AU7	AU12	AU15	AU17	AU20	AU23	AU24	AU25
Anger	N	P	N	P	N	N	P	N	P	P	N
Fear	P	P	N	N	N	N	N	P	N	N	P
Happiness	N	N	P	N	P	N	N	N	N	N	P
Sadness	P	P	N	N	N	P	P	N	N	N	N
Neutral	N	N	N	N	N	N	N	N	N	N	N

At the DBN's fourth level are the nodes associated with variables that probabilistically reflect the strength of the evidences (here is not relevant whether they are positive or negative evidences). The variables associated to these nodes are, respectively, *EH-AU1* ∈ *{small, moderate, big}*, *EH-AU4* ∈ *{small, moderate, big}*, *EH-AU6* ∈ *{small, moderate, big}*, *EH-AU7* ∈ *{small, moderate, big}* , *EH-AU12* ∈ *{small, moderate, big}* , *EH-AU15* ∈ *{small, moderate, big}* , *EH-AU17* ∈ *{small, moderate, big}* , *EH-AU20* ∈ *{small, moderate, big}* , *EH-AU23* ∈ *{small, moderate, big}* , *EH-AU24* ∈ *{small, moderate, big}* and *EH-AU25* ∈ *{small, moderate, big}*.

It is through the nodes of the fifth level that information is propagated between time slices. In Fig. 3 this propagation, from past or to future, is represented by dashed arrows, and dark nodes are those of a previous time slice (*t-1*). As an example, *EH-AU1 State(t)*∈ *{minimum, low, medium, high, maximum}* is a variable associated to one node of this fifth level in present. The functionality of the fifth level nodes is to combine / fuse probabilistically, through inertia, information coming from the low level in present time slice with that from the previous instant. After the fusion, the information is used in the present by the high level nodes and is made available to the next time slice to be fused therein.

In the sixth level of the DBN are the nodes associated with variables collecting the evidences provided by the sensors. For example, *EH-AU1 Sensor* ∈ *{minimum, low, medium, high, maximum}*, is one of those variables.

4   Discussion of Results and Critical View

Fig. 4 presents some results obtained by the proposed technique to identify the head orientation when the human is facing the AMA directly. In image (a) is showed a scene in our laboratory with the human face segmented. From (c) to (g) are the synthesized face images after the application of the 3D transformation and, from (j) to (n), the correspondent NGDHs. The *pseudomean* probability increases as the synthesized image becomes more similar to a frontal face, as it is observable at the histograms. In (h) is illustrated graphically the output as a line segment drawn superimposed to the segmented face. The angle of this segment, referenced to the image vertical axis, corresponds to the real human head orientation. In this case a vertical segment means a frontal face.

Even when the human is not facing the AMA, always one of the synthesized images presents a near frontal face and the real orientation can be found.

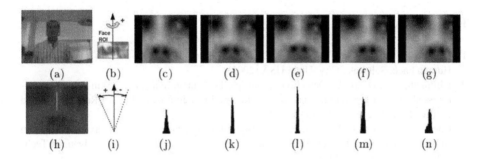

Fig. 4. Working principles of the technique to find the real head orientation. In (a), image of a scene with a frontal face segmented. In (b) is defined the positive direction of the rotations used to synthesize images. Synthesized images after applying a 3D rotation with an angle of (c) *-30°*, (d) *-15°*, (e) *0°*, (f) *+15°* and (g) *+30°*. NGDHs of the synthetic images generated for an angle of (j) *-30°*, (k) *-15°*, (l) *0°*, (m) *+15°* and (n) *+30°*. In (h) is presented the output: a vertical line segment means a *0°* head orientation. In (i) is defined the vertical axis reference of the output image.

The implementation of the presented DBN architecture is actually under test. Reaching conclusions based on negative evidences is something that should be done with special care because it can lead to mistakes. However, unlike other types of classifiers, Bayesian networks can treat negative evidences naturally and correctly through *priors* values near zero. Anyway, in the proposed method, the classification is done using mainly the positive evidences. The two main exceptions are *neutral* and *other* emotional states.

5   Conclusions and Further Work

In this paper is proposed a human face focus of attention technique and a Dynamic Bayesian Network structure to classify facial expressions. Both are to incorporate in an autonomous mobile agent whose high level architecture is also proposed here.

The focus of attention technique has a good performance, is fast and easy to implement. In the future we intend to use it as a valuable help to automatically extract facial feature points without the use of a complex 3D model. Before that, the technique will be validated more rigorously attaching a inertial sensor to the human head and comparing its outputs with that of the proposed method.

The proposed DBN uses explicitly two types of evidences (negative and positive) and the temporal information is propagated at a low level. The preliminary tests done with the DBN showed that it has great potentialities. We intend to build a simpler version of the proposed DBN (using only positive evidences) and, comparing the two versions, prove the real advantages incoming by the use of negative evidences.

Acknowledgments. The authors gratefully acknowledge support from EC-contract number BACS FP6-IST-027140, the contribution of the Institute of Systems and Robotics at Coimbra University and reviewers' comments.

References

1. Ekman, P., Friesen, W.V., Hager, J.C.: Facial Action Coding System - The Manual. A Human Face. Salt Lake City, Utah, USA (2002)
2. Hiremath, P.S., Danti, A.: Detection of multiple faces in an image using skin color information and lines-of-separability face model. International Journal of Pattern Recognition and Artificial Intelligence 20(1), 39–69 (2006)
3. Chen, X., Flynn, P.J., Bowyer, K.W.: Fully automated facial symmetry axis detection in frontal color images. In: 4th IEEE Workshop on Automatic Identification Advanced Technologies, pp. 106–111 (2005)
4. Nakao, N., Ohyama, W., Wakabayashi, T., Kimura, F.: Automatic detection of facial midline and its contributions to facial feature extraction. Electronic Letters on Computer Vision and Image Analysis 6(3), 55–66 (2008)
5. Datcu, D., Rothkrantz, L.J.M.: Automatic recognition of facial expressions using bayesian belief networks. In: 2004 IEEE International Conference on Systems, Man & Cybernetics, October 2004, pp. 10–13 (2004)
6. Zhang, Y., Ji, Q.: Active and dynamic information fusion for facial expression understanding from image sequences. IEEE Transactions on Pattern Analysis and Machine Intelligence 27(5), 699–714 (2005)
7. Viola, P., Jones, M.: Robust real-time face detection. International Journal of Computer Vision 57(2), 137–154 (2004)

Using Eye Blinking for EOG-Based Robot Control

Mihai Duguleana and Gheorghe Mogan

Transylvania University of Brasov, Product Design and Robotics Department,
Bulevardul Eroilor, nr. 29, Brasov, Romania
{Mihai.Duguleana,Mogan}@unitbv.ro

Abstract. This paper proposes a new approach to real-time robot controlling by integrating an Electrooculography (EOG) measuring device within human-robot interaction (HRI). Our study focuses on controlling robots using EOG for fulfilling elementary robot activities such as basic motor movements and environment interaction. A new EOG-based HRI paradigm has been developed on the specific defined problem of eye blinking. The resulted model is tested using biometric capturing equipment. We propose a simple algorithm for real-time identification and processing of signals produced by eyes during blinking phases. We present the experimental setup and the results of the experiment. We conclude by listing further research issues.

Keywords: Electrooculography, robot, control, human-robot interaction, eye blink.

1 Introduction

Robot control is one of the key fields in Robotics. Efficient alternative controlling capabilities are important for motor-disabled persons, elderly people and patients suffering from several types of Sclerosis or other diseases that affect hand and facial muscles. Using information from multiple sensor devices will also increase the quality of HRI when applying sensor-fusion.

Human eye movements have been recently used with success in human-computer interaction by several researchers [1], [3], [6] and [7]. Most of the applications based on this kind of feedback are conducted in fields like Virtual Reality, Robotics and Biomedicine.

Eye movements can be recorded in 3 ways: with magnetic coils, using video processing or using EOG [6]. Video processing and EOG are most used techniques, however, although video processing requirements are very easy to fulfill (just a quality camera), EOG tends to produce more quality outputs in terms of speed and error. While in the video-based approach, the camera scans for the eyes of the subject and measures the movement using powerful yet time consuming image processing libraries, in the EOG approach, a simple low cost device can use one or two pairs of electrodes to measure the resting potential of the retina. This potential is the result of eyeball movement within the conducting environment of the skull and it varies proportional to the amplitude of eye movements [1].

L.M. Camarinha-Matos, P. Pereira, and L. Ribeiro (Eds.): DoCEIS 2010, IFIP AICT 314, pp. 343–350, 2010.
© IFIP International Federation for Information Processing 2010

Several other researchers have been conducting related studies to the subject of our paper. In order to use EOG, some researchers have been able to reduce noise in EOG recordings by filtering the heart beating pollution from the output signal and by eliminating the drift that appears randomly when the subject is moving his eyes [6], to minimize the signal differences between different testing subjects or to eliminate certain signals [4] and to control wheelchairs and other mobile robots [1].

Different types of signals have been identified for each of the following actions: blinking, horizontal and vertical saccadic motions or winking [7].

There are also available comparisons between different EOG devices and their efficiency or between measuring methods such as EOG, EEG and EMG [3]. The research question which we approach is whether robust robot control in real time using EOG can be achieved.

In this paper, we focus on developing a simple motor controlling application for commanding the grasping modules of a humanoid robot using EOG. We propose a new algorithm for blinking detection in real-time EOG applications. Furthermore, we describe in the "Experimental Setup" section the equipment we have used for conducting our research and conclude in the last section with implementation issues and further research problems.

2 Contribution to Technological Innovation

Although there have been several attempts to clearly delimitate a good interaction model between humans and robots using EOG information, most of the literature focuses on offline control and saccadic eye movements processing [2]. Most of the experiments are based on EOG devices that require skin preparation (skin scrubbing) and the appliance of conducting gel between the electrode surface and the skin of the subject. We present a system the uses dry electrodes and wireless technology for communicating with the processing unit, thus speeding up the testing process and increasing the flexibility of this solution.

We foresee the implementation of a fully functional EOG-based device that could be used in industrial environment for integrating people with disabilities into the work field or for achieving more precise robot control as one of the practical technological applications that can be developed based on the results presented this paper.

2.1 EOG-Based Robot Commanding Paradigm

Having eye blinking the only form of input increases the robustness of the system. We propose a new commanding paradigm for real-time control with eye blinking in an EOG-based HRI (see Fig. 1).

The EOG device mounted on the subject's head sends amplified data to the computer unit. Considering the continuous attribute of the experiment, we split the application into 2 threads. In the signal processing module, the data is processed and the result is sent to the state handler. Several filters (like noise, drift and other biometric algorithms) are contributing to robust eye blinking identification.

Depending on the state of the robot and on the previous data received by the state handler, this module accesses predefined commands of the robot. The handler consists of 2 states: the waiting state and the active state. One may choose to let the robot finishing its previous tasks before engaging into other new activities, or to override these with the new received command. As data is continuously received from the signal processing module, some commands that are quickly assessed may have a certain initial value that may change its meaning when receiving new information.

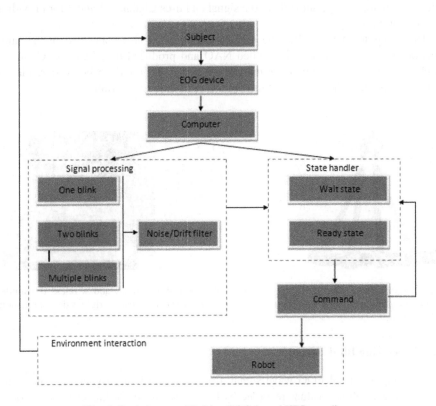

Fig. 1. Real-time eye blinking EOG-based HRI paradigm

In the first part of this section we describe the experimental equipment used for completing our study. We then present the algorithm used for detecting eye blinking. We end this section with a critical analysis of experiment results.

2.2 Experimental Setup

We are using for this experiment an EOG solution from Starlab Company. The wireless electro-physiology sensor system (presented in the left side of Fig. 2) is mounted on the subject's head; 2 of the electrodes are placed on the sides, the other 2 above each eye and the Driven Right Leg (DRL) circuit (the reference) on the right ear of the subject (center Fig. 2). DRL circuit is particularly important because it influences the quality of measurements. We are using for DRL conductive gel to increase the common-mode rejection ratio (CMRR) and to improve the noise immunity [5].

When blinking, humans use their facial muscles. Because of this, the EOG blinking signal is very strong, thus allowing us to mount the electrodes in approximate positions without having to worry about data loss.

The EOG wireless device sends data to a USB modem connected to our computer. The Enobio application auto-filters the signal and uses Channels 2 and 3 for providing EOG information.

The computer that handles the entire experiment is also connected in the same network with a humanoid robot called NAO and produced by Aldebaran Company (right side of Fig. 2). We will command the hand grippers of the robot, differentiating between left and right motors by blinking once or blinking two times.

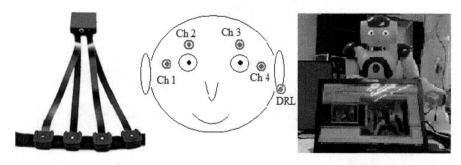

Fig. 2. Experiment setup. Left side – EOG device with 4 electrodes and wireless transmitter (*Enobio equipment*), center – Enobio electrodes setup (*head scheme*), right side – humanoid robot (*Nao*).

2.3 Processing Blink Signal

Considering a normal EOG wave signal, the event of a blink triggers a peak occurrence in the amplitude values recorded by Enobio software, far higher than any other possible noise that the EOG measurement might have if the blink wouldn't exist. As seen in Fig. 3, an average blink lasts between 100ms and 200ms (these values vary depending on the subject's bio-attributes, fatigue level, eye health and other factors) and reaches up to a 400μV (a 250-300μV in average) maximum before returning to the mean voltage level that was recorded before blinking.

Using the above observations, we may detect blinks by adding a preset minimum threshold which should filter most of the noise and false peaks. Unfortunately, there are some cases in which the signal wave experiences a drift - sometimes the voltage increases with similar values like the ones recorded from blinks. We can further filter these cases by setting a maximum threshold and calculating difference between the minimum values recorded before and after peak occurrence. When implementing these restrictions in real time, we apply the following algorithm written in pseudo-code:

```
while receiving_data
{
    get_data;
    decode_data;
    if check_time_from_last_blink = ok
    {
        if is_minimum_since_last_t_ms
        {
            get_maximum_on_t+T_ms_interval;
            get_time_of_maximum;
            if maximum > min_thres and maximum <
            max_thres
            {
                get_min_before_time_of_maxim;
                if
                compare_min_before_time_of_maximum
                _with_current_data = ok
                {
                    BLINK;
                    retain_time_of_blink;
                }
            }
        }
    }
}
```

The algorithm searches for amplitude points recorded at the end of a peak, after a certain period from the last acknowledged blink, to ensure that we do not count twice the same recording. If local minimum is found, we sequentially check for the maximum value recorded within a proper time interval, compare it with minimum (240μV) and maximum thresholds (450μV), search for the minimum value recorded before the occurrence of maximum and compare it with current data to eliminate drift errors. In the event of a valid result (i.e. a maximum 100 μV difference between the 2 minimums), we compute the command and retain the occurrence time.

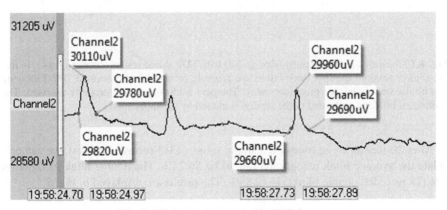

Fig. 3. Blink signals recorded in EDF format

In order to differentiate between one and multiple blinks, we will use the time retained from the last acknowledged blink. Two or more blinks occur continuously, one wave after another. We expect i.e. to record two blinks within a maximum 500ms timeframe. We will set this interval to be the waiting period after which we decide if the subject has blinked once or twice.

2.4 Discussion of Results

We compare the data received from Enobio device and processed by our application with the data saved by Enobio in EDF format, available the end of each session. The differences are presented in Fig. 4.

The main problem faced by real-time computing is the processing time. Intel processors (as any other processor) execute instructions once every few milliseconds, depending on their clock frequency and their interruption rate. We can try to increase the interrupt rate granularity using Microsoft Windows Multimedia SDK (for Win 32 systems), thus improving the preciseness of our system, but this comes with a severe power cost. The algorithm used for data decoding and processing also requires a few milliseconds, as well as receiving data from the wireless modem. Summing up all these times, our system (Intel Core 2 Duo T9300, 2.50 GHz, 2GB DDR2 SDRAM, Window Vista) works with data received every 15 to 20ms. This limitation has serious impact on the recorded wave. There are cases when blinks are missed, or data is seriously affected.

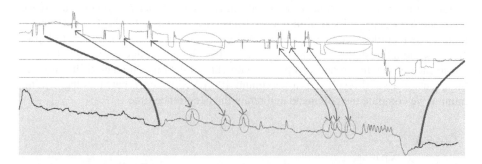

Fig. 4. Comparing recorded results (*first graph*) with EDF stored results (*bottom graph*). In this experiment session, the first three blinks are properly recorded and processed. The following two blinks are missed due processor delay. The next 3 blinks are also properly assessed. The continuous blinking at the end of the session is missed by the application.

After 20 measuring sessions on a single subject (313 recorded blinks), we can calculate the average blink recognition rate to be 56.23%. The double blink recognition rate (28 recorded double blinks) is 42.85%. The results are displayed in Fig. 5.

3   Conclusions and Further Work

Integrating the proposed EOG-based HRI paradigm for real-time robot controlling in real life can be both useful and time-saving. The main result is that people with severe movement-disabilities will be able to have an efficient interaction with environment. Although the implementation of the described paradigm requires bypassing issues like the need of complete redesign of the living environment, control with eye blinking can be achieved. After extending the symbolic functions presented in our experiment, persons with paralyzed facial muscles will be able to use robots to fulfill a wide variety of tasks.

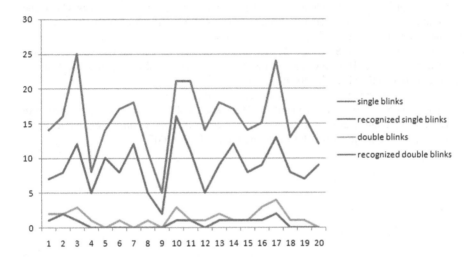

Fig. 5. Analyzing the recognition rates for single and double blinks, over a dataset of 20 test sessions. On the OX axis is displayed the session number and on the OY axis, the number of occurrences.

The experiment results depend with the system on which we run the application. Further work will be conducted into performing the experiment on different hardware and software platforms.

The computation times need to be lowered as much as possible. Further work will be conducted into improving the communication between the EOG equipment and the processing unit, optimizing the source code of the application and reconsidering the thresholds values to more precise ones, obtained after statistically analyzing data from multiple sessions.

Acknowledgments. This paper is supported by the Sectoral Operational Programme Human Resources Development (SOP HRD), financed from the European Social Fund and by the Romanian Government under the contract number POS-DRU/6/1.5/S/6 and by the national research grant ID_775/2009. The experiments were conducted at Italian Institute of Technology (IIT), Italy.

References

1. Barea, R., Boquete, L., Lopez, E., Mazo, M.: Guidance of a Wheelchair Using Electrooculography. In: Proceeding of the 3rd International Multiconference on Circuits, Systems, Communications and Computers (1999)
2. Choudhury, S.R., Venkataramanan, S., Nemade, H.B., Sahambi, J.S.: Design and Development of a Novel EOG Biopotential Amplifier. International Journal of Bioelectromagnetism 7(1), 271–274 (2005)
3. Grave de Peralta Menendez, R., Noirhomme, Q., Cincotti, F., Mattia, D., Aloise, F., Andino, S.G.: Modern Electrophysiological Methods for Brain-Computer Interfaces. Computational Intelligence and Neuroscience Journal 2007 (2007)
4. Manoilov, P., Borodzhieva, A.: An Algorithm for Eye-Blinking Artefacts Duration Determination. In: Proceedings of the Fourth International Bulgarian-Greek Conference Computer Science 2008, Part 1, Kavala, Greece, vol. 1, pp. 846–850 (2008)
5. Starlab Enobio, http://starlab.es/products/enobio
6. Usakli, A.B., Gurcan, S., Aloise, F., Vecchiato Babiloni, F.: On The Use of Electrooculogram For Efficient Human Computer Interfaces. Computational Intelligence and Neuroscience Journal, article in press (2009),
   http://www.hindawi.com/journals/cin/aip.html
7. Youngmin, K., Nakju, L.D., Youngil, Y., Wan, K.C.: Robust Discrimination Method of the Electrooculogram Signals for Human-Computer Interaction Controlling Mobile Robot. Intelligent Automation and Soft Computing Journal 13(3) (2007)

Bio-inspired Binocular Disparity with Position-Shift Receptive Field

Fernanda da C. e C. Faria, Jorge Batista, and Helder Araújo

Institute of Systems and Robotics,
Department of Electrical Engineering and Computers, University of Coimbra – Polo II,
3030-290 Coimbra, Portugal
{fernanda,batista,helder}@isr.uc.pt

Abstract. Depth perception starts with the binocular interaction receptive fields of simple cells modeled by two Gabor functions followed by a half-squaring function. Simple cells do not have reliable disparity computation. Complex cells combine two simple cells in quadrature. They are better adapted to encode disparity information. The image disparity can be determined by fixing the receptive field in one eye and varying it in the other. Pooling information of spatial frequency and orientation is very important to improve the quality of results of real world stereograms. In this work, a bio-inspired method to calculate binocular disparity based on the energy model for depth perception of real world images is described and implemented. The performance of the proposed method is also evaluated in what concerns the algorithm computational cost, root-mean-square error and percentage of wrongly matched pixels.

Keywords: Depth perception, Binocular disparity, Bio-inspired stereo vision, Energy model.

1 Introduction

In the literature several methods to compute the binocular disparity are described such as statistical approaches, probabilistic approaches and artificial neural networks [13]. The focus of this work is on the application of bio-inspired models.

The brain combines information from both eyes and constructs a visual world that is perceived as single and three dimensional. Primary visual cortex (V1) is the first site at which single neurons can be activated by stimuli in both eyes. Primary visual cortex neurons encode information specifically about the relationship between the images in the two eyes [1]-[4].

Biologically plausible models for stereo vision inspired in the visual cortex employ receptive field (RF) profiles of binocular cells for disparity computation. A region of a scene that is visible by left and right eyes is named binocular view field. All points in the binocular view field have different positions in the left and right eyes [2], [4], [5]. Binocular disparities are the small positional differences between the images from the left and right eyes. The slightly different viewpoint is due the horizontal separation of the eyes in the head. Depth perception is deduced through binocular disparity [2]-[4].

L.M. Camarinha-Matos, P. Pereira, and L. Ribeiro (Eds.): DoCEIS 2010, IFIP AICT 314, pp. 351–358, 2010.
© IFIP International Federation for Information Processing 2010

Stereoscopic vision at the neuronal level based on events within the primary visual cortex can be studied through two subdivisions of cortical cells, named simple cells and complex cells. Simple cells are composed of orientation selective RFs that have spatially separate regions. These regions are mutually antagonistic, i.e., they respond to either ON (excitatory) or OFF (inhibitory) to a stimulus [3], [5]-[9]. The receptive fields of binocular simple cells are selective to binocular disparity and they are also affected by several stimulus parameters, such as [2], [4], [5]: position, contrast polarity, spatial frequency and orientation. The other type of V1 cells, complex cells, are composed of orientation selective RFs and respond to a stimulus anywhere within the RF, i.e., there is not spatially separate regions. Complex cells are not sensitive to changes in stimulus position and contrast polarity. The fact that they do not suffer from the influence of irrelevant parameters makes them well adapted to encode disparity information [3]-[6].

The binocular energy model is a model for disparity-selective complex cells based on a combination of simple-cell subunits. Binocular interaction RFs of a simple cell is described as the product of left and right eye RFs. This interaction can be demonstrated by a linear binocular filter followed by a half-power function [2], [4], [10], [11].

This work describes a bio-inspired method to calculate binocular disparity based on energy model for depth perception of real world images [10]-[11].

2   Contribution to Technological Innovation

Visual perception is essential for many applications, especially in Robotics. For example, in applications related to human-robot interaction, the machine needs to cope with and share the human environment in a friendly way. For applications such as assistants in surgery, service robots, caretakers for the elderly and disabled people, a technological solution is necessary requiring advanced perception capabilities as well as advanced skills that allow a robot to perform the desired tasks.

The properties of a scene analyzed by a robot head can involve tracking movements, focusing by vergence and 3D perception of the scene structure. The relative orientation of the eyes, the target location and depth are important for surveillance activities [15] [16].

The algorithm presented in this paper is a preliminary work related to the development of bio-inspired visual perception modules for robotic heads. The model created is based on two algorithms [10], [11]. The principal idea is to develop a faster algorithm to compute disparity maps employing the concepts of energy model for real world stereograms.

3   Stereoscopic Model

Binocular disparity forms the basis of stereoscopic depth perception. The binocular energy model is based on a combination of simple cells. Each complex cell is the linear combination of the outputs of four simple type subunits. A typical binocular simple cell is identical to two Gabor functions (equation 1), one for each of its receptive fields in the left and the right retinas [10].

$$g(x, y, \phi) = \exp\left(-\frac{x'^2 - y'^2}{2\sigma^2}\right) \cos(\omega x' - \phi) \tag{1}$$

where ω is the cell preferred spatial frequency ($2\pi f$), θ is its preferred orientation, ϕ is its phase, $x'=x cos(\theta)+y sin(\theta)$ and $y'=y cos(\theta)-x sin(\theta)$. The standard deviation σ is computed as follows:

$$\sigma = \frac{\sqrt{\ln 2}}{2\pi f} \times \frac{2^{1.5} + 1}{2^{1.5} - 1} \tag{2}$$

where the half-maximum bandwidth is 1.5 octaves [10].

The left and right RFs are shifted in position (equations 3 and 4 – the receptive field is fixed in one eye and varying it in the other) [11].

$$g_l(x, y) = g(x, y, \phi) \tag{3}$$

$$g_r(x, y) = g(x + d, y, \phi) \tag{4}$$

where d is a positional difference between the left and right eyes Gabor functions.

The response of a simple cell can be determined by first filtering, for each eye, the retinal image by the corresponding receptive field profile (equation 5), and then adding the two contributions from the two eyes (equation 6) [12].

$$L = \int_{-\infty}^{+\infty} I_l(x, y) g_l(x, y) \, dx \, dy \tag{5}$$

$$S = L + R \tag{6}$$

The response of a complex cell can be modeled by summing the squared outputs of a quadrature pair of simple cells, i.e., their spatial phases differ by 90 degrees while all the other parameters of the cells are identical (equation 7). The combination of simple cells in quadrature eliminates the Fourier phase dependence. Therefore, complex cells encode reliable disparity information [7], [9], [12].

$$C = S_1^2 + S_2^2 \tag{7}$$

Briefly, the process of depth perception begins with the binocular interaction RFs of simple cells. They can be modeled by two Gabor functions followed by a half-squaring function. Simple cells depend on the Fourier phase of the stimulus. As a result they do not perform a reliable disparity computation. Complex cells combine two simple cells in quadrature and eliminate the Fourier phase dependence. They are better adapted to encode disparity information than simple cells.

3.1 Computing Disparity

To compute the image disparity, the most responsive complex cell at each spatial location is selected at zero phase disparity for the first spatial frequency (f). We use 6 spatial
frequencies (0.5, 1.0, 2.0, 4.0, 8.0 and 16.0 cycles per degree) and 6 RF orientations (30,
60, 90, 120, 150 and 180 degrees). Next the disparity responses of the complex cells
population with the fixed f are computed, for the full range of the positional differences
(d) for each θ. Complex cells at a local maximum or a local minimum are selected and if
it is not the first spatial frequency f, then the selected complex cell is the cell with the
closest filtered d value computed. If spatial frequency $f = 0.5$, then the selected complex
cell is the one with the biggest d value. Another situation is when a local maximum or a
local minimum does not exist then the d value is -99. The value -99 means that the d
value will be ignored in the pooling final disparity map. The result images and the filtered images are saved. A 5x5 median filter is used. The size of the receptive field decreases when f increases. The range of values for d is split into several steps. The steps
have a small and fixed size. Fig. 1 shows a block diagram of the algorithm.

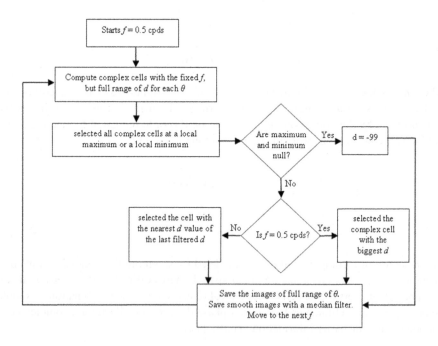

Fig. 1. Block diagram of the algorithm

The outputs of the algorithm are 36 images (6 spatial frequencies and 6 orientations) that will be pooled for the computation of the final disparity map. The images
employed in the pooling are the images saved without filtering. The values of the
filtered images are used only during the process of selection of d (Fig. 1).

3.2 Pooling

A disparity map created by pooling the cells with multiple spatial frequencies and orientations produces results that are more reliable and accurate than those that would be obtained without the pooling step. The pooling is the same method described in [10] where each spatial position of the 36 disparity maps with different spatial frequencies and orientations are combined to compute the average. The resulting average is compared with each spatial position of all maps and the position whose value is farthest from the mean is removed. The process is repeated until the total of spatial positions is reduced by half.

4 Evaluation Methodology and Results

The algorithm evaluation was done employing two quantitative measures of fit quality: root-mean-square error (R) and percentage of wrongly matched pixels (B) [13]. R is computed using equation 8,

$$R = \sqrt{\frac{1}{N} \sum_{(x,y)} |d_C(x, y) - d_T(x, y)|^2}$$ (8)

where d_C is the computed disparity map, d_T is the ground truth map and N is the total number of pixels.

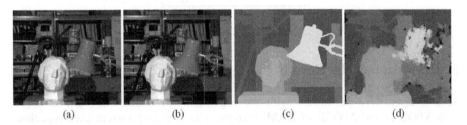

Fig. 2. (a) Left image; (b) right image; (c) the ground truth disparity map; (d) the estimated disparity map

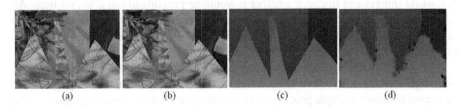

Fig. 3. (a) Left image; (b) right image; (c) the ground truth disparity map; (d) the estimated disparity map

(a)   (b)   (c)

Fig. 4. (a) Left image; (b) right image; (c) the estimated disparity map

Equation 9 is used to calculated B with a disparity error $\delta_d = 1$.

$$B = \frac{1}{N} \sum_{(x,y)} (\mid d_C(x, y) - d_T(x, y) \mid > \delta_d), \tag{9}$$

Fig. 2 and Fig. 3 show the resulting disparity maps for the images from the Middlebury stereo repository [13] (http://cat.middlebury.edu/stereo). Fig. 4 also presents an output disparity map for the method described in section 3.

Table 1 shows the results of root-mean-square error (R) and the percentage of wrongly matched pixels (B) to Figures 2 (d) and 3 (d). Errors of table 1 are only evaluated in non-occluded regions [13] (http://cat.middlebury.edu/stereo).

Table 1. Evaluation results

	R	B
Fig.2 (d)	2.0	20
Fig.3 (d)	1.5	11

5   Discussion of the Results

Several tests were performed with the algorithm described, using a Pentium 4 with 3.00GHz and 2.00GB of RAM memory. The operating system used was Suse Linux 10.

The algorithm proposed by Chen and Qian [11] (using a coarse-to-fine approach) was implemented in C++ and tested with the goal of analyzing its performance with real world images and to check whether it would be possible to run it in real-time. All functions that are used to perform convolution were implemented in the frequency domain to allow a decrease in the processing time. However, in spite of several optimizations, it was not possible to obtain real-time performance.

The coarse-to-fine algorithm spent approximately twenty seven minutes to process an image with 256x256 pixels (Fig. 4. (a) and (b)). The coarse-to-fine algorithm can be improved using multiple processors and a library with multithreading support. The algorithm proposed by Read and Cumming [10], was also implemented in C++. However its processing time was higher than the processing time of the coarse-to-fine algorithm. The test with the images presented in Fig. 4. (a) and (b) required five days and nineteen hours of running time.

The proposed algorithm in this work required 7 minutes and 33 seconds to obtain the disparity map of Fig. 4 (c). For Fig. 2 (d) the algorithm spent 8 min and 45 sec. and for Fig. 3. (d) the disparity map was computed in 6 min. and 20 sec. The method described method is based partially on the algorithms presented in [10] and [11].

The root-mean-square error and the percentage of bad matching pixels presented in table 1 are similar to the results shown in [10] but do not have yet the precision of stereo algorithms in 13 (http://cat.middlebury.edu/stereo).

6 Conclusion and Future Work

The estimation of disparity maps using the energy model is slow. Real images are inherently complex due to the non-uniformity of the disparity values. This problem can be handled by pooling images with different orientations and spatial frequencies.

On the other hand, pooling requires additional processing time. One alternative to develop a real time system (using models of populations of cortical neurons) is to employ DSPs and FPGA chips [14].

As future work, we intend to improve the precision of the algorithm and its suitability for tracking applications. Depth accuracy is crucial for binocular vergence control.

References

1. Cumming, B.G., DeAngelis, G.C.: The Physiology of Stereopsis. Annual Review of Neuroscience 24, 203–238 (2001)
2. Anzai, A., Ohzawa, I., Freeman, R.D.: Neural Mechanisms for Processing Binocular Information. I. Simple Cells. Journal of Neurophysiology 82, 891–908 (1999)
3. Parker, A.J.: Binocular Depth Perception and the Cerebral Cortex. Nature Reviews. Neuroscience 8, 379–391 (2007)
4. Qian, N.: Computing Stereo Disparity and Motion with Known Binocular Cell Properties. Neural Computation 6, 390–404 (1994)
5. Ohzawa, I., DeAngelis, G.C., Freeman, R.D.: Stereoscopic Depth Discrimination in the Visual Cortex: Neurons Ideally Suited as Disparity Detectors. Science 249, 1037–1041 (1990)
6. Hubel, D.H., Wiesel, T.N.: Receptive Fields, Binocular Interaction, and Functional Architecture in the Cat's Visual Cortex. J. Physiol. 160, 106–154 (1962)
7. Qian, N.: Binocular Disparity and the Perception of Depth. Neuron 18(3), 359–368 (1997)
8. Ohzawa, I., DeAngelis, G., Freeman, R.: Encoding of Binocular Disparity by Simple Cells in the Cat's Visual Cortex. J. Neurophysiol. 75, 1779–1805 (1996)
9. Read, J.: Early Computational Processing in Binocular Vision and Depth Perception. Progress in Biophysics and Molecular Biology 87, 77–108 (2005)
10. Read, J.C.A., Cumming, B.G.: Sensors for Impossible Stimuli Solve the Stereo Correspondence Problem. Nature Neuroscience 10(10), 1322–1328 (2007)
11. Chen, Y., Qian, N.: A Coarse-to-Fine Disparity Energy Model with Both Phase-Shift and Position-Shift Receptive Field Mechanisms. Neural Computation 16, 1545–1577 (2004)
12. Qian, N., Zhu, Y.: Physiological Computation of Binocular Disparity. Vision Research 37(13), 1811–1827 (1997)

13. Scharstein, D., Szeliski, R.: A Taxonomy and Evaluation of Dense Two-frame Stereo Correspondence Algorithms. Int. J. Comput. Vis. 47, 7–42 (2002)
14. Tsang, E.K.C., Lam, S.Y.M., Meng, Y., Shi, B.E.: Neuromorphic Implementation of Active Gaze and Vergence Control. In: ISCAS - IEEE Intl. Symp. on Circuits and Systems, pp. 1076–1079 (2008)
15. Batista, J., Peixoto, P., Araújo, H.: A Focusing-by-Vergence System Controlled by Retinal Motion Disparity. In: ICRA – Proc. of the IEEE International Conference on Robotics and Automation, San Francisco, CA, pp. 3209–3214 (2000)
16. Batista, J., Peixoto, P., Araújo, H.: Binocular Tracking and Accommodation controlled by Retinal Motion Flow. In: ICPR – Proc. of the Int. Conference on Pattern Recognition, Barcelona, Spain, vol. 1, pp. 171–174 (2000)

Part 12

Signal Processing - I

Fractional Filters: An Optimization Approach

Carlos Matos[1] and Manuel Duarte Ortigueira[2]

[1] UNINOVA and Escola Superior de Tecnologia, Instituto Politécnico de Setúbal, Portugal
cmatos@est.ips.pt,
[2] UNINOVA/DEE Campus da FCT da UNL, Quinta da Torre, 2825-114
Monte da Caparica, Portugal
mdo@fct.unl.pt

Abstract. The design and optimization of fractional filters is considered in this paper. Some of the classic filter architectures are presented and their performances relatively to an ideal amplitude spectrum evaluated. The fractional filters are designed using the differential evolution optimization algorithm for computing their parameters. To evaluate the performances of all the filters the quadratic error between the computed amplitude is calculated against an ideal (goal) response. The fractional filters have a better behavior, both in the pass and reject-band.

Keywords: Fractional Filters, Fractional Derivative, Optimization.

1 Introduction

The importance of filters in signal processing and other engineering areas is unquestionable. Continuous time filters are widely used functional blocks, from simple anti-aliasing filters preceding ADCs to high-spec channel-select filters in integrated RF transceivers. Four classical classes of filters are currently used: Butterworth, Chebyshev, elliptic and Bessel. Even in the integer order case, filter design is challenging, mainly when the system has to meet a wide set of constrains [1]. Most tools for filter design are based on the transfer functions of the above classes, which impose only requirements related to the magnitude or phase responses.

The design of fractional filters was considered for low orders, [7] and [8]. Here, we will consider the problem with all the generality.

We are dealing essentially with an optimization problem that we will face by using the differential evolution (DE) algorithm [2]. DE is a stochastic, population-based optimization algorithm.

With this algorithm we were able to design fractional filters. To do it we used the poles and zeros as design parameters, together with the fractional order, α. This inserts in the problem a new parameter – the fractional derivative order – that gives a new degree of freedom. This may increase the computational burden associated with the optimization algorithm, but leads to more flexible solutions.

The papers outlines as follows. In section 2 we summarize the contribution to technological innovation of this work. In section 3 we describe the main characteristics of

L.M. Camarinha-Matos, P. Pereira, and L. Ribeiro (Eds.): DoCEIS 2010, IFIP AICT 314, pp. 361–366, 2010.
© IFIP International Federation for Information Processing 2010

the filters. The optimization algorithm is described shortly in section 4 after which we present the simulation results. Finally we will present some conclusions.

2   Contribution to Technological Innovation

This algorithm opens a way to the design of fractional filters, it allows the calculus and optimization of all the design parameters, including the fractional parameter.

Fractional filters better approximate the ideal response than the classical ones. Their applicability in Industrial Control Systems can be very wide.

The presented results are an incentive in itself to fractional capacitor manufacturers and filter designers, allowing the generalised use of fractional filters and the use of this technology.

3   Integer Order Filters

3.1   Specification of the Filter

The specifications for a low pass filter are expressed in figure 1. The specifications of the other kinds of filters are similar. So, we will not consider them. Usually we fix the band pass (BP) amplitude equal to 1. The obtained filter will have amplitude oscillations in the interval

[1-δ_p, 1+δ_p]. Other interesting values are:

δ_s – amplitude of stop band ripple

ω_c - pass band edge frequency

ω_s - stop band edge frequency

$\Delta\omega_t$ – width of the transition band: $\Delta\omega_t = \omega_s - \omega_c$

A_p – band-pass attenuation

$$A_p = 20 \text{Log} \frac{1+\delta_p}{1-\delta_p} \qquad (1)$$

A_s – stop-band attenuation

For other kinds of filters the specifications are similar.

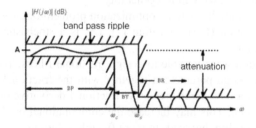

Fig. 1. Specifications of a low pass filter

In the presented work we considered the filter specifications as described in figure 2.

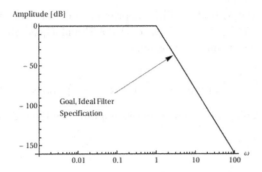

Fig. 2. Specifications of an ideal low pass filter

4   Simulation Results

The Genetic Differential Evolution Algorithm was introduced by [5]. It was developed to optimize real parameters of a real valued function. It finds the true global minimum, regardless of the initial parameters, It has fast convergence and it uses a small set of control parameters.

Applying (DE) algorithm to fractional filter design, will lead to filters with minimum quadratic error to a defined goal. The minimization of the quadratic error of the frequency response, supply us with the values of the zeroes, poles and fractional order α.

3rd Order Integer Low-Pass Filter

Suppose that we want to approximate the ideal low pass filter defined by:

$$\begin{cases} 1 & \text{if } 0 \leq \omega \leq 1 \\ -20\text{Log}(\omega^3) & \text{if } \omega > 1 \end{cases} \tag{2}$$

With the usual 3rd order Low-Pass filters, Butterworth, Bessel, Elliptic and Chebyshev. The quadratic error of these filters compared to the ideal response, for $\omega \in\,]0,10]$ is: Butterworth: 1.90658, Bessel: 18.4252, Elliptic: 5649.03, Chebyshev: 282.28

3rd Order Fractional Filter

We define the fractional Butterworth filter, α the fractional parameter, as:

$$H(s) = \frac{1}{s^{3\alpha} + 2s^{2\alpha} + 2s^{\alpha} + 1} \tag{3}$$

First we will use a 3rd order all-pole fractional filter (2). We impose that we have two complex conjugate poles and a real pole. The optimization algorithm is intended to calculate the poles and α that minimize the quadratic error using the genetic differential evolution algorithm.

For the above defined ideal filter approximation, we obtained, Pole 1 = -0.386955±0.890131, Pole 2 = -1.13249, α = 1.00031 and a quadratic error: 0.331989

The fractional transfer function is given by:

$$H(s) = \frac{1}{s^{3.00094} + 1.9064s^{2.00063} + 1.818s^{1.00031} + 1.06688} \tag{4}$$

The responses are depicted in figure 3 for the amplitude and figure 4 for the phase.

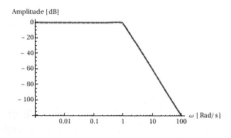
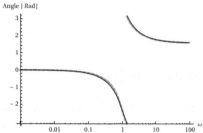

Fig. 3. Amplitude response of 3rd order fractional filter. Goal in solid Black and designed in dashed gray.

Fig. 4. Phase response of 3rd order fractional filter (dashed gray) and 3rd order LP Butterworth (solid black)

The parameter α is very close to 1 as the filter, a 3rd order is very close to the integer response given by the Butterworth filter.

Now we are going to use the same 3rd order fractional filter to approximate an ideal 4th order Low-Pass filter defined by:

$$\begin{cases} 1 & \text{if } 0 \le \omega \le 1 \\ -20Log(\omega^4) & \text{if } \omega > 1 \end{cases} \tag{5}$$

Proceeding as above we calculate α and the poles:

Pole 1 = -0.0000449527+ j0.817145, Pole2 = -1.67915, α = 1.34776 with a quadratic error of: 24.6592. And the transfer function is:

$$H(s) = \frac{1}{s^{4.043} + 1.679s^{2.696} + .668s^{1.348} + 1.121} \tag{6}$$

This is a case where α>1, because the ideal filter decay is bigger than the integer Butterworth capacity. The responses are depicted in figure 5 for the amplitude and figure 6 for the phase.

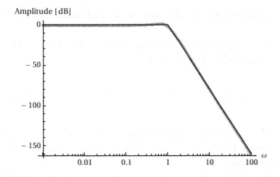

Fig. 5. Amplitudes of fractional 3rd order fractional low pass filter (dashed grey) and ideal 4th order LP response (solid black)

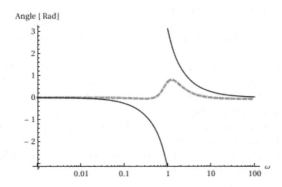

Fig. 6. Phase response of 3rd order fractional Low Pass filter (dashed grey) compared with Butterworth (solid black)

5 Conclusions

We just considered the design of fractional filters and compared their performances with similar classic filters, from the point of view of the amplitude spectrum. The fractional filters approximate much better the ideal filter than the classic ones.

One rule of design should be starting by the use of the fractional filter derived from the integer that better approximates the goal. In our study, we used Butterworth filters as the starting point. We demonstrated that if the integer filter order is smaller than the needed response α will be bigger than one, on the other hand, if we start with an integer filter that has an order higher than needed then α will be smaller than one.

We have shown that the fractional filters outperform the integer ones. By changing poles location and finding a suitable α a fractional filter can perform as a higher or lower order integer filter with advantages. One of the main advantages is that we can have a smaller quadratic error between the goal ideal filter and the designed filter. Another important advantage is that a N order fractional filter with α>1 performs as an integer filter of order>N, so we can have a filter of order>N but with the complexity of a N order.

The same fractional approach will be applied to other type of classical filters and the results will be presented in future work.

References

1. Damera-Venkata, N., Evans, B.L.: An automated framework for multicriteria optimization of analog filter designs. IEEE Transactions on Circuits and Systems – II: Analog and Digital Signal Processing 46(8), 981–990 (1999)
2. Haupt, R.L., Haupt, S.E.: Practical Genetic Algorithms, 2nd edn. John Wiley & Sons, Inc., New Jersey (2004)
3. Nedelea, L., Topa, M., Neag, M.: Computer-Aided Network Function Approximation for Multicriteria Filter Design. In: SCS 2003 - International Symposium on Signals, Circuits and Systems, Iaşi, Romania, pp. 81–84 (2003)
4. Ortigueira, M.D.: A coherent approach to non integer order derivatives. Signal Processing Special Section: Fractional Calculus Applications in Signals and Systems 10, 2505–2515 (2006)
5. Ortigueira, M.D.: Introduction to Fractional Signal Processing. Part 2: Discrete-Time Systems. In: IEE Proc. On Vision, Image and Signal Processing, vol. (1), pp. 71–78 (2000)
6. Price, K.V., Storn, R.M., Lampinene, J.A.: Differential Evolution: A Practical Approach to Global Optimization. Springer, Berlin (2005)
7. Radwan, A.G., Soliman, A.M., Elwakil, A.S.: First Order Filters Generalized to the Fractional Domain. Journal of Circuits, Systems and Computers 17(1), 55–66 (2008)
8. Radwan, A.G., Elwakil, A.S., Soliman, A.M.: On the Generalizations of Second-Order Filters to the Fractional-Order Domain (2009)

MicroECG: An Integrated Platform for the Cardiac Arrythmia Detection and Characterization

Bruno Nascimento[1], Arnaldo Batista[1], Luis Brandão Alves[2],
Manuel Ortigueira[1], and Raul Rato[1]

[1] Dept. of Electrical Engineering, Universidade Nova de Lisboa, Faculty of Sciences
and Technology, Quinta da Torre, 2825-516 Monte da Caparica, Portugal
brunonascimento@netcabo.pt, agb@fct.unl.pt, mdo@fct.unl.pt,
rtr@fct.unl.pt
[2] Department of Cardiology of Hospital Garcia de Orta,
Almada, Portugal
brandaoalves@gmail.com

Abstract. A software tool for the analysis of the High-Resolution Electrocardiogram (HR-ECG) for Arrhythmia detection is introduced. New algorithms based on Wavelet analysis are presented and compared with the classic Simson protocol over the P and QRS segments of the Electrocardiogram (EEG). A novel procedure based on a two step wavelet analysis and synthesis is performed in order to obtain a frequency description of the P, T or QRS segments. This frequency "signature" is useful for the detection of otherwise asymptomatic Arrhythmia patients. The tool has been developed in Matlab, and deployed for a standalone C application.

Keywords: Cardiac Arrhythmia, Fibrillation, Wavelets and Time-Frequency.

1 Introduction

Atrial fibrillation is the most common sustained heart arrhythmia. It is estimated to occur in more than 0.4 percent of the adult population and perhaps as many as 10 percent of the population who are 60 years or older [1]. Atrial arrhythmia may be transient or persistent. While most atrial arrhythmia occurs in individuals having other forms of underlying heart disease, some atrial arrhythmias occur independently. While atrial arrhythmias do not directly cause death as frequently as ventricular arrhythmias, they increase the risk factor for a number of other diseases such as strokes, thrombosis, atherosclerosis, systemic and cerebral embolism and cause a number of additional medical problems [2]. A two-step wavelet method is introduced for the detection and reconstruction of the cardiac micro-potentials [3] that account for the atrial and ventricular arrhythmia [4]. These algorithms are incorporated in a software platform tool (MicroECG) for the integrated High Resolution Electrocardiogram (HR-ECG) processing. A continuous wavelet method is herein applied for the detection of the micro potentials and a wavelet packet methodology for the reconstruction of these signals. MicroECG includes the following pre-processing tools: QRS detection, versatile peak detection, signal averaging or beat-by-beat analysis and ECG delineation

L.M. Camarinha-Matos, P. Pereira, and L. Ribeiro (Eds.): DoCEIS 2010, IFIP AICT 314, pp. 367–373, 2010.

with wavelet processes [5] [6]. These pre-processing tools are presented to the medical user or researcher in an intuitive and user-friendly interface where all the parameters can be viewed and changed. After this classical pre-processing is performed, an innovative wavelet methodology is applied in two steps. The first step consists in the application of the continuous wavelet transformation for the micro potentials detection via time-frequency scalograms. The next step includes the wavelet packet transform applied to the user selection in the scalogram plane in order to obtain both the reconstructed micro potentials and a frequency signature for each patient. This frequency signature contains information about the micro potentials presence in the patient's HR-ECG [7]. This presence is confirmed by higher frequency components. This procedure is user selected and is applied to the P-wave or the QRS complex. Fig. 1 shows a screen-shot of the *MicroECG* user interface presenting the Frank leads [8] automatically delineated ECG [9]. The system is versatile to the user and offers the pre-processing tools necessary to the wavelet processing [10].

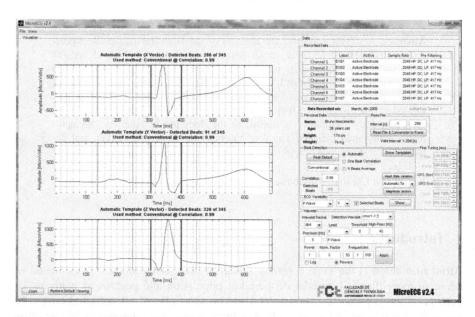

Fig. 1. A screen-shot of the *MicroECG* user interface showing the Frank leads automatically delineated ECG. The user can change a significant number of parameters.

2   Contribution to Technological Innovation

In this paper we present a tool with the following advanced features:

1. Incorporation under the same roof all the processing steps necessary to the high resolution HR-ECG processing thus saving the user all the time consuming pre - processing procedures.
2. User selection of all the HR-ECG analysis parameters.

3. Innovative wavelet packet methodology for the detection and reconstruction of micro-potentials.
4. User driven (mouse-click) selection of signal features in the wavelet time-scale plan for subsequent reconstruction.
5. Cardiac micro-potential syntheses and representation.

3 Methods and Results

A. Continuous Wavelet transform

The continuous wavelet transform (CWT) is based on a set of analyzing *wavelets* [11] that allow the decomposition of an electrocardiographic signal in a series of coefficients. Each wavelet used to analyze a signal has its own duration, temporal localization and frequency band. The resulting coefficients from the application of a continuous wavelet transformation corresponds to a measure of the components, on a given temporal and frequency band, of the HR-ECG segment under study. The resulting coefficients are obtained through two major steps:

1. The multiplication of an analyzing wavelet and the HR-ECG segment.
2. The calculation of the degree of correlation between the two signals above. This transformation is given by:

$$C(a,b) = \frac{1}{\sqrt{a}} \int ECG(t)\Psi\left(\frac{t-b}{a}\right).dt \tag{1}$$

where **a** is the scale, **b** is the temporal segment, **ECG (t)** is the electrocardiogram and **Ψ** is the analyzing wavelet.

The P-wave scalogram shows an intense component below the 80 Hz mark and a weak component signal post this mark. Figure 2 shows the scalogram for a 40 Hz high-pass filtered simulated ECG signal with a micro-potential between 33 and 54.ms. [12] The rounded whiter patch represents micro-potential energy The colour intensity of the scalogram is proportional to the degree of correlation between the filtered signal and the detection wavelet at play. This means that the lighter zone in the scalogram represents the area where the signal is highly matched the detection wavelet [13]. It is known by the authors' experience that the detection wavelet cmor1-1.5 (Complex Morlet Wavelet) produces the best results regarding the detection of late potentials in the HR-ECG data, so it is set by default in the MicroECG software.

B. Discrete wavelet transform

Unlike the CWT, the Discrete Wavelet Transform (DWT) allows for signal reconstruction. Calculating wavelet coefficients at every possible scale produces a redundant signal representation. If the scales are based on powers of two — so-called *dyadic* grid — then the analysis will be much more efficient. This is known as the DWT. As seen in Fig. 3, the approximations (cA_n) are the high-scale, low-frequency components of the signal. The details (cD_n) are the low-scale, high-frequency components. The decomposition process can be iterated, with successive approximations

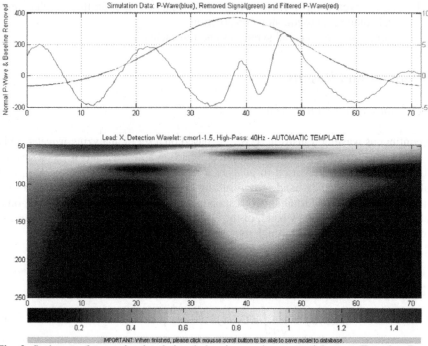

Fig. 2. Scalogram from a simulated signal showing a micro-potential event. Top plot: P wave with 380 µV amplitude and the same wave after filtering with micro-potential around 33 and 54 ms, and around 12 µV amplitude.

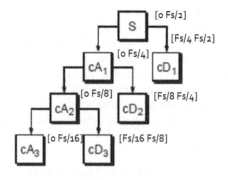

Fig. 3. Wavelet decomposition tree

being decomposed in turn, so that one signal is broken down into many lower resolution components. This is called the *wavelet decomposition tree*.

Since the analysis process is iterative, in theory it can be continued indefinitely. In reality, the decomposition can proceed only until the individual details consist of a single sample or pixel.

C. Wavelet packet transform

The Discrete Wavelet Packet Transform (DWPT) offers a more complex and flexible analysis, because the details as well as the approximations are split.

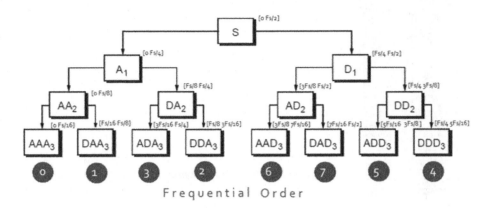

Fig. 4. Wavelet packet decomposition

The difference between DWT and DWPT is that the former presents the same frequency resolution in all the nodes in the same level, since the signal's approximation and detail nodes are all split into two new signals, instead of only the approximation node being split as it happens in the DWT as seen in Fig. 4. Therefore the DWPT turns out to be more efficient to study high resolution cases because there is no loss of resolution in the frequency axis. Another important thing to take notice is that in the final level of this multi-level decomposition "tree" there are the coefficients that can be used to reconstruct the original signal. However these coefficients or "leaves" of this "tree" are in no sequential order in terms of frequency, and one most take notice of this fact if signal reconstruction from this coefficients is required.

In *MicroECG*, these decomposition levels are calculated via the length of the signal and its sampling frequency. The number of "leaves" of this wavelet packet decomposition "tree" is always a power of 2, for example, if a number of 8 levels are calculated there will be 256 "leaves" or coefficients in the end. However, all these 256 "leaves" will be shown only if the user selects all frequencies to be analyzed from zero to the Nyquist frequency. If the user only selects a sub-set of the frequencies available to be analyzed the 256 "leaves" will be reduced accordingly. For better exemplify these same principles, Fig. 5 is shown where the micro-potential lies around 33-44ms with less than 10μV amplitude and bandwidth between 65 and 187 Hz.

Figure 6 shows the colour maps DPWT energy map of: Top: a patient with Paroxistic Atrial Fibrillation; Bottom: a normal subject. Lighter colour means increased node energy, therefore indicating micro-potential activity.

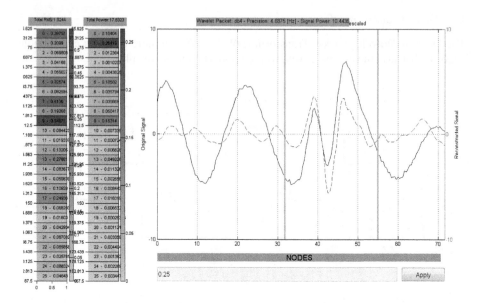

Fig. 5. DPWT reconstruction for the micro-potential of Fig. 2 (dashed) and original filtered P wave. The micro-potential lies around 33-44ms with less than 10μV amplitude and bandwidth between 65 and 187 Hz.

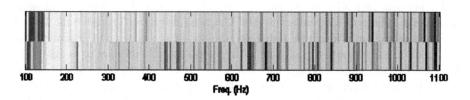

Fig. 6. DPWT energy map of: Top: a patient with Paroxistic Atrial Fibrillation; Bottom: a normal subject

4   Conclusions and Future Work

The DWPT is a promising tool in the detection of small amplitude, short lived signals present in the HR-ECG. A spectral signature is obtained and the reconstruction of the micro-potentials is possible through the selection of the most energetic nodes. In this work, interesting results have been obtained with simulated data, and will now progress with real data from patients with Paroxistic Atrial Fibrillation. The *MicroECG* system will serve as a platform for this research work relieving the user from the time consuming pre-processing steps along with all the wavelet algorithms. This platform is design to be flexible and open to improvements.

References

1. Cox, J.L., et al.: Electrophysiology, Pacing and Arrhythmia, Operations for Atrial Fibrillation. Clin. Cardiol. 14, 827–834 (1991)
2. Chang, Y.U., et al.: National Implications for Rhythm Management and Stroke Prevention: the AnTicoagulation and Risk Factors. Atrial Fibrillation (ATRIA) Study, JAMA 285, 2370–2375 (2001)
3. Kuchar, D., Thorburn, C., Sammel, F.: Late potentials detected after myocardial infarction. Natural history and prognostic significance. Circulation 6, 1280–1289 (1986)
4. Zandi, A.S., Moradi, M.H.: Quantitative evaluation of a wavelet-based method in ventricular late potential detection. The Journal of Pattern Recognition Society (2006)
5. Daubechies, I.: Ten Lectures on Wavelets. Society for Industrial and Applied Mathematics (1992)
6. Malmivuo, J., Plonsey, R.: Bioelectromagnetism - Principles and Applications of Bioelectric and Biomagnetic Fields. Oxford University Press, New York (1995)
7. Berbari, E.J., Steinberg, J.S.: A practical guide to the use of the high-resolution electrocardiography. Wiley-Blackwell (2000)
8. Frank, E.: An accurate, clinically practical system for spatial vectorcardiography. Circulation 13, 737–749 (1956)
9. Almeida, R., Martínez, J.P.: Multilead ECG Delineation Using Spatially Projected Leads From Wavelet Transform Loops. IEEE Transactions on Biomedical Engineering 56(8) (2009)
10. Tompkins, W.J.: Biomedical Digital Signal Processing: C Language Examples and Laboratory Experiments for the IBM PC. Prentice Hall, Englewood Cliffs (1993)
11. Couderc, J.P., Zareba, W.: Contribution of wavelets to the non-invasive Electrocardiology. In: ANE, pp. 54–62 (1993)
12. Afonso, V., Tompkins, W., Nguyen, T., Luo, S.: ECG beat detection using filter banks. Trans. Biomed. Eng. 46(2), 192–202 (1999)
13. Natwong, B., Sooraksa, P.: Wavelet Entropy Analysis of the High Resolution ECG, Industrial Electronics and Applications. In: 1ST IEEE Conference (2006)

A Contribution for the Automatic Sleep Classification Based on the Itakura-Saito Spectral Distance

Eduardo Cardoso[1], Arnaldo Batista[1], Rui Rodrigues[2], Manuel Ortigueira[1], Cristina Bárbara[3], Cristina Martinho[3], and Raul Rato[1]

[1] Dept. of Electrical Enginnering, Faculty of Sciences and Technology –University Nova of Lisbon, Campus de Caparica, 2825-516 Portugal
agb@fct.unl.pt
[2] Dept. of Mathmatics, Faculty of Sciences and Technology –University Nova of Lisbon, Campus de Caparica, 2825-516 Portugal
[3] Hospital Pulido Valente; Laboratory of Sleep Patologies of the Pneumology Department

Abstract. Sleep staging is a crucial step before the scoring the sleep apnoea, in subjects that are tested for this condition. These patients undergo a whole night polysomnography recording that includes EEG, EOG, ECG, EMG and respiratory signals. Sleep staging refers to the quantification of its depth. Despite the commercial sleep software being able to stage the sleep, there is a general lack of confidence amongst health practitioners of these machine results. Generally the sleep scoring is done over the visual inspection of the overnight patient EEG recording, which takes the attention of an expert medical practitioner over a couple of hours. This contributes to a waiting list of two years for patients of the Portuguese Health Service. In this work we have used a spectral comparison method called Itakura distance to be able to make a distinction between sleepy and awake epochs in a night EEG recording, therefore automatically doing the staging. We have used the data from 20 patients of Hospital Pulido Valente, which had been previously visually expert scored. Our technique results were promising, in a way that Itakura distance can, by itself, distinguish with a good degree of certainty the N2, N3 and awake states. Pre-processing stages for artefact reduction and baseline removal using Wavelets were applied.

Keywords: Sleep Staging; EEG signal processing; AR modelling; Itakura-Saito Distance.

1 Introduction

According to the new criteria based on the Rechtschaffen and Kales(R&K) rules, the human sleep is divided in two phases, the rapid eye movement (REM) and the non-rapid eye movement (NREM).sleep [1]. The NREM is divided into three stages, N1 N2 and N3, being N3 the deepest state of sleep. The various states are distinguished on the basis of pattern changes in the electroencephalogram (EEG), electromyogram (EMG) and electro-oculogram (EOG). The depth of non-REM sleep stages are arranged from the lighter to the deepest, as follows: N1, N2 and N3. The awake state is characterized by alpha frequencies ($8 - 13Hz$), to score an epoch as awake is just necessary that over

L.M. Camarinha-Matos, P. Pereira, and L. Ribeiro (Eds.): DoCEIS 2010, IFIP AICT 314, pp. 374–381, 2010.
© IFIP International Federation for Information Processing 2010

50% of the epoch has alpha rhythm. The REM state has low chin EMG tone, saw-tooth waves, trains of sharply contoured or triangular, often serrated, 2-6 Hz waves maximal in amplitude and symmetrical EOG deflections. The N1 is characterized by mixed frequency activity (4-7 Hz) and low amplitude waves and slow eye movement. Following the N1 is N2 when spindles or K-complexes disassociated with arousals occur. A spindle is a train of distinct waves with frequency 11-16 Hz (most commonly 12-14 Hz) with duration 0.5 seconds, usually maximal in amplitude in central derivations. K-complex is a well-delineated negative sharp wave immediately followed by a positive component standing out from the background EEG, with total duration around 0.5 seconds, usually maximal in amplitude when recorded from frontal derivations. For an arousal to be associated with a K complex, it must begin no more than 1 second after the termination of the K complex. The N3 stage shows waves of frequency 0.5-2Hz and peak-to-peak amplitude higher than 75 μV, when these waves occupy more than 20 to 50% of the 30 seconds epoch, this is scored as N3.

The five stages of sleep, including their repetition, occur cyclically in a normal subject. The first sleep cycle which ends after the conclusion of the first REM stage, usually lasts for about 100 minutes. Each subsequent cycle lasts longer, as its respective closing REM stage extends in duration. So a subject with a regular sleep can complete five cycles in a typical sleep nigh. This sleep cycle is variable, influenced by several agents such as sleep deprivation, frequently changing sleep schedules, stress and environment effects. Another factor that affects the sleep cycle is age: during infancy and childhood the percentage of REM sleep is highest, decreasing with age [2]. Figure 1 shows the sleep cycles in childhood, early adulthood and old age [3]. Figure 2 shows the relative distribution of the wake, REM and Slow wave sleep (N3) along age [4]. REM period decreases and stabilizes at around 16 years of age, while the awaking period steadily increases with age. REM sleep is associated with the development of the brain in the early life.

The aim of our work is to contribute to the automatic sleep classification using the EEG signal (C3-A2) signal and the Itakura-Saito [5] spectral distance estimator. A spectral template for the wake state is firstly obtained. This template is then compared with all the spectral representations of all night epochs. Without any further processing a hypnogram is obtained where N2, N3 and wake states are distinguishable. However N1 and REM stages are often indistinguishable, requiring other detection strategies, namely using the EOG. This scoring falls in the category of a continuous unsupervised sleep staging for an all night session.

2 Contribution to Technological Innovation

This paper presents the following main contributions to innovation:

1. An automated process to the calculation of the awake spectrum template based on the spectrogram and the AR modeling. This procedure is adequate for a unsupervised sleep classification scheme.
2. Validation of the ISD as a tool for the Sleep Classification.

Implementation of a software tool that incorporates the developed algorithms in a user friendly interface (*SleepLab*).

3 Materials and Methods

Sleep EEG data from Hospital Pulido Valente was used in this work. EEG signals were recorded at a rate of 100Hz. Visual sleep scoring of sleep stages were scored by Hospital experts, according to Rechtschaffen & Kales based on 30-second epochs. These hypnograms stand as our reference.

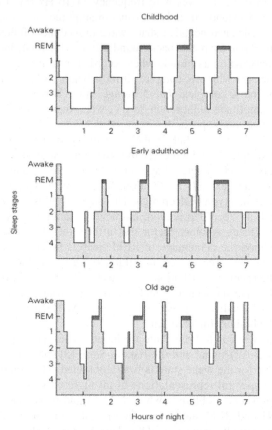

Fig. 1. Reference hypnograms for childhood, early adulthood and old age [3]

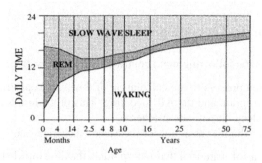

Fig. 2. Wake, REM and deep sleep time along age [4]

3.1 Pre-processing

We have dealt with signal saturation commonly occurring in continuous EEG recordings by replacing each of these epochs by the previous one, a procedure also used in the visual scoring. Baseline removal was performed through wavelet filtering. Movement artefacts that lead to abnormal signal amplitudes were dealt in the same way as in saturation cases. In all cases the affected epochs were replaced by the previous ones, a procedure also used in the visual scoring.

3.2 Awake Template Estimation

An awake template is required for the purpose of the spectral similarity test. Awake epochs were obtained via the power spectrum (Welch method) of each epoch, and then selecting the epochs whose power spectrum peak lie between 8 and 11 Hz, and is above a selected threshold. Due to spindle activity and other EEG components, this power peak must be predominant in order for the epoch classified as awake. An autoregressive (AR) spectral estimation of all the awake classified epochs are calculated, and their mean represents the awake template. Figure 3 represents the power spectrum of the template (solid) and of a sleep epoch (solid) relative to a study patient. The power spectrum of the EEG epochs typically exhibit two main peaks.

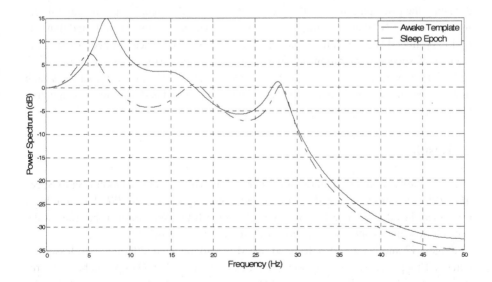

Fig. 3. Spectrum of the obtained EEG awake template (solid) and a sleep epoch for the same patient (dash). See text.

Its relative location and value varies according to the sleep/awake state. The order of the AR model has been estimated based on three factors: the Minimum Description Length (MDL), the Final Prediction Error (FPE) and the Akaike Information Criterion (AIC). All this factors pointed out to an optimal model order of 6 [6] [7].

3.3 Itakura-Saito Distance

This tool [5] [8] is used to compare each EEG epoch with the mentioned template, using their spectra, since the Euclidian distance is inadequate for this case. In this study we have used AR modelling for obtaining the spectra [9][10]. The Itakura-Saito spectral distance (ISD) d_{IS} is defined by the general expression:

$$d_{IS} = \int_{-\pi}^{\pi} \left[\frac{|X(\omega)|^2}{|S(\omega)|^2} + \log\left(\frac{|S(\omega)|^2}{|X(\omega)|^2} \right) - 1 \right] \frac{d\omega}{2\pi} \tag{1}$$

where $S(\omega)$ is the spectrum of the epoch under study and $X(\omega)$ is the template spectrum. This distance is sensible to the relative spectra amplitudes which can be a benefit since some sleep staging can be performed based o the EEG amplitude, namely the higher amplitudes normally present in the N3. However this becomes drawback if the EEG also has amplitude fluctuations due, for instance, to electrode displacement. To overcome this, we have normalized all the spectra to have unity gain, at zero frequency, being the price paid for this to reduce sensibility to the signal amplitude and therefore decreasing N3 detection rate. After some experimentation we have found that this option produced better results in our cases. Itakura-Saito distance has been used in the context of speech recognition and measures the dissimilarity of two spectra $S(\omega)$ and $X(\omega)$, having the functions peaks a predominant weight in the d_{IS} value, which makes sense in our case where peaks in certain frequency bands define the respective sleep stage.

4 Results

Figure 4 shows a patient hypnogram expert scored (blue) and the Itakura-Saito Spectral (ISD) distances obtained as described above (green). The ISD has not been processed, besides a 4 coefficient moving average filter. We confirm that the awake states follow the hypnogram therefore validating our template.

Stages N2 and N3 are also detected. REM is also detected although with lesser accuracy. This patient, as most of the others, exhibit only a few N1 epochs being therefore not possible to fully assess the ISD to detect this state. It is also patent that the ISD plot allows for the evaluation of the way the sleep state continuously progress from stage to stage, unlike the visual scoring that produces discrete stage transitions. Figure 5 shows the mean and standard deviation of the ISD values for each visual

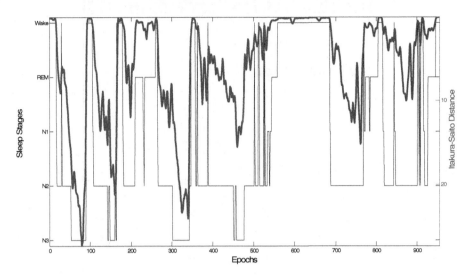

Fig. 4. Visually scored hypnogram (blue) and ISD automatic scoring (green). See text.

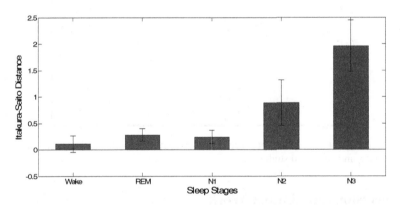

Fig. 5. Mean and standard deviation of the ISD for each visually scored stage. See text.

scored stage, for the same patient. As expected *ISD* is lower in the awake state and higher in the N3 state. N1 and REM stages are similar spectral wise, which can be seen in this figure.

A software tool named *SleepLab* was developed in *Matlab* [11] to streamline the data pre-processing, template estimation and Itakura-Saito distance. The user interface is shown in Figure 6. Other versions of the Itakura distance are also obtained for comparison purposes. This platform is opened to future developments as *ICA (Independent Component Analysis)* to remove the EOG artifacts, and sleep spindle detection. This is an open platform that will include newer developments.

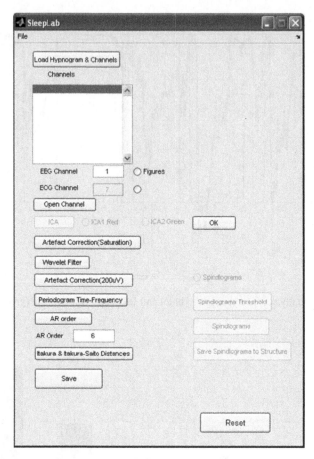

Fig. 6. A screen-shot of the user interface. The *Save* button exports all the results and models for comparison and statistical studies.

5 Conclusions and Future Work

Continuous EEG signal analysis for automatic sleep classification is a difficult task. This kind of signal is typically affected by the usual artifacts related to the patient unpredictable movements and possible electrode displacements during the sleep period. We have introduced an automatic procedure to obtain the awake template using the spectrogram of all the night´s epochs, which is computationally very efficient and essential for the ISD calculation. We have used the ISD formulation (distortion measure) which we have found to produce better results than the gain-optimized Itakura-Saito distortion measure generally used [4]. It is still unclear which of the distortion measures better suits the sleep scoring via EEG signal analysis, and we intend to continue the research in order to differentiate and assess the different spectral distances measures for this task. In this work the ISD produced automatic hypnograms that could detect the awake, N2 and N3 states. The assessment of the N1 is compromised by the fact that this state is relatively rare among the tested patients. The REM is identical to the N1, spectral wise, and therefore requires other features to be automatically detected, namely the EOG.

We also intend to submit the *ISD* obtained results to a Neuro-Fuzzy classifier, as this seems to be an obvious step to follow. Furthermore, we plan to use the EOG as a classifier of the REM stage and apply further artifact removing techniques such as ICA. EMG chin activity is planned to be introduced as an important indicator of sleep deepness.

References

1. Akaike, H.: Power spectrum estimation through autoregressive model fitting. Annals of the Institute of Statistical Mathematics 21, 407–419 (1969)
2. Ebrahimi, F., et al.: Assessment of Itakura Distance as a valuable feature for computer-aided classification of sleep stages. In: Conference Information: 29th Annual International Conference of the IEEE-Engineering-in-Medicine-and-Biology-Society, vol. 1-16, pp. 3300–3303 (2007)
3. Estrada, E., Nazeran, H., Nava, P.: Itakura Distance: A useful similarity measure between EEG and EOG signals in computer-aided classification of sleep stages. In: 27th Annual International Conference of the IEEE-Engineering-in-Medicine-and-Biology-Society, vol. 1-7, pp. 1189–1192 (2005)
4. Gray, R., et al.: Distortion Measures for Speech Processing. IEEE Transactions on Acoustics, Speech and Signal Processing 28, 367–376 (1980)
5. Iber, C., et al.: The American Academy of Sleep Medicine Manual for the Scoring of Sleep and Associated Events (2007)
6. Kandel, E., Schwartz, J., Jessell, T.: Principles of Neural Science (2001)
7. Kay, S.: Modern Spectral Estimation: Theory and Application (1999)
8. Nicolau, M., et al.: Why we sleep: the evolutionary pathway to the mammalian sleep. Progress in Neurobiology 62, 379–406 (2000)
9. Rechtschaffen, A., Siegel, J.: Sleep and Dreaming. Principles of Neuroscience (2000)
10. Soong, F., Sondhi, M.: A Frequency-Weighted Itakura Spectral Distortion Measure and It's Application to Speech Recognition in Noise. In: IEEE International Conference Acoustics, Speech and Signal Processing, vol. 12, pp. 625–628 (1987)
11. Matlab Signal Procssing Tollbox. Inc., Matworks

Part 13

Signal Processing - II

Controlled Invariant Polyhedral Sets for Constrained Discrete-Time Descriptor Systems

José Mario Araújo[1] and Carlos Eduardo Trabuco Dórea[2]

[1] Instituto Federal da Bahia, Departamento de Tecnologia em Eletro-Eletrônica, Rua Emídio dos Santos, S/N, Barbalho, Salvador-BA, Brazil
jomario@ifba.edu.br
[2] Universidade Federal da Bahia, Escola Politécnica, Depto. de Engenharia Elétrica,
Rua Aristides Novis, 2, Federação, Salvador-BA, Brazil
cetdorea@ufba.br

Abstract. This paper addresses the problem of constructing controlled invariant polyhedral sets for linear discrete-time descriptor systems subject to state and control constraints and persistent disturbances. Regardless the large number of contributions on set invariance for linear systems in the standard form, there are few works dealing with set invariance properties in the case of descriptor systems. Here, assuming regularity and causality of the descriptor system, the state equations are written in such way that standard algorithms can be directly applied. Moreover, state and control constraints can be enforced through a piecewise linear delayed state feedback. A numerical example is presented to illustrate these ideas.

Keywords: Descriptor systems, set invariance, constraints.

1 Introduction

Descriptor systems is an important class of linear systems, also called generalized state space, or singular systems and yet implicit systems when algebraic equations are present. Very important works have built a rich theoretical and applied framework on the subject [1], [2], [3], [4] and [5]. The design of constrained control systems is very useful in practice, since certain requirements of supply or safety impose limits on physical quantities. The use of the set-invariance concept is a efficient way of dealing with constrained control systems (see [6], [7] and [8] and references therein). Several works concerning constrained control for standard state-space systems can be found in the literature [9], [10] and [11]. For the class of descriptor linear systems, however, the contributions on the characterization of controlled invariance over polyhedral sets are not so numerous. Some important works on positive invariance under linear pole placement design can be found on literature [12], [13], [14], [15] and [16]. However, the use of linear feedback may lead to very conservative solutions, not coping with severe control constraints or high amplitude disturbances. In this note, controlled

L.M. Camarinha-Matos, P. Pereira, and L. Ribeiro (Eds.): DoCEIS 2010, IFIP AICT 314, pp. 385–392, 2010.

invariance of polyhedral sets for discrete time linear descriptor systems is analyzed. By assuming that the system is regular and causal, the state equation can be rewritten in an augmented form which gives the possibility of applying available methods for characterization of controlled invariance for polyhedral sets in standard linear systems. A delayed state-feedback control law can then be synthesized to enforce the constraints. A numerical example is presented in order to illustrate the effectiveness of the proposal.

2 Contribution for Technological Innovation

Descriptor systems arise from a diversity of areas, such economics, chemical and electrical [1]. The control of this class of models is very important, since a series of requirements of quality, reliability and safety are involved. In many cases, physical constraints are inherent, and comprising operational limits of supply/safety. The set-invariance for control under constraints is well developed for systems in the classical state representation. For descriptor model a few works have contributed in this aspect. The present paper tries to rise new ideas in this direction.

3 Preliminaries

The nth-dimensional system under study is in the form of a perturbed descriptor state-space representation:

$$Ex(k+1) = Ax(k) + Bu(k) + Dd(k) \tag{1}$$

in which $x \in \Re^n, u \in \Re^m, d \in \Re^p$. The disturbance amplitude is supposed to be bounded for all instants k. When $rank(E) = q < n$, without loss of generality, the state vector can be partitioned:

$$x(k+1) = \begin{bmatrix} x_1(k+1) \\ x_2(k+1) \end{bmatrix} \tag{2}$$

and the system matrices can be written:

$$E = \begin{bmatrix} I_q & 0 \\ 0 & 0 \end{bmatrix}, A = \begin{bmatrix} A_{11} & A_{12} \\ A_{21} & A_{22} \end{bmatrix}, B = \begin{bmatrix} B_1 \\ B_2 \end{bmatrix}, D = \begin{bmatrix} D_1 \\ D_2 \end{bmatrix} \tag{3}$$

The hypothesis that the system is causal assures that A_{22} is invertible [4]. In this case, manipulations on the systems matrices leads to the form:

$$x(k+1) = \tilde{A}x(k) + \tilde{B}u(k) + \tilde{C}u(k+1) + \tilde{D} \begin{bmatrix} d(k) \\ d(k+1) \end{bmatrix} \tag{4}$$

in which

$$\tilde{A} = \begin{bmatrix} A_{11} - A_{12}A_{22}^{-1}A_{21} & 0 \\ -A_{22}^{-1}A_{21}(A_{11} - A_{12}A_{22}^{-1}A_{21}) & 0 \end{bmatrix}, \tilde{B} = \begin{bmatrix} B_1 - A_{12}A_{22}^{-1}B_2 \\ -A_{22}^{-1}A_{21}(B_1 - A_{12}A_{22}^{-1}B_2) \end{bmatrix}$$

$$\tilde{C} = \begin{bmatrix} 0 \\ -A_{22}^{-1}B_2 \end{bmatrix}, \tilde{D} = \begin{bmatrix} D_1 - A_{12}A_{22}^{-1}D_2 & 0 \\ -A_{22}^{-1}A_{21}(D_1 - A_{12}A_{22}^{-1}) & -A_{22}^{-1}D_2 \end{bmatrix}$$

Now, one can see that one-step forward terms in control input and in disturbance appear. This is not a problem for the disturbance, since it is not measured. For the control input, it is convenient to consider it as another state variable. The augmented state vector is then:

$$\chi(k+1) = \begin{bmatrix} x(k+1) \\ u(k+1) \end{bmatrix} \tag{5}$$

The augmented state equation are now given as:

$$\chi(k+1) = \begin{bmatrix} \tilde{A} & \tilde{B}+\tilde{C} \\ 0 & I \end{bmatrix}\chi(k) + \begin{bmatrix} \tilde{C} \\ I \end{bmatrix}\Delta u(k+1) + \begin{bmatrix} \tilde{D} \\ 0 \end{bmatrix}\begin{bmatrix} d(k) \\ d(k+1) \end{bmatrix} \tag{6}$$

In which $\Delta u(k+1) = u(k+1)-u(k)$. This is a standard state-space model with state vector $\begin{bmatrix} x^T(k) & u^T(k) \end{bmatrix}^T$ and bounded disturbance $\begin{bmatrix} d^T(k) & d^T(k+1) \end{bmatrix}^T$, and application of well-established algorithms for standard systems is straightforward. It should be noticed that this extended system has $n+m$ eigenvalues: (i) q finite eigenvalues of (1); (ii) $n-q$ eigenvalues equal to 0 corresponding to infinite eigenvalues of (1); and m eigenvalues equal to 1 corresponding to the control input dynamics. In the next section, this representation will be useful for the characterization of controlled invariance of polyhedral sets that represent constraints on state variables and control inputs.

4 Solution of Constrained Control Problem

4.1 Controlled Invariance

Assume that system (1) is subject to the following state and control constraints:

$$x(k) \in \Omega = \{x : Gx \leq \rho\}, u(k) \in \mathcal{U} = \{u : Uu \leq v\}, \Delta u(k) \in \Delta\mathcal{V} = \{\Delta u : L\Delta u \leq \varphi\} \tag{7}$$

The disturbance is supposed to be bounded as follows:

$$d(k) \in \mathcal{D} = \{d : Vd \leq \mu\} \tag{8}$$

Considering the augmented representation, the constraints on state and control can be written as:

$$\chi(k) \in \Gamma = \{\chi : \mathcal{G}\chi \le \rho\}, \mathcal{G} = \begin{bmatrix} G & 0 \\ 0 & U \end{bmatrix}, \rho = \begin{bmatrix} \rho \\ \upsilon \end{bmatrix}$$

and the bounds on the disturbance as:

$$\begin{bmatrix} d(k) \\ d(k+1) \end{bmatrix} \in \Psi = \{d : \mathcal{V}d \le \bar{\mu}\}, \mathcal{V} = \begin{bmatrix} V & 0 \\ 0 & V \end{bmatrix}, \bar{\mu} = \begin{bmatrix} \mu \\ \mu \end{bmatrix}$$

The goal now is to construct a control law which enforces the constraints, for all disturbances in Ψ. Such a construction will be based on the following concept [9]:

Definition 4.1. A set is λ-contractive controlled invariant with respect to system (6) and constraints (7),(8) if for any $\chi(k) \in \Gamma$, $\exists \Delta u$ such that

$$\chi(k+1) = \begin{bmatrix} \tilde{A} & \tilde{B} + \tilde{C} \\ 0 & I \end{bmatrix} \chi(k) + \begin{bmatrix} \tilde{C} \\ I \end{bmatrix} \Delta u(k+1) + \begin{bmatrix} \tilde{D} \\ 0 \end{bmatrix} \begin{bmatrix} d(k) \\ d(k+1) \end{bmatrix} \in \lambda\Gamma \quad \text{with } 0 < \lambda \le 1.$$

The constrained control problem can then be solved by computing Γ^*, the maximal controlled invariant set contained in Γ [8,9]. Hence, if the initial state is consistent with the algebraic equation:

$$0 = A_{21}x_1(0) + A_{22}x_2(0) + B_2u(0) + D_2d(0) \tag{9}$$

and $\chi(k) \in \Gamma^*$ then there exists $\Delta u(k) \in \Delta \mathcal{V}$ such that $\chi(k+1) \in \lambda\Gamma^*, \forall d(k) \in \mathcal{D}$. As a consequence, if $\chi(0) \in \Gamma^*$, then $\exists \Delta u(k+1)$ such that $\chi(k) \in \Gamma^* \forall k$ and $\forall d(k) \in \mathcal{D}$. Moreover, if $d(k) = 0, \chi(k) \in \lambda^k\Gamma^{*k}$, thus if $\lambda < 1$, $\chi(k) \rightarrow 0$ when $k \rightarrow \infty$, guaranteeing asymptotic stability.

Once the maximal controlled invariant is obtained, a piecewise linear control law can be computed that assures the respect to constraints [9]:

$$\Delta u(k+1) = \phi[\chi(k)] = \phi[x(k), u(k)] \tag{10}$$

One can see that such control law is delayed with respect to the augmented state vector.

4.2 Admissible Initial Conditions

In the previous subsection, the issue of consistency of initial conditions was mentioned. The control law (10) enforces state and control constraints as long as the initial state satisfies $\chi(0) \in \Gamma^*$. However, differently from standard linear systems, $\chi(0)$ may not be consistent, i.e., may not satisfy the algebraic equation (9). In this case, a jump can occur for $k = 0$ and this is unpredictable due the disturbance $d(0)$. Let $x(0^+)$ be the state after the jump. The dynamic part of state vector does not experiment jumps in $k = 0$. It can be verified by changing the representation of (1) into a canonical representation where the dynamic and algebraic equations are decoupled [14]. Hence $x_1(0^+) = x_1(0)$. The algebraic portion can be made explicit from (9):

$$x_2(0^+) = -A_{22}^{-1}A_{21}x_1(0) - A_{22}^{-1}B_2u(0) - A_{22}^{-1}D_2d(0) \tag{11}$$

The consistency of the initial condition can be treated on the basis of the following definition.

Definition 4.2. Consider the set Γ^*, controlled invariant with respect to the system (6) and constraints (7),(8). The set of admissible initial states is defined by:
$\Lambda_{ad} = \{x(0) \in \Omega : \exists u(0) \in \mathcal{U} : x(0^+) \in \Gamma^*, \forall d(0) \in \mathcal{D}\}$.

Let now Γ^* be the polyhedral set $\Gamma^* = \{x : G^*x \le \rho^*\}$. In this case, the set of admissible initial states is also a polyhedron, given by the set of $x(0) = \begin{bmatrix} x_1(0)^T & x_2(0)^T \end{bmatrix}^T$ such that $\exists u(0)$ which satisfies, $\forall Vd(0) \le \mu$:

$$\begin{bmatrix} G^* \begin{bmatrix} I \\ -A_{22}^{-1}A_{21} \end{bmatrix} \\ 0 \end{bmatrix} x_1(0) + \begin{bmatrix} G^* \begin{bmatrix} 0 \\ -A_{22}^{-1}B_2 \end{bmatrix} \\ U \end{bmatrix} u(0) + \begin{bmatrix} G^* \begin{bmatrix} 0 \\ -A_{22}^{-1}D_2 \end{bmatrix} \\ 0 \end{bmatrix} d(0) \le \begin{bmatrix} \rho^* \\ v \end{bmatrix} \tag{12}$$

Since $d(0)$ is not measured, its influence can be taken into account by considering the worst case row-by-row. Define then the vector:

$$\sigma_i = \max_{Vd \le \mu} \left\{ \left[-G^* \begin{bmatrix} 0 \\ -A_{22}^{-1}D_2 \\ 0 \end{bmatrix} \right] d \right\}_i \tag{13}$$

The variable $u(0)$ can be eliminated by a projection computed like in [8], resulting in the following polyhedron on x_1:

$$\Lambda_{x_1} = \{x_1(0) : H_1x_1(0) \le h_1\} \tag{14}$$

The set of admissible initial states is then given by:

$$\Lambda_{ad} = \left\{ x(0) : \begin{bmatrix} [H_1 & 0] \\ G \end{bmatrix} x(0) \le \begin{bmatrix} h_1 \\ \rho \end{bmatrix} \right\} \tag{15}$$

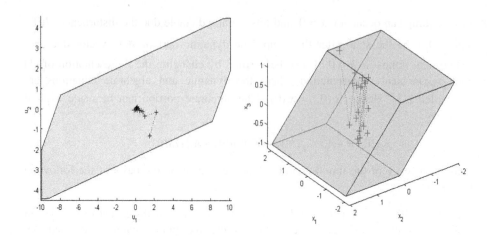

Fig. 1. Projection onto the control space (a) and the state space (b) of the controlled invariant polyhedron computed with $\gamma = 1$, together with a control and a state trajectory

5 Numerical Example

Consider the same system used in [13, 14, 15]:

$$E = \begin{bmatrix} 1 & 0 & 0 \\ 0 & 1 & 0 \\ 0 & 0 & 0 \end{bmatrix}, A = \begin{bmatrix} 1.2 & 0 & 0 \\ -1 & -0.7 & -1 \\ 2 & -0.5 & -1.2 \end{bmatrix}, B = \begin{bmatrix} 0 & 1 \\ 1 & -1 \\ 0.5 & 2 \end{bmatrix}, D = \begin{bmatrix} 0 \\ 1 \\ 1 \end{bmatrix}$$

The following state and control constraints (7),(8) are imposed: $|G_s x| \le \rho_s, |u_i| \le 10, i = 1, 2$ with

$$G_s = \begin{bmatrix} 0 & 1 & 0.9318 \\ -1 & 0 & -0.1164 \\ 0 & 0 & 1 \end{bmatrix}, \rho_s = \begin{bmatrix} 1 \\ 2 \\ 1 \end{bmatrix}$$

The disturbances are bounded as $|d(k)| \le \gamma$. By application of the algorithm proposed in [8], it was verified that the maximal controlled invariant polyhedron contained in the set of constraints, with a contraction rate $\lambda = 0.99$, is non-empty for $\gamma \le \gamma_{max} = 1.082115$.

Figure 1 shows the controlled invariant polyhedron for $\gamma = 1$ projected onto control and state spaces, where it can be noticed that the original polyhedron of the constraints in states is itself controlled invariant. These results are better than those obtained by the pole placement control law proposed in [14], where $\gamma_{max} = 0.208815$. A piecewise control law that enforces the constraints can be computed as in [9]. However, it turns out that for this example, with $\gamma = 1$, invariance of Ω under control constraints can be achieved by a linear feedback $\Delta u(k+1) = F\chi(k) = F_1 x(k) + F_2 u(k)$ computed by linear programming as in [10, 11], leading to

$$F = \begin{bmatrix} 0.9370 & 0.7409 & 0 & -0.8944 & -0.4852 \\ -0.7146 & 0.1915 & 0 & -0.0385 & -1.8254 \end{bmatrix}.$$

It should be noticed that due to the null column in F, the closed-loop augmented systems has: (i) 4 finite eigenvalues in 0.6663, -0.4669, -0.0329, 0.0305, and (ii) 1 eigenvalue equal to 0, corresponding to the infinite pole of (1). Its confirms stability of the system under closed-loop.

The set of admissible initial states coincides with the initial polyhedron. A simulation was carried out with initial conditions $x(0) = \begin{bmatrix} 1.649 & -0.2354 & 0 \end{bmatrix}^T$, $x(0^+) = \begin{bmatrix} 1.649 & -0.2354 & 1 \end{bmatrix}^T$. The initial control input $u(0)$ was then computed in order to guarantee $x(0^+) \in \Gamma^*$, resulting in $u(0) = \begin{bmatrix} 1.5 & -1.344 \end{bmatrix}^T$ The simulated trajectories with random disturbances are depicted in figure 1.

6 Conclusions and Future Works

A characterization of controlled invariance of polyhedral sets was proposed for descriptor linear discrete time systems, based on an augmented state-space representation in the form of a classical linear system. Under this representation, standard algorithms can be used to compute controlled invariant sets. Then, a delayed state feedback law can be synthesized to solve a control problem under state and control constraints for systems subject to bounded disturbances. Through a numerical example, it was shown that the proposed controller can outperform linear ones proposed in literature. Future works will focus the study of the solution to the problem by means of static and dynamic output feedback laws, already characterized in [17] for classical linear systems. The design of a control law for simultaneous regularization and constraints satisfaction will be also investigated.

Acknowledgments. The Authors would like to thank to their Institutions and to PROAP/CAPES for financial support.

References

1. Luenberger, D.G.: Time-invariant descriptor systems. Automatica 14(5), 473–480 (1978)
2. Yip, E.L., Sincovec, R.F.: Solvability, controllability, and observability of continuous descriptor systems. IEEE T Automat. Contr. 26(3), 702–707 (1981)
3. Cobb, D.: Feedback and pole placement in descriptor variable systems. Int. J. Control 33(6), 1135–1146 (1981)
4. Dai, L.: Singular control systems. Springer, New York (1989)
5. Lewis, F.: A survey of linear singular systems. Circ. Syst. Signal Pr. 5(1), 5–36 (1986)
6. Blanchini, F.: Set invariance in control. Automatica 35(11), 1747–1767 (1999)

7. Dórea, C.E.T., Hennet, J.C.: (A,B)-invariance conditions of polyhedral domains for continuous-time systems. European Journal of Control 5(1), 70–81 (1999)
8. Dorea, C.E.T., Hennet, J.C.: (A,B)-invariant polyhedral sets of linear discrete-time systems. J. Optimiz. Theroy App. 103(3), 521–542 (1999)
9. Blanchini, F.: Ultimate boundedness control for uncertain discrete-time systemsvia set-induced Lyapunov functions. IEEE T Automat. Contr. 39(2), 428–433 (1994)
10. Vassilaki, M., Hennet, J.C., Bitsoris, G.: Feedback control in linear discrete-time systems under state and control constraints. Int. J. Control 47(6), 1727–1735 (1988)
11. Vassilaki, M., Bitsoris, G.: Constrained regulation of linear continuous-time dynamical systems. Syst. Control Lett. 13, 247–252 (1989)
12. Georgiou, G., Krikelis, N.J.: A design approach for constrained regulation in discrete singular systems. Syst. Control Lett., 297–304 (1991)
13. Tarbouriech, S., Castelan, E.B.: Positively invariant-sets for singular discrete-time systems. International Journal of Systems Science 24(9), 1687–1705 (1993)
14. Castelan, E.B., Tarbouriech, S.: Simple and weak D-invariant polyhedral sets for discrete-time singular systems. Controle e Automacao 14(4), 339–347 (2003)
15. Tarbouriech, S., Castelan, E.B.: An eigenstructure assignment approach for constrained linear continuous-time systems. S yst. Control Lett. 24, 333–343 (1995)
16. Lin, Z., Lv, L.: Set invariance conditions for singular linear systems subject to actuator saturation. IEEE T Automat. Contr. 52(12), 2351–2355 (2007)
17. Dórea, C.E.T.: Output-feedback controlled invariant polyhedra for constrained linear systems. To appear in Proceedings of 48th CDC, pp. 1–6 (2009)

Using Human Dynamics to Improve Operator Performance

Rui Antunes[1,2], Fernando V. Coito[1], and Hermínio Duarte-Ramos[1]

[1] Faculdade de Ciências e Tecnologia da Universidade Nova de Lisboa
2829-516 Caparica, Portugal
{rui.mantunes,fjvc,hdr}@fct.unl.pt
[2] Escola Superior de Tecnologia de Setúbal do Instituto Politécnico de Setúbal
2910-761 Estefanilha, Setúbal, Portugal
rui.antunes@estsetubal.ips.pt

Abstract. Traditionally Man-Machine Interfaces (MMI) are concerned with the ergonomic aspects of the operation, often disregarding other aspects on how humans learn and use machines. The explicit use of the operator dynamics characterization for the definition of the Human-in-the-Loop control system may allow an improved performance for manual control systems. The proposed human model depends on the activity to be performed and the mechanical Man-Machine Interface. As a first approach for model development, a number of 1-D manual tracking experiments were evaluated, using an analog Joystick. A simple linear human model was obtained and used to design an improved closed-loop control structure. This paper describes practical aspects of an ongoing PhD work on cognitive control in Human-Machine systems.

Keywords: Human Dynamics, Man-Machine Interfaces, Human-in-the-Loop Control, Manual Tracking Systems.

1 Introduction

Our life is enhanced by mechatronics products, comprising Man-Machine Interfaces. However, ordinary machines are not usually designed to assist human to improve one's skill, and in many cases much time and effort are needed for an operator to be trained. One of the main reasons is because machines usually don't change regardless of the human skill, often requiring a long operator training stage.

An important goal is to create and develop intelligent mechatronics systems, capable of adapting themselves to the level of the skill/dexterity of the operators who use them, considering not only the ergonomic aspects of the operation, but also the way humans learn and use machines[1]. This brings along a new concept for manual control

---

[1] A Human-Machine mechatronics system that has the function to assist the human operator is usually called Human Adaptive Mechatronics (HAM).

L.M. Camarinha-Matos, P. Pereira, and L. Ribeiro (Eds.): DoCEIS 2010, IFIP AICT 314, pp. 393–400, 2010.

engineering on Human-Machine systems that inevitably have to consider human in the closed-loop. Recent demands in many areas, for more precision, accuracy and safety (such as in medicine, biotechnology, robotics, transports, entertainment, space, nanotechnology, ocean, disaster site and factory), led to a new need for the development of HAM systems [1].

2   Contribution to Technological Innovation

The purpose of this paper is to present a contribution on human operator modeling for control applications purposes. The inclusion of the operator model on the development of Man-Machine interface devices leads to improved performance on manually controlled operations, as well as easier operation and a reduced training stage.

As a first approach for model development nonparametric system models are used. The models may be obtained from frequency, transient and spectral analysis. The scope of this document is centered on frequency analysis, which proved to be adequate for the development of operator models that, in spite of their simplicity, lead to a good performance. In the sequel, the modeling procedure will de described. The other approaches have also been evaluated but fall beyond the scope of this paper.

A real-time simulation experiment was developed for evaluating skill on predefined closed-loop Human-Machine systems, as a special tool to measure the overall performance. An effort performance measure is also proposed, based on human lazy strategies.

3   State-of-the-Art / Related Literature

It is a key idea that we need to model human behavior, and, so far, many models of the human controller have been proposed.

In 1940's Tustin tried to introduce a human control model using a transfer function to model human action, proposing a linear servo control. In the 1960's Ragazzini modeled a human as a PID controller and showed that humans are time-variant systems having randomness, stating also that the differences among individuals should be addressed. In 1970 Kleinman et al. studied the dynamics of pilots. The transfer function of a pilot was considered as the cascade of the reaction lags/delays attributed to the neuromuscular human system. A method to compensate the time-delay, using a Smith predictor, was described. Anil proposed in 1976 that the human controller could be described both as time-delay and a Kalman filter.

Kawato introduced later in the 1990's the feedback error learning model, which assumes that human has inverse and forward models of the dynamics of the movements, and that the brain, by learning, tends to change human's model from feedback to feedforward. More recently, Wolpert and Kawato improved the feedback error learning model to a module selection and identification control (MOSAIC), by expanding the inverse model into a controller and the forward model into a predictor.

HAM research [2], [3] is being promoted now in some countries, mainly at Japan and UK. Latest developments include studying the brain activity at particular

Brodmann's areas using near-infrared spectroscopy [4], and the manipulation of human behavior by distorted dynamics vision [5].

4 Research Contribution and Innovation

Several methodologies can be carried out to obtain an LTI model. In this work, special focus is given on improved frequency analysis [6], for obtaining Human-Machine linear models from 1-D manual tracking experiences. However, two major points must be stressed over human operator modeling:

1) The operator behavior can not be fully captured through a simple dynamic model, or even a set of such models. Thus, the objective of the models developed is not to replicate human behavior, but only to capture enough information to compensate the drawbacks inherent to the human operator dynamics.

2) It is difficult, if not impossible, to experimentally obtain an open-loop operator model. In any experiment the operator closes the loop between sensing and acting. Hence, to obtain the operator "true" model it is necessary to extract it from the close loop data.

4.1 Frequency Analysis

Consider a one-dimensional input signal, to be tracked, $x(t)$, built from a sum of N sinusoids at pre-defined multiple frequencies. Assume that the one-dimensional input normalized signal has duration T, and $y(t)$ is the correspondent LTI system output. Such signals may be written as:

$$x(t) = \sum_{k=1}^{N} x_k(t) = \sum_{k=1}^{N} a_k \sin(\omega_k t) \quad \max\{|x(t)|\} = 1 \; , \; x(t=0) = 0 \; . \tag{1}$$

$$y(t) = \sum_{k=1}^{N} y_k(t) = \sum_{k=1}^{N} b_k \sin(\omega_k t + \varphi_k) \; . \tag{2}$$

For each applied frequency, the I/O response may be obtained through the following scheme:

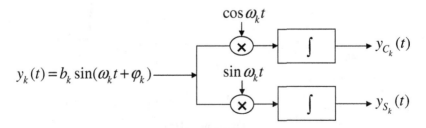

Fig. 1. Frequency analysis *block diagram* for each k-multiple frequency

By performing the integration along time T (a multiple of the sinusoid period, $T = \dfrac{k2\pi}{\omega}$), leads to:

$$y_{C_k}(T) = \int_0^T b_k \sin(\omega_k t + \varphi_k)\cos\omega_k t\, dt \qquad y_{C_k}(T) = \frac{b_k T}{2}\sin\varphi_k \ . \qquad (3,4)$$

$$y_{S_k}(T) = \int_0^T b_k \sin(\omega_k t + \varphi_k)\sin\omega_k t\, dt \qquad y_{S_k}(T) = \frac{b_k T}{2}\cos\varphi_k \ . \qquad (5,6)$$

$$b_k = \frac{2}{T}\sqrt{y_{C_k}{}^2(T) + y_{S_k}{}^2(T)} \quad \text{and} \quad \varphi_k = \arctan\!\left(\frac{y_{C_k}(T)}{y_{S_k}(T)}\right) . \qquad (7,8)$$

which corresponds to the operator closed-loop frequency response.

For each multiple input frequency, a corresponding magnitude was settled to build a human feasible manual tracking input signal. Figure 2 shows the magnitude Bode plot of the input signal $x(t)$ created for the manual tracking experiments (made with a commercial Joystick).

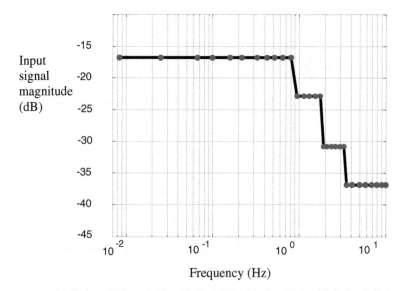

Fig. 2. Input signal magnitude based on the N=30 frequencies sum, ranging 0.0083Hz to 10Hz

4.2 Modeling Human Behavior

One hundred tracking time-trials, with $T=120$ seconds duration each, were obtained for the same participant with no history of neurological deficits. At least, a minimum 10 minute rest was given between trials, that all, lasted for 3 weeks.

A sample of a trial for the input $x(t)$ is presented *below*, in figure 4:

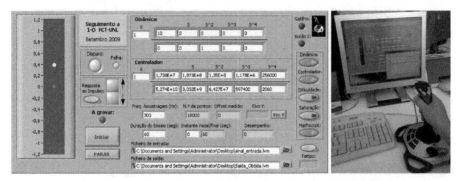

Fig. 3. LabVIEW developed application for the manual tracking experiences (*left*). Manual tracking time-trial using Logitech's Extreme 3D Pro. 8-bit analog Joystick (*right*).

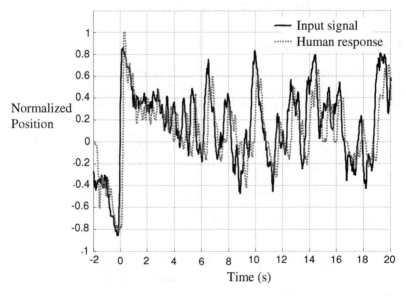

Fig. 4. A 1-D manual tracking sample (*first 20 seconds*) at 100Hz sampling rate. The *input signal is null* at 0 and at 120 seconds ($t=0$, T).

One hundred open-loop linear models for the same individual were obtained, from the closed-loop time-trials, by inverse manipulation. The $\pm 2\sigma$ limits were calculated (assuming a normal unimodal symmetrical distribution, approx. 95 of the models fits inside). A 3 stable pole open-loop nominal model was proposed, based on magnitude:

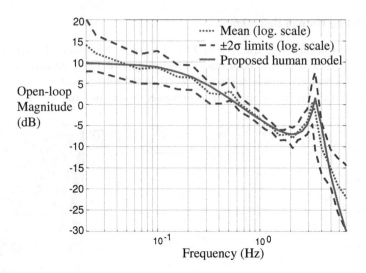

Fig. 5. *Proposed human model* open-loop magnitude Bode plot, ranging between *0.02Hz and 7Hz*, based on 100 1-D manual tracking experiments

$$H(s) = \frac{2060}{s^3 + 4.5s^2 + 527s + 679} . \qquad (9)$$

4.3 Controller Design Strategy

Three controllers are proposed to control an unstable *P(s)* dynamics. The first (*C1*) is a classical phase-shift compensator. The second (*C2*) considers human as a static gain only, and the third controller (*C3*) is obtained from the human model:

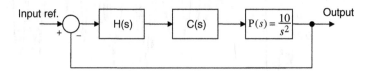

Fig. 6. *Block diagram* for the *closed-loop physical system* to be controlled

$$C_1(s) = \frac{0.5s + 0.05}{s + 50} \qquad C_2(s) = \frac{C_1(s)}{ko} = \frac{679}{2060} \cdot \frac{0.5s + 0.05}{s + 50} . \qquad (10, 11)$$

$$C_3(s) = \frac{C_1(s)}{H_1(s)} = \frac{256000s^4 + 1.178e006s^3 + 1.35e008s^2 + 1.873e008s + 1.738e007}{2060s^4 + 597400s^3 + 6.427e007s^2 + 3.032e009s + 5.274e010} . \qquad (12)$$

Where *H1(s)* presents the same frequency behavior as (9), but includes an additional term (with unity static gain), in order to allow the implementation of *C3(s)*.

5   Discussion of Results and Critical View

This section presents obtained experimental results, with *C1*, *C2* and *C3* controllers:

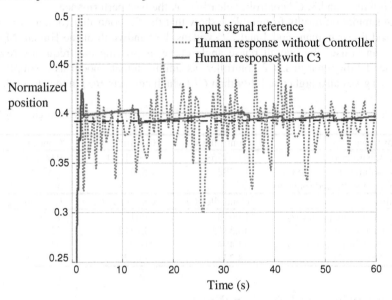

Fig. 7. *Human step response* for two closed-loop control systems (*without controller, and with C3 developed controller*), with *P(s)* dynamics, at 300Hz sample rate. *Input reference is 0.3925.*

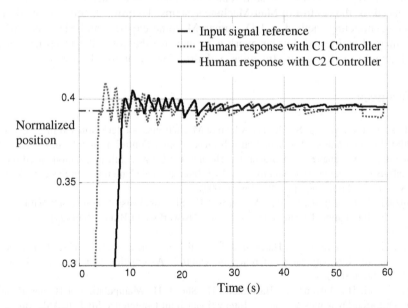

Fig. 8. Detailed human step response for two closed-loop control systems (with C1 and C2 controllers), with P(s) dynamics, at 300Hz sample rate. Input reference is 0.3925.

Manual step performance was measured on a double-integrator $P(s)$ unstable process, considering the reference mean square error, for acuity, and the mean stabilized duration (related with human's lazy strategies, within ±0.0035 from input reference). From figures 7 and 8, $C3$ controller clearly took the best performance.

The simulation results from table 1 show that the $C3$ controller (obtained from the proposed linear human model and $C1$) widens the bandwidth of the Human-Machine system and raises the overall phase angle curve, improving the frequency response and the stability margins. $C2$ controller, assuming human model as a simple static gain (ko) gives also higher stability than $C1$ (which neglects $H(s)$ in the closed-loop).

Table 1. Step response manual performance (in 60 seconds) and stability margins, for P(s)

Performance:	Controller $C1$	Controller $C2$	Controller $C3$
Mean square error	0.0045634	0.0091764	0.0016567
Mean stabilized duration (s)	1.5382	1.5542	5.5260
Number of stabilized sequences	24	20	5
Stability:	Controller $C1$	Controller $C2$	Controller $C3$
Gain Margin Frequency (Hz)	1.0618	1.0618	4.6104
Gain Margin (dB)	40.5313	50.1712	52.1004
Phase Margin Frequency (Hz)	0.0494	0.0202	0.0202
Phase Margin (°)	58.2328	45.9675	51.4105

6   Conclusions and Further Work

In this paper, some HAM research topics that take human factor into account were introduced for the control of Man-Machine systems. To prove the effectiveness of the proposed modeling method, a 1-D Human-Machine experimental SISO system was implemented and tested. Further work is to improve the controller robustness and to develop multi-model design strategies, and also to move on to 2-D systems.

References

1. Harashima, F., Suzuki, S.: Human Adaptive Mechatronics - Interaction and Intelligence. In: 9th IEEE International Workshop on Advanced Motion Control, Istanbul, pp. 1–8 (2006)
2. Suzuki, S., Watanabe, Y., Igarashi, H., Hidaka, K.: Human skill elucidation based on gaze analysis for dynamic manipulation. In: IEEE International Conference on Systems, Man and Cybernetics, Montreal, pp. 2989–2994 (2007)
3. Suzuki, S., Harashima, F., Pan, Y., Furuta, K.: Skill analysis of human in machine operation. In: International Conference on Neural Networks and Brain, Beijing, pp. 1556–1561 (2005)
4. Suzuki, S., Kobayashi, H., Harashima, F.: Brain monitoring analysis of skill on voluntary motion. In: International Conference on Control, Automation and Systems, Seoul, pp. 1178–1182 (2007)
5. Kobayashi, H., Ohyama, Y., Hashimoto, H., She, J.-H.: Manipulation of Human Behavior by Distorted Dynamics Vision. In: International Joint Conference SICE-ICASE, Busan, pp. 4446–4450 (2006)
6. Söderström, T., Stoica, P.: System Identification. Prentice-Hall, Englewood Cliffs (1989)

Railscan: A Tool for the Detection and Quantification of Rail Corrugation

Rui Gomes[1], Arnaldo Batista[1], Manuel Ortigueira[1],
Raul Rato[1], and Marco Baldeiras[2]

[1] Department of Electrical Engineering, Universidade Nova de Lisboa, Portugal
agb@fct.unl.pt
[2] Refer, Rede Ferroviária Nacional, EP
mlbaldeiras@refer.pt

Abstract. Rail corrugation is a phenomenon that leads to a waving in the rails with wavelengths typically between *3 cm* and *100 cm* and amplitude levels of several microns. The genesis of this waving is complex. Rail corrugation is a recognized problem that leads to excess vibration on the rails and vehicles to a point of reducing their life span and compromising safety. In urban areas excess vibration noise is also a problem. A software tool was developed to analyze accelerometer signals acquired in the boggies of rail vehicles in order to quantify the rail corrugation according to their frequency and amplitude. A wavelet packet methodology was used in this work and compared with the One Third Octave Filter (OTOF) power representations, which is currently used in the industry. It is shown that the former produces better results.

Keywords: Rail Corrugation, Wavelets, Time-Frequency.

1   Introduction

Rail corrugation is a problem extensively felt by railway companies. This phenomenon is due to the railway traffic conditions that produce corrugation wavelengths in the railhead between 3cm and 100cm [1]. These rail irregularities are a matter of concern due to excess vibration loads in the vehicles and noise. Vibration may compromise safety and reduce the life span of the equipment, therefore requiring some type of rail maintenance. Early detection of the phenomenon to improve rail security and for economical reasons is a desired goal.

Corrugation measurement may be done using the *direct* and the *indirect* approach [2], [3]. In this work an *indirect* measurement approach in which the corrugation levels are obtained through the signals from axle-box accelerometers [3].

In this paper is presented a software tool, *RailScan* that integrates under the same *roof* the necessary signal processing steps and procedures for the rail corrugation detection and quantification using the EN ISO 3095 parameters, exploring the wavelet's superior ability for non-stationary signal analysis.

The *RailScan* user interface is designed to allow for the system parameters to be modified and adjusted for research purposes. The results are presented in a series of interactive results representations. The results numerical values may be exported for

L.M. Camarinha-Matos, P. Pereira, and L. Ribeiro (Eds.): DoCEIS 2010, IFIP AICT 314, pp. 401–408, 2010.
© IFIP International Federation for Information Processing 2010

later comparative analysis. The software has been developed in *Matlab* [4]. *RailScan* corrugation signal analysis includes: 1. Time-scale representation with user selected wavelets; 2. Base-line removal; 3. Mouse driven feature selection in the Time-Scale plan; 4. Wavelet-Packet implementation that results in power spectrum in the corrugation wavelengths, rail corrugation localization in the rail and its signal recovering in selected wavelet nodes; 5 .One Third Octave Filter (OTOF) power representations.

2 Contribution to Technological Innovation

Wavelet analysis is herein used as a tool for the analysis on the vibration signals due to the rail corrugation, following a new trend [1] in this research area. Wavelet analysis has been proved to be more adequate for the processing of non-stationary signals, such as these, for which the classical Fourier analysis presents limited results. However, the application of this tool lacks standardization procedures and overall validation. This work is a contribution for that goal, also being a preparation for the implementation of a version of the EN ISO 3095 with wavelets.

3 Methods

RailScan uses *the Continuous Wavelet Transform* (CWT) and the *Wavelet Packet Transform*, to analyze the axle-box accelerometer data. These methods will be described in this section. It should be emphasized that the CWT is used in the *RailScan* interface with a mouse driven selection tool to analyze user elected signal details, which is not represented were for lack of space.

A. *Continuous Wavelet Transform*
The Continuous Wavelet Transform is used in this work to perform time-scale analysis of corrugation signals. This is done multiplying a signal $x(t)$ by scaled and translated versions of $\psi(\tau)$ the mother wavelet:

$$CWT_x^{\psi}(\tau,s) = \frac{1}{\sqrt{|s|}} \int x(t)\psi^*\left(\frac{t-\tau}{s}\right)dt . \tag{1}$$

CWT is a function of two variables, the scale s and position τ which is related with the localization of the Wavelet, as the wavelet is shifted through the signal. The scale parameter can be seen as a scale in a map, larger scale show global views and smaller scales show detailed information of a hidden pattern in a signal [5]. A time-scale signal representation is obtained where features are exposed and localized both in time and in the frequency, since scale can be converted to frequency. *RailScan* interface allows for the user to mouse select features in the time-scale plan and then automatically to synthesize the underling signal using *Wavelet Packets*, within the selected frequency boundaries. The synthesized signal may be the corrugation component which has been recovered from the whole signal, for analysis purposes. In this work it was found that the application of the complex Morlet wavelet gives better results for the real corrugation tested signals.

B. Wavelet Packets

The CWT is generally a representation with a high degree of redundancy that doesn't allow for signal reconstruction, but permits time-scale signal representations with a user defined frequency resolution. However, the Discrete Wavelet Transform (DWT) allows for multiresolution signal reconstruction, although its time-scale representation being defined for consecutive frequencies that are a power of two related, in consecutive levels. This constraint may be avoided if the Wavelet Packet Transform (WPT) is used. The general representation of the wavelet tree of a second order, three levels Wavelet Packet tree is shown in Figure 1. The filters sequence has been altered in order to give the last tree nodes (the tree *leaves*) a frequencial order. The last line numbers sequence represents the nodes natural order. A_1 stands for signal approximation in level 1 due to the Low Pass (LP) filtering, and D_1 stands for signal detail in level 1 due to the High Pass (HP) filtering level 1. Likewise DA_2, for instance stands for the detail of approximation signal A_1. For the other nodes the same rule is applied.

The *leaves* frequency nodes progress linearly between zero and the Nyquist frequency, a feature that makes the Wavelet Packet transform a desirable tool in this application. The frequency resolution may be increased, and is limited by the signal length. Of course time resolution decreases in the leave's nodes, as frequency resolution increases.

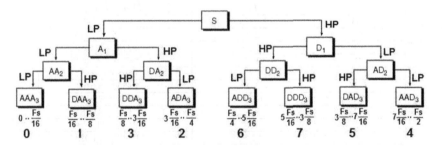

Fig. 1. Wavelet tree with level 3 decomposition (in the frequencial order)

A scheme was used with 64 leaves which cover the corrugation wavelength band with enough resolution. For this a six level WPT is implemented with a precision of 3.9 Hz. Applying expression (7) with $v=1m/s$ the wavelength scale is obtained as shown in Fig. 3 (horizontal axis). The *Daubechies D10* wavelet was used [5].

C. One Third Octave Filter (OTOF)

The European Standard EN ISO 3095 [2] was followed in this work, regarding the indirect measurement of the corrugation level. This chapter includes the case of the data being acquired with an axle-box accelerometer. Accordingly, the OTOF is used to identify the frequencies contents of the vibration due to corrugation, in a predefined scale [2] shown in the first column of Table 1. This procedure will allow for result comparison between the classical OTOF spectra and the one derived from Wavelet Packets application.

A series of band-pass filters for each central frequency (f_c) are defined, for each the lower cutoff frequency (f_{lcut}) and higher cutoff frequency (f_{hcut}) is give by the expressions:

$$f_{lcut} = \frac{1}{10^{\frac{1}{20}} \cdot f_c}.$$

(5)

$$f_{hcut}t = 10^{\frac{1}{20}} \cdot f_c.$$

(6)

$$f = \frac{v}{\lambda}.$$

(7)

Using expression (7) the pre-defined ISO wavelengths (for $v=1$ m/s) were converted to frequencies. Third order Butterworth filters are defined as in [6]. Table 1 contains the OTOF bands for the 23 steps according to [6].

Table 1. One third octave band structure

Wavelength (m) λ	Central frequency (Hz) f_c	One third octave band (Hz) f_{lcut} - f_{hcut}
0.63	1.5873	1.4147 - 1.7810
0.5	2.0	1.7825 - 2.2440
0.4	2.5	2.2281 - 2.8050
0.315	3.1746	2.8294 - 3.5620
0.25	4.0	3.5650 - 4.4881
0.2	5.0	4.4563 - 5.6101
0.16	6.25	5.5703 - 7.0126
0.125	8.0	7.1300 - 8.9761
0.1	10.0	8.9125 - 11.2202
0.08	12.5	11.1406 - 14.0252
0.063	15.8730	14.1468 - 17.8098
0.05	20.0	17.8250 - 22.4404
0.04	25.0	22.2813 - 28.0505
0.0315	31.7460	28.2937 - 35.6196
0.025	40.0	35.6500 - 44.8807
0.02	50.0	44.5625 - 56.1009
0.016	62.5	55.7032 - 70.1262
0.00125	80.0	71.3001 - 89.7615
0.001	100.0	89.1251 - 112.2018
0.008	125.0	111.4064 - 140.2523
0.0063	158.7302	141.4684 - 178.0982
0.005	200.0	178.2502 - 224.4037
0.004	250.0	222.8127 - 280.5046
0.00315	317.4603	282.9368 - 356.1963

For frequencies close to zero or the Nyquist value an interpolation factor is applied to the data to improve filter stability. For each band the resulting filtered signal power is obtained to be compared with the pre-defined ISO power values [2]. Following the

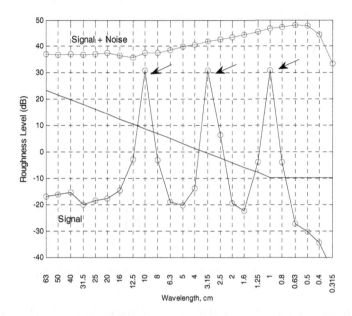

Fig. 2. Power Spectrum of the Roughness Level, 1/3 Octave Power Spectrum for simulated signal and simulated sinal added to noise

mentioned ISO rule the rail roughness limit spectrum is represented in Fig. 2 by the solid line.

D. Pre Processing

For the wavelet processing, the higher wavelength band extends to infinity. Since the corrugation signal may contain higher energetic long wavelengths components that would result in power peaks, which would hide the power in the interest bands, a base line removal step is required. Having in account that the higher *ISO* wavelength value is *0.63 m* and the long wavelength corrugation extends to *1.00 m* [1], the data is filtered with a *wavelet packet* filter to remove signal components with wavelengths higher than *1.00 m.*

The *wavelet packet* filter was implemented using the reconstruction of the signal associated to the few base-line nodes and then subtracting this residue from the original corrugation signal. Since only a few nodes are involved, the resulting algorithm is rather fast. Moreover, the *wavelet packet* frequency structure allows for a flexible selection of the cutoff frequency value.

4   Application to a Simulated Signal

A simulated corrugation signal with three sinusoids corresponding to a *1000 m* rail section, with sampling frequency of *500 Hz* at an average speed of *1 m/s* is obtained:

$$y(n) = A\left[sen(2\pi f_1 n_1) + sen(2\pi f_2 n_2) + sen(2\pi f_3 n_3)\right] \times N \qquad (5)$$

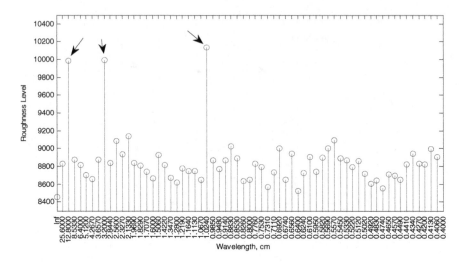

Fig. 3. Power Spectrum of the Roughness Level, Wavelet Packet Spectrum for signal + noise

With f_1 corresponding to 10 Hz (λ=10cm), f_2 corresponding to 33.33 Hz (λ=3cm) and f_3 corresponding to 100 Hz (λ=1cm), $n_1 \in [1,125000]$, $n_2 \in [187500,312500]$, $n_3 \in [375000,500001]$ and $A=100 \ \mu m$ being the corrugation amplitude value. A random noise N with zero mean and standard deviation of $150 \ \mu m$ is added. Fig. 2 shows that the noise added signal in the *OTOF* power spectrum no longer shows the signal components (arrow marked) whereas in fig. 3 plot (*WPT*) the peaks are clearly detected (arrow marked).

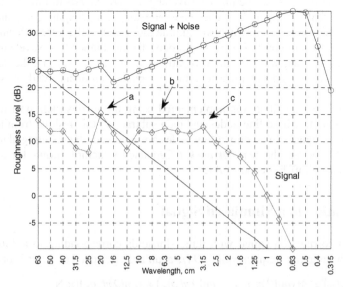

Fig. 4. Power Spectrum of the Roughness Level, 1/3 Octave Power Spectrum

5 Application to a Corrugation Signal

Fig. 4 shows the *OTOF* power spectrum of a real corrugation signal and the spectrum of the same signal added to a simulated noise of standard deviation of *135 μm*. The noisy signal spectrum no longer detects the relevant components *b* and *c*. However the WPT plot, in Fig. 5, detects components *b* and *c,* with component *a* clearer defined. This shows the superior detection ability of the WPT algorithm.

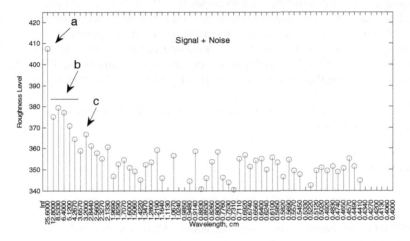

Fig. 5. Power Spectrum of the Roughness Level, Wavelet Packet Spectrum for signal + noise

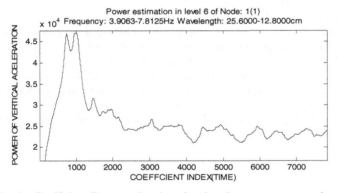

Fig. 6. Wavelet Coefficient Power estimation showing that excess corrugation in the wavelength *25.6-12.8 cm* band exists, in the rail track between *61 and 157 m,* see text

6 Corrugation Spatial Localization

One of the advantages of the Wavelet Transform is the ability of the time localization along with the frequency (scale) description. This feature is used in the *WPT* to locate in the rail, the places where corrugation in a particular wavelength occurs [7], an information important for railway companies that will then perform some type of remediation procedures [8]. Fig. 6 shows that corrugation power in the wave-length band *25.6-12.8 cm* is higher between wavelet coefficients 481 and 1226 which corresponds to the rail track between 61 and 157 m.

7 Conclusions and Further Developments

Wavelet analysis has produced promising results both for simulated data and corrugation detection for accelerometer signals acquired in the axle-box of a railway vehicle. Wavelets outperform the classical *OTOF* method for signals contaminated with high levels of noise. This feature seems important in the development of portable in-vehicle corrugation detectors as well as improved accelerometer data analysis. For future work it is planned to represent wavelet analysis results in the *EN ISO 3095* representation, as well as address issues of standardization and referencing.

Acknowledgements. The collaboration of Dr. Stuart Grassie of Railmeasurement in this work is acknowledge.

References

1. Grassie, S.L.: Measurement of railhead longitudinal profiles: a comparison between different techniques. Wear 191, 245–251 (1996)
2. prEN ISO 3095: Railway applications – Acoustics – Measurements of noise emitted by railbound vehicles
3. Verheijen, E.: E, A survey on roughness measurements. Journal of Sound and Vibration 293, 784–794 (2006)
4. Matworks Inc., Natick, MA 01760-2098
5. Daubechies, I.: Ten Lectures on Wavelets, Society for Industrial and Applied Mathematics
6. ANSI/ASA S1.11-1986(R1998) American National Standard Specifications for Octave-Band and Fractional-Octave-Band Analog and Digital Filters
7. Caprioli, A., Cigada, A., Raveglia, D.: Rail inspection in track maintenance: a benchmark between the wavelet approach and the more conventional Fourier analysis. Mechanical System and Signal Processing 21, 631–652 (2007)
8. Grassie, S.L.: Rail Corrugation: advances in measurement, understanding and treatment. Wear 258, 1224–1234 (2005)

Active System for Electromagnetic Perturbation Monitoring in Vehicles

Adrian Marian Matoi and Elena Helerea

Transilvania University of Brasov, Eroilor Bvd. 29, 500036 Brasov, Romania
matoi@unitbv.ro, helerea@unitbv.ro

Abstract. Nowadays electromagnetic environment is rapidly expanding in frequency domain and wireless services extend in terms of covered area. European electromagnetic compatibility regulations refer to limit values regarding emissions, as well as procedures for determining susceptibility of the vehicle. Approval procedure for a series of cars is based on determining emissions/immunity level for a few vehicles picked randomly from the entire series, supposing that entire vehicle series is compliant. During immunity assessment, the vehicle is not subjected to real perturbation sources, but exposed to electric/magnetic fields generated by laboratory equipment. Since current approach takes into account only partially real situation regarding perturbation sources, this paper proposes an active system for determining electromagnetic parameters of vehicle's environment, that implements a logical diagram for measurement, satisfying the imposed requirements. This new and original solution is useful for EMC assessment of hybrid and electrical vehicles.

Keywords: Electromagnetic environment, electromagnetic emissions, European legislation, automotive safety, active measurement system.

1 Introduction

Modern vehicles are based on a large number of command and control systems, data acquisition and processing units. Output data from certain systems represent input data for others. Based on data received from sensors, actuators control input/output parameters for different systems, directly or through feedback loops [1]. According to the controlled system, sensors and actuators can be considered critical elements for vehicle functioning. Due to the complexity and number of sensors/actuators, processing and command units, electromagnetic compatibility (EMC) problems have diversified in two directions:

- Signal integrity and implicitly, the integrity of data transmitted between units is affected by perturbation sources situated in their electromagnetic environment;
- Besides existing electromagnetic noise, vehicles raise the perturbation level of the electromagnetic environment.

Nowadays EMC testing methods for vehicles imply basically measuring emissions level and applying an electromagnetic field on the vehicle to check its immunity, in an anechoic chamber or free space [2]. The development and testing of safety-related and

L.M. Camarinha-Matos, P. Pereira, and L. Ribeiro (Eds.): DoCEIS 2010, IFIP AICT 314, pp. 409–416, 2010.

safety critical systems has received considerable attention from the technical, academic and standards-making safety community in recent years, since safety methodology and its development in other standards show a lack in understanding the correct way to deal with this issue [3].

Current paper presents the concept of a real time emissions measurement system designed to be mounted in vehicles. The proposed system is described and experimental determinations under different conditions are performed.

2   Contribution to Technological Innovation

Technological innovation is the key factor for the development of a knowledge based society. Nowadays requirements related to a proper functioning of vehicles impose the development of innovative techniques and systems for automotive EMC assessment.

The paper contributes to technological innovation through the design and implementation of a new active system for electromagnetic perturbation monitoring in vehicles. This system is capable to measure the parameters of electromagnetic environment from the vehicle, automatic adjust measurement system's parameters and warn the driver in case of EMC limit overpass, increasing therefore the functional safety of the vehicle.

3   EMC Automotive Testing Methods Analysis

The increase of electric and electronic devices involved in technical domains, including automotive, has led to the development of a large number of EMC testing methods [2], [3], [4], [5], [6]. The requirements for engine vehicles regarding EMC are stated in 2004/104/EC EU directive, covering both emissions and immunity, for vehicles produced/traded in EU. The requirements refer both to radiated and conducted perturbation.

Electric and electronic systems functioning at frequencies higher than 30 MHz (or whose harmonics are higher than 30 MHz) are considered possible radiation sources. In the far field region, electromagnetic field can be characterized either by electric field strength or by magnetic field strength that are coupled by medium's wave impedance [7]. Since electric field strength measurement is more precise in high frequency domain and magnetic field strength can be determined from wave's impedance formula, electromagnetic field is characterized by electric field strength. Due to the large number of electronic components functioning at high frequencies, in the following are analyzed the requirements regarding radiated emissions of vehicles and electronic subassemblies (ESA).

3.1   Emissions

In order to determine emissions radiated by ESAs, a series of settings have to be performed. Recommended environment is an anechoic chamber or an open space, 'quiet' from electromagnetic point of view [2]. In order to obtain conclusive results, an offset in amount of 6 dB is defined between noise level and limit line for the measured device. Resolution bandwidth of the spectrum analyzer is 120 kHz, for the entire frequency domain: 30 MHz-1 GHz.

For narrowband perturbation measurement, an average detector is utilized. The distance between measurement antenna and ESA is 3 m.

In comparison to ESAs, the emissions from vehicles are measured at a distance of 10 m, utilizing a 'quasi-peak' detector for broadband emissions and an average detector for narrowband emissions. Limit lines for both broadband and narrowband emissions from vehicles are presented in Fig. 1.

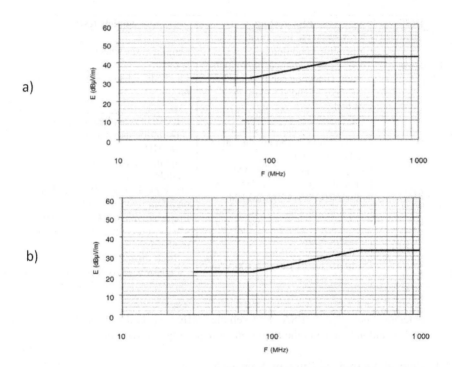

Fig. 1. Electromagnetic emission limit lines for vehicles according to 2004/104/EC directive: a) broadband; b) narrowband [2]

The module of electric field strength in frequency domain 75 – 400 MHz:

$$E = 32 + 15,13 \log(F/75) \tag{1}$$

in the case of broadband emissions and:

$$E = 22 + 15,13 \log(F/75) \tag{2}$$

in the case of narrowband emissions, where: E – electric field strength module [dB$_{mV/m}$], F – frequency [MHz]. Broadband signal is considered the signal whose frequency bandwidth is larger than bandwidth of the measurement device [7]. The limit line for narrowband emissions is more restrictive than the one for broadband emissions.

3.2 Immunity

Testing methods for immunity of vehicles and their ESAs are also specified in the directive. It consists of exposing the vehicle and its separate ESAs to electromagnetic fields and verifying their functionality during exposure. Device under test (DUT) state and testing conditions for both vehicle and ESAs are specified in Table 1.

Table 1. Testing conditions for automotive ESAs and vehicles according to 2004/104/EC directive

DUT	ESA testing	Vehicle testing
1. State of DUT	- switched on, in normal operating conditions - if the ESA contains more units, interconnection cables should be the ones intended for use in vehicle	- engine turns wheels at a 50 km/h speed - all EMC related equipment turned on
2. Testing conditions	- the field is applied using the substitution method in the range 20 – 2000 MHz - applied signal is: 80%AM modulation, 1 kHz in frequency range 20 - 800 MHz and PM modulation, t on 577ms, period 4600 ms in frequency range 800 – 2000 MHz - dwell time: 250 ms - highest severity level 100 V/m	- the field is applied using the substitution method in the range 20 – 2000 MHz - applied signal is: 80%AM modulation, 1 kHz in frequency range 20 - 800 MHz and PM modulation, t on 577ms, period 4600 ms in frequency range 800 – 2000 MHz - only vertical polarization testing is required - dwell time: 250 ms - highest severity level 100 V/m

The testing methods for ESAs and vehicles differ especially through distance between DUT and antenna and the requirement regarding polarization of the test field.

3.3 Critical Analysis of Current Approach

Although EMC testing technique has advanced, there are still some aspects that have to be taken into account for EMC assessment:

- From an entire vehicle series produced, only a couple are EMC tested;
- Tests are performed in a laboratory or "quiet" free space, where perturbation sources are artificially simulated;
- Electromagnetic environment is rapidly evolving regarding number and type of perturbation sources [8];
- Mobility of sources is not taken into account, far field and near field conditions not being therefore considered.

EMC achievement method for vehicles could be improved by installing an EMC monitoring system on each vehicle capable to:

- Measure and process parameters of electromagnetic environment;
- Adjust system's measuring parameters actively;
- Warn the driver in case of detecting powerful perturbation sources, capable to affect vehicle's functionality;
- Interact with communication and control systems of the vehicle, in order to increase the safety level when necessary.

4 Active System for EMC Monitoring of Vehicle's Environment

4.1 The System Concept

The concept has been developed to overpass existing limitations. Logical diagram of the system is presented in Fig. 2.

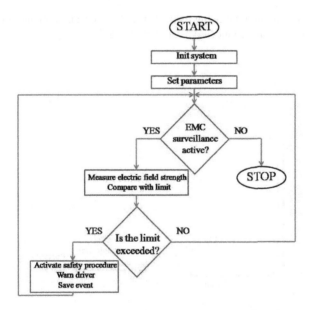

Fig. 2. Active electromagnetic emission measurement system logical diagram

The measurement system has the following functions:

- To initiate the software platform, allowing to measure and process data related to electromagnetic field parameters;
- Set the parameters of devices, like: type of measurement, frequency domain, resolution bandwidth, threshold, limit line and so on;
- Check if EMC surveillance is activated by the command computer or the driver;
- Perform field measurement and compare it to the pre-established limit line;
- In case the limit is exceeded, the system activates a safety procedure through the command computer of the vehicle, warns the driver and saves data like position of

the vehicle (supposing that the vehicle has a GPS system), time and values that exceed the limit line.

A good functioning of the system implies a bidirectional connection between the EMC surveillance system and command computer of the vehicle that can be achieved, for example, by means of a bus system or a modern interface like USB. The major advantage of this implementation is the flexibility concerning measurement parameters, interconnectivity, upgrades and implementation of future standards regarding EMC requirements. The safety of passengers and other participants to the traffic is increased considerably both by warning the driver in case of unexpected high field strength and activating safety procedures like: increasing voltage on communication bus lines, activating a supplementary communication system for safety related devices of the vehicle (steering, braking, engine control).

4.2 Implementation of the System

The concept has been implemented using a spectrum analyzer, antenna and a portable computer. The components are connected as shown in Fig. 3.

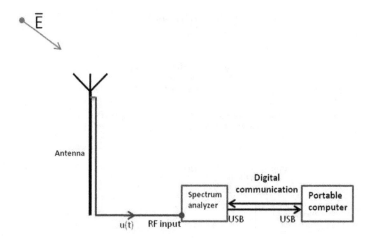

Fig. 3. Components connection diagram

The components of the system are:

- AAronia Spectran HF 6080 spectrum analyzer having the following characteristics: frequency domain: 10 MHz- 8 GHz; Resolution bandwidth: 1 kHz – 50 MHz; Input signal range: -160 dBm – +10 dBm; Accuracy: +/- 2 dB; Portable (battery), USB connection port.
- AAronia Hyperlog 7060 electric field measurement antenna having the following parameters: Directional; Factory calibration frequency range: 700 MHz - 6 GHz; Gain: typically 5 dBi; Antenna factor: 26 – 41dB/m.
- HP Compaq 6710b portable computer running the measurement software.

5   Experimental Determinations

Measurements have been performed in order to determine whether the system is able to detect in real time perturbation sources, while the vehicle is running. The system has been mounted in an ALFA Romeo 156 vehicle. The antenna has been placed on the top of the vehicle/ inside the passenger's compartment. The measurement software has been started and measurements have been performed while the vehicle was driven inside and outside Brasov city. Measurement system's parameters were: Frequency domain: 80 MHz – 8 GHz; Resolution bandwidth: 1 MHz, due to the wide frequency domain; Scanning time: 50 ms; Peak detector.

In Fig. 4 is shown one of the performed measurements, when the antenna was placed inside passenger's compartment.

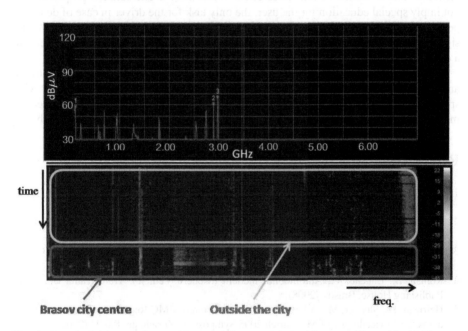

Fig. 4. Electric field strength surveillance while a vehicle is driven outside and inside Brasov city

The experimental determinations show that the number of electromagnetic field sources is larger inside Brasov city in comparison to its surroundings. Highly populated areas have the following characteristics from electromagnetic environment's point of view: available communication services are various and numerous (and offer broadband services), radio and TV antennas are situated in the vicinity and the number of mobile perturbation sources (cellular phones, vehicles) is higher.

6 Conclusions

The evolution of electromagnetic environment imposes an active method for monitoring its parameters and adjusting the running conditions of the vehicles, in order to increase passengers and traffic safety.

The developed active system for electromagnetic perturbation monitoring is capable to measure and process data related to vehicle's electromagnetic environment in real time, increasing therefore the safety of vehicle's functioning. Unpredicted perturbation sources are detected and data regarding their parameters would be available in case the pre-established limit lines are exceeded.

Although the prices of EMC equipment have been high until recently, modern technology will allow a good integration cost - low cost spectrum analyzers are already available on the market - taking into consideration the advance of EMC measurement technique and reduction of integrated circuits dimensions. The solution proposed does not imply special education for the user, the only task for the driver in case of detecting perturbing fields being to stop the vehicle (the user can be warned by a visual/audio signal). The system is capable to automatically save data about events and transfer it to a computer when the periodical service is attended.

Performance can be increased by including in the measurement system an isotropic antenna and a parallel processing spectrum analyzer. The development of a wide spread EMC measurement system will allow a better characterization of the electromagnetic environment. Position of the measurement antenna remains an open subject.

References

1. Ribbens, W.B.: Understanding Automotive Electronics, 6th edn. Newnes Publishing House, USA (2003)
2. European Union Commission: Commission directive 2004/104/EC, Official Journal of the European Union (2004)
3. Armstrong, K.: Review of Progress with EMC-Related Functional Safety. In: 2003 IEEE Symposium on EMC proceedings (2003)
4. Roman, B., Enache, V.: Automobilul modern (Modern Vehicle). Transilvania University Publishing House, Brasov (2008)
5. Heirman, D., Stecher, M.: A History of the Evolution of EMC Regulatory Bodies and Standards. In: Proceedings of EMC Zurich 2005 Symposium, Zurich, pp. 83–94 (2005)
6. O'Hara, M.: A generic automotive (TIER1) EMC Test Standard, In: Proceedings of Automotive EMC 2006 Driving the New Directive Conference, Birmingham (2006)
7. Williams, T.: EMC for Product Designers, 4th edn. Newness Publishing House, Cornwall (2007)
8. Costea, M.: Methods and Proceedures for Assurance of EM Imunity/Metode şi Mijloace de Asigurare a Imunităţii Electromagnetice/. AGIR Publishing House, Bucharest (2006)

Part 14

Advances in Energy Systems

Energy Consumption Monitoring System for Large Complexes

André Jorge, João Guerreiro, Pedro Pereira, João Martins, and Luís Gomes

UNINOVA – CTS
Universidade Nova de Lisboa - Faculdade de Ciências e Tecnologia
Monte da Caparica, Portugal
andrejorge77@gmail.com, joaocaguerreiro@gmail.com,
{pmrp,jf.martins}@fct.unl.pt, lugo@uninova.pt

Abstract. This paper describes the development of an open source system for monitoring and data acquisition of several energy analyzers. The developed system is based on a computer with Internet/Intranet connection by means of RS485 using Modbus RTU as communication protocol. The monitoring/metering system was developed for large building complexes and was validated in the Faculdade de Ciências e Tecnologia University campus. The system considers two distinct applications. The first one allows the user to verify, in real time, the energy consumption of any department in the complex, produce load diagrams, tables and print, email or save all available data. The second application keeps records of active/reactive energy consumption in order to verify the existence of some anomalous situation, and also monthly charge energy consumption to each corresponding department.

Keywords: Power Meter, Power Analyzer, Energy Efficient Buildings, Modbus Protocol.

1 Introduction

Environmental conservation has become a very important issue. The use of renewable energies has experienced a significant growth from the crisis of the oil in the 70's, in which renewable forms of energy started to be considered as a potentially alternative to the oil producing finite resources of the Earth [1]. Recent European Community Directives point to an energy consumption reduction, leading to an annual improvement in energy efficiency of around 6 per cent in 2012. Strict regulations, regarding power consumption and energy efficiency, have been set to preserve the environment. To fulfill energy conservation goals, it will be helpful if consumers could assess their energy load diagram so that they can plan/re-plan their energy consumption profile. Unstable global energy supplies, increasing load demands and increasing environment concerns are forcing energy producers and consumers to re-evaluate the energy usage paradigm. An energy monitoring system is an essential tool to help consumers understanding their energy usage profile and the associated environment impact and

L.M. Camarinha-Matos, P. Pereira, and L. Ribeiro (Eds.): DoCEIS 2010, IFIP AICT 314, pp. 419–426, 2010.
© IFIP International Federation for Information Processing 2010

providing an instrument to re-shape their energy load diagram and, consequently, reduce its inherent costs. The developed system helps and instructs people to use their energy in a better way.

The efficient use of energy has direct consequences for the users, such as consumption and inherent costs reduction. Several strategies can be taken to fulfill these objectives: load shifting, automatic load control, energy storage, autonomous generation, and renewable energy usage. Nevertheless, in order to implement any of those strategies it is fundamental to accurately know the load diagram and load profile of each user. There are some commercial tools that can be used to monitor energy consumption and perform power management analysis, however when large complexes, with hundreds of metering points, are considered they become extremely expensive. In [2], Yeardy et al. present another tool for power consumption measurement, showing some results.

The main purpose of the present work is the development of a open source distributed metering system, with an innovative user interface and communication tool, that allows the analysis and study of energy load profile, applied to large complexes. The system was successfully installed in the campus of the Faculty of Science and Technology (Universidade Nova de Lisboa), Portugal. The campus comprises several buildings' departments occupying a total area of 30ha. The development system proposes a method to circumvent the limitations placed by the Modbus protocol [3][4] (as the typical series communication structure, improving the transmission rate), acquire energy consumption data, produce load diagrams for each user in the complex facility (allowing users to evaluate potential interventions in order to reduce consumption and minimize waste and load peaks), calculate the energy consumption costs associated with each department, maintain monthly costs accounting records, and provide detailed information on the validity of best rates solutions. The development of the system was based on three phases:

1. Development of the network communication tools;
2. Development of the real time analyses software package;
3. Development of the energy recording, taxing and analysis software package;

The last package is essential for organizing the energy cost distribution between all campus' departments, and help each one of them establishing solutions that should be adopted in order to solve the problem of excessive energy consumption [5].

2   Contribution to Technological Innovation

Current energy consumption is based on conventional data logging systems, which involves two major problems; (i) is the fact that retrieving the energy consumption data is not conventional, (ii) the cost of energy consumption monitoring systems is high. Smart-meters offers a possible solution, however they are often proprietary equipment with dedicated protocols. The solution presented here is an open-source energy monitoring system that skirts the above barriers by also being cheap and robust.

3 Modbus Protocol

Modbus is an open protocol used in Industrial Automation Systems (IAS) as well as in Building Management Systems (BMS). The Modbus protocol was created in 1979 by Modicon, a company of Schneider Electric Group. In 2004 this group decided to offer Modbus as a public protocol and by that reason, the Modbus-IDA community appeared [6]. Since 1979 Modbus protocol rapidly became an industrial standard and has been implemented by hundreds of manufacturers in various applications and industrial segments. Its popularity has increased due to its simplicity of implementation and availability of free source code in the Internet. Modbus is an application-layer messaging protocol, positioned at level 7 of the OSI model and provides client/server communication between devices connected on different types of buses or networks.

The devices connected to a Modbus network interact through a master-slave scheme where only the master can start the conversation and the slave responds by sending the information requested by the master or performing the task set for him.

Serial Modbus connections can use two basic transmission modes, namely ASCII (American Standard Code for Information Interchange) or RTU (remote terminal unit). The transmission mode in serial communications defines the way the Modbus messages are encoded. Using Modbus/ASCII, the messages use plain ASCII format, while when using Modbus/RTU format a compressed format is used. This binary encoding makes the message unreadable by humans when monitoring, but have a severe impact in terms of reducing the size of each message, which allows for more data exchange in the same time frame.

4 Network Hardware Description

Fig. 1 presents proposed network topology, composed by the following main devices:

- PD8 (RS-485/Ethernet Converter)
- UPT210 Universal Power Transducer
- CT (50:5 current transformer)

The PD8 (RS-485/Ethernet Converter) converter allows transmitting data from/to master devices through an Ethernet data network, to/from devices equipped with an RS-485 interface. The converter is available in two versions concerning its operation mode: Real-Port network service and serial bridge with UDP protocol. In our particular case, the converter is operating with Real-Port Network service because a computer was needed to log the information provided by the UPT210. The converter used in this mode enables to co-operate only with one master computer at a time. In this case, for using a PD8 converter to serve Modbus protocol, a PC is needed to control break time intervals between received transmission characters.

UPT210 Universal Power Transducer is a digital meter able to measure the electrical parameters on three-phase systems. It provides accurate measurements even by distorted waveform. An LCD display provides the three-phase quantities. The working parameters can be easily set up by instrument keypad. UPT210 is a compact, cost effective meter operating both as a stand-alone device and as an integral part of a more extensive energy monitoring and management network. It replaces multiple analogue meters as well as single function meters such as voltmeters, ammeters, wattmeters, varmeters, frequency-meters, power factor-meters, energy-meters, etc.

The current transformer (CT) is used for measurement of electric currents. When current in a circuit is too high to directly apply to measuring instruments, a current transformer produces a reduced current accurately proportional to the current in the circuit (in this case, 50:5 CT), which can be conveniently connected to measuring and recording instruments. The current transformer also isolates the measuring instruments from what may be very high voltage in the primary circuit.

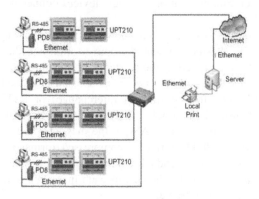

Fig. 1. Network topology

5   Network Implementation Details

In this section, we will step through each part of the network implementation, which is broken down in two main areas: Master implementation and Slave implementation.

The first one, Master implementation, is composed by a computer running a monitor program, having as main tasks to control break time intervals between received and transmitted message, gather information from all the transducers and analyze the collected data.

Using a computer as the system brain, allows to employ meters without local memory, which are cheaper compared with those with it, and from a single place can collect all the data, making unnecessary any human resources to do this job.

The second area, concerns all the physical devices in the neighbourhood of the place where power consumption is going to be measured. This includes several power transducers and a PD8 converter which allows the communication between the local network or internet and the devices equipped with RS-485 interface.

The system can be implemented either in a local network or using internet for remote access, as shown in Fig. 2. In this work, the system was tested in a local network.

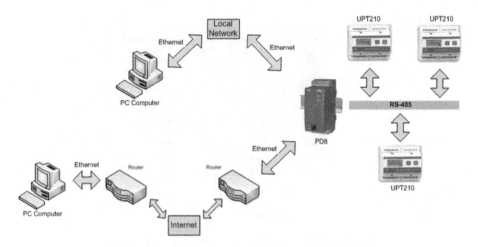

Fig. 2. System configuration using a local network or internet

5 Monitoring Software

The proposed monitoring software consists of two distinct applications:

- Real-time analysis
- Collect and record data

5.1 Real-Time Analysis Application

The developed software has the aim to make real-time analysis of all the parameters that characterize the electric network, such as voltage, current, power, active and reactive energy. The measured values can be used to build graphics load for later analysis of energy consumption in a given period of time, stored in a file, the functionality is also available in print, or simply sending the data to the mail of the person responsible for examine any issue that may exist for example.

This package can only make a connection to a single analyzer simultaneously due to the protocol limitations, which requires the reservation of a communication port on the computer for each device. On must note that this feature makes sense, because only then one can perform real-time analysis. If not the time of the n-scan counters implemented in line would suffer from such a delay that would be relevant to the energy analysis performed by this package. Fig. 3 gives an overview of the application, where a screen shot of the system acquisition is shown.

5.2 Collect and Record Data Application

The second application has the goal of recording all the values of active and reactive power and/or energy of each analyzer, which could be connected to the Internet or connected to a local network. In the first case, a single server is capable to collect all the data from n analyzers (UPT210) connected to m converters (PD8). A sampling

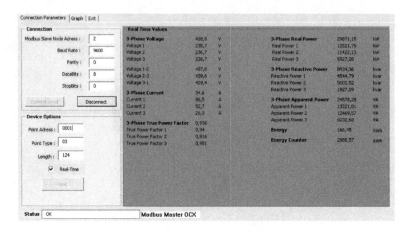

Fig. 3. Snapshot of the Real-Time implemented program

time of 10 msec per analyzer was considered. In the second case, each local network, if there is more than one, needs a server. The application collects and records the values of energy of each analyzer considering 24 hours intervals.

If there's the need to produce a energy bill for each department associated with a specific analyzer, the server has full knowledge of what the devices contained in each network in order to be made a comparison of consumption not only from month to month but between equipments. In this perspective, it can easily detect undesired events as wasteful consumption of energy or leakage. This package has the ability to adjust the energy consumption to the rates imposed by the energy supplier. In the Portuguese case, automatic adjust to the four periods of the year as well to the different daily periods.

The previous rules were employed because, in this particular project, the system was implemented in our Institution, which is supplied by a 15 kV medium voltage power system.

6   Energy Consumption Analysis in Large Complexes

This developed software package reports the consumption of a number of unlimited measurement points located in one or several complexes. Allows measuring the real costs incurred in the various sectors, departments, or even in critical equipments, with immediate benefits to users:

- Increase the transparency of energy taxation increasing the knowledge within the cost of their activities;
- Adjust the tariff policy and decide further investments in new equipment.

The user gains a powerful tool that allows benchmarking to compare the consumption of installations, equipment with other similar services, forcing those responsible for each department or sector to eliminate the observed deviations, leading to an efficient energy usage.

This software package enables record viewing in a graphic and/or table format. It contains tools that easily allow the identification of particular power contributions and its peak value, contributions to the overall consumption of energy, and the causes of energy consumption over periods of several hours of charging.

The feature Real-Time Monitoring has some advantages that should be taken into consideration. The energy service provider usually performs monthly readings of the consumed energy or simply esteems it if the installations are small (and only charge back about 15 days later). It can run more than 6 weeks until the client is aware of its consumption and detect any abnormal behavior. To efficiently manage energy resources is important to have the knowledge of the consumption evolution in a daily and weekly basis. This is easily achieved with the developed system.

For large complexes, with several power meters, the traditional manual solution has a high cost because it requires staff to make the "journey" from meter to meter, recording the readings and entering them into a computer application for analysis. The developed system does it automatically, without the need of human intervention and with lower expenses. Fig. 4 presents the evolution of the active power for two days of consumption in the Electrical Engineering Department.

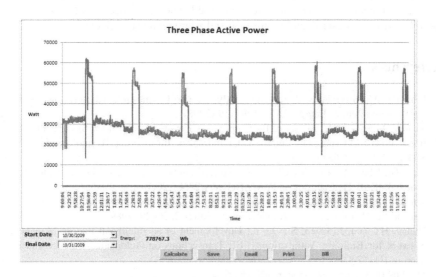

Fig. 4. Evolution of the average power

The developed software package easily adds data referring to multiple points of energy consumption. This feature makes possible to dynamically manage the consumption of a department or even a single activity, even when spread over multiple locations or buildings. The subsequent analysis of the amounts charged will help the user to optimize the consumption and pricing profile, thereby reducing the value of the energy invoice.

7 Conclusions

This paper presented an energy monitoring low cost system suitable to use in large complexes, with several departments/buildings far apart. Several commercial tools are available but they become extremely expensive for large complexes with a huge amount of metering points.

The great advantage of the developed system is the use of the Modbus RTU protocol, considering the physical implementation done through Ethernet, which enables the implementation of this system in large complexes, bypassing the need to establish cabling in the whole complex area, which was practically impossible in the considered implementation.

The industrial implementation of these systems usually has the configuration RS-232 to RS-485 network, stating the need of a computer in each network implemented. In this case several networks need just one computer to monitor all meters in all departments. The system also includes an analyses software package, which is very useful for energy consumption monitoring and suitable for establishing energy management policies.

The system is accessible to every industrial or commercial facility since it uses a reduced cost platform. To accomplish that, a RS-485/Ethernet converter, power meters and a standard personal computer were used. The developed monitoring system is flexible, presents a user friendly interface and a large data storage capacity.

References

1. Elhadidy, M., Shaahid, S.: Parametric Study of Hybrid (wind+solar+diesel) power generating Systems. Renew. Energy 21(2), 129–139 (2000)
2. Yeardy, M., Sweeney, J., Swan, B., Culp, C.: A Low-Cost Embedded System for Internet Based Power Measurement. International Journal of Information Technology & Decision Making 2(4), 669–681 (2003)
3. Liao, G., Chen, Y., Lu, W., Cheng, T.: Toward Authenticating the Master in the Modbus Protocol. IEEE Transactions on Power Delivery 23(4) (2008)
4. Smith, H., Modzelewski, T.: Enhancing Energy Management Systems with Advanced RTU Capabilities. IEEE Computer Applications in Power 2, 26–29 (1989)
5. Huang, H., Yen, J., Chen, S., Ou, F.: Development of an Intelligent Energy Management Network for Building Automation. IEEE Transactions on Automation Science and Engineering 1(1) (2004)
6. Modbus-IDA, http://www.modbus.org

High Temperature Superconducting Fault Current Limiters as Enabling Technology in Electrical Grids with Increased Distributed Generation Penetration

João Murta Pina[1], Mário Ventim Neves[1], Alfredo Álvarez[2],
and Amadeu Leão Rodrigues[1]

[1] Centre of Technology and Systems,
Faculdade de Ciências e Tecnologia, Nova University of Lisbon
Monte de Caparica, 2829-516 Caparica, Portugal
jmmp@fct.unl.pt, ventim@uninova.pt, leao@uninova.pt
[2] "Benito Mahedero" Group of Electrical Applications of Superconductors,
Escuela de Ingenierías Industriales, University of Extremadura
Avenida de Elvas s/n, 06006 Badajoz, Spain
aalvarez@unex.es

Abstract. Amongst applications of high temperature superconductors, fault current limiters are foreseen as one of the most promising in power systems. Several topologies have been developed in the last years, taking advantage of different superconductors' properties. Increasing distributed generation (DG) penetration, based on renewable energy, adds new short-circuit sources to electrical grids, which brings several energy quality and protection issues. Superconducting fault current limiters can obviate these problems, representing thus an enabling technology for DG penetration. In this paper current limiter topologies are presented, its operations principles, strengths and weaknesses, in the context of these DG grids. In the end, future trends are discussed.

Keywords: Superconducting fault current limiters, distributed generation.

1 Introduction

In the past years, several reasons justified the increasing penetration of dispersed, embedded or distributed generation (DG) in electrical grids. Amongst these highlights common demand on greenhouse emissions reduction by the use of renewable energy sources; energy efficiency and rational energy use; diversification of energy sources [1]; availability, short construction times and cheap small generator plants; and the advantages of placing generators near consumers decreasing transmission costs [2]. Nevertheless these favorable aspects, DG still raises several relevant technical questions [3], [4], as network voltage changes (e.g. in partially loaded grids with high renewable generation); power quality issues (e.g. harmonics due to static converters); and conflicts with network protections. The latter relates with increase in short-circuit current levels and grid switchgears' selectivity issues, amongst others.

Restrictions arising from protections conflicts usually prevent additional DG penetration [5]. Adding new rotating generators (e.g. wind turbines) may increase dramatically

L.M. Camarinha-Matos, P. Pereira, and L. Ribeiro (Eds.): DoCEIS 2010, IFIP AICT 314, pp. 427–434, 2010.
© IFIP International Federation for Information Processing 2010

fault levels, as resulting short-circuit currents consist on phasor sum of original fault currents and new DG generators' fault currents [5]. The latter are not considered when grids protections are originally designed. Simulations found in the literature [3], [6], demonstrate that adding DG generators increases considerably fault levels which can exceed the current interrupting capacity of the existing switchgears.

An obvious solution to the above problem is to upgrade grid switchgears, adapting their rating to the new levels, but this may turn economically unfeasible. Reducing new generators fault contributions may be achieved by introducing impedances (transformers or reactors) between these and the corresponding grid, which increases losses. Explosive fuses may also be used but these must be replaced after a fault. In recent years, new technologies appeared, as solid state fault current limiters [7], which have high semiconductors losses and are costly, or high temperature superconducting fault current limiters (SFCL). The latter are detailed in the paper.

Next section addresses authors' contribution to technological innovation. High temperature superconducting (HTS) materials are introduced and SFCL classified according to its characteristics and operation principle. Resistive and inductive types are explained in later sections. Future trends and conclusions are drawn in the end.

2 Contributions to Technological Innovation

The vision of future electric grids envisages coexistence of distributed and central generation, energy storage and bidirectional energy flow, between grid and consumers/producers. SFCL are a promising technology in such environment, addressing issues as safety or power quality. It is thus relevant to develop analysis tools for their dynamic behavior, and authors built such a straightforward algorithm for one type of those limiters (inductive), based on the individual analysis of device's elements (HTS and iron core) [8]. It builds FCL's hysteresis cycle, allowing simulating grids' currents and correctly dimensioning switchgears or transformers.

3 High Temperature Superconducting Fault Current Limiters

Superconducting materials are natural fault current limiters, often recognized as one of its most promising power application. In superconducting state they carry high current densities (up to 10^4 A/mm^2) with negligible losses. Under a fault, current density increases. The material loses superconductivity and becomes resistive, limiting current. Once fault suppressed, it returns naturally to the superconducting state. This is the principle of the resistive SFCL, detailed in Section 3. These devices use material non linear resistivity in superconducting/normal state transition.

3.1 High Temperature Superconducting Materials

The main macroscopic properties of the first discovered superconducting materials (superconductivity was discovered by the Dutch physicist Kamerlingh Onnes in mercury, in 1911) were the abrupt loss of electrical resistivity under a certain critical temperature and the exclusion of magnetic flux from the material (Meissner effect). For decades, superconductors' highest critical temperature was around 20 K, so they had to be cooled with liquid helium (boiling temperature 4.22 K) in expensive cryogenic systems. The discovery of superconductivity in ceramic copper oxides, as $YBa_2Cu_3O_x$, boosted this temperature to above liquid nitrogen boiling temperature, 77 K, reducing dramatically cryogenics' cost. In these high temperature superconductors, magnetic flux is not completely expelled from material's core, rather penetrates it in quantized amounts known as fluxoids in the so called mixed state. The transition from superconducting to normal state, known as quench, depends on the values of current density, temperature and flux density in the material.

3.2 Classification of Superconducting Fault Current Limiters

SFCL may be classified according to the way they are introduced in the grid, their use of quench, or employment of iron cores, amongst others.

Single-phase SFCLs' classification is presented in Fig. 1. It depends on how the devices are inserted in the grid: in series (resistive), magnetically linked (inductive) or through a rectifier bridge (rectifier). In this paper resistive and inductive topologies are presented. The rectifier SFCL was abandoned due to high voltage failures and high losses on the semiconductor elements used.

Three-phase SFCLs are the most important devices in power applications. They are built by three single-phase modules or using an exclusive three-phase design [9]. Although the latter approach uses less HTS material than three single-phase SFCL modules, a fault in one phase affects the remaining ones and this device is restricted to symmetric loads (e.g. motors). Thus, this approach is not presented in the paper.

4 Resistive Type Fault Current Limiter

The resistive SFCL is represented in Fig. 2. It is built, in its most basic form, by an HTS element in series with the grid, with a shunt resistance, R_s, described later.

4.1 Operation Principle

In normal grid operation, the SFCL has negligible impedance and associated losses, being electrically invisible to the grid [10]. Under a fault, the current exceeds HTS's critical value, leading to quench. HTS's impedance rises abruptly, limiting current.

Reference [11] proposes a simple qualitative explanation for the resistive SFCL behavior under a fault, based on the analysis of the curve that relates electrical field, E, with current density, J, in HTS materials, see Fig. 3 and Fig. 4:

- If HTS length is "high", E is "low" so as J and ohmic losses. The heat produced is dissipated by the cryogenic system and material's temperature remains constant. Although this represents the ideal behavior of the SFCL, the amount of bulk HTS used (up to hundreds of meters [12]) may turn it unfeasible.
- If HTS length is "low", E and J are "high". Thus, the initial current peak may not be sufficiently limited. Losses are "high" and HTS fast heating may not be absorbed by cryogenics, which can lead to material's collapse.
- In a "moderate" length HTS, E, J and losses are also "moderate". In this case there is an HTS slow heating.

The shunt resistance R_s protects HTS material against hot spots formation, i.e. regions that enter normal state, increasing locally their resistivity and temperature and degrading the material. R_s provides an alternative low resistance path for current.

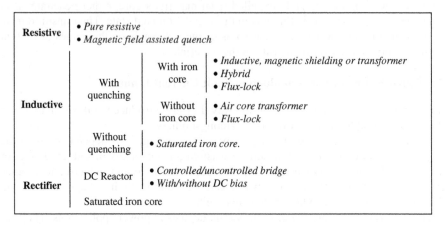

Fig. 1. Classification of single-phase superconducting fault current limiters

4.2 Resistive SFCL Demonstrators

Under the framework of CURL 10 project [13] a three-phase 10 kV/10 MVA was build with superconducting bifilar coils as limiting elements. The system operated in field conditions in RWE company's electric grid in Netphen, Germany, coupling two 10 kV buses. Yet, no fault occurred in that period. This concept evolved to magnetic field assisted quench SFCL, referred in the last section.

A limiter using thin film HTS was successfully tested in a 14 kV single-phase grid [14]. 10 kA prospective current is limited to 445 A in the first peak and previously to less than 140 A. Although operation is demonstrated, thin films' high cost, namely for transmission grids with large number of elements, lead to abandoning this approach.

The New Energy and Industrial Technology Development Organization, NEDO, is developing a resistive limiter based on HTS coated conductors. In a 3.8 kV single-phase grid, a 17 kA prospective current is limited to 700 A [15].

4.3 Conclusions

Resistive SFCL allows fast limiting action, in less than half cycle, since HTS element is in series with the grid. It is also a compact device. Yet, several elements must be series connected in order to achieve desired limiting performance, degrading quench homogeneity which can lead to material's destruction. Current leads are also needed, to make current transition from room to cryogenic environment. Recovery time is usually in the order of a few seconds [11]. Devices demonstrated their technical viability in medium voltage distribution networks, usually associated with DG.

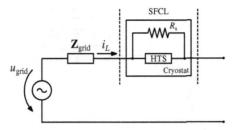

Fig. 2. Resistive superconducting fault current limiter electrical diagram

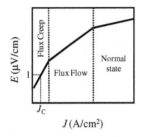

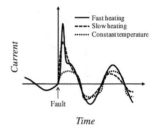

Fig. 3. HTS E-J qualitative dependence. The 1 µV/cm criterion defines critical current density, J_c, below which the material is in the superconducting state. Above J_c and below normal state, the material is in the mixed state.

Fig. 4. Different types of response under fault in resistive SFCL with distinct lengths (adapted from [11])

5 Inductive Type Fault Current Limiter

The inductive type SFCL, introduced in [16], is magnetically linked with the power line, behaving as a current transformer with short-circuited secondary, see Fig. 5. The primary is fed by the power line, while the secondary is built by an HTS element, usually a cylinder or a stack of cylinders. The primary and secondary concentrically embrace an iron core forming a closed or open path for magnetic flux.

5.1 Operation Principle

In normal operation, the primary's magnetic flux induces currents in the HTS that shield magnetically the iron core, leading to a negligible primary's linked flux (no flux lines penetrate the core) and consequently to negligible impedance (only related to leakage), see Fig. 6. Under a fault, line current increases abruptly and the HTS is no longer able to shield flux. It finds a preferential path through iron where it is amplified, see Fig. 7. Primary's linked flux increases by some orders of magnitude, increasing inductance and limiting current. Current evolution is represented in Fig. 8. Limitation is visible in the first half cycle, although it gets more effective after that.

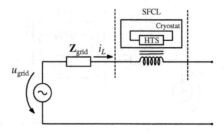

Fig. 5. Inductive superconducting fault current limiter electrical diagram

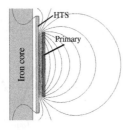 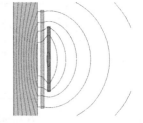

Fig. 6. Axisymmetric representation of an inductive SFCL in normal operation. Primary's flux is shielded from iron core by HTS induced currents.

Fig. 7. SFCL under a fault. Flux penetrates iron core, increasing device's impedance.

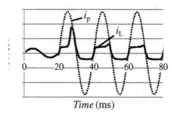

Fig. 8. Evolution of current in the circuit, i_L, under a fault, applied at 20 ms. Prospective current, i_p, is also shown. Results are taken from [8].

5.2 Inductive SFCL Demonstrators

The most relevant demonstrator found in the literature was implemented by ABB Company, namely a three-phase 10.5 kV/1.2 MVA built in a three leg core [17]. In laboratory, 60 kA prospective currents were limited to 700 A in the first half cycle and to less than 250 A after 50 ms. After 6 months of operation in Kraftwerk am Löentsch hydroelectric plant, Swiss, the device "...*did not face any major problems*". The re-cooling time for the material was in the order of two to ten seconds.

5.3 Conclusions

The inductive SFCL has some important advantages compared with the resistive one. Current leads, source of ohmic losses, are dispensable, limiting impedance is easily adjusted through primary turns, and hot spots are easily suppressed by cryogenics. Yet, it has considerable weight and volume due to iron cores. Large bulk superconductors are also hard to produce in good homogeneity conditions. Nevertheless, technical viability in distribution networks is demonstrated.

6 Future Trends and Conclusions

Resistive SFCL are object of great research due to their compactness. Yet, hot spot formation is a major issue, as it might irreversibly damage HTS elements. A novel design called magnetic field assisted quench is being developed in the framework of CULT 110 project [18], using applied field's quench dependence. HTS element is placed inside a conventional coil and these are shunted. In normal operation, current flows through the "zero" impedance element. Under a fault, a voltage is developed at its terminals. Part of the current deviates to the coil, originating magnetic flux that forces homogeneous and fast quench, avoiding hot spots.

Although less compact, robustness of inductive SFCL makes them attractive in distribution networks, where DG is applied. The algorithm developed by the authors [8] is thus of utmost relevance.

SFCL limit DG short-circuit currents, allowing its increasing penetration. Although cryogenics is still the most relevant technical challenge in superconductivity, it can be diluted if other HTS technologies are present, as lossless superconducting transformers, flywheels (energy is stored in a rotating mass, using HTS bearings to avoid contact) and SMES (superconducting magnetic energy storage, energy is stored in the magnetic field of an HTS coil). The last ones are related with energy storage and power quality, key issue in the advent of future electric grids, relying on DG, energy storage and bidirectional energy flow and complying with strict standards.

References

1. CIGRE Sudy Committee 37-23: Impact of increasing contributions of dispersed generation on the power systems. Technical report, CIGRE (1999)
2. CIRED Working Group 04: Dispersed generation. Preliminary report, CIRED Conference, Nice, France (1999)
3. Conti, S.: Analysis of distribution network protection issues in presence of dispersed generation. Electrical Power Systems Research 79, 49–56 (2009)
4. Jenkins, N., Allan, R., Crossley, P., Kirschen, D., Strbac, G.: Embedded Generation. The Institution of Engineering and Technology, London (2000)
5. Boutsika, T., Papathanassiou, S.: Short-circuit calculations in networks with distributed generation. Electrical Power Systems Research 78, 1181–1191 (2008)
6. Tran-Quoc, T., Andrieu, C., Hadjsaid, N.: Technical impacts of small distributed generation units on LV networks. IEEE Power Engineering Society General Meeting 4, 2459–2464 (2003)

7. Kunde, K., Kleimaier, M., Klingbeil, L.: Integration of fast acting electronic fault current limiters (EFCL) in medium voltage systems. In: CIRED 17th International Conference on Electricity Distribution, Barcelona, Spain (2003)
8. Pina, J., Suárez, P., Ventim Neves, M., Álvarez, A., Leão Rodrigues, A.: Reverse Engineering of Inductive Fault Current Limiters. Accepted for publication. In: 9th European Conference on Applied Superconductivity, EUCAS 2009, Dresden, Germany (2009)
9. Sato, T., Yamaguchi, M., Fukui, S., Watanabe, Y., Matsumura, T., Shimizu, H.: A Study on DC S/N Transition Type Superconducting Fault Current Limiting Interrupter. IEEE Trans. App. Superconductivity 13, 2088–2091 (2003)
10. Noe, M., Juengst, K.-P., Werfel, F., Cowey, L., Wolf, A., Elschner, S.: Investigation of high-Tc bulk material for its use in resistive superconducting fault current limiters. IEEE Trans. App. Superconductivity 11, 1960–1963 (2001)
11. Paul, W., Chen, M., Lakner, M., Rhyner, J., Braun, D., Lanz, W.: Fault current limiter based on high temperature superconductors - different concepts, test results, simulations, applications. Physica C 354, 27–33 (2001)
12. Shimizu, H., Yokomizu, Y., Matsumura, T., Murayama, N.: Proposal of Flux Flow Resistance Type Fault Current Limiter using Bi2223 High Tc Superconducting Bulk. IEEE Trans. App. Superconductivity 12, 876–879 (2002)
13. Bock, J., Breuer, F., Walter, H., Elschner, S., Kleimaier, M., Kreutz, R., Noe, M.: CURL 10: Development and Field-Test of a 10 kV/10 MVA Resistive Current Limiter Based on Bulk MCP-BSCCO 2212. IEEE Trans. App. Superconductivity 15, 1955–1960 (2005)
14. Sim, J., Park, K., Kim, H., Kang, J., Lee, B., Kim, H., Oh, I., Hyun, O.: 14 kV single-phase superconducting fault current limiter based on YBCO films. Cryogenics 47, 183–188 (2007)
15. Yazawa, T., Koyanagi, K., Takahashi, M., Ono, M., Toba, K., Takigami, H., Urata, M., Iijima, Y., Saito, T., Ameniya, N., Shiohara, Y.: Superconducting fault current limiter using high-resistive YBCO tapes. Physica C 468, 2046–2049 (2008)
16. Bashkirov, Y., Fleishman, L., Patsayeva, T., Sobolev, A., Vdovin, A.: Current-limiting reactor based on high-Tc superconductors. IEEE Trans. Magnet. 27, 1089–1092 (1991)
17. Paul, W., Lakner, M., Rhyner, J., Unternährer, P., Baumann, T., Chen, M., Windnhorn, L., Guérig, A.: Test of 1.2 MVA high-Tc superconducting fault current limiter. Superconductor Science and Technology 10, 914–918 (1997)
18. Elschner, S., Breuer, F., Walter, H., Stemmle, M., Bock, J.: HTS Components for High Voltage Resistive Current Limiters Based on a Magnetic Field Triggered Concept. IEEE Trans. App. Superconductivity 17, 1772–1775 (2007)

On the Mineral and Vegetal Oils Used as Electroinsulation in Transformers

Mariana Şerban, Livia Sângeorzan, and Elena Helerea

Transilvania University of Brasov,
29 Eroilor Str., 500036 Brasov, Romania
helerea@unitbv.ro

Abstract. Due to the relatively large availability and reduced price, the mineral transformer oils are widely used as electrical insulating liquids. However, mineral oil drastically degrades over time in service. New efforts were made to improve mineral oils characteristics, and other types of liquids like vegetal oils are proposed. This paper deals with new comparative tests on mineral and vegetal oils using as indicator the electric strength. The samples of non-additive mineral oil type TR 30 and vegetal oils of rape, sunflower and corn have been tested with increasing voltage of 60 Hz using different electrodes. The obtained data have been statistical processed. The analyze shows different average values of electrical strength for the different type of sample. New method of testing through electrical breakdown is proposed. Experimental data confirms that it is possible to use as electroinsulation organic vegetal oils in power transformers.

Keywords: Mineral oil, vegetal oil, electrical breakdown testing, statistic processing, electrode effect.

1 Introduction

Intensification of global warming, leading to environmental destruction, implicitly human health, and acute crisis of raw materials and energy have increased. In recent years new researches to find clean alternative green energy resources, replacing non-renewable resources with new renewable and environmentally friendly resources have been developed.

The global crisis of raw material resources, including oil resources, negatively affects the energy industry [1]. One research direction is to improve the performance of high power electrical transformers, and in particular, of electrical insulation systems. Replacing oil as feedstock for the manufacture of transformer oil should meet the requirements imposed on electrical insulation of high voltage insulation of power transformers [2]. One possibility is to use vegetal oils which are both clean and renewable [3]. There are different variants of oil research, seeking practical solutions to the partial or total replacement of mineral oils with other oils, such as the plant oils [4]. Condition assessment of aging and the estimation of the lifetime average insulation systems used in high power equipment, is today an important research objective for producers and users [5], [6].

L.M. Camarinha-Matos, P. Pereira, and L. Ribeiro (Eds.): DoCEIS 2010, IFIP AICT 314, pp. 435–442, 2010.

This paper makes reference to the comparative analysis of traditional vegetal oils and minerals and determines some of their alternative use in high power transformers. The aim is to develop a testing methodology based on nondestructive insulating oils methods that allow comparative analysis between different types of electrical insulating oils.

2   Contribution to Technological Innovation

Current challenges related to implementing strategies for sustainable development of human society require the development of new technological innovations. Energy is highly relevant in this respect, to increase energy efficiency and to reduce consumption of scarce raw materials.

In the transport of electricity domain, the issue is diverse, lifetime supply systems and electricity supply being directly linked to good operating condition of high power transformers. The possibilities of replacing the transformer mineral oil, polluting, other dielectric materials such as liquid vegetable oils from plants, green, clean and renewable are under research. The characteristics of the insulation used, in particular transformer oil, establish the good function of the transformer. There are standard methods for determining the characteristics of transformer oil.

Other aspects are that, the current conditions have changed:

✓   have appeared new types of oils, namely the inclusion of categories of vegetable oils in study of transformer insulation;

✓   regulating devices firms proposed building test equipment according to specific standards, which do not meet specific conditions (which are very different from the request insulation);

✓   insulating oil stiffness values as a parameter characteristic of electrical resistance applications depend on a number of intrinsic and extrinsic factors, which are not always specify the companies producing electrical insulating oils;

✓   data processing methods usually statistical distribution of normal type, not always applicable in the case of variable data strings.

This paper proposes an experimental analysis for different types of electrical insulating oils - mineral and vegetal - to optimize the dielectric rigidity test methodology and establish the optimal matrix properties necessary in comparative tests of insulating oils.

3   Challenges on Electrical Transformer Oils

The insulating oil has a dual role in the complex system of electrical insulation system of power transformers, as a cooling medium and as a medium of electrical insulation. Characteristic of the insulation, in particular of transformer oil, is to largely maintain the good functioning of the transformer.

Mineral oils are a very complex mixture, which can reach about 2900 types of molecules of paraffin, naphthen and aromatic hydrocarbons, their properties can vary greatly from one batch to another, even if they come from the same batch and even the same name.

Efforts are being made today for rapid and effective establishment of criteria for comparing electrical characteristics of the different types of oils that could run for classes of oils used in electrical insulation systems [2].

The lifetime of transformer oil and its technical performance of operation, depend primarily on its initial quality and then on the operating conditions. As the adverse effects on the ability of insulation occur almost immediately after using the new oil refinery delivered, a special attention was paid to a set of defining characteristics of new oil and control methods of these features, before oil supply to the recipient.

The results of fast quality control methods of electrical oils, are unusually reported. The possibility of developing methods for determining the basic indicators of insulating oils - like dielectric loss angle tangent, or tangent of δ, and stiffness are continuously studied and modern models are being tried to be advantageous in terms of price and cost [1], [2].

It was found that one of the main causes of decline of oil dielectrics electrical parameters (such as modification of loss angle tangent of the dielectric rigidity or other physic - chemical, organic acid, water content, etc.) is the formation of free radicals causing the formation of colloidal structures which disturb electrical insulating performance [4].

Similar concerns are found in other countries (USA, England, Belgium, etc.) the specialized technical literature noting that manufacturers use different processes transformer oil refinery to produce products similar to those already known [3]. The power transformers in the Romanian power system use only mineral insulating oil, resulting from refining crude oils selected for this purpose, in most cases being used transformer oil type TR 30 (non-additive oil) and, type TR 25 A (additive oil).

As the current conditions have changed a new approach is acquired to replace the liquid electrical insulation materials with newer more efficient ones. There are studies about the possibilities of replacing the transformer mineral oil, with other dielectric materials such as liquid vegetal oils from plants, green, clean and renewable.

There are also the standard methods for determining the characteristics of transformer oil [5]. Some firms propose building test equipment according to specific standards, but not always they meet specific conditions (which are very different from the request insulation).

It notes also that the insulating oil electric strength, as a parameter characteristic of electrical insulating capacity, depends on a number of intrinsic and extrinsic factors, which are not always specified by the companies producing electrical insulating oils.

Data processing methods, usually with statistical distribution of normal type, are not always applicable in the case of variable data strings.

4 Experimental Data

Measurements were carried out to determine the electric breakdown voltage of different samples of mineral and vegetal oils: non-additive TR 30 oil, sunflower, corn and rapeseed oils.

The Megger AF 60/2 equipment has been used (Fig. 1). The electrodes of test vessel have different shapes: plane, sphere and semi-sphere, and could be set at different distances. A magnetic stirring could be produced by a rotating magnetic field, controlled by software. A thermometer of BK PRECISION 710 type measures the temperature of the oil and the ambient environment.

Fig. 1. Equipment for oil electrical breakdown testing

Samples of oil have been subjected to increasing voltage up to breakdown of sample, with a rate of 2.5 kV/s and frequency of 61.8 Hz. A distance of 1 mm between electrodes for each type of electrodes - plane, calotte and sphere - has been fixed. The volume of oil used in each test subject to breakdown was 300 cm³. The temperature of oil and ambient environment was of 25-28°C. The results of breakdown voltage have been saved by a non-volatile memory.

5 Proceeding of Data and Results

Measured data were statistically processed. Various statistic parameters have been calculated and histograms have been plotted to reveal the distribution of these measurements. Date proceeding was made using the software Statistics.

5.1 Statistical Distributions

Statistical distribution laws, which provide theoretical models as an approximation of measured values for random variables, have been analyzed.

The normal distribution function is determined by the following formula:

$$f(x) = \frac{1}{\sigma\sqrt{2\pi}} e^{-\frac{(x-m)^2}{2\sigma^2}}, \tag{1}$$

where: μ is the mean, σ is the standard deviation, e is Euler's constant.

The lognormal distribution is often used in simulation of variables. In general, if x is a sample with a normal distribution, then $y = e^x$ is a sample with a lognormal distribution. Thus, the lognormal distribution is defined as:

$$f(x) = \frac{1}{x \cdot \sigma \cdot \sqrt{2\pi}} e^{-\left[\frac{(\ln(x)-\mu)^2}{2\sigma^2}\right]} \tag{2}$$

where: μ is the estimated population mean, σ is the estimated population standard deviation.

The Gamma distribution is defined as:

$$f(x) = \left[\frac{1}{\Gamma(\alpha) \cdot \beta^\alpha} e \right] \cdot x^{\alpha-1} \cdot e^{-\frac{x}{\beta}} \tag{3}$$

where: Γ is the Gamma function of argument alpha, α is the so-called shape parameter, and β is the so-called scale parameter. For $\alpha = 1$, the exponential distribution is obtained.

The Weibull distribution is commonly used in lifetime random data analysis. The Weibull distribution takes values in the range $x \geq 0$ and has one scale parameter, β, and one shape parameter, α, both of which must be positive.

5.2 Concordance Tests and Variability Coefficient

The coefficient of variation V is a synthetic indicator of random data variations and brings information on the homogeneity of the studied lot of samples.

As the percentage ratio between standard deviation and arithmetic mean, coefficient of variation V can range between 0-100 %. If the coefficient of variation tends to zero is considered a low variation, a corporate uniform and averaged a high degree of representativeness. If the coefficient of variation tends to 100 %, is considered an intense change, and a heterogeneous community with a low average of representativeness. Thus 4 thresholds of representativeness could be considered:

✓ 0<V<17%   - mean is strictly representative (has high homogeneity).

✓ 17%<V<35%   - mean is moderately representative (less homogeneous).

✓ 35%<V<50%   - mean is broadly representative (less homogeneous).

✓ V>50%   - mean unrepresentative (lack of homogeneity).

An important aspect of the description of the variables is the shape of its distribution, which shows how frequent the values are from different ranges of the variable. Typically a researcher is interested in how well the distribution can be approximated by the normal distribution. Some precise information can be obtained by performing one of the tests of normality to determine the probability that the sample came from a normal distributed population of observations. However, none of these tests can entirely substitute for a visual examination of the data using a histogram. The graph allows the evaluation of the normality of the empirical distribution because it also shows the normal curve superimposed over the histogram. It also allows the examination of various aspects of the distribution qualitatively.

The concordance tests verify if the empirical distribution differs a lot or does not differ from the proposed theoretical distribution. The Kolmogorov-Smirnov test, Shapiro-Wilks'W test, χ^2 test are the most used as concordance tests [7].

5.3 Results of Breakdown Voltage Tests

The empirical distribution parameters calculated for the four types of random variables data - voltage breakdown of TR 30 mineral oil, sun flower oil, corn oil, rapeseed oil - tested with sphere, plan and calotte electrodes – are given in Table 1, Table 2 and Table 3.

Table 1. Empirical parameters and estimated parameters of the distribution statistical lows obtained for the series of variables of breakdown voltage (kV) for Mineral Oil, Sun Flower Oil, Corn Oil, Rapeseed Oil, with sphere-sphere electrodes

Empirical Distribution Parameters (Sphere electrodes)	Type of Random Variables			
	Mineral Oil TR 30	Sun Flower Oil SFO	Corn Oil CO	Rapeseed Oil RO
Sample, N	99	99	99	99
Mean, μ, kV	17.66	16.77	20.08	18.83
Variances, σ^2	19.29	38.83	46.10	36.86
Standard deviation	4.39	6.23	6.78	6.07
Median, kV	17.70	16.60	19.80	19.00
Variability coef,%	33.80	32.23	24.86	37.13
Shapiro-Wilk	0.9874	0.9803	0.9742	0.9925
Kolmogorov test	0,0688	0,0563	0,0353	0,0606
Normal Distribution, $N(\mu, \sigma^2)$	N(17,66; 4.3917)	N(16,7788; 6.23)	N(20,0828; 6.79)	N(18,8374; 6.07)
Lognormal Distribution Log ($\lg \mu, \sigma^2$)	Log(2.8385; 0.264)	Log(2.7496; 0.4147)	Log(2.9161; 0.471)	Log(2.8685; 0.4123)
Gamma Distribution, $G(\alpha, \beta)$	G(1.1492; 15.3585)	G(2.5387; 6.6093)	G(3.2768; 6.1289)	G(2.4815; 7.591)

Table 2. Empirical parameters and estimated parameters of the distribution statistical lows obtained for the series of variables of breakdown voltage (kV) for Mineral Oil, Sun Flower Oil, Corn Oil, Rapeseed Oil, with plan-plan electrodes

Empirical Distribution Parameters (Plan electrodes)	Type of Random Variables			
	Mineral Oil TR 30	Sun Flower Oil SFO	Corn Oil CO	Rapeseed Oil RO
Sample, N	99	99	99	99
Mean, μ, kV	14.00	24.54	19.95	23.03
Variances, σ^2	19.28	38.82	46.09	36.86
Standard deviation	4.39	6.23	6.78	6.07
Median, kV	14.55	23.40	11.65	25.25
Variability coef.,%	23.70	13.57	19.61	11.70
Shapiro-Wilk	0.9874	0.9803	0.9742	0.9925
Kolmogorov test	0.0688	0.0563	0.0353	0.0606
Normal Distribution, $N(\mu, \sigma^2)$	N(17.66; 4.3917)	N(16.7788; 6.23)	N(20.0828; 6.79)	N(18.8374; 6.07)
Lognormal Distribution Log ($\lg \mu, \sigma^2$)	Log(2,6082; 0.2617)	Log(3,1899; 0.1515)	Log(2,7213; 0.2012)	Log(3.1296; 0.1276)
Gamma Distribution, $G(\alpha, \beta)$	G(0.8744; 16.0219)	G(0.5144; 47.7115)	G(0.6045; 25.6447)	G(0.3483; 66.156)

In the Table 1 and Table 2 are shown the values of variance coefficient V for all types of oils is between 17-38 % for the voltage breakdown tests with sphere and plane electrodes. The data illustrate that oil samples are not very homogeneous. These values highlight the fact that during the tests these types of oils change their structure.

The oils ages after the 99 breakthroughs. This shows that in this case the arithmetic mean is not representative. A test with 99 successive electric breakdowns should not be representative for the initial characterization of the insulation oils. The data of Table 3 show the variance coefficient V for mineral oil of 17.43 % for tests with calotte electrodes, which indicates a high uniformity and highlights the fact that the oil has not changed the structure.

Table 3. Empirical parameters and estimated parameters of the distribution statistical lows obtained for the series of variables of breakdown voltage (kV) for Mineral Oil, Sun Flower Oil, Corn Oil, Rapeseed Oil, with calotte -calotte electrodes

Empirical Distribution Parameters (Sphere electrodes)	Type of Random Variables			
	Mineral Oil TR 30	Sun Flower Oil SFO	Corn Oil CO	Rapeseed Oil RO
Sample, N	99	99	99	99
Mean, μ, kV	16.04	20.08	18.83	17.66
Variances, σ^2	7.82	36.86	19.28	36.86
Standard deviation	2.79	6.07	4.39	6.07
Median, kV	16.20	15.30	15.65	14.25
Variability coef,%	17.43	33.80	32.23	24.86
Shapiro-Wilk	0.9239	0.9742	0.8572	0.9874
Kolmogorov test	0.1194	0.0563	0.0353	0.0606
Normal Distribution, $N(\mu, \sigma^2)$	N(16.1222; 2.8907)	N(20.0828; 6.7895)	N(18.8374; 6.0713)	N(17.6616; 4.3917)
Lognormal Distribution Log (lg μ, σ^2)	Log(2.7604; 0.2132)	Log(2.9161; 0.471)	Log(2.8685; 0.4123)	Log(2.8385; 0.264)
Gamma Distribution, $G(\alpha, \beta)$	G(0.6353; 25.3759)	G(3.2768; 6.1289)	G(2.4815; 7.591)	G(1.1492; 15,3685)

6 Conclusion and Future Work

The experimental data regarding the electric breakdown of electroinsulating oils are useful in comparative analyze of new type of oils. Research conducted for the purposes of insulating mineral oil replacement potential were targeted and vegetable oils of different types and grades, which shows similarity with the characteristics of these oils as insulating mineral oil currently used. Experimental data shows that there is compatibility of vegetable oils can be used as substitutes for mineral insulating oils.

Analysis of the experimental data illustrated that there is a normal distribution of values of each type of mineral oil and vegetable. Checking the values of some key statistical parameters lead to the formulation of the following observations:

    ✓   Median and module are not significantly different from that of the arithmetic mean;
    ✓   Frequency distribution of rapeseed oil has two maximum;
    ✓   The coefficient of asymmetry is a relatively large value.

Because of the obtained asymmetry and the existence of two levels in the histograms the measurement batch of 99 tests was performed again, with new oil samples. Main statistical parameters values obtained for the new values do not differ significantly from those measured earlier.

Thus, the researches in this area have been exhausted and that they should continue to complete the final conclusions of the possibility to use organic vegetable oils as substitutes for mineral insulating oils. New research should be done relative to the type of electrodes used in ac breakdown oil testing.

References

1. Şerban, M., Helerea, E.: The Use of Vegetable Ecological Insulating Oils of High Power Transformer. In: Proceeding of International Conference (BENA) Environmental Pollution and its Impact on Public Health, pp. 120–126. Transilvania University of Brasov Press (2008)
2. Helerea, E., Munteanu, A., Serban, M.: Aspects Regarding the Monitoring and the Life Extension of Electroinsulating Oils Used in High Voltage Systems. In: Proceeding of the BRAMAT International Conference, pp. 134–138. Transilvania University of Brasov Press (2007)
3. Lvov, M.Y., Chichinskii, M.I.: Rated Indices for Evaluating the Winding Insulation Wear of Power Transformers. Power Technology and Engineering 36(5) (2002)
4. Sangeorzan, L., Helerea, E., Veştemean, D., Clotea, L.: A Statistical Approach on Load Distribution for an Industrial System. In: Optimization of Electrical and Electronic Equipments, Brasov (1998)
5. Forster, E.O., Yamashita, H., Mazzetti, C., Pompili, M., Caroli, L., Patrissi, S.: The Effect of the Electrode Gap on Breakdown in Liquid Dielectrics. IEEE-Transactions on Dielectrics and Electrical Insulation 1(3), 440–448 (1994)
6. Burnet, N.: It's a challenge for Farmers and Rape Energy Specialists. Synchronous Press, Cluj-Napoca (2004)
7. Constantinescu, I., Golumbovici, D., Militaru, C.: Processing Experimental Data with Digital Computers. Technical Publishing House, Bucuresti (1980)

Interconnections between Reliability, Maintenance and Availability

Catalin Mihai, Sorin Abagiu, Larisa Zoitanu, and Elena Helerea

Transilvania University of Brasov,
29, Eroilor Str., Brasov, Romania
catalin.mihai@electricats.ro

Abstract. The assurance of power quality depends on factors which influence the performances of the availability: the reliability and its support – the maintenance. This paper deals with the interactions between the indicators of reliability, maintenance, availability and with the methods for the calculation of the reliability indicators. For an overhead line of 110 kV the characteristics of the reliability of the system are determined by modeling and analyzing its functionality by the Markov process of continuous time. The value of the availability index and the maintenance function function contributes to ascertain for the studied case that the value of the availability coefficient has the same value with the probability of success and the probability of repairing an equipment is closely connected to the maintenance function.

Keywords: Reliability, maintenance, availability, Markov process, electric lines.

1 Introduction

The equipment used on the power systems is relatively old and increases the financial effort for their maintenance.

Therefore appear features of the electrical systems that are closely interrelated, such as: reliability, availability and maintenance, their interactions determining the qualitative and quantitative aspects of the analyzed system, its safe operation.

The reliability, as a feature of the system in fulfilling the specific functions in a certain period of time, continues to be the subject of many researches [1],[5],[7] and [10]. There are many papers [2],[8],[12] and [13] that have as a research subject the maintenance, their goal being to determine the optimum technical – organisational actions to maintain or to repair the system functionality. Concerning the system availability, there is analysed from this point of view: the system capacity of fulfilling its function in a certain moment within a period of time.

Taking in account the necessities for an increasing quality of the delivered electrical energy, there emerges the importance of a new approach in dealing with the aspects of reliability, availability and maintenance, in order to develop efficient methods for calculating the parameters/characteristics in relation with the operation time.

This paper analyses the connections between reliability, availability, maintenance and the "Markov chains" is the proposed method for determining the indicators of the

L.M. Camarinha-Matos, P. Pereira, and L. Ribeiro (Eds.): DoCEIS 2010, IFIP AICT 314, pp. 443–450, 2010.

correlation between reliability, availability maintenance and the probability of failure for an overhead line of 110 kV.

2 Contribution to Technological Innovation

The evaluation of repairing probability for equipment, that can be integrated rapidly in the maintenance program of studied systems, represents an innovation in technical domain based on the analysis of reliability indicators, contributing to implementation of the integrated concept reliability, maintenance and availability.

3 Characteristics Measures for Reliability, Maintenance and Availability

The safe operation of a technical system is defined by the totality of characteristics, Reliability, Maintenance and Availability.

The function of Reliability is defined by the relation:

$$R(t) = e^{-\int_0^t z(t)\cdot dt} \tag{1}$$

where $z(t)$ - rate of failure is defined like the probability of uninterrupted operation until the moment of time t.

The relation (1) applies to any law of distribution of operation time. For the exponential repartition of operation time, the rate of failure is: $z(t) = \lambda(t) = \lambda = const.$ It results:

$$R(t) = e^{-\lambda(t)\cdot t} \tag{2}$$

Maintainability (M) represents a safety function and consists in the probability for an installation (or an equipment) to re-enter into operation after a certain time when the maintenance actions were made [1].

The maintenance function is defined by the relation:

$$M = 1 - e^{-\mu t} \tag{3}$$

where: μ is the intensity of repair, representing the probability that for a device which was faulty at the moment t, to be repaired in the next very short period of time. For an exponential repartition of the repairing periods: $\mu(t) = const.$

3.1 Reliability Measures

Reliability measures of repairable systems can be categorized into three groups [3]:

- o   Measures based on the system's first failure,
- o   Steady-state measures,
- o   Time-specific measures.

As time advances progresses, the repairable system reaches a steady-state condition. This means that certain estimates of system measures do not change with time. These measures include availability, mean time between failures MTBF, mean time to failure MTTF, mean time to repair MTTR, and the expected number of failures per unit time (failure frequency). The following relations are well known:

$$MTBF = \frac{1}{\mu(\infty)}$$

$$MTTF = \frac{A(\infty)}{\mu(\infty)} \qquad (4)$$

$$MTRF = \frac{1 - A(\infty)}{\mu(\infty)}.$$

Here $A(\infty)$ and $v(\infty)$ are respectively the steady-state availability and failure frequency of the system. Therefore,

MTTF, MTTR, and MTBF can easily be found from the steady-state availability and failure frequency.

In Fig. 1 there are shown the links between Reliability, Maintenance, Availability.

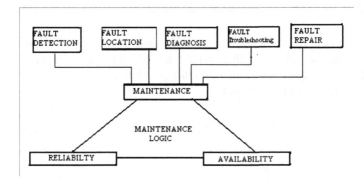

Fig. 1. Connections between reliability, maintenance and availability

Analyzing Fig. 1, it can underline that the reliability of a system is characterized by the set of measures that give information on the performance of the system functionality in a period of time.

4   Calculation of System Reliability Indicators: Case Study

It consider the case of a 110 kV overhead power line shown in (Fig.2), with repair and failure intensities used in the design and provided by the Normative [9].

It aims at determining the characteristics of system analysis and adopting a model of its operation using continuous time Markov processes that can be used for operation and maintenance services of overhead power line owner.

Fig. 2. The scheme of supply of a consumer to 20 kV through 110 kV overhead line

In Table 1 There are listed the average values cited in technical literature [6] for the following parameters: the intensity of failure, the intensity of repair for a 110 kV installation.

Table 1. Intensities of repair and failure in installations of 110 kV

Elements of overhead power line	Intensity of failure λ_i [year^{-1}]	Intensity of repair μ_i [year^{-1}]
Collector bar	1,3x10-2	175,2
Breaker line cell	3x10-2	175,2
Transformer 110 kV/MV	2x10-2	21,0
110 kV overhead line	1,3x10-2	547,5
Bar and line separator	0,4x10-2	438

Being a serial system components, to study some elements of the scheme is considered a system of 7 elements characterized by indicators of reliability λi and μi. In such a scheme, failure of any of the items that goes into them has the effect of removing all successful schemes in the state.

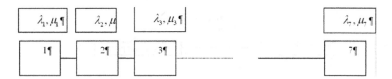

Fig. 3. Equivalent scheme for calculating the reliability indicators of 7 elements connected in series

The schema elements can be considered dependent or independent, the states which may take different elements of the scheme. If the items are functionally dependent, the number of states is equal to (n +1).

- in state 0   - all elements are in operation,
- in state 1   - element 1 is defective,
- in state n   - element 2 is defective.

There is no possibility of transition from states with a defective component in states with two defective elements or states with two defective elements in states with three defective elements, since at the failure of one element, the scheme is decommissioned, therefore there is assumed that the other elements can not be damaged.

States denomination:

-successful state (all elements in service):   0
-failure state: 1, 2, 3,...,7.

Transition graph for a system with elements in series is shown in Figure 4.

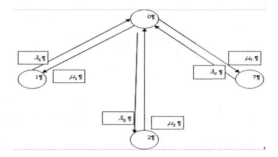

Fig. 4. Graphical representation of transitions for the series schedule

4.1 Calculation and Analysis of Reliability Measures

Based on the analysis of state transitions [11] has made the transition intensities matrix. Transition intensities matrix, column matrix of absolute probability and matrix equation of state of absolute possibility tending to constant values independent of time.

If the system with n elements series, matrices are given below:

$$
\begin{bmatrix}
-\sum_{1}^{n}\lambda_i & \mu_1 & \cdots & \mu_n \\
\lambda_i & -\mu_1 & \cdots & 0 \\
\cdots & \cdots & \cdots & \cdots \\
\lambda_n & 0 & \cdots & -\mu_n
\end{bmatrix}
\begin{bmatrix}
P_0 \\
P_1 \\
\cdots \\
P_n
\end{bmatrix} = 0
\tag{5}
$$

Calculation of success and failure probabilities is carried out by solving the relation (5), where P0 is the probability for the system to be in working order, P1-P7 corresponding to 7 states of transition. In this case:

$$
P_i = \frac{\lambda_i}{\mu_i} \cdot P_0 =
\begin{cases}
0,007 \cdot 10^{-2}; \\
0,00089 \cdot 10^{-2}; \\
0,016 \cdot 10^{2}; \\
0,0089 \cdot 10^{-2}; \\
0,0006 \cdot 10^{-2}; \\
0,016 \cdot 10^{-2}; \\
0,089 \cdot 10^{-2}
\end{cases}
\tag{6}
$$

$$
P_0 = \frac{1}{1+\sum \dfrac{\lambda_i}{\mu_i}} = 0,998
$$

;

For an operation time planned for the $Tp = 8200$ h/year the following measures are calculated:

Probability of success:

$$P_S = P_0 = 0,998 \tag{7}$$

Probability of rejection:

$$P_R = \sum_1^7 P_i = 0,002 \tag{8}$$

Mean total success time:

$$M[\alpha(T_p) = P_s T_p = \frac{1}{1+\sum_1^7 \frac{\lambda_i}{\mu_i}} T_p = 0,998 \cdot 8200 = 8183,6 \quad h/year \tag{9}$$

Mean total failure time:

$$M[\beta(T_p) = P_R T_p = \frac{\sum_1^7 \frac{\lambda_i}{\mu_i}}{1+\sum_1^7 \frac{\lambda_i}{\mu_i}} T_p = 0,002 \cdot 8200 = 16,4 \quad h/year \tag{10}$$

Mean number of damages:

$$M[\nu(T_p)] = \sum P_i \sum q_{0j} T_p = P_0 \sum q_{0j} T_p = P_0 \left(\lambda_i + ... + \lambda_n\right) T_p = \frac{T_p \sum \lambda_i}{1+\sum \frac{\lambda_i}{\mu_i}} \tag{11}$$

$$= 0,998 \cdot 14 \cdot 10^{-2} \cdot 0,936 = 0,13$$

Mean duration of a successful state:

$$M[(T_f)] = \frac{M[\alpha(T_p)]}{M[\beta(T_p)]} = \frac{1}{\sum \lambda_i} = \frac{1}{14 \cdot 10^{-2}} \quad year \tag{12}$$

Mean duration of continuous operation (a state of failure):

$$M[(T_d)] = MTBF = \frac{M[\beta(T_p)]}{M[\nu(T_p)]} = \frac{\sum \frac{\lambda_i}{\mu_i}}{\sum \lambda_i} = 0,0087 \quad year \tag{13}$$

Since the system is studied with a series structure is inferred that the failure of any component of the system generates damage of the entire line. Therefore, it is of tantamount importance to have a system with intensity of repair and an intensity of failure, such as:

$$\lambda_e = \frac{1}{M[T_p]} = \sum \lambda_i = 0,14 \quad year^{-1}$$

$$\mu_e = \frac{1}{M[T_d]} = \frac{\sum \lambda_i}{\sum \frac{\lambda_i}{\mu_i}} = 114,75 \quad year^{-1} \tag{14}$$

Determination of Availability and Maintenance Functions

To write the coefficient of availability and maintenance function will be used for repair and failure, the intensities equivalent to the system analyzed.

$$M[T_d] = \frac{1}{\mu_e} = \frac{1}{114,75} \cdot 8760 = 60,518 \quad days$$

$$A = \frac{\mu_e}{\lambda_e + \mu_e} = \frac{114,75}{114,75 + 0,14} = 0,998 \tag{15}$$

Maintainability function is:

$$M = 1 - e^{-\mu_e t} \tag{16}$$

After analysis, we have the following cases presented in Table 2.

Table 2. Probability of repair of overhead line

Time required for repair [h]	Probability to be repaired [%]
$t = 1$	1.6%
$t = 24$	32.73 %
$t = 48$	54.75 %
$t = 200$	96.32 %

It is noted that for the time to repair the overhead line of 110 kV, for $t = 1\ h$, the probability for that line to be repaired is 1.6%, and the acceptable probability (96.32%) repair for overhead line studied, leads to a minimum for 8 days.

5 Conclusions

The method used for determining the characteristics of reliability is easy to apply and almost draw up and provided maintenance plans and procedures and likewise and maintenance programs related equipment or systems studied.

The case study was performed with the parameters of professional norms, which is useful for design calculations.

For operating systems is useful to introduce the value of operating parameters that may substantiate more rigorous maintenance plans.

Calculated data were compared with data mining from SC Electrica SA (Electricity Distribution Company from Romania) and they are the values around which confirms the validity of the calculation.

References

1. Nitu, V.I., Ionescu, C.: Fiabilitatea in energetica. Editura Didactica si Pedagogica, Bucuresti, (1980)
2. McMahon B.: Reliability and maintenance practices for australian and new zealand transmission lines, 'The Reliability of Transmission and Distribution Equipment', 2S37, Conference Publication No. 406 (1995)
3. Jacob D., Amari S. V., Analysis of Complex Repairable Systems, RAMS, IEEE (2005)
4. Mettas, A.: Reliability Predictions based on Customer Usage Stress Profiles, IEEE, RAMS (2005)
5. Martinescu, I., Popescu, I.: Analiza fiabilitatii si securitatii sistemelor. Editura Universitatii Transilvania Brasov, Brasov (2002)
6. Nitu, V.I.: Fiabilitate, disponibilitate, mentenanta in energetica. Editura Tehnica Bucuresti, (1987)
7. Mihoc, Gh., Muja, A., Diatcu, E.: Bazele matematice ale teoriei fiabilității. Editura. Dacia, Cluj – Napoca (1976)
8. Boşianu, L.: Fiabilitate şi mentenanţă – îndrumar de lucrări practice. Institutul Politehnic Bucuresti (1992)
9. NTE 005/06/00: Normativ privind metodele şi elementele de calcul al siguranţei în funcţionare a instalaţiilor electrice.
10. Stillman, R.: Power Line Maintenance with Minimal Repair and Replacement. In: IEEE Proceedings Annual Reliability and Maintainability Symposium (2003)
11. Kececioglu, D.: Reliability Engineering Handbook, vol. 2, DEStech Publication Inc., Pennsylvania USA (2002)
12. Rigler, D. M., Hodgkins, W. R, Allan, R. N.: Quantitative reliability analysisof distribution systems: repair times. In: Power Engineering Journal (1997)
13. Fulvio E. O.: An Optimal Sparing Model for the Operational Avdability toApproach the Inherent Availability. In: Proceedings Annual Reliability and Maintainability Symposium (2001)

Part 15

Dedicated Energy Systems

Evaluation of Supercapacitors Effects on Hybrid Energy Systems for Automotive

Carmen Lungoci and Elena Helerea

Department of Electrical Engineering, Transilvania University of Brasov,
1-3 Politehnicii Street, Brasov, Romania
lungoci@unitbv.ro

Abstract. This work aims at evaluating the effects of the supercapacitors presence in hybrid energy systems used in automotive. The design and the electrical schema of a hybrid energy system that contains batteries and supercapacitors and propel a synchronous motor are purposed. The motor operating regime is described, detailing the drive evolution of the cycle speed imposed. In these conditions, to model the systems behavior, simulations developed in Matlab/Simulink environment are carried out. Two energies management strategies for the ensemble energy system-motor are implemented. Simulations are done and the energy management is discussed, making the comparative analyses. Applying a current control strategy on the supercapacitors, under two working conditions, functional diagrams are showed and compared. The results obtained highlight the advantages of the supercapacitors.

Keywords: Supercapacitors, energy systems, energy management, automotive, simulations.

1 Introduction

Nowadays, in transport the use of hybrid energy systems represents an important current topic [1] [2]. In a hybrid vehicle, the most utilized batteries are the Ni-Mh and Li-Ion, presenting advantages due to their technology. But energy recovery using a traditional system composed by batteries (SB) is a constraint. The weight, volume and the price of the batteries reduce the efficiency of the system. From this reason, there are many researches to optimize the architecture and the structure of an energy system [3][4].

The useful strategy adopted is an energy system containing many energy sources. Among the existing solutions, the hybrid energy system using batteries and supercapacitors (SBSC) is proposed and analyzed. This work is aims to develop a SBSC system for electrical traction. The architecture of this system is proposed and the studies regarding the structure, functionality and modeling on it are presented. Using the models for the elements components of the system, developed by the authors in the previous papers, the modeling and simulations are realized, in order to obtain the electrical parameters: current, power, energy, in the test conditions of functioning, imposed by a proposed drive cycle. The necessary power resulted is ensured by

L.M. Camarinha-Matos, P. Pereira, and L. Ribeiro (Eds.): DoCEIS 2010, IFIP AICT 314, pp. 453–460, 2010.
© IFIP International Federation for Information Processing 2010

the hybrid energy system, applying two energy management strategies. In this way, the effects brings by the supercapacitors presence in the energy system are finally underlined.

2 Contribution to Technological Innovation

The automotive field requires new technological innovations regarding energy demands inside of subsystems. This trend is putting increasing pressure on energy systems from a vehicle to be efficient and run for long periods. From technical point of vu, they must be able to store and deliver enough energy and power.

Batteries are preferred for most applications because of their superior capability to store energy. The disadvantage consist is the poor ability to deliver power.

Supercapacitors offer a combination of high power and good energy performance parameters with commercial relevance. They are very high surface area activated carbon capacitors that use a molecule-thin layer of electrolyte [5]. This new technology gives them the property to storage energy proportional to the charge surface area. So, they are able to hold a very high charge which can be released in a controlled manner.

Taking in account the batteries and the supercapacitors properties, there is a strong trend in automotive towards hybridizing both energy sources, making the energy system more highly and efficient functional from the point of vu of the energy management. The last technological advances in the applications to automobiles are based on this ability of supercapacitors to complete with the batteries.

3 State of Art

In hybrid vehicles, the load profile is characterized by a low value of a main power with big picks of power requested in transient regimes. In these conditions, a hybrid energy system that contains supercapacitors near batteries (SBSC) ensures performing answers of power, higher like in SB systems.

There are researchers which evaluated the effects of the supercapacitors in the hybrid energy systems and they developed and realized practically the SBSC systems [4] [5].

The studies from the literature proved the advantages of SBSC systems use, in which batteries ensure a constant voltage and the role of supercapacitors is to deliver/storage the transient picks of power.

In order to optimize the structure, to improve the functionality and to grow the energy efficiency of the SBSC systems used in automotive, new analyses are necessary, the improvement of the existing models is required and the development of new models is expected.

4 Research Contribution and Innovation

In the present research improvements on the energy systems used in automotive are proposed. The main objectives of this work are:

- To present the ensemble hybrid (batteries-supercapacitors)-synchronous motor;
- To simulate the functioning regimes under different running conditions;
- To implement two energies management in order to highlight the contribution of the supercapacitors in automotive presented system.

2.1 System Description

The architecture of the proposed supply/propulsion system consists of a batteries pack and a supercapacitors pack, being utilized in a hybrid vehicle (Fig. 1). The battery pack is directly connected to the DC bus, providing a constant voltage for the system. Mechanical load of the system is represented by the inertia and brakes of the vehicle. Propulsion is ensured by MSA traction motor. The DC/AC inverter, coupled to MSA, transforms the electrical DC power provided on the bus into AC power and controls its parameters.

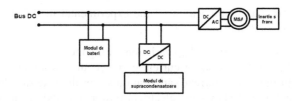

Fig. 1. Architecture of the power system used in hybrid electrical vehicle

The power supplying the inverter is delivered by the both: main and the secondary power source. Supercapacitors pack represents the secondary power source, ensuring optimal performance for the motor in punctual operation regimes. The bidirectional DC/DC converter connects the supercapacitors pack to DC bus, controlling current flow and allowing energy recovery while breaking. The functioning regimes of the motor are modeled according to the proposed running drive cycle – 3ECE. The entire power demand by the motor is ensured by the batteries and supercapacitors pack, designed according to the speed cycle.

The aim of simulations is to obtain a quick and consistent response to transient power requests from the motor, in order to obtain a high energy efficiency of the entire system. The model used for simulations includes a batteries pack consisting of 23 elements, providing a constant voltage in amount of 280V. Supercapacitors pack introduced in the simulation model has the following parameters: total capacity in amount of 5.8 F, voltage across terminals 150 V and internal resistance 0.19 Ω. Electrical propulsion motor is a permanent magnet synchronous motor, with the following parameters: $U_n = 230$ V; $I_n = 42,9$ A; $M_n = 35$ Nm; $n_n = 3300$ rpm; $P_n = 12,1$ kW. Energy efficiency is to be determined in simulations, by analyzing obtained responses.

Two energy management strategies are presented:

1. The necessary of the electrical power requested by the motor is entirely ensured by the batteries (SB system), during the drive cycle period;
2. The same necessary of power is ensured by the batteries and the supercapacitors.

The energy management is treated, observing the temporal responses obtained by simulations under the under drive cycle conditions for each case above. Running cycles set (3ECE) is composed from several European urban running cycles, containing different acceleration, constant speed and breaking phases. There are presented three levels of rotational speed for the motor: 1100 rot/min, 2200 rot/min, 3300 rot/min, the motor dynamics having easy accelerations and breakings.

2.3 Energy Management Using SB

The following work assumptions have been considered:

- The unique energy source used is the pack of batteries;
- The entire electrical power requested by the motor is ensured by the batteries and the braking energy of the motor is completely taken by the batteries;
- The model of batteries is an internal resistance in series with an electromotive voltage source;
- For the synchronous motor was used the experimental model developed by the authors and detailed in [6].

In Fig. 2 the necessary of current (I_{bus}) variation during the 3ECE cycle is presented. It can be observed the many peaks of current corresponding when crossing to another level of speed. In Fig. 3 the current variation curve on the batteries during the same cycle are obtained. Fig. 4 shows the electrical power required by the traction motor during the cycle and Fig. 5 presents the power electrical variation at the pack of batteries in the same period. Graphics shows that during the running cycle, batteries must ensure all the power picks required by the motor, which implies their overload.

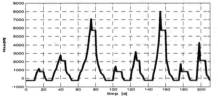
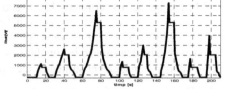

Fig. 2. Motor current I_{bus} during 3ECE cycle   **Fig. 3.** Current I_{bat} of batteries during cycle

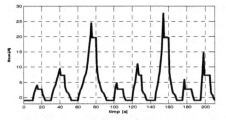

Fig. 4. Electrical motor power P_{bus} **Fig. 5.** Electrical batteries power P_{bat}

On the other hand, the batteries must take the entire breaking power reinserted by the motor in the DC bus, which is practically impossible. The SB system is not sufficient to ensure the motor functionality, being required to use a hybrid energy system, like SBSC, that can answer efficiently of the dynamics of the motor.

2.4 Energy Management Using SBSC

The electrical model of the supercapacitors used in simulations is composed by a variable capacity in series with a resistance. The pack of batteries is simple modeled by an ideal voltage source. The synchronous motor has the experimental model detailed by the authors in the previous works [6]. The functioning regimes of the motor are given by the running drive cycle 3ECE. The power control principle utilized for this SBSC, which establishes the contribution of each source in supplying the motor, is based on the separation of medium power demand from the transitory power demand and consists of a first order low pass filtering function. The filter is applied to the current supplying the motor obtaining a reference output current for controlling the supercapacitors pack. In order to implement control strategy for the supercapacitors pack, the transfer function of a first order filter has been utilized. To highlight the filter action on the system functionality, the time constant will take two values: first, 3 s, than simulations are repeated for value of 6 s. Simulations has been done using the Matlab Simulink software.

The motor current is in Fig. 6. In Fig. 7 is layout the current variation that must be ensured by the pack of batteries, when using the constant time filter $\tau = 3$ s. In Fig. 8 is shown the variation of the current when $\tau = 6$ s. Fig. 10 shows the reference current applied to the pack of supercapacitors for $\tau = 3$s, and in Fig. 11 for time constant $\tau = 6$ s. The reference current is resulted after the filter at the converter entry, when batteries and supercapacitors are used together.

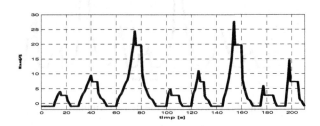

Fig. 6. Current I_{bus} at the traction motor

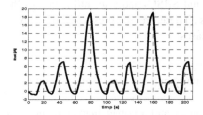

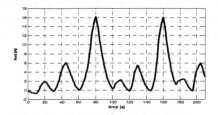

Fig. 7. Batteries current I_{bat} for $\tau = 3$ s   **Fig. 8.** Batteries current I_{bat} for $\tau = 6$ s

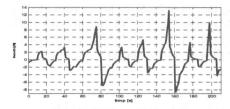
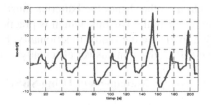

Fig. 9. Reference converter current, $\tau = 3$ s   **Fig. 10.** Reference converter current, $\tau = 6$ s

The graphics prove an important filter of the current delivered by the batteries. Supercapacitors take efficiently the power picks and batteries are smoothed. Graphics prove a better management of current sharing on both energy sources, which ensures together the necessary of electrical energy of the motor.

5   Discussions of Results

In this section, a comparative analyze of graphics in both energy management strategies is done. The power variation curves for the ensemble SBSC-synchronous motor are detailed. In Fig. 11 is represented the requested power by the motor.

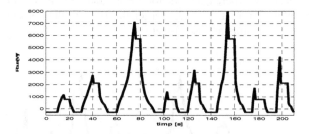

Fig. 11. Power P_{bus} at the motor terminals

In Fig. 12, Fig. 13 and Fig. 14 are analyzed the results obtained after the utilization of both energy management strategies (SB and SBSC) and after utilization of the power control strategy on the supercapacitors. Therefore, is presented the power variation on the batteries terminals in the three cases:

1. using SB like energy management strategy;
2. using SBSC like energy management strategy and a power management strategy with a filter having $\tau = 3$ s;
3. using SBSC like energy management strategy and a power management strategy with a filter having $\tau = 6$ s.

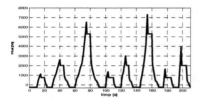

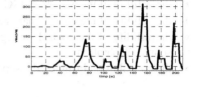

Fig. 12. Batteries power P_{bat}, SB-motor

Fig. 13. Batteries energy W_{bat}, SB-motor

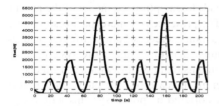

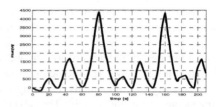

Fig. 14. Batteries power P_{bat} ,SBSC-motor, with filter constant $\tau = 3s$

Fig. 15 Batteries power P_{bat}, SBSC-motor, with filter constant $\tau = 6s$

The energy management is underlined from the energy variation curves resulted from simulations in the Fig. 13, Fig. 16 and Fig. 17.

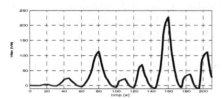

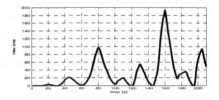

Fig. 16. Batteries energy W_{bat}, SBSC motor, $\tau = 3s$

Fig. 17. Batteries energy W_{bat}, SBSC motor, $\tau = 6s$

Comparing the graphics obtained, it can be deduced:

1. When using SB systems, power and energy on batteries have high values and high picks, that crave for batteries;
2. Using SBSC systems, the transient picks of power and energy on batteries are smoothed;
3. Growing-up the time constant value of the filter used for power control strategy on supercapacitors, the power/energy on batteries becomes smaller and smoother.

Therefore the contribution of the supercapacitors in the energy deliver/storage processes became more important and the system energy efficiency is improved.

Simulations effected highlight the effects of supercapacitors in the hybrid energy system used in automotive. With this research there are certified:

- the validity of the SB and SBSC system models;
- the validity of the energy management strategy with SBSC;
- the validity of the control strategy of the supercapacitors pack based on power sources separation;
- the contribution bring by the supercapacitors in hybrid energy systems.

6 Conclusions and Further Works

The use of SBSC as power control strategy leads to an optimized model of the propulsion system, in accordance to requirements. The presence of supercapacitors in power supply/recovery systems used for electric traction increases battery lifetime and allows a fair design in terms of weight and volume. Therefore, the entire system can be design at lower power requirements, power dimensioning being separate from energy dimensioning of components, ensuring therefore increase of efficiency, reduction of dimensions, costs and weight. The advantages offered by power systems with batteries and supercapacitors recommend them for applications in transportation, especially where high power peaks are required.

The paper presented an analysis regarding power control and energy management when utilizing SB and than a SBSC-synchronous motor system, in functioning conditions imposed by standard 3ECE running cycles.

A command strategy has been implemented for the supercapacitors pack in order to optimize system performance and energy efficiency.

Results of the analysis prove that supercapacitors particularly reduce current peaks applied to/from the battery and improve acceleration characteristics, range and efficiency of the vehicle, especially when the running cycle determines a lot of current peaks.

For the future, experimental results are expected and new models for the components of system will be implemented.

References

1. Chan, C., Chan, K.: Modern Electric Vehicle Technology. Oxford University Press, Oxford (2006)
2. Yap, H., Schofield, C., Bingham, C.: Hybrid energy/power sources for electric vehicle traction systems: The Institution of Electrical of Electrical Engineers. Michael Faradya House, Stevenage, SGI 2AY (2004)
3. Steiner, M., Scholten, J.: Energy storage on board of railway vehicles. In: ESSCAP, Belfort, France (2004)
4. Livint, G., Gaiginschi, R., Horga, V., Drosescu, R., Chiriac, G.: Vehicuel electrice hibride. Venus, Iasi (2006)
5. Lungoci, C., Mailat, A., Helerea, E.: Eco-design of a hybrid energy system for electric vehicles. In: 2nd International Conference on Sustainable energy, Brasov, pp. 438–446 (2008)
6. Lungoci, C., Bouquain, D., Miraoui, A., Helerea, E.: Modular test bench for a hybrid electric vehicle with multiples energy sources. In: 11th IEEE International Conference on Optimization of Electrical and Electronic Equipment, Brasov, pp. 299–306 (2008)

Characteristics of the PTC Heater Used
in Automotive HVAC Systems

Radu Musat and Elena Helerea

Department of Electrical Engineering, Faculty of Electrical Engineering and
Computer Science, *Transilvania* University of Brasov,
29 Eroilor Str., 500036 Brasov, Romania
r_musat@yahoo.com, helerea@unitbv.ro

Abstract. The present heating method which uses the cooling system of the internal combustion engine of the vehicle takes a lot of time to heat the interior air. In order to improve the heating process, auxiliary devices are required. The new innovative techniques propose as auxiliary heating device positive temperature coefficient heaters. For a better control of the temperature, the parameters of these devices should be known. This paper deals with a detailed description of the new types of positive temperature coefficient heaters used in automotive field. The test bench system developed for determining the parameters and characteristics of the positive temperature coefficient heater is described. The obtained data of the thermal resistance and voltage-current characteristics are used for controlling the temperature in order to design and control the positive temperature coefficient heaters properly.

Keywords: PTC heater, HVAC, thermal comfort, vehicle, characteristics.

1 Introduction

The passenger's thermal comfort inside a vehicle is ensured by using heating, ventilating and air conditioning (HVAC) systems.

Modern internal combustion engines (ICE) with fossil fuels offer improved efficiency and dissipate less heat to the cooling system of the engine. On cold days, these engines produce little heat excess and are unable to provide the amount of heat for warming the vehicle interior up to a comfortable level [12].

In the automotive field, different technologies are available to provide the heat and to quickly ensure the passenger's thermal comfort. The conventional heating system uses the heat loss produced by ICE, which is transferred to the cooling system and then used for heating the vehicle interior air. This conventional heating method has disadvantages: it loses about 60 % of the heat and the interior air temperature increases slowly. To improve the conventional heating method, auxiliary heating devices are required [16].

This paper describes and analyses an auxiliary heating device proposed to be used in the automotive field. Also, a test bench system is developed for determining the parameters and characteristics of the positive temperature coefficient (PTC) heater.

L.M. Camarinha-Matos, P. Pereira, and L. Ribeiro (Eds.): DoCEIS 2010, IFIP AICT 314, pp. 461–468, 2010.

The obtained data of the thermal-resistance $R = f(T)$ and the voltage-current $U = f(I)$ characteristics will be used for controlling the temperature in order to design the PTC heater for vehicle thermal comfort system.

2 Contribution to Technological Innovation

In the paper an innovative technique is proposed: a PTC heater is used as auxiliary heating device because of the specific thermal and electrical properties: thermal self-regulation, high responding time, quickly removing the condensed drops from the windscreen and improving the visibility through it.

Based on the experimental results described in the paper, a model and simulation of the PTC heater are proposed. An integration of the PTC model in the vehicle heating diagram for overall heating process simulation will be made in order to design and control optimally a PTC heater.

3 State of the Art and Existing Problems

Since the 1990's, research has been developed regarding the auxiliary heaters that warm up the interior air as soon as the vehicle is started [18-21]. There have been difficulties as regards the fact that the auxiliary heaters demand a large quantity of energy, and consequently they operate only when the engine is running, which increases the fuel consumption and the pollution.

After the significant increase in the fuel prices in 2006, much automotive research has shown renewed interest in fuel-efficient vehicles. In gasoline-fuelled vehicles, about 40% of fuel energy is wasted in exhaust heat, while 30% of energy is transferred through the engine coolant. Because of that, these engines produce little heat excess, especially in winter time, in city traffic and traffic jams, and they are unable to warm quickly the passenger compartment to a comfortable level [12].

Various vehicle models from leading manufacturers around the world are now equipped with PTC auxiliary heaters. In 2007, 65% of all diesel vehicles in Europe were equipped with an auxiliary heater and this is expected to rise to 90% by 2010. It is obvious that PTC heaters will not be limited to diesel vehicles but will be also used in gasoline-powered ones as well [13].

Commonly used PTC materials include high density polyethylene (filled with graphite), polymeric and titanate ceramic materials (which work by grain boundary effects). PTC heaters based on barium titanate ceramic ($BaTiO_3$), having high resistance and power-dissipation characteristics, are mostly used in automotive industry [1], [2], [5], [7], [8].

Several authors have studied the resistance – temperature dependency of PTC heaters [3], [5], [6], [11], [15]. Over the years, various theoretical and experimental models have been developed to describe the PTC heater effect, e.g. in semiconducting $BaTiO_3$, such as Heywang (the most accepted model), Jonker and Wang [4], [6], [7].

A comparative analysis between PTC thermistors and heaters sustains the development of new heating solutions.

4 PTC Thermistors and Heaters

PTC thermistors have specific features: thermal self-regulating and efficient energy consumption, no danger of fire since there are no glowing parts, no excess temperature protection required, no smell, no radiation and oxidation, fast thermal response time, temperature setting from +50 °C to + 320 °C, compact design and long life service [10].

PTC thermistors have a wide variety of applications, which can be divided into two distinct categories [22]. The first category utilizes the resistance-temperature or voltage-current characteristics of the PTC thermistor. These are known as self heated applications and include: self-regulating heaters, PTC over-current protectors, time delay, motor starting etc. The second category comprises zero power or sensing applications (e.g. temperature sensors and control) [17].

The PTC thermistor has a low value of electrical resistance at low temperatures. When a voltage is applied to the cold elements, a high current is generated and the value of resistance rises with the temperature. As soon as the current flows through the device, the elements warm up by electrical dissipation until a steady state is reached and the resistive elements have reached their working temperature. This triggers the reduction of the electric current because the electric charge is unable to cross the boundaries of the tiny crystals at high temperatures. For this reason, the manufacturers of auxiliary heaters propose the use of the PTC thermistor principle [18], [19], [20], [21].

The PTC heater is mounted inside the HVAC system, after the heat exchanger. In Fig. 1, there is illustrated the position of the PTC heater and the air flow inside the HVAC system.

The PTC heater is connected to the vehicle electrical system and it is controlled by the Engine Control Module (ECM), HVAC control panel and relays [9]. In Fig. 2 there is illustrated the PTC heater control diagram.

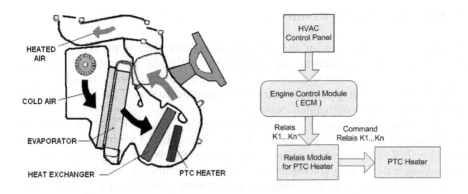

Fig. 1. HVAC system   **Fig. 2.** PTC heater control diagram

The PTC heater, illustrated in Fig. 3, consists of a moulded plastic plate (1), an electrical connector (2) and heating resistive elements with fins (3). The PTC heating resistive elements (Fig. 4) consist of small metallised ceramic plates (1), which are layered alternately along the unit core with aluminium radiator elements (2). These layers are held together by spring elements in a frame. The aluminium elements ensure the electrical contacts and transfer the heat to the passing heater air flow [14].

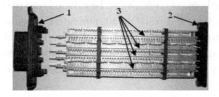 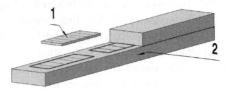

Fig. 3. PTC heater components   **Fig. 4.** PTC heating resistive elements

The heating resistive elements are separated in different heating circuits in order to adapt the heating power to different requirements and they act as positive temperature coefficient resistors. The maximum value of the temperature of the elements is around 165 °C, if no air flows through the heating system [12].

The heating elements are switched progressively in order to reduce the demand factor of the generator, to prevent load dumps and ECM problems caused by high currents.

The PTC heater operates only: (i) at low external temperatures; (ii) when insufficient heat is supplied by ICE cooling system; (iii) at reduced loads of the generator.

The total electrical power consumption for a PTC heater ranges between 900 W and 2000 W, depending on the air volume of the vehicle interior. Vehicles equipped with PTC heater are fitted with a more powerful generator.

5   Experiments and Results

In order to model and simulate the processes which take place in the HVAC system, data related to the characteristics of the auxiliary heating devices are required. For a PTC heater, it is important to analyze and measure the temperature – resistance characteristics and the voltage-current characteristic in order to design the PTC heater and to determine the optimal thermal comfort.

To measure and obtain the temperature-resistance curves, $R = f(T)$, a test bench was developed. The test bench, illustrated in Fig. 5, consists of a heating camera (type Carbolite PF/200), a cooling camera (type Derby DK 9620), temperature sensors (placed inside the heating/cooling camera) and a data acquisition system.

To measure and obtain the voltage-current characteristics $U = f(I)$, a test bench was also developed. The test bench, illustrated in Fig. 6, consists of a battery (type Rombat Pilot Diesel Hybrid, 12V / 77Ah), an ammeter, a voltmeter, temperature sensors (placed on PTC heating elements) and a data acquisition system.

All the acquired data are processed by means of MATLAB tool.

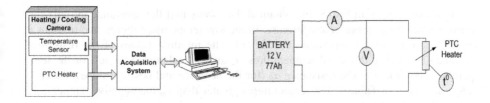

Fig. 5. Test bench scheme implementation for thermal resistance characteristics

Fig. 6. Measurement scheme for determining $U = f(I)$ characteristics

To make the experiments, a 1000 W / 13.5 V PTC heater sample was used. This heater consists of four power stages (two stages of 333 W and two stages of 166 W). In Fig. 7, there is illustrated the electrical diagram for the PTC heater sample.

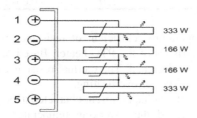

Fig. 7. Electrical diagram of the PTC heater sample

In Fig. 8 and Fig. 9, there are illustrated the experimental results representing the characteristics $R = f(T)$ and $U = f(I)$, for each stage.

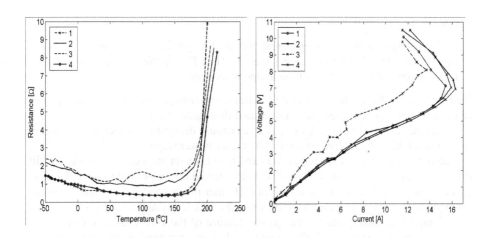

Fig. 8. Thermal resistance characteristics

Fig. 9. Voltage-current characteristics

As it can be seen in Fig. 8, the obtained data show that the resistance initially decreases with the increase in temperature. In the low temperature region, the resistance curve has a negative temperature coefficient. The minimal values of the resistance obtained at specific threshold temperatures, T_t and the calculated values for the temperature coefficient of the resistance α_R (for the negative and positive slope), for each stage are given in Table 1. For temperatures greater than T_t, the negative temperature coefficient is changed to a positive one.

Table 1. The values of the resistance R, the threshold temperatures T_t. and the temperature coefficient of the resistance α_R for each stage.

Stage	R [Ω]	T_t [°C]	α_{R-} [K^{-1}]	α_{R+} [K^{-1}]
1	0.367	120	- 0.0044	+ 0.937
2	0.895	110	- 0.0037	+ 0.285
3	1.34	130	- 0.0024	+ 0.211
4	0.35	130	- 0.0042	+ 0.984

The values of the temperature coefficient of resistance require specific thermal regulating process characteristics of the PTC heater. Based on these coefficients, the PTC heaters can be properly designed. The thermal resistance characteristic is appropriate for preventing the PTC heater overheating.

As it is shown in Fig. 9, the voltage-current characteristics are linear until the PTC heating elements have reached their working temperature and a steady state is reached. After these values, the electrical current drastically decreases.

Warming up of the PTC heater depends on the electrical power inside the elements and can be described with the following relationship:

$$U(I) \cdot I(t) = \frac{U^2(t)}{R(T,t)} \cdot \delta \cdot (T - T_A) + C_{PTC} \cdot \frac{dT}{dt} \; . \tag{1}$$

where:

$U(t)$ – voltage supply; $I(t)$ – electrical current through the PTC heater; δ – heat dissipation of PTC; T – present temperature of PTC; T_A – ambient temperature; C_{PTC} – heat capacity of PTC; dT/dt – time temperature variation.

Based on the voltage and current data values, the dissipation power – temperature characteristics for each stage are obtained and illustrated in Fig. 10.

As it can be seen in Fig. 10, there is a maximum dissipation power corresponding to the threshold temperatures for each PTC heater power stage.

The obtained values of the parameters and the characteristics can be compared with those from specialty literature. The PTC heater tested above proved to have the same characteristics with those from a typical PTC thermistor model. The developed test bench allows testing these characteristics rapidly, efficiently and accurately.

The high responding time is the typical feature of the PTC heater. This is useful after the vehicle is started: till the engine reaches its operating temperature, the conventional heating system does not supply the necessary heat for the interior air. This additional heat can practically be accounted to the PTC heater.

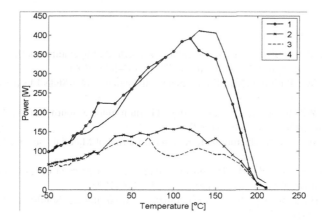

Fig. 10. Dissipation power – temperature characteristics for PTC heater sample

6   Conclusion and Future Work

This paper deals with an analysis on auxiliary heating devices used in vehicle thermal comfort systems. A test bench system was developed for determining the parameters and characteristics of PTC heater and measurement data were processed.

Based on the experimental results described in the paper, a model and simulation of the PTC heater was developed. An integration of the PTC model in the vehicle heating diagram for overall heating process simulation is to be made.

The PTC heaters are necessary in some conditions (e.g. winter time) to increase the passenger's thermal comfort. The PTC heaters are ideal for thermal comfort control due to their capacity of thermal self-regulating and high responding time.

The challenge is that the PTC heater demands a large quantity of electrical current, so it operates only when the engine is running and thus increases the fuel consumption and the pollution.

New higher capacities of PTC heater would be possible with a 42 V vehicle wiring system. The transition to 42 V voltages, the decentralisation of power distribution and the development of more complex energy sources will provide new innovative systems to supply PTC heaters properly.

Since vehicles are getting more efficient, they free less heat for the heating system; thus, by including auxiliary devices consuming electric energy, the heating time will be improved and the engine efficiency increased. The electric energy is taken from the engine through the generator/battery system, which reduces the overall efficiency of the vehicle. Consequently, an adequate energy balance and management should be accomplished.

Increasing the overall efficiency is the main objective in any PTC heater design and can be achieved by different techniques, such as: improving the technology of materials, manufacture and control processes.

References

1. Amin, A.: Piezoresistivity in semiconducting positive temperature coefficient ceramics. Journal of the American Ceramic Society 72(3), 369–376 (1989)
2. Heywang, W.: Bariumtitanat als Sperrschichthalbleiter. Solid-State Electronics 3, 51–58 (1961)
3. Heywang, W.: Resistivity anomaly in doped barium titanate. Journal of the American Ceramic Society 47(10), 484–490 (1964)
4. Heywang, W.: Semiconducting barium titanate. Journal of Materials Science 6, 1214–1224 (1971)
5. Huybrechts, B., Ishizaki, H.: The positive temperature coefficient of resistivity in barium titanate. Journal of Materials Science 30, 2463–2474 (1995)
6. Jonker, G.H.: Some aspects of semiconducting barium titanate. Solid-State Electronics 7, 895–903 (1964)
7. Wang, D.Y.: Electrical properties of PTC barium titanate. Journal of the American Ceramic Society 73(3), 669–677 (1990)
8. Mamunya, Y.P., Muzychenko, Y.V.: PTC effect and structure of polymer composite. Journal of Polymer Engineering and Science 47, 34–42 (2007)
9. Amsel, C., Schoenen, R.: Use of CAE-Methods to analyse the influence of new electrical systems behaviour on tomorrow's 42V. Institut für Kraftfahrwesen, Aachen (2001)
10. Jones, L., Kinsman, K.: PTC Thermistor Introduction. Compliance Engineering Magazine (2002)
11. Schedel, R.: New PTC Heaters Control High Voltages in Hybrid and Electric Vehicles. Eberspaecher Magazine (2009)
12. Daly, S.: Automotive air conditioning and climate control systems. Elsevier, Oxford (2006)
13. Ehsani, M., Gao, Y.: Modern Electric, Hybrid Electric, and Fuel Cell Vehicles – Fundamentals, Theory, and Design. CRC Press, Washington (2005)
14. Stone, R.: Introduction to Internal Combustion Engines, 3rd edn. SAE International and MacMillan Press, USA (1999)
15. Apostol, I., Helerea, E.: Obtaining the High Performance PTC Thermistors based on Barium Titanate. In: Proceeding of the 11th International Conference on Optimization of Electric and Electronic Equipment – Optim. 2008, Brasov, pp. 119–123 (2008)
16. Kassakian, J.G., Perreault, D.J.: The Future of Electronics in Automobiles. In: Proceeding of ISPSD, pp. 15–19. IEEE Explore, Los Alamitos (2001)
17. Spectrum Sensors & Control Inc., Advanced Thermal Products Division, http://www.specsensors.com
18. Denso Corporation, http://www.globaldenso.com
19. Behr Hella Service GmbH, http://www.behrhellaservice.com
20. Valeo Termico SA, http://www.valeo.com
21. Eberspaecher electronics GmbH, http://www.eberspaecher.com
22. Advanced thermal Products Inc., http://www.atpsensor.com

Fuel Cell Systems for Telecommunications

Eunice Ribeiro[1], António Cardoso[1], and Chiara Boccaletti[2]

[1] University of Coimbra, FCTUC/IT
Department of Electrical and Computer Engineering
Pólo II – Pinhal de Marrocos, P – 3000-290, Coimbra, Portugal
Tel.:/Fax: +351 239 796 232/247
eribeiro@co.it.pt, ajmcardoso@ieee.org
[2] Sapienza University of Rome
Department of Electrical Engineering
Via Eudossiana, 18, 00184 Rome, Italy
Tel.: (+39) -06-44585762; Fax: (+39)-06-4883235
chiara.boccaletti@uniroma1.it

Abstract. Standalone power systems for telecommunications are becoming an emergent need, due to environmental problems and their current tendency to be localized in remote places. Along with photovoltaic and wind generators, fuel cells are one of the most mature technologies to be employed in this kind of systems. As they are expensive and complex systems, it is important to simulate their behaviour to study different operating modes. This paper intends to propose a simulation of a fuel cell system with a voltage-fed full-bridge converter in the Matlab-Simulink© environment fulfilling the strict telecommunications equipment requirements.

Keywords: Telecommunications power system, fuel cell, dc-dc converter.

1 Introduction

Due to the attention to environmental concerns that has been increasing at a worldwide level and the proliferation of telecommunications equipment in remote places, one of the best choices for the future of the telecommunications power supply systems is based on renewable energies applied to stand-alone power systems. This kind of power systems combines a set of different renewable energies to guarantee an autonomous and sustainable operation with a reduced need of maintenance, suitable for supplying remote telecommunications equipment. The majority of standalone power systems are based on wind and photovoltaic generators. These kinds of generators are intermittent and, consequently, it is necessary to include energy storage systems to balance the energy production during periods of low solar radiation or wind speed.

In combination with solar or wind generators, fuel cells associated to electrolyzers and hydrogen tanks are a good solution to store energy, as an alternative to the most standard batteries, because they increase the system availability while reducing its maintenance costs.

L.M. Camarinha-Matos, P. Pereira, and L. Ribeiro (Eds.): DoCEIS 2010, IFIP AICT 314, pp. 469–476, 2010.
© IFIP International Federation for Information Processing 2010

This paper intends to present the simulation of a fuel cell system operation, where the included DC-DC converter plays a very important role to fulfill the telecommunications equipment requirements. The simulation has been performed as closely as possible to actual conditions, using dynamic models of fuel cells. Different operating modes are studied and compared to the telecommunications requirements verifying the excellent performance of the fuel cell to supply this kind of equipments.

2   Contribution to Technological Innovation

Since telecommunications equipments are being organized in dispersed networks, reliable remote power solutions are emerging as a critical need, where a backup system like a fuel cell combined with an electrolyzer and a hydrogen tank has a vital role. The proposed simulation permits to improve the application of fuel cells as a backup in these kinds of systems, since the power electronics interface simulation is included and different modes of operation can be designed and studied in advance.

The DC-DC converter employed in this simulation is different from the usual ones, which are simple topologies without galvanic isolation [1-6]. Indeed, in order to fulfill the telecommunications equipment requirements, galvanic isolation is required. At low power levels, simple, non-isolated topologies are commonly used, such as buck, boost and buck-boost [7]. Their topologies include an electronic switch, an inductor to store energy, and a flywheel diode [8]. The electronic switch commutation is controlled in order to maintain the required load voltage. The flywheel diode carries the current during that part of switching cycle when the electronic switch is off.

Higher levels of power (above 1 kW) require isolated topologies, e. g. flyback, forward, push-pull, half-bridge and full-bridge. These are more complex topologies, but, once again, the load voltage depends on the switching control of the electronic switches [8]. Fuel cells brought other challenges to power electronics like the need for low input current ripple, in order to reduce the ripple of the stack voltage and this is why current-fed converters are usually specified as a good power electronics interface for them [7]. The study of these kinds of converters as power electronics interfaces between the fuel cell and the load is usually performed through analytical calculations to describe their operating behaviour [9] or simulations with usual DC voltage sources instead of fuel cell system models as this paper proposes [10]. The advantages of such a study are obvious. Fuel cell systems are expensive and complex and, therefore, they need to be carefully designed and studied before their implementation, especially for high power applications or critical applications where uninterruptible power is required.

The converter chosen for this system was the voltage-fed full-bridge converter. According to [11], where a mathematical analysis is presented as a criterion to choose the most efficient and appropriated DC-DC converter for fuel cells applications, the voltage-fed full-bridge converter is the most efficient DC-DC converter with galvanic isolation and it needs the least core cross section of the transformer. The input current ripple is low [7].

3   Fuel Cell System Simulation

The aim of the proposed simulation is to study the dynamic performance of a fuel cell system composed only by a fuel cell carefully dimensioned and a power electronics interface capable of maintaining the required telecommunications equipment voltage. As it was already explained, telecommunications power systems must obey to strict power requirements and, due to this, power converters play a very important role in this kind of systems. The importance of the power converters simulation increases when a not yet consolidated technology to produce electrical power, such as fuel cells, is used.

The fuel cell model and its parameters were taken from [1-6] and they have been used to simulate innumerous standalone applications like portable equipments (laptops, for example) [1], residential houses [2, 3], vehicles [4], and hybrid power generation plants [5, 6]. The model has been implemented in the Matlab-Simulink© environment, as shown in Fig.1.

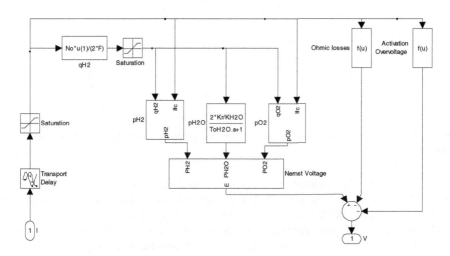

Fig. 1. Fuel cell system Simulink© model

The required amount of hydrogen q_{H_2} [kmol (s)$^{-1}$] that is consumed by the fuel cell is related to the stack current I (A) by [1-6]:

$$q_{H_2} = \frac{N_o I}{2F} \tag{1}$$

where N_o is the number of cells in series in the stack and F is the Faraday's constant.

This value allows calculating the partial pressure of hydrogen (p_{H_2}), oxygen (p_{O_2}) and water (p_{H_2O}), which are important to obtain the Nernst voltage, given by:

$$E = N_o \left[E_o + \frac{RT}{2F} \log \left[\frac{P_{H_2} \sqrt{P_{O_2}}}{P_{H_2O}} \right] \right]$$ (2)

where E_o is the no-load voltage [V], R is the universal gas constant and T is the stack temperature [K].

The stack output voltage V is

$$V = E - B \ln (C \times I) - R \times I$$ (3)

where B and C are constants to simulate the activation overvoltage in the fuel cell system [1-6] and R is the internal resistance of the fuel cell stack [Ω].

The whole simulation system is presented in Fig. 2.

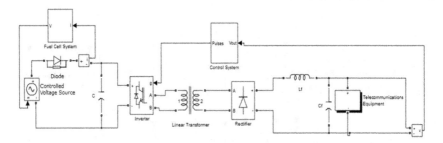

Fig. 2. Fuel cell system Simulink$^\copyright$ model with power electronics interface and telecommunication equipment

The modeled telecommunication equipment is a Radio Base Station (RBS). The model includes resistances and switches aiming to simulate load variations, as shown in Fig. 3. A typical RBS load has a nominal power of 3 kW and an overload (until 4 kW) is imposed to study the transient behaviour of the system in case of load variations. Its nominal operating voltage range is 48 V and the operating voltage ranges from 42.75 V to 56.7 V [12].

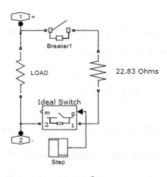

Fig. 3. Simulink$^\copyright$ load model

4   Simulation Results

The dynamic performance of the fuel cell is tested under a load variation of 33%, applied between 0.3 and 0.6 seconds, which is shown in Fig. 4.

In Fig. 5, the output stack voltage is shown and a voltage ripple of 1.5 V is visible. During the increase of power, the voltage ripple also increases to 2 V. As it can be seen in Fig. 6, the voltage is always kept under the required levels for telecommunications equipment with a reduced ripple of 0.4 V, even in presence of the transients

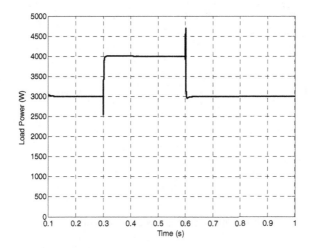

Fig. 4. Simulink© load model: Load Power

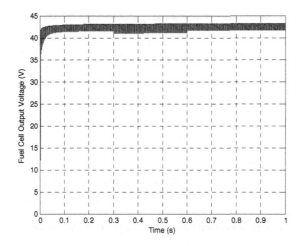

Fig. 5. Simulink© load model: Fuel Cell Output Voltage

caused by the turn-on of the system or the power variations. A LC filter was used, with a capacitor of 200 μF and an inductance of 2 mH. When the load power increases, the voltage reduces to 37.6 V during the 15 ms transient as it can be seen in detail in Fig. 7. At 0.6 seconds, an overvoltage of 60.7 V is caused by the load power decreasing again to the nominal value (Fig. 8). Also this transient takes 15 ms.

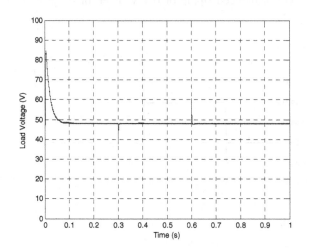

Fig. 6. Simulink© load model: Load Voltage

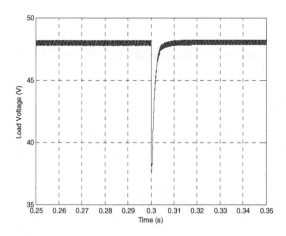

Fig. 7. Simulink© load model: snapshot of Load Voltage curve

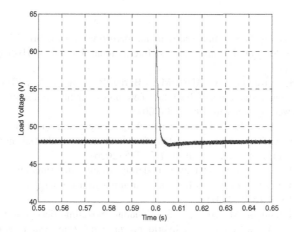

Fig. 8. Simulink© load model: snapshot of Load Voltage curve

5   Conclusion

Telecommunications equipments are strictly exigent on their requirements, such as establishing dc nominal voltage, keeping voltage at its operating level and assuring a reduced ripple and noise in voltage and current waveforms. The presented results of the simulation show how effective the chosen fuel cell system is in fulfilling the load requirements. The present work permits to improve the application of fuel cells as a backup device, since the power electronics interface simulation is included and different modes of operation can be designed and studied in advance.

Directions for future work, include the implementation of a complete standalone power system model of which the fuel cell system will be a part. Mathematical models of the different system components (photovoltaic and wind generators) will be interconnected and a supervisory control system will be developed to define the interaction among them. The most important objective of this control system is to supply the load at its full demand while monitoring the pressure in the hydrogen storage tank. To design such a control system is a challenging task that requires the definition of monitoring key system parameters to be compared one with another to transmit the precise commands, allowing the accomplishment of the load requirements. The conceived fuel cell system model already takes these parameters into account. Further work will be done to achieve a more complex and reliable system. For example, a supercapacitor could be added to the fuel cell system in order to improve its dynamic response.

Acknowledgments. This work was partly supported by Fundação para a Ciência e a Tecnologia (FCT) under Project No. SFRH/BD/47741/2008 and Project No. SFRH/BSAB/950/2009.

References

1. Yalcinoz, T., Alam, M.S.: Improved dynamic performance of hybrid PEM fuel cells and ultracapacitors for portable applications. International Journal of Hydrogen Energy 33, 1932–1940 (2008)
2. El-Sharkh, M.Y., Rahman, A., Alam, M.S., Byrne, P.C., Sakla, A.A., Thomas, T.: A dynamic model for a stand-alone PEM fuel cell power plant for residential applications. Journal of Power Sources 138, 199–204 (2004)
3. Uzunoglu, M., Alam, M.S.: Dynamic modeling, design, and simulation of a combined PEM fuel cell and ultracapacitor system for stand-alone residential applications. IEEE Transactions on Energy Conversion 21, 767–775 (2006)
4. Uzunoglu, M., Alam, M.S.: Dynamic modeling, design and simulation of a PEM fuel cell/ultra-capacitor hybrid system for vehicular applications. Energy Conversion and Management 48, 1544–1553 (2007)
5. Onar, O.C., Uzunoglu, M., Alam, M.S.: Dynamic modeling, design and simulation of a wind/fuel cell/ultra-capacitor-based hybrid power generation system. Journal of Power Sources 161, 707–722 (2006)
6. Uzunoglu, M., Onar, O.C., Alam, M.S.: Modeling, control and simulation of a PV/FC/UC based hybrid power generation system for stand-alone applications. Renewable Energy 34, 509–520 (2009)
7. Kirubakaran, A., Jain, S., Nema, R.K.: A review on fuel cell technologies and power electronic interface. Renewable and Sustainable Energy Reviews 13, 2430–2440 (2009)
8. Mohan, N., Undeland, M., Robbins, W.: Power Electronics Converters, Applications and Design. John Wiley & Sons, USA (2003)
9. Averberg, A., Mertens, A.: Analysis of a voltage-fed full bridge DC-DC converter in fuel cell systems. In: Power Elecronics Specialists Conference, pp. 281–292 (2007)
10. Kovacevic, G., Tenconi, A., Bojoi, R.: Advanced DC-DC converter for power conditioning in hydrogen fuel cell systems. International Journal of Hydrogen Energy 33, 3215–3219 (2008)
11. Krykunov, O.: Comparison of the DC-DC converters for fuel cell applications. International Journal of Electrical, Computer, and Systems Engineering 1, 71–79 (2007)
12. Reeve, D.W.: DC Power System Design for Telecommunications. John Wiley and Sons, USA (2007)

Hybrid Photovoltaic-Thermal Collectors: A Review

Figueiredo Ramos[1], António Cardoso[2], and Adérito Alcaso[1]

[1] Polytechnic Institute of Guarda, School of Technology and Management, Portugal
{framos,aderitona}@ipg.pt
[2] University of Coimbra, FCTUC/IT, Department of Electrical
and Computer Engineering, Portugal
ajmcardoso@ieee.org

Abstract. Solar energy can be converted directly into electric and thermal energy through photovoltaic cells and thermal collectors, respectively. However this conversion, in particular the photovoltaic, has a reduced efficiency. A solution proposed to increase this efficiency is with the hybrid solar structure, which consists in the junction of the photovoltaic panel and the thermal collector in a single module. The interest on these solar systems led the International Energy Agency to create a "Task" on this subject. This paper presents a review of the research in this area, presenting the definitions of the related collectors and results of their characteristics, as well as some ideas for future studies.

Keywords: Hybrid photovoltaic/thermal (PV/T) collector, photovoltaic (PV), thermal (TH), heat transfer, efficiency.

1 Introduction

At the beginning of the XXI century the energy issues have been occupying a central place in the international concerns. These concerns are related to ecological aspects, namely climatic concerns with the global heating and climate changes, economic aspects, tied to the scarcity of resources of fossil origin and geopolitical aspects, regarding the difficulty of energy transportation mainly through politically unstable zones.

Due to the vital importance of the energy sector in the countries economies and from all the issues mentioned above, it is necessary to establish new energy and environmental politics in order to find a balance between the environmental, technical and economical viability of energy production and consumption, promoting thus a sustainable development.

The European Union (EU), geographic area that is strongly dependent on external primary energy, considers that, relatively to the energy sources, a strong increase of renewable energies in global energy production is desirable, in order to reach a 15% contribution until 2010. The concerns of the EU on energy and environmental politics integration are reported in the new "Energy Politics for the Europe". This politic proposal must be the basic instrument for the reduction of the Greenhouse Gases and the increment of the energy production with renewable sources, among others. Also in Portugal, the Government has defined the "National Strategy for the Energy" to promote energy production on the basis of renewable sources, with the capacity of exploration in the country, being the solar energy one of them.

L.M. Camarinha-Matos, P. Pereira, and L. Ribeiro (Eds.): DoCEIS 2010, IFIP AICT 314, pp. 477–484, 2010.

The technology associated with the exploitation of solar energy, namely the independent photovoltaic and thermal systems, for conversion of the solar radiation into electric and thermal energy, respectively, is already a mature technology. However, one of the inconveniences associated to this traditional technology, particularly the photovoltaic one, is its low efficiency, leading necessarily to great areas of implantation for these systems, which is a major limitation. That is particularly important in applications where the availability of free lands is more limited. Moreover, the solar radiation increases the temperature of photovoltaic cells, decreasing their efficiency, and the natural convection cooling of these modules, due to climatic conditions, is not enough to reduce the temperature in order obtain a desired maximal efficiency. To surpass these inconveniences, investigators had considered the integration of the thermal and photovoltaic systems in a single device for conversion of solar energy with simultaneous production and consumption of electric and thermal energy. The goal of this integration is to generate more energy per unit area than with the photovoltaic panel and the thermal collector, installed independently. These devices of solar co-generation are called "Photovoltaic-Thermal" collectors/panels or "PV/T". In contrast to the independent photovoltaic and thermal solar systems, the hybrid devices have not reached yet a technological maturity and are still being studied. By recognizing their potentialities, the International Energy Agency has created a task, "Task 35 - Solar PV/Thermal Systems", whose aim is to increase the common knowledge of the PV/T solar systems, the promotion of their development, the market introduction of these solar systems with quality and commercial competitiveness and also contributing to the standardization of functional tests and surveillance of commercial characteristics of these systems in the construction sector. Under supervision of Task 35 some publications were developed [1-3] being foreseen for publication in 2009 a final report, with the goal of presenting all the information about the PV/T solar systems.

2   Contribution to Technological Innovation

In this paper, a review of the research on PV/T collectors and their application in heat and electricity production will be presented, illustrating their potentialities.

The performance of PV/T collectors depends on many variables, being the temperature one of the most important, and, although promising, there is not yet a consensus about the viability of this technology and its application, since it can differs from region to region. For example, in the northern countries, with lesser solar radiation, the PV/T collectors can be used, to a large extent, integrated in buildings to lower the temperature of the PV modules and to supply hot air for preheating of interior spaces. In countries with warmer climate, as it is the case of the Mediterranean countries, the PV/T collectors can be used, for the most part, to lower the temperature of PV modules and heating domestic waters.

More research is needed, namely regarding modelling, structure dimensioning and topology aspects. A setup is being developed in order to experimentally validate this research, which will also comprises a modelling and computational simulation based on techniques of distributed parameters and finite elements, in order to obtain a better temperature distribution in the PV/T.

3 PV/T Collector Types

Different possibilities are described in the literature for the construction of a PV/T. The basic structure uses a thermal fluid for cooling photovoltaic cells, allowing the increase of their conversion efficiency and recovering some of the various heat losses that in another way would be simply transmitted to the environment. This allows the production of thermal energy and its direct application in domestic water heating, swimming pools or drying substances, among others.

The PV/T collectors can be classified primarily with regard to the existence, or not, of auxiliary mechanisms for concentration of the solar radiation. The collectors with concentrators use reflective devices in order to increase the amount of solar radiation in a small area (in the PV face). The collectors without concentrators are of flat type, like usual PV panels, and the solar radiation directly reaches the area of the collector. The collectors are still classified in accordance with the existence of a solar tracking system and the type of thermal fluid that can either be liquid (water) or gas (air).

Regarding the concentrating type, some authors [4], [5] had developed PV/T collectors that consist of a parabolic reflective surface that concentrates more solar energy in the photovoltaic cells, whose material must support the high working temperatures of these collectors in the receiving area. In the backs of the photovoltaic arrangement, the thermal fluid (normally water with antifreezing characteristics) cools the PV cell taking out the heat for the production of thermal energy. Other authors [6] developed a structure with a different version of concentrating PV/T, as shown in Fig. 1, with a system composed by two parabolic mirrors. In this system, that must include a solar tracker, the first mirror concentrates the solar radiation of small wavelength in photovoltaic cells for production of electric energy, whereas the second parabolic receives the radiation with higher wavelength that however crossed the first mirror and that later will be reflected in a pipe that has a fluid in its interior, that serves as a way of thermal transference. This system, according to its authors, proved to be efficient and economically competitive as compared to the traditional power plants.

With respect to flat-type PV/T collectors, more often used than the concentrating ones, these are similar to common thermal collectors and photovoltaic panels, which are cheaper although less efficient. The flat PV/T collector is usually constituted by the PV component, whose material is the conventional doped crystalline silicon, and the TH component, joined each other, being the later behind the first one. This PV/T module can be glassed or not, i.e. it can include or not, in its structure, a glass placed above the photovoltaic cells.

Fig. 2 shows the structure of a typical flat plate PV/T collector showing the PV module, the heat extraction equipment - metallic plate constituted by pipes that absorb heat and functions as a cooling system of the PV module attached to it - the glass cover and the thermal isolation that has a function of preventing great heat losses through the equipment walls. These collectors are suitable for roof installation or other areas of easy access, not only because they allow an easy and adjusted integration in constructions, but also because they occupy less space than the photovoltaic and thermal modules used separately.

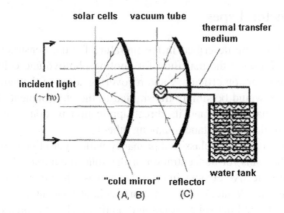

Fig. 1. A schematic structure of a concentrating PV/T collector [6]

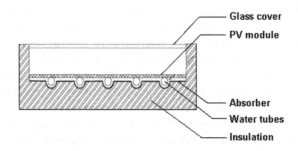

Fig. 2. Cross section of a flat plate PV/T collector

The flat plate PV/T collectors can be divided in two types: water and air, depending on what fluid passes through the pipes. When using water it is usually associated to another liquid with antifreezing characteristics, so that it does not freeze so easily when the environment reaches negative temperatures, preventing damages in the system. According to the typical PV/T collector shown on Fig.2, there are authors [7], [8] that propose the air as a thermal fluid, showing that for the same amount of solar radiation, the efficiency of the photovoltaic module is always lower than the thermal module and also that the increase of solar radiation results in an increase of the efficiency of the two modules, PV and TH.

Other authors [9-12] analysed a PV/T collector with water as thermal fluid and multicrystaline silicon PV panel, with and without a glass cover. They had stated that using this cover in a collector increases the thermal efficiency, but reduces the electric efficiency due to the additional losses by reflection. These authors also consider the choice of the thermal fluid as one of the most important selections to make, having the liquid ones (water) a better performance than the air collectors.

The evaluation of the PV/T systems and their application areas are analyzed in [13]. The authors consider that thanks to the use of PV/T collectors, which they call as solar co-generation technology, there are some practical and technical improvements regarding the installation of PV and TH systems separately. These improvements are:

a lesser installation area, reduced installation costs and the fact that PV and TH modules use different parts of the solar spectrum (PV - wavelength of the visible one; TH - wavelength of the infrared one), making the flat PV/T hybrid technology well adjusted to explore both radiations, due to the fact that the silicon, main component used in the PV cells, is partially transparent to the infrared radiation. It is important that the PV/T collector absorbs the maximum radiation that it receives, using for this a good PV and a thermal plate with a great absorption of heat.

4   PV/T Collectors Performance

A realistic system for the simultaneous conversion of the solar radiation in electric and thermal energy through the PV/T is schematized in Fig. 3. Apart from the PV/T collector, that converts the solar radiation, the system includes a possible pump and hot water storage for the thermal system, and a charge controller, a battery and a DC/AC converter, for the electric system. There is also a supervision and control system of the conversion process.

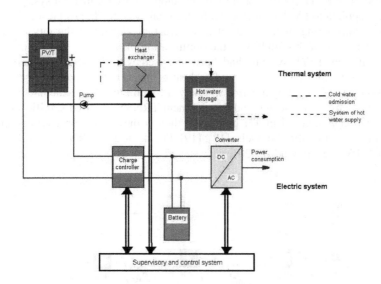

Fig. 3. Block diagram of PV/T system

The performance of PV/T system depends on factors like the temperature of the thermal fluid, the amount of the mass flow of this fluid, the number of glass covers, the configuration of the thermal flat plate module and the supervisory and control system.

In the analysis of a PV/T collector [14] it was reported that the reduction of the temperature verified in PV module, due to the thermal fluid, was superior to 10 °C which implied an increase of about 5% in the photovoltaic efficiency.

As stated before, in a flat PV/T collector without additional glass cover the electric efficiency is bigger than with a covering glass. In this case the PV module can even reach a bigger temperature than a conventional PV panel and there is an increase of reflected radiation on the top of the collector. To reduce the verified reflection the glass cover must be highly transparent to the solar radiation [15].

When the thermal resistance between PV and TH modules increases, this implies the existence of a great difference in temperatures - high temperature gradient - between them, leading to the increase of thermal losses and a reduction of PV performance. In PV/T collectors the thermal efficiency increases with increased heat transfer coefficients, that is, with the reduction of thermal resistance. With glass covers the thermal efficiency of the collector is bigger.

5   Modelling and Simulation

The modelling of a PV/T system can be based on the known base models of the PV and TH modules, with an additional path between them. The model can then be implemented in a software package. The majority of studies used the TRNSYS (The Transient Energy System Simulation Tool) simulation program or the MAT-LAB/SIMULINK. TRNSYS was initially developed only for thermal systems but has been also applied to PV/T collectors with electrical systems. In [16] a simulation was presented considering meteorological data of a typical year of the city of Nicosia, Cyprus. The goal of this study was the optimization of the water flow in the system. In [17] different PV/T systems had been analysed with TNRSYS, namely for the cases of water heating in a house and preheat of the ventilation air in a school. The simulation was executed by a period of one year, with typical climatic data from Holland. For the areas of research and development TRNSYS is used significantly when the simulation is focused in TH part, even though the simulation environment also allows the inclusion of PV models, [18], [19]. Fig. 4 shows a TRNSYS model used to simulate a PV/T solar window [20].

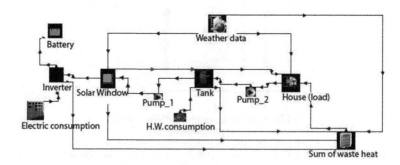

Fig. 4. Block diagram of a PV/T TRNSYS model [21]

In [21] a PV/T system was analysed, in this case, with MATLAB/SIMULINK and the obtained results were compared with the experimental ones, concluding that the considered system was possible, although needing more research.

6 Conclusions

This work has presented a review of the available literature on PV/T collectors, mainly of flat plate type. The results show that the PV/T efficiency is sensitive to many variables and a more detailed study seems to be necessary in order to obtain an optimal PV/T collector with improved efficiency and reduced costs, in order to be economically competitive.

Acknowledgement. This work was supported in part by the Portuguese Foundation for Science and Technology (FCT) under Project N° SFRH/BD/50276/2009 and Project N° SFRH/BSAB/950/2009.

References

1. PV/T Collectors: Technologies Combine to Increase Output. IEA SHC Solar Update Newsletter, Document Number DE2-4 (2006)
2. Hansen, J., Sorensen, H.: IEA SHC Task 35 PV/Thermal Solar Systems. World Renewable Energy Congress, Document Number DE2-3, Firenze, Italy (2006)
3. Zondag, H.A.: Commercially Available PV/T Products. Document Number DA2-1 (2006)
4. Coventry, J.S.: Performance of a Concentrating Photovoltaic/Thermal Solar Collector. Solar Energy 78, 211–222 (2005)
5. Smeltink, J.F.H., Blakers, A.W.: 40 kW PV Thermal Roof Mounted Concentrator System. In: 4th World Conference on Photovoltaic Energy Conversion, Waikoloa, HI (2006)
6. Yang, M., Izumi, H., Sato, M., Matsunaga, S., Takamoto, T., Tsuzuki, K., Amono, T., Yamaguchi, M.: A 3kW PV-Thermal System for Home Use. In: Twenty-Sixth IEEE Photovoltaic Specialists Conference, Anaheim, CA (1997)
7. Bhargava, A.K., Garg, H.P., Agarwal, R.K.: Study of a Hybrid Solar System - Solar Air Heater Combined with Solar Cells. Energy Convers. Mgmt. 31(5), 471–479 (1991)
8. Aste, N., Beccali, M., Chiesa, G.: Experimental Evaluation of the Performance of a Prototype Hybrid Solar Photovoltaic-Thermal (PV/T) Air Collector for the Integration in Sloped Roof. In: Proceedings of EPIC 2002 AIVC, Lyon, France (2002)
9. Tripanagnostopoulos, Y., Souliotis, M., Battisti, R., Corrado, A.: Application Aspects of Hybrid PV/T Solar Systems. In: ISES Solar World Congress, Goteborg, Sweden (2003)
10. Zondag, H.A., van Helden, W.G.J., Elswijk, M.J., Bakker, M.: PV-Thermal collector development - an overview of the lessons learnt. In: 19th European PV Solar Energy Conference and Exhibition, Paris, France (2004)
11. Zondag, H.A., Jong, M.J.M., Helden, W.G.J.: Development and Applications for PV Thermal. In: 17th European Photovoltaic Solar Energy Conference, Munchen, Germany (2001)
12. Zondag, H.A., van Helden, W.G.J.: PV-Thermal Domestic Systems. In: 3rd World Conference on Photovoltaic Energy Conversion, Osaka, Japan (2003)
13. Elia, S., Tiberi, V.: Dimensioning and Efficiency Evaluation of Hybrid Solar Systems for Energy Production. Thermal Science 12(3), 127–138 (2008)
14. Vandaele, W.P., Bloem, J.J., Zaaiman, W.J.: Combined heat and power from hybrid photovoltaic building integrated components: results from overall performance assessment. In: 2nd World Conference and Exhibition on Photovoltaic Energy Conversion, Wien (1998)
15. Furbo, S., Shah, J.J.: Solar Energy 74, 513–523 (2003)

16. Kalogirou, S.A.: Use of TRNSYS for modelling and simulation of a hybrid PV-thermal solar system for Cyprus. Renewable Energy 23, 247–260 (2001)
17. Jong, M.J.M.: System Studies on Combined PV/Thermal Panels. In: Elftes Symposium Thermisch Solarenergie, Germany (May 2001)
18. Energia Solar Térmica - Manual Sobre Tecnologias, Projecto e Instalação. Comissão Europeia, programa ALTENER (2004)
19. Energia Fotovoltaica - Manual Sobre Tecnologias, Projecto e Instalação. Comissão Europeia, programa ALTENER (2004)
20. Davidsson, H., Perers, B., Karlsson, B.: Performance of a multifunctional PV/T Hybrid Solar Window. Passivhus Norden, Trondheim (2008)
21. Járdán, R.K., Nagy, I., Barabás, R.: Control of a Combined Photovoltaic/Thermal Energy System. In: ICIT 2003, Maribor, Slovenia (2003)

Part 16

Advances in Electrical Machinery

Study of AC Losses in Superconducting Electrical Components for Electrical System Design

José-María Ceballos, Alfredo Alvarez, and Pilar Suarez

"Benito Mahedero" Group of Electrical Applications of Superconductors,
Industrial Engineering School, University of Extremadura
Apartado 382, Avenida de Elvas s/n
06071 Badajoz, Spain
jmceba@unex.es, aalvarez@unex.es, psuarez@unex.es

Abstract. An experimental rig allowing us to perform AC loss measurements, on short (10 cm) tape samples of high-temperature superconductor Bi-2223/Ag, was designed and tested.We propose a new set-up in order to determine AC losses in multilayer superconducting coils. We made a comparative AC losses study of an isolated tape and of the same tape in the same conditions except for the proximity of another tape, with and without current, located just over the first one. We present a serial of results obtains from different tapes, first we used multifilament BSCCO tape (1G) and YBCO tape (2G) with ferromagnetic substrate.

Keywords: AC losses, Superconductivity, Bi-2223 tapes, YBCO tapes, Superconducting coils.

1 Introduction

The purpose of the work was to study, characterize, and measure the different components of AC losses in superconductors that are part of such electrical systems as transformers, electrical motors, etc.

Firstly, we present a serial of experiments consisted in the evaluation of a single tape carrying current in a possible external magnetic field, obtained in collaboration with the *Superconductor Physics Department* within the *Institute of Electrical Engineering* from *Slovak Academy of Sciences*.

Finally, we focused in a tape as part of a multilayer coil, because this is the most usual way that the tape is used in electrical systems. The behavior of each section of tape is different from of an isolated piece because of the influence of the superconducting layer wound just next to it.

In order to analyze the different components of the AC loss including the influence of one section of tape by another wound together with it, we made a comparative study of an isolated tape and of the same tape in the same conditions except for the proximity of another tape, with and without current, located just over the first one.

L.M. Camarinha-Matos, P. Pereira, and L. Ribeiro (Eds.): DoCEIS 2010, IFIP AICT 314, pp. 487–494, 2010.
© IFIP International Federation for Information Processing 2010

2 Contribution to Technological Innovation

The study of AC losses under the simultaneous action of the transport AC current and the external AC magnetic field is of prime importance for the reliable prediction of dissipation in electric power devices such as motors/generators, transformers and transmission cables. The reason for such a study is because, if the study of losses is an important part of the design of any electrical application, in superconducting electrical systems losses determine not only their efficiency but also the capacity of the corresponding cooling system.

3 Experimental

We carried out two different serial of experiments in order to determinate the AC losses in a sample of superconducting tape.

In the first one, we tried to find the contribution of the external magnetic field to the AC transport losses.

In the second one, we found the influence of the presence of nearby tapes on the AC losses in a single tape.

3.1 Transport Losses in a Single Tape with External Magnetic Field

For this experiment, the setup consists on an isolated tape feeding with a wide range of transport current and exposed, simultaneously to an external magnetic field (Fig. 1 shows a scheme of this configuration).

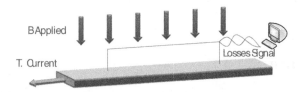

B Applied

T. Current

Losses Signal

Fig. 1. Experimental arrangement for the measure of the transport losses in a single tape with external magnetic field

The main aim of this serial of experiment was to determine, by an electromagnetic method, the AC loss in a superconducting wire transporting the AC current $I_T = \sqrt{2}I_{rms}$ $cos(2\pi f t)$ while exposed to the AC magnetic field $B_{ext} = \sqrt{2}B_{rms} \, cos(2\pi f t + \varphi)$.

In particular, the dependence on the phase shift φ between I_T and B_{ext} has been investigated.

To carry out this method, one has to resolve two main problems:

a) An independent supply of current into the sample and in the AC field magnet winding is necessary to keep the values of I_{rms} and B_{rms} constant while changing the phase difference.

b) The distinction between the dissipation covered by the power supply for I_T and the one delivered by the energizing system of the AC magnet is necessary to avoid a double count of dissipation in loss registration.

For measurement of transport loss the loop perpendicular to the wide face of the tape is used. AC loss per unit of length is determined by formula:

$$P_T = I_T*V_T/L \qquad (1)$$

Where I_T is the RMS value of transport current, V_T is the part of RMS value of voltage from measuring loop which is in phase with transport current, and L is loop length. Perpendicular arrangement reduces the false voltage signal induced by external field. Fine compensation of the remaining false voltage is performed with the help of an adjustable mutual inductance linked to AC magnet current. Similar compensation is used in the case of the magnetization loss measurement, but linked now to the sample current. By this way the false signals were reduced satisfactory.

All the experiment with this set-up was implemented at frequency of 72Hz. The characteristics of the tape analyzed in this experiment are shown in table 1.

Table 1. Characteristics of the tape under test

High Strength American Superconductor			
Type	1G	**Width (mm)**	4.2 (+/- 0.2mm)
Superconductor	Bi(Pb)-2223	**Thickness (µm)**	0.31 (+/- 0.02mm)
Fabrication Tech	PIT	$I_c(A)$	120A
Matrix	Silver Alloy	**Reinforcement**	Stainless Steel

3.2 Transport Losses in a Single Tape under the Influence of Another Tape

In many applications of superconducting tape in electrical devices, the tape must be wound in multilayer coils as in figure 2. In such a case, every piece of tape is located very close to some other piece, in the next layer, along the coil. The proximity of these two parts of the circuit adds a new component (not necessarily positive) in the total loss of the multilayer coil that does not exist in the tape or single-layer coil loss. Therefore, we can divide the loss into 3 components:

a) The transport loss, P_N, which can be calculated by the Norris equation [1].

b) The magnetic loss, P_{mag}, due to the global magnetic field created by the complete coil.

c) The local loss, P_{loc}, due to the proximity of turns in the same position of consecutive layers. So, the total loss, P_T , can be written as follows:

$$P_T = P_N + P_{mag} + P_{loc} \qquad (2)$$

To evaluate the new component of the loss, P_{loc}, we designed and carried out the experiment described below.

Figure 3 shows the arrangement of the tapes for the measurement of the losses. In this case, the tape is not bent as in a coil, and therefore $P_{mag} = 0$ (no global magnetic field has to be taken into account). The electrical method is used to determine the losses in the longer tape through the measurement of the voltage between taps on the tape (see figure 3, circuits *CI* and *CO*) or the *emf* in a *contact-less loop* (circuits *CLI* and *CLO*) [2].

Fig. 2. Multi-layer coils carrying the same or different current in each layer. The proximity of the tapes in the same position of consecutive layers makes the AC loss different from in a single layer coil.

Fig. 3. Experimental arrangement of the tape (the longer) for the measurement of the losses both under and outside the influence of another tape (the shorter) very close to the former.

The shorter tape is located over the *CI* and *CLI* circuits, leaving the *CO* a *CLO* circuits outside its influence. The current I_L in the longer tape and I_S in the shorter one are independent but in phase for this study.

The measuring equipment picks up the waveforms of the currents through two Hall current probes, and the waveforms of the tap and loop voltages through four measurement amplifiers that filter and adapt the signals to be read by a data acquisition board (DAQ). All the waveforms have a whole number of periods (typically 5) at a frequency f, of 100 Hz.

The characteristics of the different tapes under test are summarized in table 2.

Table 2. Characteristics of tapes under test

	1G Samples	2G Samples
Superconductor	Bi(Pb)-2223	YBCO
Fabrication Tech	PIT	MOD/RABiTS
Matrix	Silver Alloy	-----
Thickness (μm)	230 ± 10	150 ± 20
Thickness (μm)	4.20 ± 0.10	4.40 ± 0.15
I$_c$(A)	95	75

4 Results and Discussion

4.1 Transport Losses in a Single Tape with External Magnetic Field

In figure 4, the dependence of transport loss P_T as a function of the amplitude of the magnetic field is displayed.

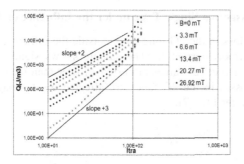

Fig. 4. Transport losses dependence with the amplitude of the perpendicular magnetic field (B) for different transport currents (Itra)

As we can see exits a strong dependence in the losses respect to the amplitude of the magnetic field.

The slope in the behavior of the transport losses change dramatically when a perpendicular magnetic field is applied.

We can also observe that this slope is even higher when the superconductor became to be saturated and the current starts to flow through the silver matrix [3].

In figure 5, the dependence of transport loss P_T as a function of the phase shift between the transport current and magnetic field is displayed.

Although we initially supposed that the maximum of the losses occurs when the transport current and external field are in phase, as we can see in the figure 6, it seems that the maximum of losses occurs in a range of shift angles between 30°-50°, depending of the amplitude of the external magnetic field. The more the magnetic field amplitude increase, the more angle of the maximum of the losses, as we can see in the figure 6, in which we present the variation of transport losses with fixed current (34A) under different field amplitudes. These transport losses have been normalized to the maximum.

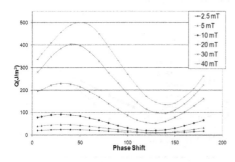

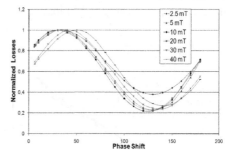

Fig. 5. Transport losses dependence with the phase shift in degrees, between transport current (34A) and magnetic field for different amplitudes of the magnetic field.

Fig. 6. Normalized to the maximum transport losses dependence with the phase shift between transport current (34A) and magnetic field for different amplitudes of the magnetic field

4.2 Transport Losses in a Single Tape under the Influence of Another Tape

Figure 7 shows the loss in the 2G long tape, outside the influence of the shorter, as a function of the transport current I_L. The sample shows significantly higher losses compared with the theoretical values at currents lower than the critical current. This indicates that the losses in the 2G tapes are affected by the magnetic losses in the ferromagnetic substrates [4, 5-7].

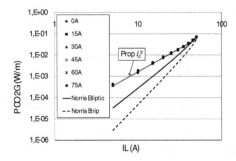

Fig. 7. Losses outside the influence of the short tape (probe CO) for different currents I_S (from 0 to 75 A) in 2G sample. This loss corresponds to the transport loss in a 2G single tape at currents lower than critical current. It is been that the experimental measurements follow an I_L^2 dependence [8].

In Fig. 8 we have plotted the experimental data of losses in 2G sample and the sum with Norris's models with ferromagnetic losses. *FM1* corresponds to data from [4, 6] and *FM2* corresponds to data from [5, 6]. In general, the addition of the ferromagnetic losses *FM1* or *FM2* to the Norris Elliptical losses improves considerably the agreement with our experimental measurements as in [6]. However, our measurements fit to "*FM2* + Norris Elliptic" for all values of I_L but only fit to "*FM1* + Norris Elliptic" for $I_L > 25$ A.

In Fig. 9 a comparison of losses between 1G and 2G tapes for $I < I_c$ is shown and we can see a significant difference between them but the most important one is the different slopes because of FM losses.

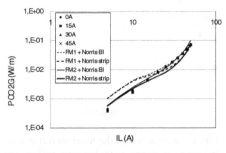
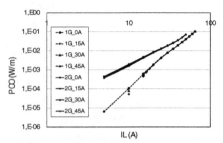

Fig. 8. Comparison between loss in 2G sample and theoretical curve making into account ferromagnetic losses in the substrate (FM) at values lower than the critical current

Fig. 9. Comparison between losses in 1G and 2G tapes measured through the probe *CO*. These losses correspond to the transport losses in each single tape.

The results for 1G setup show an expected behavior that is, the losses in probe *CI* increase when I_S increase concluding that the presence of consecutive superconducting layers affect to AC losses of the neighboring layers due to the dependence of the critical current with the transport current through the two tapes [9], but for 2G setup we can see in the figure 10 a different and interesting behavior. When I_S increase below I_c the losses in the long tape decrease but when I_S increase above I_c the losses in the long tape increase. Figure 11 shows a scheme of our arrangement to give a possible explanation of this effect.

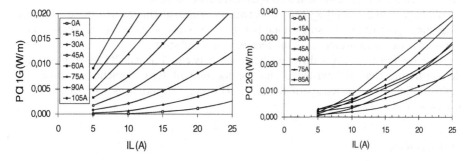

Fig. 10. Losses under the influence of the 1G and 2G short tape (probe CI) for different currents IS (from 0 to 105 A in the 1G tape and from 0 to 85A in the 2G tape)

 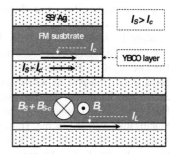

Fig. 11. Scheme of our arrangement. The right figure correspond to the case for $I_S < I_c$ and the left one is drawn the case for $I_S > I_c$. In both of them are the short and the long tapes. Spots represent Ag layers and stain steel covers, grey color represent FM substrates and white color represent YBCO layers. The layers are not at scale.

The short tape *FM* substrate and the conducting layers (Ag layer and stainless steel coverts) are located between short and long tapes YBCO layers. So when $I_S < I_c$, the magnetic field cause by I_S in the long tape FM substrate reduces the magnetic field in the same substrate due to I_L. This effect is stronger when I_S increases producing a reduction of the losses in the long tape. However, when $I_S > I_c$, the current $(I_S - I_c)$ goes through the conducting layers increasing the magnetic field in the long tape FM substrate and the losses in the long tape [10].

5 Conclusions

An experimental set-up for the measurement of AC loss under the simultaneous action of the transport current and the magnetic field shifted in phase was developed and tested.

The results clearly show that the maximum loss is not at zero phase shift, and its position depends on the magnitude of the current and field.

Two similar arrangements for 1G and 2G assembled tapes have been constructed and studied in order to establish a comparison between them.

We have found a good agreement between our measurements and those estimated from bibliography for 2G single tape but it is necessary to carry on the study taking our own losses measurements in the ferromagnetic substrate.

Also we have shown a different behavior between 1G and 2G assembled tapes demonstrating that the existence and the location of ferromagnetic substrates are highly influent on the losses of the tapes. However, experiences with different 2G samples must be realized.

References

1. Norris, W.T.: Calculation of Hysteresis Losses on Hard Superconductors Carrying AC: Isolated Conductors and Edges of Thin Sheets. J. Phys. D, Appl. Phys. 3, 489–507 (1970)
2. Frolek, L., Souc, J., Laudis, A., Kovác, P., Husek, I.: Partitioning of Transport AC Loss in a Superconducting Tape into Magnetic and Resistive Components. IEEE Trans. Appl. Supercond. 11, 2967 (2001)
3. Gömöry, F., Janíková, E., Souc, J.: Resistive Losses in a High-Tc Wire Carrying AC Current Larger than Ic. Supercond. Sci. Technol. 15, 1345–1352 (2002)
4. Duckworth, R.C., Thompsom, J.R., Gouge, M.J., Lue, J.W., Ijaduola, A.O., Yu, D., Verebelyi, D.T.: Transport AC Losses Studies of YBCO Coated Conductors With Nickel Alloy Substrates. Supercond. Sci. Technol. 16, 1294–1298 (2003)
5. Duckworth, R.C., Gouge, M.J., Lue, J.W., Thieme, C.L.H., Verebelyi, D.T.: Substrate and Stabilization Effects on the Transport AC Losses in YBCO Coated Conductors. IEEE Trans. Appl. Supercond. 15, 1583–1586 (2005)
6. Gianni, L., Bindi, M., Fontana, F., Ginocchio, S., Martini, L., Perini, E., Zanella, S.: Transport AC Losses in YBCO Coated Conductors. IEEE Trans. Appl. Supercond. 16, 147–149 (2006)
7. Majoros, M., Ye, L., Velichko, A.V., Coombs, T.A., Sumption, M.D., Collings, E.W.: Transport AC Losses in YBCO Coated Conductors. Supercond. Sci. Technol. 20, 299–304 (2007)
8. Stravrev, S., Grilli, F., Dutoit, B., Ashworth, S.P.: Comparison of the AC Losses BSCCO and YBCO Conductors by Means of Numerical Analysis. Supercond. Sci. Technol. 18, 1300–1312 (2005)
9. Suarez, P., Alvarez, A., Perez, B., Ceballos, J.M.: Influence of the Current Through One Turn of a Multilayer Coil on the Nearest Turn in a Consecutive Layer. Journal of Physics, Conference Series 97, 012058 (2008)
10. Suarez, P., Alvarez, A., Ceballos, J.M., Perez, B.: Losses in 2G Tapes Wound Close Together: Comparison with Similar 1G Tape Configurations. IEEE Transactions on Applied Superconductivity 19, 2395–2398 (2009)

Robust Position Control of a DC Motor
by Sliding Mode

Gabriela Mamani[1], Jonathan Becedas[2], and Vicente Feliu Batlle[1]

[1] Universidad de Castilla-La Mancha, E.T.S.I. Industriales,
Av. Camilo José Cela S/N, Ciudad Real, Spain
{glmamani,Vicente.Feliu}@uclm.es
[2] Department of Engineering, University of Leicester, LE1 7RH, Leicester, United Kingdom
jbr6@le.ac.uk

Abstract. The position of the DC motor is controlled by using a continuous sliding mode control (SMC), which is highly robust to the Coulomb friction torque and to high unknown payload variations, which involve changes in the rotational inertia of the motor shaft. The main contribution of the work is the experimentation of a SMC control which does not requires the knowledge of the payload variation range, i.e., the system is quite robust to any unknown change in the payload mass value.

Keywords: Robust control, sliding mode control, DC motor.

1 Introduction

Many of the developed controllers depend strongly on the exact modelling of the mechanical system. Any change in the plant parameters reduces the controller performance, making the system lose the desired specifications. The discrepancies between the actual plant and the mathematical model may be due to un-modelled dynamic, variation in system parameters or the approximation of complex plant behaviour by a straightforward model. We must ensure that the resulting controller has the ability to produce the required performance levels in practice despite such plant/model mismatches. This has led to an intense interest in the development of so-called robust control methods which seek to solve this problem. One particular approach to robust controller design is sliding model control methodology.

Several SMC approaches have been applied to different types of motors. The authors in [1] apply discrete time sliding-mode methodology in order to develop an induction motor position controller. In [2] an adaptive observer and a higher order sliding-mode framework are combined to control induction motors without mechanical sensors. In [3] the sliding-mode approach is developed to control an induction motor fed by a three-level voltage source inverter. In the paper of [4] discuss current decoupling and controller design for sensorless vector-controlled induction motor drives. They present a method, which does not require speed estimation, for

L.M. Camarinha-Matos, P. Pereira, and L. Ribeiro (Eds.): DoCEIS 2010, IFIP AICT 314, pp. 495–504, 2010.
© IFIP International Federation for Information Processing 2010

decoupled current control based on integral sliding mode. Another contribution concerned with electric drive control is the paper by [5], which presents a cascade control scheme, based on multiple instances of a second-order SMC algorithm for the speed/position control of permanent-magnet motors.

A (SMC) design methodology based on the control law described in [6] and [7] is applied here to a DC servo motor model. A rigorous interpretation of the relationship between the equivalent control law and the low frequency components of the discontinuous control action maintaining a sliding motion is described in [8].

2   Contributions to Technological Innovation

This work presents an easily implemented robust controller applied to DC motor model, since the motor is the basis of many applications in present-day industry, as is the case of manipulator robots. A simple demonstration of the control method's robustness to variations in the inertia is provided. The analysis presented shows that the system correctly performs for any type of payload and for any variation in it. Unlike other existing control methods in which to define the range in which the inertia may vary is necessary, in this paper this is not, which permits greater versatility and security upon its implementation in any type of electro-mechanical systems. Moreover the control method is robust to Coulomb friction, one of the non-linear types of friction which is still of current scientific interest since it affects the control accuracy

3   Modeling of the DC Motor Model and Problem Statement

A common electromechanical actuator in many control systems is constituted by the DC motor [9]. We can write its dynamic equation by using Newton's Second law:

$$kV = J\ddot{\theta}_m + v\dot{\theta}_m + \hat{\Gamma}_{Coul}(\dot{\theta}_m) \tag{1}$$

Where θ_m is the angular position of the motor (rad). $\ddot{\theta}_m$ stands for the acceleration of the motor (rad/s^2) and $\dot{\theta}_m$ is the velocity (rad/s). J is the unknown inertia of the motor $(kg \cdot m^2)$, v is the viscous friction coefficient $(N \cdot m \cdot s)$ and $\hat{\Gamma}_{Coul}$ is the unknown friction torque $(N \cdot m)$. This nonlinear friction term is considered as a perturbation. When the motor rotates $(\dot{\theta}_m \neq 0)$ this only depends on the sign of the angular velocity of the motor: $\hat{\Gamma}_{Coul} = \xi sign(\dot{\theta}_m)$ with ξ an unknown constant value, denoted as Coulomb friction coefficient $(N \cdot m)$. When the velocity is zero $(\dot{\theta}_m = 0)$ the friction opposes to the torque produced by the input voltage, depending on its sign: $\hat{\Gamma}_{Coul} = \xi sign(V)$. The parameter k is the electromechanical constant of the motor $(N \cdot m / V)$. The constant factor n is the reduction ratio of the motor gear; thus $\theta_m = \hat{\theta}_m / n$ and $\Gamma_{Coul} = \hat{\Gamma}_{Coul} n$, note that the magnitude seen from the motor side of the gear are written with an upper hat and the magnitude seen from the other side of the gear are written with standard letters. V is the motor input voltage (V) acting as the control variable for the system. This is the input to a servo-amplifier, which controls the input current to the motor by means of an internally PI current controller. The electrical dynamic can be neglected because this is much faster than the mechanical dynamic of the motor.

The motor angle $\theta_m(t)$ is measured by an incremental encoder and is used in this feedback control. The design requirement is to regulate the motor position $\theta_m(t)$ to track a given smooth reference trajectory $\theta_m^*(t)$. The unmeasured state is estimated by computing a finite number of time derivatives of output signal.

The nominal system equation of the motor dynamics (1) can be written in state-space form as

$$\dot{x}(t) = \begin{bmatrix} 0 & 1 \\ 0 & -\dfrac{v}{J} \end{bmatrix} x(t) + \begin{bmatrix} 0 \\ \dfrac{k}{Jn} \end{bmatrix} u(t) - \begin{bmatrix} 0 \\ 1 \end{bmatrix} \mu sign(\dot{\theta}_m) \qquad (2)$$

With $\mu = \dfrac{\xi}{Jn} (\dfrac{N \cdot m}{kg \cdot m^2})$.

Note that the uncertainty represented by $\mu sign(\dot{\theta}_m)$ acts in the input channel (i.e. in the second of the pair of the differential equations). The variable structure control system with a sliding mode have the ability to completely reject the effect of the bounded uncertainty acting in the input channels which is referred to as matched uncertainty, (see [8]).

4   Sliding Mode Control: State Feedback

Consider the following state representation of an uncertain Linear Time Invariant (LTI) dynamic system $\forall t \geq 0$

$$\dot{x}(t) = Ax(t) + Bu(t) + f_m(t, x, u) \qquad (3)$$

$$y(t) = Cx(t) \qquad (4)$$

Where the state $x \in \mathfrak{R}^n$, $A \in \mathfrak{R}^{n \times n}$, $B \in \mathfrak{R}^{n \times m}$ and $C \in \mathfrak{R}^{p \times m}$ with $1 \leq m \leq n$. The variables $u \in \mathfrak{R}^m$ and $y \in \mathfrak{R}^p$ will be refereed to as the input and output respectively. The matrices A, B, C will be termed the system, input and output distribution matrices respectively. The uncertain vector function $f_m(t,x,u)$ represents the lumped sum of matched nonlinearities and/or uncertainties. In this paper, the following is assumed:

A.1: The pair **A, B** is controllable.
A.2: The input distribution matrix **B** is full rank.

As is well known, SMC design consists of a two-step procedure. The first one is the description of the control objective in terms of a space state surface (called the sliding surface). The surface choice is developed such that the system trajectories satisfy the performance specifications, when the sliding variable lies on the sliding surface. The second step (controller design) is represented by the definition of a control action which steers the state trajectories onto the sliding surface, after a finite transient.

4.1 Sliding Surface Design

By assumption $rank(B) = m$, then an orthogonal similarity transformation $x \rightarrow T_r x = z$ exists such that the state and input matrices have the following structure:

$$T_r A T_r^T = \begin{bmatrix} A_{11} & A_{12} \\ A_{21} & A_{22} \end{bmatrix}, T_r B = \begin{bmatrix} 0 \\ B_2 \end{bmatrix} \tag{5}$$

Where $A_{11} \in \Re^{(n-m)\times(n-m)}$, $A_{12} \in \Re^{(n-m)\times m}$, $A_{21} \in \Re^{m\times(n-m)}$, $A_{22} \in \Re^{m\times m}$ and $B_2 \in \Re^{m\times m}$ are assumed to be known constant matrices. The square matrix B_2 is non-singular because the input distribution matrix is assumed to be of full rank. The new coordinates are defined as $z = \begin{bmatrix} z_1 & z_2 \end{bmatrix}^T$, where $z_1 \in \Re^{n-m}$ and $z_2 \in \Re^m$.

The sliding surface design σ

$$\sigma = \{x \in \Re^n : s(t) = Sx(t) = 0 \tag{6}$$

where $s(t) \in \Re^m$ is the switching function and $S \in \Re^{m\times m}$ is the switching gain matrix to be designed.

If $s(t) = 0$, and $z_2(t)$ in term of $z_1(t)$ yields $z_2(t) = -Mz_1(t)$. Define the gain matrix M as

$$M = S_2^{-1} S_1 \tag{7}$$

where $S_1 \in \Re^{m\times(n-m)}$ and $S_2 \in \Re^{m\times m}$ has the property $\det(S_2) \neq 0$.

Hence, the reduced-order sliding mode dynamic is given by

$$\dot{z}_1(t) = (A_{11} - A_{12}M)z_1(t) \tag{8}$$

In the context of designing a regulator, the matrix governing the sliding motion $(A_{11} - A_{12}M)$ must have stable eigenvalues. The switching surface design problem can therefore be considered to be one of choosing a state feedback matrix M to stabilize the reduced order system (A_{11}, A_{12}). Therefore, to find a gain matrix M by using any available linear state feedback method will always be possible, e.g. pole placement, quadratic minimization or direct eigenstructure assignment (more details of this approach can be found in [8].

4.2 Control Law Design

A common control structure is divided into two parts:

$$u(t) = u_l(t) + u_n(t) \tag{9}$$

where $u_l(t)$ is a state feedback control law, often the nominal equivalent control $(u_{eq}(t))$ and $u_n(t)$ is a discontinuous or switched component.

The control signal is assumed to have the following form, [8]:

$$u(t) = -(SB)^{-1}SAx(t) + u_n(t) \tag{10}$$

The nonlinear component is given by $u_n(t) = \rho sign(s(t))$ where the signum function exhibits the property that $ssign(s) = |s|$. In order to smooth the control action, a small positive scalar, γ is added to the denominator of the control law to yield

$$u_n(t) = \rho \frac{s}{|s| + \gamma} \tag{11}$$

The scalar function ρ, which depend only on the magnitude of the uncertainty and satisfies the η - reachability condition, [8].

5 Experiments

The experimental platform consists of a three legged metallic chassis that supports an Harmonic Drive mini servo DC motor RH-8D-6006-E036AL-SP(N) which has a reduction relation $n = 50$, an electromechanical constant $k = 0.21(N \cdot m/V)$ an inertia $J = 6.87 \cdot 10^{-5}(kg \cdot m^2)$, viscous friction $v = 1.041 \cdot 10^{-3}(N \cdot m \cdot s)$ and Coulomb friction coefficient $\xi = \mu n J = 0.119(N \cdot m)$. The frame makes the stable and free rotation of the motor around the vertical axis of the platform possible. The motor shaft is capable of turning either right or left around the Z axis. Furthermore, a servo-amplifier is used to supply the DC motor. This amplifier accepts control inputs from the computer in the range $[-10,10](V)]$. Finally, the sensor system is integrated by an encoder embedded in the motor, which allows us to know the motor position with a precision of $7 \cdot 10^{-5}(rad)$. The sample interval in the signals processing support was set at $T = 1 \cdot 10^{-3}(s)$. The real time experiments are carried out under the Real Time Workshop®, which allows us to generate and execute C code from SIMULINK® models and embedded MATLAB® code. The controller is implemented in a PC with the real time software. A data acquisition card is used to establish the communication with the real platform: execution of the control law and reading of the sensorial system described above.

5.1 Experimental Results

The demonstration of the robustness with regard to payload changes is carried out by changing the ratio between the inertia value used to design the control algorithm, J_a, and the real value of the motor, $J : \delta = J_a / J$. The experiments are developed by changing this ratio from $\delta = 20$ to $\delta = 1/20$. Fig. 1 depicts the results when $1 \leq \delta \leq 20$. The signals θ_m to θ_{m7} correspond to the different values of δ ,(see first and second column of Table 1; the third column represents the percentage of J whit regard to J_a). Note that the control the control is robust with regard to the inertia change: the controller never becomes unstable and the steady state error is null. Nevertheless, the trajectory tracking error increases when the inertia of the motor decreases with regard to that used to design the control. Observe that when $\delta = 1$, i.e. $J_a = J$ the delay of the trajectory θ_m with regard to the reference θ_m^* is insignificant, and when that ratio increases from 2 to 20, the delay is more notorious. Nevertheless, the system is always stable and the steady state error is null, which demonstrates the robustness of the control law.

The maximum trajectory tracking errors in each trajectory
$(\theta_m$ to $\theta_{m7})\varepsilon\% = (\left|\dfrac{\theta_m^* - \theta_m}{\Theta}\right|)$, where Θ represents the amplitude of the signal

θ_m^* (in this case $\Theta = 1(rad)$), are represented in the fourth column of Table 1. Note that the error $\varepsilon\%$ increases if δ increases. Such values vary from 2.25%, for θ_m, to 80.84%, for θ_{m7}. Note that the steady state error is null in both cases, although the maximum trajectory tracking error $\varepsilon\%$ increases with the δ value.

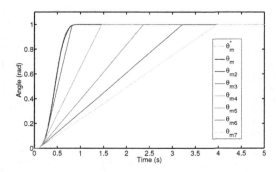

Fig. 1. Results when $1 \leq \delta \leq 20$

Table 1. Result 1

Signal	δ	$J = \% J_a$	$\varepsilon\%$
θ_m	1	100%	2.25
θ_{m2}	2	50%	2.92
θ_{m3}	3	33.33%	18.13
θ_{m4}	5	25%	51.78
θ_{m5}	10	10%	69.20
θ_{m6}	15	6.67%	76.74
θ_{m7}	20	5%	80.84

Fig. 2 shows the experimental results obtained when $1/20 \leq \delta \leq 1$. In this case, the signals θ_{m8} to θ_{m13} correspond to those experiments carried out with δ varying between the values of 1 and $1/20$. This signifies that in the following experiments the real inertia of the motor is from 1 to 20 times greater than the controller design inertia, or that it is the same to increase the inertia of the motor shaft. The first and second column of Table 2 depicts the correspondence between the signals θ_m to θ_{m13} with regard to the ratio δ. The third column of this table shows the percentage $\dfrac{J}{J_a} \cdot 100$. Note that the most unfavourable case $\delta = 1/20$ corresponds to inertia of the motor which is 20 times greater than the controller design inertia. Observe that the trajectories θ_m to θ_{m13} are superimposed on the reference trajectory θ_m^*. All the trajectories have null steady state error and the trajectory tracking errors $\varepsilon\%$ do not increase (see fourth column of Table 2).

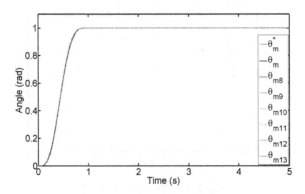

Fig. 2. Results when $1/20 \leq \delta \leq 1$

Table 2. Result 2

Signal	δ	$J = \% J_a$	$\varepsilon\%$
θ_m	1	100%	2.25
θ_{m8} , . . .	1/2	200%	2.18
θ_{m9}	1/3	300%	2.24
θ_{m10}	1/5	500%	2.21
θ_{m11}	1/10	1000%	2.21
θ_{m12}	1/15	1500%	2.18
θ_{m13}	1/20	2000%	2.15

These results permit us to affirm that the trajectory tracking error is almost the same for all cases in which $J \geq J_a$, and these errors correspond to that obtained when $J = J_a$.

This demonstrates the good performance of the presented method, which can be used in experimental platforms for trajectory tracking tasks in which the payload may change. Such a robustness is obtained in these experiments for very extreme cases $J_a \geq J \geq J_a$, which means that there is no boundary in the δ value, with the exception of physical limitations such as the saturation of the servo-amplifier, i.e. the maximum and minimum δ values are given by the maximum voltage value supported by the servo-amplifier (in these experiments $10(V)$ which is delimited for every application.

The authors want to highlight that due to the (SMC) nature is that of a switch changing from one state to the other, the control action signals has not been included, because the control action presents a high frequency chattering effect which makes quite difficult the visualization. Since the nature of this paper is wanted to be maintained essentially practical and experimental by the authors, theoretical analysis of the system under the effect of the different types of noise has not been included. Nevertheless, notice that the results are obtained from a real platform, means that the sensors measurement and the system dynamics are affected by unstructured noise. Even in presence of these types of noise the control system works properly with high accuracy as shown with these experimental results, which demonstrate a high robustness to unstructured measurement and system noises.

6 Conclusion

A SMC based on the equivalent control approach has been presented and designed for the DC motor model. This approach allows matched uncertainties in DC motor model to be dealt with. These results advise the use of a control scheme insensitive to payload variations, to fulfil the requirements imposed to the system for the whole range of inertias due to the controller design does not require bounded uncertainties. Further computer simulations and experiments were carried out to test the robustness property of the SMC, considering different combination of uncertain parameters. The experimental results demonstrate the good performance of the method: the responses of the control system in trajectory tracking tasks are quite fast and the steady state errors are null. Therefore, in light of the experimental results obtained, we demonstrate that the SMC control method proposed in this paper solves the problem of high payload changes in DC motors and electromechanical actuators, since the control design is robust with regard to the friction in the motor dynamics and high varying payloads with no restriction in the variation, i.e. this method does not requires the *a priori* knowledge of the varying range of the load, being this, the main contribution of this work. Furthermore, the control law is very well suited for trajectory tracking tasks with. This characteristic makes the control here designed able to control robot manipulators, in which the trajectory tracking is an essential problem since the accelerations must be slow enough not to damage the electrical actuators nor the mechanical structure and joints.

On the other hand, a chattering reduction technique is part of the future research to be done and also the design and development of a sliding mode controller to solve the tracking problem of an uncertain very lightweight single-link flexible arm with high varying payload

Acknowledgments. This research was supported by the Spanish Government Research Programme via Project Ref.: PBI-05-057, by the Consejería de Educación y Ciencia de la Junta de Comunidades de Castilla-La Mancha and European Social Fund.

References

1. Veselic, B., Perunicic-Drazenovic, B., Milosavljevic, C.: High-Performance Position Control of Induction Motor Using Discrete-Time Sliding-Mode Control. IEEE Transactions on Industrial Electronics 55(11), 3809–3817 (2008)
2. Traore, D., Plestan, F., Glumineau, A., De Leon, J.: Sensorless Induction Motor: High-Order Sliding-Mode Controller and Adaptive Interconnected Observer. IEEE Transactions on Industrial Electronics 55(11), 3818–3827 (2008)

3. Ryvkin, S., Schmidt-Obermoeller, R., Steimel, A.: Sliding-Mode-Based Control for a Three-Level Inverter Drive. IEEE Transactions on Industrial Electronics 55(11), 3828–3835 (2008)
4. Comanescu, M., Xu, L., Batzel, T.D.: Decoupled Current Control of Sensorless Induction-Motor Drives by Integral Sliding Mode. IEEE Transactions on Industrial Electronics 55(11), 3836–3845 (2008)
5. Pisano, A., Davila, A., Fridman, L., Usai, E.: Cascade Control of PM DC Drives Via Second-Order Sliding-Mode Technique. IEEE Transactions on Industrial Electronics 55(11), 3846–3854 (2008)
6. Young, K.D., Utkin, V.I., Ozguner, U.: A Control Engineers Guide to Sliding Mode Control. IEEE Transactions on Control Systems Technology 7(3), 328–342 (1999)
7. Edwards, C., Spurgeon, S.K.: Sliding Mode Control -Theory and Applications. Taylor and Francis, U.K. (1998)
8. Utkin, V.: Sliding Modes in Control Optimization. Springer, Berlin (1992)
9. Begamudre, R.D.: Electro-Mechanical Energy Conversion with Dynamics of Machines. Wiley, New York (1998)

Disc Motor: Conventional and Superconductor Simulated Results Analysis

David Inácio[1], João Martins[1], Mário Ventim Neves[1], Alfredo Álvarez[2],
and Amadeu Leão Rodrigues[1]

[1] CTS/UNINOVA, Faculty of Sciences and Technology – Universidade Nova de Lisboa,
Quinta da Torre, 2829-516 Caparica, Portugal
[2] Departament of Electrical Engineering, Escuela de Ingenierias Industriales, Universidad de
Extremadura, E-06006 Badajoz, Spain

Abstract. Taking into consideration the development and integration of electrical machines with lower dimensions and higher performance, this paper presents the design and development of a three-phase axial flux disc motor, with 50 Hz frequency supply. It is made with two conventional semi-stators and a rotor, which can be implemented with a conventional aluminum disc or a high temperature-superconducting disc. The analysis of the motor characteristics is done with a 2D commercial finite elements package, being the modeling performed as a linear motor. The obtained results allow concluding that the superconductor motor provides a higher force than the conventional one. The conventional disc motor presents an asynchronous behavior, like a conventional induction motor, while the superconductor motor presents both synchronous and asynchronous behaviors.

Keywords: Axial disc motor; Superconductivity; HTS; YBCO; Finite elements program.

1 Introduction

The development and research of lower size electrical machines with higher performance has become a fundamental issue in the electrical machines community. With applications in many systems, the development and improvement of traction electrical motors presents one of the nowadays biggest challenges. Being the automobile the principal means of transport used in the world, they have deserved higher attention. Some countries, such as Portugal, promote and ensure financial advantages to users that acquire electrical vehicles. The integration of electrical motors in the active production of movement in a vehicle, instead of fuel motors, is the main challenge face to the various automobile's constructors, forcing them to establish lines of ecological vehicles, hybrids and fully electric, essential for environmental preservation. The electrical motors development is also "forced" by the increasing fuel prices and by the CO_2 limited emissions, imposed by the European Commission. These actions and incentives were the starting point for a all new ecological journey, where the simultaneous use of combustion and electrical motors makes possible the simultaneous reduction of CO_2 emissions and fuel consumption, desired in the actual economical crisis. On the other hand the production of fully electric cars has also become an

L.M. Camarinha-Matos, P. Pereira, and L. Ribeiro (Eds.): DoCEIS 2010, IFIP AICT 314, pp. 505–512, 2010.

important objective integrating, for the example, the use of hydrogen based power supplies [1][2] or renewable energies, such as photovoltaic [3].

The discovery of high temperature superconductor – HTS – materials along with their characteristics [4], has improved the development and integration of superconducting electric motors and superconductivity in various systems replacing conventional motors. Those superconducting motors are applied in different systems: measurement instruments (Superconducting Quantum Interference Devices [5]), electronics [6], train motors and technology [7], ships [8], vehicles [9] and small airplanes [10]. The use of HTS materials provides the achievement of smaller and lighter electrical vehicles. Fuel cells and hydrogen technology can also be integrated, where the low temperature of liquid hydrogen can cool down the HTS elements of the traction motor, making them superconductors. This integration can rise some security aspects that must be overcome with the correct development and improvement of such systems, in order to ensure the safety of users of these vehicles [11].

2   Contributions to Technological Innovation

This paper compares the performance of two disc motors: a conventional one and a HTS one. From the obtained results, one can observe that the superconductor motor develops a higher force than its equivalent aluminum motor. Furthermore, a technological important feature, the HTS motor present synchronous behavior while the conventional present asynchronous behavior.

3   Superconductivity

The high temperature superconductor – HTS - materials present zero resistance only in stationary conditions. In alternate field applications HTS material presents losses. The HTS materials are subject to penetration of quantized flux within the superconductor sample through the cores of current vortices [13]. These vortices consist of a magnetic flux cylindrical core aligned with the applied magnetic field, with a distance equal to the coherence length ξ. This core is surrounded by a cylinder of supercurrents that flow in a vortex ring with a thickness equal to the London penetration depth λ.

The vortices are distributed in a cantered hexagonal geometry, as presented in Fig. 1, which appears in the superconductor from the edges to the centre. The vortices

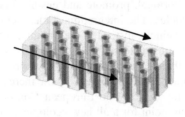

Fig. 1. Vortices dynamics in a superconductor sample

are subject to the Lorentz force that tends to move them. Accordingly to Maxwell Law, an electric field (1) is induced due to the magnetic field variation inside the vortices within the superconductor.

$$\vec{E} = \vec{B} \times \vec{v} \tag{1}$$

In (1), $\vec{B}$ denotes the magnetic field and $\vec{v}$ the vortices displacement speed. Current densities J are induced in HTS material and there are resistive losses, proportional to the product of the induced current density by the electric field created. According to Barnes [25], these losses are proportional to torque by a factor of 2π. For pure superconductor materials the variation of applied magnetic field in a superconductor makes the vortices traveling freely by the sample. When the superconducting materials present impurities or defects, the vortices are subject to the pinning flux, the vortices stay trapped in impurities or imperfections (pinning centers) and the magnetic behavior of the sample depends on its magnetic history, independent of time. For higher pinning is need higher current density to Lorentz force win the pinning force, causing more losses and torque.

4 Electric Disc Motors

The first developed electrical machine was the primitive axial flux machine, built by Faraday. Since then, the constant development of radial flow electric machines has made it to prevail on axial flow, and around 1900 was already used in large scale. At that time, the study and development of electric machines was influenced by the materials and manufacturing processes available. Even before 1980 the axial flux machinery begun to have great applicability in low speed applications. The expensive production of axial flux induction motors was a factor that limited the use of such motors, such as the fact that the faulty construction of the rotor limited the speed of the machine [12].

Today is possible to build axial flux motors with relatively low weight, low volume and with excellent mechanical and dynamic performance, which makes the axial flux induction machine a solution in several applications.

Disc motors using HTS materials have been used mainly in two topologies: disc motors where the rotor elements of superconducting materials act as magnets [14] or motors where the rotor is a single superconductor disc presenting hysteresis behaviour composed, for example, by YBCO [15] or BSCCO [16].

With the first topology the motor presents behaviour similar to a synchronous motor, while with the second one presents a more complex behaviour. Experimental results for a rotoric ring (cylinder) [17] or for a disc [18] in the HTS hysteresis motors show this dual behaviour. This does not happen when one has a rotoric ring with low electrical conductivity, as in ferromagnetic materials, due to the characteristics of pinning that HTS materials present and due to the dynamics of vortices in this type of material [19]. The stators of the disc motor can be conventional ones, composed by copper windings and steel, or superconductor ones, when high current densities are required [19].

The disc motors have been elected to be used in electric vehicles that use fuel-cell technology [20]. The liquid hydrogen used as fuel cells, could also be used [11] to cool the HTS materials in the rotor disc of the motor installed on the electric vehicle.

Currently there are essentially three categories of machines optimized with super-conductor materials: hysteresis, reluctance and trapped field motors [21], [22], [23]. Theoretically, the torque produced from an HTS machine is three to five times higher than the torque obtained for the same conventional machine, made by conventional materials [24].

5 Developed Motor

5.1 Topology

The built disc motor is composed by two semi-stators with 24 slots and 24 conventional cooper windings each one, a steel shaft, a rotor consisting of an aluminum disc or a YBCO disc, two support bearings and fixing screws. Fig. 2 shows the built motor.

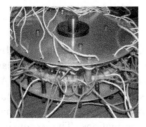  

Complete motor.   Conventional rotor with shaft.   Superconductor rotor.

Fig. 2. Built disc motor

The spacing between the semi-stators and rotor should be as small as possible to assure lower dispersion in the flux produced by the coils of semi-stators, ensuring a higher torque. In the mechanical connection between the semi-stator paramagnetic material (mica) high magnetic reluctance screws were used, in order to cancel the magnetic connection between semi-stators. A system that ensures the adjustment nuts of airgap was also integrated.

5.2 Characteristics

This motor, when the rotor is composed of aluminum, has an asynchronous behavior, functioning as a conventional induction motor.

The operation of this motor is quite similar to the drum induction motor, where the flux, coming from one semi-stator, penetrates the rotor disc perpendicularly and closes itself onto the other semi-stator. The disc motor in study has the electrical circuit on the side of the stator, with 24 independent coils, and the rotor consists of an aluminum disc. The stator coils create a magnetic rotating field making the aluminum rotor "feel" a variable inductive magnetic field. Thus, electromotive forces will be induced on the disc giving origin to currents in the rotor disc. The induced currents produce an electromagnetic torque, T_{elect}, which places the rotor to rotate.

When the rotor is composed of HTS materials it presents a complex behavior, showing both synchronous and asynchronous behaviors [25]. At startup, the stator rotating field magnetizes the rotor HTS materials and, in this rotor magnetization process, vortices are induced in the HTS material. These vortices traveling in the HTS disc and can be subject to pinning centers, that pinning them, magnetizing the rotor and creating a field in the rotor that, in steady state, presents a constant phase relatively to the rotating field created by the stator. The interaction between these two fields origins a motor torque that presents an amplitude equal to the product of the amplitudes of two fields with the phase between them (2).

$$T = B_{max} \times H_{max} \times \sin\left(\alpha_B \,{}^\wedge \alpha_H\right). \tag{2}$$

5.3 Simulations

The motor described above was simulated with a commercial finite elements software package, FLUX2D®. In this package, the non-HTS material parameterization was made with same materials already included, like copper, aluminum and steel. In this program, the material parameterization was made with same materials that were parameterized, like the copper, the aluminum and the steel. For the HTS materials, namely YBCO, the parameterization was based using the E-J power law (3).

$$\rho(E,B) = \frac{E_c^{\frac{1}{n(B)}}}{J_c(B)} |E|^{\frac{n(B)-1}{n(B)}} + \rho_0, \tag{3}$$

J_c denotes the critical current density, E_c the critical electric field, n the exponent and ρ_0 the resistivity. The following parameter values, available from the used software package, were used for the HTS material (YBCO): $E_c = 10^{-4}$ V/m (Critical Electric Field); $J_{c0} = 4,4 \times 10^6$ A/mm^{-2} (Critical Current Density); $B_0 = 10^6$ T (Magnetic Induction Field); $n_0 = 15$ (Exponent); $\rho_0 = 10^{-13}$ Ωm (Additional resistivity).

The analysis of the motor characteristics is done with FLUX2D®, being the modeling performed as a linear motor. The obtained results are presented below. The flux lines resulting from the supply of the coils in the stator are shown in Fig. 3. It can be seen that, for a linear stator with identical dimensions to the cylindrical motor designed, two magnetic poles are created magnetizing the rotor.

The current density distribution analysis over the airgap shows, as expected, a sinusoidal distribution with two poles, as presented in Fig. 4.

Fig. 3. Flux lines produced by the semi-stators supply

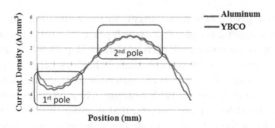

Fig. 4. Simulated current density distribution over the airgap

The results presented in Fig. 5 and Fig. 6 allows concluding that the motors present the expected behavior. Fig. 5 shows the force, for both motors in a no-load condition. The motor with the aluminum rotor presents an asynchronous behavior.

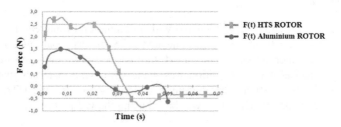

Fig. 5. Comparison of longitudinal force time evolution between the simulated obtained characteristics for motors without load

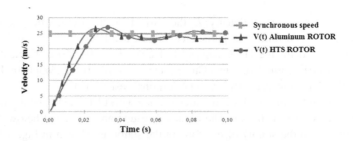

Fig. 6. Comparison of longitudinal force time evolution between the simulated obtained characteristics for motors without load

In Fig. 6 is possible to observe that the aluminum rotor motor, in steady state, does not achieve synchronous linear speed (approximately 25 m/s for an effective length stator of 0,495 m, a frequency of 50 Hz and 2 poles). The HTS rotor motor behaves like a synchronous motor. In steady state, as shown in Fig. 6, it can be seen that it does achieve synchronous speed, behaving as an asynchronous motor when not in steady state. Two important characteristics of the HTS motor can be observed in above figures. The HTS linear motor presents a higher force than the conventional aluminum motor and also presents dual synchronous and asynchronous behavior.

Running this motor from start up to steady state, it behaves like an asynchronous motor, working with slip until it reaches the steady state. After reaching the steady state condition the rotor rotates with synchronous speed, acting like a permanent magnet motor.

6 Conclusions and Future Work

From the obtained results it is possible conclude that the conventional disc motor behaves like an induction motor, with asynchronous behavior while the HTS disc motor presents asynchronous and synchronous behaviors. During asynchronous regime, the magnetization of the superconductor, by the rotating field created in the stator, induces currents in superconducting materials, which establish a magnetic flux that, reacting with the stator flux give rise to an electromagnetic torque, proportional to the losses. In steady state operation, the motor torque is null due the synchronism between the field created by the stator and the field resulting in the rotor. Both fluxes are synchronous thus no flux variation exists and no losses are created.

From the Flux2D® obtained results it can be seen that the HTS motor presents a higher force than the equivalent aluminum motor. However, the obtained force in the simulated HTS disc motor has not been as superior as in the aluminum disc motor. Possible causes may be the simplified simulation problem, a godless accurate parameterization of the materials in the finite element package and the use of a simulated linear motor instead a rotary motor.

Future work considers improving the material parameters in the finite elements program, and develops a more realistic simulation of this linear motor in order to obtain an approach of the electromagnetic characteristic of disc motor. Another approach is the study of this motor considering the load and/or speed variation.

Acknowledgements. Authors would like to thank CTS (Centre for Technology and Systems) of UNINOVA (Institute of New Technologies) for financial supporting this work.

References

1. Barclay, F.: Fuel Cells, Engines and Hydrogen. Wiley, Chichester (2006)
2. Thomas, C., James, B., Lomax Jr., F., Kuhn Jr., I.: Fuel options for fuel cells vehicle: hydrogen, methanol or gasoline? International Journal of Hydrogen Energy 25, 551–567 (2000)
3. Solar electrical vehicles information,
   http://www.solarelectricalvehicles.com
4. Superconductivity information, http://superconductors.org/
5. Casas, J., Miyamoto, N., Nakane, H., Goto, E.: Performance of a double SQUID Magnometer. IEEE Transactions on Magnetics 27(2) (1991)
6. Van Duzer, T.: Superconductor Electronic Device Applications. IEEF Journal of Quantum Electronics 15(II) (1989)
7. MAGLEB Official Website information, http://www.smtdc.com

8. Snitchler, G., Gamble, B., Kalsi, S.: The performance of a 5 MW high temperature super-conductor ship propulsion motor. IEEE Transactions on Superconductivity 15(2) (2005)
9. Sumitomo Electric information,
   http://global-sei.com/super/topics_e/index.html
10. Electromechanical Systems Applied Superconductivity information,
    http://www.masbret.com/UAPT.html
11. Thomas, C., James, B., Lomax Jr., F., Kuhn Jr., I.: Int. Journal of Hydrogen Energy 25(6, 1), 551–567 (2000)
12. Axial flux technology information,
    http://www.axcomotors.com/axial-flux_technology.html
13. Abrikosov, A.: Zh. Eskp. Teor. Fiz. 35, 1442; Sov. Phys. JETP 5, 1174 (1957)
14. Marquez, I., Granardos, X., Obradors, X., Pallares, J., Bosch, R.: IEEE Transactions of Applied Superconductivity 9(2), 1249–1252 (1999)
15. Álvarez, A., Suárez, P., Cáceres, D., Granados, X., Péres, B., Ceballos, J.: Disk-shaped superconducting rotor for an axial flux induction motor. Physica C 398, 157–160 (2004)
16. Nakamura, T., Jung, H., Muta, I., Hoshino, T.: Synchronization of an axial-type Bi-2223 bulk motor operated in liquid nitrogen. Supercond. Sci. Technol. 17(11), 1319–1323 (2004)
17. Tsuboi, Y., Ohsaki, H.: Torque characteristics of a motor using bulk superconductors in the rotor in the transient phase. IEEE Trans. Applied Supercond. 13, 2210–2213 (2003)
18. Álvarez, A., Suárez, P., Cáceres, D., Cordero, E., Ceballos, J., Péres, B.: Disk-shaped Superconducting Rotor under a Rotating Magnetic Field: Speed Dependence. IEEE Trans. Applied Supercond. 15(2), 2174–2177 (2005)
19. Álvarez, A., Suárez, P., Cáceres, D., Granados, X., Obradors, X., Bosch, R., Cordero, E., Péres, B., Caballero, A., Blanco, J.: Superconducting armature for induction motor of axial flux based on YBCO bulks. Physica C 372–376(3), 1517–1519 (2002)
20. Rahman, K., Patel, N., Ward, T., Nagashima, J., Caricchi, F., Crescimbini, F.: Application of Direct Drive Wheel Motor for Fuel Cell Electric and Hybrid Electric Vehicle Propulsion System. In: Conference Record IEEE 39th Industry Application Conference, vol. 3 (2004)
21. Match, L.: Electromagnetic an Electromechanical Machines. Wiley & Sons, Chichester (1986)
22. McCulloch, M., Dew-Hughes, D.: Brushless Ac machines with high temperatures superconducting rotors. Material Sciences and Engineering 53(1-2), 211–215 (2000)
23. Barnes, G., McCulloch, M., Dew-Hughes, D.: Applications and Modelling of Bulk HTS in Brushless AC Machines. Supercond. Sci. Technol. 13, 875–878 (2000)
24. Bondrea, N., Leão Rodrigues, A.: Torque comparison of an eight-pole permanent magnet excited and a high temperature superconductor disc motor. In: Proceedings of the 4th International Workshop on Processing and Applications of Superconducting (RE)BCO Large Grain Materials PASREG 2003, Jena, Germany (2003)
25. Barnes, G.: Computational modelling for type-II superconductivity and the investigation of high temperature superconducting electrical machines, Ph.D. Thesis, Oxford Univ. (2000)

Part 17

Electronic Circuits Layout and Optimization

GADISI – Genetic Algorithms Applied to the Automatic Design of Integrated Spiral Inductors

Pedro Pereira, M. Helena Fino, Fernando Coito, and Mário Ventim-Neves

Faculdade de Ciências e Tecnologia – Universidade Nova de Lisboa,
2829-516 Caparica, Portugal
pmrp@fct.unl.pt, hfino@ieee.org, fjvc@fct.unl.pt,
ventim@uninova.pt

Abstract. This work introduces a tool for the optimization of CMOS integrated spiral inductors. The main objective of this tool is to offer designers a first approach for the determination of the inductor layout parameters. The core of the tool is a Genetic Algorithm (GA) optimization procedure where technology constraints on the inductor layout parameters are considered. Further constraints regarding inductor design heuristics are also accounted for. Since the layout parameters are inherently discrete due to technology and topology constraints, discrete variable optimization techniques are used. The Matlab GA toolbox is used and the modifications on the GA functions, yielding technology feasible solutions is presented. For the sake of efficiency and simplicity the pi-model is used for characterizing the inductor. The validity of the design results obtained with the tool, is checked against circuit simulation with ASITIC.

Keywords: Discrete-Variable Optimization, Genetic Algorithm, Spiral Inductor Design.

1 Introduction

The rapid growth and reduced cost of communication systems operating at high frequencies, has motivated the development of devices with a large number of elements implemented in integrated circuit. In the particular case of RF transceivers, voltage controlled oscillators (VCOs) are responsible for the purity of the signal generated. For these applications LC-VCOs are often chosen due to their phase-noise behaviour. The performance of the LC-VCOs is well determined by the quality factor of the spiral inductor.

For the design of spiral inductors, designers usually adopt methodologies based on either pre-characterized inductor designs or ad hoc techniques [1]. In either case designing a spiral inductor involves the determination of multiple correlated variables. Due to the complexity of the design, optimization-based techniques have been proposed [2], [3] and [4]. In these approaches, however, continuous variable optimization techniques are employed and constraints are considered only on the bounding values for the inductor layout parameters. Technology-constrains regarding the discrete nature of the variables is dealt in a subsequent procedure where the layout

L.M. Camarinha-Matos, P. Pereira, and L. Ribeiro (Eds.): DoCEIS 2010, IFIP AICT 314, pp. 515–522, 2010.

parameters obtained from optimization are rounded to the nearest technology feasible value. This methodology usually yields sub-optimum solutions where the correlation of the parameters obtained is not granted.

During the last years GAs have been widely used in circuit design [5] and [6]. This paper introduces a GA tool for the optimization-based design of spiral inductors. In this tool the solution is obtained considering user-defined constraints in the design, reflecting a discretization of the variable values according to the technology used. Further constraints imposing bounds on the ratio between design variables are also accounted for as a way of supporting design heuristics. The tool offers the possibility to choose the performance parameter to be optimized, such as maximizing the quality factor, Q, at a given operation frequency, or the minimization of the area occupied by the device. The tool was developed in Matlab and the GA optimization toolbox was used. The validity of the solution obtained is checked against results from simulation with ASITIC simulator.

2   Contribution to Technological Innovation

The main objective of the optimization based tool presented is to generate the geometrical layout parameters of integrated spiral inductors. For this purpose two main concerns were considered. On one hand a technology–aware methodology is adopted where the discrete nature of the variables is accounted for as a way of restricting the search space to those points allowed by the technology. Further constraints arising from heuristic design rules are also considered. On the other hand the necessity for obtaining solutions in an efficient way led to the use of the inductor physical model, instead of using a simulation based approach.

2.1   Planar Spiral Inductor Pi-Model

The efficiency of the optimization tool is obtained through the use of an inductor model. For the sake of simplicity the pi-model, illustrated in Fig. 1.a., is adopted.

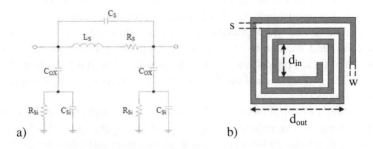

Fig. 1. a) Planar inductor pi-model; b) Layout of a square inductor

For the evaluation of the inductance, Ls, several approaches have been proposed, based on a fitting process to values obtained experimentally [7], or through physics-based equations [8]. In this tool the Modified Wheeler formula is used [7], where

$$L_s = k_1 \mu_0 n^2 d_{avg} / (1 + k_2 \rho), \tag{1}$$

given that

$$\rho = (d_{out} - d_{in}) / (d_{out} - d_{in}), \tag{2.a}$$

$$d_{avg} = 0.5 (d_{out} + d_{in}), \tag{2.b}$$

$$d_{out} = d_{in} + 2 n w + 2 (n-1) s. \tag{2.c}$$

where, n is the number of turns, s is the track to track distance, and w is the track width, as represented in Fig. 1.b. Finally, k_1 and k_2, are coefficients allowing the model to be adapted to several inductor shapes [7]. The evaluation of R_s, $R_{si}C_s$, C_{ox}, and C_{si}, is obtained with equations in [9] and [10].

2.2 Genetic Algorithms Applied to Integrated Inductor Design

Genetic Algorithms (GAs) are a stochastic search method that mimics the natural biological evolution, operating on a population of potential solutions, applying the principle of survival of the fittest to produce better and better approximations to a solution. GAs can be applied to any problem that can be formulated as function optimization problems. As a result, they are applied to non-linear problems, defined on discrete, continuous or mixed search spaces, constrained or unconstrained. Besides that, GAs are conceptually simple and have proved to be robust to dynamic changes.

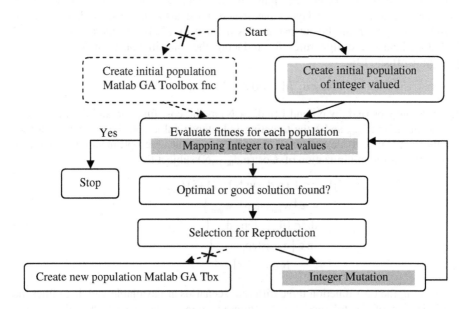

Fig. 2. Simple Genetic Algorithm flowchart

The main advantages of using GAs in optimization problems instead of the more traditional search and optimization methods reside in the fact that they search a population of points in parallel instead of a single point, thus making results less sensitive to the point chosen. Furthermore, GAs do not require derivative information or previous knowledge, they handle noisy functions well, and are resistant to becoming trapped in local optima [11].

The optimization tool developed was implemented with the Matlab GA toolbox. Since this toolbox shows several limitations for discrete optimization problems, where each variable has an imposed step-size, three functions were developed. The flowchart showing the process of GA is represented in Fig. 2, where the additional functions, are shown with a dark background.

3   Optimization Methodology for Inductor Design

The methodology adopted aims to achieve a technology/topology-aware solution, where constraints are mandatory. Regarding the number of turns, n, it was considered to have a minimum value of 1.5 and subsequent values are obtained with an unitary increment, i.e.,

$$n \in [1.5, 2.5, 3.5, ...[\, , \tag{3}$$

Due to the inductor model considered the shape of the inductor must account for square, hexagonal and octagonal topologies. On what concerns the technological constraints, minimum values for the track width, w, for the track-to-track spacing, s, and for in input diameter, d_{in}, must be defined. Technology-depend minimum increment values for these layout parameters must also be considered. Finally the correlation between the layout parameters defined by (4) is considered, as a way of including heuristic design rules for reducing the parasitic phenomena due to the proximity effect [12].

$$0.2 < d_{in} / d_{out} < 0.8 \, , \; d_{in} > 5w \, . \tag{4}$$

If we define $Cost(n, d_{in}, w, N)$ and $L(n, d_{in}, w, N)$ as the cost function and the inductance of the spiral, and L_{exp} and δ the targeting inductance value and the tolerance allowed for the inductance to deviate from the targeting value, the optimization problem is formulated as the minimization of $Cost(n, d_{in}, w, N)$ subject to

$$
\begin{aligned}
(1-\delta) L_{exp} &\leq L(n, d_{in}, w, N) \leq (1+\delta) L_{exp} \\
w &\in [w_{min} : step_w : w_{max}] \\
d_{in} &\in [d_{min} : step_d : d_{max}] \\
n &\in [n_{min} : step_n : n_{max}] \\
N &\in [2, 4, 8]
\end{aligned}
\tag{5}
$$

Concerning the cost function three different scenarios are available yielding either the minimization of the tolerance, δ, the minimization of the device area, d_{out}, or the maximization of the quality factor, for a predefined frequency of operation and a maximum output diameter, d_{out} [13]. For the pi-model, the expression of the quality factor becomes [14]

$$Q=(\omega L_s/R_s)\cdot\left(R_p\Bigg/\left(R_p+\left[\left(\frac{\omega L_s}{R_s}\right)^2+1\right]R_s\right)\right)\cdot\left(1-\left(C_p\,R_s^2/L_s\right)-\omega^2L_sC_p\right). \qquad (6)$$

Where

$$R_p=\left(1/\omega^2C_{ox}^2R_{si}\right)+\left(R_{si}\left(C_{ox}+C_{si}\right)^2/C_{ox}^2\right) \qquad (7)$$

$$C_p=C_{ox}\left(1+\omega^2\left(C_{ox}+C_{si}\right)C_{si}R_{si}^2\right)\Big/1+\omega^2\left(C_{ox}+C_{si}\right)^2R_{si}^2 \qquad (8)$$

For the inductor design, the GA procedure starts with the creation of the initial population, where each individual is composed by four variables (w,d,n,N), representing the layout geometry parameters. The initial population is randomly created, but the individual's genes must obey to variable boundaries. Represented in Fig. 2 an alternative functions for creating an integer-valued population is used.

```
function Population =
integer_pop(GenomeLength,FitnessFcn,options)
totalpopulation = sum(options.PopulationSize);
range = options.PopInitRange;
lowerBound= range(1,:);
span = range(2,:) - lowerBound;
% ROUND fun guarantee that individuals are integers
Population = repmat(lowerBound,totalpopulation,1) + ...
     round(repmat(span,totalpopulation,1) .*
     rand(totalpopulation,GenomeLength));
% End of creation function
```

The population is converted to real values and then evaluated through the objective function. In this function each individual is evaluated according to the constraints imposed and if it is not compliant, a penalty is applied so that it shows a very low probability of being elected for the next population. The algorithm stops here, if termination conditions are verified.

The next step accounts for the generation of a new population. Here selection and reproduction functions are used. For the selection the roulette wheel method is chosen. Afterwards, reproduction (or mutation) is made. Due to the difficulty of Matlab in dealing with real-valued population with predefined step-size, a mutation function was defined, allowing the creation of a new population of integer-valued individuals.

```
function mutationChildren =
integer_mutation(parents,options,GenomeLength, ...
     FitnessFcn,state,thisScore,thisPopulation)
shrink = 0.1;
scale = 1.0;
scale = scale - shrink * scale * ...
state.Generation/options.Generations;
```

```
range = options.PopInitRange;
lowerBound = range(1,:);
upperBound = range(2,:);
scale = scale * (upperBound - lowerBound);
mutationPop = length(parents);
mutationChildren = repmat(lowerBound,mutationPop,1) ...
    + round(repmat(scale,mutationPop,1) .* ...
    rand(mutationPop,GenomeLength));
% End of mutation function
```

4 Results

The results presented in this section spotlight the ability of the developed GA-based tool to achieve optimal design of spiral inductors. The design of 7 nH inductor for an operation frequency of 0.8 GHz is addressed, where the technological parameters shown in Table 1 are used to evaluate R_{si}, C_s, C_{ox} and C_{si}. The determination of the layout parameters is done according to the constraints represented in Table 2. Also a minimum space between tracks of 1.5 µm and a maximum tolerance δ of 2.5%, are assumed.

In this section, three examples are addressed. In example A, the inductor layout parameters minimizing the tolerance, δ, are computed; example B deals with designing an inductor with the smallest device area. Finally in example C an inductor with maximum quality factor, given a maximum output diameter of 500 µm is obtained. In examples B and C the tolerance, δ, is an additional constraint, with maximum value of 2.5%. The results obtained are presented in Table 3.

Table 1. Technological parameters

Parameter	Value	Parameter	Value
ε_o	8.85e-12	t_{ox} (µm)	600
ε_r	1.0	C_{sub} (F/m^2)	4.0e-6
σ (Ωm)	1 / 2.65e-8	G_{sub} (S/m^2)	2.43e+5

Table 2. Design Constraints

Parameter	Min	Step	Max
w (µm)	5.0	0.25	50.0
d_{in} (µm)	20.0	0.25	250.0
n	1.5	1.0	15.5

Regarding the results in Table 3, for the working example A, we should mention that several different results can be obtained for the same goal. This means that there is a grid of solutions that match the objective. On the other hand for examples B and C the use of a maximum tolerance, δ, as an additional restriction, leads to the

Table 3. Optimization results

	w(μm)	d_{in}(μm)	n	N_{side}	d_{out}(μm)	L_{tool}(nH)	δ(%)	Q_{tool}
A	11.00	149.50	4.5	4	259.00	7.00	0.0	3.90
B	5.50	48.50	7.5	4	150.50	6.83	2.42	2.35
C	34.75	176.25	4.5	8	499.50	7.17	2.42	9.19

Table 4. Comparison of results between evaluated and simulated

	L_{tool}(nH)	L_{Asitic}(nH)	Error (%)	Q_{tool}(nH)	Q_{Asitic}(nH)	Error (%)
A	7.00	6.97	0.43	3.90	3.83	1.82
B	6.83	6.73	1.49	2.35	2.30	2.17
C	7.17	7.01	2.23	9.19	8.65	6.24

optimum result shown. It is also possible to conclude that there is a commitment between Q and d_{out}, i.e., when maximizing Q, the largest area is chosen. The validity of these results was checked against simulation with ASITIC yielding results shown in Table 4.

5 Conclusions

This paper introduces a tool for the determination of the layout parameters of CMOS spiral inductors. In this tool a GA optimization methodology is adopted, where constraints on the values of the variables representing the layout parameters are used. These constraints regard not only a limitation on the maximum/minimum values of the variables but also a discretization on their values. This enables the generation of the best solution for the technology used. Further constraints imposing predefined correlation between layout parameters are considered as a way of implementing heuristic design rules. Three working examples showing the design of an inductor for different optimization goals were shown. The solutions obtained are in good accuracy when compared to simulation results, with errors below 7%.

The evolution of the tool to a multi-objective optimization will be addressed, allowing designers to have a better understanding of the solution space, and to choose the best solution. The main limitation of the work proposed resides in the applicability of the tool to higher frequencies. This limitation is inherent to the pi-model used for the integrated inductor. The inclusion of more appropriate high frequency model will be considered as a continuation of the work proposed.

References

1. Hamm, D.: Design of Integrated LC VVCOs. In: Toumazou, C., Moschytz, G., Gilbert, B. (eds.) Trade-offs in Analog Circuit Design, ch. 18, pp. 517–589. Kluwer Academic Publishers, Dordrecht (2002)
2. Nieuwoudt, A., Massoud, Y.: Multi-level Approach for Integrated Spiral Inductor Optimization. In: Design Automation Conference, pp. 648–651 (2005)

3. Allstot, D., Choi, K., Park, J.: Parasitic-Aware Optimization of CMOS RF Circuits. Kluwer Academic Publishers, Dordrecht (2003)
4. Chan, T., Lu, H., Zeng, J., Chen, C.: LTCC Spiral Inductor Modeling, Synthesis and Optimization. In: ASPDAC 2008, pp. 768–771 (2008)
5. Stelmack, M., Nakashima, N., Batill, S.: Genetic Algorithms for Mixed Discrete/ Continuous Optimization in Multidisciplinary Design. In: Symposium on Multidisciplinary Analysis and Optimization (1998)
6. Wankhede, M., Deshmukh, A.: Optimization of Cell-based VLSI Circuit Design using a Genetic Algorithm: Design Approach. In: Proceedings of the International MultiConference of Engineers and Computer Scientists (2009) ISBN 978-988-17012-7-5
7. Mohan, S., Hershenson, M., Boyd, S., Lee, T.: Simple Accurate Expressions for Planar Spiral Inductances. IEEE Journal of Solid-State Circuits 34 (1999)
8. Jenei, S., Nauwelaers, B., Decoutere, S.: Physics-Based Closed-Form Inductance Expression for Compact Modelling of Integrated Spiral Inductors. IEEE J. Solid-State Circuits 37, 77–80 (2002)
9. Choi, Y., Yoon, J.: Experimental Analysis of the Effect of Metal Thickness on the Quality Factor in Integrated Spiral Inductors for RF ICs. IEEE Electron Device Lett. 25, 76–79 (2004)
10. Murphy, O.: Advanced Physical Modelling of Multilayer Inductors for CMOS RF Front-End Applications. PhD Thesis, University College Cork - National University of Ireland (2005)
11. Sivanandam, S., Deepa, S.: Introduction to Genetic Algorithms. Springer, Heidelberg (2008)
12. Aguilera, J., Berenguer, R.: Design and Test of Integrated Inductors for RF Applications. Kluwer Academic Publishers, Dordrecht (2004)
13. Pereira, P., Fino, M.H., Coito, F., Ventim-Neves, M.: ADISI – An efficient tool for the automatic design of integrated spiral inductor. In: 16th IEEE International Conference on Electronics, Circuits and Systems – IEEE ICECS 2009, Hammamet – Tunisia (December 2009) (accepted for publication)
14. Yue, C., Wong, S.: Design Strategy of On-Chip Inductors for Highly Integrated RF Systems. In: Proceedings of the 1999 Design Automation Conference, pp. 982–987 (1999)

Test Based on Built-In Current Sensors for Mixed-Signal Circuits

Román Mozuelos, Yolanda Lechuga, Mar Martínez, and Salvador Bracho

Microelectronic Engineeering Group, University of Cantabria, ETSIIT,
Av. Los Castros s/n, 39005 Santander, Spain
{Roman.Mozuelos,Yolanda.Lechuga,Mar.Martinez,
Salvador.Bracho}@unican.es

Abstract. This paper presents a test methodology for mixed-signal circuits. The test approach uses a built-in sensor to analyze the dynamic current supply of the circuit under test. This current sensor emphasizes the highest harmonics of the dynamic current of the circuit under test when the current to voltage conversion is done. The goodness of the test method is analyzed first by means of a fault simulation and afterwards through the experimental data obtained from several benchmark circuits.

Keywords: Dynamic current test, Built-in current sensor, Design for test, Mixed–signal circuit.

1 Introduction

The increase of mixed signal applications, with integrated circuits containing both analog and digital sections, motivates the development of design-for-test approaches for testing analog macros embedded in digital systems. The success of supply current monitoring (I_{DD}) in digital CMOS integrated circuits has prompted researches to investigate the feasibility of I_{DD} as a testing methodology for analog modules [1].

A survey of I_{DD} test methodologies, both quiescent and transient, can be found in [2]. All of them require precise measurements to be effective. Traditionally the current measurement is performed externally to the chip. However, to enhance the precision and to increase the sampling rate may require the use of suitable built-in current sensor circuits (BICS) to measure the current inside the chip [3].

The design of these BICS relies on the voltage drop across a resistance, induced by the dynamic supply current, in order to generate the fault signal. This current is captured in the sensor directly [4] or through current mirrors [5]. Sometimes, the charge accumulated in a capacitor is used to detect the shape of the dynamic current of the circuits with faults [6].

The paper is organised as follows. Section 2 highlights the contribution to technological innovation. Section 3 presents the I_{DDX} test method. Section 4 analyses the efficiency of the test method by means of a fault evaluation. Section 5 shows measured data from the benchmark circuits. Finally, the discussion and the conclusions are presented.

L.M. Camarinha-Matos, P. Pereira, and L. Ribeiro (Eds.): DoCEIS 2010, IFIP AICT 314, pp. 523–530, 2010.

2 Contribution to Technological Innovation

This work proposes a new test method based on the analysis of the circuit dynamic current (I_{DDX}), both quiescent and transient, for the verification of digital, analog and mixed-signal circuits. The structural test method aims to reduce the test time and the complexity of the measurement equipment commonly used in mixed-signal tests.

3 Dynamic Current Test Method

In order to process accurately the information contained in the dynamic current that goes across the circuit under test (CUT), the measurement is performed by a built-in current sensor circuit (BICS) integrated within the CUT. Thus, it minimizes the distortion effect of the capacitances and inductances associated with the input/output pads, the circuit package and the elements of the printed circuit board.

The BICS output provides a sequence of digital pulses whose width reflects the amplitude and duration of the dynamic current. Defective circuits are exposed comparing the BICS output waveform of the CUT with the expected one for the fault-free circuit.

The test setup, besides providing the CUT stimulus, requires a digital signature analyzer to process the BICS output. This low cost equipment can be as simple as an integrator, a counter or a memory.

3.1 Built-In Current Sensor

In the mixed signal circuit, the current across the digital logic is sampled in series by a BICS placed in the power supply path between the CUT ground (Virtual_GND) and the chip pin (GND) (figure 1). The sampling element is a MOSFET transistor because it is able to accept large current transients without introducing a significant voltage drop and, at the same time, it is sensitive to the small quiescent currents [7].

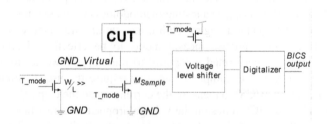

Fig. 1. BICS to analyse the dynamic current through the digital logic

However, this measurement strategy would degrade the performance of the analog blocks due to the reduction of their effective voltage supply. Therefore, in this case, the current is replicated by placing additional branches to the current mirrors of the circuits, taking advantage of the widely use of these basic build blocks in analog design [8].

In both cases, the sampled current is converted to voltage, then amplified and finally digitalized by a window comparator made of CMOS digital gates.

Under faulty conditions, the normal values of the analog circuit current may be increased, decreased or more generally distorted. Some of these faults do not produce a significant change in the quiescent current. However, they can affect the relationship of the harmonic components of the current waveform, causing a change in the slope of transient of the dynamic supply current [9].

So, we have designed a novel built-in current sensor circuit with the goal to emphasize the high-frequency components of the current when the current to voltage conversion is done. It uses the principle that a capacitor placed at the output port of a gyrator behaves like an inductance at the input port.

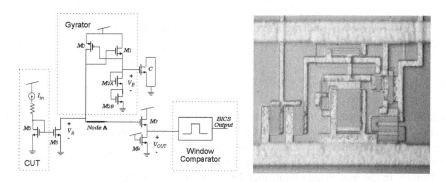

Fig. 2. Proposed Built-In current sensor (a) Scheme and (b) die photograph

The circuit relies on the inverted back-to-back connection of active devices to implement the basic gyrator behaviour. The transconductance sources are done with two transistors, an NMOS (M0) and a PMOS (M1), connected as it is shown in figure 2a. Transistors M2 bias M0 and M1 in the saturation region. The capacitor (C) is achieved by means of the gate capacitance of another NMOS transistor [10].

A prototype, without the window comparator, has been fabricated with the Austria MicroSystem (AMS) 0.6 µm technology to characterise the frequency response of the circuit. The chip photograph can be seen in figure 2b.

Figure 3 displays the experimental measurements of the circuit tranresistance (v_{OUT} vs. i_{IN}). The left graph shows a good agreement among the theoretical calculus using the small signal model of the circuit, the layout simulation with the AMS 0.6µm technological transistor models and the data measured from a fabricated chip.

The circuit behaviour emulates an inductance with one series and one parallel stray resistor, where the BICS sensitivity to the high frequency components of the current can be appreciated in the abrupt change of the circuit output voltage (lower graph of figure 3b) when a current pulse is injected at the BICS input (upper graph of figure 3b). The quiescent change of the voltage, after the current stabilization, is smaller and it is given by the low frequency impedance of the circuit.

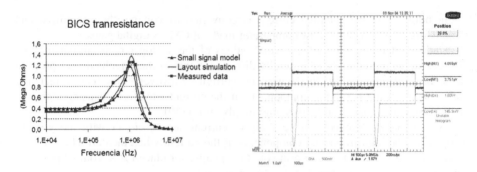

Fig. 3. BICS tranimpedance measure: (a) frequency and (b) transient responses

The BICS design is quite sensitive to process spread attributable to the transistor implementation of the capacitor.

4   Fault Evaluation

A fault simulation has been carried out to check the efficiency of the test method. The process consists on the analysis of CUT behaviour when we include the electrical abstraction of a fabrication defect (known as fault) and the comparison of the circuit performance with expect for the fault-free one.

Defects in the integrated circuit materials commonly give rise to catastrophic faults [11]. In this work, we have considered short circuits between the transistor terminals, gate oxide shorts (GOS) and large deviations of the passive components (figure 4).

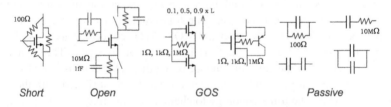

Fig. 4. Catastrophic transistor fault model

The fault model includes soft opens due to cracks in the interconnection lines, where there is still a small current flow due to the quantum phenomenon of the tunnel effect. Hard opens, especially the open gate defect, due to the complete disconnection of the line strongly depends on the technology and physical topology of the circuit and are more difficult to model in an initial stage of the circuit analysis [12].

The I_{DDX} test method uses the width of the digital pulses that appear at the sensor output for each transition of the CUT inputs to expose the defective circuits. In order to get an estimation of the goodness of the proposed test approach, the fault coverage obtained through the BICS output is compared with other more traditional structural tests. They are the quiescent current (I_{DDQ} test) and the DC voltage at the circuit outputs.

The threshold detection limit can be established through a Montecarlo simulation taking into account the process spread, or by means of the comparison with the measures taken from a well-known good circuit (golden device). These limits include a 100ns resolution in the pulse width of the BICS digital output, a 5μA variation in the I_{DDQ} of the CMOS logic, a change in the logic state of the digital outputs, and a 10mV deviation for the expected voltage at the analog block output.

Several benchmark circuits, both digital and analog, have been designed and fabricated to carry out the test evaluation. The digital module includes combinational logic cells and sequential memory registers. The BICS is placed between the CUT ground and the ground package pin [13].

The analog block is an operational amplifier in a voltage follower configuration. The current through the differential stage of the operational amplifiers is sampled by a new transistor added to the current mirror. As these circuits are usually connected in feedback configurations, the sampled current is sensitive not only to the differential stage and the bias network but also to the output stage.

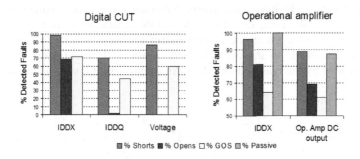

Fig. 5. Fault coverage of the digital logic and the operational amplifier

Figure 5 shows the fault coverage obtained in the test evaluation. The detected faults are classified according to their type (shorts, opens, GOS and passive components) and the detection methodology applied. Our dynamic current test approach is shown in the left hand columns (I_{DDX}) and the reference structural tests in the right ones. Quiescent current (I_{DDQ}) and voltage test (*Voltage*) for the digital logic together with the operational amplifier DC output voltage (*Op. Amp. DC output*).

It can be appreciated a larger fault coverage from the I_{DDX} method. The reason is that some faults are detected through the change in the duration of the transient current in spite of not modifying the quiescent current or the DC voltage of the CUT (*I_{DDQ} or DC Voltage*) [8][9].

5   Experimental Measurements

The test method has been experimentally validated through the design and fabrication of the benchmark circuits with the implementation of the BICS.

Figure 6 shows a measure of the BICS that analyzes the current through the digital logic. The sensor generates pulses proportional to the CUT dynamic current when a transition happens at the circuit inputs or at the clock signal.

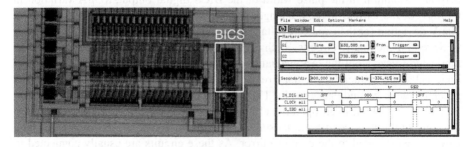

Fig. 6. Digital logic and BICS (a) chip photograph and (b) measured waveforms

Three faults have been integrated within the manufactured operational amplifier (figure 7). All the faults have a parametric behaviour as they are implemented by an NMOS transistor (W=1µm, L=80µm) whose ON resistance is over 250 KΩ. The faults emulate a mismatch on the current mirror transistors of the differential stage (F1), an oxide pinhole in the compensation capacitor (F2) and a deviation in the current provided by the bias network (F3). An analog multiplexer selects each time a fault.

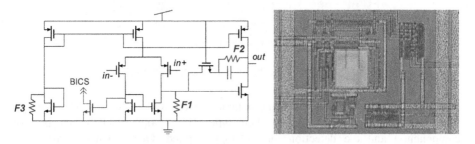

Fig. 7. Operational amplifier with injected faults (a) schematic and (b) chip photograph

The operational amplifier is configured as voltage follower in this experiment. The input and the output voltages are displayed on the upper part of figure 8 graphs for the fault-free and two faulty conditions. The BICS waveforms are displayed on the lower part of figure 8 graphs. Although the three faults produce small variations on the DC levels at the operational amplifier output, almost negligible in F3, all of them induce a large change in the pulse width of the BICS, consequently they are easily detectable with the proposed test method [14].

The same measured values for gain, offset voltage and slew-rate in two versions of the operational amplifier, one alone and the other with the BICS, allows appreciating the minimal influence of the sensor in the CUT performance.

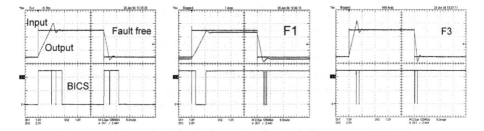

Fig. 8. Measured waveforms of the CUT and BICS output

The influence of the process spread in the BICS behaviour can be notice in table 1. It shows the Montecarlo simulation of the fabricated circuit. The large standard deviation of the BICS pulse width has to be taken into account to set the boundary limits for the pass/fail flag. To obtain these values it may be necessary to know precisely the fabrication parameters or to use a golden device as reference. In spite of this dispersion, the BICS output allows a clear discrimination between the fault-free circuit and the defective ones.

Table 1. Montecarlo simulation of the pulse width of the BICS output

BICS Output	Typical value	Mean value	Standard deviation
Fault free	2.67 us	3.28 us	1.46 us
F1	18.85 us	15.86 us	5.82 us
F2	13.29 us	12.58 us	2.61 us
F3	19.84 us	19.66 us	0.81 us

6 Discussion of Results

The proposed I_{DDX} test method provides a better fault coverage figure than the one obtained from a more traditional structural DC tests used as reference. Although, sometimes it is still necessary to characterize the functional performance of the mixed signal circuits before shipment due to customer or manufacturer necessities, the reduced test time and lower requirements of the test equipment makes this structural I_{DDX} test suitable for its application at the wafer level allowing an easy discrimination of the chips before their inclusion in the system package.

7 Conclusions and Further Work

This work proposes a new test method for mixed-signal circuits based on the analysis of the circuit dynamic current (I_{DDX}), both quiescent and transient.

The structural test uses a built-in current sensor to sample the dynamic current through selected branches of the CUT. The BICS was designed to prioritise the information obtained from the highest frequency components of the current.

The future development of this work should study the correlation between the BICS output and the functional performance of the CUT to relate the structural fault detection of the proposed I_{DDX} test with the test process yield.

The test method can be extended to a full BIST structure. To achieve this, the output signal processing must be included within the chip. It will be also necessary to allow the user to set the threshold limit that classifies the circuit as defective and to standardize the communication between the BICS and the test system.

Acknowledgments. This work was funded by the Project TEC2007-65588/MIC and by the Franco-Spanish Integrated Action "Integrated test of high-speed operation data converters" (2007-2008).

References

1. Robson, M., Russell, G.: Current Monitoring Technique for Testing Embedded Analogue Functions in Mixed-Signal ICs. Electronics Letters 32, 796–798 (1996)
2. Sabade, S., Walker, D.M.H.: IDDX-Based Test Methods: A Survey. ACM Transactions on Design Automation of Electronic Systems 9, 159–198 (2004)
3. Alorda, B., Canals, V., Segura, J.: A two-level Power-Grid Model for Transient Current Testing Evaluation. J. Electronic Testing 20(5), 543–552 (2004)
4. Maidon, Y., Deval, Y., Begueret, J.B., Tomas, J., Dom, J.P.: 3.3V CMOS Built-In Current Sensor. IEE Electronics Letters 33, 345–346 (1997)
5. Stopjaková, V., Manhaeve, H., Sidiropulos, M.: On-Chip Transient Current Monitor for Testing of Low-Voltage CMOS IC. In: Proceedings of Design, Automation and Test in Europe, pp. 538–542 (1999)
6. Segura, J., De Paul, I., Roca, M., Isern, E., Hawkins, C.J.: Experimental Analysis of Transient Current Testing Based on Charge Observation. Electronic Letter 35, 441–447 (1999)
7. Mozuelos, R., Peláez, N., Martínez, M., Bracho, S.: Built-in Current Sensor in Mixed Circuit Test Based on Dynamic Power Supply Consumption. In: IEEE International On-Line Testing Workshop, pp. 25–28 (1996)
8. Mozuelos, R., Martínez, M., Bracho, S.: Built-In Sensor Based on the Time Variation of the Transient Current Supply in Analogue Circuits. In: XVI Conference on Design of Circuits and Integrated Systems, pp. 630–635 (2001)
9. Lechuga, Y., Mozuelos, R., Martínez, M., Bracho, S.: Built-in Dynamic Current Sensor for Hard to Detect Faults in Mixed Signal ICs. In: Design, Automation and Test in Europe Conference and Exhibition, pp. 205–211 (2002)
10. Lechuga, Y., Mozuelos, R., Martínez, M., Bracho, S.: Built-in Sensor based on Current Supply High-Frequency Behaviour. IEE Electronics Letters 39, 775–777 (2003)
11. Segura, J., Hawkins, C.: CMOS Electronics: How it Works, How it Fails. IEEE Press, Los Alamitos (2004)
12. Arumí, D., Rodríguez-Montañés, R., Figueras, J.: Experimental Characterization of CMOS Interconnect Open Defects. IEEE Transactions on Computer-Aided Design of Integrated Circuits and Systems 27, 123–136 (2008)
13. Olbrich, T., Mozuelos, R., Richardson, A., Bracho, S.: Design-for-Test (DfT) Study in a Current Mode DAC. In: IEE Proceedings Circuits, Devices and Systems, vol. 143, pp. 374–379 (1996)
14. Mozuelos, R., Lechuga, Y., Allende, M.A., Martínez, M., Bracho, S.: Experimental Evaluation of a Built-in Current Sensor for Analog Circuits. In: Design of Circuits and Integrated Systems Conference, pp. 96–100 (2004)

Structural DfT Strategy for High-Speed ADCs

Yolanda Lechuga, Roman Mozuelos, Mar Martínez, and Salvador Bracho

Microelectronics Engineering Group
University of Cantabria Av. de los Castros s/n
39005 Santander, Spain
{yolanda.lechuga,roman.mozuelos,mar.martinez,
salvador.bracho}@unican.es

Abstract. This paper presents a Design-for-Test (DfT) approach for folded ADCs. A sensor DfT circuit is designed to sample several internal ADC test points at the same time, so that, by computing the relative deviation among them the presence of defects can be detected. A fault evaluation is done considering a behavioral model to compare the coverage of the proposed test approach with a functional test. Afterwards, a fault simulation is used on a transistor level implementation of the ADC to establish the optimum threshold limits for the DfT circuit that maximize the fault coverage figure.

Keywords: Folding and interpolated A/D converters, Design-for-Test, Circuit simulation, Behavioral modeling, Simulink environment.

1 Introduction

Nowadays, the analogue-to-digital converter is a common block in mixed-mode circuits. Embedded ADCs are used in a wide range of applications such as satellite receivers, new generation DVD players, interfaces with storage elements such as computer hard-disks, or the emerging ultra-wide band radio technology. These converters demand high performance to be suitable for the digital telecommunication market, which requires low linearity errors, high speed and low power consumption (battery-powered devices). Low-power performance leads to explore other suitable architectures featuring low-to-moderate resolution in addition to the flash ADC topology. Folding and interpolating techniques are proposed [1-3] as this type of ADC has the advantage of small number of comparators and chip area while the operating speed is the same that of the flash type.

To better explore the design options, and to preliminary evaluate any test approach, it is advisable to perform an analysis at the system behavioural level before starting at transistor level [4]. Behavioural simulators work much faster and it is possible to use the electrical design parameters (gain, bandwidth, offset, parasitic elements) for building the behavioural model; in order to estimate the effects of the injected faults on the specifications of the data converter. In that sense, a system implementation on the MATLAB/SIMULINK environment provides a significant number of advantages.

L.M. Camarinha-Matos, P. Pereira, and L. Ribeiro (Eds.): DoCEIS 2010, IFIP AICT 314, pp. 531–538, 2010.

Traditionally, ADCs are characterized through a specification test, based on a parameter characterization that requires expensive instruments to accurately measure analog signals [5]. To overcome problems related to functional testing, different BIST (Built-in Self Test) techniques have been proposed. They use internally generated or analyzed signals to translate on-chip the methods used in the functional tests [6-9].

The use of structural fault-model testing has been recognized as a promising alternative or addition to specification testing [10]. Some Design-for-Test (DfT) techniques do not attempt to extract the ADC performances to identify the defective circuits, but use a fault model to describe the electrical faulty behavior of a real defect. Therefore the effectiveness of the test technique can be estimated by analyzing the fault coverage figure.

This paper is organized as follows: Section 2 summarizes the original contributions of this work. Section 3 briefly describes the architecture of the folded and interpolated ADC used as benchmark circuit, as well as the electrical parameters chosen to build its behavioural model. Section 4 presents the proposed structural design-for-test method. Section 5 describes the fault evaluation performed to check the test goodness on the behavioural model, and also on a transistor level implementation of the ADC. The paper finishes in Section 6 with the conclusions.

2   Contribution to Technological Innovation

This work proposes a structural DfT method that monitors some internal test points to extract information about the ADC behaviour. The voltage deviation among these test points is the parameter chosen to infer the presence of a defect in the CUT.

We take advantage of a behavioral description of both the folded and interpolated converter and the design-for-test approach to allow a fast evaluation of the influence of the circuit parameter deviations on the DfT fault coverage and to establish a relationship with the converter performances.

A CAT platform has been used for fault injection and simulation [11], in order to set the optimum threshold voltage that results in maximum fault coverage. The paper is going to be focused in the fault evaluation process of the DfT approach, including a detailed description of the circuit modules necessaries to implement it.

3   Folded and Interpolated A/D Converter and Behavioral Model

The folded and interpolated (FI) A/D converter architecture divides the codification process in two steps performed in parallel: a coarse encoder for the most significant bits and a fine subsystem for the least significant bits [1-3]. It uses an analog preprocessing in the form of a "folding amplifier" (FB) to significantly reduce the number of comparators required to the fine subsystem with regard to a flash ADC.

The block diagram of a 6-bit folded A/D converter implementation is shown in Fig. 1. This circuit uses a resistive reference ladder to obtain 20 voltage references to feed the preamplifier array. A preamplifier block, senses the difference between the

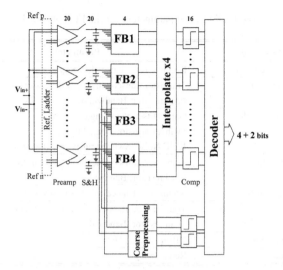

Fig. 1. Block diagram of the folded A/D converter

differential input signal *(Vip, Vin)* and a differential threshold *(Vrp, Vrn)* to produce a differential signal that later drives the folder blocks.

The folded A/D converter uses a distributed implementation of the track-and-hold (S&H) function to ease the synchronization between the coarse and fine bits.

The most popular method of producing folding signals involves the use of coupled differential pairs in the folder circuit. A folding degree of 4 was chosen for our application. An interpolation network, usually made of a string of equal resistors, produces additional folding signals without requiring additional folder blocks allowing the reduction of the ADC complexity and power consumption. It also performs an averaging that reduces the offset requirements of the comparators [3].

The analog coarse preprocessing circuit generates analog versions of the two MSBs. Both are generated by means of combination of the output signals of the S&H stages, so folding is not only used in the fine converter but also in the coarse one.

The differential outputs of the interpolation network and the coarse preprocessing block are digitalized by a set of 18 comparators. Then, the decoder uses the cyclic thermometric code provided by the 16 comparators of the fine converter and the 2 bits of the comparators of the coarse block to encode the 6-bit output and to obtain the overflow and underflow signals.

The converter behavior has been modeled by using the MATLAB/SIMULINK environment. The model allows the inclusion of the main sources of distortion in the converter blocks as a set of parameters to take into account the current-voltage relationship between the circuit inputs and outputs.

Table 1 summarizes the MATLAB/SIMULINK models of the converter blocks with their main high level parameters.

Table 1. High-level parameters for the FI ADC blocks

ADC Block	Parameter
Reference Ladder	Nominal resistance value, Sigma variance
Preamplifier	Transistor transconductance, Bias current
	Load resistor, Bandwidth
Sample and Hold	Gain, Offset, Sampling capacitor
	Switch transistor areas, Jitter
	KT/C Noise, Switch transistor conductances
Folder Block	Transistor transconductance, Bias current
	Load resistor, Bandwidth
Interpolate Network	Nominal resistance value, Sigma variance
Coarse ADC	Transistor transconductance, Bias current
	Load resistor, Bandwidth
Comparator	Offset voltage, Hysteresis
Digital encoder	Redundancy

4 DfT Approach

The proposed method is based on a structural test that provides a digital go/nogo output to be used as interface with a low cost ATE. To diminish the process parameter spread, instead of analyzing the voltage values of the converter internal nodes, we are going to focus on the relative variations that appear among them.

The voltage difference between $\Delta V_1 = [V_{SH}(i) - V_{SH}(i+1)]$ and $\Delta V_2 = [V_{SH}(i+1) - V_{SH}(i+2)]$ is computed by means of a differential difference amplifier (DDA) whose transference function implements (1).

$$\Delta V_{out} = A_{VDDA} \cdot [(V_{SH}(i) - V_{SH}(i+1)) - (V_{SH}(i+1) - V_{SH}(i+2))] \tag{1}$$

Where ΔV_{out} is the output of the DDA, A_{VDDA} is the DDA voltage gain, and $V_{SH}(i)$ are the output voltages, either positive or negative, of the S&H block number "i".

In order to simplify the DfT, the circuit is designed to give zero volts at the DDA output for the fault-free ADC. Thus, any deviation at the DDA output above a voltage limit would indicate the presence of a fault in the ADC. This threshold voltage has to be chosen to accommodate the measurement resolution, noise, temperature and process variations. The comparison of the DDA output with the threshold voltage is done by two differential pair comparators (DPC), to detect both positive and negative increments on ΔV_{out}.

The DDA output only will be zero volts if the transfer function of the three preamplifiers connected to the S&H modules is linear. As it happens for a limited range of the ADC input voltage, the DfT uses two additional comparators to discriminate the opportunity window where the DDA has to be evaluated.

The proposed method uses a five signal test bus to connect to the DfT the three signals sampled by the DDA plus the two additional signals needed by the comparators to establish the sampling window (Fig. 2).

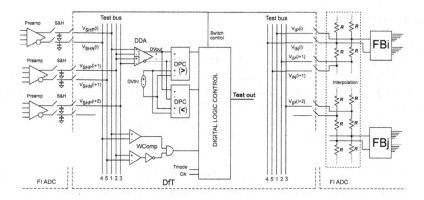

Fig. 2. Simplified scheme of the proposed Design-for-Test structure

The digital logic control propagates a start pulse using an own test clock. First, it connects the positive outputs of the S&H number 1, 2 and 3 (V_{SHP1}-V_{SHP2}-V_{SHP3}) and wait for the window comparators, connected to the positive and negative outputs of the S&H numbers 1 and 2 (V_{SHP1}-V_{SHN1} and V_{SHP2}-V_{SHN2}), to detect an ADC input voltage that corresponds with the linear range of preamplifiers 1-3. Then, the control circuit allows the DDA output processing by the DPC to detect the presence of a defect in the ADC. If the differential pair comparators are both zero the control circuit provides another test clock pulse to start the second measurement, and the process is repeated until all the S&H modules are evaluated.

After the S&H outputs, the DfT analyses the 16 differential outputs of the interpolated network. Finally, the DfT is connected to the outputs of the coarse preprocessing blocks. In this module, the positive and negative outputs of each amplifier are connected to two DDA inputs; meanwhile, the third input is tied to a reference voltage.

5   Test Evaluation Results

The fault evaluation method consists on injecting faults in one of the modules analyzed by the DfT, meanwhile the remaining ones are considered fault-free. First, the positive outputs of the modules and then the negative ones are processed to obtain the digital outputs of the differential pair comparators *DPC(>)* & *DPC(<)* (Fig. 2).

Fault simulation analysis has been done with a fast ramp and a sinewave input stimulus comprising, both of them, the limits of the ADC full scale. The sinewave input is used for computing the main specifications of the ADC by traditional functional test routines. For the DfT evaluation (fast ramp as input stimulus) only a few codes have been computed during each input transition. One important advantage of this input vector is that it has no linearity requirements, so it could be easily generated on-chip, to convert the DfT implementation into a full BIST structure.

5.1 Behavioral Model

The fault coverage results from the proposed structural DfT are compared to a functional test based in the estimation of the SINAD degradation. Table 2 summarises this fault coverage comparison. The table shows the deviation in each parameter that induces a degradation of three dBs at the converter SINAD and the deviation of the parameter that provokes a voltage at the differential difference amplifier of 100 mV. Some parameters that do not induce a high enough change in the ADC SINAD or in the DfT voltage are labelled by "----" in Table 2.

Table 2. Fault detection on the ADC building blocks of the behavioral model

ADC Block	Model Parameter	SINAD	DfT
Reference Ladder	ΔR_{REF}	> 35 %	> 20 %
Preamplifier	ΔR_L	> 20 %	> 5 %
	$\Delta \beta_n$	----	----
	ΔI_{BIAS}	----	> 20 %
	BW	$< 5 \cdot f_{in}$	$< 7 \cdot f_{in}$
Sample & Hold	Aperture Time	> 5 % of TCLK	> 10 % of TCLK
	Jitter	> 2 % of TCLK	> 1 % of TCLK
Folder Block	ΔR_L	> 5 %	> 5 %
	$\Delta \beta_n$	----	----
	ΔI_{BIAS}	> 15 %	> 55 %
	BW	$< 7 \cdot f_{in}$	$< 3 \cdot f_{in}$
Interpolated Network	ΔR_{INTERP}	----	> 300 %
Coarse Preprocessing	ΔR_L	> 75 %	> 10 %
	$\Delta \beta_n$	----	> 200 %
	ΔI_{BIAS}	> 250 %	> 10 %

The SINAD measurement and the DfT circuit detect some faults easily. For instance, deviations of the nominal value of one resistor of the reference ladder and the interpolating network, deviations in the load resistor of the preamplifiers and folder blocks, the reduction of the bandwidth of one of the folder blocks, or jitter in the sample and hold modules. The other two parameters used in the preamplifier behavioural description, transistor β_n and differential pair bias current, I_{Bias}, have a relatively small influence on the converter SINAD because they induce a very small change in the zero crossings of the preamplifier outputs. The DfT can detect deviations on the differential bias current, but not in the transistor β_n because the DfT evaluation is restricted to the CUT linear region.

Table 2 also shows that the DfT tolerance to the aperture time is worse than the SINAD limit, due to all S&H switches being affected by aperture time in the same way, effect that the DfT circuit can not detect easily.

5.2 Transistor Level Implementation

A transistor level implementation of the FI ADC has been developed using the UMC 0.13μm technology. We have injected catastrophic faults into two critical blocks of this circuit (preamplifiers and folder blocks) to evaluate the optimum threshold limit for the DfT that permits to obtain a fault coverage higher than 99%.

The following catastrophic fault model has been used: Three short faults have been included for each transistor. They interconnect the drain, source and gate terminals with different resistance values. The open source and drain faults are placed in series with the two transistor terminals. As far as the open gate faults is concerned, the fault model used forces the transistor to be open, although floating gate voltage would depend on coupling capacitances with adjacent lines, that influence the electrical behaviour of the defective line [12]. Since data from the layout are needed to evaluate coupling capacitances, the simulations of open gate faults are planned to be repeated as future work, once circuit layout is finished.

For fault injection and simulation, we have used the Computer-Aided-Test (CAT) platform [11], integrated in the Cadence Design Framework Environment. It has been developed for the evaluation of test techniques for mixed-signal and RF circuits, and it includes tools for fault simulation, test generation and test optimization.

For the preamplifiers, a total amount of 1,160 catastrophic faults have been simulated (20 times 58 faults per preamplifier), and all of them can be detected by the DfT using a threshold voltage of 100 mV. As far as the open faults is concerned, open drain faults in the differential pair transistors with DC input are more difficult to be detected for the corner preamplifiers (Preamp1 and Preamp20, Fig. 1). In these cases the DfT can detect open faults with an equivalent resistance higher than 40kΩ, whereas, for the rest of open drain and source faults, a threshold voltage of 100 mV is enough to detect faults with an equivalent resistance higher than 10kΩ.

For the folder blocks, 496 catastrophic faults have been simulated (4 times 124 faults per folder block). In this case, all the short and open faults injected in the middle folder blocks (FB2 and FB3, Fig. 1) can be detected using a threshold voltage of 100 mV. For the corner folder blocks (FB1 and FB4, Fig. 1), four DS shorts, four open drain faults, four open source faults and two open gate faults cannot be detected. For these undetectable faults DDA outputs are very close to the 100 mV threshold voltage, thus, probably they could be detected by increasing DDA gain.

In summary, we have obtained an overall fault coverage of 99.15% using a threshold voltage of 100mV. And this fault coverage could even be enhanced, if needed, for the analysis of other ADC blocks, by simply modifying the DDA gain.

5   Conclusions and Further Work

This paper presents a DfT approach for folding and interpolated ADCs. It analyses internal ADC nodes to compare relative deviations among them and, thus, the defects on the CUT can be detected.

A behavioral modeling of the ADC and the DfT has been done in MAT-LAB/SIMULINK to facilitate the analysis of the proposed test approach.

The detection threshold level to be used by the DfT to considerer a circuit defective is established by means a fault simulation using a CAT platform.

The proposed approach is intended for embedded modules, it also lowers the test time as only a few ADC samples are necessary for the DfT. However as a structural test, it does not provide information about the ADC performances.

As future work, we plan to check the ability of the DfT to detect simulated GOS (Gate Oxide Shorts) and parametric faults in all the ADC blocks, as well as experimentally on a prototype, where it will be necessary to establish the DfT circuit impact on the ADC performance. Finally, it is interesting to study how to complement this test strategy with other methods based on digital or supply current measurements, in order to increase fault coverage by including faults inside the comparators.

Acknowledgments. This work was funded by the Project TEC2007-65588/MIC and by the Franco-Spanish Integrated Action "Integrated test of high-speed operation data converters" (2007-2008).

References

1. Pan, H., Abidi, A.A.: Signal folding in A/D converters. IEEE Transactions on Circuits and Systems I: Regular Papers 51(1), 3–14 (2004)
2. Nauta, B., Venes, A.G.W.: A 70-MS/s 110-mW 8-bit CMOS folding and interpolation A/D converter. IEEE J. Solid-State Circuits 30, 1302–1308 (1995)
3. Venes, A.G.W., Van-de-Plassche, R.J.: An 80-MHz, 80-mW, 8-b CMOS folding A/D converter with distributed track-and-hold preprocessing. IEEE Journal of Solid-State Circuits 31(12), 1846–1853 (1996)
4. Maloberti, F., Estrada, P., Malcovati, P., Valero, A.: Behavioral modeling and simulation of data converters. In: IMEKO 2000 (2000)
5. Huertas, J.L.: Test and Design-for-Testability in Mixed-Signal Integrated Circuits. Kluwer Academic Publishers, Dordrecht (2004)
6. Arabi, K., Kaminska, I., Rzeszut, J.: BIST for D/A and A/D converters. IEEE Design & Test of Computers 13(4), 40–49 (1996)
7. Frisch, A., Almy, T.: HABIST: histogram-based analog built in self test. In: International Test Conference, pp. 760–767 (1997)
8. Azais, F., et al.: Implementation of a Linear Histogram BIST for ADCs. In: Design Automation and Test in Europe, pp. 590–595. IEEE CS Press, Los Alamitos (2001)
9. Huertas, G., Vázquez, D., Rueda, A., Huertas, J.L.: Oscillation-Based Test in Mixed-Signal Circuits. Springer, Heidelberg (2006)
10. Zjajo, A., de Gyvez, J.P., Gronthoud, G.: A quasi-static approach for detection and simulation of parametric faults in analog and mixed-signal circuits. In: IEEE International Mixed-Signal Testing Workshop, pp. 155–164 (2005)
11. Bounceur, A., Mir, S., Rolíndez, L., Simeu, E.: VLSI-SoC: Research trends in VLSI and Systems on Chip. In: CAT platform for analogue and mixed-signal test evaluation and optimization. IFIP International Federation for Information Processing, vol. 249, pp. 281–300. Springer, Heidelberg (2007)
12. Arumí, D., Rodríguez-Montañés, R., Figueras, J.: Experimental Characterization of CMOS Interconnect Open Defects. IEEE Transactions on Computer-Aided Design of Integrated Circuits and Systems 27(1), 123–136 (2008)

Part 18

Microelectronic Circuits Design

A CMOS Inverter-Based Self-biased Fully Differential Amplifier

José Rui Custódio, Michael Figueiredo, Edinei Santin, and João Goes

Department of Electrical Engineering, Faculty of Sciences and Technology, Universidade Nova de Lisboa, 2825-114 Monte de Caparica, Portugal
jrui.custodio@gmail.com, mf@uninova.pt, e.santin@fct.unl.pt, jg@uninova.pt

Abstract. A CMOS self-biased fully differential amplifier is presented. Due to the self-biasing structure of the amplifier and its associated negative feedback, the amplifier is compensated to achieve low sensitivity to process, supply voltage and temperature (PVT) variations. The output common-mode voltage of the amplifier is adjusted through the same biasing voltages provided by the common-mode feedback (CMFB) circuit. The amplifier core is based on a simple structure that uses two CMOS inverters to amplify the input differential signal. Despite its simple structure, the proposed amplifier is attractive to a wide range of applications, specially those requiring low power and small silicon area. As two examples, a sample-and-hold circuit and a second order multi-bit sigma-delta modulator either employing the proposed amplifier are presented. Besides these application examples, a set of amplifier performance parameters is given.

Keywords: Fully-differential amplifier, inverter-based amplification, low power, self-biasing.

1 Introduction

The complementary fully differential amplifier has a wide range of applications in both the analog and digital domain. This type of amplifier may be used in applications where a wide input signal range is necessary, such as filters, voltage comparators, low voltage differential-signalling (LVDS) systems, and TTL-to-CMOS buffers. Examples of single-ended versions of this type of amplifier have been proposed in [1]. Besides a fully complementary structure, the amplifiers in [1] use a self-biasing method which avoids using separate biasing circuits to bias the amplifier. The advantages of self-biasing techniques are well-known: they simplify the implementation of amplifiers by removing amplifier biasing circuitry, thus saving power and die area; they enable circuits to be insensitive to process, supply voltage, temperature (PVT) and parameter variations; circuits employing these techniques are capable of supplying switching currents greater than the quiescent bias currents [1].

Similar to the amplifiers in [1], a single-ended self-biased amplifier was proposed in [2]. As in all single-ended amplifiers, they suffer from the lack of common-mode (CM) rejection and are highly sensitive to surrounding noisy circuitry. Although die area is practically doubled, the benefits of fully differential circuits outrun their disadvantages, thus it is always a better option than their single-ended counterpart.

L.M. Camarinha-Matos, P. Pereira, and L. Ribeiro (Eds.): DoCEIS 2010, IFIP AICT 314, pp. 541–548, 2010.
© IFIP International Federation for Information Processing 2010

Fully differential self-biased amplifiers have already been proposed, such as, a folded cascode CMOS opamp (with and without gain boosting) [3], a class AB amplifier [4], and an LVDS signal receiver [5]. The amplifier reported in [4] is a pseudo-differential amplifier that relies on a complex active common-mode feedback (CMFB) network which has a separate biasing circuit, thus, is not completely self-biased. The LVDS signal receiver from [5] uses a continuous time CMFB circuit with resistors, thus lowering the achievable gain.

The objective of this brief is to propose a simple CMOS inverter-based self-biased fully differential amplifier with constant DC gain over PVT variations for a wide range of applications. Basically this circuit is a differential version of the amplifier proposed in [1], where self-biasing and output common-mode adjustment is realized through a switched-capacitor (SC) CMFB network.

This paper is organized as follows. Section 2 debates on the contribution of technologic innovation introduced by the proposed circuit. The theory of operation and design analysis of the amplifier is described in Section 3. This section also proposes a design methodology. Application examples in a sample-and-hold amplifier and a sigma-delta ($\Sigma\Delta$) modulator with simulation results are shown in Section 4. The paper is completed with a section dedicated to the conclusions.

2   Contribution to Technological Innovation

It is well-known that circuits employing self-biasing are less sensitive to PVT variations [1]. In fact, these circuits have the advantage of being able to reestablish their nominal operating point after a perturbation in the operation. As a result, the yield of the designed circuits is improved substantially. Also, self-biased circuits do not necessitate dedicated biasing circuitry, and thus power and area are lowered.

Another desired characteristic of a circuit is the capability of being implemented differentially. Fully differential circuits suppress even-order harmonic distortion and are more robust to extrinsic (surrounding) noise. This is a major concern in mixed-signal circuits, where the noise from digital circuitry is coupled into the sensitive analog blocks via the substrate and supply lines. Implementation simplicity (in terms of structure, number of devices, and layout effort) is another issue, since, generally, it leads to circuits consuming less power and area, presenting low noise, and easy to be laid out.

In this work we present a CMOS inverter-based self-biased fully-differential amplifier with the innovation of using a simple SC CMFB circuit to both control the output CM voltage and bias the amplifier. The proposed amplifier accomplishes the above mentioned characteristics and is well suited for a broad range of applications as will be demonstrated.

3   Inverter-Based Self-biased Fully Differential Amplifier

3.1   Theory of Operation

The proposed amplifier, illustrated in Fig. 1, comprises two input CMOS inverters (M_2, M_3) and two voltage controlled resistors (VCR) M_1 and M_4, biased in the boundary of the saturation and triode regions (it is very difficult to bias both these transistors simultaneously in the saturation region). A simple SC CMFB circuit comprising only two capacitors (C_{CM}) and five switches is used to properly adjust the output common-mode voltage to about $V_{DD}/2$ and, on the other hand, to provide closed-loop control (self-biasing) of the amplifier. The VCRs, M_1 and M_4, have their gate voltages controlled by the output of the SC CMFB circuit, V_{CM}. M_1 and M_4 together with V_{CM} are connected to the input inverters in a negative feedback loop reducing the effect of PVT variations on the amplifier's DC gain. As an example of compensation, if V_{DD} increases, the source-gate voltage in PMOS device M_1, V_{SGP1}, also increases producing an increase in the bias current I_D. This increase will change proportionally the current in the two input inverters, increasing the output CM voltage. As a consequence, the CMFB circuit will produce a higher V_{CM} output control voltage (assuming that V_{CMI} is constant and provided by a bandgap circuit) forcing V_{GSP1} to remain constant, thus compensating the V_{DD} variation. Process and temperature variations have similar compensations through the negative-feedback loop. As will be seen in the following sub-section, the DC gain, A_{VO}, is approximately the ratio of a transconductance by an output conductance, gm/gds. The DC gain is maintained constant because variations in gm ($\pm$ 30%) are accompanied by similar variations in gds, thus their ratio has variations less than 7 % over PVT variations.

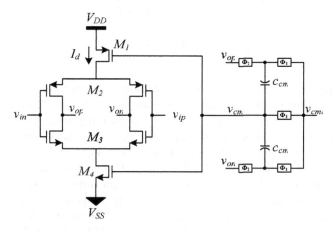

Fig. 1. Schematic of the fully-differential single-stage self-biased amplifier with the SC CMFB circuit

3.2 Design Analysis

Performing a small signal analysis followed by a Y-parameter simplification of the amplifier it is possible to obtain the amplifier's transfer function, given by,

$$A_V \cong \frac{s \cdot (cgd_2 + cgd_3) - gm_3 - gm_2}{s \cdot (cgd_2 + cgd_3 + C_L + C_{CM}) + gds_2 + gds_3} \tag{1}$$

Equation (2) presents the amplifier's DC gain. Some assumptions have been made, namely, $gm_3 \cong k \cdot gm_2 = k \cdot gm$ ($k = \mu_N/\mu_P$), $b_{ef2} \cong b_{ef3} = b_{ef}$ ($b_{ef} \cong 0.85$) and $gds_2 \cong gds_3 = gds$. μ_N and μ_P represent the mobilities of the NMOS and PMOS transistors, respectively. b_{ef} represents the gm degradation in devices M_2 and M_3 due to body-effect. Special care should be taken when considering a value for b_{ef}, as it may vary with the operating region of each transistor.

$$A_{V0} \cong \frac{b_{ef} \cdot gm \cdot (1+k)}{2 \cdot gds} \tag{2}$$

It should be noticed that (1) represents the gain of a standard inverter input amplifier, in other words, no parameters of devices M_1 and M_4 appear in the transfer function.

From (1) it is also possible to obtain expressions for the dominant pole frequency (BW), gain-bandwidth product (GBW), and the unity gain frequency (UGF), which are important performance parameters in opamp circuits. The following equations respectively represent the mentioned performance parameters. Parasitic capacitor $cgd = cgd_2 = cgd_3$ and C_L represents the output load capacitance.

$$f_{pole} = BW = \frac{2 \cdot gds}{C_L + C_{CM} + 2 \cdot cgd} \tag{3}$$

$$GBW = A_{V0} \times BW = \frac{b_{ef} \cdot gm \cdot (1+k)}{C_L + C_{CM} + 2 \cdot cgd} \tag{4}$$

$$UGF = \frac{b_{ef} \cdot gm \cdot (1+k) - 2 \cdot gds}{C_L + C_{CM}} \tag{5}$$

By considering the DC gain and GBW as initial specifications for the opamp, a possible design procedure would be to use (4) to obtain the gm that satisfies the GBW for a given effective load ($C_{eff} = C_L + C_{CM} + 2cgd$), and then to employ (2) to find the gds that satisfies the A_{V0} requirement. The drain currents for M_2 and M_3 can be calculated using gm and a given drain-source saturation voltage, $V_{DSsat} = V_{GS} - V_T \geq 100$ mV. Finally, M_2 and M_3 should be sized to be in saturation and to have an adequate gds (adjusted by the channel lengths). Multiplying the drain current of M_2 (or M_3) by two (to account for both current paths, differential) it is possible to size M_1 and M_4 in the triode/saturation boundary region for a $V_{DSsat} \geq 100$ mV ($V_{DSsat1,4}$ should not be large to avoid degrading output swing). Some care should be taken in the sizing of the transistors to guarantee the desired output common-mode voltage, power budget, output swing and PVT and mismatch insensitivity.

4 Simulation Results

This section presents simulation results of the proposed amplifier for two target applications. Firstly, the amplifier is applied in a sample-and-hold amplifier (SHA) intended for the front-end stage of a low resolution, high speed pipelined analog-to-digital converter (ADC). Secondly, the proposed amplifier is used in a multi-bit $\Sigma\Delta$ modulator targeted at hearing aid devices. Both amplifiers were designed in a 130 nm high speed 1.2 V CMOS technology (L_{min} = 120 nm). The mobility and threshold parameters (Level 2), K_N, K_P, V_{TN} and V_{TP} of the devices are, respectively, 525 μAV^{-2}, 145 μAV^{-2}, 0.38 V and -0.33 V. For V_{cmi}, 550 mV was used.

4.1 Application in a Sample-and-Hold Amplifier

An interesting application for the proposed amplifier is in a SHA as depicted in Fig. 2. This SHA was successfully applied in the front-end stage of a low resolution (7 bit) and high speed (500 MS/s) pipelined ADC. As a result, the basic specifications of the amplifier, such as DC gain (A_{V0}) and GBW, should be large enough to accommodate these requirements. Furthermore, the power consumption must be kept as low as possible to avoid degradation in the ADC performance.

With these prerequisites in mind and by using the proposed design procedure as an initial step followed by electrical simulations for sizing refinements (this includes typical and, at least, process corners), the transistors are sized as reported in Table 1.

Table 1. Feature size of the transistors for the sample-and-hold amplifier

Transistor	W (μm) / L (μm)
M_1	47 / 0.18
M_2	32 / 0.16
M_3	32 / 0.16
M_4	32 / 0.50

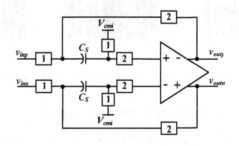

Fig. 2. Complete electrical schematic of the sample-and-hold amplifier

To evaluate the overall performance and robustness of the designed amplifier, its key parameters are simulated for different PVT corners according to Table 2. At typical conditions (Ct), the amplifier dissipates 0.9 mW and achieves a DC gain of 25.8 dB with a GBW larger than 2.88 GHz (for an effective load capacitance of 0.5 fF). The results for the other PVT corners are shown in Fig. 3. It should be noted that, although the GBW and the static power vary considerably, the DC gain varies less than ±0.75 dB considering all corners. These results were expected and clearly indicate the contribution of self-biasing in reducing amplifier sensitivity to PVT variations, concerning the DC gain.

Table 2. List of PVT corners used in the electrical simulations

Corner	Process	Supply Voltage	Temperature
Ct	TT	1.2	27
C1	TT	1.14	27
C2	TT	1.26	27
C3	SS	1.14	-40
C4	SS	1.14	85
C5	SS	1.26	-40
C6	SS	1.26	85
C7	FF	1.14	-40
C8	FF	1.14	85
C9	FF	1.26	-40
C10	FF	1.26	85

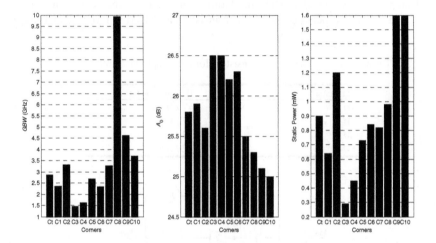

Fig. 3. GBW, A_0, and static power of the amplifier for PVT corners listed in Table 2

4.2 Application in a Multi-bit Sigma-Delta Modulator

The proposed amplifier was also applied to a second-order four-bit $\Sigma\Delta$ modulator as shown in Fig. 4. In this context, the amplifier is employed to realize a low power SC integrator, which is one of the key elements that determine the global performance of the $\Sigma\Delta$ modulator. This modulator is intended for hearing aids, and, therefore, it requires a dynamic range of about 96 dB with a peak signal-to-(noise plus distortion) ratio (SNDR) above 60 dB. Additionally, the signal bandwidth is 20 kHz. These specifications are met using a second-order four-bit $\Sigma\Delta$ modulator with nonlinear digital-to-analog converters with an oversampling ratio of 32.

The most stringent requirements are needed in the first integrator, which results in a higher complex amplifier design than necessary for the second integrator. It was verified by high level simulations that a minimum DC gain of 40 dB in the amplifier of the first integrator is enough to achieve the target dynamic range of 96 dB. In addition, the amplifier needs to settle its output with an error lower than 10 bit of resolution required for 60 dB of SNDR when operated at 1.28 MHz sampling frequency. This is achieved with a GBW higher than 8.4 MHz. To meet all these specifications the amplifier is sized following the same procedure described earlier and the results are shown in Table 3.

Table 3. Feature size of the transistors for the amplifier of the first integrator

Transistor	W (μm) / L (μm)
M_1	8.5 / 1.2
M_2	15 / 0.8
M_3	16 / 1.3
M_4	7.75 / 4.5

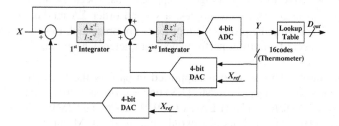

Fig. 4. Complete block diagram of the second-order four-bit ΣΔ modulator

The performance of the amplifier was verified through different PVT corners simulations as indicated in Table 2. The amplifier achieves a DC gain of 42.9 dB with a GBW larger than 8.4 MHz (for an effective load capacitance of 10 pF) dissipating only 41 μW at typical operation. The results for the remaining corners are depicted in Fig. 5. As in the previous example, we can note that the DC gain varies less than ±1.5 dB considering all corners.

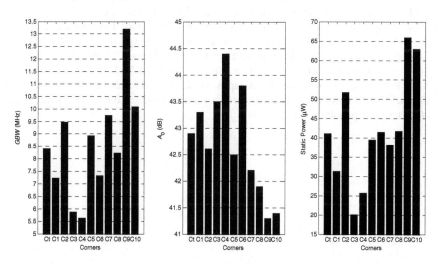

Fig. 5. GBW, A_0, and static power of the amplifier for PVT corners listed in Table 2

5 Conclusions

A CMOS self-biased fully differential amplifier was presented. In order to generate the biasing voltages of the amplifier, a CMFB is employed. The CMFB circuit, based on an SC network, uses the amplifier's outputs to derive the mentioned voltages, hence the designation, self-biased amplifier. Due to the self-biasing structure of the amplifier and its associated negative feedback, the amplifier is compensated to achieve low sensitivity to PVT variations. The output common-mode voltage of the amplifier is adjusted through the same biasing voltages provided by the CMFB circuit. The amplifier core is based on a simple structure that uses two CMOS inverters to amplify the input differential signal. Despite its simple structure, the proposed amplifier is attractive to a wide range of applications, specially those requiring low power and small area. As two examples, a second order $\Sigma\Delta$ modulator and a SHA circuit either employing the proposed amplifier were presented. Besides these application examples, a set of amplifier performance parameters was given.

Acknowledgments. This work was supported in part by the Portuguese Foundation for Science and Technology (FCT/MCTES) under projects SPEED (PTDC/EEAELC/66857/2006), LEADER (PTDC/EEA-ELC/69791/2006) and IMPACT (PTDC/EEA-ELC/101421/2008). The authors also would like to thank Marta Kordasz for implementing an opamp transfer function extractor program based on Y-parameters, which greatly reduced circuit analysis time.

References

1. Bazes, M.: Two Novel Fully Complementary Self-Biased CMOS Differential Amplifiers. J. of Solid-State Circuits 26, 165–168 (1991)
2. Zhu, Z., Liu, Y., Yang, Y.: A High Speed Self-biased CMOS Amplifier IP core. In: Proc. IEEE International Workshop on VLSI Design and Video Technology, pp. 6–9 (2005)
3. Mandal, P., Visvanathan, V.: A Self-Biased High Performance Folded Cascode CMOS Op-Amp. In: Proc. 10th International Conference on VLSI Design, pp. 429–434 (1997)
4. Giustolisi, G., Grasso, A.D., Pennisi, S.: High-Drive and Linear CMOS Class-AB Pseudo-Differential Amplifier. IEEE Trans. on Circuits and Systems II 54(2), 112–116 (2007)
5. Xiao, P., Kuchta, D., Stawiasz, K., Ainspan, H., Choi, J.-H., Shin, H.: A 500 Mb/s, 20-Channel CMOS Laser Diode Array Driver for a Parallel Optical Bus. IEEE ISSCC Digest of Technical Papers 467, 250–251 (1997)

Reconfigurable Circuits Using Magnetic Tunneling Junction Memories

Victor Silva, Jorge Fernandes, and Horácio Neto

INESC-ID / IST / UTL, Technical University of Lisbon, Portugal
{vicant,jorge.fernandes,hcn}@inesc-id.pt

Abstract. This paper presents the first results of our work to research and develop new reconfigurable circuits and topologies based on Magnetic RAM (MRAM) memory elements. This work proposes a coarse-grained reconfigurable array using MRAM. A coarse-grained array, where each reconfigurable element computes on 4-bit or larger input words, is more suitable to execute data-oriented algorithms and is more able to exploit large amounts of operation-level parallelism than common fine-grained architectures. The architecture is organized as a one-dimensional array of programmable ALU and the configuration bits are stored in MRAM. MRAM provide non-volatility with cell areas and with access speeds comparable to those of SRAM and with lower process complexity than FLASH memory. MRAM can also be efficiently organized as multi-context memories.

Keywords: MRAM. Reconfigurable Hardware. Coarse-grained array. Programmable ALU. Multi-context.

1 Introduction

The field of reconfigurable computing has been, so far, dominated by fine-grained Field Programmable Gate Arrays (FPGA). Nevertheless, FPGA have substantial drawbacks. Since most FPGA are SRAM based, their volatility makes FPGA unappealing for applications that require reduced parts count and small footprint or rapid availability of logic or high security [1]. FPGA also have a large routing overhead due to their bit-level nature, demand large configuration memories for both processing units and routing switches and require large configuration times that make runtime reconfiguration practically unfeasible.

Reconfigurable arrays (RA) try to overcome the disadvantages of Field Programmable Gate Array (FPGA) based computing solutions by providing multiple bit-wide data-paths and complex operators instead of bit-level configurability. The wider data-paths allow for the efficient implementation of complex operators in silicon. Thus, RA offer lower overhead, exploit better operation level parallelism and are better suited for data-oriented algorithms [2].

This work proposes a MTJ-based coarse-grained reconfigurable array. The reconfigurable architecture proposed is organized as a 1-dimensional coarse-grained array. The basic processing elements (PE) are arithmetic and logic function units 4 or more

L.M. Camarinha-Matos, P. Pereira, and L. Ribeiro (Eds.): DoCEIS 2010, IFIP AICT 314, pp. 549–558, 2010.

bits wide. The operation to be executed by each PE is controlled by the MRAM bits. The array is run-time reconfigurable. The MTJ structures can be rewritten while the circuit is in execution, and therefore a new reconfiguration can be loaded while the current application is running.

A number of architectural and circuit solutions are being studied, implemented and evaluated. The fundamental components of the RA have already been designed and electrically simulated. The results of the electrical simulations were on line with expectations.

A scaled down version of a coarse-grained reconfigurable array using TAS-MRAM was designed and a first prototype has been sent for fabrication and is expected to be delivered in a few weeks. This prototype will be further processed at INESC-MN facilities to lay out the layers that will form the MTJs.

2   Contribution to Technological Innovation

This work aims to answer a number of open research questions, such as:

- Is it possible to cost effectively deal with FPGA inherent volatility?
- Is there an alternative reconfigurable architectural model to the nasty FPGA bit-level architectural model?
- Is it possible to have it all, a non volatile reconfigurable device that it is more oriented for data intensive algorithms?

Magnetic RAM (MRAM) technology offers a solution to the intrinsic volatility of SRAM, with low reading and writing times, virtual limitless re-programmability and almost no area overhead compared with other technologies such as FLASH [3],[4].

At the architectural level, reconfigurable arrays (RA) try to overcome the disadvantages of FPGA based computing solutions by providing multiple bit-wide data-paths and complex operators instead of bit-level configurability. RA wider data-paths allow for the efficient implementation of complex operators in silicon. Thus, RA offer lower overhead, exploit better operation level parallelism and are better suited for data-oriented algorithms.

The objective of this research and development is, therefore, to design and develop a reconfigurable array architecture based on MRAM. This kind of device enjoys the advantage of non volatility due to be based on MRAM and at the same time offers the computational advantages that RA have over FPGA.

The use of magnetic tunneling junction (MTJ) memory cells in run-time reconfigurable hardware devices is a very promising technological solution and an emergent area of research. At the architectural level and in order to meet the increased computational requirements of data-intensive applications, reconfigurable devices are starting to evolve to coarse-grained compositions of functional units or program controlled processors, that are more able to improve performance and energy efficiency. The combination of these two aspects, as proposed in this research, can therefore provide a main contribution to technological innovation in the area of reconfigurable computing.

3   State of the Art

Since the 1990s, a number of architectures have been proposed and designed [2], [5], [6], [7], [8]. These architectures can be classified according to their basic interconnect structure, granularity and reconfiguration model. Practically all of the proposed architectures are SRAM-based and none of these is MRAM-based.

The predominant architectural arrangement has been a 2-D array or mesh, although some of the works, see for example [7], [8] have demonstrated that 1-dimensional coarse-grained linear array architectures can provide high-performance for specific application domains.

MRAM have so far been exclusively employed as elements on fine-grained FPGA look alike solutions, such as Look Up Tables (LUT) [3], [4], [9], [10], [11], [12] and no works have been published on MRAM-based coarse-grained reconfigurable arrays.

The most common MRAM cells consist of Magnetic Tunneling Junctions (MTJ) vertically integrated with silicon CMOS transistors as depicted on Fig. 1. A MTJ cell is conceptually made of two thin ferromagnetic layers separated by an ultra thin non-magnetic oxide layer [3], [4], [9]. Magnetic remanence of the ferromagnetic elements provides for non-volatility.

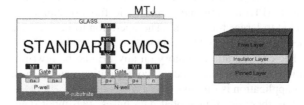

Fig. 1. Left: MTJ requires a few steps above standard CMOS. Right: Magnetic Tunnel Junction Structure.

The relative magnetic orientation of these layers defines two different values of equivalent resistance Rp (low resistance), when the free layer and the pinned layer are oriented to the same direction, and Rap (high resistance), when the free layer and the pinned layer are oriented in opposite direction. These different values of equivalent resistance can be employed as state variables to represent the logic states '0' and '1'.

This resistance can be evaluated by sending current through the junction and measuring the voltages at the nodes of the MTJ. A structure is required to determine whether the junction is on a low resistivity configuration or in a high resistivity configuration.

To write information in a MTJ, a magnetic field is applied through the junction in order to force the change on the magnetic orientation of the free layer. The strength and nature of the required magnetic field depends on the writing approach. Currently, there are 3 writing approaches known as Field Induced Magnetic Switching (FIMS) [3], [4], [9], Thermally Assisted Switching (TAS) [10], [11] and Spin Transfer Torque (STT) [12].

Most MRAM produced so far are FIMS-based, but their size has been limited to 16Mb [13] because this technique has major drawbacks such as its susceptibility to soft errors due to write selectivity, its lower scalability and its high current consumption. The TAS and STT approaches have been recently proposed to overcome the above mentioned issues. The TAS approach was preferred due to its weaker demands from the material point of view.

The TAS approach requires one bidirectional current to create the magnetic field. A local current (for each junction) is then used to enhance the effectiveness of the aforementioned magnetic field by momentarily heating the junction by Joule effect. This heating will unpin the free layer.

4   Research Contribution and Innovation

To the authors' knowledge, this is the first R&D work where a MRAM based coarse grained reconfigurable array is proposed and a proof of concept prototype is developed and manufactured. Also, the proposed design employs a TAS writing based MRAM instead of the more conventional FIMS writing based MRAM.

The reconfigurable architecture proposed in this work [14] is organized as a 1-dimensional coarse-grained array. By providing a not too complex but very effective architecture organization 1-dimensional arrays are a good option to permit full characterization of the MRAM-based run-time reconfigurable technology. The basic processing elements (PE) are arithmetic and logic function units 4-bit wide (which can be easily scaled to larger bit-widths). The operation to be executed by each PE is controlled by the respective MRAM configuration memory bits. The array is run-time reconfigurable. The configuration memory on any PE can be rewritten while the circuit is in execution, and therefore a new reconfiguration can be loaded into any PE while the current application is running.

For computation, there are four global data buses, two input data buses and two output data buses, see Fig. 2. The A bus and the B bus feed the rALU with its operands. The S bus and the Carry out bus deliver the result of the logical-arithmetic operation executed and its eventual carry out. The exclusive access to the global data buses for each rALU is ensured by 16 selector signals, Sel(k), one for each rALU.

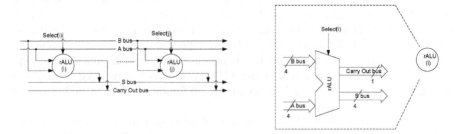

Fig. 2. General Computational Architecture

For configuration, there is one input global bus, as shown in Fig. 3. The Conf bus carries the data that will be stored on the MTJ to be used later on for configuration, thus supporting shallow dynamic re-configurability.

Sixteen selector signals determine which rALU(k) configuration memory will be written. The configuration memory contains the information that defines the ALU functionality. This configuration memory is made of an array of identical TAS-MRAM cells as the one depicted on Fig. 3.

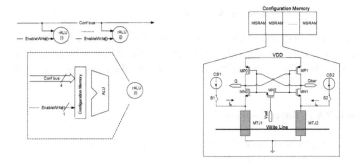

Fig. 3. Left: Configuration Architecture. Right: Configuration memory structure.

4.1 Datapath Unit

The data-path unit is implemented in a bit slice fashion. Since this module is implemented in full custom, a bit slice style makes it easier to change the available data-path width.

The 4 bit ALU is made by the concatenation of 4 identical data-path slices as the one depicted on Fig. 4. The less significant carry in bit can be set to '0' or '1' while the remaining carries in are connected to their direct predecessor lower order bit slice carry out. As shown in Fig. 4, the function computed by the ALU depends on the values of the five multiplexers selector values. These values depend on the data stored in the memory configuration bits and their values are easily generated from Fig. 4.

The adder is implemented as a classic Ripple Carry Adder. An adder-subtracter is implemented by adding a XOR gate to the adder input port A and by selectively setting the adder input port Carry In with a logic '1'.

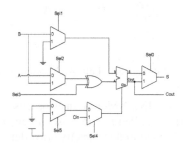

Fig. 4. Data path bit slice structure

The XOR and MUX designs are implemented using transmission gates, because of simplicity of implementation. The implementation of the arithmetic-logic functions takes advantage of the adder defining equations (1)-(2).

$$S = A \cdot B + A \cdot Cin + B \cdot Cin ,$$ (1)

$$Cout = A \text{ xor } B \text{ xor } Cin .$$ (2)

For example, the operation AND is implemented by selecting the adder-subtrater output S, given by equation (1) and setting the adder-subtracter Carry-in input signal to logic '0'. This is accomplished by setting the controls signals, Sel0-Sel5 to logic '0'.

4.2 TAS-MRAM Based Storage Cell

Two circuit designs have been evaluated for the TAS-MRAM based storage cell [10], [11]. These circuits, as shown in Fig. 5 consist of:

- An Unbalanced Flip Flop (UFF) used as a sense amplifier.
- Two MTJ cells (MTJ1 and MTJ2).
- Two unidirectional current sources CS1 and CS2. These two current sources are responsible for the Joule effect on each MTJ.
- A write line that is employed to propagate the external magnetic field in either direction. This line is common to all storage cells.
- Two PMOS isolation transistors (for architecture 2).

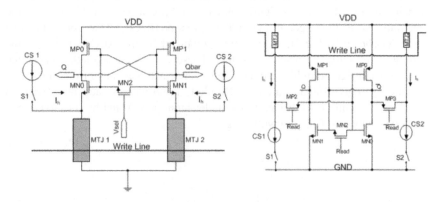

Fig. 5. TAS-MRAM based storage cell. Left Architecture 1. Right: Architecture 2.

During the read phase, the MN2 NMOS transistor acts as a short circuit, thus, the two cross-coupled inverters are pulled to a meta-stable operating state. The resistance value of each of the MTJ coupled to its respective inverter will move away the meta-stable operating point from one of the stable states and bring it closer to the other. So, when the Vsel/Read signal is released, the structure will move to the closest stable state. Afterwards, new information can be stored into the MTJ without altering the value stored in the UFF.

Due to the number of arithmetic-logic functions available on each ALU, a cluster of four memory bits is assigned to each individual ALU. Since the cluster size is small, the four control signals required are generated at the same writing cycle.

The inner working of the UFF coupled with MTJs provides the required support for run-time reconfiguration. So it is possible to write a new plane of configuration while the rALU is operating at full speed.

4.3 Bidirectional Current Generator

A bidirectional current generator capable of delivering a current higher than 20 mA has been designed to provide the current that is necessary to generate the bidirectional magnetic field responsible for switching the magnetic orientation of the MTJ's free layer and therefore write new information on the MTJ.

In order to better characterize the MTJ behavior, a digital controlled current source is used in association with a digital controlled current sink, see Fig. 6. The bidirectional current is shared among all TAS-MRAM storage cells, and therefore only one generator is required for the whole set of MTJ. The writing operation require 2 steps, in the first step the current flows in a direction that will allow writing a logical '1' on a given memory cell and in the second step, the current that flows in the write line will reverse its direction in order to allow writing a '0' in another memory cell.

Both Rbias1 and Rbias2 resistance are external and they are employed to change the intensity of the currents that passed across the current source and across the current sink respectively.

The switches S1 and S2 operate in complementary fashion. Their purpose is to turn on and turn off the current source as required by the logic responsible for the configuration. The switches S3 and S4 operates in complementary fashion and are responsible for turning off or on the current sink as required by the logic responsible for the configuration.

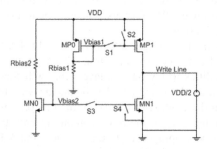
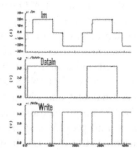

Fig. 6. Left: Bidirectional current generator. Right: Bidirectional current generator electrical behavior.

4.4 Unidirectional Current Generator

A unidirectional current generator able to deliver at least 1mA has been designed to provide the local current to momentarily heat each junction by Joule effect, as required by the TAS approach.

In order to facilitate the characterization of the MTJ behavior, a digital controlled current source has been designed, as depicted in Fig. 7. The unidirectional current generator is split into a front- end and a back-end. The Front-end is made of a resistance (Rbias3) and a PMOS transistor (MP0) while the back-end is made of switches (S1 and S2) and two identical PMOS transistor (MP1 and MP2). The front-end is shared among the whole set of unidirectional current generators while there is one back-end module associated with each memory cell pair of MTJ.

Rbias3 is an external resistance that is employed to bias the back-end's driver transistors (MP1 and MP2). The switches S1 and S2 operate in complementary fashion. Their purpose is to turn on and turn off the PMOS driver transistors (MP1 and MP2). The aforementioned switches are opened and closed depending on the value of an internal generated digital control signal.

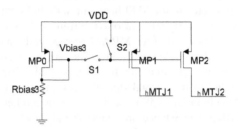

Fig. 7. Unidirectional current generator

5   Discussion of Results and Critical View

In order to fulfill our goal several architectural and circuits solutions are being studied, implemented and evaluated. The core blocks have already been designed for AMS 0.35µm 4-Metal CMOS process technology and have been electrical simulated with a set of stimuli pre and post-layout under PVT corners. The electrical responses of the core blocks were on line with expectations.

An initial proof of concept coarse-grained reconfigurable array using TAS-MRAM was designed and a first prototype has been sent for fabrication. This prototype will be further processed at INESC-MN facilities to lay out the layers that will form the MTJs. A final test and characterization of the design will validate the viability of TAS-MRAM based memory element in the context of coarse grained reconfigurable computing and provide a study of the inner core of the basic computing unit, the re-configurable ALU (rALU). It will also be employed to figure out how the MRAM configuration memory and the reconfigurable ALU fit together.

The circuit implements 1 of the 16 rALU that are part of the initial architecture as depicted on Fig. 2. Each ALU is capable of supporting up to 16 different operations, thus a four MRAM bit configuration memory is associated to each ALU. It is the information stored on the configuration memory that selects which operation will be carried out.

Both storage-cell circuits were simulated pre and post-layout under the same conditions, including the same set of AMS recommended PVT corners. Both performed as expected, however, architecture 1 has been preferred over architecture 2 because it requires a lower TMR. The TMR (Tunneling Magneto Resistance) is defined by the ratio between the two MTJ equivalent resistances (TMR = $\Delta R/R$) and is a critical factor for the viability of the MRAM. According to the post-layout simulation results, architecture 2 requires a TMR of at least 40% while architecture 1 requires a TMR of 30%. On both cases the value of Rp was set to $1k\Omega$.

The whole MRAM rALU was electrical simulated post-layout under an extensive set of stimuli. In order to mitigate the ground and power supply bounce without increasing the number of both power supply pads and ground pads, external semi rings with multiple metal pads to reduce the inductance due to the bonding wires for power and ground have been connected to their respective power and ground pads. The same procedure was performed to the auxiliary voltage reference source VDD/2.

6 Conclusions and Further Work

As mentioned in section 4 and as far as the authors are aware this is the first proposal of a TAS-MRAM based coarse grained reconfigurable array. This research aims to provide a new approach to overcome the problems due to volatility that make FPGA less appealing for many applications, while maintaining the advantages inherent to coarse grain level operators. Further, it offers an open door to a very cost effective partial and full run time reconfigurability.

A scaled down prototype was sent for manufacturing at Austria Microsystems in late June 2009 and samples have been received in October 2009. A PCB board will now be designed for further evaluation and analysis of this prototype.

There are still many open questions for further work, either at circuit level or at the architectural level. For multi-context reconfiguration, further research is necessary to evaluate which of the storage cell architecture developed is more adequate for multiple planes of configuration and if there is one optimum number of configuration planes. It is also important to find if those results are fully technology scalable.

From the architectural point of view, future research should consider issues such as a fixed interconnect structure versus a fully reconfigurable one, handshake mechanisms or level of homogeneity among functional units.

Acknowledgments. We acknowledge the major contribution to this work from our partners of INESC-MN. This work is partially supported by the Portuguese Foundation for Science and Technology (FCT) through Project MRAM (PTDC/EEA-ELC/72933/2006).

References

1. Third Generation Non-Volatile FPGAs Enable System on Chip Functionality. White Paper, Lattice Semiconductor Corporation (2007)
2. Nageldinger, U.: Coarse-grained Reconfigurable Architectures Design Space Exploration. Ph.D Dissertation, C.S Department, University of Kaiserslautern (2001)
3. Bruchon, N., Cambon, G., Torres, L., Sassatelli, G.: Magnetic remanent memory structures for dynamically reconfigurable FPGA. In: International Conference on Field Programmable Logic and Applications, pp. 687–690. IEEE, Los Alamitos (2005)

4. Bruchon, N., Torres, L., Sassatelli, G., Cambon, G.: Magnetic tunnelling junction based FPGA. In: 2006 ACM/SIGDA 14th International Symposium on Field Programmable Gate Arrays, pp. 123–130. ACM, New York (2006)
5. Hartenstein, R.: A Decade of Reconfigurable Computing: a Visionary Retrospective. In: Conference on Design, Automation and Test in Europe, pp. 642–649. IEEE, Los Alamitos (2001)
6. Zain-ul-Abdin, Svensson, B.: Evolution in architectures and programming methodologies of coarse-grained reconfigurable computing. Microprocessors and Microsystems 33(3), 161–178 (2009)
7. Ebeling, C.: The General Rapid Architecture Description. Tech. Rep. UW-CSE-02-06-02, University of Washington (2002)
8. Goldstein, S.C., Schmit, H., Moe, M., Budiu, M., Cadambi, S., Taylor, R.R., Laufer, R.: PipeRench: A Coprocessor for Streaming Multimedia Acceleration. In: 26th International Symposium on Computer Architecture (ISCA 1999), pp. 28–39. IEEE, Los Alamitos (1999)
9. Bruchon, N., Torres, L., Sassatelli, G., Cambon, G.: New non-volatile FPGA concept using Magnetic Tunneling Junction. In: IEEE Computer Society Annual Symposium on VLSI: Emerging VLSI Technologies and Architectures (ISVLSI 2006), pp. 269–276. IEEE, Los Alamitos (2006)
10. Zhao, W., Belhaire, E., Dieny, B., Prenat, G., Chappert, C.: TAS-MRAM based Non-volatile FPGA logic circuit. In: International Conference on Field-Programmable Technology (ICFPT 2007), pp. 153–160. IEEE, Los Alamitos (2007)
11. Guillemenet, Y., Torres, L., Sassatelli, G., Bruchon, N., Hassoune, I.: A non-volatile run-time FPGA using thermally assisted switching MRAMS. In: International Conference on Field-Programmable Logic and Applications (FPL 2008), pp. 421–426. IEEE, Los Alamitos (2008)
12. Zhao, W., Belhaire, E., Mistral, Q., Nicolle, E., Devolder, T., Chappert, C.: Integration of Spin-RAM technology in FPGA circuits. In: 8th International Conference on Solid-State and Integrated Circuit Technology (ICSICT 2006), pp. 799–802. IEEE, Los Alamitos (2006)
13. DeBrosse, J., Arndt, C., Barwin, C., Bette, A., Gogl, D., Gow, E., Hoenigschmid, H., Lammers, S., Lamorey, M., Lu, Y., Maffitt, T., Maloney, K., Obermeyer, W., Sturm, A., Viehmann, H., Willmott, D., Wood, M., Gallagher, W.J., Mueller, G., Sitaram, A.R.: A 16Mb MRAM featuring bootstrapped write drivers. In: 2004 Symposium on VLSI Circuits, pp. 454–457. IEEE, Los Alamitos (2004)
14. Silva, V., Oliveira, L.B., Fernandes, J.R., Véstias, M.P., Neto, H.C.: Run-Time Reconfigurable Array using Magnetic RAM. In: 12th EUROMICRO Conference on Digital System Design, DSD 2009 (2009)

A New Automated Trigger Circuit for a
Pulsed Nd: YAG Laser

Fatah Almabouada, Djelloul Louhibi, Abderrahmane Haddouche,
Abdelkader Noukaz, and Ramdan Beggar

Centre de Développement des Technologies Avancées,
Division des Milieux Ionisés & Laser
BP 17, Cité du 20 août 1956, Baba Hassen, Algiers, Algeria
falmabouada@yahoo.fr

Abstract. The power supply of flash lamp-pumped a Nd: YAG solid-state laser
basically consists of a trigger circuit which initiate the ionization of the gas into
the lamp, a simmer circuit that keeps the ionized gas with a low-level dc current
and a main discharge circuit where a storage capacitor is discharged into a flash
lamp to pump the Nd:YAG laser. The impedance of the flash lamp presents a
nonlinear variation and the gas deionization which can occur between two
pulses laser, leading to another manual triggering operation. To overcome this
operation, we give in this paper a new automated trigger circuit activated by a
delivered signal from the simmer circuit. This circuit is simple for implementation and need just few components. It has been simulated by PSpice software
and validated by experimental results.

Keywords: Flash lamp, solid-state laser, simmer circuit, trigger circuit.

1 Introduction

Pulsed Xenon flash lamps are gas-discharge devices designed to produce a pulsed
radiation. They convert the electrical energy to the optical radiation. This intense
pulse of radiant energy is used in many applications. In our case these devices are
used for pumping solid-state lasers.

One of the principle diagrams of the power supply circuit of a pulsed flash lamp is
the simmer mode operation as shown in Fig. 1. This mode has a several advantages
and one of them is the increasing of the flash lamp lifetime.

The power supply performs a number of functions:

- The external trigger circuit provides a high voltage pulse around 20 kV to initiate
the ionization of the gas. The secondary of the trigger transformer is connected to a
wire which is wrapped around the lamp [1]-[2].

- The simmer circuit maintains a partial steady-state ionization by establishing and
maintaining a low-current dc arc between the lamp electrodes.

L.M. Camarinha-Matos, P. Pereira, and L. Ribeiro (Eds.): DoCEIS 2010, IFIP AICT 314, pp. 559–566, 2010.

- The charging unit is used to charge the storage capacitor C. The charging must be completed within the inter-pulse time of the laser. The principal capacitor discharge through the flash is ensured by an electronic switch. The capacitor C, the inductor L and the impedance R of the flash lamp constitute the circuit that provides the desired shape pulse during the discharge. The operation of the laser and the flash lamp characteristic, allow to fix the values of C and L [2].

During the operation of the laser, the lamp gas can be deionized between two laser pulses obliging to trigger again which is a drawback because in our previous work the triggering operation was activated by a manual command.

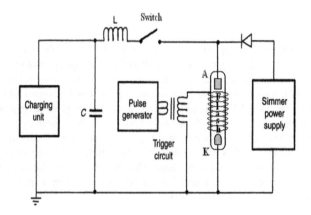

Fig. 1. Principle diagram of the flash tube excitation circuit

2   Contribution to Technological Innovation

This work is an innovation in the electronic command of a trigger circuit used to energize the flash lamp. In our contribution the command trigger is automated by a circuit which isn't complex and uses little components. Several works were done in this field [3] and where the trigger is activated at each laser pulse which is a disadvantage because that decreases the flash lamp lifetime [2].

3   Simmer and Trigger Circuit

3.1   Simmer Circuit

After the triggering, the flash lamp impedance R varies in a nonlinear way where its measured value is given within 1 kΩ and 17 kΩ [4]. This variation is represented by the electrical characteristic of specified flash lamp as illustrated in Fig. 2.

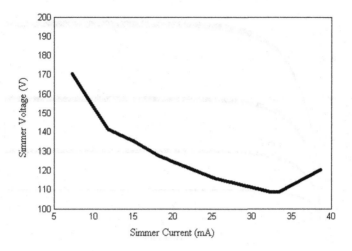

Fig. 2. Electrical characteristic of the flash lamp (Flash-Heraeus Noblelight Ltd. Model: P537)

The simmer circuit will be able to follow this variation. The proposed simmer uses a voltage multiplier which is supplied by 200 V as an alternative voltage given by a switch mode power supply. This voltage multiplier delivers 1.2 kV and 100 mA when a flash lamp is non-ignited. At the ionized state, these values vary in accordance with the flash lamp resistor load [5].

Before the experimental step, all the simulated results of designed circuits have simulated using the Pspice simulator.

The simulated simmer circuit is represented in Fig. 3, V1 is equal to 200 V and the resistor R10 represents the flash lamp resistor taking several values. The simulated results of the simmer voltage are given for several values of R in Fig. 4.

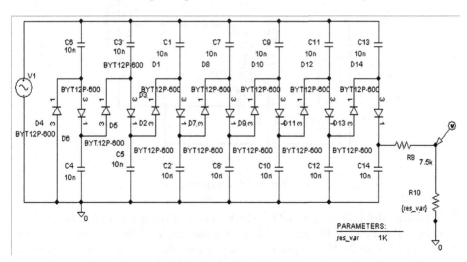

Fig. 3. Simmer circuit

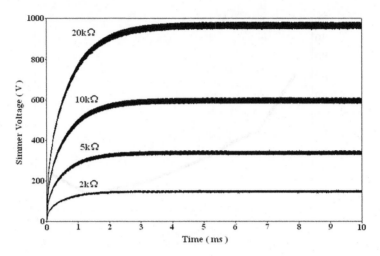

Fig. 4. Variations of the Simmer voltage versus the flash resistor

3.2 Trigger Circuit

In our previous work we developed a trigger circuit activated by a manual command [6]. This trigger (Fig. 5) is a flyback converter [7] using a commercial high voltage transformer (THT model: HR6060). The user has just to push the manual button (S) to supply pulse duration T_1 to the switching transistor (T), adjusted by R1 and C1 of the monostable MC4538, which will be sufficient to produce the high output voltage (V_{HT}).

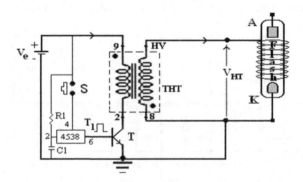

Fig. 5. Trigger circuit

In general, the THT is supplied by 120 V (Ve) as a voltage at 15.625 kHz (64 µs) allowing pulse duration T_1 equal to 32 µs for a duty cycle of 50%. In our case, a low voltage of 12 V to 24 V is applied for a safety use; therefore the pulse duration T_1 should be adjusted in order to have the same high voltage in the output. For this purpose, the relation between the parameters is expressed by [7]:

$$T_1 = (L_p/V_e)I_{pmax} .   (1)$$

where L_P is the primary inductance and I_{Pmax} is the maximum primary current.

For Ve=12 V we must increase T_1 at 320 μs for obtaining the same I_{pmax}.

The circuit was simulated and tested experimentally. The experimental result is given by Fig. 6. To avoid the manual triggering after the deionization of the gas, the useful idea is to automate the command of this trigger circuit.

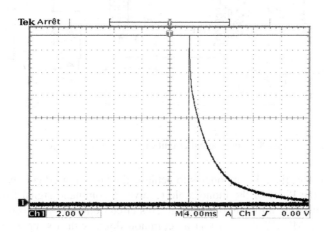

Fig. 6. The triggering pulse (*trace vertical: 2kV/div*)

3.3 Simmer Command for Triggering

For the automated command, the command signal is generated by the simmer circuit depending of the ionized state. When the simmer output is around 1.2 kV corresponding to the flash lamp non-ignited state, a pulse voltage is required for the monostable in order to generate the trigger pulse. For the ignited state, the simmer circuit has a small voltage value which is not sufficient to command the monostable. The complete simmer-trigger schematic enclosing the command signal is illustrated in Fig. 7.

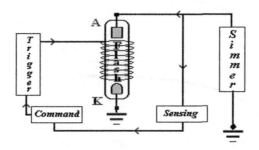

Fig. 7. Simmer-trigger schematic enclosing the command signal

4 Experimental Circuit

The Fig. 8 shows the experimental circuit.

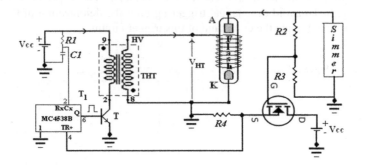

Fig. 8. Experimental circuit of the automated trigger

Fig. 8 describes the all components to achieve the last reported command function. Furthermore, the Pin 4 of the monostable receives a command signal from the additional circuit used to automate our trigger. This circuit employs a resistor divider and an IGBT (or a MOSFET transistor) as common drain with a simple resistor at its source. For the deionized gas state, the resistor divider (R2, R3) gives a sufficient voltage to the gate of the IGBT which works in the switch-on mode. In this case, the IGBT switches to the minimum required voltage (3 V) used by the Pin 4 in order to offer the desired T_1 from the monostable. In the ionized gas state, the resistor divider can not fulfill the voltage condition keeping the IGBT in the switch-off mode.

The simulated results of the monostable input voltage (Pin4) and the simmer voltage verify the behavior of the additional circuit for the automated case as shown in Fig. 9. These results are in good accordance with the experimental results given in the Fig. 10.

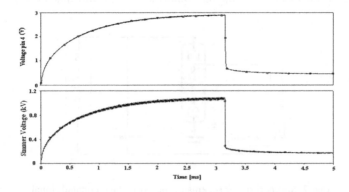

Fig. 9. Simulated results of the simmer voltage and the monostable voltage (pin4)

Fig. 11 represents the experimental behavior of the simmer voltage and the high voltage triggering pulse. It is observed that when the simmer voltage reaches its high value, the trigger circuit delivers the triggering pulse for gas ionization into the flash lamp. At this moment, the simmer voltage drops down to its small value. The circuit was tested with a Xenon flash lamp: Flash-Heraeus Noblelight Ltd. Model: P537 which is used to pump the Nd: YAG laser.

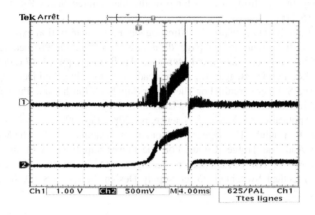

Fig. 10. The simmer voltage (lower trace vertical: 500V/div) and the voltage pin 4 (*upper trace vertical: 1V/div*)

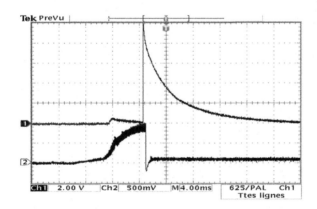

Fig. 11. The trigger pulse (upper trace vertical: 2kV/div) and the simmer voltage (*lower trace vertical: 500V/div*)

5 Conclusion

In this article, an automated trigger circuit has been developed in order to overcome the manual triggering when the deionized flash lamp gas can occur. The command circuit is simply implemented using available components allowing a quick maintenance. The experimental results are in good agreement as obtained in simulation.

References

1. Hook, W.R., Dishington, R.H., Hilberg, R.P.: Xenon Flashlamp Triggering for Laser Applications. IEEE Trans. Electron Device ED-19(3), 308–314 (1972)
2. Koechener, W.: Solid-state Laser Engineering, 6th Revised and updated edn. Springer, Heidelberg (2006)
3. Changaris, D.G., Louisville, K.Y. (US), Zinner, W.S.: New Albany, IN (US): Method and circuit for repetitively firing a flash lamp or the like. United States Patent 6,965,203 B2 (November 15, 2005)
4. Beggar, R., Louhibi, D., Noukaz, A., Almabouada, F.: Caractérisation expérimentale d'une lampe flash utilisée pour le pompage d'un laser à solide. In: Proceeding SENALAP: Quatrième Séminaire National sur le Laser et ses Applications, pp. 14–17 (2008)
5. Noukaz, A., Louhibi, D., Beggar, R., Almabouada, F.: Modelling And Development Of The Command And Simmer Circuits For The Power Supply Of Flash Lamp Pumped Solid-State Lasers. In: AIP Conference Proceedings LAPAMS: First International Conference on Laser and Plasma Applications in Materials Science, pp. 208–211 (2008)
6. Almabouada, F., Louhibi, D., Beggar, R., Noukaz, A., Haddouche, A.: The Main Discharge Transformer And The Trigger Circuit For The Power Supply Of A Flash Lamp-Pumped Solid State Laser. In: AIP Conference Proceedings LAPAMS, pp. 192–195 (2008)
7. Brown, M.: Practical Switching Power Supply Design. Series in Solid State Electronics, Motorola, pp. 29–34 (1991)

Author Index